THE COLLECTED WRITINGS
OF SAMSON OCCOM,
MOHEGAN

THE COLLECTED WRITINGS OF SAMSON OCCOM, MOHEGAN

Leadership and Literature in Eighteenth-Century Native America

Edited by
JOANNA BROOKS

Foreword by
ROBERT WARRIOR

OXFORD
UNIVERSITY PRESS
2006

OXFORD
UNIVERSITY PRESS

Oxford University Press, Inc., publishes works that further
Oxford University's objective of excellence
in research, scholarship, and education.

Oxford   New York
Auckland   Bangkok   Bogotá   Buenos Aires   Cape Town   Chennai
Dar es Salaam   Delhi   Hong Kong   Istanbul   Karachi   Kolkata
Kuala Lumpur   Madrid   Melbourne   Mexico City   Mumbai   Nairobi
São Paulo   Shanghai   Singapore   Taipei   Tokyo   Toronto

Published by Oxford University Press, Inc.
198 Madison Avenue, New York, New York, 10016

www.oup.com

Oxford is a registered trademark of Oxford University Press

Library of Congress Cataloging-in-Publication Data
Occom, Samson, 1723–1792
The collected writings of Samson Occom, Mohegan /
edited by Joanna Brooks.
p.   cm.
ISBN-13 978-0-19-517083-2

1. Occom, Samson, 1723–1792—Diaries. 2. Occom, Samson,
1723–1792—Correspondence. 3. Mohegan Indians—Biography.
4. Indian civic leaders—New England—Biography. 5. Indian
religious leaders—New England—Biography. 6. Preaching—Early
works to 1800. 7. Indians of North America—
Missions—New England. 8. Indians of North America—New
England—Religion. I. Brooks, Joanna, 1971– II. Title.
E99.M83023 2006
974.004'973092—dc22
[B]   2006000068

Printed in the United States of America
on acid-free paper

FOREWORD

Robert Warrior

Samson Occom, best known for being the protégé of Dartmouth College founder Eleazar Wheelock and for being the author of a short autobiography that has become standard fare in many Native American and American literature classrooms, is finally getting his full due as a writer, leader, and historical figure, thanks in no small part to the painstaking efforts of Joanna Brooks in bringing this volume to light. Native American studies scholars, Americanists in literary and historical studies, scholars of religion and missions, and many others who encounter Occom's work in these pages stand to gain new, robust insight into heretofore opaque instances of eighteenth-century Native American agency, intellectual production, and writerliness. Because of Occom's significance and the completeness of Brooks's work, this volume and the history it documents seem destined to be important scholarly landmarks.

Occom's 1768 autobiography, which has been so crucial to his recovery, is also a deceptive marker of who Occom was and what he believed. Students in my own classes usually appreciate the critical edge Occom brings to the antiracist conclusion of the autobiography, which you can read in the prose section of this volume, but they also are typically put off by his diffidence, disappointed in both his Christian piety and his concomitant lack of a traditional Mohegan spirituality, and befuddled by his eighteenth-century rhetorical conventions. Some undergraduates in my classes—this is especially true of my Native students—never see past Occom's repeated referral to himself as a heathen and think of him as a dupe of his Christian handlers.

Occom's best-selling 1772 *Sermon on the Execution of Moses Paul* has become more widely known in recent years and presents a different angle on Occom, one that highlight's Occom's incisiveness as a social critic of the systemic problems Native people in his era faced. Still, the sermon's strong strains of moralism and triumphant Christianity can buttress, rather than challenge, a view of Occom as a cold-souled Calvinist who seemed never to miss an opportunity to scold sinners, warn of the dangers of unbelief, and at least flirt with capitulation to the structures and ideologies that were spelling ruin for Native American communities in his time.

The sermons, letters, political documents, hymns, and other writings Brooks has collected here under one cover, however, provide ample proof that Samson Occom was a much more complex figure than most readers of only the short narrative and the Moses Paul sermon have perceived. While his piety and commitment to proselytizing other Indians remain a consistent theme through most of these writings,

Occom also appears as a trusted political leader of tribal communities and a fierce advocate for amelioration of injustices among the Mohegans and others. He also comes across as a beloved spiritual leader among an extensive intertribal community of Native people. More, he was a person held in high regard in his time, with friends and associates in the upper economic strata in New England and Great Britain.

Brooks presents these writings by type, each of which presents a different perspective on Occom. The letters reveal him as a man deeply concerned with his family, faithful to his circle of devout Calvinists on both sides of the Atlantic, and capable (though probably not as often as many might wish) of indignation when mistreated or taken advantage of. His occasional prose includes material that shows his respect for and commitment to traditional forms of indigenous knowledge. The journals, though primarily concerned with documenting the movements and activities of Occom's travels, are remarkable for the record they provide of the daunting challenges of getting around New England, Great Britian, and Iroquoia in that era— usually on a shoestring. The surviving sermons, which are a tiny fraction of the thousands Occom appears to have preached, show the straightforward missionary Christian theology he professed. The petitions and other political documents Occom wrote for the Mohegans and others are vistas into the political mind of indigenous people encountering the available, quite narrow routes of redress in eighteenth-century New England. The hymns, along with documenting the importance of hymn singing in the development of eighteenth-century indigenous missions, also show Occom's musical talent and round out a portrait of Occom in his fullness and complexity. All the documents reveal the depth with which Occom and other New England Native people were marked not just by race and growing marginalization but also by chronic, deep poverty.

In her introduction, Brooks details the many facets of Occom's life and places him in the context of his times in New England. Here, I will make three observations about how these writings point us toward a new, deeper understanding of Occom's importance to New England Native history and the ongoing history of written Native intellectual work.

First, Occom comes across in these writings as a traveler, of his Native world, of the circuit of his faith, and to points across the Atlantic. His world was one in which travel was prohibitive in many ways, and most people in New England never made it very far from the places they were born. Even immigrants to the colonies most likely stayed put once they arrived. Occom, then, with his movements from place to place, including his eighteen-month sojourn in England and Scotland to raise money for Eleazar Wheelock's college, was likely one of the most well-traveled people in whatever company he was in.

Though he does not write about them except in a general way, his encounters in England and Scotland exposed him to a full range of clergy and other elite people there. Staying in their homes, dining at their tables, and soliciting their funds for Wheelock's college must have taught him an immense amount about human nature, much of it apparently not that pleasant to him. Still, the metropolitan perspective he must have gained on the British outpost in which he had spent his life must have impacted how he considered the world of New England.

I would be surprised if the high and mighty of white society back home in the colonies—including Wheelock, who was already taking his college in a direction away from its commitment to Native education by the time Occom got back—did not seem at times unsophisticated to the sojourner, which is perhaps behind Occom's newfound critical boldness upon his return to New England. I would venture to say that the wisdom of his later years came at least in part from the opportunity his travels gave him to see the world in its interconnected largeness.

The second observation I want to make has to do with a perception I have that Occom's writing brightens when he spends time in Native communities or when he travels with David Fowler and other Christian Indian leaders. Occom provides glimpses of the sense of camaraderie Occom and this nascent Native Christian leadership shared. Their lives featured a noticeable lack of many material things, but between the lines one can see that one thing they did have was each other. Occom, Fowler, and the other Native Christians who founded the historic Brotherton settlement in the latter part of the eighteenth century did so for political, economic, and religious reasons. But surely they also did it because of their affection for each other and the joy they shared in simply being together, which is reflected in these writings.

One reason that recent readings of Occom have been so impoverished, I would offer, is that he has been considered as a lone figure rather than as someone standing for and standing amid an extensive social network. Certainly, he must have spent long seasons confronting isolation and loneliness. But he also participated in generational, communal struggles for justice and one intertribal movement in the founding of Brotherton, which predictably created a deep sense of collective action, work, and togetherness. The best readings of Occom's work, including those by Jace Weaver, Lisa Brooks, and Sean Teuton, find these threads. The documents collected here should make Occom's life of shared struggle available to even more scholars and students.

The last observation I offer regarding Occom and what we learn from him in these documents has to do with what I call a fundamental orientation to the future that he evinces throughout his writings. Amid chronic poverty and impossible political odds, Occom and those he worked alongside must have maintained an amazingly tight focus on how their communities and their progeny might continue. Far from being focused either on otherworldly rewards or a pathway into the trappings of life in white society, Occom works consistently and tirelessly to advance the claims of his own tribal nation and others, create institutions through which the next generation of Native leadership could emerge, and heal the damage caused by generations of oppression.

Leadership, as these writings attest, is hard, but the future is one of the things that seems to keep people like Occom going. Being a leader requires long hours, attention to the needs of others when one might want more to attend to the needs of oneself or one's family. Occom makes personal sacrifices again and again as he wends his way through New England to visit communities, represent tribal interests, or keep track of the efforts with which he associated himself. He lived to see few of the lasting results of his decades of work, but the Mohegans are now one of the most culturally and politically intact groups of Natives in New England, and Dartmouth, two centuries after Wheelock's betrayal of Occom and subsequent neglect of the education of Native students, has established itself as an important center for Native American higher education. The future, it turns out, was worth the trouble.

For everything positive these writings reveal, however, it is also clear that Occom was far from perfect. In spite of the complexity that emerges in these writings, he remains liable to the criticism that his commitment to Christianity made him vulnerable to a triumphalist Christian interpretation of New England history. It certainly committed him to a deeply patriarchal institution that excluded the overt leadership of women, including his sister, Lucy Occom Tantaquidgeon.

Though quite vocal in his opposition to slavery, he also worked actively against the inclusion of Afro-Mohegans in the political and social world of his tribal nation. That same tribal nation was born, I think it is important to add, in the divide-and-conquer crucible of Puritan colonialism, and the Mohegans participated with their colonizers in the decimation of those from whom they divided, the Pequots, during the massacre at Mystic in 1637 and the subsequent Pequot War. While Occom himself was not responsible for the divide or for Mohegan cooperation with the British in the destruction of their Pequot relatives, the conditions under which Occom and other Mohegan leaders worked in the eighteenth century were in many ways defined in that earlier era; the pragmatism that helped guarantee their survival and eventual resurgence, then, was not without problems.

Fortunately for all of us, success in intellectual work does not require perfection, and judging historical figures like Occom need not mean he should be defined by his failings, even if it is worth keeping in mind the ways Occom limited himself through his own blindness to injustice. Foibles and all, Occom's contribution to the history of Native New England and to Native intellectual history and writing remain.

Encountering this world-traveling Native intellectual who found joy and hope for the future in working alongside other Natives is a rare treat for me as a historian of Native writing and intellectualism. It cements Occom's place of importance in that history. His affection for and correspondence with Phillis Wheatley, referred to herein, is a stunning reminder that Native American written intellectual work has contemporaneous roots with a comparable African-American history. Further, Occom paves the way for the more interpretive, but less documented, work and life of William Apess in the 1820s and 1830s. He prefigures the travels abroad (especially to England, but to other places, as well) of George Copway, John Joseph Mathews, D'Arcy McNickle, Gerald Vizenor, and others. His love of community and the future will later be seen in the lives and works of the best and brightest lights in Native intellectual history, including Gertrude Simmons Bonnin (Zitkala-Sa), Ruth Muskrat Bronson, Clyde Warrior, Joy Harjo, Simon Ortiz, and others.

The publication of this volume, then, including the tremendous work Joanna Brooks has done in making it happen, is a wonderful thing. It is a testament of hope, and a witness to why the unfolding of Native intellectual history is so important and interesting to chart. Across more than two centuries, Samson Occom demonstrates once and for all his courage, tenacity, and intelligence in having left behind this trail that we can now follow. The rest is up to us.

Acknowledgments

Financial support from the National Endowment for the Humanities, the American Philosophical Society's Phillips Native American Research Fund, and the University of Texas at Austin sustained my work on this edition of the writings of Samson Occom. I am also grateful for the generosity of Dartmouth College, the Connecticut Historical Society, the New London County Historical Society, the Beinecke Library at Yale University, the University of Georgia, the Newberry Library, the Huntington Library, the Mashantucket Pequot Research Center, and the Library of Congress in permitting manuscripts from their collections to be reprinted. At Dartmouth College, Phillip Cronenwett, former manuscripts curator, provided crucial support at an early phase of the project, as did Connecticut Historical Society Library director Nancy Milnor. Sarah Hartwell, Barbara Krieger, and other staff members made my time at the Dartmouth Rauner Special Collections Library both productive and pleasant. Marci Vail at the Long Island Collection of the East Hampton Library also assisted my research.

I would like to express my gratitude to leaders and members of the Mohegan and Brotherton tribes who have graciously fielded my inquiries and encouraged my research. Mohegan historian Melissa Tantaquidgeon Zobel generously made copies of my transcripts of the Occom archive available to the Tribal Council, Historical Preservation Department, Tribal Publications Department, Chief of Staff's Office, and Education Department, helping me carry out my responsibilities to return this body of knowledge to its communities of origin. I appreciate also warm and helpful responses to my work from tribal archivist Faith Davison and Council of Elders vice-chairman Joseph Gray. Tribal linguist Stephanie Fielding has been exceptionally generous in providing translations of Mohegan-Pequot-Montauk words appearing in Occom's writings. I thank her for her spirited feedback and insights. Special acknowledgment is also due to Will Ottery, Jim Ottery, and June Ezold, all descendents of Samson Occom. Will Ottery and the late Rudi Ottery especially deserve recognition for their groundbreaking genealogical research in Native New England, which appears in *A Man Called Samson*. Will Ottery was kind enough to send me a copy of the book and to discuss Samson Occom with me by phone.

Emily Baker served as my editorial assistant throughout the crucial middle phases of this project. This edition owes much to her superbly meticulous work. I am grateful to her for keeping the project afloat during a very eventful year.

Robert Warrior provided guidance and encouragement at an early stage of the project and contributed the gracious foreword to this volume. LaVonne Ruoff has also been an example and an inspiration to me. Paula Gunn Allen and Greg Sarris were my first teachers in American Indian literature at UCLA. Bernd Peyer, Laura Murray, and Hilary Wyss also deserve my thanks for their own groundbreaking work on Occom, Joseph Johnson, and Native New England. The visionary scholarship of Lisa Brooks has influenced tremendously my own thoughts on Occom. I thank her as well for being a friendly and receptive correspondent during this project.

Friends and comrades in the fields of early American studies and early Native American studies especially have offered sustaining encouragement during what has felt at times like a monumental undertaking. Hilary Wyss and Kristina Bross especially deserve my gratitude for their always seasonable advice and feedback. I would also like to acknowledge the friendship and collegiality of Bryan Waterman, Eric Slauter, Scotti Parrish, Elizabeth Dillon, Eric Wertheimer, Stephanie Fitzgerald, Meredith Neuman, Lisa Gordis, Betty Donahue, Phil Round, Christopher Looby, Lisa Logan, Denise Askin, and April Langley.

My graduate students at the University of Texas served as my ideal test audience for this volume: Jodi Relyea, Sylvia Gale, Emily Baker, Caroline Wiggington, Amanda Moulder, Katy Young, Anthony Fassi, Noah Mass, Heidi Juel, and Jeremy Dean. Their enthusiastic responses to Occom and his writings renewed my courage in the final stages of the project.

In preparing Occom's mountain of manuscripts for publication, I have incurred many debts to family, friends, and coworkers. Caroline Herring, a true friend, trekked to the Library of Congress during an especially rainy winter to check my transcript of an Occom manuscript. Blanca Madriz provided crucial physical support in the nick of time in copying and mailing this massive manuscript.

Colleagues and friends at the University of Texas have sustained me, my family, and my work during a very eventful two years. It was Michael Winship who first encouraged me to undertake this project. Lisa Moore, Madge Darlington, Jim Lee, Julie Cho, Ann Cvetkovich, Neville Hoad, James Cox, Domino Perez, Shirley Thompson, Steve Marshall, and Jennifer Wilks helped keep love alive in so many ways—with home cooking, humor, collective childcare, spiritual wisdom, scholarly acumen, insight, humor, style, grace, sarcasm, honesty, loyalty, and perspective.

As always, I owe Michele Brooks thanks for her expert genealogical research assistance, as well as for teaching me to love and listen to the past.

I began work on this project about the same time that Ella America Brooks-Kamper was conceived, and I concluded just weeks before the anticipated arrival of Rosa Lucille Brooks-Kamper. Ella, as a spirited, loving, resilient, hilarious two-year-old, it appears that your in utero exposure to so much eighteenth-century manuscript did you no harm. May the same be true for our beautiful Rosa. My husband, David Kamper, has traveled, shared, talked, thought, and (best of all) laughed with me every step of the way during these wild couple of years. David, you make everything possible for me.

Contents

Petitions and Tribal Documents

Sermons

A Note on the Texts

This collection brings together for the first time the known published works and surviving manuscripts of the eighteenth-century Mohegan writer Samson Occom. The Occom archive comprises in total more than 1,000 holograph manuscript pages of letters, diaries, sermons, hymns, petitions, and other prose writings. Dartmouth College and the Connecticut Historical Society hold the largest collections of Occom manuscripts, while smaller collections and individual documents can also be found at the New London County Historical Society, the Library of Congress, the Mashantucket Pequot Museum and Research Center, the Newberry Library, and the University of Georgia. At Dartmouth College, Occom's diaries, sermons, and prose writings are housed in a special vault collection in the Rauner Special Collections Library, while his letters are catalogued among the Eleazar Wheelock Papers, which were collated under the direction of librarian Edward Connery Lathem in the 1970s. A typescript of Occom's diaries was prepared and donated to Dartmouth College in 1974 by the Dartmouth College Class of 1911. Microfilm editions of the Dartmouth College Eleazar Wheelock Papers and the Connecticut Historical Society Samson Occom Papers are also available.

Aside from those letters received and preserved by recipients such as Eleazar Wheelock, it is unclear how most of Occom's writings survived and came into the possession of these libraries. Some sources suggest that Occom's son-in-law Anthony Paul inherited the books and papers Occom kept at his New York home; it is possible that Benoni Occom inherited the books and papers his father left behind in Mohegan. A writing desk from the Occom home at Mohegan is said to have come into the possession of the Connecticut Historical Society. Perhaps this desk also contained some of Occom's papers. Neither the Connecticut Historical Society nor Dartmouth has records of how they came into the possession of large bodies of Occom's manuscripts.

I have designed this collection mindful of the needs and concerns of scholars and students in the fields of literature, history, American studies, and Native American studies. My goal has been to make available as much of the Occom archive as possible in an accessible, reliable scholarly edition. This process has necessarily entailed many decisions about text selection and presentation.

This edition has been prepared in accordance with the guidelines of the Modern Language Association Committee on Scholarly Editions. It offers letter-faithful transcriptions of Occom's manuscripts and transcribed reprints of his published writings. All transcriptions have been checked for accuracy against imprint and manuscript originals. Occom's original capitalization, spelling, grammar, and punctuation have been retained, except for instances in his published writings that I have judged to be the result of printers' errors, which have been silently corrected.

In developing a system of annotation, my goal has been to supply contextual information to support the interpretation and comprehension of Occom's writings in a way that does not overwhelm the primary texts themselves. Available biographical information for named individuals appears in the glossary of names at the end of the volume rather than in the footnotes.

The Collected Writings of Samson Occom, Mohegan presents diaries compiled by Occom over the course of more than fifty years. Manuscript evidence suggests that Occom composed installments in his diaries from brief daily notes of his itineraries and transactions. Dartmouth College holds one notebook of these daily notes for the dates December 16–18, 1787, February 24–April 6, 1788, and January 1–February 22, 1788. Because these notes do not differ substantially from the diaries, I have not reproduced them here. I have also chosen not to reprint an account book documenting Occom's income and expenses in Montauk in 1761.

This collection features twenty integral sermons by Samson Occom. The Dartmouth Occom Vault collection also contains four undated sermon fragments by Occom that I have not included here, as well as six sermons and sermon fragments that I have determined (primarily on the basis of orthography) were not written by Occom and consequently have not included in this collection:

- "Sermon No. 13" on 2 Corinthians 13:2; dated "Middlef^d Jan. 3. 1762," "Sharon M. J 1762," "Haveshill [17]64," "Gorham July 17. L.D. 1766 with variations and additions."
- "No. 25" on Romans 7:12, dated "Attleboro 26th Sept 1762," "Newbury 4 Octr L. D. 1762," "Geo. Town 30 Octr 1763."
- "Sermon no. 57" on Psalms 11:7, dated "9 July 18, 1762."
- Sermon fragment, opening phrase "of Life; & to complete the System of destruction," undated but probably composed after 1783.
- Sermon fragment, opening phrase "III. To shew why ye Serv^{ts} of ye L. J. C do earnestly desire," undated.
- Sermon fragment, opening phrase "versal whether it extends to all the command of God holy law," undated.

Samson Occom has been credited with the authorship of dozens of hymns. I have been able to verify his composition of only the six hymn-texts reprinted here. Modern bibliographers have sometimes attributed to Occom "The Unknown World," which appears in *A Choice Collection of Hymns and Sacred Songs* (1774), but this poem was in fact written by Laurence Sterne. "A Sailor's Acknowledgement," which appears with "The Unknown World" in *A Remarkable Prophecy* (Boston, 1798), has also been credited to Occom, but there is no evidence to support this conjecture. Consequently, neither "The Unknown World" nor "A Sailor's Acknowledgment" appears in this volume.

Some manuscripts in the Dartmouth Occom Vault Collection—a few diaries as well as the 1768 manuscript autobiography—were emended by William Allen when he compiled his unpublished biography of Occom in 1859. Allen attempted to modernize and regularize Occom's spelling, punctuation, and grammar, marking his corrections on the originals in black ink; he also underlined in black ink the names and places of persons in the diaries. My transcriptions of Occom's diaries and his 1768 autobiography represent my best efforts to reconstruct the original holograph manuscript text. The edition of the 1768 autobiography transcribed and published by Bernd Peyer in 1982 and now widely anthologized includes many of Allen's emendations; Peyer also omitted passages lined out by Occom. I have excluded Allen's emendations and restored Occom's lined-out passages in strikethrough type.

This edition was prepared in accordance with the following rules of transcription, formatting, and emendation:

- Interlineations have been inserted into the text and marked between two carets, except for interlineations resulting from line breaks, which have been silently inserted into the text.
- Original paragraphing has been retained, although the format has been standardized to the modern indent.
- Original capitalization has been retained, even though it has sometimes been difficult to accurately distinguish upper-case and lower-case, especially for the letters "w," "v," and "g."
- Original abbreviations and contractions have been retained.
- Original underlines have been retained and are represented here in italics.
- Long dashes as punctuation have been retained.
- Cancelled passages have been retained in strikethrough type.
- Superscript letters have been retained in superscript type.
- Terminal punctuation has been supplied in brackets where necessary to aid comprehension.
- Where conjectural interpolation is possible, illegible words and letters or words and letters missing due to manuscript damage have been supplied in brackets followed by question marks. Where conjecture is not reasonably certain, damaged or illegible words and letters are represented by bracketed ellipses: "[. . .]".
- Words intentionally omitted or left blank in the original manuscript are represented by empty brackets: "[ ]".
- For letters, the placement of datelines, salutations, and closings has been standardized. Missing date and place information have been supplied, if possible, in brackets. Conjectural place and date information has been marked with question marks.
- For letters, text appearing in the margins or on envelopes has been transcribed after the document in a note.
- Marginalia appearing on the covers of journals has not been transcribed.

In preparing this edition, I have tried to be mindful of my responsibilities to acknowledge and work respectfully with the tribal communities represented in this body of writing, especially the Mohegan and Brotherton tribes. I have given complete transcripts of Occom's writings to Mohegan tribal historian Melissa Fawcett

Tantaquidgeon, archivist Faith Davison, and linguist Stephanie Fielding. Tantaquidgeon graciously made these transcripts available to the Mohegan Tribal Council of Elders, Tribal Council, Education Department, Tribal Publications Department,
and Historical Preservation Department; through her, I invited feedback and advice
from tribal members as I prepared the scholarly apparatus for the volume. I have also
sent complete transcripts of Occom's writings to Brotherton tribal chair Theodore
Stephenson, former Brotherton tribal chair and Occom descendant June Ezold, and
Occom descendents Will Ottery and Jim Ottery. Copies of this volume will be donated to the Mohegan and Brotherton tribes. I would like to acknowledge the often
unrecognized efforts of generations of American Indian writers, historians, and ge-
nealogists in compiling and preserving tribal histories. It is my hope that this collection can serve to bring Occom's literary legacy home from the archives to its tribal
communities and thus in a small way contribute to the important work of intellectual and cultural repatriation now taking place in tribal communities across North
America.

CHRONOLOGY

1723   Samson Occom born to Sarah and Joshua Occom (or Ockham) at Mohegan.

1739   The Great Awakening comes to Mohegan territory.

1741   New Light itinerant James Davenport visits Norwich, Connecticut, in August; Occom hears him preach and experiences spiritual stirrings.

1742   Occom selected as a councilor to Mohegan sachem Ben Uncas II.

1743   Joshua Occom dies. Samson Occom attends hearings of the Mason-Mohegan land case in Norwich. On December 6, he travels to the home of Eleazar Wheelock in Lebanon Crank, Connecticut, where he begins a college-preparatory course of study. During his four years with Wheelock, Occom visits and facilitates worship meetings in neighboring Native communities.

1747   Occom terminates his studies with Wheelock in November; during the winter, he keeps school at New London, Connecticut.

1748   Preparing for enrollment at Yale, Occom studies Latin, Greek, and Hebrew with Benjamin Pomeroy at Hebron, Connecticut, during the spring and summer. In November and December, he visits Boston and Natick, Massachusetts, where he lodges with Native elder Joseph Ephraim.

1749   Occom embarks on a summer fishing expedition to Montauk, Long Island. Officially released from his studies on account of debilitating eyestrain, in November, Occom establishes a school for thirty students at Montauk.

1751   Occom marries Mary Fowler (Montaukett) in the fall, and the couple establishes their home among the Montaukett people.

1752   First child, Mary, born to Samson and Mary Occom.

1753   Second child, Aaron, born.

1754   Third child, Tabitha, born. Samson Occom undertakes a course of study in traditional herbal medicine from Ocus (Montaukett).

1755   Fourth child, Olive, born. With the encouragement of Aaron Burr and the New York Commissioners of the Scotch Society for Propagating Christian Knowledge, Occom attempts a visit to the Lenape and the Iroquois. His visit is interrupted by the onset of the Seven Years' War.

1756   Samuel Buell and Eleazar Wheelock seek financial relief for Occom, who has struggled to meet the needs of his growing family and fallen into debt due to poor pay and unfair treatment from his missionary sponsors. In November, the Boston Board of Commissioners of the London Society for Propagating the Gospel recommends Occom's ordination.

1757   Fifth child, Christiana, born. Occom examined for ordination on July 13 at Lebanon, Connecticut, by Benjamin Pomeroy, Nathan Strong, Stephen White, Samuel Moseley, and Eleazar Wheelock.

1758   Presbyterian minister Samuel Davies of Virginia recruits Occom for a mission among the Cherokee. Occom's ordination referred to the Long Island Presbytery.

1759   Occom examined and ordained by the Suffolk, Long Island, Presbytery on August 29 and 30. Samuel Buell delivers the ordination sermon.

1760   Samson and Mary Fowler Occom take their oldest son, Aaron, to Moor's Indian Charity School in April. Occom and David Fowler visit New England Native communities during the fall. In November, Occom is recruited by the New York Commissioners of the Scotch Society for Propagating Christian Knowledge to undertake a mission among the Oneida.

1761   Occom and David Fowler leave Montauk in May. In June, they arrive at Oneida, bearing the recommendation of Sir William Johnson. Occom spends nine weeks preaching and establishing a school; he also recruits three Mohawk young men—Center, Ngeyes, and Joseph Brant—to attend Moor's Indian Charity School. At a farewell ceremony on September 18, Occom receives a wampum belt from the Oneida. He baptizes three Oneida converts and preaches a farewell sermon on September 20. Occom arrives home at Montauk on October 22. Sixth child, Talitha, born.

1762   In May, Occom returns to Oneida, where he finds the people in desperate economic circumstances due to war and an early frost the previous growing season. He returns to Montauk in the fall.

1763   Seventh child, Benoni, born. In May, Occom embarks on his third Oneida mission, but he and fellow Mohegan minister Samuel Ashpo are forced to return from New York by the outbreak of Pontiac's War. Occom travels to Mohegan in December to select a homesite.

1764   Occom accompanies George Whitefield on a preaching tour of New England until February. The Boston Board of Commissioners subsequently appoints him as a missionary among the Niantic and Mohegan. In March, Occom, his wife, and seven young children move their household across the Long Island Sound from Montauk to Mohegan, losing some of their possessions in the crossing. Political trouble erupts at Mohegan in April and May, when Ben Uncas III leases out tribal lands without the consent of his councilors. Occom takes part in an effort to reconstitute the tribal government. His preaching at Mohegan draws parishioners away from the white minister David Jewett, who criticizes Occom for his political activities. In August, Wheelock obtains a commission from the Connecticut Board of Correspondents ordering Occom to undertake another mission among the Iroquois, but the mission fails due to lack of funding.

1765   On March 12, Occom is brought before the Connecticut Board of Correspondents on charges of misconduct and heresy for his involvement in Mohegan political affairs, especially the Mohegan-Mason land case. Occom apologizes under pressure from Wheelock and is exonerated. After spending the summer among the Iroquois, Occom leaves Mohegan in November for a two-and-a-half-year fund-raising mission for Moor's Indian Charity School. Occom and white minister Nathaniel Whitaker embark from Boston harbor for London on December 23, amid controversy about the fund-raising effort and Occom's identity as a Mohegan convert.

1766   Occom and Whitaker land at Bricksham, England, on February 3; on February 16, Occom preaches his first sermon in England at George Whitefield's Tabernacle in London. During his tour of England, Occom is introduced to nobles and prominent religious figures, attends King George II in his robing room at the Parliament House, visits the Tower of London and Westminster Abbey, and is invited to take Anglican orders. In November, back at Mohegan, Mary Occom sends her son Aaron to Moor's Indian Charity School.

1767   Occom and Whitaker tour Scotland in the spring. On May 16 at Edinburgh, Occom displays the wampum belt and recites the speech given him by the Oneida; he is offered an honorary doctorate in divinity by the University of Edinburgh. Occom and Whitaker visit Ireland in July.

1768   While Whitaker sails for home on March 2, Occom remains in England to testify in another hearing of the Mohegan-Mason land case. He arrives home at Mohegan by early June to find his family in financial straits. That summer, Occom receives a number of visitors, including a delegation of Oneida, and renews his ties to neighboring Native communities in southern New England. In September, Occom composes a second draft of his autobiography.

1769   Eighth child, Theodosia, born. Suffering from poor health and a debilitating shoulder injury, Occom is unable to travel. In January, he confesses being "shamefully over taken With Strong Drink" to the Connecticut Correspondents. Controversial Mohegan sachem Ben Uncas III dies in May. Occom and others protest at the funeral, and the tribe refuses to name a new sachem. In November, the Long Island Presbytery acquits Occom of public drunkenness.

1770   Eleazar Wheelock relocates Moor's Indian Charity School to Hanover, New Hampshire.

1771   Ninth child, Lemuel Fowler, born. Aaron Occom dies at Mohegan in February. Wheelock writes Occom to accuse him of repeated bouts of intemperance; Occom accuses Wheelock of betraying the Native educational mission of Moor's Indian Charity School and breaks ties with him in July.

1772   Occom declines invitations to accompany white missionaries among the Lenape, choosing instead to remain home, recover his health, and attend to the needs of his own family. Occom renews his connections with John Thornton and other sympathetic English trustees of the former Moor's Indian Charity School, who offer him moral and financial support. On September 2 at New Haven, Occom delivers an execution sermon on behalf of Moses Paul, a Wampanoag man convicted on murder charges. The first edition of Occom's *Sermon, Preached at the Execution of Moses Paul* is published on October 31; three additional editions (one in broadside) appear by the end of the year.

1773   As demand for his execution sermon continues to grow, Occom attains public celebrity among Native and white people. He receives numerous invitations to preach and enjoys improved health. On March 13 at Mohegan, Occom attends the initial organizational meeting of the Brotherton movement, including members of the Mohegan, Pequot, Niantic, Montuakett, Farmington, and Narragansett communities. He preaches in southern New England Indian towns throughout the summer. Joseph Johnson (Mohegan), the leader of the Brotherton movement, marries Tabitha Occom in December.

1774   Tenth child, Andrew Gifford, born. Joseph Johnson completes land negotiations with the Oneida on behalf of the Brotherton effort, as enthusiasm for the movement continues to grow among Native peoples in southern New England. Occom publishes his *Collection of Hymns and Spiritual Songs* on April 6. In July, he and David Fowler set out for Oneida territory to survey the newly granted Brotherton lands.

1775   In January and February, Occom preaches in Connecticut and southeastern New York. The first wave of emigrants leaves for Brotherton in April. Olive Occom marries Solomon Adams on April 13. Emigration to Brotherton is interrupted by the onset of the American War of Independence.

1777   During wartime, Occom preaches itinerantly in Rhode Island, Connecticut, and Massachusetts.

1780   Occom suffers a crippling hip injury when he slips on the ice in February. His resulting lameness and wartime hardships place Occom's family once again in difficult economic straits.

1784   Emigration to Brotherton resumes at the end of the war. Occom accompanies a party of migrants including the families of his brother-in-law Jacob Fowler and his daughter Christiana Occom Paul to Brotherton in May. He returns to Mohegan in early June.

1785   Occom preaches among southern New England Indian towns during a summer revival season. He departs Mohegan for New York on September 22 and arrives at Brotherton on October 24. On November 7 and 8, he participates in the formal political organization of Brotherton.

1786   Occom arrives back at Mohegan in February. After spending the spring and early summer at home, he returns to Oneida territory in July. He ministers and counsels the people of Brotherton and New Stockbridge for the next five months, as emigration from New England continues. On October 16–18, Occom participates in discussions with Oneida leaders about the status of the Brotherton land grant. He departs for Mohegan on November 9.

1787   Occom reaches Mohegan on January 4. He spends the winter and spring visiting local Native communities and attending to tribal business. In April, he travels to Long Island to attend a meeting of the Long Island Presbytery and to visit with the Montaukett and Shinnecock tribes. He embarks again for Oneida in May, arriving in early July. Brotherton and New Stockbridge residents clear a homesite for Occom. On August 27, New Stockbridgers issue a written invitation to Occom to live among them as their minister; controversy consequently ensues when John Sergeant, Jr., arrives in September from Stockbridge, Massachusetts, to resume his ministry among the Mahican.

Occom leaves Brotherton on November 13, traveling southward through New York and New Jersey.

1788 Occom visits Princeton College and Lenape communities in New Jersey on his way to Philadelphia, where he joins Peter Poquunnuppeet and David Fowler on a tour to raise funds for churches and schools at Brotherton and New Stockbridge. He returns home to Mohegan in late March. Occom sets out once again for Oneida territory on May 26, arriving in July. In September, the Oneida sign the Treaty of Fort Schuyler, which results in the loss of millions of acres to the state of New York but reserves small tracts for the New Stockbridge and Brotherton communities.

1789 In February, the New York Assembly passes "An Act for the Sale and Disposition of Lands," which confirms and orders an official survey of the Brotherton reservation and places some restrictions on white leasing of Brotherton lands. In May, Samson and Mary Fowler Occom move their household from Mohegan to Brotherton. Occom visits Mohegan in October and November.

1790 Occom's son Lemuel Fowler dies at Mohegan by drowning. Controversy at Brotherton intensifies over the disposition of tribal lands. Occom fiercely opposes the leasing of tribal lands to whites; he is criticized and ridiculed at Brotherton town meetings by counterfactional leader Elijah Wampy (or Wympy).

1791 Despairing the loss of about 2,000 acres of Brotherton lands, including common groves and cedar swamps, in January, Occom petitions the New York Assembly to revoke altogether the authority of Brotherton residents to lease lands to whites. On February 21, the Assembly passes "An Act for the Relief of the Indians Residing in Brothertown and New Stockbridge," vesting powers to lease lots in an elected tribal council. Occom moves his family to New Stockbridge in December.

1792 On April 12, the New York Assembly authorizes a May date for the ejection of whites from illegitimately leased Brotherton lands. Samson Occom dies at New Stockbridge on July 14. Three hundred Native people attend his funeral on July 15.

ABBREVIATIONS

CC	Samson Occom, *A Choice Collection of Hymns and Spiritual Songs*, New London, Connecticut: Timothy Green, 1774
CHS	Samson Occom Papers, Connecticut Historical Society, Hartford, Connecticut
CHS-M	Samson Occom Papers microfilm reel, Connecticut Historical Society, Hartford, Connecticut
DCA	Dartmouth College Archives, Dartmouth College, Hanover, New Hampshire
DHSS	*Divine Hymns, or Spiritual Songs, for the use of religious assemblies and private Christians: being a collection by Joshua Smith, Samson Ockum and others.* Troy, New York: Moffit & Lyon, 1803
HM	Huntington Manuscript, Huntington Library, San Marino, California
LOC	Library of Congress, Washington, D.C.
MPMRC	Mashantucket Pequot Museum and Research Center, Mashantucket, Connecticut
Newberry	Newberry Library, Chicago, Illinois
NLCHS	New London County Historical Society, New London, Connecticut
Rauner	Rauner Special Collections, Dartmouth College, Hanover, New Hampshire
UG	University of Georgia, Hargrett Rare Book and Manuscript Library, Athens, Georgia
WJP	*Sir William Johnson Papers*, ed. Milton W. Hamilton, 14 volumes (Albany: The University of the State of New York, 1962)
WJM	Sir William Johnson Manuscripts, 26 volumes, New York State Library, Albany, New York

The Collected Writings of Samson Occom, Mohegan

"This Indian World"

An Introduction to the Writings of Samson Occom

For decades, the round box fashioned from the bark of an elm tree and entwined with elaborately carved vines, leaves, and dotted lines was catalogued among the holdings of the Peabody Essex Museum in Salem, Massachusetts, as a typical example of early Native New England handicraft. But emissaries of the Mohegan Nation who visited the museum in 1995 to survey its holdings for possible repatriation saw something more: an important document of a pivotal moment in their tribal history. They took photographs of the elm bark box back to Mohegan territory in Connecticut, to the home of tribal medicine woman Gladys Tantaquidgeon, then 96 years old. Tantaquidgeon recognized in its carved dots and lines traditional symbols of Mohegan migration, and she searched deep within the collective memory of the tribe to remember the particular migration story this box had been carved to record. It was fashioned in the 1780s or 1790s, she recalled, by Mohegan migrants to a new pantribal settlement at Brotherton, New York. The Mohegan minister Samson Occom sent the box from Brotherton back home to his sister Lucy Occom Tantaquidgeon at Mohegan, hoping that the carvings might communicate to Lucy and other Mohegans the fates and sentiments of the migrants who had set out for Oneida territory in the 1770s and 1780s to secure a future free from white encroachment. Samson Occom served as a spiritual and political leader of the pantribal Brotherton movement; he and his wife, Mary Fowler Occom, emigrated to New York in 1789. Lucy Occom Tantaquidgeon continued to live at Mohegan, occupying a key parcel of traditional territory and defending Mohegan political and cultural traditions as white encroachment continued into the nineteenth century.[1]

During his lifetime, Samson Occom (1723–1792) witnessed the colonial infiltration and disruption of traditional tribal sachemships and the erosion of tribal territories. With dedication and vision, in collaboration with members of tribal communities throughout New England and beyond, he worked to reestablish indigenous traditions of collective self-governance and to revive spirituality among aggrieved Native communities. Occom believed that English-language literacy and New Light

---

1. Tantaquidgeon Zobel, *Medicine*, 135–136. A note on terminology: here and throughout the introduction, I use the term "pantribal" to designate indigenous intellectual, cultural, and political forms that entail a blending of specific tribal features into new supratribal forms of "Indianness." I will use the term "intertribal" to describe new developments within tribal communities emerging from lateral interactions with other indigenous peoples.

Christianity could potentially serve to bolster Native peoples' political autonomy and spiritual well-being. Consequently, he sought out a college-preparatory education from the Congregational minister Eleazar Wheelock, recruited other Native students to attend Wheelock's Moor's Indian Charity School, and became a beloved preacher and spiritual leader among New England and Long Island Native communities. When Wheelock abandoned his commitment to Native education and reconstituted Moor's Indian Charity School as Dartmouth College in 1771, Occom broke ties with his former mentor and committed the last decades of his life to the Native-led Brotherton movement. Contemporary Mohegan and Brotherton tribes now remember Occom as an important ancestor, while literary scholars recognize him as a pioneering Native American writer and a progenitor of Native American literature.

Over the past century, scholarship on Samson Occom has emphasized his adoption of Euro-American cultural forms such as Christianity and written English, sometimes portraying him as a successful product of the English "civilizing" mission. The elm bark box he carved for his sister Lucy serves as a powerful reminder that the story of Samson Occom extends far beyond the familiar story of his relationships to Eleazar Wheelock, Moor's Indian Charity School, and other white colonial institutions. From his birth to a traditional Mohegan family, through his adult service as a tribal councillor, through the end of his life in the all-Native township at Brotherton, New York, Occom thought of himself first as a Mohegan with profound responsibilities to his own tribal community and to American Indian people in general. He was an herbal doctor, a hunter, a fisherman, a father, a husband, a tribal leader, and an intertribal political figure as well as an ordained Presbyterian minister, a schoolteacher, and an itinerant preacher. His efforts to maintain his relationship with his sister Lucy and other Mohegan who did not migrate to Brotherton demonstrate Occom's abiding commitment to Native kinship traditions and his continuing fluency in Native cultural forms. He could write a letter, preach a sermon, or tell a story by carving a box. After all, carving—like wampum, quillwork, and painting—was just another form of writing for Native peoples, and each form of writing had its own particular powers and nuances, its connections to complex matrices of feeling and tradition. Occom's elm bark box reminds us that English-language literacy did not cancel out other forms of Native writing. It emblematizes the fullness, the richness, and the complexity of the thought-worlds inhabited by Occom and other early American Indian writers and intellectuals.

The Collected Writings of Samson Occom, Mohegan offers an unprecedented view into Occom's cultural and intellectual universe from the perspective of his surviving literary archive. Over the course of almost five decades—from his first independent efforts to teach himself English in the 1730s to his death in July 1792—Samson Occom time and time again took up his quill pen and faced the page. He wrote under the careful eye of Eleazar Wheelock; in the wigwam that served as his home among the Long Island Montaukett; in the two-story wood-frame house he built for his large family at Mohegan, Connecticut; during preaching tours of Iroquoia, England, Scotland, and Ireland; in roadside taverns and private homes where he lodged during his frequent foot travels between New England and New York; and in the homes raised for him at Brotherton and New Stockbridge, New York, by fellow refugee Christian Indians. Despite difficult conditions familiar to itinerant preachers, as well as those specific to American Indians living in hostile economic and political circumstances, he steadily built an incomparable archive comprising about one thousand holograph manuscript pages of diaries, letters, sermons, autobiographies, ethnographies, and hymns. It is the largest extant body of writing produced by an American Indian author before Santee Sioux intellectual Charles Eastman (1858–1939) began his writing career in the early twentieth century.

The Occom archive includes six occasional prose pieces that provide striking glimpses into the lives and thoughts of colonial-era Northeastern Native peoples. Three of these were composed during the 1750s and 1760s, when Occom lived as a teacher and minister among the Montaukett people of Long Island. At Montauk, Occom transcribed the conversion experience of a young woman named Temperance Hannibal (Hannabal), compiled a manual of traditional herbal medicine, and produced an ethnography of Montaukett lifeways. During the late 1760s, Occom wrote two brief autobiographies to defend himself against charges of racial imposture and to demand compensation for his labors from sponsoring New England missionary societies: the more extensive "Short Narrative" (1768) has been widely anthologized as a representative work of early American Indian literature. Occom's prose writings also include a meditative essay reflecting on "The most remarkable and Strange State Situation and Appearence of Indian Tribes in this Great Continent" (1783). Wrote Occom:

> The Most Learned, Polite, and Rich Nations of the World, I find them to be the Most Tyranacal, Cruel, and inhuman oppressors of their Fellow Creatures in the World, these make all the confusions and distructions among the Nations of the Whole World, . . . Indians, So Called, in this most extensive Continent, are Universally Poor . . . Yet in general they kind to one another, and are not given to Lying, Cheating, and Steeling.

Seventy-six surviving letters written by Occom track his growth from his early tutelage under Eleazar Wheelock through his emergence as a public figure and an intertribal political and spiritual leader. These include letters to Native American family and friends, sponsoring missionary societies and religious bodies, prominent ministers such as Samuel Buell and Eleazar Wheelock, and other notable colonial and early national figures such as Susannah Wheatley, slave-mistress to the pioneering African-American poet Phillis Wheatley. (Phillis Wheatley and Samson Occom also corresponded directly with each other, as is evidenced in one surviving letter addressed from Wheatley to Occom on February 11, 1774, and subsequently published in colonial newspapers. In this letter, Wheatley thanks Occom for his letter "respecting the negroes" and his "vindication of their natural rights"; she also articulates her own powerful critique of slavery and the hypocrisy of the struggle for "liberty" from British "oppression" in light of American slaveholding. Unfortunately, Occom's side of this historic exchange between two early American intellectuals of color does not survive.) Letters written during Occom's English travels reveal the vulnerability, loneliness, isolation, and sadness he experienced when he was away from his family, tribal community, and homelands. After his return to

Mohegan, in 1771, Occom rejected Wheelock for abandoning his commitments to Native education and reconstituting Moor's Indian Charity School as Dartmouth College. He wrote:

> I am very Jealous that instead of your Semenary Becoming alma Mater, she will be too alba mater to Suckle the Tawnees, . . . I verily thought once that your In-stitution was Intended Purely for the poor Indians with this thought I Cheer-fully Ventur'd my Body & Soul, left my Country my poor young Family all my friends and Relations, to sail over the Boisterous Seas to England, to help for-ward your School, Hoping, that it may be a lasting Benefet to my poor Tawnee Brethren [. . .] I was quite Willing to become a Gazing Stock, Yea Even a Laugh-ing Stock, in Strange Countries to Promote your Cause—. . . I went, purely for the poor Indians, and I Should be as ready as ever to promote your School acording to my poor Abilities ^if^ I Coud be Convincd by ocular Demonstration, that your pure Intention is to help the poor helpless Indians, but as long as you have no Indians, I am full of Doubts,—. . . Many gentlemen in England and in this Coun-try too, Say if ^you^ had not this Indian Buck you woud not Collected a quarter of the Money you did—

Letters written in the final years of Occom's life document his continuing efforts to see to the survival of the Brotherton Indian community, as well as his deepening concern for the situation of American Indians in general. He wrote in 1788:

> I am Now fully Convinc'd, that the Indians must have Teach[ers] of their own Coular or Nation,— They have very great and reveted Prejudice against the White People, and they have too much good reason for it—. . . I think they are now in a Most Deplorable Condition and Situation, it Seems that Heaven and Earth, are in Combination against us, I am, Some Times, upon the Borders of Desperation and much Discouragd with my poor Brethren, I often groan, and Say with myself, before I am aware of it, O Strange, O Strange, Why are we thus—and my mind very ^is much^ overwhelmed at Times,—But When I Con-sider the Promises of God in his Book my Mind is little revivd again.

Thirteen petitions written in the hand of Samson Occom are also numbered among his collected writings. These include legal statements drafted by Occom with and on behalf of the Mohegan, Niantic, Mahican-Stockbridge,[2] Montaukett, Shin-

---

2. Although often confused with the Mohegan tribe of eastern Connecticut, the Mahican people constitute a separate and distinctive tribal nation with its own history, language, and traditions. The historical Mahican were Algonkian-descended peoples of western Massachusetts and east-ern New York; their traditional territory ranged from the Housatonic River in the east to the Hudson River Valley in the west. Some Mahicans formed a settlement at Stockbridge, Massa-chusetts, where they received Protestant missionaries; members of this community became known as Stockbridge Indians. Under pressure from white encroachment, many Stockbridgers removed to New Stockbridge, New York, in the 1770s and 1780s. In the 1820s and 1830s, New Stockbridgers moved west again to the traditional territory of the Munsee people in Shawano County, Wisconsin, and became known as Stockbridge-Munsee Indians. Today, this federally recognized tribal nation calls itself the Mohican tribe.

necock, and Brotherton tribes addressed to colonial overseers, state governments, and the United States Congress. Occom used his literacy and his position of authority as a public figure to interject the collective voice, perspective, and concerns of tribal communities into often unfair and imbalanced legal processes. Petitions drafted by Occom served as written vehicles for tribal oral histories recounting the colonization of the Americas from an authoritative Native perspective. In petitions representing the land concerns of the Montaukett and Brotherton tribes to the State of New York and the United States Congress, Occom described North America as "this Boundless continent" and "this Indian world," documenting an indigenous view of the political geography of the Americas.

Twenty surviving sermons written by Occom between 1759 and 1792 are also collected here. These include his landmark *Sermon at the Execution of Moses Paul* (1772), which appeared in nineteen editions during the eighteenth and nineteenth centuries and has been recovered to contemporary literary anthologies. Moses Paul (Wampanoag) recruited Occom specifically to publicize the racial injustice of his murder trial and subsequent execution, and record crowds attended Occom's sermon at New Haven on September 2, 1772. Notes and texts for an additional nineteen surviving sermons also appear in this collection. Sermons dating from the 1750s and 1760s show that early in his career Occom typically relied on a biblical text and a simple outline of numbered applications. In his later years, Occom developed a more elaborate style that allowed him to connect scripture to contemporary social and political contexts. For example, in 1787, Occom used Native communities as exemplars of the charitable love commanded in Luke 10:27, "Thou shalt love thy neighbor as thyself":

> The Savage Indians, as they are so calld, are very kind to one another, and they are kind to Strangers;—But I find amongst those who are Calld Christians, Void of Natural affection, according to their Conduct in the World,—and what Shall we say of you or think of you, or what do you think of yourselves; You that are Slavekeepers, do you Love God, and do you Love your Neighbour, your Neighbour Negroe as Yourself, are you willing to be Slaves yourselves, and your Children to be Slaves too . . . I must Conclude, that Slavekeepers must keep Slaves against their own Light and understanding and they that will keep Slaves and plead for it, are not Neighbours to anyone, and Consequently they are not Lovers of God, They are no Christians, they are unbelievers, yea they are ungenteel, and inhumane.

Occom preached against slavery, criticized slaveholding ministers, and urged churches to refuse communion with slaveholders. His later sermons document Occom's awareness of his unique situation as a person of color with significant public authority, and his willingness to use this authority to condemn the inhumanity and evil of empire. In addition to writing sermons, Occom was also an accomplished hymnodist and editor. In 1774, he published *A Choice Collection of Hymns and Spiritual Songs*, a hymnal designed to serve a strong regional culture of hymn singing in Native New England, especially among the peoples affiliated with the Brotherton movement. Occom's hymnal also won broad popularity among New Light Christians from New

Hampshire to Virginia: throughout the late eighteenth and nineteenth centuries, original Occom compositions were adopted and reprinted in dozens of American hymnals.

Finally, the Occom archive includes twenty-four hand-sewn manuscript diaries spanning almost five decades from 1743 to 1792. These journals chronicle Occom's career as a missionary, itinerant, tribal councillor, and intertribal leader; political and social affairs among the Mohegan; interactions with Hudson River Valley Dutch communities and Montaukett, Pequot, Niantic, Farmington, Stockbridge, Delaware, and Oneida peoples; and travels throughout England and the Northeast, including visits to Iroquoia, London, New York City, and Philadelphia. Occom approached journal writing primarily as a professional exercise: as a way to account for his ministerial labors and responsibilities. However, his journals also constitute an important source of historical information about the Mohegan and Brotherton communities, offering firsthand accounts of events such as the political organization of Brotherton on November 7, 1785:

> Now we proceeded to form into a Body Politick—We Named our Town by the Name of Brotherton, in Indian Eeyawquittoowauconnuck . . . Concluded to live in Peace, and in Friendship and to go on in all their Public Concerns in Harmony both in their Religious and Temporal Concerns, and every one to bear his part of Public Charges in the Town,—They desired me to be a Teacher amongst them, I Consented to Spend Some of my remaining with them, and make this Town my Home and Center—

Occasionally, the diaries permit us profoundly personal glimpses into Occom's spiritual life. This memorable entry from April 2, 1786, records Occom's comforting nighttime vision of his dear friend the celebrity English itinerant George Whitefield, who had died in 1770:

> Last Night I had a remarkable Dream about Mr Whitefield, I thought he was preaching as he use to, when he was alive, I thought he was at a certain place where there was a great Number of Indians and Some White People—and I had been Preaching, and he came to me, and took hold of my wright Hand and he put his face to my face, and rub'd his face to mine and Said,—I am glad that you preach the Excellency of Jesus Christ yet, and Said, go on and the Lord be with thee, we Shall now Soon done. and then he Stretchd himself upon the ground flat on his face and reachd his hands forward, and mad a mark with his Hand, and Said I will out doe and over reach all Sinners, and I thought he Barked like a Dog, with a Thundering Voice—

In addition to these otherworldly moments, Occom's journals finally offer us an extensive document of the daily textures, the quotidian pleasures and hardships, of life in early American tribal communities.

The publication of the surviving Occom archive increases exponentially the known and available extent of American Indian writing before 1800. To face this mountain of manuscript, now in print, is to come to terms with how much we have to learn about Native peoples in the era of colonization as complex, multidimensional human beings. It has long been assumed that Occom can be adequately understood based on his slim autobiographical narrative of 1768 and his furious, merciful execution sermon of 1772. On the basis of these two pieces of writing, a consensus view once developed of Occom as a missionary apologist for Christian imperialism. But like the elm bark box he carved for his sister Lucy, this massive body of writing compels us to revisit and reimagine Occom, his mind, his heart, and his world. It permits us a vision of Native life and community unavailable in white-authored ethnographies, histories, missionary tracts, letters, and diaries from the colonial and early national eras. In these letters, sermons, prose essays, petitions, and diaries, in details mundane and sublime, we can glimpse a fuller range of intellectual, political, spiritual, cultural, and social movement among Native peoples in early America. In their mass, variety, and particularity, the writings of Samson Occom help us to imagine what Occom called "this Indian world": the vastness of indigenous America on its own terms.

When Samson Occom drafted a brief autobiography in 1765, he declared himself firmly rooted in the political and spiritual terrain of "this Indian world." "I Was Born a Heathen in Mmoyanheeunnuck alias Mohegan in N. London North America," he wrote, using his indigenous language to indicate his tribal community. According to tribal tradition, the Mohegan people trace their roots to the wolf clan of the Lenni Lenape, which migrated from its mid-Atlantic homelands in present-day Delaware, New Jersey, New York, and Pennsylvania to Lake Champlain, New York, and finally to southeastern Connecticut. Upon their arrival in New England, according to Mohegan tribal historian Melissa Tantaquidgeon Zobel, the people were given the name "Pequot," meaning invaders, by neighboring New England tribes. In about 1635, a splinter group led by Uncas separated itself from the main Pequot community in order to establish a new settlement at Shantok on the western bank of the Thames River. There, Uncas and his followers declared themselves "Mohegans," meaning "wolf people."[3]

The Mohegan quickly capitalized on their advantageous territorial situation on the Thames River and the Long Island Sound, establishing themselves as powerful players in the political-economic networks of the wampum trade. Under the leadership of Uncas, they also developed extensive kinship ties with neighboring Narragansett, Pequot, and Niantic communities. The incursion of English and Dutch colonists into the indigenous economies of southern New England created tremendous new intertribal tensions, imbalances, and conflicts. In the face of these new pressures, Uncas sought to maintain the political advantage of the Mohegan not only by cultivating kinship networks through strategic tribal intermarriage but by forming alliances with the English as well. Uncas's decision to ally with colonial invaders proved costly for Native New England, both to the well-being of rival tribes and to

3. Tantaquidgeon Zobel, *Lasting,* 12; Tantaquidgeon Zobel, *Medicine,* 27; Oberg, 48–49; L. Brooks, 112; L. Murray, *To Do Good,* 31–33. Some university-based historians and anthropologists have rejected the traditional Mohegan account of their own origins, instead positioning the Mohegan as an autochthonous people of New England. See Oberg, 18–20.

the long-term interests of the Mohegan. During the infamously brutal Pequot War of 1636–1637, Mohegans collaborated with the English in the destruction of the Pequots. On May 26, 1637, two hundred Mohegans and Narragansetts joined the English in a gruesome attack on a fortified Pequot encampment at Mystic. More than four hundred Pequot men, women, and children were killed, many of them burned alive as the English and their Mohegan and Narragansett allies set fire to the Pequot fort. History records that some Mohegan and Narragansett participants in the Pequot Massacre protested the brutality of the attack to the English military leader John Underhill. Even after witnessing firsthand and contributing to the carnage of colonial warfare, leaders of the Mohegan tribe continued to cultivate strategic alliances with the English against their indigenous neighbors. In 1643, Uncas betrayed the Narragansett leader Miantonomi, first delivering him as a captive to the English and then having him killed at the historic site of Uncas Leap on the Yantic River.[4]

Tactical alliance with the English did not protect Mohegan territory against colonial expropriation. After the Pequot War, pressure from the colony of Connecticut and individual English settlers to acquire Mohegan lands increased exponentially. Uncas did his best to defend his people and their territory by affixing his mark to a tangle of deeds, agreements, and treaties. (Contemporary historians are still struggling to untangle and understand the implications of this set of documents.) He also engaged Major John Mason, a trusted personal ally during the Pequot War, as a legal advocate for the Mohegan in their land concerns. Continuing his longtime strategy of allying with the English and believing that Mason as a literate Englishman enjoyed a significant advantage in legal dealings with the colony, Uncas formally initiated a trustee relationship with Mason in 1640. Uncas authorized him to found the town of Norwich, Connecticut, on nine square miles of Mohegan territory, reserving fishing rights to the Mohegan. In 1659, Uncas significantly expanded Mason's role as a trustee by deeding him all Mohegan lands, but the very next year, in 1660, Connecticut governor John Winthrop, Jr., pressured Mason to convey his trusteeship to the colony. Even as the colony compromised the autonomy of Mason's role as trustee, the Mohegan and Mason continued to recognize and affirm their mutual trust through a series of legal agreements that accorded Mason streams of revenue from Mohegan land sales and rents. Mohegan people relied increasingly on land sales for income during the late seventeenth century, as they found their traditional sources of revenue from the fur and wampum trades diminishing and their hunting and fishing greatly compromised by colonial incursion. Amid these escalating territorial pressures, in 1671, Mason wisely honored his trust by reserving a plot of land "eight thousand by four thousand feet" for perpetual use by the collective Mohegan tribe. These so-called sequestered lands came to form the core of a new Mohegan homeland.[5]

4. Oberg, 34–45, 52–55, 77–82, 87–109; L. Brooks, 116–119; Tantaquidgeon Zobel, *Lasting*, 13–14; Tantaquidgeon Zobel, *Medicine*, 27–28. On the Pequot War, see Cave, Hauptman, Salisbury, Oberg, 63–72.

5. L. Murray, *To Do Good*, 33; St. Jean, 373–378; Peyer, *Tutor'd*, 62; Oberg, 89–90, 154–156, 165–166.

During the late seventeenth and early eighteenth centuries, the colony of Connecticut adopted increasingly aggressive measures to advance the expropriation of Mohegan lands by individual white landowners. After the death of Uncas in 1683, Uncas's son Owaneco and John Mason's son Samuel attempted to maintain the Mohegan-Mason trust relationship. However, Connecticut governor Fitz-John Winthrop openly disregarded both the colony's historical agreements with Uncas and the advocacy of the Mason family. Tensions crested in the winter of 1703, when the colony forcibly expelled Mohegan families from their planting grounds at Massapeaugue. With the aid of the Mason family, Mohegans appealed their dispossession to the English Crown and to an appointed Royal Commission. The commission ruled in favor of the tribe. Nonetheless, the General Court of the Colony of Connecticut in 1721 upheld the expropriation of the Mohegan hunting grounds and asserted the ultimate authority of the colony to determine the disposition of Mohegan lands. Effectively, the Mason-Mohegan trust was at an end. To complicate matters further, when Owaneco's son Caesar died in 1723, the colony backed the passage of the sachemship to Caesar's son Ben Uncas, rather than to Mahomet, the rightful heir according to traditional tribal rules of succession.[6]

In the long run, Uncas's political strategy of cultivated alliance with colonial interests may have backfired by undermining Mohegan autonomy and making the community even more susceptible to outside interference. The dissolution of the Mohegan-Mason trust and the manipulation of the tribal sachemship crippled the legal ability of the Mohegan people to act collectively in defense of their own territory. Thus, the colony of Connecticut instituted a shift in Mohegan territory from a collective to a proprietary land system, a shift with deeply harmful consequences for Mohegan tribal life. Historian Jean O'Brien has closely charted a similar process of "dispossession by degrees" in her study of the seventeenth- and eighteenth-century Native community at nearby Natick, Massachusetts. At Natick, white settlers displaced Native residents through "the excruciating workings of business as usual": a steady, multifaceted encircling of legal, political, economic, cultural, and entrepreneurial pressures backed implicitly (if not openly) by the military force of the colony. She writes:

> For Indians, land meant homeland, which conferred identity in a corporate and religious sense, and it contained the crucial kinship networks that inscribed their relationships on the land. As English colonization proceeded, land also became a commodity for Indians. Eventually, it became a source of social welfare, which completed the process of dispossession in Natick. But . . . [they] remained in their ancestral territory, migratory and occupying marginal places that the colonizers permitted them as indentured servants, wage laborers, soldiers, mariners, and itinerant sellers of baskets and brooms. (211)

The impacts of colonization on traditional subsistence and trade economies made Native individuals and families especially vulnerable to the pressure to sell lands for

6. L. Brooks, 125, 131; DeForest, 315; L. Murray, *To Do Good*, 33–34; Peyer, *Tutor'd*, 62–63; Oberg, 208–209.

money. Land sales, in turn, contributed to the dissolution of the place-based kinship and intertribal networks that economically, culturally, spiritually, and politically sustained tribal communities. The increasing vulnerability of tribal governments to colonial manipulation further exacerbated the vulnerability of tribal territories and tribal members. These changes spiraled and reverberated through every dimension of Mohegan life. Limited access to traditional hunting and planting grounds changed the way Mohegans worked, worshiped, celebrated, dressed, and ate; hungry Mohegan people left their homes seeking employment as laborers, sailors, or domestic servants; dispersion threatened the continuity of Mohegan language, ritual, and traditional knowledge.[7]

Samson Occom was born at Mohegan in 1723 during this time of tremendous change and uncertainty. The year of Occom's birth was the same year the colony of Connecticut infiltrated the Mohegan sachemship, backing the passage of the office to Ben Uncas instead of Mahomet, the rightful traditionary heir; in 1726, the colony supported Ben Uncas's son Ben Uncas II as sachem rather than Mahomet's son John. The dispute over the sachemship created a deep rift among the Mohegan people, splitting them into two camps: supporters of Ben Uncas and Ben Uncas II at Ben's Town, supporters of Mahomet and John Uncas at John's Town. Samson Occom grew up at Ben's Town with his Mohegan father, Joshua Ockham or Occom; his mother, Sarah Samson, the descendent of a powerful Pequot family; his half-brother, Joshua; his brother, Jonathan; and his sisters, Lucy and Sarah.[8]

Even as colonial pressures encircled and dispersed Mohegan people, Occom was reared in a household committed to Mohegan traditional life. "My Parents were altogether Heathens, and I Was Educated by them in their Heathenish Notions," Occom wrote in 1765. "Our Indians regarded not the Christian Religion, they Woud persist in their Heathenish ways, and my Parents in perticular were very Strong in the Customs of their fore Fathers, and they led a wandring Life up and down in the Wilderness, for my Father was a great Hunter." Joshua Occom taught his son hunting and fishing skills that Samson would both rely on for subsistence and relish for pleasure until the end his life. Samson also grew up mindful of the traditional festival cycles of the Mohegan year, the central event being the fall Wigwam festival, a celebration of the harvest with a ritual pounding of corn into *yokeag*. Christianity made very slow inroads at Mohegan: Mohegans had rejected the missionary efforts of both James Fitch, appointed by the colony in 1671, and Experience Mayhew, who came to Mohegan in 1714. In 1732, Thomas Peguun, an indigenous man from Natick, Massachusetts, visited Mohegan as a missionary, creating long-standing kinship ties between the Mohegan and Natick peoples. The colony of Connecticut appointed Jonathan Barber as a schoolmaster at Mohegan in 1733. Occom later remembered that Barber "went about among the Indian Wigwams, and where ever he Coud find

---

7. O'Brien, 9, 211.

8. Tantaquidgeon Zobel, *Lasting*, 18; L. Brooks, 133, 137; L. Murray, *To Do Good*, 36–37; Ottery, 34–35; Love, *Occom*, 22–23. There has been some dispute over whether Sarah Wyacks or Wyoggs was in fact the sister of Samson Occom. An August 2, 1763, letter from Sarah to Samson (CHS) seems to verify the relationship.

the Indian Child^n, woud make them read—but the Children Usd to take Care to keep out of his way;—and he Us'd to Catch me Some times and make me Say over my Letters, and I believe I learnt Some of them, But this was Soon over too." Only when the wave of evangelicalism we now call the Great Awakening crested in Connecticut in the late 1730s and early 1740s did Mohegan people begin to take an interest in Christianity. Occom recalls:

> When I was 16 years of age, we heard a Strange Rumor among the English, that there were Extraordinary Ministers Preaching from Place to Place and a Strange Concern among the White People—this was in the Spring of the Year. But we Saw nothing of these things, till Some Time in the Summer, when Some Ministers began to visit us and Preach the Word of god; and the Common People also Came freequently and exhorted us to the things of god.

After 1739, twenty-one Mohegans, including Samson Occom's mother Sarah, Samuel Ashpo, and Henry Quaquaquid, joined the New London congregation of Rev. David Jewett. Occom himself was converted under the preaching of the radical evangelist John Davenport in 1741.[9]

The Great Awakening sparked a distinctive culture of Christian Indian separatism in Southern New England. Native people recognized coherent elements of New Light and traditional belief and created separate Indian churches that allowed them to exercise their spiritual gifts and powers without white supervision. Samuel Niles (Narragansett) established a separatist church when Congregationalists at Charlestown, Rhode Island, excommunicated him for preaching without a license. More than one hundred Narragansetts followed Niles, arranged for his ordination by three Moravian Indians, and built their own meeting-house. Niles also pastored residents of nearby Niantic, Pequot, Montaukett, and Mohegan communities. At Mohegan, Samuel Ashpo left the church of David Jewett and established a separate Indian congregation in the early 1740s. Jewett was correctly perceived to be sympathetic to the landed interests of the colony, and the separatist Ashpo church served as an important seat of power for the tribe's traditionalist–John's Town faction. During the formative early years of his conversion, Samson Occom witnessed in the leadership of Samuel Ashpo and Samuel Niles the potential of separatist Christianity as an instrument for advancing the spiritual and political autonomy of Native people.

Samson Occom also witnessed firsthand the deliberations of the Mohegan tribal council. His father served Ben Uncas II as a tribal councillor, and Samson was also appointed to the council on July 1, 1742. He was then nineteen years old. He joined the council at a time when Mohegans were once again renewing political and legal efforts to reclaim their territory. In 1743, after petitioning King George II to restore their traditional land base, the Mohegan tribe, with the assistance of the Mason family and attorney William Bollan, took their suit to court in the colonies. The so-called Mason Case was a contest between competing interpretations of legal documents:

---

9. DeForest, 277; L. Murray, *To Do Good,* 40; Richardson, 25; Peyer, *Tutor'd,* 63–64; Love, *Occom,* 24–34; Allen, 161.

Connecticut argued that a deed signed by Uncas in 1640 and a 1681 treaty conveyed Mohegan lands to the colony, while Bollan and the Mohegan held that these deeds and treaties in fact placed the lands in trust. A few of the noteworthy jurists assembled to hear the case, including Daniel Horsmandsen, chief justice of New York, agreed with the Mohegan, but the majority ruled in favor of the colony.[10]

During the summer of 1743, Occom himself attended hearings of the Mason land case held in Norwich. He heard William Bollan argue the illegitimacy of Ben Uncas II and expose the colony's strategic manipulation of Mohegan illiteracy in land dealings. He saw for himself the historical vulnerability of the tribal sachemship to outside influence and corruption and the power of written English-language instruments in matters concerning Mohegan territory. Occom realized, as Lisa Brooks writes, "that the best route to protecting their lands was for the Mohegans to acquire the power of literacy for themselves." Sometime that same year, in 1743, Joshua Occom died, fully ushering Samson into his responsibilities as an adult male member of his family, kinship network, and tribe. These weighty new responsibilities and his sense of the imperilment of Mohegan territory generated in Occom "a great Inclination," as he himself described it, to improve his reading and writing skills.

After the end of fall hunting and the harvest ceremonial season, on December 6, 1743, Samson Occom traveled to the home of the Rev. Eleazar Wheelock, at Lebanon Crank, in the heart of Mohegan territory. Wheelock, a Yale-educated Congregationalist minister penalized for his itinerant preaching during the Great Awakening, home-schooled young white men as a way of supplementing his suffering ministerial income. As Samson Occom recounts in his 1768 autobiography, his mother knew Wheelock through her work in Lebanon as a domestic laborer:

> At this Time my Poor Mother was going to Lebanon, and having had Some Knowledge of Mr *Wheelock* and hearing he had a Number of English ^youth^ under his Tuition, I had a great Inclination to go to him and be with ^him^ a week or a Fortnight, and Desired my Mother to Ask Mr Wheelock, Whether he woud take me a little while to Instruct me in Readings Mother did So, and When She Came Back, She Said Mr Wheelock wanted to See me as Soon as possible,—So I went up, thinking I Shoud be back again in a few Days; when I got up there, he received me with kindness and Compassion and in Stead of Staying a Fortnight or 3 Weeks, I Spent 4 Years with him.—

Between 1743 and 1747, Occom learned English, Hebrew, Greek, and Latin under the direction of Wheelock, who anticipated that Occom would soon study at his alma mater, Yale College. Indeed, as Occom's friend and mentor the Rev. Samuel Buell noted, Occom "was so well fitted for Admittance into College (which was designed) that he doubtless would have entered upon his Second year at his first admission." However, terrible eyestrain prevented Occom from matriculating at Yale, and he instead continued his preparation for the ministry under Benjamin Pomeroy

10. Peyer, "Samson Occom," 209; L. Brooks, 128, 137–138; L. Murray, *To Do Good,* 35; Love, *Occom,* 120–121; Oberg, 210–213.

at Hebron, Connecticut, in 1748. That fall, Occom obtained a copy of John Eliot's Massachusetts-language *Indian Bible* (1685). It seems clear that Occom completed his ministerial studies with an awareness of New England missionary history, a sense of his own responsibility to Native peoples, and the examples of Samuel Ashpo and Samuel Niles firmly in mind.[11]

At the conclusion of his studies, in the summer of 1749, Occom traveled to Montauk, Long Island, with a Mohegan fishing expedition. The Montaukett and Mohegan shared a common language, common kinship ties, and a long history of trade relations on the Long Island Sound. Rather than seek out a ministerial post or missionary assignment from Wheelock, Samson Occom proposed to the Montaukett the prospect of his usefulness as a schoolteacher or minister among them. In November 1749, Occom returned to Montauk with the permission of the tribe and a half-year commission as a teacher from the Boston Board of Commissioners of the Scotch Society for Propagating the Gospel, the missionary society that had underwritten his education and that would continue to provide him very limited financial support during his time at Montauk. He established a school for about thirty boys and girls from Montauk, Shinnecock, and neighboring white communities. Demonstrating his commitment to his host community, Occom also established a lasting home for himself with the tribe by marrying his Montaukett former pupil Mary Fowler in 1751. Mary was a strong-minded young woman from the well-placed Fowler and Pharoah families and a descendent of the seventeenth-century sachem Wyendanche. In deciding to marry, the couple flouted Wheelock's injunction that Occom avoid any "ingagements" that might "interfere" with the "Grand Design" of his missionary sponsors. They also openly resisted colonial laws that forbade exogamous marriage among the Montaukett and other tribal communities, laws designed by the colony of New York to hasten indigenous population decline. For Samson and Mary Fowler Occom, the decision to marry was the first of many courageous stands the couple would take against a colonial culture hostile to the well-being of indigenous families. They established a traditional home in a wigwam at Montauk, where in addition to his responsibilities as minister and schoolteacher, Samson learned Montaukett herbal medicine and served as a healer, judge, and counselor to the Montaukett and Shinnecock. By 1755, the couple had four young children. Struggling to survive on a meager annual stipend, Occom supported his household by farming, fishing, hunting, working wood, and binding books. He also welcomed Native students from southern New England to attend his Montauk school.[12]

While Occom was at Montauk, Eleazar Wheelock developed his own plan for teaching and evangelizing the Native people of New England and beyond. Inspired by what he perceived to be his own "success" in the education of Samson Occom, Wheelock developed a "great design," detailed in a letter to George Whitefield:

11. Buell, vii; Eels, "Indian Missions" (1939), 101; Item, Rauner Vertical File (VF).

12. Peyer, *Tutor'd*, 66; DCA 749506, 761225; Love, *Occom*, 44–45. On New England Indian pupils at Occom's Montauk school, see the letter from Occom's "cousin" William Sobuck, of Lyme, Connecticut, September 12, 1757, who asks Occom to send home his son Enoch (DCA 757512).

To take of their own Children, (two or three of a Tribe, that they may not Loose their own Language) and give them an Education among ourselves, under the Tuition, & Guidance, of a godly, & Skillful Master; Where they may, not only, have means to make them Schollars, but the best Means to Make them Christians indeed, and as many as Shall appear to be gracious, and Whose Parts and Tempers invite us to it, to fit them for the Gospel Ministry among their respective Tribes.

Wheelock believed that converting Native Americans was a critical part of the English civilizing mission in Iroquoia, and he felt strongly that Native missionaries could be trained to take the place of English missionaries, with better success. It was Wheelock's thinking that Native missionaries would not face the same "insuperable" difficulties of acquiring Native languages and learning Native cultural norms. They would be better accustomed to the hardships of life in the "wilderness," and they would expect less compensation for their labors from missionary societies. Beginning in 1754, Wheelock recruited about one hundred Native American students—young men and women—to attend his Moor's Indian Charity School at Lebanon. His first pupils were young Lenape men sent from New Jersey by the missionary John Brainerd. Other notable students included Samson Occom's brothers-in-law David and Jacob Fowler (Montaukett), Samuel Ashpo (Mohegan), Joseph Johnson (Mohegan), and Joseph Brant (Mohawk). White missionaries Samuel Kirkland, David McClure, and David Avery also attended Moor's Indian Charity School. Until 1762, Wheelock gave all of his students a college-preparatory education, including courses of study in scripture, theology, Latin, and Greek. However, facing criticism from sponsoring missionary societies that "Indians will not be so proper for these Purposes, as Persons Selected from Among the English," Wheelock retooled the Moor's curriculum to focus more on preparing his students for the practical aspects of their future duties as missionaries and schoolmasters, small farmers, and domestic servants. Native pupils and their parents also criticized the Moor's "design," especially when they learned that Wheelock was benefiting from the labor of his Native pupils in the course of their "training" as farmhands and domestic servants. Some Native parents withdrew their children, and many Native pupils fled the school during its almost fifteen years of operation at Lebanon. Even so, Moor's Indian Charity School served a vital role in fostering new intertribal connections between young Algonkian, Lenape, and Iroquois men and women, connections that would deepen over time into important political relationships. As would American Indian boarding schools in the late nineteenth and early twentieth centuries, Moor's Indian Charity School served as a cradle for intertribal political consciousness.[13]

Wheelock and his ministerial colleagues eagerly sought to draw Samson Occom away from his responsibilities and family at Montauk into their "great" missionary

13. DCA 762412.1, DCA 756201; L. Murray, *To Do Good*, 53; Love, *Occom*, 56–81; Peyer, *Tutor'd*, 60–61. Wheelock documented and promoted his plans for Moor's Indian Charity School and Dartmouth College in a series of narratives published between 1763 and 1773.

"design." In 1755, Aaron Burr and the New York Correspondents of the Scotch Society for Propagating Christian Knowledge recruited Occom to visit the Lenape and Iroquois, but his travels were interrupted by the onset of the Seven Years' War, the military contest between rival imperial powers France and Great Britain and their respective European and indigenous American allies over North American territory. Three years later, in 1758, the Presbyterian minister Samuel Davies of Virginia proposed that Occom go as a missionary among the Cherokee and recommended his ordination in preparation for this mission. Occom was examined and ordained by the Presbytery of Long Island, under the direction of his friend Samuel Buell, on August 29 and 30, 1759. However, the proposed mission to the Cherokee never materialized. Instead, the New York Correspondents called Occom and his brother-in-law David Fowler, a former student at Moor's Indian Charity School, to undertake a mission among the Six Nations from June to November 1761. As commissioned, Occom and Fowler established a school at Oneida, and they recruited three young Mohawk men—Joseph Brant, Center, and Ngeyes—to attend Moor's Indian Charity School.

Occom's mission to Iroquoia also fulfilled indigenous political purposes never envisioned by his sponsors. During his missionary travels, Occom refreshed historical alliances between the Mohegan and Mohawk, and he established new diplomatic relations with Sir William Johnson, the Mohawk-acculturated British superintendent of Indian affairs. He met with the Oneida in council and received from them a wampum belt, initiating a political relationship that, like their ties to William Johnson, would be of abiding consequence to the Native peoples of southern New England.[14] Occom returned to Oneida country in 1762 and again in 1763, as did his fellow Mohegan, the New Light separatist leader Samuel Ashpo. Lisa Brooks makes the important observation that "education flowed both ways" for Occom, Ashpo, and the Iroquois. She writes:

> While Occom, Ashpo, and their successors taught reading, writing, and the principles of Christianity, they learned Iroquois language and diplomacy, as well as the limits of their own religious beliefs. . . . The Algonquians who served as teachers in the Iroquoian missions also learned a great deal about the circumstances that Indian people shared, including dispossession. . . . The shared experience of colonization provided a common ground on which Iroquois and Algonquians alike could come to comprehend the intricate nature of the colonial system and the potential routes of resistance for Indian people.

Occom's missions to the Oneida between 1761 and 1763 gave him a powerful new perspective on the difficult situation of his own Mohegan and other New England tribes, as well as new alliances and new tactics to mobilize on their behalf.[15]

---

14. Significantly, Occom memorized the Oneida council's speech, but did not record it in his journals. Instead, he related it to Wheelock, who transcribed it in a letter (DCA 761625.1) and later published it in his 1767 Narrative (27). The speech was reprinted in the Hartford, Connecticut, Courant on October 12, 1767 (2, 1).

15. DCA 758554, DCA 761530; Love, Occom, 48–49, 83–95; L. Brooks, 147–150.

Perhaps it was this new political perspective, these new insights into the problems of the Mohegan and all Native peoples that inspired Samson Occom to plan his return from Montauk to his home community. In December 1763, he picked out a homesite on his father's homestead at Mohegan, about one mile north of Uncas Hill. Occom, his wife, and their seven young children made a difficult canoe crossing of the Long Island Sound in March 1764, losing some of their household possessions during the trip. That same month, sachem Ben Uncas III met alone with the colonial overseers of the Mohegan tribe; without the consent of his council, Uncas leased out Mohegan lands to a white farmer. Members of both the Ben's Town and John's Town factions perceived Uncas's actions as the last in a mounting sequence of abuses of power by the sachem, an open gesture of disregard for the tribal council, and a grave violation of traditional norms of collectivity and consensus in governance. Occom immediately joined the campaign to reconstitute the tribal council and to recall Ben Uncas III to his responsibilities. He explained in a May 7, 1764, letter to Wheelock:

> We are in great confusions, and I am affraid we Shall find Great Trouble, Ben-Uncas [III] has Cast off his Councel, he has leas'd out a farm without [one?] of his Councel, and has done many things before now, Contrary to the minds of his Councel, and Contrary to our agreement,—and we have also renounc'd him—And we are very much Griev'd with what our [Seers] have done—

Their colonial guardians or overseers, Occom further charged in a 1764 letter to Sir William Johnson, designed to "render [the Mohegan] Cyphers in our own land" and "us'd Ben Uncas as a tool in this design." Mohegans no longer wanted their land held in trust and administered by the colony of Connecticut; the newly reconstituted tribal council sought to own and govern tribal lands autonomously. Also in the spring of 1764, Occom led the tribe in seeking the dismissal of their schoolmaster Robert McClelland, who was publicly charged with incompetence, with abuses of power, and with systematically preferring white to Native students. Occom also openly criticized David Jewett, the appointed white minister to the Mohegan, for being in league with the colony, and some of Jewett's followers left the New London church to attend Occom's meetings. In late 1764, Samson Occom wrote a letter to King George II recalling the historic alliance of the Mohegan and the English and decrying the almost total encroachment on Mohegan lands by English settlers. Within months of his return to Mohegan, Occom was fully immersed in the tribe's renewed efforts toward self-determination in matters of land, education, religion, and governance.[16]

In these efforts, Occom of course did not act alone: he allied with Henry Quaquaquid, Samuel Ashpo, and many other Mohegan men and women from both Ben's and John's Towns. But for his activism Occom was singled out and threatened by officials of both church and colony. Ben Uncas III portrayed Occom as a dangerous troublemaker to colonial authorities. David Jewett reported him to the Boston Board of Commissioners, which withdrew the small salary it had awarded Occom for preaching to the Mohegan and Niantic. In March 1765, the board conducted a formal hear-

16. Ottery, 35; L. Brooks, 146, 151; Peyer, *Tutor'd*, 72; DCA 764472.1.

ing into Occom's political activities. Even Eleazar Wheelock thought the charges against Occom were overblown and prejudicial; still, he pressured Occom to answer them publicly. The board extracted from Occom a confession that his activism albeit "a natural & civil Right" and a "Duty" was "imprudent" and "offensive to the public." Occom reportedly recanted his confession a few months later. By the summer of 1765, he returned to Oneida territory where he resumed his ongoing conversation with William Johnson about Mohegan affairs.[17]

That fall, Occom agreed to leave his concerns at Mohegan and undertake a two-and-a-half-year fund-raising mission to Great Britain in support of Moor's Indian Charity School. Even though he carried with him letters of recommendation and endorsements from William Johnson and prominent men of church and colony from New England, New York, New Jersey, and Pennsylvania, tremendous controversy surrounded Occom's identity. The Boston Board of Commissioners, already suspicious of Occom and resentful of Wheelock, whom they perceived as an interloper in their domain, openly questioned whether or not Occom was, as he had been represented, brought up in traditional Native ways *and* lately converted to Christianity. Was he, in fact, both truly "Indian" and truly "Christian?" For many New England minds, it was impossible to reconcile the two. Compounding matters was the issue that Occom's tribal identity had been misrepresented as "Mohawk" in publicity surrounding his departure. Andrew Oliver, secretary for the Boston Board, demanded to know of Wheelock: was Occom "a Mohawk Indian lately converted from Heathenism, and in a short space of time fitted for the Ministry by Mr Wheelock?" Wheelock wrote his own account of Occom's education, which he sent with Occom as a letter of recommendation. Occom wrote his own short autobiography a few weeks before his departure from Boston on December 23, 1765.[18]

Occom and his missionary companion, Rev. Nathaniel Whitaker of Norwich, Connecticut, arrived in England in February 1766. Over the next two years, they traveled throughout England, Ireland, and Scotland, raising more than 13,000 pounds for Wheelock's school. Celebrity evangelist George Whitefield hosted Occom's debut sermon at the Whitefield Tabernacle on February 16, and introduced him to leading figures of British society and ministry, including the Countess of Huntington, Lord Dartmouth, and John Newton. Dartmouth and Whitefield both encouraged Occom to obtain Native crafts and curiosities to be given as gifts to English patrons and used to advance the fund-raising effort. Although Occom did carry to Scotland the wampum belt once given him by the Oneida, his surviving sermon notes, letters, and diaries suggest that Occom did not focus on cultivating this public ethnographic appeal. He instead focused his sermons on basic gospel themes. Received affectionately by many of his English auditors, Occom still was made to feel at times like an object of scrutiny and derision. On June 23, 1766, he recorded in his diary that the "Stage Players" of London "had been Mimicking of me in their Plays, lately.

17. Blodgett, 77–83; DCA 765304, 765114.3, 765212.10; L. Brooks, 153; Love, *Occom*, 123–129; Peyer, *Tutor'd*, 72–74.

18. Hartford, Connecticut, *Courant* May 5, 1766, 3:1; DCA 765617; Richardson, 292; Love, *Occom*, 130–136.

—I never thought I Shou'd ever come that Honor." In 1767, Occom was the subject of an exposé in "a Grub-street penny Paper," as Wheelock was informed by one of his English correspondents. Occom's letters home reflect his deep loneliness and heartsickness in being away from Mohegan, where his wife struggled to keep the family fed as Wheelock and Occom's sponsors failed in their promises of financial support. Mohegan political concerns also tugged at Occom. During the last months of Occom's mission, Samuel Mason came to England to pursue another appeal of the Mason land case. Against Wheelock's urgings to stay out of the business, Occom remained in England two weeks longer than Nathaniel Whitaker to testify in the case. He arrived back in Boston in late May or early June 1768.[19]

Occom spent the summer and fall of 1768 attempting to repair his home, rescue his household finances, and restore his familial relationships at Mohegan. He also renewed his relationships to the Native communities among whom he had preached: in July, Occom received an Oneida delegation bearing an invitation to visit; he also preached at Pequot, Niantic, and other nearby Indian towns. But even as he made himself once again home at Mohegan, Occom was still troubled by the controversy that surrounded his English tour, especially by continuing insinuations from the Boston Board of Commissioners that their financial support for his education had been misplaced and abused. In September, Occom sat down at the writing desk in his Mohegan home to begin a second draft of his autobiography:

> Having Seen and heard Several Representations, in England and Scotland, made by Some gentlemen in America, Concerning me, and finding many gross Mistakes in their Account,—I thought it my Duty to give a Short Plain and Honest Account of myself, that those who may hereafter see it, may know the Truth Concerning me.—Tho' it is against my mind to give a History of myself & publish it Whilst I am alive, Yet to do Justice to my Self, and to those who may desire to know Something concerning me—and for the Honor of Religion, I will Venture to give a Short Narritive of my Life.—

The short manuscript autobiography Occom produced that fall survives as a classic of early American Indian literature. It is clear from Occom's prefacing remarks that he himself wrote his narrative not as a voluntary or creative expression of his personhood, not even as a dutiful record of his conversion, but rather as a defense against what had stretched into an almost five-year period of public scrutiny and disputation of his character. Occom hoped that he could use writing to set the record straight. It was because he believed in the power of English-language literacy to improve the well-being of tribal communities that he sought out study with Eleazar Wheelock, took on duties as a schoolmaster at Montauk, and traveled to Britain as a fundraiser for Moor's Indian Charity School. He believed that the design of Moor's Indian Charity School—despite its obvious failings—had as good a potential as any plan to advance Native English-language literacy by training Native

19. Richardson provides the fullest account of Occom's travels in Great Britain. See, especially, Richardson, 92n4, 219, 303–304. See also Blodgett, 84–104; Love, *Occom*, 136–151; Peyer, *Tutor'd*, 74–76.

schoolmasters and ministers to take their place among tribal communities. Even as he believed in the power of writing, Occom also grappled with the warped textures of power it could perpetrate, from the tangle of deeds and treaties amassed during the Mason land case and the abusively patronizing epistolary disciplines foisted upon his students by Eleazar Wheelock to the trials of character imposed upon him by the Boston Board of Commissioners. His autobiography was an attempt to intervene decisively in the growing body of discourse about his identity and reputation.

Difficult years followed Samson Occom's return from Great Britain. In January 1769, he wrote to the Connecticut Correspondents of the Scotch Society to confess his "being shamefully over taken With Strong Drink." He addressed a similar confession to the Long Island Presbytery, which conducted its own inquiry into the matter and later exonerated him. Still, Wheelock seized upon this opportunity to chastise his former student. "I dont remember that I have been overtaken with strong drink this winter," Occom briskly answered back. "But many White people make no bones of it to call me a drunkard, and I expected it, as I have many enemies round about here, yea they call me a lyar and rogue and what not, and they curse & damn me to the lowest Hell." That same winter, Samson and Mary Occom welcomed their eighth child, a daughter named Theodosia. It must have a difficult time to welcome a new life into the household, an especially hungry wintering season. The family, as usual, was in difficult financial straits. Occom had sustained a crippling shoulder injury that made it too painful for him to travel and probably impossible for him to hunt, farm, fish, or otherwise feed his children. And in the middle of these private struggles, Occom received another delegation of Oneida leaders, who this time traveled to retrieve their children from Moor's Indian Charity School. Occom himself had recruited those students, just as he had expended two and a half painful and virtually uncompensated years of his life raising funds for Wheelock's school. "I never was so discouraged as I am now," Occom admitted to Wheelock on March 17, 1769. The season culminated in May 1769 with the death of Ben Uncas III. Occom and other Mohegans used the occasion of Ben Uncas's funeral to register a final protest against the controversial colony-backed sachem. According to some reports, Occom and his cohort walked out during the funeral service; others say that Occom and fellow pallbearers dropped the casket of Ben Uncas III on the ground, refusing to facilitate his burial in the royal grounds at Norwich. Protesting the colony's corruption of the sachemship, the Mohegan people did not appoint a successor.[20]

At the same time, deep fissures emerged in Occom's relationship to his longtime mentor Eleazar Wheelock. Ever since Occom's return from Great Britain, Wheelock had urged him to once again leave his family and undertake another mission to Iroquoia. When Occom refused, Wheelock accused him of pride. For his part, Occom grew more openly critical of the way Wheelock was conducting Moor's Indian Charity School, turning away Native students in favor of whites and refocusing his Native pupils' curriculum on more rudimentary skills befitting schoolmasters, farmers, and artisans rather than ministers or scholars. In August 1770, Wheelock relocated

20. DCA 769209.2; Tantaquidgeon Zobel, *Lasting*, 40; L. Murray, *To Do Good*, 38; Richardson, 349, 352; Love, *Occom*, 152–168; Peyer, *Tutor'd*, 77–82.

the school to Hanover, New Hampshire. A few months later, in a January 1771 letter accusing Occom of "repeated & aggravated" intemperance, Wheelock lamented
that too many of his Native pupils had brought him such disappointment. Occom
fiercely rebuked Wheelock in a letter dated July 24, 1771. Occom's long tutelage to
Eleazar Wheelock and his willingness to put "Body & Soul" in service of Wheelock's
"Great Design" had finally come to an end.[21]

Failed time and time again by Wheelock, scrutinized and discriminated against
by his sponsoring missionary societies, Occom reexamined his relationship to the
established schools and churches that directed his early career. He developed a new
sense of his independent authority and public profile. The Occom home received "a
great Number of Visitors Continually from all quarters[;] there has not been one
Week nor 3 Days I can remember in the Year past, but that we have had Some
Stranger or other," Occom wrote to Susannah Wheatley on March 5, 1771. "My
being acquainted with the World in Some Measure, has made my House a Sort of an
Asylum for Strangers both English and Indians, far and near." White missionaries
solicited his assistance in their ministerial endeavors, believing that Occom's "Influence" could pacify the "prejudices" of Native proselytes further westward. But
Occom politely declined their invitations. Instead, he focused his labors on spiritual
revitalization closer to home, among the Native peoples of southern New England.
Occom hosted singing meetings and wrote abroad to obtain hymnals and other religious books for Native Christians. He established new networks of financial and
political support beyond Wheelock's control and influence. In John Thornton in
particular, Occom found a loyal friend. Thornton, an officer of the English trust of
Moor's Indian Charity School, believed that Occom had been misused by Wheelock
and treated as a "Scapegoat," and he obtained fifty pounds of debt relief for Occom
in 1772. Occom emerged from this difficult period with a new appreciation for his
own powers independent of Wheelock, a renewed political vision, and a strengthened resolve to serve Native communities on his own terms and to use his celebrity
to advance their concerns. Undoubtedly, Mary Fowler Occom played an important
role in anchoring him at home among Native communities. According to two missionaries who visited the Occom home, Mary dressed in traditional style; if Samson
spoke to her in English, the English-literate Mary responded to him in Mohegan-
Pequot-Montauk. In her resolve, we sense her remarkable striving to protect her
household against the colonial economic, religious, and political powers arrayed
against indigenous families.[22]

Opportunity to enact publicly this new resolve to speak to and for Native
peoples came in June 1772, when Occom received a letter from a Wampanoag man
named Moses Paul, who was awaiting execution for the December 1771 murder of a
white man named Moses Cook at a Bethany, Connecticut, tavern. Paul, who had appealed his sentence alleging the racial bias of the all-white jury, invited Occom to

21. DCA 771122; Richardson, 354–355.

22. Richardson, 359; DCA 772328. John Thornton's letters to Occom during this time appear in
      "Sketch of the Life of Samson Occom," *The Religious Intelligencer* 7.26 (November 23, 1822):
      409–415.

preach at his execution: "Considering that we are of the same nation, I have a particular desire that you should preach to me upon that occasion." On September 4, at the Brick Meeting House in New Haven, Occom preached from Romans 6:23, "The wages of sin is death." A "very great Concourse of People" gathered "as much excited to hear Mr. Occum preach, as to see the Execution, altho there has not been one in this Town, since the year 1749," the Hartford, Connecticut, *Courant* reported. Reversing the racial spectacle of the execution, Occom charged that all present— "Indians, English, and Negroes"—were sinners in need of redemption. He also used the occasion to speak directly to Native people, exhorting them to temperance, implicitly comparing the destructive effects of colonialism, including the introduction of alcohol and the destruction of Native subsistence economies, to the nature of sin itself. Native peoples, he urged, might save their lives through collective spiritual regeneration. *A Sermon, Preached at the Execution of Moses Paul, an Indian* was first published on October 31, 1772. It subsequently went through nineteen editions, ranking Occom as the sixth leading author in the American colonies during the 1770s. In addition to its print circulation, Occom's sermon circulated orally in Native communities. Occom's future son-in-law Joseph Johnson recorded in his journal reading the sermon aloud to his Native students at Farmington, Connecticut.[23] The *Sermon, Preached at the Execution of Moses Paul* marks a turning point in the public career of Samson Occom. It is the first recorded occasion when Occom speaks publicly as a Native minister to Native audiences about specifically Native concerns.

Occom's celebrity grew throughout New England in the months following the execution of Moses Paul. "I have Continual Calls to Preach," he wrote to John Moorhead in April 1773, "both by the English and Indians, and I Preach 4 or 5 Times every week." Exemplary of the invitations Occom received is this from Benjamin Bellknap and Joseph Borden of Johnston, Rhode Island, who wrote: "We are Distitute of a preacher of the Gospel in the meeting house . . . and we having had the favour of reading your Sermon on the Execution of Moses Paul, has greatly convinced us of the necessity of the Gospel be preached among us, and we earnestly Desire you, to Come to us as Soon as you Can." Even as his public profile continued to grow, Occom remained most concerned with issues close to home. In January 1773, the protracted Mohegan-Mason case was decided in favor of the colony and the suit finally dismissed. Occom wrote to Samuel Buell:

> The grand Controversy, Which has Subsisted between the Colony of Connecticut and the Mohegan Indians ^above 70 years^ we hear is finally Decided, and it is in Favour of the Colony, I believe it is a pure Favour; I am afraid the Poor Indians will never Stand a good Chance with the English, in their Land Controversies because they are very Poor they have no Money, Money is almighty now a Days, and the Indians have no Learning, no Wit nor Couning the English have all.

23. Occom's *Sermon* was not the first English-language publication by a Native American. Joseph Johnson published a letter to Moses Paul months earlier in the Connecticut *Journal*. Chamberlain, 445, 415n3; L. Murray, 187; Peyer, *Tutor'd*, 91–96; *Courant*, September 8, 1772, 3, 2.

The Mohegan tribal sachemship had been infiltrated and functionally destroyed. Mohegan claims to their own traditional territories had been effectively terminated by the colony of Connecticut. Many Native communities in New England faced the almost total disruption of their autonomous economic, political, and cultural lives.[24]

In the face of this upheaval, men, women, and children from the Montaukett, Mohegan, Pequot, Narragansett, Niantic, and Farmington communities met at Mohegan on March 13, 1773, to envision for themselves a new future: a new pantribal settlement, to be called "Brotherton," united around principles of self-determination and Christian worship. Many of the Native men and women involved in the founding of the Brotherton movement were religious separatists and veterans of local Native struggles for defense of territory and tribal autonomy. Joseph Johnson, David and Jacob Fowler, and Samson Occom had traveled extensively among southern New England communities, as well as among the Oneida and other Iroquois tribes. Traditional relationships of kinship, exchange, and political alliance, as well as these newer missionary networks, laid the groundwork for Brotherton. What additionally distinguished the founding of Brotherton from other Christian Indian towns such as Natick, Massachusetts, or Brotherton, New Jersey, was that the movement did not originate with white missionaries but among Native peoples themselves. Eleazar Wheelock had in 1767 envisioned establishing a "town of Christianized Indians" in the "heart of yᵉ Indian country" to attract greater interest among western tribes. Wheelock would have liked to claim Brotherton as his own, but his name appears nowhere in the records of its organization. Rather, it was the Mohegan schoolmaster Joseph Johnson and the Native community at Farmington who led and directed the Brotherton movement through its early phases. It was the people of Farmington who in October and December 1773 invited and exhorted "All our Indian Brethren, at Mohegan, Nihantuck, Pequot, Stonington, Narragansett, and Montauk" to continue the discussions begun in March. Joseph Johnson coordinated the diplomatic aspects of the effort, conducting crucial land negotiations with the Oneida in 1774 and soliciting assistance from Indian superintendents Sir William Johnson and Guy Johnson, as well as governors and colonial assemblies. Occom served as an elder statesman, advocate, and spiritual advisor for the effort. "I am promoting the thing and encouraging the Indians all I can," he wrote on November 10, 1773, "and if they succeed I shall go with them with all my Heart."[25] Occom made a distinctive contribution toward a common religious culture at Brotherton by compiling and publishing his *Collection of Hymns and Sacred Songs* in 1774. He designed the hymnal, which featured some of his own original hymn-texts, to sustain and advance a strong culture of hymn singing and singing-meetings that had developed among the Christian Indians of southern New England. Hymns from Occom's oft-reprinted *Collection* were both embraced by Native Christians at Brotherton and, eventually, absorbed into the canon of American hymnody.[26]

---

24. Bellknap and Borden to Occom, May 4, 1773 (CHS); L. Murray, *To Do Good,* 39.

25. DCA 767602.1; Peyer, *Tutor'd,* 82–84; L. Murray, *To Do Good,* 174, 203–204, 255–285; Wonderley, "Brothertown," 464; Love, *Occom,* 210. On the contexts for the founding of Brotherton, see Love, *Occom,* 188–230; L. Murray, *To Do Good,* 168–174; Wyss, 123–153.

26. See J. Brooks, "Six Hymns" and *American Lazarus.*

On October 4, 1774, the Oneida granted a bounded plot of about six square miles to the Brotherton tribes, and the first party of Brotherton emigrants ventured up to Oneida territory in March 1775. Most were from Montaukett or Farmington. This initial phase of emigration, however, was interrupted by the onset of the American War of Independence. Despite strong patriot sentiments and high enlistment rates among New England Indians, Occom himself insisted that Native people were "neither Whigs nor Tories." Even as Occom advised the Oneida and other Native tribes "not to entermeddle in these Quarrils among the White People," the war wrought tremendous destruction in Indian country: Native towns were ravaged, Native food stores plundered, Native orchards burned, and Native governments disrupted. Iroquois territory was hit especially hard. About forty people at the fledgling Brotherton settlement retreated to Stockbridge, Massachusetts, where they waited out the hostilities. "This war has been the most Distructive to poor Indians of any wars that ever happend in my Day, both as to their Spiritual and Temporal Injoyments," Occom lamented in 1783.[27]

Even as it brought destruction to Native towns and communities, the Revolutionary War led to an upsurge in pan-Indian political consciousness and mobilization. Many Native peoples fled destruction in their home territories and migrated to Iroquoia, even as the Iroquois themselves struggled to recover from massive losses of life, property, planting fields, orchards, and food stores. Emigration to Brotherton also resumed after the end of the war. On May 8, 1784, Occom accompanied one of the first postwar parties of emigrants, including his brother-in-law Jacob Fowler, his daughter Christiana Occom Paul, and their families on a voyage up the Hudson River to Brotherton. Brotherton settlers returning from their wartime sanctuary at Stockbridge, Massachusetts, were joined by a new movement of Stockbridge Indians who sought to escape aggressive white encroachment on their Massachusetts township by establishing the community of New Stockbridge, six miles from Brotherton. By 1785, the population of Brotherton reached 200, while 400 Native emigrants lived at New Stockbridge. Both settlements struggled to survive amid the general poverty and famine of the postwar period. With no financial support from white patrons or religious societies, and little money of their own, Brotherton residents eked out a marginal subsistence by farming and fishing. On Monday, November 7, 1785, Occom attended the historic organizational meeting of Brotherton, or *Eeyaw-quittoowauconnuck*,[28] where he promised to "make this Town my Home and Center." Although Samson and Mary Fowler Occom did not in fact move their household from Mohegan until May 1789, Occom kept his promise to make the town his "Center." Despite persistent hip and back pain stemming from earlier injuries, he spent the years 1785 to 1789 in almost constant transit between Mohegan and Brotherton,

27. L. Murray, *To Do Good*, 242–243, 265; Love, *Occom*, 222, 231–232; Wonderley, "Brothertown," 465, 469; Calloway, 34; Tantaquidgeon Zobel, *Lasting*, 19.

28. Mohegan tribal linguist Stephanie Fielding believes that "Eeyawquittoowauconuck" (written as <iyáhqituwôkanuk> in contemporary orthography) translates as "he does so like someone looking in a certain direction or a certain way." Phrased differently, this meaning might indicate a group united by a distinctive shared perspective.

where he preached, advised, and counseled the community in it spiritual and political affairs.[29]

Almost immediately following its political organization, the Brotherton community came into dispute with the Oneida over the legal disposition and allotment of Brotherton lands. The Oneida faced tremendous territorial pressures in the post–Revolutionary War period as the state of New York aggressively expropriated millions of acres of Native lands for white occupation through the Treaty of Fort Herkimer (1785) and the Treaty of Fort Schuyler (1788). In October 1786, Oneida tribal leaders pressured Brotherton residents to relinquish their bounded 1774 allotment and to "live at large" on Oneida territory. As veterans of protracted legal land battles such as the Mohegan-Mason case, Brotherton founders vested their security in the legal documentation of specific land claims. The Oneida may have believed that bounded lands such as those granted to Brotherton residents were particularly vulnerable to purchase, leasing, squatting, seizure for debt repayment, seizure for fine repayment, and other paralegal and extralegal land acquisition techniques. Additionally, Oneida historian Anthony Wonderley suggests that the Oneida may have been motivated to renegotiate their land allotments to Brotherton as a form of retribution for the Brotherton settlers' retreat during the Revolutionary War and their failure to stand with and fight alongside the Oneida. Occom attended some of the meetings with the Oneida, and he, along with other Brotherton leaders, refused to accede to the Oneida's requests.[30]

Another threat to Brotherton's allotted land base came from within the community, as a party of impoverished settlers led by Elijah Wampy (or Wympy) began to lease tribal lands to whites. Fierce factionalism developed around the land leasing issue, erupting on at least one occasion into open physical violence. Occom, who had witnessed the tremendous costs of leasing under the sachemship of Ben Uncas II at Mohegan, ardently opposed the actions of the Wampy party, and he sought out a series of legal remedies to protect Brotherton lands. On February 25, 1789, the New York State Assembly passed an act that confirmed 27 square miles as territory of the Brotherton Indians, ordered an official survey of the land, and restricted the term of leases at Brotherton to ten years. Occom returned to the assembly in February 1791 with a petition to revoke altogether the authority of Brotherton tribal members to lease lands to white settlers. The assembly responded by passing "An Act for the Relief of the Indians Residing in Brothertown and New Stockbridge" on February 21, 1791, which vested powers to apportion and lease lots in an elected tribal council and directed revenue streams from leases toward town improvements and education. Even as the tribe lost about 2,000 acres through the leasing activities of the Wampy party, Occom's actions were not received without controversy at Brotherton. In tribal meetings, Elijah Wampy mocked Occom and openly challenged his authority

---

29. Dowd, 93, 103; Wonderley, "Brothertown," 466.

30. Wonderley, "Brothertown," 475–476. On Oneida land controversies and treaties, see Lehman; Wonderley, "Good Peter"; Wonderley, "Brothertown"; Hauptman, *Conspiracy;* Campisi and Hauptman; Hauptman and McLester.

to act on behalf of the tribe in its political affairs. Out of frustration, Occom moved his household from Brotherton to New Stockbridge in December 1791.[31]

At Brotherton just as at Mohegan, Occom's insistence on Native governance and autonomy was construed by his rivals and opponents as anti-white sentiment. Occom did not apologize for Native resentment of the criminal violence and conquest perpetrated by white colonists. As he wrote in November 1791, if Native peoples "have very great and reveted Prejudice against the White People," "they have too much good reason for it." In his private writings and sermons, Occom celebrated the humanity and customary generosity of Indian people, even as he mourned the tremendous losses sustained under colonialism. In his public practice, he remained committed to the idea that Indians were best positioned to lead, teach, and minister to other Indians. When the white minister John Sergeant, Jr., relocated his church from Stockbridge, Massachusetts, to New Stockbridge in 1788, Occom engaged him in open debate and competed for parishioners. He entered into a similar competition for Native souls with white minister Samuel Kirkland. Kirkland wrote of Occom in May 1792:

> There is no Indian, in the compass of my knowledge ([Joseph] Brant only excepted) who has more inveterate prejudices against white people than Mr. Occom. Altho his education & professional calling in most cases restrains them. [B]ut in certain companies, & on certain occasions, they will break out & induce him to inculcate sentiments not only derogatory from that national character, which is due to the white people, but injurious to the real interest of the indians, & such as tend to sour their minds & rivet their prejudices.

Even a party of Stockbridge Indians wrote to Kirkland to complain that Occom had "alionate[d] the affections of our poor ignorant people from white people in general and Ministers in particular. Furthermore, we have thought and so believe that Mr Occom has gone out of the line of his duty in meddling too much with our civil government." To the end of his life, Occom remained committed to a vision of autonomous Native leadership that did not separate spiritual from political concerns.[32]

Samson Occom died on July 14, 1792, near his home at New Stockbridge. According to published reports of his death, he collapsed while gathering cedar for a woodworking project. Three hundred Native people from Oneida, New Stockbridge, and Brotherton attended his funeral the next day, where his erstwhile rival Samuel Kirkland preached from Matthew 24:44: "Therefore be ye also ready: for in such an hour as ye think not the Son of man cometh." Kirkland's choice of text suggests that Occom's death at sixty-nine years old came as a sudden blow to the Brotherton and New Stockbridge communities. Occom was survived by his wife and at least seven of his children.[33]

Although the community continued its efforts to preserve its land base and political autonomy, within ten years of Occom's death, white settlers outnumbered

31. Peyer, *Tutor'd*, 86–87; Love, *Occom*, 287–289.

32. Wyss, 144, 147.

33. Peyer, *Tutor'd*, 88; Sprague, 194; Love, *Occom*, 294–298.

Brotherton Indians on Brotherton lands by a five-to-one ratio. In 1818, Brotherton Indians joined their Oneida and Stockbridge neighbors under the leadership of Hendrick Aupaumut (Mahican-Stockbridge) in planning a removal to Wisconsin. Treaties with the U.S. government and the Ho-Chunk and Winnebago tribes resulted in the allocation of 23,040 acres as "Brothertown Township," in Calumet County, Wisconsin, in 1831. In 1839, the Brothertown Indians sought and obtained legal title to their lands as well as U.S. citizenship. Even though the federal government assumed that the conferral of citizenship then constituted the abolition of tribal nation-state status, Brothertown tribal members did not abandon their traditions of self-governance. Throughout the twentieth century, they organized to reclaim lands lost to white encroachment, and after 1978 began a campaign to regain their status as a federally recognized tribe. Many tribal members continue to reside in the Fond du Lac, Wisconsin, area, where they continue their efforts toward federal recognition.[34]

After the departure of Samson Occom and other participants in the Brotherton movement, the Mohegan tribe continued to repair its traditional forms of self-government from centuries of colonial disruption. Samson's sister Lucy Occom Tantaquidgeon did not migrate to upstate New York, but instead stayed at home in Uncasville, Connecticut, and assumed a leading role in tribal affairs. What happened at Mohegan during the late eighteenth and early nineteenth centuries matches what historians have observed happened among the Choctaw, Creek, and other Removal-era tribal communities: female-headed tribal factions tended to resist removal from traditional lands, even when it cost them formal recognition from the federal government; male-headed tribal factions developed male-focused tribal governance and land ownership systems recognized as legitimate by federal Indian overseers and broader Euro-American society. In 1831, during the Jacksonian era of Indian Removal, Lucy Occom Tantaquidgeon, her daughter Lucy Tantaquidgeon Teecomwas, and her granddaughter Cynthia Teecomwas Hoscoat deeded a plot of land on Mohegan Hill to tribal ownership for the building of a community church. These women understood that it would be strategically important to the continuance of the Mohegan on traditional lands to escape removal by demonstrating themselves a "Christianized" people. The Mohegan Congregational Church has remained a key venue of tribal political, social, and cultural life ever since. Even when tribal treaty relationships with the federal government were terminated in the 1860s and 1870s, the Mohegan Congregational Church remained a key venue of tribal political, social, and cultural life. The half-acre on which the church stands is the only plot of land that remained continuously in tribal ownership. Proving their relationship to that plot of land and proving the line of leadership that began with Lucy Occom was crucial to the Mohegan tribe's successful petition for reinstatement of federal recognition in 1994.[35]

When the Mohegan tribe prepared its petition for federal recognition in the 1970s and 1980s, tribal intellectuals remembered the contribution of Samson Occom to the

---

34. Love, *Occom*, 290–293, 316–331; Wonderley, "Brothertown," 481, 483.

35. Tantaquidgeon Zobel, *Lasting*, 21, 22–27, 47–48, 54–55; *Medicine Trail*, 12, 15, 24–25.

preservation of self-governance during an especially difficult era in their history. The federal government demands proof of "continuous" self-governance within the tribe; however, as tribal historian Melissa Tantaquidgeon Zobel noted, colonial authorities had purposely disrupted tribal governments, driving traditional forms of leadership into hiding or into assuming new forms unrecognizable to outsiders. She further argued that the legal definitions and benchmarks of continuous tribal governance established by the federal government do not reflect the way tribal communities understand the structure of authority in their own communities. Tantaquidgeon Zobel wrote, "The historical pattern of manipulation by non-Indian governing bodies of their native counterparts suggests that the implementation of a sociocultural framework is preferable to a political one when judging the continuity of Native leadership . . . Sociocultural leaders (such as herbal healers, oral historians, and craftspeople) persevere long after political rulers have been silenced." She consequently proposed that the continuity of tribal authority could be tracked through "sociocultural" rather than "political" authorities. Occom stood in the breach during the colonial dismantling of the political Mohegan sachemship and helped establish a new line of "sociocultural authority" through tribal councils and churches to preserve the identity and sovereignty of the tribe. During the years when the Connecticut General Assembly denied the legitimacy of the Mohegan tribal sachem in favor of Ben Uncas III, it was Samson Occom who strove to maintain "sociocultural lifeways" and "ushered in an era in which the sociocultural leader would reign supreme." Today, the Mohegan continue to remember Occom as giving the tribe a "reputation for being Christianized, which helped them avoid later relocation" during the era of Indian Removal.[36]

It is instructive to compare the ways Samson Occom has been remembered by his own people as a defender of traditional governance with the ways he has been remembered and reconstructed by historians over the past 150 years. Scholarship has often emphasized Occom's Christianity and his relationships to Eleazar Wheelock and Dartmouth College over his ongoing tribal relationships, portraying him as an exemplary (if culturally conflicted) Christian Indian convert. In 1859, the Congregational minister William Allen (1784–1868), former president of Bowdoin College and compiler of the *American Biographical Dictionary,* made a first attempt at writing a biography of Samson Occom. Allen's manuscript "Memoirs of Samson Occom, the Mohegan Indian Missionary, Including His own Journal of many Years, With Specimens of his Sermons, and various Notices Relating to the Indians of his Tribe" includes transcriptions of large sections of Occom's diaries, four sermons, and historical and biographical commentary. It appears to have been prepared for publication but never came to press. William DeLoss Love (1851–1918), a graduate of Samuel Kirkland's Hamilton College, Congregationalist minister, and historian,

---

36. Tantaquidgeon Zobel, "Rooted"; "Samson Occom," *The Mohegan Tribe: Heritage,* www.mohegan .nsn.us/heritage/SamsonOccum.aspx (April 19, 2005). It should be noted, as well, that different Native communities in the Northeast remember Samson Occom differently. Some regret his cooperation with Wheelock in recruiting dozens of young people from Iroquois tribes away from their tribal communities for missionary education.

published *Samson Occom and the Christian Indians of New England* in 1899. Not sur-
prisingly, Love's biography of Occom is imbued with the Christian concerns of its
author and the ethnocentric sensibilities of its time. Still, it has remained the standard biographical work on Occom and an indispensable resource for Occom scholars
for more than a century, thanks to Love's extensive research in Occom's letters and
diaries and other primary documents of Brotherton genealogy and tribal history.

At the turn of the century, Samson Occom was remembered largely in his connection to Dartmouth College. In 1904, the great Santee Sioux intellectual and writer
Charles Eastman (Ohiyesa) (1858–1939), an 1887 Dartmouth graduate, was asked to
return to his alma mater to play the role of Samson Occom in a commemorative university celebration. Before an audience of assembled dignitaries, including the sixth
Earl of Dartmouth, Eastman reenacted the scene in December 1743 when Occom first
met Eleazar Wheelock in Lebanon, Connecticut. He also staged a tableau of Occom's
1766 debut sermon at the London tabernacle of George Whitefield. At the time of
this celebration, Charles Eastman was the last Native American known to have
graduated from Dartmouth. Even as the college neglected its foundational commitments to American Indian education in the early twentieth century, it continued to
celebrate Occom's memory by publishing three monographs about Occom and other
Native students at Moor's Indian Charity School—James Dow McCallum, *The Letters of Eleazar Wheelock's Indians* (1932); Leon Richardson, *An Indian Preacher in
England* (1933); and Harold Blodgett, *Samson Occom* (1935). Like Love's 1899 biography, these three works have deeply informed contemporary scholarship on
Occom and other early American Indian writers.

Occom's name and legacy flickered in and out of popular memory throughout
the middle decades of the twentieth century. In 1943, the Los Angeles–based California Shipbuilding Company, founded by John McCone, later a director of the
Central Intelligence Agency, christened a Liberator warship the *Samson Occom*.
Shinnecock author Lois Marie Hunter also remembered Occom in her local history
The Shinnecock Indians (1950). On June 20, 1970, the Montauk Historical Society
celebrated "Samson Occom Day." A decade later, Dartmouth College, in connection
with a revived commitment to Native American students and Native American
studies, used the name, image, and historical fundraising achievements of Samson
Occom to raise an additional $500,000 for the college endowment between 1980 and
1982. At the very moment Dartmouth fund-raisers in Hanover, New Hampshire, resurrected Occom as an emblem of the college's past and future, Mohegan historians
at Mohegan, two hundred miles away, were reconstructing their own very different
memory of Occom as a pivotal figure in the past and future of the tribe.[37]

Scholarly interest in Samson Occom did not revive until the growth of ethnohistory and the disciplinary emergence of American Indian literary studies in the
1970s and 1980s. Ethnohistory encompassed new efforts to understand colonization
not as simple conquest but rather as a complex set of encounters that required of
both Native peoples and European colonists strategic negotiations, adaptations, and

37. Norwich, Connecticut, *Bulletin* (September 4, 1943), Item, Rauner VF; Hunter, 31–33; Long Island *Press* (June 14, 1970), 18, Item, Rauner VF.

accommodations. But one of the limits of ethnohistory is that it tends to privilege sites of white-Indian contact as the determining contexts for American Indian history. Consequently, ethnohistorian James Axtell remembered Occom primarily in connection with Eleazar Wheelock's experiment at Moor's Indian Charity School as an emblem of apologetic acculturation. Scholars of American Indian literature rediscovered Samson Occom in the early 1980s as part of the effort to reconstruct a genealogy of American Indian writing. German scholar Bernd Peyer rediscovered Occom's short autobiographical narrative in the Dartmouth archives and first republished it in his anthology *The Elders Wrote: An Anthology of Early Prose by North American Indians, 1768–1931* (1982). Peyer identified Occom as the "'father' of modern Native American literature." Occom's monumental *A Sermon, Preached at the Execution of Moses Paul, an Indian* (1772) was reintroduced to scholarship in 1992 by the literary historian LaVonne Brown Ruoff. According to Ruoff, the *Sermon* was "probably the first book published in English by an American Indian." She aptly characterized Occom's rhetorical effort as a "delicate task" and a "balancing act" that appealed to both white and Indian audiences and that exemplifies for literary scholars "how an Indian author adapted Western European theology and a literary genre for his own purposes." First appearing in the journal *Studies in American Indian Literature,* the *Sermon* and the short autobiographical narrative subsequently appeared in the *Heath Anthology of American Literature* and eventually in other American literature anthologies as well.[38]

As Occom joined an expanding canon of early American literature, literary scholars approached his writings through the interpretive frameworks of multiculturalism, focusing on questions of identity formation, racial authenticity, and intercultural contact. Early criticism concentrated on his conflicted interfaces with institutions like Moor's Indian Charity School, white mentors like Eleazar Wheelock, and the white audiences for his printed writings. Consequently, Occom came to be viewed primarily as an intermediary between traditional Mohegan culture and white society. Margaret Connell Szasz, for example, characterized him as a stereotype-rending "cultural broker moving between Indian and non-Indian worlds" and an "intercultural eighteenth-century American" (61). David Murray and Arnold Krupat emphasized Occom's strategic adoption of discourses that appealed to white audiences in order to win attention and respect within the broader public sphere. Other scholars have represented Occom's cultural situation as a disorienting or confusing liminality between white and Indian worlds. There is in this strand of scholarship a quiet implication that Occom adopted English-language literacy and Christianity at the expense of his own wholeness or at some cost to Mohegan oral tradition and culture.[39]

A key problem in this now-conventional approach to Occom is the tendency to focus on his 1768 autobiography to the neglect of his much broader archive. Regrettably, the autobiography is now the only text by Occom to appear in most major

38. Peyer, "Samson Occom," 215; Ruoff, 78–81.

39. Szasz, 78; Krupat, *Voice in the Margin,* 141; D. Murray, *Forked,* 57. Scholarship focusing on Occom's "betweenness" includes M. Elliot; McCarthy; Elrod; D. Murray, *Forked.*

American literary anthologies, and it exerts a disproportionate influence over the way we understand Occom's life and career. The generic familiarity of the auto-biography seems to facilitate easy comparison with other late eighteenth-century autobiographies by authors such as Benjamin Franklin and Olaudah Equiano or with later works of Native American life writing. But it is hazardous to read it as a singular or definitive mapping of Occom's thoughts and feelings about himself, his tribal community, or the situation of Native people in the eighteenth century. Occom self-consciously composed this autobiography under circumstances of distrust and constraint to fulfill a discrete rhetorical purpose: to answer ongoing charges by his religious rivals and political opponents that he and Wheelock had falsified his identity as a recent convert—at once an authentic "Christian" and an authentic "Indian"—in order to bolster the fundraising mission for Moor's Indian Charity School. Focusing too closely on the autobiography distracts us from the broader body of ideas and feelings encompassed in Occom's extensive archive. Similarly, honing in on Occom's well-documented but conflicted thirty-year relationship with Eleazar Wheelock and the Moor's Indian Charity School project screens out Occom's lifelong ties to his indigenous relatives and communities, just as focusing on his tactical rhetorical gestures toward white audiences may blind us to the Native co-authors, intellectuals, readers, and hearers who constituted Occom's most important audience. This is not to say that Samson Occom did not experience suffering and loss or that the Mohegan and other New England tribal communities did not undergo significant change and privation during the late colonial and early national eras. Occom's own writings chronicle hardships and sufferings, as well as the continuities and pleasures of life in tribal communities and the multifaceted strategies, more and less successful, developed by dedicated Native leaders to envision and realize new futures for their peoples. It is more productive to read his writings not primarily as a record of the troubles of individual acculturation but as part of an ongoing in-digenous intellectual history of engagement and survival against the epic crimes of colonialism.[40]

This is the pivotal point Robert Warrior (Osage) made when he claimed Occom as an important figure for American Indian intellectual tradition in his landmark book *Tribal Secrets: Recovering American Indian Intellectual Traditions* (1995). War-rior sought to advance American Indian intellectual sovereignty by encouraging Native American scholars to recognize, engage with, and draw strength and direc-tion from the rich intellectual legacies created by Native American writers of the eighteenth, nineteenth, and twentieth centuries. "Writers going back at least as far as Samson Occom have grappled with many of the same issues that remain with us today," Warrior wrote. "Finding in their work not only resources for self-determined Native engagement but also political commitments and intellectual praxes that are at times troubling is a double-edged sword that reminds us constantly of our own challenges and fallibilities." Occom faced concerns and conditions similar to those that face contemporary American Indian intellectuals, including Euro-American land theft and genocide, destruction and usurpation of Native American territories and

40. On liminality, see Turner, 95–96.

traditions, exile, trauma, and grief. The goal of the "humanizing work of criticism," as Warrior describes it, is to realize "the fullness of [American Indian] humanity," "the fullness of our past, present, and future," through honest, courageous, compassionate engagement with the writings of these Native intellectual ancestors. To read Samson Occom in this way is to look at the expanse of his writing on its own terms. It is to grapple with its historical particularity, its generic variety, its familiarity, its foreignness, and, as we do, to confront Occom's full humanity, his contributions and his miscalculations, his strengths and weaknesses. It is to find in his writings, their faithful resolve, their unwarranted fidelities, their internal fractures, moments visionary and plodding, the expression of a full and autonomous Native thought-world at a crucial historical moment.[41]

The most compelling recent scholarship on Samson Occom follows this indigenist turn in American Indian literary criticism by paying rigorous attention to the specific tribal-historical contexts that generated his letters, sermons, petitions, and diaries. Grappling with the broader Occom archive has, in turn, led to new questions, vocabularies, and paradigms for interpretation that take us well beyond exhausted critical terms such as "identity" and "liminality." Bernd Peyer, Hilary Wyss, Dana Nelson, Laura Arnold, and I have examined Occom's efforts to adapt New Light Christianity to the cultural and political needs of the Mohegan and Brotherton communities. Lisa Brooks (Abenaki) situates Occom within a centuries-old tradition among Northeastern Native peoples of using writing to redress the shattering impacts of colonization and reconstitute Native communities in relationship to their homelands. Through collective petition writing, Brooks observes, Occom helped construct a new discourse of indigenous rights predicated on customary norms of communal responsibility emblematized in the Algonkian trope of "the common pot." She writes:

> Occom's strategy was to strengthen relationships within the larger coastal network and to reconstruct a new dish from amongst the surviving wampum-making nations, a village that could be moved along the waterways to a place with more abundant resources, away from colonial control. All of the people involved in this project were committed to the principles of Christianity that Occom had embraced as a young man, as well as to the ideals of the Common Pot.

Rather than represent Occom as an often-solitary Native author struggling to adjust to the discursive topographies of colonial power, Brooks successfully recasts the scholarly focus on Occom "as he emerged from and operated within native space." She explains:

> The emphasis on Wheelock (as if this was Occom's primary relationship) and the Indian school (as if Lebanon was his "home and center") has skewed our perceptions of the role of this colonial institution in Occom's life and in New England Indian communities. By centering other spaces, and allowing Wheelock and his school to remain in the background, I hope that I can demonstrate that

41. Warrior, 44, 122, 124.

> Wheelock's home was just one site within Occom's extensive network, and that
> the school was operating, not just as a colonial project, but as a location *within
> native space.* (emphasis added)

The life and the career of Samson Occom indeed look very different when we remember that he lived and moved within a space he called "this Indian world": physical, spiritual, and political territories inscribed by hundreds of years of indigenous
histories and relationships, histories and relationships that have ultimately absorbed and encompassed Eleazar Wheelock, Moor's Indian Charity School, English-
language literacy, and Christianity. The indigenist turn in American Indian literary
studies and the recuperation of Occom's extensive archive bring us to an exciting
moment in early Native American studies. Native and non-Native scholars are now
reading a broader range of early American Indian writings with a greater sense of
their relevance to historical and contemporary American Indian communities. Re-
membering the importance of Native communities to the life and work of Samson
Occom fosters scholarship more responsible to the concerns of contemporary indigenous peoples, including the Mohegan and Brotherton peoples who today claim
him as an ancestor.[42]

The compilation and republication of Occom's archive bears several important
implications for the way we understand Native peoples in the colonial and early national Americas. First, coming to terms with the expanse and variety of Occom's
writings impels us to reconsider how early Native writers conceived of literacy and
literary authority. Occom may have been the first but he was not the only member
of his family to learn to read and write in English. And he was not illiterate when
he arrived at Eleazar Wheelock's home in 1743. From an early age, Occom taught
himself rudiments of written English, and he was well versed in nonalphabetic literate forms such as oratory, wampum belts, and carving. Tribal councils and ceremonies also had distinctive, context-dependent compositional forms, which Occom
learned according to his position of responsibility within his family and tribe. This
sense of responsibility and these compositional sensibilities shaped to a significant
extent his adoption of the English language. Occom understood that English literacy constituted an intricate field of power, as he himself had witnessed in the trials
of the Mohegan-Mason land case in 1743. As he grew in his stature and authority as
a tribal and intertribal leader and public figure, he learned to negotiate with growing confidence these textures of power. He learned when it was possible to use an
English-language instrument like a petition to interject a collective tribal perspective
into colonial politics. He understood that his position in the public sphere sometimes required of him strategic acts of writing like his 1768 autobiography, which
contended very much against his own inclinations and habits of expression. He recognized, too, when writing had no power to provide emotional relief, as the gaps
and silences in his writings attest. In his letters, sermons, diaries, and hymns, we can
see Occom exploring the powers and limitations of alphabetic literacy to improve

42. L. Brooks, 141n68, 159.

the lives of Native people, and we can detect his hopes and frustrations in this unfolding process. In reading Occom's collected writings, we learn what it meant for a dutiful, community-minded Mohegan man to adopt alphabetic literacy in a time of incredible change and danger for New England tribal communities.

Occom's writings also give us a rich sense of the social shape of New England Native communities in the late colonial and early national eras. Historian Jean O'Brien has observed that Native people in New England formed small population "clusters" in marginal spaces by the end of the eighteenth century. In Occom's diaries, especially, we can trace his movements along kin and social networks between these clusters, which he calls Indian "towns" or Indian "places." His diaries, letters, and prose writings also give us a sense of the importance of hospitality and visiting in maintaining Native social and political networks. Occom considered generosity and hospitality to be defining characteristics of American Indian cultures. He often hosted dozens of visitors at his modest Mohegan home: "As our Custom is, we freely Entertain all Visiters," he explained in his 1768 autobiography. Recognizing Occom's commitment to maintaining these Native networks at Mohegan and beyond reminds us that a distinctive sense of indigenous space and social responsibility shaped his life and his writings, more so even than Eleazar Wheelock and Moor's Indian Charity School. Occom's writings, especially his correspondence with his wife and children, also document the struggles of indigenous families to protect themselves and safeguard their relationships against the fracturing forces of colonization.

In his sermons, letters, petitions, and prose writings, we see how Native people in the late colonial and early national eras developed articulate critiques of colonialism and rhetorics of decolonization. Despite his expressed disdain for the dress and grooming habits of the Iroquois, Occom did not believe that Europeans or Euro-Americans represented civilization. To the contrary, he often criticized the outrageous behavior of the English and American "savages" and "heathens" he encountered in cities like New York and London. His sermons offer unsparing critiques of the inhumanity and immorality of European colonialism, especially in comparison with the generosity, modesty, and reverence characteristic of many Native civilizations. Occom insisted that the Americas belonged to indigenous people. He remained throughout his life a stalwart defender of Native self-governance and territorial autonomy, even amid strong opposition from white colonial officials and factional controversy within his home Native communities. In order to combat the pervasive moral and social decay unleashed by colonialism, Occom exhorted Native peoples to exercise their powers of rational thinking. Like many other prophetic eighteenth-century Native leaders, he saw the destructive powers of alcohol and encouraged Native peoples to avoid it. Taken together, Occom's writings comprise the most extensive Native-authored commentary on colonialism to survive the colonial era.

Because Occom scholarship has tended to emphasize his affiliation with missionary projects like Moor's Indian Charity School, taking in the full expanse of his writings may lead us to reassess the connections between Native Christianity and decolonization in early America. Occom's collected writings urge a new view of how Christian Indians understood the role faith and church could play in advancing the well-being of tribal communities. Occom viewed the collective spiritual regeneration of tribal communities as a necessary component of their survival, and he understood his own often difficult spiritual path as a Christian Indian as having been divinely appointed. He and other New England Native Christian leaders like Samuel Niles, Samuel Ashpo, David Fowler, and Joseph Johnson adapted the teachings, customs, and forms of New Light Christianity to develop new venues for spiritual revitalization among Native people. In New England, separate Native churches served as venues for self-governance during a time when traditionary governmental forms had been infiltrated and disrupted by colonial agents. Factions within tribes certainly implemented different forms and aspects of Christian doctrine and practice that best allied to their respective interests: there is evidence that Christianity was used both to continue more visionary aspects of Native culture and to criticize nonassimilative cultural forms and practices. Historian Gregory Dowd has observed a similar range of religious developments among the non-Christian prophetic cultures of eighteenth-century Native America. Among the Ottawa, Delaware, Shawnee, and Cherokee, according to Dowd, new religious movements sometimes took shape in the revitalization of familiar rituals and practices, sometimes in the intertribal adoption of new religious practices, and sometimes in the prophetic revelation of new ceremonial practices. Religious movements among Native peoples encompass parallel and intertwined processes of revitalization, adaptation, and innovation that often defy simple categorization as "traditional" or "progressive," "accommodationist" or "nativist," "Christian" or "non-Christian." Acknowledging that Occom's Christianity also defies simple characterization as "assimilative" or "accommodationist" helps us to see him more accurately as a Native intellectual taking part in the broader pan-tribal revitalization movements of the late eighteenth century.

A cumulative effect of reading the Occom archive is a coming to terms with the complexity of his social, cultural, and intellectual world. Laboring to articulate the fullness and depth of life, thought, and writing in "this Indian world" is an ongoing effort of American Indian studies. For the last twenty years, American Indian literary critics, beginning with Paula Gunn Allen (Laguna Pueblo) and Elizabeth Cook-Lynn (Sioux) and continuing through Robert Warrior, Jace Weaver (Cherokee), and Craig Womack (Creek), have labored to shift frameworks for the study of American Indian literature from critical preoccupations defined by anthropological curiosity or modernist-aesthetic fascination to pan-Indian and tribal historical and cultural contexts, literary traditions, and political concerns. The goal is to see this literature on its own defining terms. Similarly, tribal-based intellectuals are working to define their own histories and communities in terms that enact their sovereign status. The present-day historian of Occom's own Mohegan tribe, Melissa Tantaquidgeon Zobel, has argued successfully that tribes must recast legal terms for winning tribal recognition from the U.S. government in their own terms. Item 83.7(c) on the federal petition form demands proof of "continuous authority" as a condition of winning tribal recognition. Tantaquidgeon Zobel asserts that because colonial governments have for hundreds of years infiltrated and disrupted tribal governments and because tribes themselves have reacted by vesting "sociocultural leaders" with authority over the life of the tribe, tribes themselves should define their sovereignty on these terms. She writes, "The critical thing to remember is not to be intimidated out of reformulating the question [of item 83.7(c) on the recognition petition] into Chiweeosk-Chiwee-Neezush (the Mohegan language equivalent of 83.7)!"[43]

Acknowledging "this Indian world" on its own terms is not about the simple additive logic of multiculturalism. It is about recognizing Native American writing as an exercise of intellectual self-determination. Robert Warrior has written, "If our struggle is anything, it is the struggle for sovereignty, and if sovereignty is anything, it is a way of life. That way of life is not a matter of defining a political ideology or having a detached discussion about the unifying structures and essences of American Indian traditions. It is a decision—a decision we make in our minds, in our hearts, and in our bodies—to be sovereign and to find out what that means in the process." Recognizing American Indian intellectual sovereignty means acceding the generative power and determining authority of distinct matrices of aesthetic, spiritual, and political principles and priorities that give shape to American Indian lives and American Indian writings. It means acknowledging that those principles and priorities constitute their own terms for theory and practice, that American Indian literature should be understood on its own inalienable grounds, grounds on which we dwell as guests or strangers.[44]

As we strive to reimagine the fullness of "this Indian world" in the colonial and early national eras, literary scholars face special challenges. One of our challenges has been confronting the continuing misapprehension that there was not significant literary activity among Native Americans until the late nineteenth or twentieth centuries, at least not enough to conduct a serious humanistic study of how Native peoples themselves textually registered and enacted their realities, perceptions of colonialism, and strategies for survival. This misapprehension results both from the purposeful destruction of indigenous libraries by European colonists and from our own privileging of alphabetic print and manuscript texts. Most of us do not yet know how to read the rich array of nonalphabetic textual forms that constitute the ancient literature of the Americas: codices, birchbark scrolls, wampum belts, quillwork, winter counts, and so on. New collaborations among art, literary, and material historians promise to bring alphabetic, ideographic, hieroglyphic, and pictographic textual forms into communication.[45]

Conventional frameworks for literary interpretation may also impede our recognition of the autonomy of indigenous thought-worlds. Comparative colonial literary studies foreground the lives and writings of European and Euro-American colonists: Anglo-American, Ibero-American, Luso-American, and Franco-American. Indigenous peoples assume the status of the territory itself, the inarticulate background, the page on which the European histories of the "New World" are written. Even a comparative formulation as helpful and ubiquitous as Mary Louise Pratt's "contact zone," which acknowledges imperialism as the imposition of radical power "asymetries," tends to negate the specific intellectual and spiritual contents of "this Indian world." Indeed, thinking about indigenous territory—*Indian Country*—as a "contact

43. Tantaquidegon Zobel, "Rooted," 53.
44. Warrior, 123.
45. On nonalphabetic indigenous textual forms, see Boone, Boone and Mignolo, and Wyss and Bross.

zone" assumes that North and South American geographical spaces are empty of power, that historical time is universal and homogenous, and that the effects of colonialism are primarily anthropomorphic. This does not necessarily square with indigenous views of space, time, or personhood, which hold that the land itself generates specific matrices of power, vectors of time, and human communities. Thus, even the notion of the "contact zone" does not acknowledge the priority, fullness, and autonomy of "this Indian world."

The limitations of conventional comparative study in admitting the integrity of indigenous life and thought-worlds has been described by colonial Latin Americanist Jose Rabasa as "the problem of the background." Rabasa observes that conventional comparison assumes the universality of Euro-American intellectual "backgrounds" as frameworks for analysis. Doing so cancels out the distinctive conceptual and perceptual frameworks of indigenous civilizations. He explains:

> What indigenous peoples think about the intrusion in their territories, the extraction of their knowledge, and strategies they develop to make sense of this Euroamerican process of appropriation is systematically excluded from the discussion. Our limitations are partly due to our inability to (re)cognize the background and the framework *from which* and *against which* Indians make sense of Euroamerican appropriations. In fact, the assumption that an all-encompassing single background ultimately makes sense of indigenous perspectives systematically negates Indian conceptualizations. (10–11)

Without underestimating the globalizing reach of European systems of thought and language, it is possible to train ourselves to acknowledge indigenous backgrounds— indigenous systems of thought and language—that preceded and in many cases have survived and absorbed Euro-American thought and culture. Learning to acknowledge the precedence of indigenous thought-worlds requires, first, that we defamiliarize ourselves with our most immediate and comfortable registers of critical inquiry, especially those critical registers that presume a comparative transparency across cultural domains. Second, we can learn to work more deeply in indigenous textual forms, even those that challenge conventional alphabetic notions of the literary. The challenge of "reading" let alone "understanding" Native oral traditions and nonalphabetic forms like codices, wampum belts, quillwork, birchbark scrolls, and winter counts reminds us that these texts emerge from distinctive thought-worlds not reducible to our own, powerful and autonomous thought-worlds that enact different modes of relationship to time, space, place, power, and personhood. Confronting the difficulty of reading and understanding indigenous texts is important to developing a responsible intellectual orientation to the colonial Americas, as well as a concomitant sense of the richness, integrity, and power of the thought domains that constitute "this Indian world."

There is no easy way forward. Learning to acknowledge the precedence of "this Indian world" entails a profound shift in our habits of thought, a revisiting of familiar assumptions about the places we live and the realities we inhabit. Reading or attempting to read the truly expansive literary legacies of the indigenous Americas is one way to face the limits of our privileged thought domains. We can reckon with the richly composite pictographic-ideographic textures of the Mixtec codices. We can confront the Incan writer Guaman Pomo de Ayala's monumental seventeenth-century letter to the king of Spain, the 1179-page, 397-drawing *Nueva Coronica y buen gobierno*. But until now there has been no "big book" of Native North American writing from the colonial era to confront us with comparable mass and complexity. This compilation and republication of Samson Occom's massive manuscript archive challenges us to revisit people and places we thought we knew. The historic span, generic breadth, range of concerns, and depth of detail encompassed in Occom's writings force us to move beyond narrow and familiar paradigms of inquiry to a new grappling with early American Indian writing on its own generic, aesthetic, and functional terms.

Samson Occom was first a Mohegan and second a founding member of the Brotherton tribe. His thought-world was rooted in tribal territories, tribal histories, kin networks, political responsibilities and obligations, ceremonial and planting cycles, and understandings of space, time, and personhood he learned first from his father, Joshua; his mother, Sarah; their relatives; and their broader tribal community. What he experienced as a teenager during the Great Awakening and what he learned as a young man from Eleazar Wheelock he reckoned with and adopted into this Native thought-world, even as this thought-world itself evolved with the changing circumstances of the Mohegan people and their kin. Occom did not believe that Christianity canceled tribal thought-worlds: "God made me an Indian," he declared in his 1768 autobiography. God made "this Indian world" for Indians, he declared in petitions he wrote on behalf of the Montaukett and Brotherton tribes. Reenvisioning the story of Samson Occom bears significant implications for the way we understand the shape and determining principles of Native American literature: from its beginnings, Native American writing has been shaped by a sense of responsibility to the well-being of tribal communities; a situatedness in networks of obligation, stewardship, and relationship; and a consciousness of the meaningfulness of tribal lands. These are the principles that shaped both the archive of Samson Occom and "this Indian world" he so faithfully inhabited.

PROSE

The occasional writings of Samson Occom provide us rare insights into the intellectual, spiritual, and cultural lives of Northeastern Native peoples in the eighteenth century. Most surviving accounts of American Indian life from this historical period were composed by European visitors to the American colonies or white settler-colonists; these documents often tell us more about the culturally specific preoccupations and prejudices or the political motives of their authors than they do about the indigenous peoples they purport to represent. Occom belonged to the communities he wrote about. Having been reared as a traditional Mohegan, he certainly understood that documenting the ceremonial life and customs of the Montauketts and Mohegans entailed specific cautions and obligations. He wrote about forces of tradition and change from the viewpoint of an intertribal political figure acutely engaged in the day-to-day business of survival in a rapidly changing world. Finally, Occom also understood that his unique position as an ordained Native American Presbyterian minister devolved upon him the often uncomfortable burden of being viewed by his white-majority audiences as a representative of all Indian people. Awareness of these intersecting tribal, intertribal, and colonial situations and their respective rhetorical demands shape the prose writings of Samson Occom.

Three of the prose pieces collected in this section were written during the decade Occom spent with the Montaukett tribal community of Long Island. Occom first came to Montauk in 1749 with a Mohegan fishing expedition; he subsequently found a place for himself as the community's first Native American minister and schoolmaster. White minister Azariah Horton recommended to local missionary societies that Occom be recognized as his successor. In 1751, Occom married Mary Fowler, the daughter of James Fowler (Shinnecock) and Betty Pharoah Fowler (Montaukett), a member of the powerful Pharoah family and a descendent of the seventeenth-century sachem Wyendanche. In 1754, the Montauketts experienced a powerful religious revival that appears to have touched some tribal members unconvinced by Horton and other white missionaries. During this season, Occom recorded the conversion narrative of a Montaukett woman named Temperance Hannibal (Hannabal). Hannibal family members beginning with "Hannabole Indian sore hand" or "Hannibal H Indian" appear in colonial documents from the early eighteenth century. David Hannibal followed David Fowler as a schoolmaster at Montauk in 1770; at least one Hannibal emigrated to Brotherton, while most of the family remained with the Long Island community.[1] This relation of experience by Temperance Hannibal is a rare eighteenth-century autobiographical narrative by a Native American woman. Occom probably encouraged Hannibal to give this relation as a prerequisite for joining the church at Montauk. The extent of his involvement as an amanuensis in shaping the form and content of her expression is unknown.

Occom also developed a close relationship with a Montaukett man named Ocus, who taught him more than fifty traditional herbs and root medicines useful for a wide range of ailments and purposes, from treating burns and digestive complaints to serving reproductive health and contraception. Ocus also taught Occom how to treat the eyestrain that plagued him during his study with Eleazar Wheelock. Occom's journals reveal that he occasionally practiced medicine throughout his life. Herbal medicine continued as an important element of Montaukett traditional life, transmitted through nineteenth- and twentieth-century practitioners Eliza Beaman, George Fowler, and Pocahontas Pharoah.[2] The late Mohegan tribal elder Gladys Tantaquidgeon was also an expert in herbal medicines. Her book *Folk Medicine of the Delaware and Related Algonkian Indians,* compiled from research Tantaquidgeon conducted while studying anthropology at the University of Pennsylvania and first published in 1928, documents several cures similar to those learned by Samson Occom in the eighteenth century.

In 1761, Occom composed an ethnographic account of Montaukett customs and lifeways, including ceremonies of naming, marriage, and burial, from interviews with elders, as well as his own observations of tribal life. His original purpose and audience is unknown, but the manuscript eventually came into the hands of John Devotion, a Congregationalist minister of Westbrook, Connecticut, who passed it on to Yale University president Ezra Stiles. It was published in the *Collections of the Massachusetts Historical Society* in 1809. Contemporary historians and ethnographers have relied upon this rare eighteenth-century account of Montaukett community life. Occom here acknowledges the power even of practices such as poisoning which he felt obliged as a Christian to reject. He wrote of Montaukett poisoners, "I don't see for my part, why it is not as true, as the English or other nation's witchcraft, but is a great mystery of darkness."

Occom is best known for the narrative of his life, conversion, and early ministry he wrote in the late 1760s. A short first draft of this autobiography was composed by Occom in Boston on November 28, 1765, as he prepared to depart on a three-year fund-raising tour of England as an emissary for Moor's Indian Charity School. Despite his recent ordination by the Long Island Presbytery and even though American Indians had been traveling to Europe as tribal emissaries for more than a century, the plan to send Occom was met with great controversy. Eleazar Wheelock's rivals on the Boston board of the Society for Propagating the Gospel (SPG) especially accused Wheelock and Occom of misrepresenting his identity as a recently converted Mohegan, and they demanded more credit for their role in funding a portion of Occom's education. In a December 6, 1765, letter to Wheelock, Occom wrote: "The

1. Rabito-Wyppensenwah, 349–350.
2. Rabito-Wyppensenwah and Abiuso, 586.

Honrable Commis^rs here are still very ^Strong^ in their oppossition to your Scheem, they think it is nothing but a Shame to Send me over the great Water, they Say it is to Impose upon the good People, they further affirm, I was bro't up Regularly and a Christian all my Days, Some Say, I cant Talk Indian, others Say I Cant read." Controversy followed Occom across the Atlantic to England, where he was received with generosity and kindness by leading religious figures like George Whitefield and John Newton and made to feel—as he later remembered—like a "gazing stocke" by the masses who gathered to see him.

Occom composed a second and more extensive version of his autobiography in September 1768. This autobiographical narrative provides a unique narrative account of Occom's upbringing, conversion, early career, and ongoing struggle to receive just compensation for his work from missionary societies, as well as some insights into how Native New England communities viewed the Great Awakening and missionary work. Now widely anthologized as a representative work of early American Indian literature, the narrative has frequently been interpreted as evidence of the conflicted identity and precarious position of the Christian Indian "between two worlds." It is important, however, to remember that Occom strategically crafted this narrative to respond to the ongoing controversy about his identity among white ministers, missionary societies, and audiences. Occom himself noted that "it is against my mind to give a History of myself ^& publish it,^" but that he did so because he felt obliged to correct "gross Mistakes" and misrepresentations of his background in publicity surrounding his tour of England. His resistance to public acts of autobiography may reflect a traditional proscription against storytelling that privileges the self over the community. Consequently, the autobiographical narrative reveals more about the constraints within which Occom worked—his white audiences' prejudicial preconceptions of "Indianness"—than it does about his own sense of himself as Christian Indian. Note, for example, that Occom *twice* repeats the detail that he lived in a "wigwam," a house "Coverd with Matts made of Flags." When he wrote this autobiography, Occom was living in a wood-frame house in Connecticut, but he understood that proving himself an Indian and vindicating his claims for just compensation meant appealing to his audience's ethnographic curiosity.

A richer, more complicated sense of how Occom viewed the situation of American Indians comes to us in a meditative essay he wrote twenty-five years later. "The most remarkable and Strange State Situation and Appearence of Indian Tribes in this Great Continent" (written in 1783 or later, but never published) compares the spiritual situation of American Indians and African Americans to Europeans and Euro-Americans. According to Occom, the institution of slavery served as proof that Euro-Americans were themselves barbaric beyond any barbarism they attributed to Native Americans. His concluding description of the worldviews and values of American Indians reflects his affection for their general benevolence, generosity, and humanity and their refusal to privilege ambition over tradition, as well as his own despair over their ever-deepening disadvantages in an environment increasingly dominated by Euro-American politics and economy.

I ∾   "TEMPERANCE HANNABAL" (1754)

[Montauk] February ye [7 or 9] AD
[1754]

Temperance Hannabal

I have been the most [wicked] wretch yt ever liv'd, yea [I thot] there was nothing in
all the Nois of Religion, and I thought and Said that the Christians Lied; I thought
it was ^best^ for me to gratify my own Inclinations———Till the Last fall, I was Sick
for Some Time, and in my Sickness, I begun to Query, What would become of my
Soul, if I Shoud Die in this State and Condition, and these thoughts threw me into
Fright, and was Concern'd for my Soul for Some Time, but as I got well of my Sickness my concern wore a way———till this Late Religious Stir[3] I bethought of my Self
again and after I had been to few meetings I found my Self a great Sinner and an undone Creature before god, yea Saw myself fit for nothing but Hell and everlasting
Distruction———and as I was at one meeting and as I was amusing and considering
my State & Condition, it threw me into Such Horror and guilt of Concience and Confusion of face, I fell into a Swoun,[4] and immediately I found my Self into great Darkness, and while I was there I heard a voice before me, Saying follow me, and I went
that way, and Immediately found my Self upon Something, I Cant Compared to nothing but to a Pole, ~~but over~~ Put over a Deep hole

[DCA Vault. Courtesy of Dartmouth College Library.]

2 ∾   "HERBS & ROOTS" (1754)

Elder Root & Sweet farm Root take a hand full of each, Put them in hot water, after
it is taken of the Fire till it is Cold[,] good for collick.[5]———1

   Sweet Farm Root & Swamp burey bark but most of the Farm, Soked in 2 Qts of
water good for Poison.[6]———2

   Elder bark that green Pounded & Mixt with Netes foot oil good for Burn———3.

---

3. *This Late Religious Stir:* The Montaukett community experienced several waves of revivalism,
   especially during the tenure of Presbyterian missionary Azariah Horton during the 1740s. A Yale-
   educated Presbyterian minister, Horton himself was deeply connected to the revivalism of the
   New Light movement, and he led a major revival at Montauk in 1741. A selection of Horton's
   Montauk missionary journals (1741–1744) was published in the New-Light magazine *The Christian Monthly History* (Strong, *Montaukett*). Other white New Lights who vied for Montaukett converts included James Davenport, the celebrity Great Awakening preacher controversial for his
   "enthusiastic" excesses, whose preaching is in part credited with inspiring the conversion of
   Samson Occom, and lay exhorter Elisha Paine (Eels, "Indian Missions" [1939], 170–174). Occom
   was the first Native American preacher stationed at Montauk.

4. *Swoun:* A swoon, or faint. These physical dimensions of the conversion experience reported by
   Temperance Hannibal are characteristic of evangelical Christianity in American Indian and
   African-American communities in the decades following the Great Awakening (1739–1744).

5. *Collick:* bowel pains.

6. *Poison:* Could indicate any harmful substance introduced to the body, or a traditional belief in
   poisoners documented by Occom in his ethnography of the Montauk (Tantaquidgeon, 108).

~~Bird~~ Burr Dock Leaf, Pounded & Mixt with fat—good for swelling.—4

Swamp Shoemake Sap good for Warts.—5.

Pecquauwoss, Some Quantity of Root, Boild in a gallon of water and take the water, and take a little bag—6

Take some Weecup and sweet Fern for the boy—

And for your Self the Same Weecup & Sweet Fern or some Sage, or Hysop—and take Some Bone and Burn it throughly and Pound it Fine and [it] about half a Spoon full at a time with a little water just before or after meal.—

And make Powder of great Centry, to take in Drink, Either Water or weak Punch.[7]—

Take some Pass Wood and some Horse Mint and Spoon full of Lime, into a Qurt of Water good for Cancer.[8]—

And take some Unicorn Root and use it as you do Centry.—

Take Some Speccle Alder and some Hysop and some Weecup, good for Saltish Humours—

of Ashes—good for Pluracy[9]—

Indian Elm good for Sore mouth—7

[Geebiyanbulk?] good for ^young^ Children that are inclining to fits. Startled.—8

[Cowachin[k]?] good for Cole[10]—9

Witch Root good for Bait for Musk—11

[Wehsuc[k]] or Bitter Root good to kill Lise—12

the Same Root with Some Powder and Salt Soked in Water and take about one Spoonfull at a time—then wet the Same in Salt Water from the Tea to Rub all over the Body for Sick—13

Master Wort good for one Sort of head ake—14

the Same Rt and the Little Sor of Willow rt ~~th~~ tak wil rt first—one ^spoon^ good for kings Evil[11]—15

Eating Rt & Poison Vine Sap—16

A Long Notched Leaf good Boil—17

Master over Witch Rt—18

A Rt for fits Pound the Rt and Soke in water about half an hour 4 Rts will doe—19

Long Fever herb take it the Leaves & throw them into hot water and Put them upon the wrsts hallow of the feet and upon the forehead—20

Indian flax Rt Boil good for Bloody flux[12]—21

---

7. *Punch:* Alcoholic drink made from wine or liquor and fruit juices.

8. *Cancer:* Term historically used to indicate an ulcer of the skin, rather than a malignant tumor.

9. *Pluracy:* Pleurisy, an inflammation of the lungs.

10. *Cole:* Probably the common cold.

11. *King's Evil:* Scrofula, a tuberculosis of the lymph nodes. The term "king's evil" refers to the popular belief dating from the reign of King Edward III, the Confessor (1044–1066), that the touch of the king could cure the disease.

12. *Bloody Flux:* Dysentery, an inflammation of the intestines.

Indian hamp good for to Draw anything out of Sores—22

Robbin Planting Soup good to Draw Corruption—23

an herb good for worm—24

Poplar Rt and teeth Rt Boild good for Rumatick[13]—25

[Secuts?] good to make one Vomit—26

[Secuts?] also good for humerous Sores[14]—27

Toad Sorril good for Bruise—28

Winter green and another herbe boild in 3 Quarts of Water till it is Consum'd to a pint and then take a jill[15] honey to it good for Throat Cankers[16]—29

an herb good to make women bear Children Prety high Stock and Long Leaves—30

wores Rt good to Draw young mens to Young women—31

a wead good to Restrain women from bearing Children—32

Horse Penroil and five fingers Leaves boild together good for Fever Ague[17]—33

An herbe good for Rattle Snakes bite—34

[Solonom?] Seal and Swamp ~~penroal~~ penroial and water Crissis Seal most boild together—good for Consumtion[18]—35

Prickly Leav'd and Thorn Rts most of the thorn boild in a bout 3 Quarts of water till Consumd to a Quart—good for Heart burn—36

An herb good for green wound a Small Slinder Stalk with Bushee top—37

another wead some what Like the other herb good for Sore Eyes Caused by Cold with a Stone heated. Put upon the hinder part the Neck—38

Water Dock Rt take and boil and take the Rt after it is boild and Pound it fine to Lay upon [lax?] Sore and Lance of the water of for it is good for it—39

Sweet flay good for Cloted Blood—40

Augeet good for bust take the Rt and Pound it in hot water and lett about a jill at once twice a Day—41

A little Sort of Indian flax for a Person to take 2 Days together that has French Pox[19] and then take Sasarfax and milk wead and Pound them together 2 thirds of the first and third of the Last—42

the Docter must take and herb and Rub his hands with it wile he is Dressing the Patien—43

Musk, with Some his fat and Furr Mixt together good for Ear ake—44

Wauhtouwox and Grape Vine Sap good for [word illegible] over the Eye—45

another herb and Sassarfax heart and Speccle beans Good for Sore Eyes—46

---

13. *Rumatick:* Rheumatic fever is a complication of strep throat causing inflammation in the joints and tissues; rheumatism also refers to any pain associated with the joints.

14. *Humerous Sores:* May refer to abscesses believed to result from an imbalance or excess of the bodily humors: phlegm, blood, yellow bile, or black bile.

15. *Jill:* Also gill, a quarter of a pint liquid measure.

16. *Canker:* Sore or abscess.

17. *Ague:* Sometimes used to refer to malaria, but here probably any fever accompanied with chills.

18. *Consumtion:* Wasting away, especially from tuberculosis.

19. *French pox:* Syphilis.

Herb good to heal brocken bones about the fingers and foot—47

Pitch Pine Budes and Small Wiled Cherry Tree but 2 third of the Latter Boild [word illegible]—good for young Women whose Flowers[20] are Stopt by weakness of Nature—48

Dears horn and [Mutlyyoubuck?], but the horn Shoud be grated mak about a jill and boil it in about 6 jills of water and Let it boil away half then the other into it goo[d] for Young Women where their Monthly Sickness[21] over flows—49

an herb boild in 2 gallon of water and boil it about half away and then Cool it, and the Put about 3 Qu[ts] of Pound it flax Sead good for to Ease Women that are in Traval[22]—50

Sweet and Spaknand and healing wead, that are bushee good to heal brocken bones about Thighs Legs and arms—51

May ye 17th AD1754

Ocus[23] has now Learnt me 52 Roots—and I have this Day Paid him in all 27 York money—God is the witness & my name ~~Samson~~

Samson Occom

[NLCHS; DCA Vault. Courtesy of Dartmouth College Library.]

3 ∽   ACCOUNT OF THE MONTAUK INDIANS, ON LONG ISLAND (1761)

An Account of the Montauk Indians, on Long-Island. By Rev. Sampson Occum, A.D. 1761.

Sir,   .

I shall give you the best account of some of the ancient customs and ways of the Montauk Indians, as memory will inform us at present.

    1. I shall begin with their MARRIAGES. They had four ways of marrying. The first is, as soon as the children are born, or presently after they are born, parents made matches for their children. The father of a male child goes to the parents of a girl, and takes with him a skin or two, such as they wore before the English came, and since they have had blankets, takes a blanket and some other presents, and delivers them to the parents of the girl, and then he will relate his business to them, and when he has done, the other party will manifest their thankfulness, if they agree in the matter; but if not, they will say nothing, but return the things, and the man must carry them elsewhere. But where there is agreement, they will proceed to accomplish the marriage. They prefix a time, and both parties will make preparations.

---

20. *Flowers:* Menstrual periods.
21. *Monthly Sickness:* Menstrual period.
22. *Traval:* Travail, or labor.
23. Ocus (Montaukett; b. 1712) appears on a 1760 muster list from Suffolk County, Long Island, New York (Rabito-Wyppensenwah and Abiuso 585).

The parents of the boy prepare cloathing, ornaments, and other presents; and the other prepare a great feast; and the relations of both parties generally join in making these preparations, and when the appointed time comes, the parents of the girl and their relations bundle up their preparations, and will call as many guests as they please. The other party also gets in readiness with their company, and all things being ready on both sides, the parents of the girl take up their child, and march with their company to the man's house, and they go in boldly without any compliments, and deliver their child to the man and his wife, and they receive their daughter in law with all imaginable joy, and the mother will suckle the young couple, the one at one breast, an the other to the other breast, and both mothers will take their turns in suckling the couple; and if the children are weaned, they must eat out of one dish;[24] and in the mean time the whole company is devouring the feast, and after the feast they will distribute the presents one to another, and this being ended they have completed the marriage; and every one returns to their wigwams, and the couple that are just married are kept at their parents' houses till they are grown up, and if they see fit to live together they will; if not, the parents can't make them to live together but they will choose other companions for themselves.

2. Parents stay till their children are grown up, and then will proceed in the same manner in marrying their children, as the former; but if the father be dead, the mother will undertake for her son; if both father and mother are dead, some near relation will undertake. There is no material difference between this and the other just mentioned. Many times the couple that are to be married never see one another till the very minute they are join'd in wedlock; in this the young man is seated in a high bench in a wigwam, and the young woman is led by the hand, by her father, or by some near relation, to the young man, and set her down by him and immediately a dish of victuals is brought at set before them, and they eat together, &c. ˙

3. Young people and others are allowed to choose companions for themselves. When a young couple conclude to have each other, they acquaint their parents of it, or near relations; and they assist them in it, they generally make a feast, &c. Sometimes the couple themselves make a small feast, and so call few neighbours to eat and drink with them.

4. The couple that are to live together make no noise about it; but the woman makes few cakes baked in ashes, and puts them in a basket and carries them to the man, and sets them down before him, and if they have been free together he is obliged to receive what is set before him, and to live together; but small provocations use to part them, and [they] marry others.

II. The way of NAMING THEIR CHILDREN. They use to make great dances or frolicks. They made great preparations for these dances, of wampum, beads, jewels, dishes, and cloathing, and liquors, &c. Sometimes two or three families join in naming their children, so make great preparation to make a great dance. When they have got all things ready, they will call their neighbours together, very often send to other

---

24. According to Abenaki scholar Lisa Brooks, the act of "eating from one dish" is a key trope of Native New England literature and culture.

towns of Indians, and when they have all got together, they will begin their dance, and to distribute their gifts, and every person that receives the gifts or liquors, gets up and pronounces the name that a child is to be called by, with a loud voice three times. But sometimes a young man or woman will be ashamed to pronounce the name, and they will get some other person to do it. Very often one family will make small preparations, and call few old people to name a child; and it was very common with them to name their children two or three times over by different names, and at different times, and old people very often gave new names to themselves.

III. Concerning their GODS. They imagined a great number of gods. There were the gods of the four corners of the earth; the god of the east, the god of the west, the god of the north, the god of the south and there was a god over their corn, another over their beans, another over their pumpkins, and squashes, &c. There was one god over their wigwams, another of the fire, another over the sea, another of the wind, one of the day, and another of the night; and there were four gods over the four parts of the year, &c. &c.

But they had a notion of one great and good God, that was over all the rest of the gods, which they called CAUHLUNTOOWUT, which signifies one that is possessed with supreme power. They also had a notion of a great evil god, which they called Mutcheshesunnetooh, which signifies evil power, who they say is mischievous, &c.

And to these gods they call for help under every difficulty, and to them they offered their sacrifices of various kinds, &c.

As for their images, they kept them as oracles. The powwaws consult these images to know the minds of their gods; for they pretend these images tell what the people should do to the gods, either to make a dance or a feast, or give something to the old people, or sacrifice to the gods.

IV. As for the POWAWS[25], they say they get their art from dreams; and one has told me they get their art from the devil, but then party by dreams or night visions, and partly by the devil's immediate appearance to them by various shapes; sometimes in the shape of one creatures, sometimes in another, sometimes by a voice, &c. and their poisoning one another, and taking out poison, they say is no imaginary thing, but real. I have heard some say, that have been poisoned, it puts them into great pain, and when a powaw takes out the poison they have found immediate relief; at other times they feel no manner of pain, but feel strangely by degrees, till they are senseless, and then they will run mad. Sometimes they would run into the water; sometimes into the fire; and at other times run up to the top of high trees and tumble down headlong to the ground, yet receive no hurt by all these. And I don't see for my part, why it is not as true, as the English or other nation's witchcraft, but is a great mystery of darkness, &c.

V. Concerning their DEAD, BURIAL, AND MOURNING. They use to wash their dead clean, and adorn them with all manner of ornaments, and paint the face of them with divers colours, and make a great lamentation over their dead. When they

---

25. *Powaw:* In *A Key into the Language of America* (1643), Roger Williams translated the Algonkian term "powwaw" as "priest" (192).

carry the corpse to the grave, the whole company, especially of the women, make a doleful and a very mournful and loud lamentation, all the way as they go to the grave, and at the grave; and they use to bury great many things with their dead, especially the things that belonged to the dead, and what they did not bury they would give away, and they would never live in a wigwam, in which any person died, but will immediately pull it down, and they generally mourned for their dead about a year, and the time they are in mourning the women kept their faces blackt with coal mixt with grease, neither would they wear fine cloathes, nor sing, nor dance, neither will the mourners mention the name by which their dead was called, nor suffer any one in the whole place to mention it till some of the relations is called by the same name; and when they put off their mourning habit, they generally made a great nightly dance. They begin it in the evening and hold it till morning.

VI. Concerning their NOTIONS OF FUTURE STATE. They believed the existence of their souls after their bodies are dead. Their souls go to the westward a great way off, where the righteous, or those who behaved themselves well in this world, will exercise themselves in pleasurable singing and dancing forever, in the presence of their Sawwonnutoh[26] or their western god, from whom they have received their beans and corn, their pumpkins, squashes, and all such things. They suppose the wicked go to the same place or country with the righteous; but they are to be exercised in some hard servile labour, or some perplexing exercise, such as fetching water in a riddle, or making a canoe with a round stone, &c.

These were common notions with all Long Island Indians.

In the year 1741 there was a general reformation among these Indians, and [they] renounced all their heathenish idolatry and superstition, and many of them became true Christians, in a judgment of charity. Many of them can read, write, and cypher well; and they have had gospel ministers to teach them from that time to this; but they are not so zealous in religion now, as they were some years ago.

NAMES	NO. IN FAMILY
Cyrus Charles	4
John Peter	3
John Peter, jun.	6
Hanabal	6
Joseph Pharaoh	5
Stephen Pharaoh	4
George Pharaoh	4
Richard Pharaoh	3
Old Ned	4
Old Pharaoh	4
Molatto Ned	4
James Fowler	8

26. *Sawwonnutoh:* Roger Williams similarly describes Narragansett belief in "Kautantowwit," "the great *South-West* God, to whose House all soules Goe, and from whom came their Corne, Beanes, as they say" (190).

Hugh	6
Nezer	9
Nimrod	15
Peggee Peter	2
Widow Rafe	2
Gid Gaunuck	2
David Ruckets	3
Widow Moll	8
Widow Jane	2
Jane Pharaoh	7
	111

[page break]

NAMES	NO. IN FAMILY
Brought over	111
Widow Betty Peter	1
Widow James	7
David Tutt	2
Widow Tutt	5
Widow Shime	7
Widow Cyrus	4
Stephen Cezer	4
Andonia Fowler	4
Widow Pegge	9
Samuel Neases	2
Roben Famely	6
Total souls	162

["A Letter from Rev. John Devotion of Saybrook, to Rev. Dr. Stiles, Inclosing Mr. Occum's Account of the Montauk Indians," from the *Collections of the Massachusetts Historical Society,* ser.1, v.10 (1809): 105–111.]

4 ∾   AUTOBIOGRAPHICAL NARRATIVE, FIRST DRAFT
(NOVEMBER 28, 1765)

Since there is great miss Representations by Some Concerning my Life and Education; I take this opportunity to ~~Inform~~ ^give^ the World in a few Words, the true Account of my Education—I Was Born a Heathen in Mmoyanheeunnuck alias Mohegan in N. London No^r^th America,[27] my Parents were altogether Heathens, and I Was Educated by them in their Heathenish Notions, tho' there was a Sermon Preach'd to our Mohegan Tribe Sometimes, but our Indians regarded not the Christian Religion, they Woud persist in their Heathenish ways, and my Parents in perticular were very Strong in the Customs of their fore Fathers, and they led a wandring

27. *N. London:* New London, Connecticut.

Life up and down in the Wilderness, for my Father was a great Hunter, thus I liv'd with them, till I was Sixteen years old, and then there was a great Stir of Religion in these Parts of the World both amongst the Indians as Well as the English,[28] and about this Time I began to think about the Christian Religion, and was under great trouble of Mind for Some Time, I thought the Religion which I heard at this Time was a new thing among mankind, Such as they never heard the like before, so Ignora^nt^ was I—and When I was Seventeen years of Age I receiv'd a Hope, and as I began to think about Religion So I began to learn to read, tho' I went to no School, till I was in my nineteenth year, and then I went to the Revd Mr Wheelocks to learning, and Spent four years there, and was very Weakly most of the Time;[29] this is the true account of my Education,

Samson Occom
Boston Novr 28 1765

[DCA 765628.1. Courtesy of Dartmouth College Library.]

5 ⁓   AUTOBIOGRAPHICAL NARRATIVE, SECOND DRAFT (SEPTEMBER 17, 1768)

Having Seen and heard Several Representations, in England and Scotland, ^made wrote^ by ^Some^ Several gentlemen in America, Concerning me, and finding many miss representations and gross Mistakes in their Account,—I thought it my Duty to give a Short Plain and Honest Account of myself, that those who may See my Account hereafter ^see it^, may know the ^Truth^ Concerning me.—

Tho' it is against my mind to give a History of myself ^& publish it^ Whilst I am alive, Yet to do Justice to my Self, and to those who may ^desire^ have ^mind^ to know Something ^concerning^ of me—and for the Honor of Religion, I will Venture to give a Short Narritive of my Life.—

From my Birth till I receivd the Christian Religion—

I was Born a Heathen and Brought up in In Heathenism till I was between 16 & 17 Years of age, at a Place Calld Mohegan in New London Connecticut, in New England,—my Parents Livd a wandering life, so ^as^ did all the Indians at Mohegan; they Chiefly Depended upon Hunting Fishing & Fowling and Claming for their Living and had no Connections with the English, excepting to [Traffic] with thim, with the in ^their^ Small Trifles,—and they Strictly maintain'd and follow'd their Heathenish Ways, Customs & Religion—tho' there was Some Preaching among ^them^ these Indians, once a Fortnight, in ye Summer Season, a Minister from N London used to Come up and the Indians Use to attend, not that they regarded the Christian Religion, But they had Blankets given to them every Fall of the Year and for these things they woud attend,—and there was a ^Sort of a^ School kept, when I was quite

---

28. Occom here and in his 1768 autobiography notes the impact of the transatlantic evangelical movement now known as the "Great Awakening" on Connecticut Native communities in about 1739. On the Great Awakening in New England, see Bushman, Gausted, Goen, and Lambert.

29. Occom suffered from several ailments, especially eye strain, which prevented him from entering Yale to prepare for the ministry (Love, *Occom*, 40).

young, but I believe there never was one that ever Learnt to read any thing,—and when I was about 10 Years of age there was ~~Sort of a School again in our Place~~ a man ^who went^ ~~used to go a~~ about among the Indian Wigwams, and where ever he Coud find the Indian Childⁿ, ~~he~~ woud make them read[30]—but the ~~Indian~~ Children Usd to take Care to keep out of his way;—and he Us'd ^to^ Catch me Some times and make me Say over my Letters, and I believe I learnt Some of them. ~~Letters,~~ But this was Soon over too— and all this Time there was ^not^ one amongst us, that made a ~~Christian~~ Profession ^of Christianity^—Neither did we Cultivate our Land, ^nor^ ~~and~~ kept any Sort of Creatures except Dogs, Which We Used in Hunting; and Dwelt in Wigwams, These are ^a^ Sort of Tents, Coverd with Matts, ~~and these Matts are~~ made of Flags—And to this Time we were ^~~generally~~^ unaquainted with the English Toung in general ^tho'^ there ^were^ a few, who understood a little of ^it^ ~~the English~~—

From the Time of our Reformation till I left Mʳ Wheelock—

When I was 16 years of age, we heard a Strange Rumor among the English, that there were Extraordinary Ministers Preaching from Place to Place and ~~that there was~~ a Strange Concern among the White People—this was in the Spring of the Year. But we Saw nothing of these things, till Some Time in the Summer, when Some Ministers began to visit us and Preach ~~to us~~ the Word of god; and the Common People ^also^ Came freequently ~~to us~~ and exhorted ^us^ to the things of god, ~~and~~ ^which^ it pleased the Ld, as I humbly hope, to Bless and Acompany ~~their Endeavours by his~~ ^with^ Divine Influences, to the Conviction and Saving Conversion of a Number of us; Amongst which, I was one that was Imprest with the things, ~~Which~~ we had heard. ~~and~~ These Preachers did not only Come to us, but we ^frequently^ went to their meetings and Churches.[31] Constantly, after I ~~found Trouble of Mind~~ ^was awakened &^ convicted,^[32] I Went to all the meetings, I ^Coud^ Come at; & ~~thus~~ Continued under Trouble of Mind about 6 months, ~~and almost as Soon as I found uneasiness in my Mind, So I~~ ^at which time I^ began to Learn the English Letters; got me a Primmer and Used to go to my English Neighbours freequently for Assistance in Reading, but went to no School, ~~and my Neighbours were very ready to help me~~— And When I was 17 years of age, ~~I hope~~ I had ^as I trust,^ a Discovery of the way of Salvation through Jesus, and was enabld to put my trust in him alone for Life & Salvation. From this Time the Distress and Burden of my mind was removd, and

30. In 1723, John Mason established a school at Mohegan that was supported by the colony and missionary societies, and a schoolhouse for Mohegan children was built in 1727. Mason's students included future sachem Ben Uncas III. During the 1730s, Samuel Avery and Jonathan Barber followed Mason as Mohegan schoolmasters, but the school failed in 1738 when community members refused to send their children amid deepening land controversies between Mason and the tribe (Love, *Occom*, 27–29).

31. During the Great Awakening, several Mohegans, including Sarah Occom, Samuel Ashpo, and Henry Quaquaquid, became members of David Jewett's North Church, at Montville, Connecticut (Love, *Occom*, 33–34).

32. Occom's cross-outs here and his use of the term "conviction" reveal his effort to represent the stages of his own conversion in accordance with accepted theological understandings of conversion morphology.

found Serenity and Pleasure of Soul, in Serving god, by this time I just began [word crossed out] to Read in the New Testament without Spelling,—and I had Stronger Desire Still to Learn to read the Word of god, and at the Same Time had an uncommon Pity and Compassion to my Poor Brethren According to the Flesh, I usd to wish, I was Capable of Instructing my poor Kindred, I use to think if I Coud once Learn to Read I Woud Instruct poor Children in Reading,—and used freequently to talk with our Indians Concerning Religion,— Thus I Continued till I was in my 19th year by this Time I Could Read a little in the Bible, at this Time my Poor Mother was going to Lebanon, and having had Some Knowledge of Mr *Wheelock* and hearing he had a Number of English ^youth^ under his Tuition,[33] I had a great Inclination to go to him and be with ^him^ a week or a Fortnight, and Desired my Mother to Ask Mr Wheelock, Whether he woud take me a little while to Instruct me in Readings Mother did So, and When She Came Back, She Said Mr Wheelock wanted to See me as Soon as possible,—So I went up, thinking I Shoud be back again in a few Days; when I got up there, he received me with kindness and Compassion and in Stead of Staying a Fortnight or 3 Weeks, I Spent 4 Years with him.—After I had been with him Some Time, he began to aquaint his Friends of my being with him, and his Intentions of Educating me, and my Circumstances,—And the good People began to give Some Assistance to Mr Wheelock, and Gave me Some old and Some New Cloaths.— Then he represted the Case to the Honorable Commissioners at Boston, Who were Commission'd by the Honorable Society in London for Propagating ye gospel among the Indians in New England and parts adjacent, and they alowed him 60£ p^r An 60£ in old Tenor, Which was about 6£ Sterling, and they Continu'd it 2 or 3: years I Cant tell exactly—While I was at Mr Wheelocks, I was very Weakly and my Health much Empard, and at the End of 4 Years, I over Straind my Eyes to Degree, I Coud not persue my Studies any Longer; and out off these 4 years, I Lost Just about one year;—And was obligd to quit my Studies.— —

From the Time I left M^r W till I went [two words crossed out] Europe.

As soon as I left Mr Wheelock, I endeavourd to find Some Employ among the Indians, went to Nahantuck,[34] thinking they may Want a School Master, but they one; then went to Naroganset,[35] and they were Indifferent about School, and went

33. Before the arrival of Samson Occom, Wheelock prepared young white men for college study and the ministry by instructing them in Latin, Greek, Hebrew, and theology. His success with Occom led Wheelock to establish Moor's Indian Charity School in 1754, recruiting several students through missionary David Brainerd, who was then preaching among the Delaware. His first Native American students—among them John Pumshire (Delaware), Jacob Woolley (Delaware), Samson Wauby (Pequot), Joseph Woolley (Delaware), and Hezekiah Calvin (Delaware)—received training in classical languages as well as English until 1762, when one of his sponsoring missionary societies discouraged this course of study as unnecessary and inappropriate (L. Murray, "Pray," 50–52; Love, *Occom*, 56–81; McClure).

34. *Nahantuck:* The Niantic tribal community, at Niantic, Connecticut. Samson Occom's aunt Hannah Justice Samson married into the Poquiantup family of Niantic, creating kinship ties between Occom and the community.

35. *Naroganset:* The Narragansett tribal community, at Charlestown, Rhode Island. Samuel Niles and James Simon, both Narragansett, led rival separatist Christian Indian congregations here in the 1740s, and several Narragansett later attended Moor's Indian Charity School.

back to Mohegan, and heard a number of our Indians were going to *Montauk,* on Long Island,—and I went with them, and the Indians there were very desirous to have me keep a School amongst them, and I Consented, and went back a while to Mohegan and Some in November I went on the Island, I think it is 17 years ago last Nov[r]. I agreed to keep a School with them Half a Year, and left it with them to give ^me^ what they Pleasd; and they took turns to Provide Food for me—I had near 30 Scholars this winter; I had evening School too for those that Coud not attend Day School—and began to Carry on their meetings, tho' they ^had^ a Minister, one M[r] *Horton,* the Scotch Society's Missionary; but he Spent, I think, two thirds of his Time at Sheenecock, 30 Miles from Montauk. We met together 3 times for Divine Worship every Sabbath and once on ^every^ Wednesday evening—I ~~to~~ read the Scriptures to them and Usd to expound upon Some perticular Passages in my own Toung;[36] Visited the Sick and attended their Burials—When the half year expird, they Desird me to Continud with them, Which I Complyd with, for another half Year, When I had fulfilled that, they were Urgent to have me Stay Longer, So I Continud till I was Married ~~amongst 'em~~, Which was about 2 years after I Went there,—

And Continud to Instruct them in the Same Manner as I did before after I was maried a while, I found there was need of a Support more than I needed, while I was Single,—and I made my Case Known to M[r] *Buell* and to M[r] *Wheelock,* and also the Needy Circumstances and the Desires of these Indians of my Continuence amongst them, and M[r] *Wheelock* and other gentlemen Represented my Circumstances and the Desires of these Indians of my Continuing amongst them, and the Commissioners were so good as to grant £15 per An. Sterling[37]—And I kept on in ^my^ Service as usual, Yea I had additional Service; I kept School as I did before and Caried on the Religious Meetings as often as ever, and attended the Sick and their Funerals, and did what Writings they wanted, and often Sat as a Judge to reconcile and Deside their Matters between them, and had visitors of Indians from all Quarters; and, as our Custom is, we freely Entertain all Visiters,—And was fetchd often from my Tribe and from others ^to^ See into their Affairs Both Religious Temporal,—Besides my Domestick Concerns,—and it Pleased the Lord to Increase my Family fast—and Soon after I was Maried, M[r] *Horton* left these Indians, and the Sheenecock Indians & after this I was Licencd to P and then I had the Whole Care of these Indians at Montauk, and ~~Used to~~ visited the Shenecock Indians often,—Used to Set out Saturdays towards Night and come back again Mondays. I have ^been^ obliged to Set out from Home after Sun Set, and Ride 30 Miles in the Night, to Preach to the^se^ Indians ~~at Shenecock~~.—And Some Indians at Shenecock Sent their Children to my School at Montauk, I kept one of them Some Time, and had a Young Man ^a^ half year from Mohegan, A Lad from Nahantuck who was with me almost a Year; [six words crossed out] and had little or nothing for Keeping them,—

My Method in the School was, as Soon as the Children got together, and ~~have~~

---

36. Mohegan-Pequot and Montauk both belong to the Eastern Algonkian language group.

37. During his first two years at Montauk, Occom received no financial support from the SPCK; Eleazar Wheelock and Solomon Williams represented Occom's time at Montauk as an unpaid leave of absence from his studies to recover his eyesight (Love, *Occom,* 44).

took their proper Seats, I Pray^e^d with them, then began to hear them, I generally began (after Some of them Coud Spell and Read,) With those that were yet in their Alphabets, So around, as they were properly Seated, till I got through, and I obligd them to Study their Books, and to help one another, When they Coud not make out a hard word they Brought to me——and I Usually heard them, in the Summer Season 8 Times a Day 4 in the morning, and in ye after Noon.——In the Winter Season 6 Time a Day, As Soon as they Coud Spell, they were obligd to Spell when ever they wanted to go out. Concluded with Prayer; I ^generally^ heard my Evening Scholars 3 ^Times^ Rou^n^d, And as they ^go^ out the School, every one, that Can Spell, is obligd to Spell a Word, and to go out Leisurely one after another,——I Catechised 3 or 4 Times a Week according to the Assembly's Shorter Catechism, and many Times Proposd Questions of my own, and in my own Tonugue,——I found ~~Som~~ Difficulty with Some Children, who were Some What Dull, Most of these Can Soon learn to Say over their Letters they Distinguish the Sounds by the Ear, but their Eyes can't Distinguish the Letters, and the Way I took to Cure em, was by ~~taking~~ making an Alphabet on Small bits of paper, and Glued them on Small Chips of Cedar, after this manner A B &c. I put these on Letters in order on a Bench, then point to one Letter and bid a Child to take notice of it, and then I order the Child to fetch me the Letter from ye Bench if it Brings the Letter, it is well, if not it must go again and again till it brings ye right L^r When they Can bring any Letters, this way, then I Just Jumble them together, and bid them to Set them in Alphabetical order, and it is a Pleasure to them; and they soon Learn their Letters this way——I freequently Discussed or Exhorted my Scholars, in Religious matters,——My Method in our Religious Meetings was this; Sabbath Mornings we Assemble together about 10: O. C. and begin with Singing; we generaly Sung Dr Watts's Psalms or Hymns, I distinctly read the Psalm or Hymn first, and then give the Meaning of it to them, after that Sing, then Pray, and Sing again after Pray^r then proceed to Read Some Sutable portion of Scripture, and So Just give the plain Sense of it, in Familiar Discourse and apply it to them, So conclude with Prayer and Singing, In the after Noon and Evening we Proceed in the Same Manner, and So in Wednesday Evening,——Some Time after Mr Horton left these Indians, there was a remarkable revival of religion among these Indians and many were hopefully Converted to the Saving knowledge of God in Jx. It is to be observed before Mr Horton left these Indians they had Some Prejudices infusd in their minds, by Some Inthusiastical Exhorters from N England, against Mr Horton, and Many of em had left him, by this means he was Discouragd; and Sued a Dismission and was dismist from these Indians,—— And being acquainted with the Enthusiasts in New England & the make and the Dispositions of the Indians, took a mild way to reclaim them, I opposd them not openly but let them go on in their way, and When ever I had an opportunity, I woud read Such passages of the Scriptures, as I thought woud confound their Notions, and I woud come to them with all Authority, Saying, thus Saith the Lord, and by this means, the Lord was pleased to Bless my poor Endeavours, and they were reclaimd, and Brought to hear most any of the ministers.——

I am now to give an Account of my Circumstances and manner of Livining, I Dwelt in a Wigwam, a Small Hutt fraimed with Small Poles and Coverd with Matts made of Flags, and I was oblig'd to move twice a Year, about 2 miles Distance, by rea-

son of the Scarcity of wood, for in one Neck of Land they Planted their Corn, and
^in^ another, they had their wood,[38] and I was obligd to hire my Corn Carted and
my Hay also,—and I got my Ground Plow'd every year, Which Cost me about 12 S
an Acre; and I kept a Cow and a Horse, for which I paid 21 S every year York currency; And went 18 Miles to Mill for every Dust of Meal we Usd in my family. I
Hired or Joined with my Neighbours to go to Mill, with a Horse or ox Cart, or on
Horse Back, and Some times ~~go~~ ^went^ my self; my Family Increasing fast, and my
Visiters also, I was obligd to Contrive every way to Support my Family; I took all
opportunities, to get Some thing to feed my Family Daily,—I Planted my own Corn,
Potatoes, and Beans; I Use to be out whoeing my Corn Some times before Sun Rise
and after my School is Dismist, and by this means I was able to raise my own Pork,
for I was alowed to keep 5 Swine,[39] Some Mornings & Evenings I woud be out with
my Hook and Line to Catch fish, and in the Fall of year and in the Spring, I usd my
Gunn, for we lived very handy for Fowl, and I was very expert with Gunn, and fed
my Family with Fowl, I Coud more than pay for my Powder & Shott with Feathers; at
other Times I Bound old Books for Easthampton People, made Wooden Spoons and
Ladles, Stockd Guns, & workd on Cedar to make Pails Piggans and Churns &c.—
Besides all these Difficulties I met with adverse Providence I bought a Mare, had it
but little while, and She fell into the Quick Sands and Died, after a while Bought
another, I kept ^her^ about half Year, and She was gone, and I never heard nor Seen
her from that Day to this, it was Supposd Some Rogue Stold her, and got another and
Dyed with a Distemper, and last of all I Bought a Young Mare, and kept her till She
had one Colt, and She broke her Leg and Died and Presently after the Colt Died also,
In the whole I Lost 5 Horse Kind; all these Losses helpd to pull me down, and by this
Time I got greatly in Debt, and acquain^t^ed my Circumstances to Some of my
Friends, and they Represented my Case to the Commissioners of Boston, and Inter-
ceeded with them for me, and they ^were^ pleased to Vote 15 [£] for my Help; and
Soon after Sent a Letter to my good Friend at N London, acquainting him, that they
had Superseded their Vote; and my Friends were so good as to represent my Needy
Circumstances Still to them, and they were so good at Last, as to Vote £15 and Sent
it, for Which I am very thankful; and ^the Rev^d^^ Mr *Buell* was ^so^ kind as to Write
in my behalf to the gentlemen of Boston; and he told me they were much Displeasd
with him, and heard also once and again, that they blaimed me for being Extravagant, I Cant Conceive how these gentle^n^ woud have me Live, I am ready to ^imputed
to^ their Ignorance, and woud wish they had Changd Circumstances with me but
one Month, that they may know, by experience What my Case really was; but I am
now fully Convincd, that it was not Ignorance, For I believe it can be provd to the
world, that these Same Gentlemen, gave a young Missionary, a Single man *one Hun-*
dred Pounds for one year, and fifty Pounds for an Interpreter, and thirty Pounds for

---

38. Under agreements signed in 1703, Montauketts were confined to "North Neck," west of the
    Great Pond also known as Montauk Lake, and "Indian Fields," to the east of the Pond (Strong,
    Montaukett Indians, 58–59).
39. The agreements of 1703 restricted the Montaukett tribe as a whole to keeping 250 hogs (Strong,
    Montaukett Indians, 58–59).

an Introducer, so it Cost them one Hundred & Eighty Pounds in one Single Year, and they Sent too where there was no Need of a Missionary,

Now You See What difference they made between ^me^ and other Missionaries; they gave me 180 Pounds for 12 years Service, which they gave for one years Service in another Mission—In my Service (I speak like a fool, but I am Constraind)[40] I was my own Interpreter. I was both a School master, and Minister to the Indians, yea I was their Ear, Eye & Hand, as Well Mouth,—I leave it with World, as wicked as it is, to Judge, whether I ought not to have had half as much, they gave a young man Just mentiond which would have been but £50 ^a^ year; and if they ought to have given me that, I am not under obligations to them, I owe them nothing at all; Now what can be the Reason? that they used me after ^this^ manner, I Cant think of any thing, but this as a Poor Indian Boy Said, Who was Bound out to an English Family, and he Usd to Drive Plow for a young man, and he Whipt and Beat him allmost every Day, and the young man found fault with him, and Complaind of him to his master and the poor Boy was Calld to answere for him ^self^ before his master,—and he was askd, what it was he did, that he was So Complaind of and beat almost every Day; he Said, he did not know, but he Supposd it was because he coud not ^drive^ any better; but says he, I Drive as well as I know ^how^; and at other Times he Beats me, because he is mind to beat me, but Says he, ^I believe^ he Beats for the most of the Time, because I am an Indian.—

So I am ready to Say, they have usd thus, because I Cant Instruct the Indians so well as other Missionaries, but I Can asure *them* I have endeavourd to teach them as well as I how—but I must Say, I believe it is because I am poor Indian. I Can't help that God has made me So; I did not make my self So.—

[DCA Vault. Courtesy of Dartmouth College Library.]

6 ∾   "THE MOST REMARKABLE AND STRANGE STATE
SITUATION AND APPEARENCE OF INDIAN TRIBES
IN THIS GREAT CONTINENT" (1783)

The most remarkable and Strange State Situation and Appearence of Indian Tribes in this Great Continent.—

Some Times I am ready to Conclude, that they are under Great Curse from God,—But When I come to look and view the nations of the World I Cant See that they are under Greater Curse than other nations, there are the Poor Negroes How long they have been in wretched and most Cruel Slavery thousands and millions of em,—and when I Come to Consider and See the Conduct of the Most Learned, Polite, and Rich Nations of the World, I find them to be the Most Tyranacal, Cruel, and inhuman oppressors of their Fellow Creatures in the World, these make all the confusions and distructions among the Nations of the Whole World, they are the Na-

40. Occom here references 2 Corinthians 11:22–23: "Are they Hebrews? so am I. Are they Israelites? so am I. Are they the seed of Abraham? so am I. Are they ministers of Christ? (I speak as a fool) I *am* more; in labours more abundant, in stripes above measure, in prisons more frequent, in deaths oft."

tions, that inslave the poor Negroes in Such Barbarous manner, as out do the Savage Indians in North America, and these are Calld Christian Nations You may See, Mr John Wesleys acount of Slave Trade⁴¹ Now lets [query]—Who is under the Greatest curse he that [inclines] to such hardness of Heart, as to exercise the utmost Cruelty upon their Fellow Crea^s or they that are thus Tormented,—As for my part I Can not See So far, as to determine who are under the Greatest Curse of all the Nations I believe all Adamites are under a Curse As for this Life, it is as nothing, it is altogether uncertain

Shall now take notice of things peculiar to the Natives of this Country.—Indians, So Called, in this most extensive Continent, are Universally Poor, they have no Notion of Laying up much for the Future, they all live from Hand to Mouth, as the Common Saying is Chiefly by Hunting Fishing and Fowling; the Women Raise little Corn, Beans, and Pompkins, and pick Wild Fruts, and do other Drudgery⁴²; those that live among or near the White People, have Learnt, Some of them, to live a little in immitation of them, but very poor Still, they are good Serv^ts to themselves, they have no Oeconomy to live; wastful and imprudent, both of time & Substance, they will wory and Toile all Day to lose two Shillings & gain Six pence, they have no Patience nor Ambistion to appear Great in the World, they have no Notion of much learning, them that have had Some Learning made Little or no good Use of it ^many have lost all their Learning^,—they Learn no trades, if any of them have Learnt, they follow it not—They have no Laws or Regulations ^Neither in^, every on des what is right in his own Eyes,—Yet in general they kind to one another, and are not given to Lying, Cheating, and Steeling much what this way ^a^ is Trifling But they are much for Drink^g Strong Drink, Yet I Cant think that it is more Natural to them ^than other N^ their manner [. . .]

[CHS folder 1.10. Samson Occom Papers, Connecticut Historical Society, Hartford, Connecticut.]

41. John Wesley published his antislavery pamphlet *Thoughts Upon Slavery* in 1774.
42. Occom here uncritically reiterates a common European and Euro-American stereotype of Native American women as drudges. The gendered division of agricultural labor he describes reflects the status of women as landowners in many tribal societies (Perdue).

LETTERS

Seventy-six letters by Samson Occom provide a remarkable window onto Occom's personal and public lives, including his family relationships and friendships, as well as his position within indigenous, domestic, and transatlantic networks of religious and political affiliation. More than in any other genre of his writing, in his letters we hear the voice of Samson Occom across a full expressive range: he is affectionate, humorous, sorrowful, searching, earnest, honest, critical, righteously indignant, sarcastic, and contemptuous. To his close friends and mentors, Occom confesses vulnerabilities, hurts, and disappointments and expresses a deep and personal faith. He wrote to Eleazar Wheelock on the eve of his departure for England, December 6, 1765:

> I have a Strugle in my Mind At times, knowing not where I am going, I dont know but I am Looking for a Spot of Ground ^where^ my Bones must be Buried, and never to See my Poor Family again, but I verely believe I am Calld of god by Strange Providence and that is Enough . . . I want nothing but the Will of God, to be Wholly Swallowed up in it.

These letters also reveal Occom's passionate, unremitting concern for the survival and well-being of Native peoples. Sometimes despairing, sometimes hopeful about the situation of tribal communities, Occom did not apologize for Native resistance to white colonization. As he wrote in a letter dated November 1791:

> Indians must have Teach[ers] of their own Coular or Nation,— They have very great and reveted Prejudice against the White People, and they have too much good reason for it—they have been imposed upon, too much, and they have been, between Contending Nations [a long] Time.

Occom's letters also provide important historical information about Moor's Indian Charity School, Mohegan tribal affairs, tensions with local whites, developing relationships with the Oneida people, the conception and organization of the Brotherton movement, the impact of the American War of Independence on Native communities, and the struggle of the Brotherton and New Stockbridge communities to preserve their autonomy against an onslaught of white encroachment in upstate New York.

Eighteenth-century America has been described as a "republic of letters." During Occom's lifetime, reading and writing personal letters assumed new value as a way for even geographically isolated Americans to cultivate a shared sense of social belonging. Itinerant ministers made extensive use of letters to communicate news of remarkable revivals across the colonies in the 1740s. Epistolary communities also took shape in exchanges of sentiment and information, especially among members of the social elite, such as John Adams, Thomas Jefferson, Abigail Adams, and Mercy Otis Warren, in the late eighteenth century. During the early years of the American War of Independence, English colonial officials sometimes intercepted American letters as sources of military and political intelligence, while American political writers used private and published correspondence to organize national politics and to model appropriate expressions of citizenship. Poor, working-class, and rural Americans also took up letter writing in the late eighteenth-century, especially in New England. In Boston, Massachusetts, the poet Phillis Wheatley maintained a thirty-year epistolary friendship with Obour Tanner of Newport, Rhode Island, constituting one of the earliest literary associations among women of color.[1]

Occom's letters document his never-ending efforts to secure decent compensation from missionary societies and other sponsors. They also chart the uneven course of his thirty-year relationship with Eleazar Wheelock. It was Wheelock who trained the young Samson Occom to observe the formal conventions of Anglo-American letter-writing when Occom was his student from 1743 to 1747. Letter writing was a crucial part of the curriculum at Moor's Indian Charity School, as surviving letters written by nineteen Native American male and female Moor's students during the 1750s and 1760s show. These letters document the complex processes of subjection through which Wheelock attempted to determine the character of his Native students by drawing them into a highly disciplined discursive field of expression and obligation. Wheelock instructed his students to call themselves his "sons." He demanded that his students write to confess their sins, report on their progress, and communicate their personal business. Letters exemplary in their piety or scriptural proficiency were sometimes forwarded to sponsors of Moor's Indian Charity School, but very few were answered by Wheelock himself. Even a favored student like David Fowler had reason to complain, "I take it very hard that I have not receiv'd one Line when others have received Folio's after Folio's" (McCallum 108). Silences and gaps in correspondence mark spaces where Wheelock affirmed his authority by withdrawing his affection, as well as spaces where Wheelock's students refused to allow his surveillance. In fact, as Laura Murray perceptively notes, the termination of correspondence with Eleazar Wheelock often constituted a declaration of independence on the part of the Indian writer.

Occom's early letters suggest that he generally accepted Wheelock's paternalistic discipline and acceded to the deferential epistolary conventions of the time. Contemporary readers have especially focused on his self-abasing closures as a sign of Occom's self-hatred. These should not be taken at face value, for as we find in later

---

1. On itinerancy and letter writing, see O'Brien and Fea. Konstantin, Gelles, Lawson, Bartram, and Shuffleton discuss the epistolary habits of early national elites. On letter writing during the American War of Independence, see Flavell, Farrell, and Jefferson and Madison. Bassard analyzes correspondence between Wheatley and Tanner.

letters—especially those written after his return from England—Occom directly communicated his rejection of Wheelock as a mentor and father figure, as well as his criticisms of the devolution of the Moor's Indian Charity School project. His July 24, 1771, letter to Wheelock is exemplary in this regard. Occom issues a frank, unapologetic judgment of Wheelock's opportunistic abandonment of his Native students:

> I am very Jealous that instead of your Semenary Becoming alma Mater, she will be too alba mater to Suckle the Tawnees, for She is already aDorn'd up too much like the Popish Virgin Mary. . . . I think your College has too much Worldly Grandure for the Poor Indians they'll never have much benefet of it,—. . . I verily thought once that your Institution was Intended Purely for the poor Indians with this thought I Cheerfully Ventur'd my Body & Soul, left my Country my poor young Family all my friends and Relations, to sail over the Boisterous Seas to England, to help forward your School, Hoping, that it may be a lasting Benefet to my poor Tawnee Brethren, With this View I went a Volunteer—I was quite Willing to become a Gazing Stock, Yea Even a Laughing Stock, in Strange Countries to Promote your Cause.

Occom's 1768 letter to Mohegan's troublemaking white schoolteacher Robert Clelland also demonstrates his ironic awareness and playful manipulation of epistolary conventions, as he signs himself "I am, sir, just what you please." As he grew in maturity, stature, and responsibility, Occom addressed his white correspondents with more assurance, boldness, and authority.

Occom also corresponded with other English-literate Native Americans. During his fundraising tour of England, Occom received "chiefly mournful" letters from his wife, Mary, who was struggling under the burdens of single-handedly maintaining the family and their homestead. His replies to her reveal the vulnerability, loneliness, and sadness Occom experienced as a consequence of his sojourn among the alien British far from his tribal community, his homelands, and his family. Witness his outpouring of feeling in this 1767 letter:

> I am Sensable of the great Burden and Care that is upon you, and I feel your Burden, Cares and Sorows. My poor Family is near and Dear to me, and you are the nearest to my Heart,—tho we are at great Distance from each other Yet you are near and Dearer to me than ever,—But it was the Call of god and nothing but the Call of god in his Devine Providence, Cou'd have Caused me to Leave my Dear Family, and it is the Call of God, that you Shoud have the Whole Care of a large Family—and let us then put our Whole trust in god, and Cast all our Burdens, upon him.

On June 24, 1780, Samson and Mary gathered their whole family together to hear them read a letter to their wayward son Benoni. For Occom, personal letters served to maintain and strengthen family ties strained by physical and emotional separation. It is important to note, though, the virtual absence of letters pertaining to the internal affairs of the Mohegan tribe. This gap suggests that either a significant body of such letters was lost or destroyed, or that tribal business was not conducted by correspondence. Even as they became literate in English and versed in the legal and governmental discourses of colonial and early national Connecticut, Occom and other Mohegan tribal leaders continued to observe the political protocols essential to and constitutive of tribal life: meeting together on traditional territorial grounds, sharing meals, and affirming relationships of status and kinship. They may have rightly feared, as well, the interception and manipulation of correspondence by colonial officials. Some letters written by Occom during his final years at Brotherton do offer a glimpse of conflicts internal to that struggling tribal settlement. These, too, suggest that in eighteenth-century American Indian communities, letter writing marked moments of strain and constraint rather than social connectedness and expressive freedom.

The seventy-six letters reprinted here probably constitute only a surviving fraction of the hundreds Occom wrote over the course of his fifty-year career. The majority of these surviving letters were saved by their recipients. Eleazar Wheelock kept twenty-four letters from Occom among his extensive personal archive, now institutionalized at Dartmouth College. Only sixteen surviving letters are drafts or sender's copies preserved by Occom himself. This suggests that Occom did not choose to or was not able to maintain a large personal archive. Steeped as he was in oral traditions of knowledge preservation, Occom may not have shared Wheelock's emphasis on written record keeping as a means of memory and institution building. It is also likely that Occom had neither the time nor the paper to compose careful letter drafts or hand-copy his own correspondence. Certainly, his frequent itinerancies and his household moves from Montauk across the Long Island Sound to Mohegan and from Mohegan to Brotherton made difficult conditions for the preservation of papers. It is important to bear in mind, then, that this body of correspondence does not reflect Occom's epistolary habits as faithfully as it does the cultural forces, institutional pressures, and historical accidents that have determined the shape of American Indian literary archives.

I ❧   TO SOLOMON WILLIAMS

Easthampton
Novr ye 1, 1752

Revd Sir

I Can never be thankful Enough to your Self Sir, for the kindness and Pity you have Shown to Such a Creature as My Self, and also that I have Such a one ^as^ your Self, to go to for Direction and help, at any time,— and I Shall trouble you with a very few Lines at this Time, Just to Let you know, that I have not Receiv'd a peney from the Gentlemen at Boston[2] neither have I receiv'd any thing from the Indians worth a telling of, these almost two Years; and I am now Driven to the want, almost, of every thing, and I owe upwards of £30 in York Money, and I think I have taken nothing Needlessly, I Send these few Lines thinking you might have receiv'd Something

---

2. *Gentlemen at Boston:* Boston officers of the Society for Propagating the Gospel in New England, a missionary society organized in the seventeenth century by the United Colonies of New England.

from the gentlemen—and I Shou'd to know [if] by M^r. Buell—This, With Sincere Duty to your Self Sir, is from your most unworthy Servant

Samson Occom

[MPMRC MSS 3; envelope text: "To the Revd Mr Solomon Williams att Lebanon in New-England These". Courtesy of the Mashantucket Pequot Museum and Research Center, Archives & Special Collections.]

2   To "Madam"

1756

Madam³

I look upon Myself of all Cretures the most indebted to God, who has call'd me out of the Grossess Paganism, where I was perishing without the least Glimpse of Gospel Light, and brought me into his marvellous Light, and dispos'd the hearts of one and another of his dear People to Shew Pitty and great Kindness to me; And express the Same in Numberless Instances. among which yours by the Rev. Mr Wheelock Must be acknowledg'd an Remembred by me with the greatest gratitude. In which, however unworthy I am you could have no other Motive but a single Regard to the Advancement of the Kingdom & Glory of the Redeemer. May God reward you out of his Immense Treasures of Rewards and Gifts. and however little you may account of it thro the greatness of your affection to Christ which will make you think little of the Most you can do for him yet it was great in the Eyes of Christ, and I Trust you are Intituled— ~~yourself~~ to the Blessedness of him that considereth the Poor. Please madam to Suffer me to beg, in addition to the Favours received, your continued Remembrance at the Throne of Divine Grace, of him who is, with the Greatest Respect

your most Obliged, Dutifull, & Obedient Servant,

Samson Occom

[Sender's copy; DCA 756900.2; appears to have been transcribed by Eleazar Wheelock. Courtesy of Dartmouth College Library.]

3   To Eleazar Wheelock

Bethlem⁴
12th Novr 1756—

Rev & Hon^d Sir

I have only a Moment Liesure to hint that when I return'd to my Indians last Fall in October I was rec^d by y^m with unfeigned Testimonies of y^r affectionate Regard and was not only useful but comfortable among them till December after when to our

---

3. *Madam:* Unknown donor to Eleazar Wheelock's school.

4. *Bethlem:* Occom probably wrote this letter from the town of Bethlehem, Connecticut. However, the content of the letter, which describes the situation of the Lenape, also raises the possibility

surprise & great unhappiness we were much discomforted by ye unexpected dis-affection of ye neighbouring Delawares below—My Indians faithfully laboured to reduce them to a good Temper [. . .] cause them to desist their Hostilities upon ye Sou[thern] Provinces, where in Conjunction with the Fren[ch] [page torn] affairs of ye Delawares was not like to be comfortably settled and y^t they could not advise me to continue with them in apparent state of [word crossed out] Things. For if I should be captivated or killed there it might be unhappy for them, as it forever deprived them of a Father and a Friend—If I should be barbarously murdered among them or fall into ye Hands of my Enimies in any respect, they said that they should never forget it—^It being only^ ~~was~~ for their Sakes that I first came into their Country and now [co]uld have no other Motive ^to^ continue among ^them^ [page torn] Providence however [crossing] wch appear against my returning to my People, they having sent to me just before I left Lake George desiring my return & advising me that it was their Opinion that I might do it safely, I [word illegible] upon and ex-pected before now to be in their Country at least had hopes [. . .][5]

[DCA 756612.3; pages torn at bottom. Courtesy of Dartmouth College Library.]

4 ❧   To Eleazar Wheelock

Easthampton
Jan^r ye 14: 1760

Revd Sir,

I am exceeding Sorry I was not at home when Mr. Hills was at my House. However I have now an opportunity with Mr Hills. But I have not Mr Kirkpatrick's and Bost-wick's Letters.[6] But I intend to Come to Mr Wheelock as soon as I Can and Bring the Letters, or Send the Coppy of the Letters by first opportunity before I Come over.

_____ I intend to take the Journey as Soon as I Can in the Spring—Sir I intend

that he wrote from Bethel, New Jersey, a Christian Indian settlement organized among the Lenape by David and John Brainerd in 1747. At this time, the Lenape community was also developing ties to Moor's Indian Charity School: John Pumshire and Jacob Woolley, both Delaware, enrolled in 1754, and Joseph Woolley and Hezekiah Calvin, also Delaware, arrived at the school in April 1757.

5. With the encouragement of Aaron Burr, Sr. (1716–1757; president of Princeton College, and son-in-law of Jonathan Edwards) and the New York Correspondents of the Society in Scotland for Propagating Christian Knowledge (SPCK), Occom attempted a visit to John Brainerd's mission among the Lenape (also known as Delawares) in New Jersey and Pennsylvania in 1755 (Love, Occom, 48). This fragmentary letter suggests that Occom also extended his travels into Six Nations territory around Lake George, New York, but was interrupted by the onset of the Seven Years' War. Mohegans, Mohawks, and Mahicans had served together as English military scouts in the Lake George area (L. Brooks, 148).

6. In November 1756, William Kirkpatrick wrote a letter to Occom inviting him to undertake missionary work among the Oneida in upstate New York; David Bostwick, president of the New York board of the Society in Scotland for the Propagation of Christian Knowledge (SPCK), also wrote to Occom promising financial support for the mission (Love, Occom, 84–85).

to ~~go~~ take David with me in this Journey, if ^he^ Can Brake off from his Study 4 or 5 Months[7] that is if there is Christians Enough upon the Main Shores to Help him, thus I must Conclude the Bearer waits,—

We are Well here at Present, as I hope these may find you—This with sincere Duty to Mr Wheelock and Madam and Sutable Respects to all is from your unworthy Servant,

Samson Occom

[Recipient's copy; DCA 761114; envelope text: "To the Revd Mr. Eleazer Wheelock; Lebanon, N. England." Courtesy of Dartmouth College Library.]

5 ◌   TO ELEAZAR WHEELOCK

New York
June ye 24: 1761

Revd Sir

We reach'd New York ye 15 In^st, and to my Surprize, the Gentlemen had Concluded, not to Send me at all, and all the Reason that they Can give is, they are affraind the Indians will kill me.[8] I told them, they Cou'd not kill ^me^ but once, and told them I intended to Proceed on my Journey, and if I Perish for want of Support, I Perish,— But I intended to use your Money, Sir, that David has with him; and When they Perceiv'd my Resolution, they Emediately Consulted the Matter, and Concluded, that I Shoud go, and ^a^ Collection Shou'd be made for me, and Recommendations Shou'd be Sent by me to Genl Amhurst and to Sir William.[9]

And the whole Matter is Acomplish'd to my Surprize beyound all my expectations, The Last Sabbath after the afterNoon Service was over; at Mr Bostwick's Congregation, they made a Collection for me and my Family's Support, and it mounted to £60:s15:d7 and Monday Evening the Baptists made a Collection for me at their Meeting House, and it Mounted to £13:0:0—And ^my^ Recommendations are done by the Most Noted Gentleman of this Place, not only to the genrals, but to other gen^n of their Aquaintance, from this City to the furthermost English Settlements,—The People are uncommonly kind to us in this great City,—But we live ^in ye Suburbs^ with one Obediah Wells an old Disciple—I am invited to the City Every Day to Dine with Some gentleman or other; Some times Two or three Invitations at once, Espicially the Minister, of all Sects and Denomina^tions^ are Extreamly Kind to me,—

7. David Fowler entered Moor's Indian Charity School on April 12, 1759 (Love, *Occom*, 64).

8. Occom embarked on his journey to the Oneida Lake region of New York at the end of the Seven Years' War, after the surrender of Canada and the end of fighting between British and French forces and their allies in North America. However, the actions of General Jeffrey Amherst, who built up British garrisons at Fort Pitt and Fort Niagara and awarded Seneca lands to his officers, incited the Six Nations to plan an uprising against the British in 1761 (Parkman, 439–440). News of increasing tensions between the Six Nations and the British probably caused Occom's sponsors to fear for his safety.

9. *Sir William:* William Johnson.

Yesterday ^3 o'c PM^ I was Intro to Wait upon his Honor, Colden,[10] President and Commander in Chief in ^the^ Province of N. York, and Wish'd me Good Success and Gave me ^good^ advice and Counsil,—I believe tomorrow Morning we Shall out from here on our way to Onoyda,

Please to remember us ^in^ your Fatherly Prayr Continually, Except Duty, and Sutable Regards to the Family from

Your Most Obedient Indian Son,
Samson Occom

The Rev^d. Mr Wheelock

I deliver'd £53: S7: d10 to Mr William Hedges of Easthampton, for the Support of my Family

S.O.

The Letters that I have to the Genrals are Sign'd by

The Hon.^bl W^m. Smith Esqr
Revd David Bostwick
M^t [PVB] Livingston
Mr David Vanhorne
Willm Livingston, Esqr

[Recipient's copy; DCA 761374; envelope text: "To the Revd Eleazer Wheelock at Lebanon N. England _____ These." Courtesy of Dartmouth College Library.]

6 ∽   TO ELEAZAR WHEELOCK

Fort Herkummer[11]
Sepr y^e 25 1761

Revd Sir

I Wrote you three Letters this Summer Past, but I have not receiv'd one Syllable, either from you or from any Body Else,— I have met with great many Diffeculties, but I have not repented of my Journey yet, I am in hopes it will be of Some Service to the Indians,—I Cant relate things in this Letter, David must make a Naration of Matters,—I am Stopt here by miss Fortune, my Mare got away from me, last Monday Night, and she is not found yet,—my Eyes are very Poor ag^ain^ I ^have^ been ^un^able to read or write this Whole Month When I shall get home or how I Cant^not^ tell

Sir, Please to except this as a token of Duty, and Sincere Respect to all, from

Your Indian Son
Samson Occom

[Recipient's copy; DCA 761525; envelope text torn. Courtesy of Dartmouth College Library.]

10. *Colden:* Cadwallader Colden.
11. *Fort Herkummer:* Fort Herkimer, New York.

7 ∽   To Eleazar Wheelock

Mohegan
May 12 1762

Revd Sir

The Com^{rs} of Boston[12] are so good as to send to Capt Shaw the other Day, that I might Draw ^upon 'em^ for ^£^20 Lawful Money, and Accordingly I have. I told Capt Shaw, the gentlemen insisted upon Seeing my Acount With Mr Hedges before they wou'd do anything to help me, &c— He said there was no need of that Now,—the gentlemen are so Kind also as to Allow me to draw upon ^them^ for the Time that I have been at Home the last Winter,—for which I return unfeign thanks and shall always look upon myself under Particular obligations to them as long as I live not only for the persent help, but for all past Favors and if they see fit to ~~help~~ Pity me in time come, it will be very Acceptable, if not I have nothing to say, but to remember past Kindness with greatful Heart—I have heard Sam Ashpo and his People together, about their Controverses, and I am afraid Sam Ashpo has took irragular Steps, I Can not receive ^him^ yet, and I will not do Contrary to my Mind,— I hope I shall find him better Next Time I See him,[13]—Sir, I hope you are all Well, I am Now at Mohegan, I came ^here^ before noon, and am going down again to New London this after Noon, to go over again to Long Island;— I Shall Set out on my Journey next Week if I Can, I beg your Continued remembrance of me—this Sir, with Sincere obediance is from your true tho' unworthy Servant

Samson Occom

[Recipient's copy; DCA 762312; envelope text: "To the Revd Eleazar Wheelock at Lebanon." Courtesy of Dartmouth College Library.]

---

12. *Com^{rs} of Boston:* Officers of the Society for Propagating the Gospel in New England.

13. These "irragular steps" Occom refers to may concern either the political or the religious affairs of Samuel Ashpo. Ashpo and his family belonged to the "John's Town" Mohegan tribal faction, which openly opposed sachem Ben Uncas III and his cooperation with colonial authorities in the distribution of Mohegan lands to white settlers. Although Occom would become more and more critical of these land dealings, his family belonged to the "Ben's Town" faction traditionally allied to the sachem. Occom's displeasure with Ashpo may indicate, as Lisa Brooks suggests, that Ashpo was again taking an active role against the sachem in the land controversy (151–152). At the same time, Ashpo was embroiled in a minor controversy concerning his authority to preach among the Native communities at Groton, Connecticut; Cheningo, New York; and Oquaga, New York. More than Occom, Ashpo sympathized with Separatist New Light factions and felt empowered to exercise authority independent of institutional sanction. In July 1762, Ashpo was examined by Wheelock and other ministers, who recommended that he be formally trained in preparation for missionary work (DCA 760601; Love, *Occom*, 76). See also DCA 764215.

8 ⌘   TO MARY FOWLER OCCOM

New York
June 1, 1763

My dr.

I am yet at N. York, & I expect to set off tomorrow in my journey[14]—Left 5 pounds with in Mr. Wells' hands—for family—as soon as grass is fit to cut—hire hands [word illegible] 5 loads of hay.

Get home [words illegible] late in the fall [words illegible] Remember God and trust in him at all times.—I am your true and loving husband.

Samson Occom

[DCA 763351—copy; not in Occom's hand. Courtesy of Dartmouth College Library.]

9 ⌘   TO ELEAZAR WHEELOCK

Mohegan
Feb. 8, 1764

Rev Sir,

I left the Rev. George Whitefield at New-London this afternoon about half after three; and he was to be at Norwich tomorrow, but I think it is impossible for him to travel the road with his carriage.[15] The roads are extraordinary bad since the storms. I believe the Whitefields will be obliged to go by water to Rhode Island at last. He wants to see you extremely. That is his greatest business to come to New London, he would have gone to Rhode Island from Long Island. And he desires you to come down to him as soon as you can possibly. I need not write more. I hope to see you in a short time.

This, with sincere service is in utmost haste,
from your ~~humble~~ ^worthless^ servant,
Samson Occom

[DCA 764158—copy; not in Occom's hand. Courtesy of Dartmouth College Library.]

14. Occom embarked on his third journey to Oneida in the spring of 1763, but returned due to the outbreak of Pontiac's War.

15. Whitefield embarked on his sixth visit to America in June 1763. He spent fall 1763 in Philadelphia and winter 1763–1764 in New York City, then traveled through Long Island, southern Connecticut (including New London, Norwich, and Lebanon, where he visited Moor's Indian Charity School), and Rhode Island in February 1764. He reached Boston at the end of February and remained there until June 1764 (Gillies, 212–213).

10 ⟆   ## TO ELEAZAR WHEELOCK

Mohegan
May 7: 1764

Revd Sir

We are in great confusions, and I am affraid we Shall find Great Trouble, Ben-Uncas[16] has Cast off his Counc^e^l, he has leas'd ^out^ a farm without [one?] of his Councel, and has done many ^things^ before now, Contrary to the minds of his Councel, and Contrary to our agreement,—and we have also renounc'd him—And we are very much Griev'd with what our [Seers] have done—[17]

I intend to Come to See Mr Wheelock in a few Days, to relate to him—

We are all Well thro' favour, Plase to except Sincere Duty and Salutations to all friends in utmost hurry from

Your unworthy Servant

Samson Occom

[Recipient's copy; envelope text: "To The Revd Mr Wheelock at Lebanon." HM 30412. This item is reproduced by permission of the Huntington Library, San Marino, California.]

11 ⟆   ## TO ELEAZAR WHEELOCK

Mohegan
August 22 1764

Revd Sir

I can Write but a Word or two in great hu^r^ry, I was at New London Monday and I Can find nothing that the Honble Commss^rs has done for me But ten Pounds Since I first went up to Onoyda, and that was ^p^aid as Salary for half years Service at Montauk—

Timber for my House is got thro' your good Influance for ^wich^ I am thankful and I hope ever Shall be both to god and man—I have many Hands to Day Both

---

16. *Ben-Uncas:* Mohegan tribal sachem Ben Uncas III.

17. On March 29 and 30, 1764, colonial overseers met alone with Mohegan sachem Ben Uncas III at Norwich, Connecticut, and obtained from him a lease for a white farmer on Mohegan lands. (Like his father Ben Uncas II, Ben Uncas III was viewed by many Mohegans as a puppet of the colony.) The sachem's endorsement of this lease violated standing agreements between the tribe and colonial overseers as to the maintenance of tribal lands. It also reflected a flagrant disrespect on the part of Ben Uncas III for traditional governmental protocols of collectivity, cooperation, and consensus. Representatives of the opposing Ben's Town and John's Town factions met together in April 1764 to constitute a new body of tribal trustees, to reaffirm protocols of collective governance, and to recall Ben Uncas III to his responsibilities, but again the sachem rebuffed his people. As Occom here relates, the Mohegan people subsequently "renounc'd" Ben Uncas III as sachem. When Ben Uncas III died in 1769, Occom and other pallbearers purposely dropped his casket on the ground to demonstrate their disgust to colonial officers at the funeral (Oberg, 210; L. Murray, *To Do Good*, 38).

P^l^owers and Seller Diggers,[18] ~~and~~ the over Seers are to meet here this Day by the order of the government to reconcile matters as I understand—

David went to Lyme last Saturday and he is not come back—

I want to ^go^ on our Journey as Soon as possable[19] We have been very Sick in my family but are now better thro' favour,—

With Sincere Service I Subscribe your worthless Servant

Samson Occom

[Recipient's copy; DCA 764472; envelope text: "To the Revd Elazer Wheelock at Lebanon." Courtesy of Dartmouth College Library.]

12   TO ELEAZAR WHEELOCK

August 1764

Revd Sir

I am Sorry you couldn't get at Least Some Money for David, it looks like Presumption for us to go on long Journey thro' Christians without Money, if it was altogether among Indian Heathen we might do well enough—But I have determined to go, tho' no White Missionary wou'd go in Such Circumstances[20]—I leave my House and ^o^ther Business to be done upon your Credit, and it will be Dear Business in the End,— if I had hired one good Carpenter and four other good Hands, my House woud have been forwarder than it is now, So the Best Ju^d^ges tell me—I have Impower'd Mr Peabody of Norwich Landing to act for me to Cary on my Business, by vertue of the Paper you Put into my Hands he is to get all the Meterials that my House will require, and to Hire Hands and to pay them at any Marchents who will except and trust to your obligation, — Besides all ^I^ have said my family now wants Cloathing— and provission they must now have, or my Business Can't go on—I have

18. Samson Occom began to build a house at Mohegan after he moved his growing family from Montauk in April 1764. Reservation maps show that the two-story wood-frame structure stood east of the Norwich–New London highway, a half-mile from the original village center, the site of the present-day Mohegan Congregational Church. Mohegans often met at Occom's home to conduct the business of the tribe, and in keeping with his customary responsibilities as a tribal elder Occom frequently entertained Native and non-Native visitors. Two of these visitors, David McClure and Levi Frisbie, reported that the finished Occom home boasted a "handsome" library, and that some rooms were "papered & painted." Eleazar Wheelock promised to pay costs of construction, but his failure to make prompt payments and supervise the building during Occom's missionary travels proved an ongoing source of contention, as subsequent letters show (Love, *Occom,* 101–102).

19. In August 13, 1764, the newly constituted Connecticut Board of Correspondents of the Society in Scotland for the Propagation of Christian Knowledge commissioned Samson Occom to go with David Fowler on a mission to the Six Nations (Love, *Occom,* 103; DCA 764463).

20. The Connecticut Board of Correspondents allocated no money for Occom's mission to upstate New York, as Wheelock errantly presumed that George Whitefield would fund the mission. Occom and Fowler set out to meet Whitefield in New York City on August 27, 1765, but returned home to Mohegan in September when Whitefield declined to pay for their mission (DCA 764505).

lately heard there is Salt meat enough at the Landing to be Sold—In a word I leave my Poor Wife and Children at your feet and ^if^ they hunger starve and die let them Die there—Sir I Shall endeavour to follow your Directions in all things—This in utmost hast and with Sincere Obedience, is from

Your Good for Nothing Indian Sarvant—
Samson Occom

[Recipient's copy; DCA 764508.3; envelope text: "To the Revd Eleazer Wheelock at Lebanon;" Wheelock also wrote on the envelope: "This Letter Came to Hand Septr 8. 1764. and is the first Intelligence I have had that his Building was not conducted prudently & Successfully & Without much cost. it is now [word crossed out] ^Friday^ Evening and next Monday Morning I am to Sot out on a Journey to Milford, & my Ingagements are Such as cant be disposed with"]

13 ⟋ TO ELEAZAR WHEELOCK

Chelsey
Oc^r 4: 1765

Revd Sir

You will See What Mr Buell has wrote to you,— I exteamly want one of your Negroes and a Yoke of oxen,—my Business is Crouding, and I want to dispatch it as fast as I can,—pray let me have a yoke of oxen, if you cant Spare a Negroe—I came home but the night before last,— I shall keep Jacob[21] a few Days to help me, In utmost hast from

your Unworthy Servant
S. Occom

[Recipient's copy; DCA 765554.2; envelope text: "To The Revd Eleazar Wheelock at Lebanon." Courtesy of Dartmouth College Library.]

14 ⟋ TO THE CONNECTICUT BOARD OF CORRESPONDENTS

Norwich
21st Novr 1765

To the Honourable Board of Correspondants in Connecticut—

Gentlemen on examination of my Acc^t. with Mr Gershom Breed I find myself Indebted to him Nine Pounds Seven Shillings & Seven Pence Lawfull Money (excluding the Acct. Hertofore exhibited to ye Revd Eleazer Wheelock) now due, which please to pay to him with Interest until paid & oblige

Y.^r hum.^l Servt
Samson Occom

[Recipient's copy; DCA 765621.3; envelope text: "Revd Samson Occum Ord.^r on th b.^d Correspond.^ts for £9.7.7 Novr 21.st 1765." Courtesy of Dartmouth College Library.]

21. *Jacob:* Jacob Fowler, brother-in-law to Samson Occom, then a student at Moor's Indian Charity School.

15 ∾   TO ELEAZAR WHEELOCK

Boston
Decr 6 1765

Rev^d and Hon^d Sir

We are yet in Boston and Mr Whetaker has Concluded to Sail from here with Capt
Marshell, the Same Ship that Mr Smith of Boston Went Home in, and We expect to
Sail next Wednesday or Thirdsday,[22]—the People here are very kind they begun
to make Preparations for our Voyge, and I dont doubt, but they will get Provisions
Enough,— The Honrable Commis^{rs} here are still very ^Strong^ in their opposition
to your Scheem, they think it is nothing but a Shame to Send me over the great
Water, they Say it is to Impose upon the good People, they further affirm, I was bro't
up Regularly and a Christian all my Days, Some Say, I cant Talk Indian, orthers Say
I Cant read[23]—In Short I believe the old Devil is in Boston to oppose our Design, but
I am in hopes, he is almost Superannuated[24] or in a Delireum—^but^ I don't think
he is worth a Minding—~~But~~ I hope the Lord of Heaven Will be With us and Assist
us in his own Cause, and in his Great Name and by your prayers we Shall overcom—
O that god wou'd give us grace and Wisdom to Conduct aright before him and be-
fore all men,—I have a Struggle in my Mind At times, knowing not where I am going,
I dont know but I am Looking for a Spot of Ground ^where^ my Bones must be
Buried, and never to See my Poor Family again, but I verely believe I am Calld of god
by Strange Providence and that is Enough, he will take Care of me if I do but put
my Whole trust in him and he will Provide for mine, I want nothing but the Will of
God, to be Wholly Swallowed up in it—I am very Sorry to see a mistake in your last
Narrative—it was the Chief Sachem his wife and 3 of their Children and ten or 11
others Came Down with Mr Kirkland, and it was the Sachem's Wife 2 of his Children
and one more Died while they were down,[25] I was at the Burying of the Sachems

---

22. Samson Occom and Nathaniel Whitaker sailed from Boston to England on December 23, 1765.
    Their departure was delayed because the packet could not obtain stamped clearance papers
    to depart, as a consequence of popular opposition to the Stamp Act, which went into effect on
    November 1, 1765 (Richardson, 79–81).

23. The Boston Commissioners of the Society for the Propagation of the Gospel in New England
    generated antipathy toward Occom's visit to England. In August, Wheelock's friend John Smith
    reported that rival missionary societies had "sent an Indian over [to England] & have ordained
    him in Bristol & he cant speak English, he is designed to ape & undermine Mr. Occum who
    is Expected & much Talkt of here" (DCA 765475.1). Other circulating rumors suggested that
    Occom lacked the proper education and sophistication, that he might use his time in England
    to intervene in the Mason land case, or that he would be lured away and ordained an Episco-
    palian (Blodgett, 87).

24. *Superannuated:* Worn out with age, disabled.

25. In *A Continuation of the Narrative of the State of the Indian Charity-School, at Lebanon, in Con-
    necticut; From Nov. 27th, 1762, to Sept. 3d, 1765* (Boston: Richard and Samuel Draper, 1765),
    Wheelock mistakenly reported that thirteen Seneca boys accompanied Kirkland on his visit to
    the Mohawk River, failing to acknowledge the sachem, his wife, and their children.

Wife, and the Nex Day Sir William[26] Condoled the Death of the Queen in a Solemn Manner according to the Indian Custom[27]—and when the Solemnity was over, Sir W^m reintroduc'd Mr Kirkland to the Sachem's Favour, ^&^ he Promis'd for himself and for his People, to be kind to him—I am affraid Sir W.^m will be disple^asd^ and may make a handle of that mistake against the Cause—I am glad to see Mr Chamberlain So Jealous but am Sorry to see his Zeal little too Warm, I hope and pray that it may Cool a little but not too Cold, Mr Chamberlain won't be displeasd with ^a^ Brotherly Freedom, he has the Same liberty, he may Use it at ^any^ Oration—Sir ^pray^ for us, and in perticular for me, and I beg the Prayers of your good People,— Sincer Duty to you & to your Spouse, and Sutable regards to the rest,

> *Your very humble Ser^nt*
> *Samson Occom*

[Recipient's copy; DCA 765656.2; envelope text: "To The Revd Eleazer Wheelock at Lebanon, Connecticut." Courtesy of Dartmouth College Library.]

16   TO NATHANIEL SHAW

Boston
Decr 17: 1765

Sir—

After Sutable Comp^lnts, I request one favour more; I promised Mr Hammond of New London North Parish, the Sum of £3: S14: 0d in Money, to be pay'd the first of next May, I dont know his Christian Name, but he is remarkably Deaf, I have Sent you ~~five~~ ^Six^ Dollars by Mr Gardner the Bearer hereof, but it is not half enough, and I Shoud be much obligated to you, if you wou'd Discharge the Debt acording to the time appointed,—and Send Word to him as Soon as you can that he may know,— We expect to Sail the last of this Week, with one Capt Marshall, my Sincere Regards to your Parents, and Comp^nts to the rest of the Family. Farewell.

> *your most obliged & very Humble Servant,*
> *Samson Occom*

[CHS folder I.2; envelope text: "To Mr Nath^ll Shaw^Jur Marchant, in N. London, Connecticut; pr Favour of Mr Gardner." Samson Occom Papers, Connecticut Historical Society, Hartford, Connecticut.]

26. *Sir William:* William Johnson
27. Ritual expressions of condolence historically have played a crucial role in Iroquois political and social life, in part as means to ensure the harmonious transition of power. Becoming versed in Iroquois customs of condolence was critical to intertribal and international diplomacy. See Fenton, Pomedi.

17 ⚬⚬   TO SAMUEL BUELL

London
March 8: 1766

My Dear Sir

I Wrote you a Long Letter a few Days ago, Which I hope you will receive, this ^is^ only to desire you, to forward the two Letters to N. London,—I have ^had^ a Cold for Some Days, but I am better now thro' gods goodness. I shall take the Small Pox monday[28]—my Hearty respects to you all,

your most Obedient
S. Occom

[CHS folder I.3; envelope text: "To the Revd Mr Samuell Buell at." Samson Occom Papers, Connecticut Historical Society, Hartford, Connecticut.]

18 ⚬⚬   TO MARY FOWLER OCCOM

London
March 11: 1766

My Dear Wife

I send you with this ^letter^ some Cloathing, for our Family, there is 9 Yards of Broad Cloth and Some Shalloon[29], to make a Sute of Cloaths for Aaron, and hat is left you may do as you Please with, you may make Blankets or Cloaks of it, —and a piece of Stuff[30] about 30 Yards and Strip'd Flannel between 30 and 40 Yards, and 38 Yards of Checker'd Linen, and about as much White Linen—they go by way of Boston. and Mr Peck will Send them to Norwich Landing to Mrs Whitaker, for her things and our things are all in one Box—By the Mercy of God I am in Good Health, and I hope and pray these may find you So—Trust in the Lord Jehovah, for in him is Everlasting Strength—About a quarter after 3: this after-Noon, I was Inoculated by Mr Whitaker, and you will Soon hear whether I am well of it or Dead with it[31]—the Cloathing is by the Revd Mr Whitefield and the Pins and Books by Madam Whitefield, and the Coffee-Pot and 3 Brass Screws by one Mr Withy,—you must never ^put^ the Pot on the fire, the Brass are to hang Cloaths on—from your Husband

Samson Occom

28. Nathaniel Whitaker inoculated Occom on March 11, 1766.

29. *Shalloon:* Woven wool fabric, often used to line clothing.

30. *Stuff:* Woven fabric.

31. The practice of inoculation consisted of the purposeful insertion of smallpox scabs into an incision in the patient's skin, causing the patient to suffer a mild case of smallpox and obtain immunity to the disease. Originally practiced in Africa and Western Asia, inoculation was adopted into Western European and Anglo-American medical repertoires in the early eighteenth century. A slave named Onesimus taught Cotton Mather about inoculation, and Mather subsequently became a major American advocate of the controversial practice.

I have also Sent 3 pair of girls Stockings and one Dozen of knives and Forks and a Picture of King & Queen—

[Recipient's copy; DCA 766211; envelope text: "to Mrs Mary Occom at Mohegan, N. London in Connecticut." Courtesy of Dartmouth College Library.]

19 ∾   TO ELEAZAR WHEELOCK

London
May 30: 1766

Rev^d & Hon^rd Sir

Pray look and See What it was the Honble Commis^rs of Boston did towards my Education, I think you kep an Acount of it, and Send Master Rudolphus to Capt Shaws of N London, to know what he Pay'd me for the Commis^rs, and how many Years he Pay'd me—and Send the Acounts with all Speed, for it is of great Consequence that we have them,—the Honble Commis^rs of Boston have Wrote against us, they Signify withall, they Supported me While I was Learning at your House, & have Supported me ever Since, and pay'd all my Debts.—and you took me away from them &c &c &c[32]—I have had a Severe turn of a Bloody Flux for a week past, but I am almost well thro' god's great goodness—my Eyes are Weak I can't ^rite^ much at this Time—I hope it is Well With you all, Dutiful Respects from your unworthy Servant

                                                            S. Occom

P.S: I have not Seen the Letter Neither can we get the Copy of it yet.

[Recipient's copy; DCA 766330; envelope text: "To the Revd Mr Eleazer Wheelock, in Lebanon in America." Courtesy of Dartmouth College Library.]

32. On October 2, 1765, Andrew Oliver (1706–1774), then secretary of the Boston Board of Commissioners of the Society for the Propagation of the Gospel in New England (SPG), wrote a letter to Jasper Mauduit, head of the London society, accusing Wheelock and Occom of failing to credit the SPG for its role in Occom's education and of misrepresenting Occom's conversion and early career. Oliver's letter insinuated that Occom was incorrectly represented as "a mohawk, very lately bro't out of gross paganism & in a very little time fitted by Mr Wheelock to be what he is" in order to "procure large contributions" for Wheelock (DCA 766367.2). The circulation of the letter among missionary societies in England and the opposition of the SPG became a source of ongoing difficulty for Wheelock, Occom, and Nathaniel Whitaker. For his part, Whitaker believed that Oliver's letter reflected the SPG's "fear of being eclipsed" by Wheelock in their efforts to evangelize American Indians (DCA 766315.2). From 1751 to 1764, the SPG sent Occom a total of £225, an amount grossly insufficient to support Occom's family, let alone to justly compensate his work as a schoolmaster and missionary, as Occom himself argued in his 1768 autobiography (Richardson 129).

20 ∾   TO MARY FOWLER OCCOM AND
             ESTHER POQUIANTUP FOWLER

1766

My dear Mary & Esther

Perhaps you may Query whether I am well; I came from home well, was by the way
well, I got over well, am received at London well, and am treated extreemly well, yea
I am Caress'd too Well,—And do you pray that I may be well; and that I may do well;
and in time return Home well,—And I hope you are well, and wish you well, and
as I think you begun well, So keep on well, that you may end well, and then all will
be well:

                                                        And so Farewell,
                                                        Samson Occom

[DCA William Allen, *Memoirs of Samson Occom*, manuscript, 121. Courtesy of Dartmouth College
Library.]

21 ∾   TO MARY FOWLER OCCOM

London
Jan^r 21: 1767

My Dear

By the goodness of God I am, and have been in good State of Health Since I Wrote
to you last, excepting Some Colds I have had Several times,—I rejoice to hear our
Family was Well, last November,—let us endeavour to put our trust in god at all
Times, I am glad to hear our Aaron is at Mr Wheelock's, let him Stay there till he
knows how to behave better[33]—and do you try to Instruct Your Girls as well as you
can,[34]—I order'd Some more money to be Sent to you, and I hope you have receiv'd
it or will receive it, pay our Debts as far as you Can—My Dear, get Some Capable
Hand to Write you Letters of thanks, to the Ladies who Wrote you Letters, and Sent
you Presents from Bristol;[35] we have return'd to London again a few Days ago, and

---

33. Aaron Occom first attended Moor's Indian Charity School from April 1760 to October 1761. He
returned to the school in December 1765 for another short residence (Love, *Occom*, 65). On April
9, 1766, Wheelock wrote Occom that Aaron was "not a good boy" and advised that he be indentured "to a good Master" (DCA 766259). Mary Occom sent Aaron back to Wheelock on November 8, 1766, to prevent him from "get[ting] Married to a Very bad Girl" and "run[ning] me
in debt by Forging orders etc" (DCA 766608.2).

34. At this time, Samson and Mary Occom had five daughters—Mary, Tabitha, Olive, Christiana,
and Talitha—of ages ranging from fifteen to five years old. A sixth daughter named Theodosia
was born in 1769.

35. This remark should not be interpreted as an indication of Mary Occom's illiteracy. Occom himself taught her to read and write during his tenure as schoolmaster at Montauk, and three letters written by Mary Occom survive in the Dartmouth College Archives (DCA 766608.2; DCA
767415; DCA 766362). Occom's request that Mary get a "capable hand" to write a letter of thanks

Shall Stay here till Spring,—my Love to you all, and to all Inquiring Friends—I am as ever, your tender and Loving Husband,

Samson Occom

[Recipient's copy; DCA 767121; envelope text: "To Mʳˢ Mary Occom at Mohegan in N. London Connecticut, N. England." Courtesy of Dartmouth College Library.]

22 ⟶   ## TO ELEAZAR WHEELOCK

London
Febʳ 12: 1767

Revᵈ & Hon.ʳᵈ Sir

It has been my Lot for a long time to have Sorrow of Heart, I have had Burden upon Burden, Trial upon Trial, Both without and within, far and Near, A General Concern is Riveted in my Heart, for my Poor Bretheren According to the Flesh, Both for their Bodies and Souls; my Relations Causes Heavyer Sorrow; Every obstruction and Discouragement to Your School, and every miss Contuct and behaviour of your Indian Scholars, Touches me to the quick; More than all these, the Consideration of my poor Family, as it were, lets my ^very^ Hearts Blood; I am ready Say, I am a Cruel Husband and Father, God has Given me a large Family, but they have no enjoyment of me, nor I them for Some Years back, and the Whole Burden and Care of a Large Family of Children lies upon my poor Wife; What adds to my Sorrowful Heart is this, that Whilest I am a Teacher to others, I have neglected my own Children, by my Perigrenations and now my Children are growing up, and are growing Wild; and the Devil has been Angry, yea he has & is Devilish Mad with me, and if he can, he will Drag all my Children into all Manner Sins and Down to Hell; But blessed be God he has provided an almighty Saviour, and all my Hope is in him, for my self and Family,—if I was not fully Perswaded and Asure'd that this Work was of god, and I had an undoubted Call of god to Come over into this Country, I wou'd not have Come over like a fool as I did, Without any Countenance from our Board, but I am Will Still to be a fool for Christ Sake—This Eleviate my Heart amidst all my Burdens, and Balances all my Sorrows at Times, or enables me to bear my Trials, that I am in the way of my Duty, and the Lord uses me in any Shape to promote his Kingdom in the World,—I am Glad, and am thankful that you have taken my Wild Son,[36] if you Can make any thing of him, I shall ^be^ happy in him, if he Inclines to Book Learning, give him Good English Education, but if not let him go to some Good Master, to Learn Joiner^s^ Trade, he Inclines to that, and if that won't do, Send him over to me, and I will give him a Way to Some gentleman here—I return you Hearty thanks for the Care you have taken of my Family,—Sir, let it suffise you, to hear of me by

---

to English well-wishers seems to suggest either that Occom desired a more polished letter than he believed his wife capable of producing, or that he knew Mary was not eager to submit to self-abasing English epistolary conventions.

36. *my Wild Son:* Aaron Occom.

Mr Whitakers Letters, there is no need of my Writing often, Since Mr Whitaker Writes So often, By the Goodness of God we Enjoy Good State of Health, M^r ^Whitefield^ is Well, as he has been these 7 Years; but Mrs Whitefield is in ^low^ State of Health, Mr John Smith is Well as Usual, and hope these may find You and Yours in good Health, Dutiful and Grateful Respects to You and Your Spouse, and Love to the rest of the Family and Scholars, and Christian respects to all Enquiring Friends I am Sir,

Your most oblig'd and Humble Servant
Samson Occom

P.S. Perhaps You may Wonder Why I Write After this manner I have receiv'd Chifely Mo^u^rnful Letters from my Wife, Yet I have not forgot the Tender Mercies of god to me and mine—

Since Capt. Shaw is backward to do for my family, I wish he had all his Due, that we may be even, if You Can Satisfy him, I Shou'd be Easy in my mind.

[Recipient's copy; DCA 767162.2; envelope text: "To the Revd Mr Wheelock at Lebanon. New England." Courtesy of Dartmouth College Library.]

23   TO MARY FOWLER OCCOM

London, Ma [page torn]

My Dear

We are this Mo [page torn] out for ^the^ Country, and Shall go [page torn] perhaps to Ireland before we re[turn to] London again, and Will be 7 or 8 [page torn] before we return, I have Sent you [se]veral things Last Year, Which I [hope?] you have receivd, and I have [page torn] Some things more, Which will [page torn] in a few Days, I Sent a Box of Books a few Days ago, and you ^will^ find a letter in it, Which gives you an Account, what will be Sent to you. The Lord be with you all Bless ye with Heavenly Blessings—

My Best Love to you
I am ever your Dear Husband
Samson Occom

[Recipient's copy; DCA 767900.12; envelope text: "To Mrs Mary Occom at Mohegan in N. London or Norwich, Connecticut by Mr Whi [ink stains]." Courtesy of Dartmouth College Library.]

24   TO MARY FOWLER OCCOM

1767

My Dear,

I wrote you a Letter a few Days ago, but I Cant be easy, unless I Write again, I am Sensable of the great Burden and Care that is upon you, and I feel your Burden, Cares and Sorows. My poor Family is near and Dear to me, and you are the nearest to my

Heart,—tho we are at great Distance from each other Yet you are near and Dearer to
me than ever,—But it was the Call of god and nothing but the Call of god in his
Devine Providence, Cou'd have Caused me to Leave my Dear Family, and it is the Call
of God, that you Shoud have the Whole Care of a large Family—and let us then put
our Whole trust in god, and Cast all our Burdens, upon him, and Do our Duty Daily,
and he will Sustain us,—I have thought Some Times lately I Shall never See all my
Family again, if I Shoud ever return home again, (I Can't refrain from Tears, Whilest
I am Writing,) But it is no Matter Where or how or When we lieve this Sinful World,
if we do but meet in a better World, let us then endeavour to Cry to God night and
Day for our Selves and for our poor Children—Be not asham'd my Dear, nor be afraid
to pray with and for our poor Children,—and pray for your Husband and I will pray
for you, Instruct our Children in the fear of god as well as you Can, and Send them
to School as much as you advisable if the School Continues, let me hear from you as
often as you can,—My love to you all, Duty to Mother,[37] and love to all Relations,
and Sutable Respects to Enquiring Friends,

> *I am as ever your tender and Loving Husband*
> *Samson Occom*

[Rauner 000800. Courtesy of Dartmouth College Library.]

25 ∾   TO ROBERT KEEN

[September 1768]

Sir

I was taken Sick as soon as I got ^aboard^ of Ship and was extreemely Bad for four
W—after that I grew better and amended very fast, and we had very Rough Pasage
and in the Height of my Sickness, we had Violent winds, as I was told, for I know
but Little of it, I was perilous for Some Days—and at the End of 8 Weeks ^by ye
goodness of God^ we arrivd at Boston, and I was Joyfully recievd by my good
Friends at Boston, I Stayd but one N at Boston, on friday in the after Noon we got a
shore, and Tuesday following about 5 in the after Noon I got Home and found my
Poor Family in good Health, the Lord be Praisd for his Tender Mercies to us—I wrote
Some Letter as Soon as I got home but had no opportunity to Send them—Since I've
been at Home I have Very Busy, Yet I have been to Several Places of Indians and they
all recive me with great affection—about 5 Weeks ago onoyda Indians Came to see
me, they manyfested great Joy at my return from England and and were ~~greatly~~ very
thankful to hear the Liberality of Christians and all receive me With gladness and
tender affection,—they are very thankful to hear the Benevolent Disposition of
Christians over the Mighty Waters, by freely Contributing of their Substance towards the Instructions of the Poor Indians in North America,—they Hope by this
Means their poor Children's Eyes may be opened, that they may See with their own

37. *Mother:* Betty Pharoah Fowler.

Eyes[38]—I had 4 Onoydas ~~and 2 Mohawks~~ Come to See me Some Time Last July, and were very glad to See me, they Said, they had heard of my arrival and they wanted to See me, and So they Came Down—and they were greatly affected to hear the good Report I gave them of the People in the old Christian Countries,— They were very urgent to have me go amongst this Summer Past, but I told them, I had been gone so Long from Home, I thought Duty to Stay at home this year, and if I liv'd to see another Spring, I woud give them a long Visit, and they went away Satisfied,—I got home near fortnit before Mr Whitaker, to the Surprize of the People round about here, When they understood, He Saild 3 weeks before me, and it was not Disagreable to my Friends,—Mr Whitaker is now in Pennsylvania I Suppose to Try to Procure Some Lands of Govern^r Pen, for the School, employed by Dr Wheelock as I suppose, for I heard nothing of it till he was gone, and then I heard it [axidentally?],[39]—I Said nothing Concerning Mr Whitaker to no Body, and I have been to Dr Wheelocks but once Since I got Home, for fear I shoud have many questions Askd me,—and now I am very glad to Hear our Honorable Trustees have wrote to Dr Wheelock Concerning Mr Whitaker, now I ~~Shall~~ am ready to Answere any Questions D^r W: may Put to me Concerning Dr Whitaker:[40]—I got the Money of Dr Wheelock, he gave me an order to Dr Lotherup, and I recived it all ~~Last lately~~ about a few Weeks ago, and Dr Wheelock was very urgent to have it, for what ^he did^ for my Family in my absence, but I Chose he Shoud Stay Longer, and Pay my old Debts first,^and ye [word illegible] wrote to Mr Broome^—I found my Debts remain on Long Island Just as I left them ^so^ tho' our Presbytery Promisd me, asistance, to Discharge My Debts in my absence, but nothing has been done—and Some Small Debts, my Wife Necisarily Contracted; and What I have expended by Hiring Labour upon my little Farm, for it has been neglected in my absence; and then I have been obligd to Buy every Mouthful of food Since I came Home; and I have had a great number of Visiters of Indians from all Quarters, and some English Friends also,—these have took all my Money away, So that Debt I owe to Dr Wheelock remains Still against ^I find my Family is very Chargable & I am [unfortunately] to Say he is unprofitable^,—you have an acount of it in one of his Letters,—The School goes on much as it has done Since we have been gone the Indians are Willing to Send their Children Still, I am Affraid the Dutch, near the Indians, and the French, are trying all they can, to Prejudice the Minds of the Indians against the School and against the English, ^but if it

---

38. Several Oneida children were recruited by Samson Occom, David Fowler, and Eleazar Wheelock's son Ralph to attend Moor's Indian Charity School: Dawet, Mundius, and Jacob enrolled in 1765, William in 1766, "Little Peter," Jacob, and three others in 1767, and a few more, including a girl named Hannah, in 1768 (Love, *Occom*, 68–69).

39. On the advice of George Whitefield, Nathaniel Whitaker proposed to Eleazar Wheelock that Moor's Indian Charity School be relocated to "a tract of land on Deleware or Susquehannah, more Southerly than Lebanon," so that the school farm might profit from shorter winters and longer growing seasons and thus become a source of income for the school (DCA 766168). Whitaker believed that the colony of Pennsylvania would grant the school four or five thousand acres, in order to advance the settlement of the frontier (DCA 766222).

40. Whitaker was thought by members of the English board of trustees of the Moor's Indian Charity School fund to have mishandled some of the donations (Love, *Occom*, 147).

is of God he will maintain it^—The State of Religion in these parts is at a Low ebb, Yet I hope the Ld has not forsaken his People, there are Some manifest Tokens of his Love amongst them—I shoud be extreamly glad, if you Can do me the favour, as to Send me half a Dozen of Small Quarto Bibles,[41] With good paint and good Papers and Binding—and Charge them upon Dr Wheelock— I am much esteemed Sir Sincere Respects to you, and yours and Dutiful Respects to our Honorable Trustees,—I am, Much esteemd Sir

Your &c

Occom

[Draft; CHS folder I.4. Samson Occom Papers, Connecticut Historical Society, Hartford, Connecticut.]

26 ∽ To Robert Keen

Mohegan
Sept. 27, 1768

Most Worthy Sir,

Doubtless you have heard of my sickness on board of ship. I was taken ill two or three days after I got on board and was severely handled by it, four weeks, to that degree, that I was in delirium for some days; the Captain expected nothing but to cast me overboard in a short time; and we had a rough passage, contrary winds most of the way over; by the goodness of God, I began to amend at the end of four weeks, and grew strong very fast. We were eight weeks tossed to and fro on the mighty ocean. On Friday, in the afternoon, we landed at Boston to our great joy and the joy of our friends: O what joy it will be to christians to arrive safely at last, at the haven of the New Jerusalem. The next morning I took horse and went on my way home-ward. Tuesday following I reached home about two o'clock, P.M. And by the infinite goodness of God, found my poor family in a good state of health, except my wife, who had been in a poor declining way above a year, and she is still in a bad state of health: she has had two sudden severe ill turns since I have been at home. A few days ago we did not expect her life many hours, but by the pure mercy of God she is now much better.

I have been to several places of Indians this summer, round about here, and they all receive me with gladness and tender affection. They are very glad to hear the benevolent dispositions of christians, over the mighty waters, by freely contribut-ing their substance towards the instruction of the poor Indians of North America. They hope by this means their poor children's eyes may be opened, that they may see with their own eyes. I had four Oneida Indians come to see me, some time last July, and they manifested thankfulness at my return. They were greatly affected to hear the good report I gave them of the people in the old christian countries,— Were very urgent to have me go amongst them this summer past, but I told them I had been gone so long from home, I thought it duty to stay at home this year, and if I

41. *Quarto Bibles:* Bibles printed on quarter-sheet pages of paper.

live to see another spring, I will give them a long visit, and they went away satisfied. I am now writing a short narrative of my life. Doctor Wheelock's school prospers as heretofore, and the Indians are still willing to send their children. I am afraid, the Dutch and French near the Indians are trying all they can to prejudice the Indians against the school and against the English: but if this work is of God, he will carry it on. I trust the Lord will not forsake his people in these parts.

Sincere respects to you and yours, and grateful respects to our worthy Trustees. I am, much esteemed Sir, your most obedient servant,

Sampson Occum

[David McClure and Elijah Parish, *Memoirs of the Rev. Eleazer Wheelock, D.D.* (Newburyport: E. Littleton & Co., 1811), 175–176.]

27 ∾   TO ELEAZAR WHEELOCK

Mohegan
Novr 12 1768

Revd Sir

I intended to come up to your House before now, but I heard, you was Coming down So far as my House, and I have been very Ill for ^Some^ Days, I have a bad pain in one of my Shoulders. I was at Dr Whitaker's last Wedness, and he informs me that you had been very ill for Some Time, and I Woud Come up next Week, but I am affraid to ride, for only riding to Norwich and Landing last Wednesday has greatly agrivated my Pain, but I intend to be up as Soon as ^I^ can; the rest of family are well, this with Duty to you and Madam, is from

your most unworthy Servant
Samson Occom

[Recipient's copy; DCA 768612.1. Courtesy of Dartmouth College Library.]

28 ∾   TO ELEAZAR WHEELOCK

Hon^d Sir

I Just now receiv'd Yours for which I return Sincere thanks,—You may depend upon See me at Norwich, at the Time appointed extraordinaries are excepted,—The Inclosd is what I shall write to Mr Keen, Concerning your School, This with Duty is from

your most unworthy Servant
S. Occom

Mohegan
Decr 28: 1768

Some Time after I wrote to you, was at Dr Wheelock's, and found myself under a mistake, for he told me, he had not receiv'd any Letter from our Honrable Trustees Since

We got home from England, and finding, he had Some Letters from England Concerning Dr Whitaker's Conduct whereby he gave a Displeasure to our most worthy
Trustees and others—and told me also, he had excluded him from Trust here—I
thought it my Duty, to relate the Whole matter to him, and he was much astonished
With it—and he Desired to know my opinion of the Honorable Trustees, and I freely
told him I look'd 'em as the most Worthy, Honest, and faithful men Disintrusted in
their Trust—I believe there is no danger of allienating his mind from the Honorable
Trustees[42]—The good old gentleman is most wore out, yet he is Steady as the Sun
he keeps on in good Works—his Confidence is in God Still—There is good News in
the Wilderness among the Onoydas, many are hopefully Turned from Darkness to
Vital Godliness—

[Enclosure; Recipient's copy; DCA 768678.4. Courtesy of Dartmouth College Library.]

29 ∾ TO ROBERT CLELLAND

1768

Sir

I wonder you Cant be easy

I wonder & am amazd that you Cant let your quiet Neibours alone, I hear and I
believe it is true, You are Continually Writing, tittles tattles making Disturbance
among your ^good^ Neighbours, and I think you may be properly Call'd a Busy
Body according to Scripture—If Mr Jewet has Calld me a Serpent I dont See that you
have any Business to Call me So—^what^ if mr Jewet Shoud kill a man, woud you
go and kill another, because he did so, if you are taking Example from Mr Jewet
Why dont you follow his good Deeds,—I heard you Calld a Thief and Lyer ~~even~~ in
your own Country even at Edenburgh ^by your own Country men^ and wou'd it be
right in me, or woud you like it, to Call you a Lyer and a Thief, and to Blaze it abroad
in Writing—& You make great Complaint and Noise of being turn'd ^out^, if you
woud but rightly you Coud not Complain of any Body —^for^ You ^yourself^ turn'd
yourself out, of your own Country, you turnd y^r Self out of our School, and you
turnd y^r Self of the Church, and You are turning yourself out of the Favour of every
Body as fast as you Can, Except them that are of your Genus—take Care that you
don't turn your Self out of Heaven—~~I hope there is money you yet and for me in~~ you
represent me to be the Vilest Creature in Mohe I own I am bad enough and too bad,
Yet I am Heartily ^glad^ that I am not ^that^ old Robert Clelland, his Sins won't be
Chargd to me and my Sins wont be Chargd to him, he must answere for his own
Works before his maker and I must answere for mine—You Signify, as if it was in
your Power to do me harm you have been trying all You Can and You may your
Worst, I am not Concernd about, but I dont Intend to Hurt You—Sir you have wrote
to me Several times & I never not wrote a Line, and you have Extorted this from me.

42. Keen was concerned that the English trustees' criticisms of Nathaniel Whitaker may have upset
Wheelock.

You need not write to me any more for will not Answere y^r Letters I wont Spend my Time and Paper about them, if you have anything to Say to me at any time Say it by Word of Mouth[43]

> I am, Sir, Just What you Please
>
> S. Occom

[Sender's copy or draft; DCA 768900.7. Courtesy of Dartmouth College Library.]

30 ∽   "THEY DON'T WANT THE INDIANS TO GO TO HEAVEN WITH THEM"

1768

Now I am in my own country, I may freely inform you of what I honestly and soberly think of the Bishops, Lord Bishops, and Archbishops of England. In my view, they don't look like Gospel Bishops or ministers of Christ. I can't find them in the Bible. I think they a good deal resemble the Anti-christian Popes. I find the Gospel Bishops resemble, in some good measure, their good Master; and they follow Him in the example He has left them. They discover meekness and humility; are gentle and kind unto all men—ready to do good unto all—they are compassionate and merciful unto the miserable, and charitable to the poor. But I did not find the Bishops of England so. Upon my word, if I never spoke the truth before, I do now. I waited on a number of Bishops, and represented to them the miserable and wretched situation of the poor Indians, who are perishing for lack of spiritual knowledge, and begged their assistance in evangelizing these poor heathen. But if you can believe me, they never gave us one single brass farthing. It seems to me that they are very indifferent whether the poor Indians go to Heaven or Hell. I can't help my thoughts; and I am apt to think they don't want the Indians to go to Heaven with them.

[William Buell Sprague, *Annals of the American Pulpit*, vol. 3 (New York: Robert Carter & Brothers, 1858), 193–194.]

43. Robert Clelland was appointed schoolmaster at Mohegan by the Boston Commissioners of the Society for the Propagation of the Gospel in New England in 1752. Along with David Jewett, the SPG-appointed minister to the Mohegan tribe, Clelland sympathized with the colony of Connecticut in the Mason land case. On April 26, 1764, Occom, on behalf of the Mohegan tribe, wrote a petition (reprinted in this collection) against Clelland, who was dismissed as schoolmaster on September 19, 1764. Apparently, Clelland continued to live at Mohegan and bore resentment toward Occom for his role in the dismissal.

31 ⌒ To the Connecticut Board of Correspondents of the Society in Scotland for Propagating Christian Knowledge (SPCK)

Mohegan
Jan. 4: 1769

Rev^d ^& Honorable^ Gentlemen

As I Stand in Connection to you, So I find it my Duty to make my Faults known to you.—I have been shamefully over taken With Strong Drink, by Which I have greatly Wounded the Cause of God, and Blemished the Pure Religion of Jesus Christ, and blackend my own Character, and ^brought a reproach on the ministry^, and ~~function~~, hurt my own Soul:—For Which as in the Sight of God, I ^am^ ashamed, I am Sorry, and Sincerely Repent—And I humbly Beg your forgiveness—and Pray ye to God for me.—I Resolve, relying ~~u~~ upon the grace of God, to keep a better guard and Watch over my Self in Time to Come & desire to be restored to the Charity of all all, who have been offended thereby,[44]

Samson Occom

[DCA 769104; envelope text: "To The Honorable Board of Correspondents of the Society in Scotland, Now Sitting at Norwich." Courtesy of Dartmouth College Library.]

32 ⌒ To the Long Island Presbytery

1769

~~Most~~ Venerable ^Sirs^ ~~Gentlemen~~

As I Stand in near Connection to ~~With~~ you, in the ^fellowship of^ the Gospel, so I find it my Indispensible Duty to make my ~~open~~ faults known unto you—I have been Shamefully over taken with Strong Drink, by Which I have greatly wounded the Cause of God, and Blemishd the Pure Religion of Jesus Christ, and Blacken my own Character & function, and Hurt my own Soul—For Which, as in the Sight of God, I am ashamed, I am Sorry, I ^Sincerely^ repent,—And ^Humbly^ beg your forgiveness,—and Pray ye to god for me—I resolve, Relying upon the grace of god, to keep

---

44. The date on this letter is questionable. Rumors that Occom had been publicly "overtaken with excessive drinking" circulated beginning in February 1769, as Eleazar Wheelock related in a March 9, 1769, letter (DCA 769209.2). Occom confessed to the Long Island Presbytery in April 1769, and the matter was resolved by the presbytery in November 1769.

a better gard and watch over myself in Time to Come—for further information I refer you to the Revd Mr Buell, and to his Letter I sent him—I am ^Revd^ Sirs[45]

yours &c

SO

[Draft; CHS folder 1.5. Samson Occom Papers, Connecticut Historical Society, Hartford, Connecticut.]

33 TO NATHANIEL CHAMPLIN

Mohegan
Feb^r 23: 1769

Sir

I have been informd of the Difference Subsisting between ^you^ and Moses Mazeen, and he has apply'd to me, for advice, and I have, ~~and~~ ^do^ advizd him to Come upon some amicable agreament ^with you^ if you are Willing,— and I think it is much the Best, I believe it is more agreable ^to god^, it is more Rational, it is Humane, it is Neighbourly and it ^is^ Christian like, and I take you to be one that fears God,— and consider Moses is one that makes no profession of Religion ^*and we Revds try to be moderate with Such^—and perhaps you may use Some as Witnesses for your, Who are Distitute of the Fear of god, and they may Sin in help^ing^ your Case, against God, Which will be ten thousand Times worse, that what either of you ^will^ Lose, and what either of you will gain, will be a fruit of Sin ^in Great Measure^, ~~I am an Enimy to Law Suits~~ and therefore I woud, (as a friend and well wisher to you) ^advise you^ to come upon Some agreable Terms with Moses;—but if you won't I can advise ^him^ to nothing, but to Defend himself as Well as he can— if you Will come upon Friendly Terms—You may Chuse your Man ~~or men, to hear the difference~~ and Moses, ^his^ to Decide the Case—and appoint ~~the~~ ^a^ Place and Time, and Mose Will meet you—let him ^have^ Timely notice—I am Sir[46]

your Sincere Friend and Well Wisher ~~Both Soul & Body~~

S.O.

45. The Long Island Presbytery meeting at Easthampton on April 12, 1769, noted that it had received this confession from Occom, acknowledged Occom's "very gloomy and desponding Frame of Mind," and appointed Samuel Buell to make a report of the events at the next meeting of the presbytery. Occom himself was present when the group met again at Bridge Hampton on November 1, 1769. The presbytery found that Occom's episode "arose not from any Degree of intemperate drinking, but from having Drank a small Quantity of Spiritous Liquor after having been all day without food" (Love, *Occom*, 163–164).

46. Occom's recommendation that Moses Mazeen (Mohegan) and Nathaniel Champlin resolve their dispute through extralegal remediation demonstrates his frustration with and distrust of the colonial court system. Since 1704, the Mohegan tribe had been embroiled in a protracted legal dispute involving lands Uncas had conveyed to his ally and tribal overseer John Mason in the 1650s and 1660s that were ultimately seized by the colony of Connecticut and deeded to white settlers. Occom himself probably attended hearings of the "Mason case" convened in Norwich, Connecticut, in 1743; those hearings were decided in favor of the colony. Appeals continued,

*and we profesors ought to be moderate with Such.

[CHS folder I.5; envelope text: "To Mʳ N. Champlin." Samson Occom Papers, Connecticut Historical Society, Hartford, Connecticut.]

34 ∽   TO ELEAZAR WHEELOCK

Mohegan
March 17, 1769

Rev Sir,

I dont remember that I have been overtaken with strong drink this winter, but many White people make no bones of it to call me a drunkard, and I expected it, as I have many enemies round about here, yea they call me a lyar and rogue and what not, and they curse & damn me to the lowest Hell.[47] I am quite out of [word illegible] sometimes—them pretended Christians are seven times worse that the Savage Indians; and yet I think I take more heed to myself than ever. I do take some strong drink sometimes, but I dont tip a quarter so much as I used to do, yea I dont keep any in my house only in extraordinary cases. I do fully determine to go into the wilderness as soon as I can, and David will go with me by your help. We are both very lame, we have no horses nor money, and he wants some clothes. He was here last week with 20 other Indians. He has a daughter born lately,[48] Deacon Hugh has some hesitation whether to send his daughter or not—he will determine in a few days. There is considerable revival of religious concern at Montauk. I intend to be at your house in a few days. I want to borrow some money of you, at least £20. I left some money at Scotland, and I wrote for it last fall, but when it will come I cant tell. I heard Bʳ Jewett is kicking up his charges to load up his old Rusty Musketoon shoot at me, but I hope he will overload, that his old musket may burst. We are by Divine favour in good state of health. Sir, this, with grateful respects, is

> *from your most unworthy servant,*
> *Samson Occom*

PS. I never was so discouraged as I am now.

[Copy; not in Occom's hand; DCA 769217.2. Courtesy of Dartmouth College Library.]

---

and the case was finally resolved, again in the colony's favor, in 1773. His reaction to the final Mason case decision appears in his 1773 letter to Samuel Buell (Oberg, 207–213; L. Murray, *To Do Good*, 33–37; Love, *Occom*, 119–123; L. Brooks, 143).

47. Occom here responds to Wheelock's letter of March 9, 1769, which relayed public reports of Occom's drunkenness.

48. Hannah Fowler was born in 1768.

35 ⌒   TO ELEAZAR WHEELOCK

Mohegan
July 1: 1769

Revd Sir

I receiv'd yours, after mr Bailey I think his Name is, was here, enquiring ^after^ Jo Johnson,—I have heard nothing about him,—I have nothing to cary me up into the Wilderness neither Money nor Horse, & I have nothing to Leave with my Family to Live on—and I have got a Lame Shoulder besides, it Broke Since I was at your House, I have been Riding to Several places of Indians lately, and I find riding hurts my Shoulders, more than any exercise, Which discourages me not a little—I heard your Mohawk and Onyda Boys dont intend to Come back to School again, Sir William, is going to Set up a School for 'em[49]—if Mr Kirtland is come home I Wish he Woud Come to See me,—I cant tell When I Shall come to See you,—My Family is well by the goodness of god, and the Indians here ^are^ Well, but Religion Decays and the Devil Reigns,—Mr Jewet I hear is as bitter against me as ever, I wonder What ails that good bad man, I have pickt up nothing against him—Please to a^c^cept grateful respects, and pray for us—I am, Revd Sir

your most obliged and very Humble Servt
S. Occom

[Recipient's copy; DCA 769401; envelope text: "To The Revd Dr Wheelock at Lebanon." Courtesy of Dartmouth College Library.]

36 ⌒   "YOUR GOOD OFFER"

Mohegan
Jan^r 15: 1770

Revd Sir

I had good opportunity to forward your Letter to Mr Wheatley[50] and I Sent one to his mother, and I have just receiv'd an Answere, one Letter from Mrs Wheatley and the other from Mr Brimmer by whom I sent the Letters—Mr Brimmer writes thus

Boston 2^d Jan^r 1770 Sir agreeable to your Desire, have waited on Mr Wheatley who has ^paid^ me Forty pounds Sterling, for which I gave him a receipt on Account of Doc^r Wheelock, inclosed you have a Letter from him, also one for Doc^r Wheelock, to which must refer you, as have given a receipt for the money it will be proper for

---

49. According to Eleazar Wheelock in his *Continuation of the Narrative of the Indian Charity-School* (1771), two Oneida men traveled to Lebanon, Connecticut, in February or March 1769 to withdraw six Oneida children from the school, ostensibly to see their families. Wheelock later heard that Oneida seers had dreamed that the Six Nations would soon be at war with the English and thus wanted their children home (15–16). Love suggests that a series of diplomatic insults and blunders made by Ralph Wheelock and other non-Native Wheelock emissaries also contributed to the withdrawal (*Occom*, 161–162).

50. *Mr Wheatley:* Nathaniel Wheatley.

you to inclose the Bill of Exchange to me in order to take up my receipt, have desired Mʳ [Knox] who takes care of my Business to pay you five or six pounds, and when you forward the Bill to take ^up^ my receipt, Shall give further Orders concerning the remainder, in the Interim remain Sir

your Hum Servᵗ
John Baker Brimmer

Mʳˢ Wheatley wrote these words

I heartily Rejoice that it is in my ^Sons^ Power to be of Service to you, he says, if Mʳ Wheelock will Draw on him, he will pay the Money, my son has wrote to Mʳ Wheelock upon that Business—When you have read Mʳ Wheatleys Letter, you will then know What to write to Mʳ Wheatley—if you Send a Bill of Exchange, or Letters, I can convey them very soon to Boston—I suppose Mʳ Brimmer is [maried] and will Stay in Boston Some Time—Thro' Divine favour my Family is well, and pray these may find you and yours in Health—⁵¹

I am, Revᵈ Sir

your most obliged Humˡ Servᵗ
Samson Occom

P.S. I was at Naroganset 3: Weeks ago, We had some Conversation Concerning your Proposal of their removing with the School, they are thankful to you for your good offer, they will Consider of it, and will let you know their Minds by and by—But I can find out, their Answere

[LOC MSS 000867]

37 ∾   TO ELEAZAR WHEELOCK

Mohegan
March 6 1770

Revᵈ Sir

I receiv'd your kind favor last Sabbath by John, at Groton Indian Town, had about 3 Minute Conversation with him, he told me nothing of the Afair you Hinted at,— I have wrote nothing of the Contents of Yours to Esqʳ Thornton⁵²—have Sent ^to^ to

---

51. Susannah Wheatley and Samson Occom belonged to the same transatlantic Calvinist evangelical networks, and they shared a common friend in George Whitefield. Occom lodged at the Wheatleys' house on King Street when he visited Boston, and Susannah Wheatley was a benefactor to the Occom family. Occom also developed an acquaintance with the poet Phyllis Wheatley; see note 67.

52. Wheelock's letter apparently does not survive. The "Afair" Occom refers to may be either strained relations between Wheelock and Samuel Kirkland, or the incorporation of Dartmouth College, which was being finalized in February and March 1770. Occom believed that the reorganization and relocation of what had once been Moor's Indian Charity School and its growing indifference to Native interests would anger the school's English trustees (DCA 769556.1; DCA 769629l; DCA 770108.1; DCA 770212.3; Blodgett, 114–115; Love, *Occom,* 157–159). See also Valone.

Boston; Some Time ago—an English Gentleman Call'd on me last Week and Lodg'd With us one Night and Stay'd most one Day, he is Just from Sir Williams, and ^was^ at Onoyda this Winter past, he tells me, the Indians there are disafected towards Mr Kirtland, more than one half at Cannowaurohary[53] don't attend his ministry—The Gentleman, I believe is a grand Man, he has a Coach of 6 at New York and 2 or 3 Servants there, and 2 are With him, he is very Inquisitive about the Indians, and What treatment they Meet with from the White People,—I have no Horse to Ride, or I Woud Soon Come up to See you,—We are Well thro' Divine Favour I am Most Kind Sir

your most obliged Humble Servant,
S. Occom

P.S. The gentle^n I mentiond has been in this Country near 2 Years and been traviling Continually, and has Visited all the Indians he Coud Come at

[Recipient's copy; DCA 770206.2; envelope text: "To The Revd Dr Wheelock." Courtesy of Dartmouth College Library.]

38 ∽   "THE FLAME OF FRIENDSHIP"

Mohegan
June 9: 1770

My Very Dear Friend

What is the Reason, that I dont hear anything at
Our Friendship I believe is grown old and Rusty
all from you, is our Friendship, which use to
We Use to Write to each other once in a While but
Subsist between us Dead, and is our former aquain
now I have ^not^ heard any thing from you a long while
tance forgot, has the Water between Long Island
Does not the Chain of Friendship want to be brightend
have Quench the Flame of Friendship, has the length
once more between us? or Shall we let the Chain
of Time & Distance blot^ed^ out all Sincere Regards, What
lie to gather more Rust and let it Rust off entirely?
If We Shoud Search and See, if there is any Spark
or Shall we begin to Scour the Goulden Chain again
of Fire of Friendship left in our Hearts, if we
I will take hold of the End that Reaches here, and will
Can find any fire, What if we Shoud Try to blow it up
begin to Pollish it with all the Tokens of due Respect to
again? and What's the Matter I hear nothing from my

53. *Cannowaurohary:* Canajoharie, New York.

you, if you will take hold of the other end that Reaches
Dear Friend your kind Husband, What woud be the
over to Long Island,—I shou'd take it very Kindly, if
Harm if you woud perswade your Husband to Come over
you Woud only let me know how you do once in a While,
once to See us, and take your Sister or Sisters with you,
and you may give me Some account of the Well fair
I have been to See you Several Times Since we have livd
of the People your Way—and What ever you Want to
over here, and the Distance from here to you is no further
relate you may do it with all freedom to me, and what
than from you to me I have measured it Several times
ever you want to know of me Shall not be withholden
What if you and your Husband shoud write to me once
from you—We are all Well in my family thro' Divine favor
if you won't Come to See us and let me understand your
—Regards to all Enquiring Friends and particular Respects
Wellfair and the Wellfair of all Friends in your Family
to your Parent[54]

> *I am, my Dear Friend, your most Obedient*
> *Samson Occom*

2 Letters in one

[CHS folder I.5. Samson Occom Papers, Connecticut Historical Society, Hartford, Connecticut.]

39 ∽   TO JOSEPH FISH

Mohegan
Nov[r] 16: 1770

Rev[d] Sir

Your Allowence, for your School Masters at Stonington Indians, is Very Small, in these Hard Times, Who ever undertakes it, must not pretend to live by it—Our School Master has £24 . . . pr. Anm—, House to live in, about 16 Acres of good Land to emprove, he has inclosed it all, and is allow'd to keep two Cows and a Horse to Run in our Common Pastures and three Swine and as Many Poltry as he has a mind and wood to Burn besides, and Yet he greatly Complain^s^ I Judge he has as good ^as £^ 32 pr A[n]—I hired Jacob Fowler to Work for me a Year, and he has above 2 Months to Work yet,—But I woud not hinder him one Day from keeping School, if he had Sutable encouragement, if the Indians Will give him his Board, he may keep your School 3 Months, and if you can agree with him to keep it Longer afterwards,

---

54. Occom here encodes his feelings in alternating lines. The recipient of this letter is probably Esther Poquiantup, wife of Jacob Fowler. Jacob Fowler also wrote to Occom in this encrypted fashion on March 27, 1772 (CHS-M 244).

I Shan't Say any thing against it—he is Well qualified to keep School among the Indians,[55] I am Revd Sir

Your unworthy Friend
Samson Occom

[Recipient's copy; DCA 770616; envelope text: "To The Revd Mr Fish at Stonington." Courtesy of
Dartmouth College Library.]

40 ◌

TO BENJAMIN FORFITT

March 4: 1771

Sir

I caried over ^to America^ a number of your Charitable Society Books and a Number of Gentleman besides put Variety of Books into my for the Indians, amon^g^st
which Several Sorts of Hymn ^& Psalms^ Books were found, and I have disposd of
them all among the poor Indians, and them most thankfully reccivd, and they have
been of great Use and Benefit to the Indians, and they Continue to Come to me from
all Quarters for Books, even to the Distance of 60 miles—The Indians are greatly Delighted and edified with Singing, it is Judgd by the White Peop in this Country, that
the Indians have most Melodious voices of any People, and Hymn and Psalm Books
woud be very acceptable amongst them as Well as other Books the Indians in their
Religious meetings round about here, Sing more than any Christians and they have
frequent meetings in all Indians Towns—[56]

As your Worthy Society[57] was formd for most Noble End, and Extensive bene-
fit amongst the Children of Benighted men, and you only want to know where to
Send your Books—I think this place Calls aloud for your most benevolent Charity—
I live near a Center of five Towns of Indians[58] and they Come to me for Books—We
Used to be Supplyd in Some measure with Books from Dr Wheelocks Indian School,

55. Fish, who was minister to the North Stonington Pequot community and the Narragansetts at
    Charlestown, Rhode Island, appointed Edward Deake as schoolmaster at Charlestown, Rhode
    Island, from 1765 to 1775. Deake's annual salary was £24. Jacob Fowler served a successful term
    as schoolmaster at Groton from winter 1770 to November 1774; his annual salary was £12. Sam-
    son Occom earned £15 each year during his tenure as schoolmaster at Montauk. As Laura Mur-
    ray observes, pay for missionaries and schoolmasters was "generally very low": an unskilled
    farm worker could earn as much as £1 a week, and a private in the army £2 a month (L. Mur-
    ray, To Do Good, 190; Simmons and Simmons, xxix; Love, Occom, 195–199).

56. Hymn singing was a beloved activity among Christian Indian towns in southern New England,
    where it served as a ritual of community celebration and reconciliation. Samson Occom and
    Joseph Johnson both wrote hymn-texts, and Occom compiled and published A Choice Collection
    of Hymns and Spiritual Songs in 1774. The preface to that work and hymns by Occom appear in
    this collection. See also J. Brooks, "Six Hymns"; American Lazarus, 51–86.

57. Forfitt was secretary of a London society that distributed books to the poor (DCA 763508.1;
    DCA 763508.2; DCA 769426.2; DCA 770212.1).

58. Five Towns of Indians: Farmington, Connecticut (Tunxis); Groton, Connecticut (Pequot); Ni-
    antic, Connecticut (Niantic); Stonington, Connecticut (Pequot); and Charlestown, Rhode Island
    (Narragansett).

but he is now removed with his School far up into the Country to the Distance of 150 miles;[59] and Boston and New York are at a great Distance from us, where I suppose your Charitable Books are Sent, and we have no benefit of them, if you will be so Condesending as to Send Some Books to me to Distribute among the poor Indians, I should be very thankful and will be faithful to my trust and will Exhort and Encourage the Indians to make good Use of them,—I think the Noble end of your Charity will be answerd in Some measure, as the Indians are poor and very ignorant and a few just emerging out of Heathenish gross Darkness and are enquiring after Divine Knowledge, I think they ought to be encour^a^gd by all means, I believe it is acceptable service to the King of Kings and all that do this Service will be reward— I had a few Little Testa^nts to Dispose of among our Young People, and were extreamly pleasing to them, they Carry them in their Pockets as vade mecum[60]—the Testaments were printed in Oxford by Thomas Baskett, I Shoud be glad of a number of them, if they are to be had[61]—Little Hymn Books Design'd for the Negroes, Printed by John Oliver in Bartholomew Close near West Smithfield,[62]—and Mr Masons Songs and Penetential Hymns[63] are very Pleasing to the Indians—Mr Gart Noell Book Seller in New York, is my good Friend, if you Send to his Care Directed to me—he will take good Care to Send them me—I take this opportunity to return most Hearty ~~thanks~~ and most Humble thanks, to your worthy and most benevolent Society, for favours already receivd by the poor Indians the Lord reward you all with Temporal & Spiritual Rewards—I have been exercis'd with Rhewmatick Pains for Some Length of Time, I am not able to do much of any thing, but the rest of my Family are well thro' the goodness of a merciful God and I hope these may find you and yours in good Health and Prosperity—Pray for us and all the poor Indians

    I am most kind Sir

your most unworthy and very Hum^l Ser^t

S. O.

[Sender's copy; CHS folder I.6; note at bottom of second page: "A coppy to Mr Forfet." Samson Occom Papers, Connecticut Historical Society, Hartford, Connecticut.]

---

59. Dartmouth College was incorporated in March 1770 and established in Hanover, New Hampshire, in October 1770 (DCA 770212.2; DCA 770551).
60. *vade mecum:* Latin phrase literally meaning "go with me," but used to describe a manual or handbook.
61. Thomas Baskett, appointed printer to King George and Oxford University, published thirty-three editions of the Bible and the New Testament at Oxford between 1743 and 1764.
62. In 1757, John Oliver (1701/2–1775) issued a catalog, *Books and Tracts, printed and sold by John Oliver, in Bartholomew Close, near West-Smithfield, London*. Occom may have discovered these hymnals in Oliver's catalog. Apparently, no copy of the hymnal survives.
63. Anglican John Mason (1646–1694) first published his *Songs of Praise* in 1683 and *Penitential Cries* in 1693; the two volumes appeared together in dozens of eighteenth-century reprints. Occom selected six hymns by Mason for republication in his own *Collection of Hymns and Spiritual Songs* (1774).

41 ∽   TO SUSANNAH WHEATLEY

Mohegan
March 5: 1771

Most kind Madam,

Your most acceptable and very animating Favour of Decr 3^d 70 Came Safely to Hand
a few Days ago, for Which I return you ten thousands Thanks—

I am in great Hopes, Your Letter to Esqr Thornton will attract Bowels of Compassion towards me and mine,[64]— And I pray the Lord to reward you & yours Bountifully in Both Worlds,— I am in greater Straights and Necessities than ever, we had
but little Corn last year and Consequently little meat, it was Dry Season with us; I
have no provisions now at all only what I buy, and I have no Money to buy with. I
am oblig'd to Sell any thing I have to get meat and Corn with, & my Family Consists
ten Souls Constantly, and a great Number of Visitors Continually from all quarters
there has not been one Week nor 3 Days I can remember in the Year past, but that
we have had Some Stranger or other—My being acquainted with the World in Some
Measure, has made my House a Sort ^of^ an Asylum for Strangers both English and
Indians, far and near, — I Labour under Bodily Indisposition Constantly near a Year,
I have not been able to do much in hand Labour, Which puts me back very much;
and on these Difficulties, my unbelieving Heart brings me upon the Borders of Discouragement ^at times^, but my Reason and better understanding tells me, this is
the Time to Trust and Hope in God, and I believe God never made any Creature with
a Mouth, but that he will provide for it in his ^own^ way and Time—and when I
Come to recollect what I have Seen in my Travels, and what I have Read also, I am
Struck with amazement and Stand Speechless; I am Sure if God Shou'd Deal with me
according to my Deserts I Shoud ^have^ nothing that is Comfortable in this World
nor in that which is to Come—How many poor Creatures have I Seen in the World as
good by Nature as I am, go almost Naked in the Severest Weather, and have no where
to Lay their Heads, and not one Mouthful of the meanest Bread that they Can Command, but are Oblig'd to go from House to House, and from Door to Door, With Tears
Streaming Down their Dirty Cheeks beging a Crum of Bread, and when they have
one mouthful given them, they know not Who will ^give^ them the next,—When
I Come to Consider how much better God has Dealt with me, I am Astonish'd at my
Self, that I have no more Sense of the Distinguishing Goodness of God to me, and to
mine—I have greatest Reason to Call upon my Soul and all that is Within ^me^ to
Bless and Praise God Night and Day; and When I Come to Consider further, how
many Holy Souls, I mean the Children ^of God^ have Sufferd, in Times ^of^ Persecution, all manner of Torments, and Depriv'd of every Comfort in this World, Yet
how ful of Praises and thanksgivings were they—Yea When I Come to trace the Son

---

64. Thornton and Wheatley became acquainted through their mutual friend George Whitefield;
both belonged to the same transatlantic network of Calvinist evangelicals. Thornton served as treas-
urer of the English trust for Moor's Indian Charity School, and after Wheatley's death took her place
as a major benefactor of the Occom family.

of the most High, from the Manger to his Cross, I am Struck Dumb, I am Confounded, I am Ashamed, I have no room to open my Mouth in a Way of Complaint, I pray God to learn me by these Small Tryals I meet with in the World to Hope and Trust in God alone, and not in the Creature—I ^Pray^ God to kill me to the World, and that he woud Kill the World to me—that I may be Dead to the World and the World to me[65]—God has Seen fit to take away my eldest Son by Death a few Weeks ago, the Lord Sanctify this afflictive Dispensation to me and to mine[66]—my Wife is not Well, and the rest of my Family are Well thro' the Goodness of God at present— I pray God these may find you and yours in Health of Body and Soul Prosperity,— my ^Wife^ Joins me in Christian Respects to you and yours—

I am, most kind madam

your most unworthy and most obliged Humble Servant
Samson Occom

P.S. Please to remember ^me^ to Phillis and the rest of your Servants. Pray Madam, what harm woud it be to Send Phillis to her Native Country as a Female Preacher to her kindred, you know Quaker Women are alow'd to preach, and why not others in an Extraordinary Case—S.O.[67]

2 P.S. Madam I have ^a^ favour to beg of you that is, to get me a Singing Book, I think it was Printed at Salem lately price, I was told 8 my Children are much Inclin'd to

---

65. *kill me to the World:* Occom here invokes the doctrine of mortification, which holds that salvation requires a putting to death of the natural, worldly self in sin as a precondition for the regeneration or rebirth of a new being in grace; see Romans 6:6–8.

66. Aaron Occom reportedly died at Mohegan in the winter of 1771, leaving behind his wife, Ann Robin (Wangunk), and a son named Aaron.

67. The pioneering black poet Phillis Wheatley developed an acquaintance with Occom during his travels to Boston. During the winter of 1773–1774, Occom apparently wrote to Phillis Wheatley expressing antislavery sentiment (the letter does not survive). Wheatley replied on February 11, 1774: "I have this day received your obliging kind epistle, and am greatly satisfied with your reasons respecting the negroes, and think highly reasonable what you offer in vindication of their natural rights: Those that invade them cannot be insensible that the divine light is chasing away the thick darkness which broods over the land of Africa; and the chaos which has reigned so long, is converting into beautiful order, and reveals more and more clearly the glorious dispensation of civil and religious liberty, which are so inseparably united, that there is little or no enjoyment of one without the other: Otherwise, perhaps, the Israelites had been less solicitous for their freedom from Egyptian slavery; I do not say they would have been contented without it, by no means; for in every human breast God has implanted a principle, which we call love of freedom; it is impatient of oppression, and pants for deliverance; and by the leave of our modern Egyptians I will assert, that the same principle lives in us. God grant deliverance in his own way and time, and get him honour upon all those whose avarice impels them to countenance and help forward the calamities of their fellow creatures. This I desire not for their hurt, but to convince them of the strange absurdity of their conduct, whose words and actions are so diametrically opposite. How well the cry for liberty, and the reverse disposition for the exercise of oppressive power over others agree—I humbly think it does not require the penetration of a philosopher to determine." Her letter appeared in the New London *Connecticut Gazette* on March 11, 1774. Samuel Hopkins also invited Wheatley to undertake a mission to Africa, but she declined, explaining that she would look like a "Barbarian" to the "Natives" because she did not know their language (Wheatley, 211).

Singing and I woud Encourage them in Time, and I will endeavour to Send you Money Some Time or other. Send by any Careful Hand to Mr. J. B. Brimmer at Norwich Landing.

yours &
S. Occom

[Recipient's copy; DCA 771205.1; envelope text: "to Mrs Susanna Wheatley In Kings Street Boston." On its back is inscribed in Wheelock's script: "Rec^d Septr 25, 1772. Why could he never write in this Strain to me when he knew me Sinking under Lab^r & trials for his nation."]

42 ∽   TO ELEAZAR WHEELOCK

Mohegan
July 24: 1771

Revd Sir

Yours of Jan^r 22 I receivd but a few Days ago, Wherein you Speak of mu^c^h Sorrow on my Account,[68] I am obliged to you So far as it is agreablc to god, You seem to think that it is a Sort of Reproof from God, that I was Left to Stray, for my Staying at Home So much, But I don't think with you,—God woud Certainly gave me Strenght Sufficient to go Such Long Journeis, but I han't been able to Ride far. Now two whole Years, and I have been Confin'd to my House good Deal this Spring, I am greatly Exercis'd with my old Pains—As to my Present Standing with the Indians, I need not Say more than this, I am as Well, if not better receivd by them than ever, if I woud only Comply with their Desire, the Indians ^at^ Mohegan, Groton, Nahanteck, Stonington, and even at Charlestown in general, woud put themselves under my Instructions—as to my [word crossed out] being under a Mistake about my and Davids going into the Wilderness I am not, I woud have gone up and David too, the Spring after I got Home from England, but you Said, you had no money to Assist me with, and you yourself Discouraged David from going,—Indeed I have always Declin'd to remove my Family into the Wilderness, but David woud have gone up to Settle there—had he a proper Encouragement he woud go now—but he will not go for What you offer—he has Some thoughts of offering his Service to the Comiss^{rs} of Boston to go into the Wilderness, if they woud give him £30 Law. per An. he woud go into the Wilderness with his Family to Settle—I am very Jealous that instead of your Semenary Becoming alma Mater, she will be too alba mater[69] to Suckle the Tawnees, for She is already aDorn'd up too much like the Popish Virgin Mary. She'll be Naturally asham'd to Suckle the Tawnees for She is already equal in Power, Honor

---

68. See Eleazar Wheelock's letter to Samson Occom, January 22, 1771 (DCA 771122). Wheelock also complained in his *Continuation of the Narrative of the Indian Charity-School* (1771) that the "bad conduct" of his Native American alumni had given him "the greatest weight of sorrow" and led him to believe that white students were better candidates for the ministry (19).

69. *alma Mater . . . alba mater:* This phrase turns on Occom's substitution of the Latin "alba mater," meaning white mother, for "alma mater," meaning mother of the soul and used colloquially to indicate the school he once attended.

and Authority to ~~and~~ any College in Europe, I think your College has too much Worldly Grandure for the Poor Indians they'll never have much benefet of it,—In So Saying I Speak the general Sentiment of Indians and English too in these parts; So many of your Missionaries and School masters and Indian Scholars Leaving You and Your Service Confirms me in this opinion,—your having So many White Scholars and So few or no Indian Scholars, gives me great Discouragement—I verily thought once that your Institution was Intended Purely for the poor Indians with this thought I Cheerfully Ventur'd my Body & Soul, left my Country my poor young Family all my friends and Relations, to sail over the Boisterous Seas to England, to help forward your School, Hoping, that it may be a lasting Benefet to my poor Tawnee Brethren, With this View I went a Volunteer—I was quite Willing to become a Gazing Stock, Yea Even a Laughing Stock, in Strange Countries to Promote your Cause—We Loudly Proclaimed before Multitudes of People from Place to Place, that there was a most glorious Prospect of Spreading the gospel of the Lord Jesus to the furthest Savage Nations in the Wilderness, thro your Institution, We told them that there were So many Missionaries & So many Schoolmasters already sent out, and a greater Number woud soon follow. But when we got Home behold all the glory had decayd and now I am afraid, we shall be Deem'd as Liars and Deceivers in Europe, unless you gather Indians quickly to your College, in great Numbers and not to have So many Whites in the Charity,—I understand you have no Indians at Present except two or three Mollatoes[70]—this I think is quite Contrary to the Minds of the Donors, We told them, that we were Beging for poor Miserable Indians,—as for my part I went, purely for the poor Indians, and I Should be as ready as ever to promote your School acording to my poor Abilities ^if^ I Coud be Convincd by ocular Demonstration, that your pure Intention is to help the poor helpless Indians, but as long as you have no Indians, I am full of Doubts,—Your writing to Esqr Thornton to my Disadvantage and not ^one^ word in my favour, gave me to think, that your Indian Scholars had reason to With Draw from You, and your Missionaries and Schol Masters too, the opinion of many white People about here is that you have been Scheeming altogether, and that it was a [Ploy] to Send me over to England, for (Say they) now they don't Care any^thing^ ab^o^ut you, you have answerd their Ends, now you may Sink or Swim it is all one to them, this makes me think of what that great man of god Said to me, Mr Whitefield, just before I left England in the ^Hearing of^ Some gentlemen—ah, Says he, you have been a fine Tool to get Money for them, but when you get home, they won't Regard you the'll Set you a Drift,—I am ready to believe it Now—I am going to Say Something further, Which is very Disagreeable Modisty woud forbid me, but I am Constraind So to Write,—Many gentlemen in England and in this Country too, Say if ^you^ had not this Indian Buck you woud

---

70. Wheelock's *Continuation of the Narrative of the Indian Charity-School* (1771) noted that enrollments of Native American young men had steadily declined from 14 in May 1768 to three in May 1770. In 1771, of twenty-four charity students at Dartmouth College, five were American Indian and one was "mix'd blood" (31): Daniel Simons or Symons (Narragansett), Abraham Simons (Narragansett; brother of Daniel), Peter Pauquunnuppeet (Stockbridge), John Konkapot (Stockbridge), Samuel Squintup, and Caleb Watts (mixed race) (Kelly 123). See Kelly for a fuller accounting of the Native enrollments at Moor's Indian Charity School and Dartmouth College.

not Collected a quarter of the Money you did, one gentleman in Particular in England Said to me, if ^he^ hadn't Seen my face he woudnt have given 5 happence but
now I have 50£ freely—This one Consideration gives me great Quietness, I think I
went to England with Honest Heart, I think I have done that which I think was my
Duty to Do—I might write more but I have no time,—I Wish I Coud give you one
Visit, to have a ful talk but you got so ^far^ up, I Shall never be able[71]—If I am under
any Mistake, Please to enlighten me,—I am better in Health than I've been and my
Family is well thro' Divine Favour. Please to ^give^ my Comp[ts] to all under your Care
and Acept Duty from

> *your most unworthy Servt,*
> *Samson Occom*

P. S. I have not wrote this Sort to any one in England, I Chuse to let you know my
mind first.

> *S.O.*

[Recipient's copy; DCA 771424. Courtesy of Dartmouth College Library.]

43 ∾   TO ELEAZAR WHEELOCK

Mohegan
July 13: 1772

Rev[d] and Hon[d] Sir

PS.

   Writing gives me but very little Satisfaction, I want to Spend 3 or 4 Days, with
you at [word illegible] and to hear and See for myself—but you have got So far the
other Side of the Globe; I am not able to bear Expences So far—and it may be of no
profet if I went; I Cant find ^out^ the Reason, Why you ^coud^ not Come to my
House, or Sent for me, when you was So near last Spring,—I suppose you[d] be glad
to know, What I owe,—it is between 66 and 70 pounds LM: My Family Charges
amount to about 20 Pounds pr An. and what my Journey expences woud be, I
can'not tell—if I Shoud go on a Mission, I Shou'd not pretend to Set out till next
Spring,—and I Shoud insist upon Davids or Jacobs going with me—I have work
enough, I might preach every Day I have So many Calls—I was at Stonington Indian
Town Yester Preaching, and there was a great num^ber^ of People, and a Solemn
Meeting we had, I believe ye Lord was there of a Truth, there was flow of Tears from
the bigest part of the People most all the afternoon, and this I have Seen in many
Places Where I have been Preaching lately Please to acept Christian Sallutations,

> *from your most unworthy Serv[t]*
> *Samson Occom*

[Recipient's copy; DCA 772413.2. Courtesy of Dartmouth College Library.]

71. Hanover, New Hampshire, is almost two hundred miles northwest of Mohegan, Connecticut.

44 ∞   To Andrew Gifford

Mohegan
October 19: 1772

Rev^d and Hon^d Sir:

Blessed be the Lord God of Heaven & Earth that he has Cast an Eye of pity on his poor Worthless Creature in his Necessitous Circumstances, and that he has put it in your Tender Heart to continue your Benevolence and Intercessions for a poor Needy Creature, both with God and Man, and you have prevailed—and Blessed be God, that by your fervent Prayers the Heart of his People are opened toward me and mine, so liberally the Lord your God whom you have been Serving all your Days, Preserved you yet more abundantly with the Divine Consolations of his spirit, and Preserved all my kind Benefactors with all the Blessing of Heaven and Earth, and the Lord Strengthen your Heart and Hands in your great and arduous Work, that many may yet be refresh'd with the Fruits of your Labour, both to their Bodies and Souls, far and near and that the Lord would Continue your Sweet and most profitable Life to an beneficial Age—(as I heard a while ago you was very Sick). Your work is not done yet, you are yet to feed your Glorious Masters feeble Lamb & Sheep.

Your Most animating and Incouraging Favour of July 18 with fifteen Pounds fifteen Shillings and two pence Ster^l found me very Sick about ten Days ago, but it was a Cordial to my Body and Soul; and I am now recovering my Health very fast thro the pure Mercy of God and all my Family is in good State of Health, thanks be to God.

I have a good news to tell you, the Lord has been among the poor Indians round about here, Several have been hopefully Converted within a year, and they are very attentive to the Word of God, I have Preached abundantly amongst them, and I hope I shall go on Preaching by Gods help.

I Return most Hearty and Unfeigned thanks ten thousand Times to my good and Most kind Benefactors who have Commited their Benefactions into your Hands. The Lord who never forgets the kindness done to the least of his poor People, Reward them a Thousand fold in this world and Everlasting Blessings in the World to Come.

My poor little Brother Jacob Fowler, he is my Wife's own Brother, and is now keeping a School among the Pequot Tribe of Indians, Left a letter with me before I was take Sick, Directed to you, which I now Send with this. He was hopefully Converted about a Year and half ago and he is warm in Religion. I wish he had Mr. Benjn French's Book on Metaphor;[72] that is the best Book for the Instruction of the Indians of Humane Composure I ever Saw, and the books and the other things you mention in your Letters and I hope and pray, that my kind Benefactors may never have any Reason to Repent of their Charity to me and mine.

---

72. Occom probably means Benjamin Keach, *Tropologia: A Key to Open Scripture Metaphors,* first published in London in 1682 and reprinted more than thirty times. See his November 10, 1773, letter to the English trust.

My greatful Compliments to all my kind Benefactors and Inquiring Friends. My Wife joins me in Dutiful Respects to you—I am, Rev^d & Hon^d Sir,

> *your Most unworthy and most obliged very Humb^{le} Servant,*
> Samson Occom

[Beinecke Rare Book and Manuscript Library, Yale University, General Collection Manuscript Miscellany Group 961, Item F-1. Courtesy of Beinecke Rare Book and Manuscript Library, Yale University.]

45 ∾   TO ELEAZAR WHEELOCK

Boston
Jan^r 27: [1773]

Rev^d & Honr^d Sir

I have only Time to let you know, that I am now in Boston, Came here, this Day a Week, and Shall Stay till nex Monday by the importunity of Friends,—I left my Family 3 Weeks next fryday in tolerable good Health thro mercy,—I am much troubled with my old ails at Times, Yet I am able to ride Short Journies, and I have work enough Preaching both among the Indians & English, and there ^is^ great attention among the People—I fully intended to Come to See you the fall past, but new difficulties Came upon me about the Time I was to set out, as soon as I am able to ride So far I will Come to See you—for I want much to See, how you Go on in the Grand Cause I Cant be easy, till I See with my Eyes, and ^not only^ hear with my Ears,—Be So good as to let me hear, Where M^r. McCluer[73] and his Collegue are and What they are a doing,—A Wampum of Friendship Flew from Massipi thro Various Tribes of Indians, Came to our Hands about Six Weeks ago, and we Receiv'd it Cordially,[74]—Several Tribes of Indians are to hold a Congress Next march at Stock-Bridge, and a grand Congress is to ^be^ at Sir William Johnsons Some Time next June or July,—and if I am able, I intend to be at Both of 'em—I am, Rev^d & Honr^d Sir

> *your most obliged and very Humb^l Servt*
> Samson Occom

P.S. Mr Peck and his Lady Send their kind regards to you and yours.

[Recipient's copy; DCA 772127.1; envelope text: "To the Revd Doc^r Wheelock President of Dartmouth College." Courtesy of Dartmouth College Library.]

---

73. *Mr Maccluer:* David McClure. In May 1772, David McClure and Levi Frisbie traveled to Mohegan to recruit Occom to participate in a mission to Delaware communities on the Muskingham River in Ohio westward. Occom was encouraged by Wheelock to participate in the mission, but declined. See DCA 772306, 772323, 772326.1, 772328.

74. Wampum belts constituted an important form of indigenous communication or textuality in the Native Northeast. Typically composed of blue and white shells drawn from the coastal waters of southern New England, wampum was utilized by Iroquois and Algonkian peoples as a communicative medium of diplomacy, kinship, and commemoration. See L. Brooks, 10–11; D. Murray, *Indian Giving,* 116–140.

46 ∾   To Samuel Buell

1773

Rev^d and much Esteemed Sir

Your most Fraternal Epistle, of Jan^r 6 Came Safly to hand two Days ago, for which I
return most Hum^bl and Hearty Thanks,—I had almost Concluded, in my Mind, that
you and the Rest of the Brethren of our Revd Resbytery had determind to forget me,
but I am thankful that I am yet rememberd by you, and I hope I am Caried as a Weak
Brother, in the Arms ^of^ Your Faith at the Throne of Grace Daily, for I greatly need
the fervent Prayers of all the Saints under the Whole Heavens, in my great Work for
I have Work enough for three four or five Ministers. I ^am^ Calld Continually from
all quarters far and near, and I am trying to Preach What I can, I am nothing weakness both Body and Soul,—I believe the Lord is moving by his Divine Spirit in the
minds of ^the^ People, in many Places where I have been Last Summer, Fall and This
Winter—

   Dear Sir, I Wish you woud Come over this Spring or Summer, if we Shoud live,
and I will go with You and Show you large Fields, White already to Harvest;[75] I am
in earnest, I am not jesting; let us yet try to do mischief to Kingdom of Satan before
We Die; You very well know the old Devil ^is^ at Enemity against us, and he will
Show us no quarters if he can Captivate ^us^ according to his Will, his desire is to
Sift us as Wheat,[76] he woud Sift out every grace of god out of our Souls, and Leave
nothing but Chafe in us. But I hope Lord is yet Praying us that our Faith fail not And
it is right, that we should be at Enmity against his Black Kingdom, and to give no
quarters to them, it is a good fight of Faith,—You was to let me know from Time to
time, the Place and Time of our Presbyterys Meetings, but you never have done it
once to my Knowledge, and if I am Blame Worthy for not attending our Prebyteries
more than I have done, I think the most of the Blame will be found at your own
Door,—How Shall I know? When and Where our next Session is to be—^for you
did not tell me^, you think I ought to attend at least once in a while, I think so too,
^I agree with you^ but you ought to inform me where to attend, and so the Ought
falls upon you at last if you wont Inform me of this Springs Session or next fall,
Blame me no more, for my non attendence—Pray Sir, So good as to inform our Rev^d
Presbytery in the next Session of the Reason of my non attendence, but if I ~~am~~ ^shall
be^ there, Ill inform 'em myself,—I was at Boston the other Day I Suppose you
heard, found my Friends very kind and affectionate towards me,—Good old M^r
Moorh[77] was better than all the Rest of the Ministers in Boston to me, He was the
only Minister in Boston that Invited me to preach in his Meeting House, ^except ~~Mr
Stillman~~^ and preachd there four Times—Mr Stillman ^a Bapt. Min^ Invited me, but
I coud not preach there I was Coming away—Since I came Home from Boston I have
been troubled with my Sores but thro' the goodness of god, I am so well as to be able

---

75. *Fields, White already to Harvest:* see John 4:35.
76. *Sift us as Wheat:* see Luke 22:31.
77. *Mr Moorh:* John Moorhead.

to ride a little; and my Family is just got thro' with Measles, thro' pure Mercy; eleven have had it, I ^was^ down with ^it^ at once,—the grand Controversy, Which has Subsisted between the Colony of Connecticut and the Mohegan Indians ^above 70 years^ we hear is finally Decided, and it is in Favour of the Colony,[78] I believe it is a pure Favour; I am afraid the Poor Indians will never Stand a good Chance with the English, in their Land Controversies because they are very Poor they have no Money, Money is almighty now a Days, and the Indians have no Learning, no Wit nor Couning the English have all,—Pray let me know Religion goes on amongst your people, and let me know also, What you think of the Noise of Religion among the Indians at Montauk, I am greatly afraid, they are imposed upon by the great Arch Enemy of Souls in a great measure,[79]—

[Draft; CHS folder I.7. Samson Occom Papers, Connecticut Historical Society, Hartford, Connecticut.]

47 ⚭   TO REV. JOHN MOORHEAD

Mohegan
April 10: 1773

Rev^d & Hon^d Sir

Since I Came Home from Boston, I have had great afl ections in my Family, my Whole family have had the Measles & were Down with it at once, and eleven have had it and thro' the pure Mercy of God, my Family is got thru' with it, except two, they are not Strong Yet, and I have had my old Sores Broke again, right on my seat, but thro the goodness of God, I am Much better, I am able to ride again a little, and I have Continual Calls to Preach, both by the English and Indians, and I Preach 4 or 5 Times every week—I have had a great Number of Visiters Since I got home from Boston I had forty at once ^in the beginning^ and I have now 12 ^with me from Long Il.^,—there seems to be a gentle moving ^of the spirit of God^ upon the Minds of the People in these parts and there is a great egerness amongst them to hear the Word of God, and there are some instances of Conversions not far from us, & Christians Seems to be more ingaged in Religion, than they have been,—I have heard ~~from~~ that Indians on Long Is^d have had a Religious Stir amongst them this Winter, and many Hopeful Conversions, and I hope it is of the right kind of Religion that they have amongst them—I woud take this opportuny to return Most Sincere and Humble ^T^ to you Sir, for your Great Condesention and Repeated kindnesses to me and Mine, Surely the Lord has put it in your tender Heart to take pityful Notice of me; and I am Sure the Lord will not forget your Benevolence towards me, tho I am the most unworthy of all his Servants,—the Lord Reward you and yrs thousandfold in

78. Occom here refers to the Mason land case. For background on the case, see note 46.

79. David McClure briefly visited Montauk in September 1773. His diary mentions no extraordinary revival, although he does indicate that the Montaukett were sometimes visited by Samuel Buell and other Long Island clergy and that they "appear to be serious and devout, and spend considerable part of their time in religious exercises" (Rabito-Wyppensenwah, "Discovering," 424).

this Life, and Spiritual Rewards Whilest you and yours are here, and Eternal Rewards hereafter forever, and the Lord Reward your Dear people for their tender compassion to me,[80] thro your means, and the Lord Remember all my Benefactors in Boston according to their kindness to poor me, it is all thro your Means that I have ^had^ many kindness shown me in Boston,—and without all doubt many poor weak Lambs of god have been greatly Refreshd Both Soul and Body, by you and by your means, and I pray God to Continue your most extensive Useful Life to unusual Length,—I beg an Intrust in your Daily Prayers for me and mine, and all Indians— I am Rev^d & Hon^d Sir Your most unworthy and most oblig^d Hum^b Servant

S.O.

[CHS folder I.7; envelope text: "To Mr Moorhead 1773." Samson Occom Papers, Connecticut Historical Society, Hartford, Connecticut.]

48 To Eleazar Wheelock

Mohegan
June 1: 1773

Rev^d and Hon^d Sir

I have Wrote to you two or three Times and I never have had one Line from you—I have had Strong inclination to Come to See you and your College—but if I have no Line from you after this, I Shall think, I am not Worthy of your Notice in the least Shape, and I Shall not Come to Trouble you nor write you any more; indeed it was taken notice of, by Respectable Gentlemen in Norwich, that you woud not come to See me nor Send for me When you was at Norwich last, and our Considerate Indians in Mohegan took offense at it, I have as much & more Concern for my poor kindred the Indians than ever; and in my apprehentions, your present Plan is not Calculated to Benefit the poor Indians, it is no ^ways^ [illegible] to them, and unless there is an alteration Sutable to the Minds of the Indians, you will never do much more good among the Indians, your First Plan was much better than the last, and you did much good in it, and if you rightly managd the Indians, your Institution woud have flourishd by this Time[81]—Pray Sir, be not angry with me but bear with me a little, and

---

80. *your Dear people:* Church of the Presbyterian Strangers (now the historic Federal Street Church).

81. Wheelock documented and promoted his plans for Moor's Indian Charity School and Dartmouth College in a series of narratives: *A Plain and Faithful Narrative of the Original Design, Rise, Progress, and Present State of the Indian Charity-School at Lebanon, in Connecticut* (Boston: Richard and Samuel Draper, 1763); *A Continuation of the Narrative of the State of the Indian Charity-School, at Lebanon, in Connecticut, from November 27th, 1762, to Sept. 3d, 1765* (Boston: Richard and Samuel Draper, 1765); *A Continuation of the Narrative of the Indian Charity-School, in Lebanon, in Connecticut; from the year 1768, to the incorporation of it with Dartmouth-College, and Removal and Settlement of it in Hanover, in the Province of New-Hampshire, 1771* (Hartford: Ebenezer Watson, 1771); *A Continuation of the Narrative of the Indian Charity-School, Begun in Lebanon, in Connecticut; Now Incorporated with Dartmouth-College, in Hanover, in the Province of New-Hampshire* (Portsmouth, NH: Daniel and Robert Fowle, 1772); and *A Continuation of the Narrative of the Indian Charity School, Begun in Lebanon, Connecticut; Now Incorporated with*

alow me to know the Dispossions of Indians as well as any Englishman—and you know I have been the best Friend to [two words crossed out] you and your Institution, and I am a great Friend to the Cause now—thro' Mercy, I enjoy a good measure of Health at Present, and my Family is well—

I am Revd Sir

Your most bliged and Very Huml Servt,

Samson Occom

[Recipient's copy; DCA 773351. Courtesy of Dartmouth College Library.]

49 ∾   TO SUSANNAH WHEATLEY

Sepr 21: 1773

Most kind Madam

I have been Constantly upon a go Since I got home from Boston, I have mist two opportunities Since a Gentleman from Boston Calld on me one Morning, I forgot to ask his name he Stayd but 3 or 4 minutes, I Sent a Verbal message by him, to let you know we were Well and I heard this Week you was very low last Week,[82]—Tuesday after I left Boston I preachd at Natick in the fore noon to a large Aditory, for a Short-Notice, the Indians there, are almost extinct,[83]—as Soon as meeting was over I went on my Way, and I was ~~Invited~~ Desir'd to Stop to Preach in many Places by the Way and I might have Stayd by the Way Preaching to this Day, but I Complyd with none,—and a Thirdsday about noon ~~I got Home~~ I reachd Home, and thro' the goodness of god I found my Family in Good State of Health, and the Same goodness we are Well to this Hour, and it is a Time of Health in our Place,—my Visitors Continue as thick as ever, I expect a great Company of Indians this Week from Several Tribes,—I Waited on Sir William ^Jhonson^ the Week before last, at Fisher Island,[84] and he appears very Friendly ~~to me~~,—I have Some Thoughts of Taking a Tour to Visit ^the^ Indians in the Wilderness this fall, if my Health will permit the Lord Support ^you^ under your great afflictions and Bless these Troubles for your Eternal good,—and the Lord remember your great kindness to me and mine and reward you a Thousand fold in Eternal rewards—I want Much to hear from your Dear Son and Phillis,—I hope in God, we Shall meet in a better World than this, where all Sin and Sorrow Shall forever Cease—I return you once more most Hearty and Sincere thanks for all the Favours you have Shown and Confer'd upon me and mine, Please to remember me to Dear Mr Wheatley and your Dear Sister Mitchel, to your other Sisters,

---

Dartmouth-College, in Hanover, in the Province of New-Hampshire (Portsmouth, NH: Daniel and Robert Fowle, 1773).

82. Susannah Wheatley was bedridden with a long illness and died on March 3, 1774.

83. *Natick:* The "praying Indian" town of Natick, Massachusetts, was organized by John Eliot in 1651.

84. Fisher Island is located east of the mouth of the Thames River, in the Long Island Sound.

to ^Miss^ Amey, and to the Little Miss,[85] and Servants,—My Wife and ^Childr^ Join me in Greatful respects to you—I am most kind Madam,

Your most obliged and very Hum Servt
Samson Occom

[DCA 773521. Courtesy of Dartmouth College Library.]

50 ∾   To the Officers of the English Trust for
         Moor's Indian Charity School

Mohegan
Novr 10: 1773

Most Worthy & Honoble Gentlemen

I feel Very Small and unworthy, to write to Such, Venerable Gentlemen as your Selves, Yet I think myself happy, that I have Liberty to Write to Your Honors—It has pleased God to Visit us with much Sickness Within the Compass of a Year, my youngest Child is very low and weak now, but the rest of us are in good State of Health at present thro' the Goodness of God, —the Doc^rs Bills amount to Considerable in my Family this Year,—Thro Divine favour I am and have been Very Well this Summer past excepting a little pain I feel on my Seat when I ride 2 or 3 days together Where it has broke Several Times With a fever Sore within 2 Years,—Yet I have been to Visit 6 Small Tribes of Indians this Summer past, the furtherest from our Place westward is about 60 miles[86] and the furtherest Easward is 30 miles,[87] and to Montauk on Long Island about 40 miles, and I have been to Natick not far from Boston about Northeast ~~from~~ 80 miles from us,—And the Indians are very Eager to hear the Word God, where ever I have been this Year and the Word has taken good effect upon many, & as I pass and repass I have preachd good deal to the White People, and the Word has taken Saving effect upon many of them as I have been Informd—I have work enough preaching, I might preach every Day, but I am obliged to Contrive a little about raising Some thing on the Land, that I might add Some thing to your kind Donation, for I have a Large Family and Constant Visiters as ever, and to depend upon my allowance altogether, woud soon run me Down Stream a great Way off, We Scarcely Drink anything else but Clear Water, I Cant afford my Family any thing else, except a little Beer some my family makes. I shoud have gone into the Wilderness this Summer past but my Family was not well, and I have no Sutable Horse to ride, I lost a good Traviling Horse Last Spring, I have been oblig'd to hire a Horse Some Times this Summer, and I have none fit to ride great ways,—I propose, God willing, to take a Tour into the Wilderness next Spring,—but it will Cost me Considerable to fit me, I must buy me a Sutable Horse, and I must Hire a faithful man to take Care of my Family Business to raise Something on the Land,—if I go which I

85. *the Little Miss:* Phillis Wheatley.
86. Farmington, Connecticut.
87. Charlestown, Rhode Island.

fully I shall take a Young Man with me, either one of my wife's Brothers, or one Joseph Johnson, Whome God I hope raise up lately by his Divine Power, 2 of em Promise exceeding Well, they begin to expound the Scriptures in their meetings among the Indians, and they are Well receiv'd, they are likely Young men, of great Natural abilities, & I Charitably hope are endowd with the True and Saving Grace of god, my mind is Strength greatly at Times ~~the~~ to think the Lord is about to raise the Young men to do great things by them in their Day and generation,—I wish they were taken notice of and Sutably encouraged, they are Poor and Young, they are keeping Schools and are Studying the Word of Daily as they have Time, they have but very Small Wages for keeping Schools,[88] they greatly need help, both to food Raiments and Books, I mentiond these Young men in Letters to Some of my Friends in London ^Some Time ago^, and they Supplyd me with Some Books, Mr Forfitt now Deceasd Sent Jacob Fowler my Wife's Brother Cruden's Concordence,[89] and Doc^r^ Gifford Sent him Keach on Metaphors,[90] Which are most needful Books for these Young men—I Wish the other Two had Same Sorts of Books and other Good Books Expositors on the Bible are very Needful—there is a motion among the tribes of Indians round about here, to unite together and Seek for a New Settlement among the Western Indians, Their view is if they can find room, to embody together both in Civil and Religious State, their Main View is, to Introduce the Religion of Jesus Christ ^by their example^—among the benighted Indians in the Wilderness, and also Introduce Agriculture amongst them,—Some Indians are Sot out last mo^n^th, into the Wilderness to Reconnoiter the Wild Indian Countries, and to See Whether there is any Room for our Indians,—If this Can be effected it Will be the likeliest way to bring the Indians ^heart^ to Consider the Christian Religion, and to bring to Husbandry—they have very Prejudice against the English ministers and all English, but if a number of [Regural] ^Indian^ Christians went amongst them and Set good Example before them they may think and be Convincd, that there was in the Christian Religion, I am promoting the thing and encouraging the Indians all I can, and if they Shall Succeed, I Shall go with them with all my Heart[91]—I will take this opportunity ^once more^ to return my Sincere and ^H^ thanks for your Great Conde-

88. At this time, Joseph Johnson was stationed as a schoolmaster at Farmington, Connecticut. He married Tabitha Occom in December 1773.

89. Alexander Cruden, *A Complete Concordance to the Holy Scriptures of the Old and New Testament, Containing I: The Appellative or Common Words; II: The Proper Names in the Scriptures, to which is Added a Concordance to the Apocrypha,* was first published in London in 1738 and reprinted several times.

90. Benjamin Keach, *Tropologia: A Key to Open Scripture Metaphors* (London: John Richardson and John Darby for Enoch Prosser, 1682).

91. The Brotherton movement began with a March 13, 1773, meeting of members of the Mohegan, Farmington, Niantic, Mashantucket Pequot, Montaukett, and Narragansett tribes at Mohegan. Joseph Johnson subsequently emerged as a leader of the movement. On October 13, 1773, the Farmington Indians, with Johnson acting as scribe, composed a message to Mohegan, Niantic, Pequot, Stonington, Narragansett, and Montaukett communities urging them to consider moving up to Mohawk territory. Two days later, representatives of the Oneidas met with Sir William Johnson, agreeing to grant the New England tribes ten square miles of land to settle on (L. Murray, *To Do Good,* 182, 198–202).

scention and kindess to me and mine in allow me fifty Pounds pr An—^I pray God
to reward you with all Necessary in this Life and eternal^ I hope you never Will have
Ocation to with draw it, by my Conduct and I hope your Pleasure will Continue in
allowing the Same in Time to Come

    I am, Most Worthy and ^most^ Hono^l Gentlemen

        Your most unworthy and most obliged and very Humble Servt
                                   Samson Occom

[Draft; CHS folder I.7. Samson Occom Papers, Connecticut Historical Society, Hartford, Connecticut.]

51 ∾   To Eleazar Wheelock

Mohegan
Janu^r 6: 1774

Revd Sir

Thro' the Goodness of a gracious and mercyful God, we are in Good State of Health
in my Family at present, after many afflictions, I have not been so well these Several
years as I have been since the last Spring to this Time, I am able to ride good deal;
and I preach five and Six Times almost every Week, and the Lord has been pleasd
to own my poor imperfect endeavours, in Some measure both among the English and
Indians,—

    Jacob Fowler and Joseph Johnson, begin to preach, and they are Well receivd,
both by the White people and Indians, if they Shall live some Time in the World and
grow in grace, they will make great Preachers—Several from the Tribes round about
here, have Joined to seek for a new Country amongst our Western Bretherin; And
Joseph Johnson and Elijah Wympy of Farming[ton], were up at Sir William Johnsons's upon the Business, last Novr and they brought down good News; The Onoydas
Chearfully Promise to give us freely, if we Will Settle among them, Ten Miles Square
of Land, and we shall Chuse the Spot ourselves[92]

    Sir William and Mr Kirkland Say, We ^can^ get 15 or 20 Square, as easy as Ten if
we need

    Four Indians are Just set out again for Onyda to have further Conference with
the Indians; Joseph Johnson is gone for Mohegan, Jacob Fowler for Groton ^&^ Montauk; Samuel Tobias for Naroganset and E[lijah] Wympy for Farmington,—And if
the Lord will Continue my Health I purpose to go up in the Spring—I hope the Lord
is about opening a Door for the gospel among the Western Tribes of Indian[s] by
their Eastern Brethren,—The Lord Will Carry [out] his own Work in his own Time
and Way,—I am [not] Discouragd yet, if one Hook will not do, we will try another—

92. Sir William Johnson and representatives of the Oneida tribe conferred about land grants to New
    England Indians in an October 15, 1773, meeting at Johnson Hall. Records of this meeting ap-
    pear in *WJP* 12:1037–1038 and McCallum, 157–158. After the death of Sir William Johnson on
    July 11, 1774, his nephew and successor as superintendent of Indian affairs, Guy Johnson, for-
    malized the Oneida land grant in a proclamation dated October 4, 1774 (*WJP* 13:683–684).

Jo[.] Johnson intends to move up there as Soon as possible if nobody else goes, he has lately took one of my Dauthers to Wife;[93] David and Jacob Fowler will go up also, and if a goodly Number will go up I shall have Inclination to go with them to begin in good ^work^ with them and to lay my Bones there—(Sir William is Heartily engag'd in the afair, we Waited upon his Honor in the beginning of the Fall, while he was at Fisher Island, and he promisd us his assistance, all in his power, and he has already taken much with the Indians to help us)— I Want to Come to See you very much, but it will Cost me too much for you ^are^ a great way off,—Sutable Respects to your Family and Duty to your Self, I am Revd Sir

your most obliged and very Hum^b Servt

Samson Occom

[Draft; CHS-M 0225–0226. Samson Occom Papers, Connecticut Historical Society, Hartford, Connecticut.]

52 ∞   TO ELEAZAR WHEELOCK

Mohegan
March 14: 1774

Rev^d and Hon^d Sir

Your kind Epistle of Feb^r 6 last, came Safely to hand a few Days ago, for which I return you Sincere Thanks,—Our Young men are return'd again from Onoyda with very agreeable News, the Indians at Onoyda Joyfully open their Arms and hearts to receive all that Will Come to Settle amongst them, they will give them as much Land as they Shall need freely, let ^it^ be more or less, they will ^give^ 10 mile 15 20 or 30 Miles Square of Land if they need,—and they Promise to Protect them that will Come to the Sheding of their own Blood, and they have already Sent out Belts of Wampum to further Nations to aquaint them, that they ^are^ about to receive their Eastern Brethren to Settle amongst them, Desiring their Friendship also ^to^ them,— a Number of old Indians will go up this Summer to Visit the Indians and to See the Country—Sir William is Heartily engag'd in the affair and I believe Sincere, he has Sent out Threatening Words to Western nations, who will not befriend the Cause, or that will offer abuse to the New Settlers[94]—David and Jacob Fowler, and Jo Johnson are much engag'd to go Westward, I hope the Lord is about to do Great Marvils by them. I hope the Lord is fiting and preparing them to Blow the Gospel Trumpet in the Wilderness—I propose one of 'em Shall go with me this Summer, if I run in Debt to fit them for the Journey—If We Come to See you this Spring, or any Time,

---

93. Tabitha Occom and Joseph Johnson were married by Ephraim Judson at Norwich, Connecticut, on December 2, 1773 (Love, *Occom*, 203; L. Murray, *To Do Good*, 205).

94. On January 13, 1774, Joseph Johnson met with William Johnson to discuss particulars of the New England Indian migration to Brotherton. Johnson issued a statement to Seneca, Onondaga, and Oneida leaders and a wampum belt to be carried by Seneca chief Kayaghoshota to these and other Native nations asking all to cooperate with and harbor no "Jealousy" toward the Brotherton settlers (*WJP* 12:1060).

you may Depend upon it, we ^Shall^ expect some of the Charity Money to bear our expences, and it will Cost good deal, for the poor Boys have no Horses and they must hire Horses, for poor David has already Distroyed his Constitution by running about a foot in the Service, and Jacob's Constitution was kill'd by your rotten Bridge at Windham, he feels the Sad Effects of it more and more especially when he travels, and Jo Johnson Shall not go so far afoot, best for him to take care of his Health in Time,—If I Shoud preach all the Way up to you to bear my expences I Cou'd not get up in two Months, and it woud ^be^ no thanks to you, my allo^we^nce is Just about half Support to my Family & Visiters last year was very expensive Year to me, we had Several Congresses at my House about Western affairs, and we had much Sickness and very Dry Summer, and very hard Succeeding Winter, I am much behind hand,—Sutable Salutations to all and Duty to yourself I am Rev^d and Hon^d Sir

Your most unworthy Servant
Samson Occom

[Recipient's copy; Newberry Ayer MS 656; envelope text: "From ^Mr^ Sampson Occom March 14th 1774." Courtesy Edward E. Ayer Collection, The Newberry Library.]

53   To Joseph Johnson

Mohegan
April 14: 1775

Dear Child

I have only Time to inform you, that thro the goodness of god we are all in good State of Health at present, and your Family is Well, and all the Indians are in good Health, I am Sorry, so few Indians are going up to Onoyda this Spring, yet I hope they will keep moving up more and more,—Let me know by the first opportunity, how the Indians apeare now towards our Indians, and if any thing is in agitation Worthy of notice let us know it,—What ever you do keep Peace among yourselves and hear to one another for your mutual good,—Take god with you in all your Concerns, let his Word be your Rule both in your Religious and Temporal Concerns, Enrich your Minds with ^the^ Word of God—Our Olive was marryed last Night to Solomon Adams.

This in Utmost hast is from your Affectionate Father

Samson Occom

[Recipient's copy; DCA 775264; envelope text: "To Mr Joseph Johnson at Onoyda—" Courtesy of Dartmouth College Library.]

54   To the Oneida Tribe

1775

Beloved Brethren

I Rejoice to hear, that you keep to your Promise, that you ^will^ not meddle with the Family Contentions of the English but will be at peace and quietness, Peace never does any hurt, Peace is from the God of Peace and Love, and therefore be at ^Peace^ among your Selves, and with all men, and the God ^of P^ will Dwell with you; Jesus Christ is the Prince of Peace he is the Peace Maker, if all Mankind in the World, Believd in Jesus Christ with all thier Hearts, there woud ^be^ no more wars they woud ^live^ as one Family in Peace—Jesus Christ, Said to his Disciples just before he left them, Peace I leave with you my Peace I give unto you, not as the World giveth give I unto you, and again, a New Command I give unto you that ye Love one another[95]— Now Consider, my Beloved Brethren who is ^the^ Author of these Bloody Wars, Will God Set his People to kill one another? You will Certainly say no, Well, Who then makes all this Mischief? Methinks I hear you all Say the Devil the Devil,—So he is, he makes all the Contentions in he sows the Seeds of Discord among the Children of men and makes all Mischief in the World,—Yet it is Wright for Peaceable to Defend themselves when Wicked People fall upon them without Reason or Cause, then they can look up to Heaven to their God, and he will help them—

I will now give you a little insight, into the Nature of the English Quarrils, over the great Waters, they got to be rich I mean the Nobles and the great, and they are very Proud and they keep the rest of their Brethren under their Feet, they make Slaves of them, the great ones have got all the Land and the rest are poor Tenants— and the People in this Country live more upon a leavel and they live happy, and the former Kings of England Use to let the People in this Country have thier Freedom and Liberty; but the present King of England wants to make them Slaves to himself, and the People in this Country don't want to be Slaves,—and so they ^are^ Come over to kill them, and the People here are obligd to Defend themselves, they dont go over the great Lake to kill them,—And now I think you must See who is the oppressor, and who are ^the^ oppressed and Now I think, if you must Join on one way or other you cant join the oppresser, but the oppressed, and God will help the oppressed—But let me Conclude with one word of Advice, Use all your Influence, to your Brethren So far as you have any Connections to keep them in Peace and quietness, and not to entermeddle in these Quarrils among the White People,[96]— The Lord Jesus Christ Says Blessed are the Peace Makers, for they Shall Called the Children of God—This with great Love is from

your True Brother
Samson Occom

[Sender's copy; CHS folder I.9; envelope text: "Coppy to the Oneidas 1775." Samson Occom Papers, Connecticut Historical Society, Hartford, Connecticut.]

95. *a New Command I give unto you:* see John 13:34.
96. Although the Oneidas initially declared their neutrality, they and other Iroquois peoples were eventually drawn into the War of American Independence. Many Iroquois honored historic alliances forged through Sir William Johnson by fighting with the British, while others, including many Oneidas, chose the Patriot side. The conflict created deep divisions among and between the member tribes of the Iroquois Confederacy, and American troops burned and plundered Iroquois towns, fields, orchards, and food-stores. See Calloway, Graymont.

55 ∽   To John Thornton

1776

Most kind Sir

Accord ^to^ your kind Direction, and permission, I Continue to Draw Bills of Exchange upon your Honor, and Shall Continue ^so^ to ^do^ ~~Draw~~, till I hear other wise from You; I hope these unnatural Wars amongst you, will not ^intirely^ Stagnate the Streems Which have run So long, to refresh the Souls of the poor ^perishing^ Indians, with Divine Knowledge,[97]—I Continue preaching as I Use to do, Constantly, thro great Necessity, I am Oblig'd to Draw again half year before Hand,—and I hope & Pray you will Still Continue your Benevolence to me; the Indians in general every Where are Peacable and Chuse, not to medle with your own Contentions and Quarrils; but I am Extreamly ^Sorry^ to See the White People on both Sides, to use their Influence with the poor Indians to get them on thier Side, I wish they ^woud^ let the ^poor^ Indians alone, What have they to do with your Quarrels, and if they Join on either side, they ought not to be Blam'd but thro Favour, there is but few, that Join on either Side,[98]—This Contention amongst you Amazes and Astonishes the poor Heathen ^in the Wild.^ They Say, there never was the like, or Such instance amongst all the Indians Tribes, they are ready to say, What? Brethren and Christians kill one another; this Quarrel is great, yea very great Stumbling Blocks before the Heathen,—Thro mercy I am and been favourd with good Measure of Health this Winter past, and the rest in my Family are in Health, tho' we have had Some Sickness this Spring, I long to hear from you,—This with greatful Respect to yourself, and the rest of the Hono^l Trustees is from

your most unworth, and most obliged and very hum Servt
Samson Occom

[DCA 776900.2. Courtesy of Dartmouth College Library.]

56 ∽   To John Thornton

Mohegan
Jan^r 1: 1777

Most Kind Sir

Your most unexpected and most acceptable, Refreshing Animating, and most Encouraging Favour of 8 May last Came Safely to Hand a few Days ago, Surely the great Lord of Heaven and Earth, has deeply Engraven in Your Tender and Benevolent

97. Occom correctly anticipated that the conflict between England and the colonies would mean the termination of financial support from British benefactors, as his letters written after the American War of Independence show.
98. On Native Americans' participation in and experience of the American War of Independence, see Calloway. Blodgett notes that at least twenty-seven Mohegans fought on the Patriot side (162).

Heart, Pity and Compassion to poor me, and to my Necessitous Family; How distrest have I been lately, not knowing how to get out of my Involvements, and to Supply the Pinching Necessities of my large Family, besides my numerous Visiters; But Blessed be God, I find now, he has heard my growning, and Saw my Distress, and he has moved your Kind Heart once more, to stretch out your most Bountiful Hand over the great Atlantic in Time of great Distress to help me out of Troubles,—The Lord be Praised, and I return you unutterable and most Humble Thanks, The Lord Your God Reward you Bountifully—

I have Drawn a Bill of Exchange upon you for the Whole of your most kind and generous Donation, Necessity urges me, and I am very Confident it will not be disagreable to your Mind; I have also Drawn on you as a Trustee two Bills, for two half years past, according to your kind Direction and permission heretofore for I have heard nothing Contrary from you till now, and Doc^r Wheelock has never told me, that the money was Exhusted, tho' I did hear Such a thing Some how; but I Saw a gentleman about a year ago, who came directly from London, and he told me, he had Interview with some of the Hon Trust and he understood them, the Money was not Expended, but they wou'd not let Doc^r Wheelock have anymore, you may ^have^ Seen the Gent^n that inform'd me, it was The Revd Doc^r Ewing of Philadelphia he had been travelling thro great Britain Soliciting the Charities of the People for a certain College.[99]—The Times are Extreamly Distressing in this part of the World, these Unnatural Wars have effected and Distrest everyone, especially the Poor, I never have had Such a Burden, I have had much Sickness in my Famil lately, and every thing extreamly Dear, especially Cloathing, O that I had old Cloaths from London, if London was not more than half so far as it is, I woud Come over to beg old Cloaths[100]— Three pounds will not purchase So much of the Necessaries of Life now, as twenty Shillings woud before these ungodly Wars took place.—And the Worst of all is, these Wars have Eat out the Vitals of Religion, especially among the White People. Some White People Say themselves, that the poor Indians have more Religion than they have, the poor Indians indeed that make a Profession of Religion, maintain thei^r^ Religion in Some measure, I preach amongst them as often as I used to do and they are much engaged in attending upon the Word of God,—And there is one good Circumstance among the Indians in genral every where, they dont Chuse to Join neither Side in this Contention, but Chuse Strict N^e^utrality, and the White Americans dont want to have them join in either, the Congress have Sent out Commissioners among the Indians, Several Times and different ways to advise them to be Easy and Quiet, not to entermeddle in the English Family Quarril—My Wife's Brother went about 600 miles Westward from this Place last Septr with a number upon this Business and is just returnd, he tells me, he saw Six Sachems altogether of different Tribes, and that was the advice to them from the Commissioners, and the Sachems promised

---

99. *a certain College:* The Newark Academy of Delaware was founded by the Irish Presbyterian Francis Alison (1705–1779) in the late 1720s, and eventually became the University of Delaware.

100. Embargos and disruptions of trade associated with the American War of Independence caused textile shortages in the new United States of America. See Griffin, Montgomery.

Strictly to observe the advice, and Indians themselves are agreeing among themselves in there different Tribes not to entermeddle with the English Contentions,—When the White People began to Inlist Soldiers about here, Some of our Lazy Indians were very ready to Inlist, but the White People would not accept of them (Be it spoken to the praise of the White People,) but Some few woud and did list after all their rejection,—Last Summer there were Some White people wanted to hire others to go in their Room, and two Indians offerd themselves; but when the Colo¹ who had care of em, Saw them, he turn'd them back again.—But the Kings officers, Some of them, I hear, have been using their Influence to engage the poor Indians on their Side;—I wish the King of Great Britain woud command all his officers in North America to let the poor miserable Indians alone; What have we to do with your Contentions?—As for Mʳ Kirkland; I hear he was among the Indians Some part of last Summer, but Where he is now, I can not Say.—These Sad Contentions have brock up all Missionaries and School Masters among the poor Indians,—I heard there was Money Enough in the Hands of the Hon¹ Scotch Society and they did ^not^ know how to lay it out, I wish they woud Consider my Case; Pray most Compassionate Sir, Interceed with them for me—I wrote them last winter, but I have had no Answere, if I should write again perhaps my Letters will never reach them in these Times.

I beg the Continuence of your fervent Prayers for me and mine and for all the poor Indians;—This, with most grateful Respects to you and your Dear Family is from

your most unworthy & most obliged and very hum¹ Servᵗ
Samson Occom

[Recipient's copy; DCA 777101; envelope text: "To John Thornton Esqʳ at Clapham near London." Courtesy of Dartmouth College Library.]

57 ॐ TO BENJAMIN LATHROP

Mohegan
Janʳ 8: 1778

Dear Sir

Since I was at your Place, I have had many [. . .] Thoughts about the work of God among the People, and [. . .] [permission?] of God, in Sufering Some things in professors [. . .] unseemly, may Discourage some young Christians [. . .] particularly it may Discourage Seekers, and harden the opposers and the Careless,—What happended to poor Brother Robin [. . .] I heard another man who was thought Converted lately [. . .] amongst you was also in a Strange Way, Such things may [. . .]ble many—But it is no Strange thing to me, I read, when [. . .] of God presented themselves before him, Satan came a [. . .] them, God permits Satan for holy and wise ends to be a [. . .] to his People, and to be where his work is,—I believe that [. . .]ings are Sufferd, that People may be very Careful, that [. . .] Shoud be very earnest and Diligent, they ^shoud^ press thro [. . .] obstecles and not to rest in any thing short of Saving trust in Jesus Christ, and to make Religion of Nothing [. . .] the Religion of the Bible, we read, the Kingdom of [. . .] men Suffereth Violence, and the Violent take it by force [. . .] Reason for it, for we have a violent and Deceitful [. . .] to oppose, we have a Violent World to oppose, and [we have] a violent Tempting Devil to Combate with, and [. . .] it also writen; Strive to enter in at the Strait Gate, for may [will] not be able to enter in,—Let the Consideration of a Formal [. . .] Dead Religion, ingage your Hearts to firvency of Religion and great Engagedness, and the Consideration of the State of hypocrites, ingage you all, to great Searchings of Heart, and make your Calling and Election Sure;[101] and let opposers Stir up to Daily Carefulness and Circumspection in all things they ^may^ have no foundation to Say anything against you; put the Lord Jesus Christ in all your ways—Live in the New [. . .] of Jesus Christ, to Love one another; Be very tender of [. . .] our Little Lambs of God, And take the Word of God to [. . .] of your Councils, let it be the only Rule of your [. . .] and manners,—I hope what is writen Love, will not [. . .] you—I propose to Set out from Home next Saturday, God [willin]g—Please to present my Love to all enquiring Christians and take as much to yourself and Family as you [. . .] your Indian Brother in the Lord Jesus

Samson Occom

P: S: The errors and mistakes in People, in their Rel[igious] Concerns, either in Principle or Practice, or the mis[takes of?] Some Professors, does not at all alter God, he is the [. . .] Commandments to every one are the Same, Heaven [is the] Same, the Bible is the Same, the ordernances of [. . .] the Same, The Devil, Hell, and Damnation are the [Same,] the greatest Concern ought to be in every one to have [. . .] Religion of the Bible Experimentally, which Woud [. . .] to the true Knowledge and Enjoyment of God thro Jesus Christ Which makes Heaven to the Soul.—and therefore let every [. . .] Strive to know God and Jesus Christ.— and let us not be Gazing upon one another till we die—I am Stop [. . .] tend upon our Tribe affairs, and I Shant set out [. . .] [Sa]turday after next—As soon as I can, (if I shall ret [. . .] I intend to Come and See you, and Join your [. . .] Worship one Sabbath more.—

S.O.

[CHS folder I.9; document torn along left side. Samson Occom Papers, Connecticut Historical Society, Hartford, Connecticut.]

58 ~   TO BENONI OCCOM

June 24, 1780

My poor Son Benoni:

You was my only hope, Comfort, and Joy, being the only Son I depended upon to manage our Business at Home—you went on very Well in your Business, and was in a likely way to prosper in the World; our Neighbours round about here, both English and Indian, look'd upon you with pleasure and admiration, especially by our Friends, and you was invied by our Enimies—But alas, how soon is my hope

---

101. *make your Calling and Election Sure:* To receive an assurance of one's salvation through perseverance in faith; see 2 Peter 1:10.

turned into almost despear, my Comfort into Misery and Grief, and my Joy into Sorrow and Mourning, and you have griev'd the Hearts of our Good Friends and Well wishers; and you have rejoic'd the Hearts of our Enimies, and they will Say, now we have got Samson Occom's Children in our Company, and they are bad as any of us and a great deal worse, and especially, Noney,[102] he woud not Come amongst us a while ago, but now he is with us, and he does just as we do and worse;—But this is not all, in doing as you have done, you have openly Dispised God your Creator and have Sind against him with a High Hand, and you have Greatly pleasd the Devil, the grand Enimy of your poor Soul and everlasting Happiness,—I never forbid you of going to a Civil Company or to Visiting your Friends and Relations even to other Towns, but of bad company, which is Ruining and Distructive both Body and Soul, Such Company I have ever warned you of.—Carousing, Drinking, Fiddling, Dancing, Cursing, Swaring, and Blaspheming the Holy Name of God, you know I hate, and I have warnd things repeatedly, and I shall never Justify Such Practices; but I have Condemned them, and I [. . .] in the presence of God, Condemn them, as [. . .] and most accursed Practices, let who [. . .] sprong from the Devil [. . .] less they are repented of—You [. . .] over ever Since you [. . .] uction to behave yourself Well, to [. . .] keep the Sabbath, and to Read your Bible and go to meeting some where and try to hear Something for yourself, and behave your Self like a Rational Creature,— But you know, you have Disregarded all my good advices and Counsels.—And especially Since last fall, you know, you have gone Contrary [to] all your own Light, Knowledge, and Understanding, against your own Conscience, which is a living Witness of God in your own Breast, and I believe you have gone on willfully, tho your Conscience has been Condemning of you for your Evil Conduct,—And now if you have any Regard for Yourself, for your Parents, your Relations and for your fellow men in the world, and above all, if you have any Regard for God, your Maker and only Preserver—Consider these things Seriously, and See Whether my Advices have not been Calculated for your best Good.—And Consider also, Whether the way you have followed of your own Choice, which ^is^ Contrary to my Mind is not the Way to Shame, Confusion and Misery,—And if you in your Serious Consideration, you find it to be the way to Distruction,—Then run from it, with good Resolution, and do better in time Come, and Mind your Business Quietly as you have done in Times past;—And then I will yet try to Contrive for your best good, so far as I am able.—You know, I have lay'd a pretty good Foundation; for you and your little Brothers to being with, we have some necessary Buildings ready, and we have Some good Land Brought under good improvement and enclosd, and we ^have^ Sufficient Husbandry Tools, and you have great Priviledges in our Land belonging to the Tribe. But if you will go on, to follow the Wicked Multitude to Evil, and will not regard [me] and your Mother, and will leave us, especially [as I] am now ^lame^; You must go upon your own wits [. . .] Act, and you must Contri[. . .] think to have any Benefits[. . .] to me;—I leave it with [. . .]ther you have not [. . .]longs to me.— And [. . .] a Criple; Reme[. . .] condemned by all men, that may understand your

---

102. *Noney:* Short for "Benoni."

Conduct,—And never think you will prosper in the World, unless there is a great alteration in you for the better—

This ^was^ read to my Son 24 of June 1780 in the hearing of my Family—on the 10 of July he concluded to stay at Home and go to ^work^ peacably on the 13 day of June I orderd my Son out House for he woud not work Steady

[CHS-M 0299–0301; torn at bottom. Samson Occom Papers, Connecticut Historical Society, Hartford, Connecticut.]

59 ◌   TO JOHN BAILEY

[June or July] 1783

Most kind and much Esteemed Sir

Your most kind and refreshing Letter, Dated Ralyal Exchange[103] Nove^r 3^d 1782 came Safely to Hand the 31: May 1783 I am extreemly Glad and am very thankful, that I hear from You and Yours once more, and that so many of you are yet in the Living and Well, Whilest thousands and thousands & millions of have been taken out of the world and are fixt in their Eternal Duration, we and so many of our Families, are Yet in our Probation State but that must come to a Period and how soon, We are kept in perfect Ignorance, and it is altogether right because it the will of God, that we may put our intire Dependence and Trust in him at all Times, it is perfectly right, that we Shoud be Ignorant of Futurities, even ^though^ pertaining to this Life. This one great thing ^we^ may know, if we truely put our Trust and Confidence in him Who knows all Things, we shall never be ashamed; but if we don't put our Trust in him we shall be ashamed eternally,—I have been lame now three years last February, I Cant ride but very little it hurts me much When I do ride, and I Cant walk without Sticks, I put out my Hip only lifting up a Tongue of a Cart one morning, Close by my Door and it was Icy and my feed Slipt under the Tongue and the end of it Catch my right knee and twisted it inwards, and put out my Hip in the twinkling of an Eye, and I sent for a Bone Setter directly and he came in about three Hours after I hurt my Self, but he Coud not help me,—(and this Spring I had a wrench in my lameness, and I have layd with up with it again, and as I grew better I had a wrench in my back and the Cramps took in it, and Continued Some Days, so that I was helpless some Days, but thro mercy, I am now better again),—As for my Familys Circumstances were never more needy than we are now, we are Monyless, bare of Clothing, nothing to eat only What we pick up from Day to Day, by my Folks making Baskets and Brooms,[104] we have had no way to get any thing, but by trying to raise Some Thing on the Land,—and last year we raised very little of any thing, We had very Severe Drough along While and Provisions of all kinds are prodigious ^Scarce^ & Dear, but why do I talk after this manner, We have not been Starvd yet, and we

103. *Ralyal Exchange:* Royal Exchange, a grand commercial center at Threadneedle and Cornhill Streets, in London.
104. The crafting and selling of baskets and brooms was a common occupation for colonial-era Native Northeasterners. For context, see Ulrich.

have not been intirely destitute of Rayment, we have abundant reason to be thankful; thousands and thousands have Sufferd, thousand Times more than we have, Since these unnatural Wars have Commenced,—My mouth is intirely Stopt, I have no room to make any Complaints of this Sort, When I Come to Consider the unspeakable Sufferings of the Just, for the unjust, he said the Foxes had holes and the Birds of the air had Nests but he had no where to lay his Head,[105] he Sufferd hunger, thirst, Cold, heat, and Storms, and was hated reviled and Persecuted, and was driven from Place and so were all his Close followers,—And wherefore doth Sinful living man Complain; a man for the punishment of his Sins—If we have our punishments only in this World, it is but a Small punishment, to what it woud be in the World of eternal punishments, and if we have all the Happiness that this World can afford and no other, it woud be altogether a miserable Happiness like a great emty Dream, as the Rich Man found himself, when awoke in the other World—he found himself stript of all his Fancied Happiness, and had no better than the Devils Fare— It is Infinitely and unspeakably better to have the Portion of Lazarus than to have Diviess Portion[106]

This war has been the most Distructive ^to poor Indians^ of any wars that ever happend in my Day, both as to their Spiritual and Temporal Injoyments—there is not one Missionary among the Indians, and I know of but ^one^ School and this in our Place,—Mr Kirkland went with an Army against the poor Indians, & he has prejudiced the minds of Indians against all Misionaries, especially against White Misionaries, Seven Times more than anything, that ever was done by the White People, or any People whatever[107]—And Doc^r Wheelocks Indian Academia or Schools are become altogether unprofitable to the poor Indians—In short he has done little or no good to the Indians with all that Money we Collected in England, Since we got home, that Money never Educated but one Indian and once Mollatoe, that is, part Negro and part Indian and there has not been one Indian in that Institution this Some Time, all that money has done, is, it ^has^ made Doctor's Family very grand in the World. The money is all drawn out of the Hands of the Hon^l Trustees long ago—in very deed, I was so displeasd with the last Plan, of the Institution, and the management of Doc^r Wheelock; I opposd him, and broke of from him, presently after I got home, told him, he never Coud do much good to the Indians with his great Plan— Mr John Wheelock is now President of that College, and I believe he has but very little Regard for the poor Indians, he may Speak or Write With Seeming ^Concern^

105. *Foxes had holes . . . lay his Head:* see Matthew 8:20.

106. For the story of Lazarus and Dives, see Luke 16:19–25.

107. The Presbyterian missionary Samuel Kirkland was a sometimes controversial figure in the Iroquois communities where he lived and worked. He was influential in winning initial support for the Patriot cause among the Oneidas and Tuscaroras; this, in turn, led to deep divisions among the Six Nations and the extinguishing of the Central Council fire at Onondaga in 1777. During the war, Kirkland also took up residence at Fort Stanwix and provided intelligence and advice to Generals Phillip Schuyler and John Sullivan, even as the Continental Army destroyed Iroquois towns (Graymont, 55–58, 101, 112; Pilkington, 120–121; Calloway, 117–121). This siding with the "Army" may in part account for Occom's disappointment in Kirkland. See also Valone, Levinson.

for the Indians under a Cloak, to get Some Thing for himself, or for the White People, for the College is become a grand College for the White People, you know and all England knows that we went through England, beging for poor Helpless Indians; not for able White People,—In very deed I have nothing to do to help that Institution; If I had Twenty Sons I woud not send one there ^to^ be educated I would ^not^ do it that Honour—Doc^r Wheelock did me great Honour, the Last Time we debated about the afair, he said these Words, I beg of you Mr Occom not to hurt the Cause, if you do no good to it, for I know you are ~~more~~ Capable to do it more hurt or good ^to it^ than any man that I know of—and I told him I was not an Enimy to the Cause, to to his plan and Management,—I told Doc^r Wheelock in our Conversations, that it look to me, in his Sending So many Missionaries and School Masters into the Wilds Just before we went over to England, was only to make a great Noise, for when we got back we had no Missionary nor one School Master in the Wilderness under him; and said to him further if I was to be in England again, I shoud not dare look any gentleman in the face, I shoud Seem to them, as if I had been telling Lies to them, When I was there before, he Said, he fully intended to go as he began—In a word, that Institution is at an End with the poor Indians, they never Will or Can reap any Benefit from it, and I woud ~~have~~ ^not Desire^ any gentleman to promote that Institution under a notion ~~to~~ of benefiting the Indians,—if I was not Consious to myself that I went to England out of Sincere Desire to Benefit my poor Brethren even after I am Dead & Buried, but I am Sadly disappointed, I Coud Wish, that I never went to England,—And there is Such gloomy aspect upon the poor Indians, that I am under great Discouragement, So that I have no heart to ask or Call upon any People for help, for them or myself, yea I dont want to Trouble any one for myself,—But it is time for ^me^ to Close,—There is a great Talk of Peace now, and I hope it is so, but there is great Confusion among the White People Yet, between Royalests, W^h^igs, and Tories, but this is none of my Business, For Indians are neither Whigs nor Tories—Through the Boundless goodness of God we are in Comfortable State of Health at ^this^ Time—This With Sincere Gratitude is from

your Very Hum^l Servt

S. O.

Benjamin[108] is in a way to Purchase his Wife

[CHS folder I.10. Samson Occom Papers, Connecticut Historical Society, Hartford, Connecticut.]

60 ∾   RECOMMENDATION OF ELIPHALET LESTER

[1783 or 1784]

To all whom it may Concern, The Subscriber Send the Greeting—

Having had a long acquaintance with the the Bearer hereof, Mr Eliphalet Lester of [words missing] and has been ordained over a People many years in the order of the

---

108. *Benjamin:* Occom may here refer to his son Benoni, who is identified in some family papers as Benjamin Nony Occom.

Regular Baptist,[109] and is ^Universaly^ ~~Well~~ Receivd and approvd by the that order of ^that^ ~~Christians~~ People, and his Moral Character is as becometh the Gospel of Jesus Christ—and as a Preacher of the Gospel, he is aprov'd and Receivd by all Experimental Christians, and he ^truely^ is of a Catholic Spirit, and he is true and Sincere Friend to the poor Indians both in their Spiritual and Temporal Concerns, and is greatly Respected and belovd by them, Where ^ever^ he is known to them—and therefore, I do Sincerely recommend him in all those Characters to the ^Brotherly and Xn^ reception of all People Where ever he may be cast in the Providence ^of God^ amongst my People—

Samson Occom

[Draft; CHS folder I.10. Samson Occom Papers, Connecticut Historical Society, Hartford, Connecticut.]

61 ∾ TO JOHN BAILEY

[1784]

Most kind Sir

I Conclude you receivd a Letter from me Within a Year, in Which I acknowledged the ^great^ kindness you bestowed upon me, for Which I once more return you most humble Thanks,—In that Letter I gave a hint of the Situation of the poor Indians, and also the State of Dr Wheelocks Indian Schools—I Shall now give you ^More full^ account ~~of the Indians~~,—there is ^the^ Most Deplorable ~~aspect~~ and Most Glomy aspect upon the Indians in this boundless Continent ^as ever was known^, as for the Indians Scatred among the English, is it a gone Case with them, they have been decreasing ever Since the Europians began to Settle this Country, and this War has been as a besom of Distruction to Sweep them ^from^ the Face of the Earth, there are but very few remaining among the English, and ^these^ remaining yet in the Land of the living, are very Careless, it Seems according to their appearance, are given up to hardness of Heart and to reprobate Mind everything that lookd well and promising, ^amongst them^ is now witherd and Died; Schools among the Indians are all Ceased and there is not one Missionary amongst them all that I know of, This Family Contention of the English, has been & is the most undoing war to the poor Indians that ever happen among them it has Stript them of every thing, both their Temporal and Spiritual Injoyments—It Seems to me, at Times that there is nothing but Wo, Wo, Wo, Writen in every Turn of the Wheel of Gods Providence against us, I am afraid we are Devoted to Distruction and Misery—^and I am Discouragd and I have^

As for Doctor Wheelocks Institution for the Indians, to me it is all a Sham, it is now become altogether Unprofittable to the poor Indians; in Short he has done little or no good to the Indians, With all that vast Sum of Money We Collected in England

109. *Regular Baptist:* Regular Baptists represented an old-line English evangelical Calvinistic Baptist profession based in Philadelphia; a Separate Baptist movement emerged in the 1740s among dissenting Protestants of New England and was transmitted to the south by New England evangelists like Shubal Stearns. Regular and Separate Baptists began to unify associationally in the 1780s.

he never has educated but two through the College, one Indian and one Mallato, and there has not been any ^Indian^ there, this Some Time, as I have been lately informd; all the good that money has done is, has made the Doctors Family Very Grand in the World In ~~Very deed~~ Truth I was so displeased With last Plan of the Institution and the management of the Doc^r, I opposed him, and ~~told him~~ broke of from him, presently after I got home from England, and told him he never Coud do much good to the Indians With his grand Plan—We talkd part of two Days upon the afair, and he tried with all his might to Convince and to Convert me to his plan but I withstood him to the last, and when he Saw he Coud not turn me, then he did me this Honour, he Said these words—Mr Occom I beg of you not to hurt the Cause if you do no good to it, for I know you are ~~more~~ Capable to do it ^more^ good or hurt than any man that I know of; I told him I was a Cordial Friend to the Cause but an Enimy to his plan ^managt^, I told him further that it looks to me, in Sendg So many Missionarys and School Masters into the Wilderness Just before We Went to England was only Huzza,[110] to make a great Noise in the World for you have not one Missionary nor one School Master under you now in the Wilderness; the answere he made to that was, I am unfortunate, I did intend to go on as I began,—I said to him also, this one Comfort I have in my own Breast, that I Went to England with a Sincere Desire to profit my poor Brethren, even after I was dead and we had good Success in Collecting Money, and now if you dont make good Use of it among the Indians you will answere for it,—Some Time before the Doc^r died, he wrote ^me^ a Letter, in Which I found this Sentense, I hope You Will live to See Scores of your Tawney Brethren Nourish'd by ~~By~~ This Alma Mater,—in answere to it, I Wrote This Sentense—I am Very Jealous that in Stead of your Institutions becoming Alma Mater to my Brethren, She will be too Alba Mater to Suckle the Tawnies, for she is already adorn'd ^up^ too much like the Popish Virgin Mary, and therefore She Will be naturally ashamd to Suckle the Tawnies—[111]

Mr John Wheelock is now President of that College and I believe he has but very little Regard for the poor Indians he may Speak or Write with Seeming Concern for them under a Cloak, to get some thing ^for^ himself or for the White People; for the College is become Very grand College for the White People; it is too grand for the poor Indians; if I had twenty Sons, I woud not send one there to be Educated ~~there~~—In Very deed, I have nothing to do to promote that Institution,—I am afraid it is an imposition upon Mankind, and I woud by no means, have any hand, in imposing upon my fellow men,—

I have lately heard, that Mr John Wheelock is gone over to France, and from thence he intends to go to England, upon the Same Business that Dr Whitaker and I were upon, When we were in England if any People should Contribute to him, I woud not have them think, that they are profiting the Indians, for I verily believe the poor Indians will get no Benefit by it—I have been acquainted with it long

---

110. *Huzza:* staged applause, hype.
111. Eleazar Wheelock died on April 24, 1779. Wheelock wrote to Occom about American Indians and the future of Dartmouth College on February 24, 1771; Occom replied in his letter of July 24, 1771.

enough to know,—I Continue lame and in Needy Circumstances, I meet with many Trials and Difficulties, but in God, I shall get thro them all in a Short Time, I hope, and be at rest—This with Grateful Respects to you and yours is from

your Very hum^l and most obliged Servt,

Samson Occom

the Indians in general who have been acquainted with Dr Wheelocks management with his Indian Schollars in his Day, and the present managers, are not pleased with them, (they do not know how to Use the Indians) indeed am afraid they are too much for Self, after grandure to themselves.—And the Indian schools being Incorporated with the College will never do Indians dont like it. Mr Kirklands going with an Army against the Western Indians was and is the greatest blow against Christianizing the Indians, that ever was ~~know~~ Struck ~~The Wars that have been~~ The Nations who are Calld Christian in their Wars against each other, and particularly by the English Quarriling amongst them selves is a great Stumbling to the Heathen Indians—and it is the Darkest Time with the poor Indians, that ever was known—And ^yet^ amidst all these Discouragements with respect to my poor Brethren, I have one hope remaining, that is, God always works like himself, he works when where and how he pleases, he often begins when everything fails, and all hope is gone, and he often Chuses unlike means and Instruments, so I hope against hope at this Time, that there will be a Gospel Day with my poor Brethren, after a long Time of Egyptian Darkness[112]—I Continue lame and under many Domestick Troubles and Difficulties and I Can't ride to go abroad, I am very much confind at home,—When my mind is Clear, I write upon Divine Subjects, I have two or three Pieces.[113]

[CHS folder I.10. Samson Occom Papers, Connecticut Historical Society, Hartford, Connecticut.]

62   To Benjamin Garrett

Mohegan
August 21: 1784

Dear Sir,

I have an opportunity to Send directly to Onoyda by my Cousin Isaac Uppuiguiyantup of Nahantick, he is going next week, old Brother Phillip Cuish was here, and took my Letters this morning, and I have mentioned you and your Design fully, and recommended you to the Indians so that there is no need of my Writing of your

---

112. *Egyptian Darkness:* Occom may have adapted this phrase from a line in Phillis Wheatley's poem "To the University of Cambridge, in New England," which appeared in her *Poems on Various Subjects Religious and Moral* (1773): "'Twas not long since I left my native shore / The land of errors, and *Egyptian* gloom" (emphasis added). It is likely that Occom, as a friend of both Phillis and Susannah Wheatley, owned a copy of the *Poems.*

113. A surviving example of Occom's writings on "Divine Subjects," entitled "The most remarkable and Strange State Situation and Appearance of Indian Tribes in this Great Continent," appears in this collection.

designed Journey.[114] I Send with this, the recommendation for you, and I think you ought to get 2 or 3 of your Brethren in the ministery to give you a Recommendation also. Nothing remain'd to Send you but my Love and you may take as much as you like, and if you don't like it you may let alone—this is from

> *your, What you please*
> *Samson Occom*

To all Christian People to Whom it may Concern The Subscriber Sendeth Greeting—

I have had a long & intimate acquaintance with Benjamin Garret, the Bearer hereof, he is a poor man, and I hope one of God's poor, and he is a temperate man, he frequently Speaks in public in Religious meetings, where the Door is open for him. And he is now on his Way to Onoyda to See his Children, and is much destitute of Journey Subsistence, and as Such I recommend him to the notice of all Christian People, Where ever in the Providence he may last,

> *Samson Occom*

[Harold Blodgett, *Samson Occom* (Hanover, NH: Dartmouth College, 1935), 175–176. © 1935 University Press of New England, Hanover, NH.]

63 ⌇   TO SOLOMON WELLES

Mohegan
September 26: 1784

Much Esteemed Sir,

I am under great obligations to you for your repeated Visits to me, my Wife tells me, You was at my House just before I got Home from Albany, and I acknowledge my Faults. I hope, I have not Committed unpardonable Sin, that I have not Wrote to you before now, which I fully intended to do, but I believe it is not too late now, is it?— I had very agreeable Voige to the Westward, the Indians I Went With Were treated With all kindness and Friendship and they had holp in many Places, especially at Albany, I never did see the Dutch People so pleased With any Indians they ever saw;[115] the Indians that were there, were all good Singers, in Psalms, Hymns and Anthems, and the People Would have them Sing every Evening, and Wanted to have meetings almost every Day, and I preached there five Times and once in the New City[116] nine Miles above Albany, and twice in New York Coming back. Certainly ther has been a Gradual Work of god in Albany in these Wais; there is great Alteration in the City, for I have been there Several Times heretofore, and they were Heathenish

---

114. Benjamin Garrett traveled to Oneida to see his son-in-law David Fowler and his daughter Hannah Garrett Fowler.
115. On historical relations between Native Americans and the Dutch settlers of New York, see Burke, Robertson.
116. Troy, New York.

Sort of People, but many of them now appear like Christians.[117] The People in Albany Collected about twenty pounds in Cash for the Indians I accompanied. There were a Number of Indians Went thro Albany a few Days before we arrived there, gone to Onyda also. And Stockbridge Indians are going up this Fall,[118] the whole lot of them, many have been up there the Summer past and Planted much Corne. And since I got Home I have had Indians from Montauk on Long Island, Nahantic, and Naroganset to see me, and they say out of each of these Places many are getting ready to move up into that Country as fast as they can. Provisions Were Very Scarce in that Country, and I deliver'd all the mony into their Hands, I put only half a Dollar into my Pocket when I left Albany, and run into Debt besides by giving my obligation to pay their Passage from New London to Albany, to the amount of 36 Spanish Mill'd Dollars, and I have not paid more than one third of it, I depended upon the Charity of God's People; I wonder whether the People of your Town[119] woud not do Some thing if Sutable application was made to them; Charity or giving of Alms is Commended and recommended thro the Bible, and it is one of the greatest Marks or Signs of true Christianity,—I have a Copy of a Letter Sent me by my good Friend Esqr Thornton of London; it was Wrote by a Certain Clergyman of the Church of England, to a Minister in Holland, I will enclose you a Copy of it, he was one of the Worst of men, till he was about 30 years of age, he even tried to believe that there was no God and Ridiculed and made jest of the Bible, and he followed the Seas, Chiefly Slave Trade; and finally in a dreadful Storm Wherein they all Expected to Sink to the Bottom, There he was made to believe that there was and is indeed and in truth a Living God; and now he is one of the best of men in the World, a minister of Jesus Christ, I have been in his Company even in his own House, he liv'd then some distance from London, and since that he has moved to London.[120]—I have got his Life, Which he Wrote himself, and I Wish it was Reprented in this Country, I never saw only mine, Sent me Since I got Home from England, it is most remarkable Life I ever read.[121] I believe it is Very Scarce in this Country; What if you should

117. Occom here describes the transformation of Dutch and other European settlers from "heathens" to "Christians."

118. In 1734–1735, the Massachusetts Commissioners of Indian Affairs organized a mission to the Mahican (also known as Housatonic) Indians at Stockbridge, Massachusetts, recruiting John Sergeant (1710–1749) and Timothy Woodbridge to serve as missionaries and schoolmasters. Stockbridge was established on the model of a New England "Praying Indian" town: Christian Mahicans moved to Stockbridge, where in exchange for ceding the rights to settle on their traditional territory along the Housatonic and Hudson Rivers, they received small farm lots with the promise of protection by the colony from white usurpation. After its initial organization, Stockbridge also welcomed refugees from Shawnee and outlying Mahican groups. From 1783 to 1788, many Stockbridgers emigrated to Oneida lands on the Oriskany River, where they founded New Stockbridge. Those who did not emigrate to New York remained in the Berkshires of Western Massachusetts. See Frazier, Wheeler.

119. Wethersfield, Connecticut.

120. Occom here describes the life of John Newton.

121. *An Authentic Narrative of Some Remarkable and Interesting Particulars in the Life of John Newton* was first published in London in 1764 and reprinted in more than a dozen editions before 1800. The first American edition was published in Philadelphia in 1783.

mention it to Some of your good Friends? and see what they would say about Print-ing it; if it was encourag'd I Would Write few Lines to introduce it to the People, and Would have the letter Printed with it—You Will be so good as to let me hear from you as soon as you can; I think it is high Time for the People of god to Stir up one another and Provoke one another to Love and to good Works, for People in general have been Slumbering and Sleeping together a long while, and it is high Time to awake for the Night is far Spent and the Day at Hand; and in the Time of Darkness the Enemy has been Very busy to Sow the Seeds of Discord and all manner of Strange and Damnable Doctrines, and it is time to See which is the right way. But I must Conclude with Sincerest Regards to you and yours,—from

Your Very Hum^l Servt

Samson Occom

[Harold Blodgett, *Samson Occom* (Hanover, NH: Dartmouth College, 1935), 178. © 1935 University Press of New England, Hanover, NH.]

64 ⚬ TO THE TRUSTEES OF EASTHAMPTON, LONG ISLAND

[1784?]

To the Hon^l Trustees of Easth[ampton]

I am Glad to hear, that the People of Easthampton are Willing to buy of Indians their Rights of Montauk,—I hope you will do Well by them, give them Something very handsome,—I believe it woud be Well ^to^ help Individuals as fast as they Will ^be^ inclin'd to go—but it woud be best, if a Number woud join together and go at once—I woud bespeak for my Mother Fowler, She is [an] old Woman, and She is going with us and I believe it will be doing good [to] help her, She will want Some thing to pay her passage to Oneida, and She Will need Provisions by the Way, and When she gets up, and Cloathing She will want also, if she had no Right in Montauk [it] woud be well to help her,—but I mean [to] give her Something very handsome [. . .] Right.—Ephraim Pharaoh and his Family and Sam Scipio and his Family, I Suppo[se] are going With us also in the Same Vesel and let them have good encour-agement by the Town—[122]

[Draft; CHS-M 0369. Samson Occom Papers, Connecticut Historical Society, Hartford, Connecticut.]

122. Historians record no formal land agreement between the Montaukett tribe, colonial overseers, and the town of Easthampton in 1784, but this letter suggests that land-eager Easthampton res-idents did offer to purchase land rights from some of the approximately thirty Montaukett who elected to migrate to Brotherton and that Occom encouraged these arrangements.

65 ∾   To Samuel Buell

[February 1786?]

Revd Sir

The fourth Day of this Month, I got home once more, from the Wilderness, was gone about eight months,—My Wife tells me, she receivd a Letter for me Some Time last fall, ordering me to be at Easthampton at a Certain Time. I Sent you a Letter last Year, soon after I got home, desiring to know, when, and where our Presbytery was to meet next, to which I've had no answere Which I Conclud you receivd in Time, for I had direct ^oppert^[123] to Send it,—and now I want to know when you meet again,—I have Strongly engaged, to go back again to Onoyda as soon as I can in the Spring; for ~~the~~ there is the most Glorious Work of God, amongst the Indians that ever was seen any where, ~~except in the Jerseys some years back~~,—It is not noisy, but very deep; Solemn and Silent, with flow of Tears; there has been Some in three or four meetings,—And there is a remarkable moving among the Dutch as ever was seen along the Mohawk River in Several Places, and the most remarkable conversions in some instances as ever was heard of, —They are so eager to hear the Word of God, was some Days obligd to preach twice a Day and whether you apoint a meeting or not, they will get together to find you, you need not look to fine them,—there are three Places in particular about Albany about 10 miles; earnestly desird and intreated to have me stay with them all Winter, from the middle meeting House, to one is 6 miles, and to the other 4. I wish you was there once, it woud make you feel 30 years younger, in Preaching the Gospel Jesus,[124]—It is a wonder, and amazing to me, that after my Dispondencies, Discouragements, and almost Desparation, should find, at Times, Some Peace Comfort and Resignation to god's Disposal,—I have made and given Satisfactory Confession of my past miss Conduct, and am Universally receivd by the Indians; so far as I am known, and generally receivd by the White People round a bout here where I am intirely known, and preach among them Continually, there are a few that have not the Spirit [page torn], Such as Mr Cook I Conclude of N. Lond north

I Conclude he said Something to you, to my Prejudice [page torn] over on the Island[125] some Time ago, he is trying to Prejudice the minds of Some People here, but get no Credit by it by what I Can learn, I am afraid he is a false Brother, he was the nearest minister to me, in the depth of my Troubles and Sorrows, and he never was that man to Come to See me to know my Troubles but as soon as I began to Strugle to get up, he was forward to keep me down if he Coud; but belive the good Lord has put forth his Arm of mercy and raise me up,—I have thought hard of it, that none of the Ministers Came to See me, but one, that was Mr Benedick of Plainfield

---

123. *oppert:* opportunity.

124. Occom's account of revival marks a significant moment of cultural and religious transition for Hudson River Valley Dutch communities: in the 1770s and 1780s, attendance at old-line, Dutch-language Dutch reformed churches declined, and English-language evangelical movements attracted new adherents. On Dutch-American religious history, see Balmer, Fabend.

125. *the Island:* Long Island.

he came I think like a brother, and 3 or 4 Separat Ministers came to Visit me, like Brothers and they endevoured to encourage and Comfort me,—I believe English Missionaries will not be so Cordially receivd by the Indians in the Wilderness as they have been, Mr Kirkland is but Colely recevd, his going with the Army against the Indians will not be easily forgot, the last war has prodigiously augmented the prejudices of the Indians, everywhere

[Draft; CHS folder I.10. Samson Occom Papers, Connecticut Historical Society, Hartford, Connecticut.]

66 ﹈   "IS THERE NO REDRESS FOR THE INDIANS?"

[1788?]

Hon^d. Sir

Brother John Dantuckquechen who brings these few lines, has had a Law Suit against him [two words illegible] upon Suspission of Debt, and he [knew nothing] about it, till it was over, it was John [word illegible] doings, he imployd one [Shoals] to Cary on the Suit, now is agreable to the Laws of this State or any State? that a [man] may be Suid, and the Case tryd & Desided, and the man that Suid knows nothing from first to last, till the Execution Comes out against him, if this will do and Countanced, by by Law, then any man draw upon account against his Neighbour Without any Dealings with him,—and Sue him, get Judgment against him,—Do you Serve one another So? if not, Why Should we be Serv'd So—is there no redress [two words illegible] for the Indians, by the Rulers, if there is none, I do declare it, I had rather be amongst the most Wild and uncultivated Indians, in the Western Wilderness,— I was so Servd last Spring just as we were Set^ing^ of for Onieda and I Coud not Stop to See further about it, I thought Sin woud be at their door, but I need Say more— Is there such a thing as delivering John from the Paw of Such unreasonable and Cruel Men?—I am Yet

your very hum^l Servt
Samson Occom

[Recipient's copy; Rauner 003111. Courtesy of Dartmouth College Library.]

67 ﹈   TO THE FRIENDS IN PHILADELPHIA

Philadelphia
Febru^r 22: 1788

All Glory, thanksgiving, and Praise be unto God, for his goodness and mercy to us, that he has inclind and opend the Hearts, and Hands of his good People in this great City, to take Freindly Notice of us, to receive us into their Houses, and to treat us with all tenderness and kindness—We feel ourselves under great and lasting Oblig-ation to the People of this place—[126]

126. Occom, David Fowler, and Peter Pauquunnuppeet visited Philadelphia from January 21, 1788, to February 22, 1788; see Occom's journal for these dates for an account of the visit.

We take this opportunity; to return our most Sincere and Humble Thanks to the Congregations that have Collected for our help—We return thanks to the Freinds,[127] we give thanks to every one that have Shown any Favour to us—we give thanks to the Little Masters who have Collected for our Little Boys in the Wilderness, we give thanks to the Young Ladies, that have Collected for our little Daughters in the woods—The Lord God of Heaven and Earth your God and our God reward and Bless you all, with all the Blessing of Heaven and Earth—and we hope and Pray—that you may never have reason to repent of your kindness to us

We Shall ever remember Philadelphia with thankfulness

We ^do^ now ask good leave to return to our Families

> *Farewell—This is from*
> *your poor Indian Friend*
> *and Brothers*

[DCA 788172. Courtesy of Dartmouth College Library.]

68   To JOHN RODGERS

May 12: 1788

Rev[d] and much Esteemed Sir:

I have been unwell more than three weeks, but thro the goodness of god, I am better, and intend to Set out for Onoyda as ^Soon as^ as I am able to travil,—I was too late for our Presbutery,—and I intended to be at our Rev[d] Synod but I have just heard by an ^Indian^ just come ^from^ Onoyda that there is to be a Councel or Treatie of Indians and English, in the begining of June,[128]—and if it be possible, I woud be there, then I may have an opportunity of Seing some of Several Tribes, and have Conversation with them, concerning Religion (Here with I send a Letter to Doc[r] Duffield in Philadelphia) I beg the favour, that you woud send it by the first opportunity) This with greatest Esteem, and gratitude is from

> *Your most obliged & Very hum[l] Serv[t]*
> *Samson Occom*

[UG Read Collection, 2.19.1; envelope text: "To Doc[r] Rodgers." Courtesy of Hargrett Rare Book and Manuscript Library / University of Georgia Libraries.]

127. *the Freinds:* the Society of Friends, or Quakers.
128. The Oneidas lost millions of acres of their territory in a series of "treaties" and land agreements devised by the state of New York from 1785 to 1846. Meetings between the Oneidas and state officials including Governor George Clinton at Fort Schuyler in 1788 led to the loss of 5 million acres under the terms of a deceptively crafted "instrument of cession," which the Oneidas signed with an understanding that the state would protect their land against speculators, but which the state enforced as an outright relinquishment of Native lands (Hauptman and McLester, 10–11, 19–37; Campisi and Hauptman, 51–54).

69 ∽   TO JEDEDIAH CHAPMAN

[June 1790]

Rev^d and Much Esteemed Sir

The Young Man, the Bearer hereof is, the man I Spoke of When I was ^at^ your House last March, he is of the Tribe of Stockbridge Indians, he has a very good Character amongst all the People where he is known;[129] he was hopefully brought to Spiritual Light and Life, going on five Years and from that Time to this, he has maintained a Steady Walk in the Religion of the Bible—He has a good Understanding naturally, but he never had but little Instruction in reading and he can read English Books well, in his way, he Can't pronounce many English proper; but I believe, you can mend him in that; he understands English, better than he Can Speak it; He is a good Speaker in Indian;—He was Born, and grew up altogether amongst the Indians, like a Wild Tree in the ~~For~~ Wilderness; but we hope, he is Cut down and we now Send him to you, to hew, and to Plain, and you may Polish him, if you think worth a While;—He was very much elivated, when I told; that there was an opening for the Instruction of our Promising Young men, and Boys; I asked him, Whether he was about marrying, he said, if he Coud be accepted, at the Academy under your Care,[130] he must not think about marying—He has a great Desire to Understand the Book of God,—We have also Sent, a Boy, with the Young man, his Father has a great Desire, that he may be Instructed in Literature and he has a great Notion of going with the Young Man he is a Modest Boy, and he has had but very little Schooling, he understands but few words of English,—But we need not Say much more about them,— But bring them, and lay them at your Door of Compassion,— they are ^truly^ like the man that fell amongst Thieves, that was Stript and Wounded, and left half Dead in the High Way,—and if the Priests & Levites, may pass by on either Side without Compassion—We hope, there may by Chance, Some Samaritans pass that Way, that may Discover them, and have Compassion on them[131]—but you will know, What to Say, and What to do about them—amongst your large Acquaintance—the Stockbridge Indians in particular were very glad, and thankful that there was such Benevolent opening, for the Instruction of Indian Youth, they ~~that~~ hope, that this may be a Door of great and a lasting good ^to^ the poor Indians, both in their Temporal and Spiritual Concerns,—I have been at Times, in very great Discouragement and Gloominess of mind, When I Consider the ^miserable^ Situation of my Brethren, there has been for a long Time, a very heavy and thick Darkness been over our Heads, yea it seems, that every thing thing has been Combining together for our destruction,—But those Clouds, may yet, be disperst, and that we may be Visited with great Light from on high and yet become a People unto God—When Doc^r Wheelocks Institution for Indians was going on, I thought we were about to be rais'd from

---

129. Occom refers to John Quinney.
130. A letter from John Quinney archived among the Samson Occom Papers at the Connecticut Historical Society tells us that Chapman ran the Orange Dale Academy in New Jersey.
131. Occom refers to the biblical parable of the good Samaritan; see Luke 10:30–37.

our Misery, but that has intirely Faild,—But who knows, ~~but~~ that this opening may be the beginning of our extraction from our Gloomy State—I believe we are Included in the Promises of the Bible, that all Nations Shall be Blesed,—This with the

[Draft; CHS folder I.13. Samson Occom Papers, Connecticut Historical Society, Hartford, Connecticut.]

70 ∾   TO BENONI OCCOM

Brotherton
Dec 1: 1790

My Son Benoni

We were in great hopes of Seeing you and Dency here ^last^ summer but we were greatly disappointed, and Since Anthony[132] has got home to Saritoga Lake, he Sent the oxen to me with a Letter, and Said he expected you and Dency there every Day.—But I have hear Young David Fowler say, You Was Yet at Mohegan when he Came a long. So we Conclude you do not intend to Come, and we think you have no regard for your Mother and I, you might ^be^ as well here or better than where You are.—Provisions of all kinds are very plenty and Cheap,—and if you will not come, do Send us Word that We may know what to depend upon.— Remember Wherever you are, you are in the presence of that God, that made you, and to him you must give an account of your Conduct and remember the Day of your Death is hastening.—We hear, by David, that there was a News that our Lemuel was Drowned,—and if you hear Certain News Send us a Letter as Soon as Possible, that we may know,[133]—and if Andrew, is gone off to sea, let us know where he ^is^ gone, and with Whom, and how long they expected to be gone,[134]—We are well at present, and we hope these Lines may find you both well—This with our Tender Love is from

Your affectionate Parents
Samson & Mary Occom

[CHS folder I.11. Samson Occom Papers, Connecticut Historical Society, Hartford, Connecticut.]

71 ∾   TO BENONI OCCOM

January 17, 1791

My Son Benoni,

I am now at Poughkesy,[135] going on to New York to attend on the Assembly, about our Land and, it is not likely, that I shall get Home, till, the latter end of Next

132. *Anthony:* Anthony Paul, Samson and Mary Fowler Occom's son-in-law.
133. *Lemuel:* Lemuel Fowler Occom, Samson and Mary Fowler Occom's son.
134. *Andrew:* Andrew Gifford Occom, Samson and Mary Fowler Occom's son.
135. *Poughkesy:* Poughkeepsie, New York

Month,[136]—and I want, if you intend to . . . up at all to Onieda to Set out, So as you may . . . there Time to Plant, etc. I Came down, I was . . . Anthony's[137] and the Children had Hooping Cough,—otherwise they were well,—And they expected . . . there, whence they live, last Fall, and they [wonder] you dont Come,—Anthony Says, you talk very Strong that you wou'd Come,—and if you dont intend to Come, Send us a Word, that we may know,—I dont expect to live but few Days longer, but you may Die before me, and therefore think of Death and remember Death comes the Judgement, and so beg of God to prepare you—This With Love to you both is from

Your Tender Father
Samson Occom

[Harold Blodgett, *Samson Occom* (Hanover, NH: Dartmouth College, 1935), 208. © 1935 University Press of New England, Hanover, NH.]

72 ∾   "SORROW FILLS OUR HEARTS"

[1791]

Brothers

We must own, that we, a number of us are ^very much^ ashamed We are grieved, and Sorrow fills our Hearts, and Some Times We are mad to see the Black Ingratitude of a N^r[138] our Indians, in abusing the Kindness and and Donations given us by our Kind ^and good^ Brothers—and we are ^very^ much displeasd ~~with~~ to ^see^ Some of our People ^dare^ to rise up against the good Laws prescribd for us by the great Assembly—But we hope, our good Brothers, will over look the mad doings of our Crazy People, and not to let the Inocent Suffer for the ^Wicked^ Doings of the Stupid Creatures—

A Mill Spot was reservd for the Benefit of the Whole Town—and that is least out—and ^~~Lands where~~ ^ ~~Pine groves also~~ and Lands where Pine Grew, intended for the Benefit of the Whole, and the Best spots of Land, are least out[139]

[Draft; CHS folder I.13. Samson Occom Papers, Connecticut Historical Society, Hartford, Connecticut.]

136. Between 1789 and 1791, a Brotherton faction led by Elijah Wampy leased to white settlers thousands of acres of lands once granted by the Oneidas, thus striking at the heart of the Brotherton endeavor. In January 1791, Occom carried a petition to the state assembly requesting that the state revoke the authority of tribal members to lease lands to white settlers; see "Brotherton Tribe to the New York State Assembly" (1791) in the petitions section of this collection. The assembly responded by passing "An Act for the Relief of the Indians Residing in Brothertown and New Stockbridge" on February 21, 1791, which vested powers to apportion and lease lots in an elected tribal council (Love, *Occom,* 287–289).

137. *Anthony's:* Anthony Paul, Samson and Mary Fowler Occom's son-in-law.

138. *N^r:* Number.

139. On the leasing controversy, see note 136.

73 ⌒   "INDIANS MUST HAVE TEACHERS OF THEIR OWN
COULAR OR NATION"

[November 1791]

Revd Sir^140

I take the Liberty to write to you a few Words by Capt Hindreck, he is one of Mauhe-qunnuck,^141 alias Stockbridge Tribe of Indians, he is a Chief Sachem of that Tri[be] and his ^a number^ Tribe is well inclin'd to the Christian Religion, and ~~are~~ they are Diligent in their Temporal Concerns; and they have determined to go on till they Shall be able to main[tain them] Selves in their Religion, and in their Temporal Concerns if they keep on as they have begun but a little While, they will be able—But they are not able to walk yet, they St[ill] Creep^142 they want a ~~little Help~~ ^to lead by the Hand a little w^, and they Can't Swim alon[e] yet, they need to have a little help, to have their Chins held up a little While, till they can Swim alone—God has blest you abundantly with the Blessing of the gospel, and with Blessings of this World, You are very strong in the Christian Religion, ^and in this world^ ~~you are~~ rich in the Gospel, ~~and we~~ are very poor, and weak, ~~and you are Rich also in this World, and we are extreamly poor,~~ Capt Hendrick has been amongst the [Wes]tern Indians, and lately just go Home, as he may Inform you, There seems to be agreable Prospect opening amongst the Wes[tern] Tribes to Introduce Civilization & Christianity. I hope the P[rayers] of Gods People, that have been put up or ascending, [. . . page torn] for the Heathen, along While, by all Christians, of all [Nations?] and Denominations will Soon be heard and Answer'd [. . .] God's Time is the Best Time—There have been some Pains to Civilize and Christianize the Indians, but all to little purpose—But I think the Time must come, when they shall beg to Jesus Christ for his Inheritance and the utermost parts of the Earth his Posistion—Capt Hendrick is Invited by Some of the Western Tribes to the Distance of 1000 Miles or near—Some of his Na[?] are there already they have there about, about 30 Years^143—I am Now fully Convinc'd, that the Indians must have Teach[ers] of their own Coular or Nation,—They have very great and reveted Prejudice against the White People, and they have too much good reason for it—they have been imposed upon, too much, and they have been, between Contending Nations [a long] Time;—In Times past they were between, the French and English,—Now, they are between the Britains and Americans and Spaniards too, and ^now^ they ^are^ set on by the Britains and Spaniards against the Americans, and when there is any Mischief [page torn . . .] any

---

140. The recipient of this letter may be Philadelphia Presbyterian minister James Sprout.

141. *Mauhequnnuck:* Mahican.

142. *Creep:* crawl.

143. Hendrick Aupaumut served as a peace emissary to a Six Nations council in 1791. In 1792 to 1793, he undertook a diplomatic mission to tribes in the Ohio Valley, which is recorded in "A Narrative of an Embassy to the Western Indians," published in *Memoirs of the Pennsylvania Historical Society* 2 (1827): 61–131. His negotiations with the Miamis, Potawatomis, Menominees, and Munsees eventually led to the emigration of New Stockbridgers to Indiana and then Wisconsin in the 1810s and 1820s (Peyer, *Tutor'd*, 111–116; Ronda and Ronda).

of them; then there is an out Cry against them [. . .] Vulgar Language is; Kill kill ~~them~~ ^em^, Damn em kill [. . .] they have been unreasonably blaimd ^you will know^ [. . .] While [. . .] Canon of the [. . .] The poor Indians were in a Miserable Situation ^before the Europians Come^; and Since the Europians have Come into this Country, they are more so, except a few that have had a little Gospel Light,—I think they are now in a Most Deplorable Condition and Situation, it Seems that Heaven and Earth, are in Combination against us, I am, Some Times, upon the Borders of Desperation and much Discouragd with my poor Brethren, I often groan, and Say with myself, before I am aware of it, O Strange, O Strange, Why are we thus—and my mind very ^is much^ overwhelmed at Times,—But When I Consider the Promises of God in his Book my Mind is little revivd again—and another Thing revives my Soul at this time, that there is an opening for the Instruction of our Promising Youth,—I was at Mr Chapmans in the N Jersey, he has the oversight and Care of Academy in Newark Mountains; and was Conversing with about our Indians, and told him we wanted to find a Place, Where we may send our Sons he readily Said, Send them to him, and he woud Instruct them in Literature, Yea Said he, if you Can Send twenty I will take them,—and so we have sent two to him last June; and I hear they do Well—but he has the Whole Burden of them Yet, as I was informd, not long Since—So I permit me to Call upon you as the Bishop of the Church of Jesus Christ In North America—Come over, or Send over to our miserable Indian Macedonia and help us,[144] for we are Dying with ^the^ Poison of Fiery Serpants, in this Wilderness, and we would have the Glorious Brazen [Serpent] to be lifted up upon the Pole of the Glorious Gospel, that [who]ever looks to him by an Ey of Faith may be saved[145]—we are [try]ing to keep a School to instruct our poor Children in Letters, and the Children learn beyond all expectation—We are poorly of it for School books, and we are Scant of it for Psalm Books for the older People—They are good Singers as any People; it woud do you good to hear them once, and they are most all Singers old and Young,—and they Want ~~in~~ Clothing, it is hard to get Clothing in this Wilderness,—and Want Husbandry Tools—Capt Hindrick will give you, their Situation and Condition—Excuse my Prolexity;[146] I intended to Say But few words; ~~This With~~, The Reason I have wrote so freely to you is because I found you, the last Time I was at Philadelphia ^and [word illegible]^ Sincere Friend to the poor Indians—This with Grateful and much Esteem is from

> *Your most unworthy Indian Brother in the Gospel of Jesus*
> *Samson Occom*

---

144. In Acts 16:9–10, Paul dreams that a Macedonian man asks him to "Come over to Macedonia, and help us" by preaching the gospel. The scripture served as a pretext for colonial American missionary activity; in fact, the seal of the Massachusetts Bay Colony featured the image of an Indian circumscribed by the words "Come over and help us."

145. In Numbers 21:6–9, when the people of Israel are afflicted by biting "fiery serpents" during their sojourn in the wilderness, Moses fashions a brass serpent on a pole, promising that whoever would look at the serpent would be healed. The brass or brazen serpent is sometimes understood as a type of Jesus Christ.

146. *Prolixity:* Verbosity; copiousness of detail.

P.S. I Rejoice to see the Albany Newspaper of ~~October 24~~, Novr 3: 1791 that at the opening of Congress the President Deliverd a Speech[147] [. . .] I find, that Overture of [. . .] Still Continued to the [. . .] are in very Deed ^Deluded^ by the Enemies of the United [. . .] Indians [. . .]

[CHS folder I.12; page torn along right edge. Samson Occom Papers, Connecticut Historical Society, Hartford, Connecticut.]

74   ## TO THE NEW STOCKBRIDGE COMMUNITY

[December 1791]

My Dear Brethren

We See that many Strange ^things^ will happen in the World Some Times Contrary to our minds, Yet agreeable at other Times much Disappointed in our acspectations,— when I thought of moving my Family that Way, I Heard Little at Brotherton, and did Stop there, and thought I Shoud move no further; But there People, there took but little notice of me, Yea a party tried to hurt me,[148] all they [Have?] there is a few, that have a good regard for me, But your Calls and Invitations grew Stronger and Stronger and your Religious engagements also grew,—and my Heart was also Drawn towards you more and more—and I found Nearness to you, and you were very near to me more and more and I Cant otherwise, but that Lord of Heaven, has brought us together,—And now, I have moved my Family amongst you, yea you have movd us amongst yourselves; and I am Thankful, you have receivd us with open Arms and Hearts,—And I take this opportunity to returnd you all; most Sincere and Hearty Thanks, for your Repeated, and Continual Kindnesses and Helps,—I hope & Shall be my Daily Request, at the Throne of grace, that the most Bountiful and Gracious God, would reward you and Bless you all, with all the Necessary Blessings of this Life, and with ^the^ Blessings of the Gospel of Jesus Christ I hope we Shall be profitable to one another as long as we Shall Live, and hope and pray, We may grow in Gospel Love and Peace—in Unity, Harmony and Gospel Fellowship—Let us, then go on in Serving the Lord our God and let us help one another in all our Concerns, May we be found to build up one another both in our Temporal and in our Religious Life, and let us try to do all the good that we are Capable of unto all men, and if it be possible let us Live in Peace with all men[149]

147. In his October 25, 1791, speech to Congress, President George Washington described diplomatic and military dealings with tribes and set forth principles for the development of federal Indian policy (Washington, 19–20).

148. Fierce factional conflicts at Brotherton developed around issues of town governance and land management. Occom's diary records that on at least one occasion, in July 1788, local tensions erupted into violence among Brotherton residents in an altercation involving Elijah Wympy, Jeremiah Tuhy, and David Fowler, Jr. It is unclear whether Occom himself was a target of physical violence, or whether his comment here that some Brotherton Indians "tried to hurt" him refers to assaults on his character or authority.

149. On the relationship between Occom and New Stockbridgers, see also the August 27, 1787, petition from members of the Mahican-Stockbridge tribe to Occom, which appears in the petitions section of this collection.

[Draft; CHS folder I.11. Samson Occom Papers, Connecticut Historical Society, Hartford, Connecticut.]

75 ⚬   "STEADY IN RELIGION"

New Stockbridge
December 26, 1791

Rev^d and Much Esteemed Sir,

I dont think I can be at the ordination in Ballstown,[150] it is a long Way, and I am old, and Lame, and I must be at the Presbytery next March at Albany, if live, and Shall be well; I want to be at the ordination,—and one or two of our men with me but it cant be so now. I am now moving my family to Munhegunnach or New-Stockbridge, I told you it was Call'd Tuscarora, but that is not the Proper name of it,—Capt. Henrick who will deliver this to you, is one of our Church; he is just come from the Westward, amongst the Indians, and he has a large Tract of Land offer'd him if he and his people woud move there. I think it woud be a fine opening for the Gospel, Our Church have willlingly and Cheerfully adopted the Confession of Faith of the Presbyterian Church of the United States in America. They joyfully put themselves under the care and inspection of Albany Presbytery—And thankfully receive the gospel fellowship open'd for them.—And from This Time, we shall look upon ourSelves, one of the least Branches of the Religious Family of the Presbyterians in America—We are trying to instruct our Children in Letters, but we are very Weak, We want a little help—one Jo Quinney keeps the School, without any Prospect of Reward, and he is our Singing Master too, and he is Instructing the People in Singing Constantly, two or three Evenings every Weeke and he demands no pay—and he and his Family are very destitute of Cloathing,—our Professors keep on Steady in Religion, and our Church and Society rather increases,—our Singers are in Want of Psalm Books—What harm woud it be, if you wou'd try to beg a few amongst your Friends and Neighbours in Albany, We Use Dr Watt's Psalms altogether—I have no more to Say, at this Time,—Pray for us—This with much Esteem, is from

your most unworthy fellow Labourer in the gospel of Jesus,
Samson Occom

P.S. Capt Hendrick is our Elder, and Joseph Quinney is our Deacon; We have but very little Business for Elder and Deacon, and think one of each is enough for the [. . .]

January 8

Sir: The foregoing was Sent by Capt Hendrick, but was oblidged, to return back, and forgot to give it to Samuel Littleman who, I Conclude Call'd upon you, in his way to New Jersey. There Seems to be a Strange inclination among the Indians, to hear the Word of God preach'd, they Came to our meets from Tuscarora, most all of them,

150. *Ballstown:* Ballston, New York.

which they never did before, and Mr. Kirklands People came very thick too and they desire, that I might Spend Some Sabbaths—great many came to our meeting to Day, tho Mr. Kirkland went there this morning, and they knew of his Coming,—Mr. Kirkland is going away again, and I Shall go to his People next Sabbath[151]—Several of them, have great Desire to Join us in full—and Some of Mr. Sargeant's people[152] are Coming to us also, and they will join us in full,—I have an Evening School for the young People, and a Number come, I am Instructing to read & to speak English proper, and come on well, I am, etc

Samson Occom

[Harold Blodgett, *Samson Occom* (Hanover, NH: Dartmouth College, 1935), 208–210. © 1935 University Press of New England, Hanover, NH.]

76 ⚬ TO NEW YORK GOVERNOR GEORGE CLINTON

[1792]

Great Sir:

I am desired by our Committee to give your Excellency a Naration of our Situation, and the doings of a party of our Indians,—We have been in very unhappy Situation a long Time.—Our People did not meet as a Town near two year, and about a year ago they met, but they were so few did nothing,—and they delayd till last October about the 10th and I was then with them, and it was a ful meeting and they tryed to Chuse a New Committee, but they Could not make out, and finally Concluded to Continue the old Committee, and Confirmed them to Continue till the next Meeting, which was to be last March and they were to Consult and [word illegible] for the good of the Town; and the^y^ were to Show their Doings at the next Town Meeting;—and Some Time last November, they met, and [Consulted?] upon Some Things, Which were hotly opposed by Elijah Wampy and Calld the Committee all to Naught, and he Started up all at once and proceeded in Opposition, and Drew a paper, and got a Number to Sign it, and Sot Some ^mens^ Names down that were no present, and they Drew a Petition and Sent a man to the Honorable Assembly with it, and they began to lease out Some Lands before they sent a man to the Assembly,—These Proceedings Stird up our Committee to look about, and they empowered me, to write a Petition also, and Sent me to present it to the most Honorable Assembly at New York, And it was graciously Answerd, for Which we are very thankful.—When Putchaker got home, he gave out, that their petition was received and approved of, and ours was rejected with Contempt, tho' he had not one Line to Show from the Assembly.—and soon after, Elijah and his party went on with all fury to lease out

---

151. *Mr Kirklands People:* Although many Oneida rejected Rev. Samuel Kirkland after he promoted land-ceding treaties with the State of New York, he still maintained influence over a Christian faction of the tribe at New Oneida or Kanonwalohale. Kirkland also preached occasionally at New Stockbridge and Brotherton. On January 10, 1792, Kirkland set out for a council at Genesee with a party of eight Oneida, Stockbridge, and Tuscarora men (Pilkington, 217).

152. *Mr Sargeant's People:* Rev. John Sergeant, Jr., established a rival congregation at New Stockbridge in 1787 (Blodgett, 200–202; Love, *Occom*, 280–282). Occom's journal entries from September 21–24, 1787, and July 26, 1788, document some of his conflicts with Sergeant.

Lands to the White People, Several hired out their Home Lots, and layd out new Lots and leased them out; before I got ^home^ they had leased out about 2000 Acres,—And they have leased out a fine grove of Pine and a Cedar Swamp which were designed to be reservd for the Use of the Whole Town.—I hear the White People have Cut down great deal of the best Pine already. One of the Indians told me, he was much in Liquor when he leased out his Lot, he woud not done Such a thing, if he was Sober, and it is thought many were so, when they lease out their Lots—Now the Lessors and the Lessees Say, that what has been done by our Indians in leasing, is done according to the Liberty given to us at the first, and their doings are Lawful, the Leases will Stand ten Years,—But I think, we never were ripe yet for Leasing, even to this Day.—For our Land never was Survey'd all round Yet; and we dont know What Quantity of Land we shall have, and when ever we Shall be ripe for leasing, it must be done in Union and good agreament of the Whole Town; but what is done is done in party, in opposistion to the Most Substantial part of the Town, against the oldest men and the first Settlers, and the most Sober and Judicious men of the Town.—But many of Wampy's party is Compos'd of Strangers, that is, they did not come from the Tribes, to whom this Land was given.—Three Families are Mixtures or Molattoes;[153] Putchaker, Who Caried their Petition to the Assembly is a Stranger, he Came from Martha's Vineyard, & he was one of the Committee, and deserte^d^ his Place and Joined Wampy,—These Strangers were taken in by Benevolence & Favour, and now they are picking out our Eyes.—

All this Time they knew I was also attending upon the Assembly Concerning our Land, Yet they Wou'd ^not^ stay to See what was done,—If, What they have done is right, I dont know what Can be wrong,—When I got home, I was amazed and Surprised beyound Measure, to See What Confusion our People were in,—And last Monday we met, and it was a ful meeting—And I produced and presented the Resolves of the Most Honorable Assembly—and we had Mr Plat a gentleman Bred at Law, and Esqr Foot was also with us; and I gave the Writing to Mr Plat, to read and to Explain to our Indians, that they ^may^ understand them, and our Committee receiv'd them with gladness and Thankfulness, and them that adhear'd to the Committee were thankful also.—But Elijah Wampy and his party made Light of them and ridiculd them Elijah asked me, who sent me to the Assembly, I told him our Committee, and he Said there was no Committee.—He said further that the first Tuesday in April was past and so nothing Can be done till next April,—Mr Plat Said, we might go on upon our Business now, and so next year we might meet punctually meet on the Day appointed, but he woud not hear, but tryed to find Fault all he can.—I hear, Elijah and his Company are about to Send another Petition to the Asembly, so Ignorant are they, they think the Honorable Assembly will Confirm their party Wicked deeds and Works.—We See the Evil effects of their doings ready.—Two Families that leased out their home Lots are gone off, and perhaps will never return back to live here again, and another unavoidable Trouble will be,—When the

---

153. From the seventeenth century onward, New England and Long Island Indians often married African-Americans. These intermarriages helped replenish tribal population losses, but they also became a source of controversy: colonial overseers sometimes instituted policies banning

White People will Come with their Families, we shall be all mixt together, our Children and their will be Quarrilling, and Will set the old Folks a Quarilly,—and they will bring their Horses, Cattle, Hogs, Sheep and Dogs, and there will be no Peace amongst us.

The Stockbridgers, Capt Hendreck, who is the Chief amongst them, tells me and his People, receive the Laws, Instructions & Directions with Joy and Gratitude.—

[Two words faded] are Majority, and we Say that we are a Majority But we

[Draft; CHS-M 359–361. Samson Occom Papers, Connecticut Historical Society, Hartford, Connecticut.]

---

or penalizing exogamous marriages in order to hasten the decline of tribal communities, while tribes themselves disagreed internally over whether mixed-race members would enjoy full status within the community. Intratribal disagreements intensified especially as economic pressures increased and territorial land bases and resources diminished, and provisions excluding the children of African–Native unions became a common feature of governmental agreements in some tribal communities. In May 1773, Samson Occom and a number of Mohegan Indians signed an agreement declaring that the children of African–Native unions would have no rights in Mohegan (Mandell 475). Land agreements between the Oneida and the Brotherton-affiliated tribes of New England and Long Island formalized in 1774 also barred the children of African-Americans or African–Native unions from land rights at Brotherton (*WJP* 13: 684). The December 5, 1789, petition to Richard Law (which appears in this collection) reflects the ongoing controversy over the position of New England Indians of African descent. On African–Native relationships, see also James Brooks, *Confounding;* Plane; and Mandell, *Behind,* 182–196.

PETITIONS AND TRIBAL DOCUMENTS

Throughout his career, Samson Occom used his literacy to help Mohegan, Brotherton, and other Native communities articulate their physical and spiritual needs, defend their traditional territories, and assert their sovereignty. Thirteen petitions and governance documents written in Occom's hand assert the positions of tribal communities on matters such as the education of Native American children, the right to appoint their own governments, and the defense of their common lands and fishing territories. By adopting the voice of "we" in these documents, Occom subsumed his individual authorship within the collective authority of the tribe. This suggests that Occom and other English-language literate American Indians of his era viewed literacy as a tool to be subscribed in the service of American Indian communities.

Five documents written by Occom on behalf of the Mohegan tribe in the 1760s and 1770s mark his role in the reconstitution of indigenous governance at Mohegan after decades of outside interference. The customary line of descent of Mohegan tribal leadership was disrupted after the death of Caesar Uncas in 1723, when colonial officers influenced the passing of the sachemship out of turn to Caeser's younger brother Ben Uncas. Following his father, Ben Uncas II was also appointed sachem over the objections of many Mohegans who supported Caeser's nephew Mahomet, next in line by traditional rules of succession. Controversy over the sachemship divided the Mohegan tribe into two factions and physical camps: "Ben's Town," composed of those who supported the colony-facilitated sachemship of Ben Uncas, Ben Uncas II, and Ben Uncas III, and "John's Town," composed of supporters of Mahomet and his chosen successor, John Uncas. Members of both factions came to a new consensus in the winter of 1763–1764, when they recognized that Ben Uncas III was abusing tribal lands and territorial resources and disregarding the advice of his counselors. Occom, whose family was traditionally allied to Ben Uncas and who had once served as a councillor to Ben Uncas II, played a leading role in facilitating this new political development, for which he was criticized by the sachem and white clergy. In early 1764, Occom wrote on behalf of the newly constituted tribal council to Sir William Johnson, the British superintendent of Indian affairs for North America and a trusted friend and advisor. Observing that their Connecticut overseers designed to "render us Cyphers in our own land" and "us'd Ben Uncas as a tool" in this design, the new Mohegan council declared that they intended to reject his sachemship and choose their own leader without colonial interference. A few months later, leading Mohegans met again to draft a petition accusing Robert Clelland of mismanaging the local school and abusing their children. When Ben Uncas III died in 1769, a new faction formed around Zachary Johnson, a former councillor to Uncas, as the new sachem. However, Occom and his cohort refused to recognize the sachemship and continued to meet in council. Governmental documents from 1773, 1774, and 1778 show that Occom and his cohort addressed collective concerns surrounding the use of common lands, including planting, grazing, fencing, leasing, and managing white tenants. Resolving to share proceeds from rents, the body declared on April 28, 1778, "we Shall look upon one another as one Family, and Will Call or look upon no one as a Stranger, but Will take one another as pure and True Mohegans," thus affirming their commitment to the communal economic values once betrayed by Ben Uncas III and subverted by colonial interference.

After the end of the Revolutionary War, Occom assisted five tribal communities—Mohegan, Niantic, Brotherton, Montaukett, and Shinnecock—in composing petitions to the states of Connecticut and New York and the United States Congress. From the seventeenth century onward, petitions served as the primary instrument through which private individuals obtained support from and directed the business of the colonial government. Petitions conventionally addressed a range of personal and public concerns, from enforcing broken contracts, resolving legal disputes, and collecting on unpaid debts to obtaining relief in times of extraordinary hardship and redressing personal injuries both petty and grave. African Americans, Native Americans, and women all made use of the petition system. For many colonial assemblies, resolving petitioners' disputes and grievances constituted the first order of business. In colonial Connecticut, for example, more legislation originated through the petition process than from any other source. The Connecticut General Assembly of 1770 acted on more than 150 petitions, while originating only fifteen laws of its own. Petitions also served as an important medium for American colonies to express grievances with the British Parliament, and the right to petition was enshrined in the Bill of Rights. Manipulating colonial models of legal intervention, Native Americans used petitions to criticize oppressive practices and policies and to assert their authority and interject their own voices, perspectives, and beliefs into often unfair and imbalanced legal and economic processes.

The four postwar tribal petitions mark a shift from earlier Native petition rhetoric that positioned Native peoples as individual pleading subjects of the British crown to a new positioning as indigenous nations. These documents insist on a government-to-government relationship between tribes and states in the early national era. Witness, for example, how the Mohegan and Niantic petition to the Connecticut Assembly specifies that the tribes are not asking the state to grant "a Priviledge, which we never had before, but a Protection in our Natural Priviledges, which the King of Heaven gave to our Fathers and to their Children forever." These petitions also reflect a widening perspective on the extensive damage wrought by English colonization. The Mohegan, Niantic, Montaukett, and Shinnecock petitions allege a history of coercion and manipulation by colonial officers, including strategic manipulation of deep differences between indigenous and English concepts of land rights. Native people understood (and still understand) themselves to be originally, intimately, and ineradicably connected to their territories; land was not something to be owned, bought, partitioned into individual plots, or sold. This indigenous sense of place is captured in the tropes "this Indian world" and "this boundless continent," both featured in the 1785 petitions. Each of these petitions also remembers Native peoples' aboriginal inhabitation of the land, its natural superabundance before colonization, and its consequent degeneration under colonial dominion. In the hands of Occom and his tribal coauthors, the petition is transformed from an instrument of individual legal redress into a venue for the assertion of collective legal subjectivity and for the expression of tribal narratives. Petitions thus belong to what Abenaki scholar Lisa Brooks has identified as a Native New England tradition of using literature to recreate a Native sense of space. They constitute an important genre of Native American literature.

The final four documents in this section demonstrate how literate Native communities strategically used written instruments to manage internal affairs. In fall 1787, members of the New Stockbridge and Brotherton tribal communities invited Occom to live among them and serve as their minister. Occom was a leading architect of the Brotherton settlement and regularly visited the community, but he and his wife Mary maintained their main residence at Mohegan. During a long visit to Brotherton-New Stockbridge, on August 27, 1787, Occom met with seven leading Mahican-Stockbridge men to craft a formal letter of invitation, declaring the will of the community that they be ministered to by "one of our own"; in November 1787, Occom again met with leading men of Brotherton and New Stockbridge to craft a fundraising letter to solicit donations from white benefactors to support his move to upstate New York. Occom, David Fowler, and Peter Pauquunnuppeet carried this letter on a fundraising tour of Pennsylvania and New Jersey in January and February 1788. These two documents reflect the growing frustration of Christian Indian communities with white ministers like Samuel Kirkland and John Sergeant, Jr., a revival of the separatist spirit characteristic of many New England Christian Indian congregations in the 1740s and 1750s, and a recommitment to the concept of Native self-governance in spiritual affairs. Writing could also be used to leverage outside intervention in matters of tribal factionalism. Writing with five other Mohegans to their legal guardian Richard Law, in 1789, Occom sought to exclude a mixed-race black Mohegan from claiming his share of territorial land rights. The status of mixed-race Native people was a subject of tremendous controversy and conflict for many tribal communities in southern New England. Finally, in 1791, Occom crafted and carried a petition to the New York State Assembly to prevent a faction of Brotherton residents led by Elijah Wimpy from indiscriminately leasing out lands to white settlers.

Perhaps more than any other form of early Native American writing, petitions and tribal governmental documents reveal the day-to-day business of Native survival in difficult, hostile, and rapidly changing circumstances. The historian Francis Jennings identified five strategies colonists used to steal Native lands: creating puppet tribal leaders, permitting white settlers to harass Indian communities and encroach on Native lands, sending armed troops to intimidate tribe members, introducing alcohol to Native communities, and levying legal fines to force Native people into debts to be repaid through land seizures. Native peoples engineered their survival through maintaining forms of self-governance and protecting tribal lands. This required

courage, constant vigilance, political sophistication, persistent attention to the detailed language of laws and treaties, rejection of alcohol and commodity consump-
tion, resistance to bribery, dedication to traditional forms of leadership, and strategic understanding of political rhetoric. In appealing to colonial, state, and national
governments and white benefactors for intervention or assistance, Occom and his
co-petitioners sometimes adopted what appears to be a posture of supplication. Certainly, their language reflects the rhetoric of colonial agents and missionaries who
repeatedly charged Native communities with being backward, degenerate, and in-
capable of self-governance. But it is also possible to read their apparently humble
tones as strategic appeals to Euro-American rhetorical customs, or as manipulations
of the trope of the poor Indian that was a mainstay of Anglo-American colonial discourse. As scholars David Murray, Jace Weaver (Cherokee), and Lisa Brooks (Abenaki)
observe, early Native American authors adopted and redirected the trope of the
poor Indian to deliver sharp criticisms of the colonial regimes that created conditions of poverty for Native peoples. Native authors like Occom also encouraged Native communities to adopt more striking and assertive political stances grounded in
their original relations to the land and their inherent rights to self-determination.

I　∞　　　MOHEGAN TRIBE TO SIR WILLIAM JOHNSON

[1764]

Hon^l Sir

These, withe true Friendship and Sincere Service, beg your Hon^rs Notice and hearing,—We bless the Supream being the Governor of all Worlds—that he has given
you great Wisdom and understandg and Sent you in these parts of the World, and
when you ~~looked all~~ ^cast your Eyes a^ round you, you Saw the Natives ^the Miserable Nations of the Land^ to be without understanding, and are liable to ^be^ imposed upon by all other Nations, and it move^d your Heart in a Way of Commisira-
tion—and ^god^ hath made you a mideator between the Natives and the other
Nations, and Now the Eyes of many Nations are upon you, for help, as the Eyes of
^helpless^ Children, to a tender Parent,—they look with ardent Desires, both from
the East and from the West, from the North and from the South,—And we think and
feel ourselves happy that Some of us have had some aquantance with your Honor,
and ^that^ we may now not only look from afar—but may nearly aproach your
Honor and ^make^ our Cries in your Ears—Sir Besides the Complants Which have
been presented before your Honor and What is brought Now from Capt Tracy[1]—We
think ~~we~~ are imposed upon by our ^over^ Seers and What our ^over^ Seers ^have^
done we take to be done by the Assembly[2]—by what they have already done we

1. *Capt Tracy:* Joseph Tracy.
2. *^over^ Seers:* The colonial Connecticut Assembly appointed a series of guardians to supervise and
   direct the territorial-legal affairs of the Mohegan tribe. Although the Mohegans under Uncas voluntarily initiated a protective legal guardianship with Major John Mason in the 1650s, granting
   Mason deeds-in-trust to Mohegan territory in exchange for his legal advocacy, the guardianship

think they want render us as Cyphers in our own land—they want to root us out of our land ^root & Branch^, they ^have^ already Proceeded with arbitrary Power over us,—and we want to know from whence they got that Power or Whither they Can Maintain such Power Jusly over us—They have indeed us'd Ben Uncas³ as a Tool in their Hands and Ben Uncas was to do nothing With out his Council While he was our Sachem ~~and Now we have Cast him of~~ ^and he has now Cast of his Councel and Will not^ and we think it but Just and Honest as you Honor may See in a Bit of Paper,— and the English intends to Continue him as a Sachem ovr us, but we have a Law and a Custom to make a Sachem over us Without the help of any People or Nation in the World, and When he makes himself ^unworthy^ of his Station we put him down—ourselves—Understand Sir, this Tribe has been in 2 parties, the Goverment Pretended to befriend the Indians, and Mʳ Mason Pretended the Same and each had a Number of Indians, and there is a few ~~of us~~ that Seems to Stand between the two parties—Deacon Henry Quaquaquid will Relate the Whole Matter to Your Honor. Sir, now we desire to know from Your Hon. Which seems to be Honest in your View, and Desire your Honors advice Where to Stear,—Some Questions we woud ask, Whether we have not Power to Stop Ben Uncas from Pastoring English Creatures, and Selling Wood or Timber and Stone, and Wither the Income of the Leased Lands ought to go to the benefit of the Whole Tribe,—and how Shouᵈ we Proceed in these Matters—and Whither it woud not be as well for ^us^ to be Without Sachem as With in Time to Come—Whether the kings Instructions Concerning Indian Lands, an't as much for us as any Tribe—Whither We Cant ^use^ the Farm which Ben Uncas leasd not alone or Whether we Cant lease it out to Whome we have a mind—⁴

[CHS folder I.2; Occom's hand. Samson Occom Papers, Connecticut Historical Society, Hartford, Connecticut.]

2 ∞ ## MOHEGAN TRIBE AGAINST ROBERT CLELLAND

Mohegan
April 26, 1764

Recollected by many of the Indians against Clelland School Master among Indians.—

I. He takes a great Number of English Children, and they take Room from Indian Children, and keep them away from the Fire in the Coldest Seasons—

---

system had been appropriated to the benefit of colonial interests by the eighteenth century (St. Jean).

3. *Ben Uncas:* Ben Uncas III.

4. Writing on behalf of a newly constituted tribal council, Samson Occom here appeals to his friend William Johnson, superintendent of Indian affairs for British North America, to advise the Mohegan as they strive to resist and repair the effects of Connecticut colonial interference in their governmental affairs. Lisa Brooks acutely observes the significance of this petition: "Mohegans had reconstituted themselves as a communal body, leaving Ben Uncas and his acquiescence to colonial control behind" (153).

2. He has no government nor Authority in his School, neither does he hear his Schollars Carefully

3. He does not Pray in his School Neither does he teach the Indian Children English Manners—

4. He was to find Dinner for Children and he turns them of with any thing—

5. He has been Away from his School Many a Day

6. He has frequently used Indian Horses without asking leave of the owners—

[CHS folder I.2; Occom's hand. Samson Occom Papers, Connecticut Historical Society, Hartford, Connecticut.]

3 ∾   MOHEGAN TRIBE STANDING AGREEMENTS

[1773]

The Heads of the Tribe met to Consult our Mohegan affairs—

1. Unanimously Agreed, that none of us as individuals Shall ever take any English Creatures into our Common Pastures or into the general Fields, for the Future, If we Take in any, it Shall be for the Whole Tribe, and the owners of the Creatures, Shall pay the Tribe in Making Stone Walls around the general Fields

The Reasons—If We Shoud let individuals Take in Creatures, every one will take in as many as they please, Squaws and all, and our Fields and Pastures woud be Crouding^ed^ full every Year and We Shoud never have feed for our own Creatures—

2. Any one may let out his or her Planting or Mowing Ground upon Shares or other Wise, for a ^Summer^ Season, but not take in Creatures to feed it, in the fall,—

3. Any one may hire out his own House and inclosed Lots, Provided the Tenant keeps within his Limitts,—

4. that as there will be always some [page torn]ing Timber and Saw Mill Logs, Such Tops will be for the Whole Tribe, they may Cut them for their own fires, or Cut them into Cordwood to Sell to the White People, allowing the Tribe one Shilling for every Cord they Sell—None Shall Sell any Wood, without any Liberty from ~~any Wood~~ the Tribe and the Overseers

5. if any one is Short of Winder Fod[d]er, and is obligd to put ^out^ his Cattle to the White People to be kept, he may pay in Summer feed in our Common Pastures, but if he falls Short, by Selling his foder, he Shant be allowd to take in Creatuers into our Common Pastures, he must pay other Wise—

6. If any one or a number fence in a bit of ground in any of our Common Pastures to Plant or Sowe, he or they Shall make good Fence, and if any Damage is done by our Creatures in them they Shall recover no Damages,—

[CHS-M 112–113; Occom's hand; upper corner of page torn. Samson Occom Papers, Connecticut Historical Society, Hartford, Connecticut.]

4 ∾   ### MOHEGAN TRIBE TO COLONIAL OVERSEER

[1774]

Hon^d Sir

You may Well remember in our last meeting with our Hon^b overseers at Mr Houghtons, it was unanimously agreed on both sides, that the English Families, in the Indian Houses should all move away this Spring, and they ~~fa~~ are late to move,—and
we left it with Mr Houghton to turn them out, or desire them to move out, and now
some of them say, the Indians are will[in]g they should Stay another year,—and we
have met together Again, to know who have given them encouragement, and there
was not one, that Spoke in their Favour, and ^I^ talk[d] with Mr Houghton Since,
and he advises, to write to your ^Honor^—and this is therefore ^to^ Desire your
Honor; to Write them Positively, to move out immediately without any further
Trouble, their Names are,—Rufus [R]ose, Daniel Miner, if these will move out, the
rest [word crossed out] will move out also, their Names are, Jhon Leach, Saml
Wheeler,—Ames—wrote in the behalf of the Mohegan Tribe of Indians,

by your Hon^rs very Hum^l Servt
Samson Occom

[Draft; CHS-M 0225–0226. Samson Occom Papers, Connecticut Historical Society, Hartford, Connecticut.]

5 ∾   ### MOHEGAN TRIBE ON RENTS

April 28: 1778

In the evening, the Tribe met together, to Consult about the Disposal of the Rent
money, and as it has been agreed Unanimously heretofore once and again, that we
Shall look upon one another as one Family, and Will Call or look upon no one as a
Stranger, but Will take one another as pure and True Mohegans; and so at this Time,
we unanimously ^agreed^ that the Money does belong to the Whole Tribe, and it
shall be dispos'd of acordingly for the Benefit of the Whole.

[CHS-M 113; Occom's hand; upper left corner page torn. Samson Occom Papers, Connecticut Historical Society, Hartford, Connecticut.]

6 ∾   ### MOHEGAN AND NIANTIC TRIBES TO THE
CONNECTICUT ASSEMBLY

[May 1785]

To the Most Honorable General Assembly of Connecticut Convened at Hartford in
May, in the Year of our Common Lord & Saviour Jesus Christ one Thousand Seven
Hundred eighty and five years:

Your steady, close and faithful friends the tribe of Mohegan, and the tribe of
Nahantick sendeth greeting. Sincere friends and brethren may talk freely together

without offence. Such we concluded, the English of Connecticut and Mohegans, and Nahanticks are—

Your Excellency may well remember, that we sent a Memorial to the General Assembly, held at New Haven last October, requesting, not a Priviledge, which we never had before, but a Protection in our Natural Priviledges, which the King of Heaven gave to our Fathers and to their Children forever. When we received an answer or grant to our petition, we were all amazed and astonished beyond measure. What? Only half a sein[5] allowed to Monooyauhegunnewuck,[6] from the best friends to the best friends? We are ready to conclude, that the meaning must be, that in time to come we must not have only one canoe, one bow, one hook and line, among two tribes, and we must have taxes imposed upon us also, &c., &c. Whilst the King of England had authority over here they order no such things upon us. Alas, where are we? If we were slaves under tyrants, we must submit; if we were captives, we must be silent, and if we were strangers, we must be contented; or if we had forfeited our priviledges at your hands by any of our agreements we should have nothing to say. Whenever we went to war against your and our enemies, one bow, and one hatchet would not do for two tribes—And what will the various tribes of Indians, of this boundless continent say, when they hear of this restraint of fishing upon us? Will they not all cry out, mmauk, mmauk,[7] these are the good that the Mohegans ever gloried and boasted of—Certainly we cannot hurt the public by fishing, we never had more than two seins in Mohegan and two in Nahantick and many times not one in Mohegan for over 15 years together, and we fish but very little in the season. We conclude your excellencies must have mistaken our request. And therefore we earnestly pray again, that the honorable Assembly would protect us in our Natural Priviledges, that none may forbid, hinder, or restrain us from fishing in any of the places where we used to fish heretofore.

Signed Samson Occom, Henry Quaquaquid, Robert Ashpo, Phillip Cuish, Joseph Uppauquiyantup, Isaac Uppauquiyantup

[DCA 785340. Courtesy of Dartmouth College Library.]

7 ⤳   BROTHERTON TRIBE TO UNITED STATES CONGRESS

Brotherton
[1785?]

To the Most August Asembly, The Congress of the Thirteen United States, in this Boundless Western New World, Now Conven'd at the City of New York—

5. *sein:* A seine is a large weighted fish net, used here to indicate an annual measure of fish permitted the Mohegan people by Connecticut colonial policy. The Thames River of Connecticut is traditional Mohegan fishing territory.

6. *Monooyauhegunnewuck:* Mohegan.

7. *mmauk, mmauk:* According to Mohegan tribal linguist Stephanie Fielding, *mmauk* may be a variant of the Mohegan word *piyamáq,* which means "fish." It is also possible that the word I have transcribed as *mmauk* is actually *nimauk,* which according to Delaware language rules for possessives would mean "our fish" (Fielding).

Your Ancient and Most true and Sincere Friends and Brethren, the aboriginal Nations of this Great Indian World,——Sendeth Greeting

We intreat that of your ~~Great~~ ^Noble^ Excellencies and Clemencies, You Would listen to us, and hear us few Words——

The Most Great, The Good and The Supream ^Spirit above^ Saw fit to Creat This World, and all Creatures and all things therein; and the Children of man to Inhabit the Earth and to enjoy, and to ^over^rule all the rest of the Creatures in this World—— and the good, and the Great ^govr^ of the Worlds,——Saw fit in his good pleasure, to Divide this World by the Great Waters, and he fenced this great Continent by the Mighty Waters, all around, and it pleased him, to Plant our fore Fathers here first, and he gave them this Boundless Continent, and it was well furnishd, and Stored with all Necessaries of Life for them, and here they have livd and Spread over the Face of this Wilderness World, no man knows ^how or^ how long,——This World was full of all manner of four footed Wild Creatures great & small both on the Land and in the Waters, and Fowls Without Number ^on the dry & in the Waters^ of all Sizes and Coulors, ~~they Darken the Air Some Times~~ and they Coverd the Face of the Earth and the Waters and our Lakes, Ponds, Rivers, Brooks, and the Seas, were all alive, and [fom'd] with Fish of every Sort and Bigness, even our Sa^n^d and Mud were well Stord with Shell Fish, besids with Variety of Creeping Shell Fish great and Small,—— and our Land and Woods were Loaded with Fruit in a boundence, there were ground Nuts and beans in the Earth and Nuts on the Trees plenty,——Thus our Forefathers lived upon the Spontaneous Produc^t^ of this Country,——and in Process of Time, The great Sovereign of the Universe, Saw fit to permit the [word crossed out] ^Brethren^ of your fore Fathers to rise up against them for their maintaining the pure Religion of Jesus Christ, and they killd many of them, and a few of them fled from the Face of their Cruel Bre[thr]en and the good Spirit above Directed their Course to the West, [an]d he brought them over into this Country, and here the Good Spirit made Room for them ^and here your Fathers found us very poor and Wild and Ignorant^ and others of their Brethren Soon Come after them, and Settle with them, and Soon Mul- tiplied, and our fore Father Sold them Lands for little or nothing our Fathers knew not the Value of Lands, for they had not other use for it only to Hunt on and to gather the Natural Fruits of it; & they have Sold all their Country, along the Sea Shore, and all our Hunting, Fishing and Fowling is now gone, our Father thought to live always by hunting, but they were greatly under a mistake for now we find our selves Stript of all our Natural Priviledges,—— ~~And Just before these~~ and Some years back we made application to our good Brethren the Onoydas for a little Room to Settle ^down^ upon, and they were So kind as freely to give us a large Tract of good Land and Several ^Families^ went up and began to Settle it and others were geting ready to move up,——And the [invy?] Which your Brethren had against for Some Time for Your Happiness you injoy in this Country, grew so hott, that your own ^king^ Sent over an Army to Supress you, by which an open Family Contention began and we were also greatly distrest, and were drove of and left our efects and lost them,—— And all the Tribes to ^which^ we belong to were warmly Engaged in Favour of the United States of America ^and our young men are^ And now Thanks be to the good Spirit above, that there is a Finis to these unhappy Wars, and we hope that it will be a long and an Honorable Peace,—And we rejoice with you and Congratulate you that after a long Strugle, Under the Tyrannic Hand of your invious Elder Brother, you have broke the Slavish Chains and the galling Yoke, and by your firmness Steadyness, Resolution and Great Courage, you have got your Freedom Liberty and Independence.—And now we hope, we wish, and pray, that you may be very good, Happy, great, and Strong People, that you may be like a Tree planted by a River, that will take deep and Strong Root;[8] that you may grow up very high towards Heaven, and your Branches may Spre^a^d Extensively Wide and be Very Fruitfull in all things that are praiseworthy—And Since the Peace have took Place a number of have got up here again, and others woud Come up also but we are So poor, we are much dishartend,—and we find that this late war has stript us of all help we use to have—All the Fountains abroad that use to water and refresh our Wilderness are Dryed up, and the Springs that use to rise near are all Ceased[9]—We have neither Missionaries nor Scholmasters amongst us,—and it is pinching Necessity that Constrains us to make our Cries for help; and we h no where to make our Cries, but to Your Excellencies Benevolence—And Therefore our ^most^ Humble Petition and Request is, this once, to help us a little, in our Settling, in this Wilderness, we extreamly want a grist mill and a Saw Mill and we very Destitute of all manner of Husbandry Tools and we Should be glad and thankfull for a little Liberary, for we would have our Children have some Learning,—our Young People are much inclined to learn

[CHS folder I.10; Occom's hand. Samson Occom Papers, Connecticut Historical Society, Hartford, Connecticut.]

8 ⟍   MONTAUKETT TRIBE TO THE STATE OF NEW YORK

[1785?]

To the Great and Most Excellent Governor, and to all the Great Men Ruling in the State of New York in North America.—

We who are known by the Name, Mmeeyautanheewuck or Montauk Indians, Humbly Send Greeting

We are very Glad and Rejoice with you that you have at last got your Freedom Liberty and Independence, from under the heavy and Gauling Yoke of Your Late King, who has tryed very hard to make you Slaves, and have kill'd great many of You, but by Your Steadiness, Boldness, and Great Courage, you have broke the Yoke and the Chain of Slavery;—Now, God Bless You, and Make you very great and good forever

---

8. *like a Tree planted by a River:* Possibly refers to Jeremiah 17:7–8, "Blessed is the man that trusteth in the Lord, and whose hope the Lord is. For he shall be as a tree planted by the waters, and that spreadeth out her roots by the river, and shall not see when heat cometh, but her leaf shall be green; and shall not be careful in the year of drought, neither shall cease from yielding fruit."

9. After the end of the American War of Independence, many British religious societies withdrew monetary support for American missionary endeavors.

We Montauk Indians, have Sot Still and have not Intermedled in this Family Contention of Yours, because we had no Business with it, and we have kept our Young men quiet as we Coud, and the People on both Sides have Usd us well in general

Now, great and good Gentlemen, we humbly Intreat your Condescention and Patience to hear us a little Concerning ourselves.—

The Great and good Spirit above, Saw fit in his good pleasure, to plant our Fore-Fathers in this great Wilderness but when and how, none knows but himself,—and he that works all things Acording to his own Mind, Saw it good to give us this great Continent & he fill'd this Indian World, with veriety, and a Prodigous Number of four footed Beasts, Fowl without number and Fish of all kinds great and Small, fill'd our Seas, Rivers, Brooks, and Ponds every where,—And it was the Pleasure of him, Who orders all things acording to his good Will, he that maketh Rich, and maketh poor, he that kills, and that maketh alive, he that raiseth up whom he will, and pulleth down ^whom^ he will; Saw fit, to keep us in Porverty, Only to live upon the Provisions he hath made already at our Hands—Thus we livd, till it pleased the great and good Governor of the World, to Send your Fathers into these goings down of the Sun, and found us Naked and very poor Destitute of every thing, that your Fathers injoyd, only this that we had good and a Large Country to live in, and well furnished with Natural Provisions, and there was not a Letter known amongst them all in this Boundless Continent.—But your Fore Fathers Came With all the Learning, Knowledge, and Understanding, that was Necessary for Mankind to make them Happy, and they knew the goodness of our Land, and they Soon began to Settle and Cultivate the land, Some they bought almost for nothing, and we suppose they took a great deal without Purchace. And our Fathers were very Ignorant and knew not the value of Land, and they Cared nothing about it, they Imagin'd, they Shoud allways live by Hunting Fishing and Fowling, and gathering Wild Fruits—But alas at this age of the World, we find and plainly see by Sad experience, that by our Fore Fathers Ignorance and Your Fathers great Knowledge, we are undone for this Life— Now only See the agreement, your Fathers and our Fathers made,—We hope you wont be angry with us in telling the The agreed that we Shoud have only two Small necks of Land to plant on, and we are not allowd to Sow Wheate, and we as a Tribe ^are^ Stinted to keep only 50 Head of Cattle, and 200 Swine and three Dogs, —Pray gentlemen take good Notice, dont this discover a profound Ignorance in our fore Fathers, indeed we Suspect, Some Times, that what little understanding they had was Drowned with hott Waters before they made these Shameful agreements, and on the other hand, don't this Show, that the English took advantage of the Ignorance of our Fore Fathers Woud they be Willing to be Servd so by us? Were we Cababale to use them So?—We fare now harder than our Fore Fathers—For all our Hunting, Fowling, and Fishing is now ^almost^ gone and our Wild Fruit is gone, What little there is left the English would Ingross or take all ^to^ themselves—and our Wood is gone and the English forbid us of geting any, where there is Some in their Claim— and if our Hogs happen to root a little the English will make us pay Damages, and they freequently Count our Cattle and Hogs,—Thus we are Usd by our English Neighbours—Pray most Noble Gentlemen Consider our Miserable Case and for God's Sake help us; For we have no where to go now, but to your Excellence for help; If we had but 150 head of Cattle and some [Sheep] and a few more Hogs we Shoud be Contented and thankful

This is all we have to Say at this Time, and Shall now wait to See your Pleasure Concerning Us—[10]

[CHS folder I.13; Occom's hand. Samson Occom Papers, Connecticut Historical Society, Hartford, Connecticut.]

9 ∾   SHINNECOCK TRIBE TO THE STATE OF NEW YORK

[1787 or 1788]

To the most Excellent and Good Governor, and all the Chief Rulers, in the State of New York—

We poor Indians, known by the Name Umshennuckoouk or Shenecuck Indians, on Long Island, Most humbly send greeting—

We desire to be permitted, to rejoice with you in your great deliverance from the Cruel Tyranny of your once King, and from the Hands of your Brethren, who are like Esau[11] and you have got your great Freedom, Liberty, and Independence, by your firm Resolution, Great Boldness, and undaunted Courage. You have now Shook off the Cruel Shackels and the hard and rough Yoke of Bondage, and now you are free People, you have your own Power in your own Hands.—

May the Great God, who has all Power, Make you very great, Strong and good forever.—

Most Noble and Great Gentlemen, we humbly beg, that you woud of your Clemency hear us a few words about our little Affairs—

The Supreme and independent Spirit above, who is the right owner and Disposer of all Worlds and all things and Creatures therein, Saw fit, to give us this great Continent to live in, and here we have been, nobody knows how long, and it pleased him also, in process of Time to Send your forefathers in this Country; and here they

---

10. A century of English encroachment on Montauk territorial lands and beaches on eastern Long Island culminated in 1703 with controversial and manipulative agreements that affirmed the colony's exclusive legal title to traditional Montaukett lands and established strict regulations for Montaukett land use, requiring Montauketts to fence in their landholdings, permitting English livestock to graze Montaukett planting fields, capping Montaukett livestock holdings at 250 hogs and 50 cattle or horses, and requiring the Montauketts to establish permanent residences at one of two sites—North Neck or Indian Fields—rather than migrate seasonally according to custom. A law passed in 1712 targeted the traditional affection of Long Island indigenous communities for keeping dogs: the colony restricted the Montaukett tribe to keep only three dogs, and historical records show that on at least two recorded occasions—in 1727 and 1742—colonial trustees sent agents to kill all dogs at Montauk except the permitted three. Similar murderous raids on communal dog populations were conducted at the nearby Shinnecock community. Occom here appeals on behalf of his Montaukett relatives—he met and married Mary Fowler when he was stationed as a missionary at Montauk in the 1750s—for relief from the state government of New York (Strong, *Montaukett Indians*, 57–58, 73; Ales, *History*, 52).

11. *Esau:* In Genesis 26–27, Esau, the eldest son of Isaac, loses his birthright to his younger twin brother, Jacob.

find our Fathers, Wild and poor, and very Ignorant; They livd altogether upon Hunting, Fishing, and Fowling, and picking wild Fruits, and they knew nothing of improving Land, and kep[t] no Tame Creatures, and indeed there was no need of it, for W^h^en they wanted Fresh meat they ^woud^ run into the Bush, and Catch wild meat enough Presently, they ^only^ kept Dogs for Hunting, and When the English Came into our Country, they found it very good Land, and they bought it all for a trifle for our Fathers were utterly Ignorant of the Value of Land, they thought their Hunting, Fishing, and Fowling woud always Continue; But alas, alas it is all ^gone^ from us, and we are now poorer than our Fathers were; We have a little bit of Land that we Call our own, but the English have got all the profet of it, they Claim all the grass and the feed, and we Cant keep any Creatures; we can only Plant a little Corn, beans and Pumpkins, and thats all, And we think, we are Usd very hard, woud they be willing to be Usd in this manner? We think it is Writen in the Good old Book, Blessed is he that Considereth the poor, and we are the most wretched poor and this the way to Consider the poor, to Strip em of every thing, And now we know it is in your Power to help us, and there fore, we are Come before your Excellency for help, for we have no where to go now for help to your Honors, and if we no help, we must die at your Feet,—We only want to keep Some Cattle, Horses, and Hogs,—[12]

We are your most unworthy Servants

Umshennuckoouk

[CHS-M 367–368; Occom's hand. Samson Occom Papers, Connecticut Historical Society, Hartford, Connecticut.]

IO ⚭ MAHICAN-STOCKBRIDGE TRIBE TO SAMSON OCCOM

Revd Mr Samson Occom
New Stockbridge
Augt 27: 1787

Brothers in the Lord

We the Muhheacunnunk Tribe will now manifest to you our opinions, Desires and ^Views^ of the Christian Religion, we believe that there is but one the only true &

---

12. Samson Occom's father-in-law, James Fowler, was Shinnecock; these kinship ties and his intermittent ministerial service to Long Island Shinnecocks in the 1760s probably positioned Occom to serve as the scribe or author of this tribal petition. In his diary, Occom recorded visits to the Shinnecock community on Long Island on April 11–12, 1787, and April 14, 1788. Shinnecock territorial rights were steadily eroded by a series of seventeenth- and eighteenth-century agreements with English settlers at Southampton, Long Island. During the Deed Panic of 1703, New York colonial agents set out to buy up all remaining Indian lands on Long Island, and Southampton town trustees reacted by securing legal title to all Shinnecock lands, but conceding to the Shinnecocks a one-thousand-year lease to the Shinnecock Hills. Under the terms of the 1703 lease, Shinnecock peoples were permitted to farm on certain portions of the land, but forbidden to create fenced plots or enclosures during six months of each year, which may have prevented their keeping livestock (Strong, "How the Land was Lost: Introduction," 59–62; "The Thousand Year Lease," 96).

living God, and that he is the maker and preserver of our Lives, and upholder of the Same, that he has Sent his only begoten Son into this World, to be the Saviour of mankind, and we believe that this god has brought us up into this Wilderness, where we might begin to Serve him in Sincerity and in Truth,—

Further we believe, that this god has raised you up, and have kept you alive until this Time, and that he has Sent You up as an Ambasador into this Wilderness upon this porpose, that you might be the first Instrument or means to Stir Up Your own Nation, to try to embrace the Whole Religion—

And the Reason, Why We have such thoughts ^is^ because we have felt a great weight of your errand, and in Coming Such a manner and from Such a quarter as we did not expect.—When we look back, and Consider What poor progress the Religion of Jesus Christ has made amongst the natives of this Continent, Notwithstanding of the great pains that have been taken with them in Some Places the Indian appeared well and promising, but Soon Decay. And now it looks very Dark upon us all helps from a Broad are gone.—And we are now brought to look about, and Consider of our Situation, and we believe that this Will be the last that god will make a Trial with us.—if this will not Set us to Contrive for our own Souls, & God will leave us to our own Distruction.—These and other Considerations Induceth us, to believe that God does require from our hands, to Contrive and try to begin to Support and maintain Religion among us.—We Therefore a number of us Cheerfully agreed to begin to persue what we b[e]lieve to be our duty Since we have felt and Experienced the goodness of God, for Raising and fiting one of our own Collour, to be Instrumental to build up the Cause and the Kingdom of our Lord Jesus Christ,—We therefore feel in Duty bound to Come to request You, to Come and Settle with us, and to take the Charge over us, and to live and die with us, in Conjunction with Brotherton, if it be agreable to them; So that we may enjoy all the Previlidges and Ordernances of the Gospel, Which our Saviour has left us in his Word.

So we the Subscribers Willingly to begin with twenty Shillings in the first year and to the proportion that we Shall increase in Number and Substance, All we Shall be able to Support you fully, so we have done at present what we fell to be our Duty, and the rest we will Submit to Gods Will and Pleasure—[13]

Joseph Sauquethquant
Hendrick Aupaumut
Joseph Quannekaunt
Peter Pohqunnuppeet
David Neshoonnahkah
John Pohpenon
John Baldwin

---

13. Occom visited the New Stockbridge and Brotherton communities several times before finally moving his permanent home among them in May 1789. This letter was drafted by Occom and the New Stockbridgers during his long visit to the region in the summer and fall of 1787, chronicled in his diary. During this same visit, residents of New Stockbridge and Brotherton cleared a homesite for Occom's family.

[CHS Folder 1.11; Occom's hand. Samson Occom Papers, Connecticut Historical Society, Hartford, Connecticut.]

II ∽ MOHICAN-STOCKBRIDGE AND BROTHERTON TRIBES TO ALL BENEVOLENT GENTLEMEN

New Stockbridge
Novr 28: 1787
Brotherton
Novr 29: 1787.

To all Benevolent Gentlemen, to who these following Lines may make their appearance.—

We who lately mov'd from Several Tribes of Indians in New-England, and Sitled here in Oneida Country.—And we also Mukheeconnuck Tribe, who lately Came from Housotonuck alias Stockbridge, and have sittled here in Oneida, And finding it our indispensible Duty to maintain the Christian Religion amongst ourselves in ^our^ Towns. And from this Consideration, Some of us disired our Dear Brother, the Revd Samson Occom, to give us a Visit, and accordingly, he Came up two years ago this Fall, and was here a few Days; and his preaching Came with great Weight upon our Minds.—And he has been here two Summers and Fall Since, And we must Confess to the Glory of God, that God has made him an Eminent Instrument amongst us, of a Great and Remarkable Reformation. And have now given him a Call to Settle amongst us, and be our Minister that we may enjoy the glorious Doctrines and ornances of the New Testament. And he has accepted our Call.—But we find our Selves very Weak, we can do but very little for him, And we want to have him live Comfortable.—

The late unhappy wars have Stript us almost Naked of everything, our Temporal enjoyments are greatly lessened, our Numbers vastly diminished, by being warmly engaged in favour of the United States.—Tho' we had no immediate Business with it, and our Spiritual enjoyments and Priviledges are all gone.—The Fountains abroad, that use to water and refresh our Wilderness and all Dryed up, and the Springs that Use to rise near are Ceased.—And we are truely like the man that fell among Theives, that was Stript, Wounded, and left half dead in the highway.[14]— And our Wheat was blasted, and our Corn and Beans were Frost bitten and kill'd this Year.—And our moving up here was Expencesive and these have brought us to great Necessity—And these things have brough us to a resolution to try to get a little help from the People of God; for the present; for we have determined to be independent as fast as we can, that we may be no longer troublesome to our good Friends.

---

14. *like the man that fell among Theives:* Refers to the New Testament story of the good Samaritan, Luke 10:30–37.

And therefore our most humble Request and Petition is, to the Friends of the Kingdom of Jesus Christ, Would take notice of us, and help us in encouraging our Dear Minister, in Communicating Such things that may Support him and his Family.—This is the most humble request and Petition of the Publicks true Friends & Brothers[15]

> *Elijah Wimpey*
> *David Fowler*
> *Joseph Shanquethquat*
> *Hendreck Aupaumut*
> *Joseph Quannekaunt*
> *Peter Pohquennuppeet*

[CHS folder I.11; Occom's hand. Samson Occom Papers, Connecticut Historical Society, Hartford, Connecticut.]

12 ⌇ SAMSON OCCOM, HENRY QUAQUAQUOD, ROBERT ASHPO, SAML ASHPO, JOHN SUPPER TO RICHARD LAW, ESQ.

Mohegan
Dec 5: 1789

Hon^d Sir

In our Overhalling the list of our Tribe we have found one Name that we Cannot find out where it came from. We find the Families of Mohegan and the Number of the Families and their Christian or given Names and Sir Names but there is one of Moses Mazzeens Family is Calld Ben but what Ben no Body can tell it is Moses Mazzeens Daughter Hannah's Son and he is Blacker than our Indians and he thinks he is from Guinny[16] partly—And the Whole Tribe objects against him and we cannot tell how his Name was put down among the Names of the Mohegan Tribe it may be this the inattention of the Tribe and now we object against his having Right amongst us—more over if he takes rite amongst us—not only guinney Children but European Children and some other Children will take rite also—and it will also give Liberty to our Daughters to borrow Children from all Quarters. And therefore we beg Your

---

15. Occom, Peter Pauquunnuppeet, and David Fowler carried this petition on a fund-raising tour of Philadelphia and New Jersey in January–February 1788. The visit is documented in Occom's diary and in his letter "To the Friends of Philadelphia," February 22, 1788.

16. *Guinny:* Guinea, a term describing the upper West coast of Africa also sometimes used in colonial America to describe African-Americans.

Hon^r would positively join us in our Objection and we desire your Hon^r to answere by a Line immediately that we may go on in our Division from[17]

> *your very Humb Serv^{ts}*
> *Samson Occom*
> *Henry his X mark Quaqudquod*
> *Robert his X mark Ashpo*
> *Saml Ashpo*
> *John his X mark Supper*

[CHS-M 0302. Samson Occom Papers, Connecticut Historical Society, Hartford, Connecticut.]

I3 ∾   ## BROTHERTON TRIBE TO THE
NEW YORK STATE ASSEMBLY

[January 1791]
To the Most Honorable Assembly in the State of New York Convend at [words missing]

Great and Good Brothers—

We your very poor and Miserable Brothers humbly beg leave to S[p]eak a few Words to you once more—You very well know, that our Brothers the Oneidas Mock'd and Deceivd us—They pretended to give us a [Tract] of Land, and we had much Trouble with them about it,—and finally they took it back again, except a little Spot, hardly big enough to Build a Wigwam on—Such a thing never was done amongst the Indians before—and you bought Some of that Land, which they gave us first—and You was so kind, Benevolent, and Mercyful to us, as freely to give us, that back, which you bought of them—For ^wich^ a Number of us are very thankful, from the Very bottom of our Hearts, for we were upon the Point of Quitting the Place, and move Some Where, we knew not where But that very Time, the Great Spirit above, put it in your Hearts to pitty us, and deliverd us from our Troubles, at that Time, and our poor Hearts were Glad, We Rejoiced, and Thought our Troubles were all over, and we Shoud have nothing to do but work on the Land Pleasure,—But alas, alas; ~~We have~~ Flods of Troubles, are Overwhelming us like Boistrous Seas in a ^great^ Storm—a great number of your People, and a Number of our People are Joining together to ruin and Destroy our Town Your People are Flatering, treating, and urging our distracted Indians, to lease Lands to them ~~to them~~, and our Crazy Indians have gone on, leasing Lands, without any regard, to old Substantial People, Without any regard to Rule or order—your People will even urge Boys ^Some in opposistion to their Fathers^ to lease Lands to them, and will take leases of any of them ~~and they will urge Boys in oposistions to their Fathers, and take leasese of them~~ Can

---

17. This petition reflects the ongoing controversy over the status of New England Indians of African descent. Tribal communities disputed the status of relationships between Native Americans and African-Americans and their children, often under the pressure of colonial policies that predicated the continuity of tribal land holdings on endogamous marriage.

this be wright? if this is Right, then not[hing] Can be wrong. We hear they have Least out 4000 A[cres] already, and they keep on ~~keep on~~ leasing now Daily,—only two Young Vagabon fellows, that never had any Settled place before, have leasd out one thousand Acres of Land or more And most of them that have been leasing Lands are poor Miserable lazy Drunken Creatures—(And ^most of^ these ^are^ Elijah Wampy's party ^them have Spent all^)—and he and his ~~party~~ ^& these^, regard not our proper Committee of ~~our~~ ^the^ Town and our Committee were the oldest Settlers, ^and oldest People^ and the most Sober Substantial Steady and Judicious People we have in the Town and ~~Elijah and his party~~ ^the aposit^ Dispise Disregard, and Laugh at the Good, kind, and Brotherly Laws, Instructions, and Directions given to us by the Great Assembly of New York State ^last Winter^—And now the White People have Come in amongst, We are all mingled together, their Children, Horses, Cattle, Hogs, and Dogs, are amongst us and ^we hear^ they begin to threten our Children; and they bring Rum, to Sell to our Indians too and Some of these Whites will Work on Sabbath Days—^this is the Example they Set us^ and We hear, how true it is we Cant Certainly Say, that if these Leases are broak ^by the Assembly^—they will kill the Damned Indians, before they will leave the Place—This in Truth is our Deplorable Situation—Some Times we think, we will ^now^ bundle up our [word illegible] and push off Some Where, for we Can not live so—But when we reconsider, we find ourselves, in Safety; we are under the Care and Protection of our good Strong Brothers, Who Will not Suffer, their poor Weak Brothers, to be abused and trampled under Foot, but will hear ^the^ Cries of their destressed Brothers, Most kind Brothers, as you have taken Notice, and heard the Complaints of other Indians, and helped them—So We most humbly beg, and Intreat, Your Benevolence, to help us, and deliver us from our Troubles ^only this once^, for it is in Your Power, only Speak a word and it Shall be done—And therefore our Most humble Request and Petition is—

That of your Goodness, Be so Compassionate as to Frustrate these most Distructive, Unrighighteous, and Unlawful Leases ~~and revoke~~ And we most humbly pray that you woud be so good as to revoke the Indulgence you granted to us, in allowing, and giving us Liberty to Lease Some Lands to the White People,—it has made a Number of your People, and a number of Indians perfectly Distracted, and we want, that these People, may Come to their right Sense and therefore, we request, that no Liberty may be given, for many Years—that our People may go to work as they out to do,[18]

[CHS folder I.13; Occom's hand. Samson Occom Papers, Connecticut Historical Society, Hartford, Connecticut.]

18. Between 1789 and 1791, a Brotherton faction led by Elijah Wampy leased thousands of acres of lands to white settlers, thus striking at the heart of the Brotherton endeavor. Occom carried this petition to the state assembly in January 1791. The assembly responded by passing "An Act for the Relief of the Indians Residing in Brothertown and New Stockbridge" on February 21, 1791, which vested powers to apportion and lease lots in an elected tribal council (Love, *Occom*, 287–289). See also letter 72, "Sorrow fills our Hearts" (1791).

SERMONS

Over the course of his thirty-year ministerial career, Samson Occom traveled and preached constantly: in England, Ireland, Scotland; in rural Massachusetts, Rhode Island, Vermont, Connecticut, New Jersey, Pennsylvania, and New York, as well as Philadelphia and New York City; among the Iroquois, Lenape, Stockbridge-Mahican, Pequot, Montaukett, and Shinnecock nations; to urban whites, blacks, and Indians; to Anglicans, Presbyterians, Baptists, Seventh-Day Baptists, Free Will Baptists, Moravians, Shakers, and Methodists, as well as the unchurched and the unbelieving. Except for his assignment to the Montaukett community at Long Island, his wintering seasons at home at Mohegan in the 1770s and 1780s, and his final years at Brotherton and New Stockbridge, he was a tireless itinerant who addressed his message to all comers: white, African American, and Native American. His diary suggests that Occom typically preached extemporaneously, working from a single scripture text and the guiding influence of the Spirit. Only twenty written sermons survive of the thousands he delivered between 1759 and 1792. These reflect his commitment to plain-style, Spirit-driven preaching: a commitment shaped by the demands of his itinerancy, his dedication to marginal and rural communities, and, especially in his later years, by his belief in a practical theology that could correct social and political ills and regenerate Native American communities.

The Great Awakening and the New Light evangelical movement strongly shaped Occom's preaching style. Occom was converted under the preaching of the infamous New Light radical James Davenport. He was trained at Moor's Indian Charity School by Davenport's brother-in-law, Eleazar Wheelock, also a committed New Light partisan penalized for his Great Awakening itinerancy. The Yale-educated Wheelock belonged to a cohort of ministers who abandoned the Anglicized and cosmopolitan elements of their training to adopt a simpler style reminiscent of seventeenth-century Puritanism: an "itinerant homiletics," as the religious historian Harry Stout has described it, which relied on a biblical text, sparely outlined points of application, and the influence of the Spirit to effect saving changes in the hearts of auditors. Especially in rural or marginal communities without established churches or settled ministers, itinerant preaching was characterized by urgency: it was the role of the preacher to serve as a conduit of the Spirit and the verbal instrument of immediate conversion, to create a spiritual opening amidst the chaos, dislocation, and confusion that characterized everyday life. Celebrity transatlantic evangelist George Whitefield, who perfected and exemplified this itinerant homiletics, was to Samson

Occom an affectionate and committed friend. Occom's diaries of his itinerancy, in turn, reflect the influence of his New Light friends and mentors. Occom faithfully characterizes his preaching by the degree of the Spirit he experienced and by the response of his audience, noting the occasions when God gave him "some sense of divine things" and "freedom of speech," or when audience members were "much affected" in their "tears" and "cries."

Although his training under Eleazar Wheelock prepared him to take his place among the entering class at Yale, Samson Occom developed his preaching style to answer the spiritual needs of broad and humble audiences, including the poor, African Americans, and Native Americans. Samuel Buell, a lifelong friend of Occom's who delivered the sermon at his ordination in 1759, offers an excellent description of this style:

> As the Matter of his Sermons is designed for the good of Souls, so his Way of Ex-
> pression is proper to that End. He uses great Plainness of Speech, and makes
> close Application of Truth to the Conscience; . . . this is not so agreeable to those,
> who are loth to have their Minds impressed with a just Sense of the Weight of
> Things eternal; nor so pleasing to them who form a Taste rather for the Flowers
> of Oratory, than for the substantial Food of the Sanctuary; yet 'tis that Method
> of preaching which is best adapted to do good to the Souls of Men . . . . Those,
> who have had Opportunity to observe, take Notice, that his Manner of Expres-
> sion, when he preaches to the *Indians*, is vastly more natural and free, clear and
> eloquent, quick and powerful, than 'tis wont to be, when he preaches to others.
> (viii–ix)

Wheelock also reported that Occom had a tremendous reputation among Native peoples as a powerful orator: "By the best Judges he is Said to be an excellent Speaker in his own Language[;] his Influence is great among the Indians."[1] By the time he traveled to England, Scotland, and Ireland on behalf of Moor's Indian Charity School between 1765 and 1768, Occom had developed greater confidence in his ability to preach before white audiences. One British observer reported that Occom "pleases in every Town & city—So much Simplicity appears in the man: So honest, guiles[s] a Temper, with Seriousness in his public Service."[2] Occom himself offered this assessment of his own preaching style in the preface to his *Sermon at the Execution of Moses Paul:*

> That the books that are in the world are written in very high and refined lan-
> guage, and the sermons that are delivered every Sabbath, in general, are in a very
> high and lofty stile so that the common people understand but little of them. But
> I think they can't help understanding my talk; it is common, plain, every-day
> talk: Little children may understand me. And poor Negroes may plainly and
> fully understand my meaning; and it may be of service to them. Again, it may in
> a particular manner be serviceable to my poor kindred the Indians.

1. DCA 765617.
2. Richardson 227.

Although he rejected "high and refined language," Occom also endorsed the use of effective metaphors in preaching, as had plain-style Puritan orators of the seventeenth century. For his part, Occom believed that Native communities, in particular, appreciated spiritual concepts presented through figurative or metaphorical language. He recommended texts like Benjamin Keach's *Tropologia: A Key to Open Scripture Metaphors* (1682) as most helpful for ministers like his brothers-in-law David and Jacob Fowler who spent their lives preaching among American Indians. His use of metaphor was remembered by the Rev. Daniel Waldo, who heard Occom preach extemporaneously in the 1770s at Franklin, Connecticut. "I was attracted, in company with many others, by his reputation as an Indian preacher, to hear him," Waldo recalled:

> His subject led him to speak somewhat at length of what he called a traditionary religion; and he told an anecdote by way of illustration. An old Indian, he said, had a knife which he kept till he wore the blade out; and then his son took it and put a new blade to the handle, and kept it till he had worn the handle out; and this process went on till the knife had had half a dozen blades, and as many handles; but still it was all the time the same knife.

Waldo described Occom's voice as "pleasant, but not very loud" and his "manner" as "serious and manly." "He was undoubtedly a man of much more than ordinary talents," Waldo concluded.[3]

Sermons preached during the early part of Occom's career, between 1759 and 1772, generally adhere to a classic Puritan formula: *opening* a scripture text through brief explication of contexts and aspects; announcing the *doctrine* presented within the text; proving this doctrine through numbered *reasons;* and concluding with improvements or *applications* designed to effect a saving change in audience members.[4] Occom's chosen scripture texts focus on the life of Christ and on the necessity of salvation. In an early sermon preached among the Montaukett on Long Island, Occom selected Ephesians 5:14, using extensive metaphors of "sleep" and "awakening" to convince his audience of the necessity of spiritual conviction and regeneration. This is the only written sermon known to have survived from his years at Montauk.

Occom preached more than three hundred sermons during his tour of England, Scotland, and Ireland as a fundraiser for Moor's Indian Charity School, from December 1765 to May 1768. His preaching won him approval and affection from the large crowds of British evangelicals who gathered to hear him: leading divines like George Whitefield, Martin Madan, and Andrew Gifford invited him to preach from their pulpits, while men and women of the working classes sent Occom admiring letters after his return to America. However, for Occom, who spent most of his career before 1765 preaching to majority Native communities, his British tour was a sometimes uncomfortable and alienating tutelage in European and Euro-American perceptions of Indians. "It Looks to me Some like a Dareing Presumtion, that I shou'd Stand before you this Day as a Teacher," he admitted in one of the three man-

---

3. Sprague 195.

4. For more on Puritan sermon formula, see Miller, ch.12; E. Elliot; Toulouse.

uscript sermons that survive from his English travels. "If it may be for Gods Glory and Honor, I think I am to ready to stand before you all, if it is only as a Spectical and a Gazing Stock." Years later, in a 1771 letter to Wheelock that criticized him for abandoning his commitment to Indian education, Occom remembered the experience more bitterly: "I was quite Willing to become a Gazing Stock, Yea Even a Laughing Stock, in Strange Countries, to Promote your Cause."

Occom's growing awareness of the racial dimension of his public office as a preacher shapes his best-known sermon: *A Sermon, Preached at the Execution of Moses Paul, an Indian.* Occom delivered the sermon at Paul's request, on the day of Paul's execution, September 2, 1772, before record crowds at the First Congregational Church in New Haven. This sermon, which appeared in nineteen eighteenth- and nineteenth-century editions and reprintings, including two Welsh-language translations in 1789 and 1827, was recovered to contemporary literary study by LaVonne Ruoff in 1992. Alongside Samuel Danforth's *A Brief Recognition of New-Englands Errand into the Wilderness* (1671) and Jonathan Edwards's *Sinners in the Hands of an Angry God* (1741), Occom's *A Sermon, Preached at the Execution of Moses Paul, an Indian* is a landmark of the American sermon tradition. As a variant of the American jeremiad, Occom's execution sermon was designed both to effect saving spiritual changes in the accused, Moses Paul, and to address general spiritual declension among the thousands who gathered to witness his execution.[5] Occom used his preaching to turn the spectacle of an Indian execution into an opportunity for indicting the inherent sinfulness of all people—white, black, and Native—and the specific spiritual destructions unleashed on indigenous communities by Euro-American influence. In *A Sermon, Preached at the Execution of Moses Paul,* Occom adapts a Euro-American genre to issue a major public statement about the spiritual consequences of colonialism.

Moses Paul (Wampanoag) had been convicted by a New Haven jury of the murder of Moses Cook, who was white, at a tavern in Bethany, Connecticut, on December 7, 1771. On June 7, 1772, ten days before Paul's originally scheduled execution, Jonathan Edwards, Jr., who had grown up at the Christian Indian mission town of Stockbridge and was fluent in the Housatonic-Mahican language, delivered a first execution sermon for Moses Paul at White Haven Church in New Haven. Taking as his text Psalms 55:23, "But thou, O God, shall bring them down into the pit of destruction: bloody and deceitful men shall not live out half their days; but I will trust in thee," Edwards offered redemption in Christ to the convicted Paul, but ultimately affirmed the justice of his sentence and the death penalty. Paul's execution was delayed by his appeals to the Connecticut General Assembly and the Superior Court, in which he alleged that racial bias had tainted his jury. On June 16, 1772, Paul wrote to Samson Occom, inviting him to give a second execution sermon: "Considering that we are of the same nation, I have a particular desire that you should preach to me upon that occasion."[6] On September 2, 1772, Occom preached from Romans 6:23: "The wages of sin is death." Using sin as a leveler of racial and class distinctions,

5. See Bosco, "Lectures" and *Humiliation.*
6. Chamberlain, 445.

Occom used the execution as an occasion to convict all present—"Indians, English, and Negroes"—as sinners in need of redemption. Without excusing Paul's assault on Moses Cook, Occom acknowledged that he had been unfairly tried. He also used the occasion to speak directly to the Native people who had gathered for the occasion. Exhorting Native people to temperance, Occom aligns discourses describing the destructive effects of alcohol introduced to Native communities by colonialism with the nature of sin itself. His parallel rhetoric implied that in the fallen world wrought by colonialism, Native peoples might save their lives through collective spiritual regeneration.

The short final section of the sermon concerning Native people and alcohol attracted a disproportionate share of public curiosity. On November 6, 1772, a broadside entitled "Mr. Occom's Address to his Indian Brethren, On the Day that Moses Paul, and Indian, was executed at New-Haven, on the 2d of September 1772, for the Murder of Moses Cook" was advertised in the *Connecticut Journal & New Haven Post-Boy*. A 1773 edition of this broadside appeared from the press of Thomas and John Fleet at the Heart and Crown in Boston. It was not composed by Samson Occom. Instead, it features a loose verse rendition of Occom's concluding temperance appeal:

> *'Tis Drunkennes, this is the Sin you know,*
> *Has been and is poor Indians overthrow . . .*
> *We've nothing valueable to our Praise,*
> *And well may other Nations on us gaze;*
> *We have no Money, Credit or a Name,*
> *But what this Sin does turn to our great Shame.*

In excerpting Occom's advice to his Native audience and omitting the broadly applicable portions of the execution sermon, especially Occom's insistence on the leveling power of sin, this verse broadside appealed to and perpetuated familiar stereotypes of Indian alcoholism. The execution of Moses Paul was not the first time in New England that Native peoples had been brought to the gallows as models of the wages of alcoholism.[7] Occom himself had been accused of alcohol misuse in 1769. (A subsequent inquest by Presbyterian Church officials cleared him of the charges.) In his condemnation in the *Sermon, Preached at the Execution of Moses Paul* of alcohol as a force destructive to Native communities, Occom did not appeal to stereotypes of Native peoples as particularly susceptible to alcohol. Instead, he positioned his voice among the voices of leaders throughout eighteenth-century Indian Country—for example, the Delaware prophet Neolin—who urged Native peoples to save their own lives by refusing alcohol.[8]

The Sermon, Preached at the Execution of Moses Paul marks a turning point in the ministerial career of Samson Occom: the first recorded occasion when Occom

---

7. See Samuel Danforth, *The Woful Effects of Drunkenness, A Sermon Preached at Bristol, Octob. 12, 1709. When Two Indians, Josias and Joseph, were Executed for Murther, Occasioned by the Drunkenness both of the Murthering & Murthered Parties* (Boston, 1710).

8. On Native temperance movements, see Mancall, *Deadly*, 101–129.

speaks as a Native minister to Native audiences about specifically Native American issues. It represents the culmination of a difficult season of soul-searching for Samson Occom, which began after his return from England in 1768 and continued until his break with Eleazar Wheelock in July 1771. During these years at Mohegan, Occom reckoned with and actively sought to resolve crippling political factionalism within his home community. He watched Wheelock abandon the Native mission of Moor's Indian Charity School and move the school to Hanover, New Hampshire, in 1770. His troubled eldest son, Aaron, once a pupil of Wheelock's, died in February 1771. Occom grappled with his relationship to the missionary societies and established churches that directed his early career. He emerged from this period with a renewed political vision and a strengthened resolve to serve Native communities and to use his growing celebrity to advance their concerns. Even as demand for his preaching grew in the months after the execution of Moses Paul, and invitations came in from dissenting and separatist church communities throughout New England, Occom prioritized Native causes. Six months after he preached at the gallows of the Wampanoag Paul, in March 1773, Occom attended the first organizational meetings of the Brotherton movement at Mohegan. *The Sermon, Preached at the Execution of Moses Paul*, then, marks Occom's public emergence as an intertribal spiritual and political leader.

Occom's decision to redefine his pastoral role in the face of political turmoil shared in a broader politicization of the American ministry in the 1770s. The American Revolution caused New England ministers especially to reflect on their responsibilities to guide their congregations by maintaining a steady narrative perspective on history. Political instability caused many ministers to experience for the first time a crisis of confidence in their ability to steadfastly interpret God's role in historical events, a crisis of confidence that, in turn, engendered changes in preaching styles and guiding theological concerns. As Donald Weber has observed, some preachers adopted more fragmentary, practical preaching styles; others dedicated themselves to patriot exhortation; and still others, like the New Divinity men, retreated into speculative dispensationalist history or the highly technical theology of human affections and volition. Occom responded differently to the troubled times of the revolutionary and early national eras. Surviving sermons show that in his later years Occom developed a more elaborate and politicized preaching style centered around a Christian indigenist worldview. He did not uncritically endorse the patriot cause, nor did he retreat into technical theology. Rather, he developed a strand of practical or applied theology that correlated sin with European colonialism and held up Native communities as exemplars of brotherly love, generosity, piety, and sexual morality.

According to Occom, European colonists introduced alcohol, sexual promiscuity, usury, slavery, and profanity to North America. Occom maintained strong antislavery beliefs and preached frequently against slaveholding during the 1780s, when antislavery sentiment was not widely vocalized even among New England clergy. In 1787, he preached:

What Shall we say of you or think of you, or what do you think of yourselves; You that are Slavekeepers, do you Love God, and do you Love your Neighbour, your Neighbour Negroe as Yourself, are you willing to be Slaves yourselves, and your Children to be Slaves too . . . I must Conclude, that Slavekeepers must keep Slaves against their own Light and understanding and they that will keep Slaves and plead for it, are not Neighbours to anyone, and Consequently they are not Lovers of God, They are no Christians, they are unbelievers, yea they are ungenteel, and inhumane.

Occom condemned ministers who participated in what he called the "fashionable practice" of slaveholding and recommended that churches refuse to admit or keep communion with slaveholders. In 1792, Occom accused Europeans of introducing venereal diseases to indigenous peoples in America and the South Pacific and prophesied "Don't you think these Heathen Indians will rise up against ^you^ at the last Day not only for this Sin but for many others also?" These later sermons by Samson Occom document his decisive break with the ministerial model and mission of Eleazar Wheelock, his awareness of his unique situation as a person of color with significant public authority, and his willingness to use this authority to condemn the inhumanity and evil of empire.

Although he preached throughout his itinerancy to white and mixed-race audiences, Occom's public preaching mission was defined by his relationship to Native American communities. When Occom passed through small towns and rural settlements in his frequent travels between Mohegan, Connecticut, and Brotherton, New York, audiences of both the faithful and the curious flocked to hear the famous Indian minister. Occom's diary shows that he relied on a healthy sense of humor to reclaim his humanity from being made a racialized "gazing stock." On October 9, 1785, near Stillwater, New York, he stopped at a private home to seek a horse to take him to a preaching appointment. The man of the house "asked me Whether I was going to hear the Strange Mi[ni]ster." Occom continues the story: "I told [the man] I Suppose I Should hear him, and then told him, the People Could not See that Strange Creature till I get there, and then he asked me whether it was I that they expected I told him Yes." With his sense of irony and his open criticism of colonialism as a sin, Occom subverted his audiences' appetite for racial spectacle. In his final years, after his family moved to Brotherton in 1789, Occom reduced his itinerancy and took his place as the settled minister for the Brotherton and New Stockbridge communities, where he preached in English, relying sometimes on Hendrick Aupaumut or Peter Pauquunnuppeet to translate for his non-English-speaking congregants. Because Occom's manuscript sermons are undated, it is impossible to know which sermons he may have preached in these Native congregations. Yet his diaries and letters from these later years demonstrate that to the end of his life Occom was dedicated to speaking words to Native audiences that could touch their hearts, redeem their difficult circumstances, and contribute to their collective spiritual well-being.

I ∞   **"SAYING WHAT THINK YE OF CHRIST" (I),**
                   MATTHEW 22:42 (1759)

1759
Matthew XXII.42

Saying what think ye of Christ

you may Remember ^in^ that many Questions were Brought to our Blessed Saviour
by Sevaral Sort of People, on Porpose to Entangle him,—but he Answeared them as
fast as they Bro't them, to there Astonishment Shame and Confusion,—and at last
he Put this Question to them, which is the most important Question in the Law and
Gospel, &c. all that I shall say from this Text is to ^give^ a short History of Christ
as he was yᵉ Promised Missiah under yᵉ old Dispensation, ~~a~~ and how yt ~~he was~~
^report^ received in the world—

> and Secondly I Shall Say I Shall Say Somthing of his Conception,
> and Thirdly I Some thing of his Birth,—
> And Fourthly Somthing of his Childhood—
> And 5ˡʸ I Shall Say Something of his Publick appearance in the world,
> and 6ˡʸ his accusation Conⁿ Ignominious Death his burial Resurrection & Acention

[CHS folder I.21; CHS-M 408–409. Samson Occom Papers, Connecticut Historical Society, Hartford,
Connecticut.]

2 ∞   **"AWAKE THOU THAT SLEEPEST,"**
                   EPHESIANS 5:14 (1760)

Montauk May ye 15 1760
Eph. 5.14

Wherefore he Saith awake thou that Sleepest and arise from the Dead and Christ
Shall give thee Light—

We may at once Perceive from these words, the Infinite goodness and Condesention of God towards us Rebeles for we have willfully Departed from god our
Maker and in Departing from him, we Depart from our own Hapiness yea we forfit
all Blessedness and every mercy, and we Can Claim nothing at the Hands of god Better than Damnation, and god might have Justly left us in our misery with everlasting
Shame and Confusion of Face, and when he had thoughts of mercy he might have
By us and Placed his love on the fallen Angels who are greater in Powcr than men
they are likelyer to Serve him Better than we: But behold his Mercy is towards the
fallen Children of Adam, and there is no other Reason Can be given Why he does
^so^, but this because he will have Mercy on whom he will have Mercy and he will
have Comp^a^ssion on whom he will have Compassion—and this his Pity to us, is
brought about in a way that Men or Angels Cou'd never find out or invent, it must
needs be in and thro' the Death of his only begoten Son here is unparallel'd Love
that God so Loved the World that he gave his only begoten Son into the World that

Whosoever believeth in Shall not Perish but have everlasting Life,[9] this is good News good News unto Miserable Children of fallen A[10]; that there is a Saviour given amighty Saviour—

and in further Speaking upon ~~these~~ ^this^ text I Shall Endeavour, as god Shall help to give the Import of it, in Several Perticulars—

and here first In general

It Plainly Implys, that man as he is fallen Creature from God, is fallen A Sleep Spiritually, he is Stupified ^thereby^ yea he is fallen Down Dead in Traspasses and in Sins——

And here I Shall endeavour to repre[t] two Sorts of People ^yt are^ in the World, and Distinguish them one from the other—the one is Believer, and ~~up~~ unbeliever, Yet Both are a Sleep,

The one is in a ~~Dead~~ Sleep, yet not in a Dead Sleep but it is a Sinful and abominable Sleep

The other is in a Dead Sleep a very Dangerous Sleep, they Lie exposd to everlasting Distruction by it—

But Secondly

This text Plainly represents unto us the Infinite Mercy of God to us; in Sending his own Dear Son to a wake us out of this Dangerous yea Distructive Sleep—

And lastly I Shall Conclude with the Improvement of the Wh^o^le

and here first—there is Such a thing as Believers being a Sleep and when they are So, they are unfit to Serve god, Yea they are Disobeying and Dishonouring of him—We Read of ten Virgens, in Mat[h] 25[11] that were Slumbering and Sleeping While the Bridegroom Taried till there was a great Cry or a Loud Call made, unto them, it Seems in Such a Language as this awake thou yt Sleepest and a Rise from the Dead ~~and Christ~~ for behold the Bridegroom Cometh go ye out to Meet him. and then when they heard this ~~Voice~~ Heavenly Voice, and understood it they emediately Rose with great Confusion and Trembling, it Seems and when they Come to look about themselves they ^found^ every thing out of order, their Lamps were unprepard they were gone out, altogether unfit to Meet the Bridegroom With—and Now there is every thing to do—and a very Short time to do it for the foreruner or the Voice of the Bridegrom is already interd into the Ears of the Virgens, he yt hath behold I Come quickly and my reward is with me to give every on an according as his Works Shall be—is now on his Way, Just at the Doors, to [reccond?] With the Virgins—O! me think there was great exercise of heart and mind among the Virgins at that Season—

and further to Ellustrate this Point of Trust, let us Compare Spiri[l] Sleep with Natural Sleep & See What resemblence there may be—and how, we know by experience and observation, that a man that is a Sleep is altogether unfit for Business at yt Season he is not Doing the least Business for him self for his Relations or his Neighbours or his King for he has Desisted and lay'd aside all Business while he Sle^e^ps—

---

9. *God so Loved the World:* John 3:16.
10. *fallen A:* Adam.
11. See Matthew 25:1–13.

So is a Christian when he is Spiritually a Sleep—

again When a man is a Sleep he is Ignorant and Sinceless of all the Carryings ^on and^ [word illegible] the World he is Ignorant of the agreable Conversation that his Neighbours have, the News from a Broad has no Affect upon him, he has no fellow feelling with his Neighbours either ^in^ Joy or Sorrow So is a Sleepey Christian. he knows not What a Sweet Conversation they Enjoy one with the other ^yt one awake^ What Trade they Cary on to Heaven, and what return they have from yt Blessed Cou^n^try, and What Fellows^h^ip Communion they have with god, or what fellowship they have one with other nor what Joys or Sorrows they meet with in their Travil—like unto Thomas &c[12]—

the means of grace have but little effect on the them—

Again a man yt is a Sleep is Defenceless, he is exposd to many Dangers he is liable to be taken by his Enemies—a solder must Watch

So is a Chr^n yt is a Sleep—they are liable to all Dangers— — — Watch and Pray—

again a man yt is a Sleep may Dream Dreams, they may have Pleasent, and frightful Dreams they may Dream of Prosperity and Peace—of Adversity and Sorrow— —

So may a Chris^n Dream many things

Now let us Bring Peter as an Instance, one yt has Slept, and See What was the fruit of his Sleep, and Also one yt has awaked out ^of^ this Sleep and What was ye fruit of it[13]

Now let us Consider the State of those yt are in a Dead Sleep—those that are unregenerate are in a Dead Sleep, Dead in Traspasses & in Sins, a very Dangerous Sleep, they are liable to all the Miseries of this life to Death it Self and to the Pains of Hell forever, and in this State and Condistion it is Impossable for them to Please god, for they have no life of Godlyness therefore they Can't do the Work of god Acceptably, they are Dead and So all their Heroices are Dead by Reason of Sin,—they have no Since of god, they have no right apprihentions of heaven or Hell, they have no fear of God, and no love to him, no love to his Word no love to his ordernaces, nor to his Commandments Laws or his Precepts yea they have Rellish for Divine things, Spiritual things are foolishness with them, the Voice of Charmers from Christ Charming Never So Wisely unto them in the Tender Bowels of Compassion move them not, and the Dreadful Thunders and Lightnings of gods Firery Law from Mount Sinai,[14] Don't make them afraid and the goodness and Mercy of god, yt Daily attends Don't Lead them to repentence, and the Judgments of God Don't make to Consider—All the Reason is because they are in ^a^ Dead Sleep, they have no heart for Heart for god or ^to^ his ways Doesn't this greatly argue the Stupidity and Deadness in Such

12. Thomas Didymus was absent when the resurrected Jesus appeared to his disciples. Not until Christ appeared again eight days later and showed him the wounds in his hands and sides was Thomas convinced of the resurrection. See John 20:19–29.

13. According to Luke 9:28–36, Peter, James, and John accompanied Jesus to the Mount of Transfiguration, but were asleep during his vision of Moses and Elias and his transfiguration. The three disciples awoke to see Jesus in his "glory" (Luke 9:32).

14. *Mount Sinai:* Mountain where God revealed the Ten Commandments to Moses (Exodus 31:18).

Souls——— and Consequently Such are in a very Danger Sleep they Liy upon very Slippery Places[15] they are liable to be Cut asunder every Moment by the Justice of God, the ax is layd to the Roott of every Tree, and every Tree yt bringeth not good fruit Shall be hewn Down and Cast in to everlasting Fire[16]— —

And Secondly and lastly this Text Represents unto us the Astonishing Love and Condesention of the Great God whose Name alone is Jehovah, in Sending his own Son into the World, after our Willful apostasie from God, that whosoever believeth in him Shou'd Perish but have everlasting Life— — here is Love indeed god ^freely^ gave his Dear Son to Sinners to Save them, and the Son freely excepts and undertakes the great work Redemption the Dear Lamb of God Leaves the Bosom of his Dear Father As it were bids farewell to all the Heavenly Hosts, and comes Down to their benighted World Cloathed with Humane Body like our own—took upon him the Iniquity of the Child[r] of men—became the Son of man that we the Sinful Child[r] of men might become the Sons of the living god—he Layd Down his Life and Died the acursed Death of the Cross yt we might be made Alive unto God—all this was done to awak those yt were Sleep, and to Raise that were Dead

2ly this Text Promises a glorious Promise of Light to them yt hear ^& obey^ the Voice of X[17] Awak those yt Sleepeth X a Rise from the Dead and X Shall give thee Light—

To Conclude

let us Improve the Whole and here first is it so as we have heard, that there is Such a thing as Chris[ns] Slumbering and Sleeping—first then examine yourself and if thou ^art^ Sleeper, ~~arise~~ hear the Voice of Christ, and obey, Arise and Trim your Lamps, and X Shall give you Light,—for all thy Work is to do and behold the Bri^d^groom Cometh. go ye out to meet him awake by a true repentance and arise by faith in Christ Hear ye Voice of God in his Word, in the Preach'd go[s18]

In his Laws Precepts and Comands—
In the gospel Institutions and ordernances—
to the Wicked
In the Curses of God Law—
In the Meltyng Invitation of ye Gospel— —
In ye Creation— —
In the Providence of god
In Mercy—in health & Prosper[t]
In Judgments, Sickness &c

O! Sleeper isn't here Enough to awake you, hear the Voice of X in these things, and arise from all Sin to Righteousness, from all ye fruits of ye Flesh to the Fruits of the Spirit, Gal 5.22 1 Cor 6.9

---

15. *Liy upon very Slippery Places:* God is praised for setting the wicked in precarious or "slippery places" (Psalms 73:18).

16. *every Tree yt bringeth not good fruit:* See Matthew 3:10, Matthew 7:19, Luke 3:9.

17. *X:* Christ.

18. *go[s]:* gospel.

Back-Sliders awake and a Rise—Luke 15[19]

and ye all Receive the Promise of Glorious Light, of Life and light at last to the Heavenly Jerusalem.

[DCA Vault. Courtesy of Dartmouth College Library.]

3 ∿   ## "TURN YE TURN FROM YOUR EVIL WAYS," EZEKIEL 33:11 (1765)

Goshen 1765[20]
Ezek 33:11

Turn ye turn ye from your Evil Ways, for Why will ye, O House of Israel—

The Whole design of the ^word^ of god is, to turn ~~him~~ ^a Sinner^ from Satan to god, from Sin to holiness, from the Kingdom of Satan to the Kingd^m of God—

In Speaking to these Words I Shall endeavour to Show Several particulars, that are Implyd and express'd in this text—

I It plainly Implys y^t man as he is a Sinner by Nature, is departing from god, in his degeneracy he is gone from his Innocency, has lost the Blessed Image of God he is gone from his love to god—he is departed from the Covenant of god—he is gone far from the Commands of god—He is Strayd from his obedience—He is Gone from his Sweet Devotions to God—He is gone from the Delight of Prayer to god—from Praise—from adoration—from Thanksgiving from Self Dedication and resignation—and as he is departed from god his Chief good—he is now placing his Affection upon Vanity—&c—

II Our text Implys, that as man is Departing from god, He is in Deaths Road the Way that they go is the way of Death to Soul & Body and they are not only in ye Way of Death, but are Spiritually Dead, they are dead to god, they have no activity towards him in a way of Love and obedience, Yet activity Enough and Enough against him, they are Dead to Communion and Enjoyment of God, they are Dead to the worship of god, they ^have^ no delight ^in^ Prayer, either in Sacred Privet or Publick, if they atend upon Some Religious Duties—they are very Cold heavy and Dead Exercises,—they are dead to the Law of god, that is, they have no Sence of the Holiness, Justness and Goodness of God's Law,—they are not Senceable, that they are under Condemnation of the Law of God, and that the Curses of the Law are out against them—They are so dead, the Thunders of Mount Sinaih, acompanied with Earth Quake, and Lighting that flashes in their Consciences, don't move them,—they are in Such love with Sin they are drunk and Stupifyed with it, and they will go on in the Practice of them, tho' God Says, in Plain plain terms the Soul yt Sins Shall die, and again Cursed is every one that Continues in all things Writen in the Book of the Law to do there—again Sinners ^y^t^ will run the Downward Road, they must Die a Miserable Death as to their their Bodies and Souls—they must be cast

---

19. *Luke 15:* A reference to the parable of the prodigal son, Luke 15:11–32.
20. *Goshen:* Probably Goshen, Connecticut.

from the Glorious Presence of god—and from evry good,—to Hell and to all Evil—
to all Eternity—

~~III Our text expressly tells us that Sinners Will their own Death, Why Will ye die~~
Again they are Dead to the Sweet Calls of the gracious Gospel of Jesus X they
have no Sence of the amazing Condesention of god in Christ, nor the Way of Salva-
tion in him—They are Dead to Heaven and Heavenly Things, the Blessedness of
Heaven—They are Dead to Hell, ie, They have no Sence of the Torments of Hell &c—
III God tells us, that Sinners Will their Death, Why Will ye Die, Saith God,—

The Way Which Sinners take is the way of Death, and it is their Voluntary
Choice, they are not forced to it by God, and neither are they Drag'd to by the
Devil—but it is their free Will & act—Adam acted Voluntarily ^in^ What he did—

IV God expressly tells us in our text and Context, that he has no Pleasure in the
Death of a Sinner, but y^t he turn and Live—God Wills the Life and Eternal Salvation of Poor Sinners turn ye turn ye for Why Will ye Die—God is Sincere, Hearty,
and Earnest in his Will, it is plainly to be Seen and under Stood by Word, which in
his Revealed Will to the Children,—in particular his amazing Will to Save Sinners—
^is^ to be Discoverd in his Sending his Dearly Beloved and only Begoten Son into
this World in a^mazing^ Manner as he Did—God from Eternity ^[willed make?]^ to
man—and he knew, Man woud Will his own Death, But god Willd his Salvation,
and god Calld a Councill in the Court of H[21] upon his Will, ~~in~~ the Days of Eternity,—
and me thinks here, we may Imagin to hear the Eternal Jehovah begining (the Heavenly Hosts being Silent and attentive) thus my Will is to make man In our Likeness
and Image,—But I know he will, Will his Death and Distruction—But I Will his
Salvation and Eternal Life,—But then, the Query ^was^ Put to the Heavenly
Worlds—Whom Shall I Send, Who will go for us—methinks the Heavenly Hosts
were Silent— — —They look upon one another— — unable to Answer Such Important Ques— — Till at Length the Lamb of God Stood forth and Answerd the
Eternal Question,—Saying ^Lord I Come^ it is Writen ~~in the Volume~~ of me in the
Volume of thy Book of Eternal Decrees I Delight to do thy Will O God,—thy Will be
done—Thy Will is my Will—Send me, and I Will go—here me thinks the Heavens
Shouted—Saying Worthy is the Lamb, to take ^ye^ Book and to Lose the Seven Seals
thereof[22]—and in the fullness of time God made man and gave him Will—his Will
was to keep his Commands for his Life and happiness forever—

But man woud not keep god's but he took his own Will, and Will'd his own
Death—But god reveald his gracious Will to him—Promisd him a Saviour from ^y^t^
time he raisd his Servants the Prophets rising Early and Sending them to Proclaim
his ~~Will~~ god Will to the Children Concerning the Mesiah—And in the fullness of
Time he did Send his Send his Son into this World—he layd a Side as it it were the
Robes of Glory, took leave of Heaven &—-Enters into this World, with a Body like
our own &c ^was an [two words illegible]^—and was here till he finish'd his great
work &c——

21. *H:* Heaven.
22. See Revelation 5:1–5.

Improvement——

Is it so as we have heard, that man by [word illegible] Strayd Creature and in a way of Death, and is not this Case with many of you in this Asembly——

Doleful Condition——

Yet hark ye hear God Calling after ye to return to him,——turn ye turn ye from your Evil ways and Querying With you for Why will ye die O of O House of Israel, give^n^ Why you Chuse to Die, you y^t^ are of the Christian Church has not god done Enough han't X Sufferd Enough han't you means Sufficient, is not Heaven Desirable—and the Company of God—and of Angels

and the Blessed Eternity—you old—Why—
has not God been Sending his Dear Servants[23]

[DCA Vault. Courtesy of Dartmouth College Library.]

4 ∽   "FIGHT THE GOOD FIGHT OF FAITH,"
1 TIMOTHY 6:12 (JULY 13, 1766)

1 Timothy 6.12

It is greatly to be observd, y^t^ Christianity is Compared, almost to every Temporal Concern of Man,

The Infinite Condesention of god is to be Seen herein, that he Shoud Level his Languge to Weak Capacities

and amongst innumerable Texts of Scripture our Text is wherein Christianity is ^fitly^ Com^d^ to a Warfare—now a Warefare is one of the greatest ^Concerns^ of this World and it is a great Concern in a Kingdom [Every] one is Concernd in it or ought to be,——

So Christianity ought to be ye Greatest and universal Concern of all Mankind of all Ranks and Degrees——

And Since the Holy Ghost has Compared his Works to our Worldly Concerns, we will Endeavour to follow his Teachings, by Comparing the Spiritual Warfare with Carnal Warfare

and here first, in a Carnal Warfare there is a Regular ^method^ to be taken &c

1   there must be a regular inlestment,——
2   a Sodier y^t^ inlest Swears a Leagiance to be true to his King
3   he forsakes all and ventures his Life in the Service

23. In this sermon, Occom takes up the theological question of the will—both the will of the individual and the will of God. Occom acquired a copy of Jonathan Edwards's *Enquiry into the Freedom of the Will* (1754) in 1760. (This book is now in the possession of the Pennypacker Long Island Collection of the East Hampton Library.) The will was also a personal preoccupation for Occom, as is reflected in his December 6, 1765, letter to Eleazar Wheelock, written on the eve of his departure for England: "I want nothing but the Will of God, to be Wholly Swallowed up in it."

4 he has rite and title to all the Provistions y^t the King has made for that purpose &c ye army is [bountyful?]

5 he Stands ready to obey all orders. ~~Stands~~ and having understood his Business he is ready to fight at the word of Command—

his Enemies many and Crafty and therefore he ought to Watch his Enemies are
Chiefly these the World the Flesh and the Devil &—
and there Some Certain Seasons when these Enemies are Busy

Inference

1 So as we have heard y^t there is a ^Spiritual^ warfare, and have you Inlested yr
Selves, how long Since you have been in this Service,—What Victories have you
obtaind—if you are the fighters be Couragious, fear not the faces of your Enemies
follow your Captain Who [two words illegible], have faith in him at all times—

2 let them that have never Inlested u^n^der the great Capt of our Salv—now be
persuaded to I

[DCA Vault; dated London, July 13, 1766 by William Allen. Courtesy of Dartmouth College Library.]

5 ∾ ## "In Christ, he is a new creature,"
2 Corinthians 5:17 (July 13, 1766)

London July 13 1766
2 Corinth 5:17
Therefore if any man be in xJ he is a new Creature: &c.

Regeneration is a doctrine much Dispised by ma^n^y, but it is a Doctrine of the
Bible, and therefore it is a Supstantial Doctrine, it is a Spiritual Doctine, and it is not
to be understood but by Spiritual understanding—I believd ^it is^ generally own'd
by those, who belived the Bible to be the word of God that we must be good some
how before we are fit to go to Heaven, and this is good Reasoning, for if we believe
Heaven to be a good Place we must be good, if it be a Holy place, we must be Holy,
if it be a pure Place, we must be pure, if it be Spiritual, we must Spiritual, or else we
can't Enjoy Heaven, yea if god be Holy, we must be holy in order to Serve him here
and in the world to come, or in other words, to Enjoy him in this World and in the
World to come—

We are ready to Conclude, that a poor Beggar, in his filthy, Ragged Garments, is
not fit to go into the Kings Palace and to Serve him there, and we Shou'd not ^like^
a Swine, in his filth to Dwell in our Houses; So an unholy Man is no man fit to Enter
into Heaven, the Habitation of God,—

And therefore we must be holy, and god has found out away for us to become
holy, and it is by being in Christ—

Now if any man be in Christ he is a New Creature, old things are passed away,
and behold all things are become new—

In further Speaking upon these words I Shall Endeavour to show by the Help of
God—

1 What it is to be ^in^ Christ—
2 Such are new Creatures
3 to Such all old thing are done away and all thing are become anew
1 Then What it is to be in Christ, to be in x is to be united to him by a living Faith, in other words to believe and receive Jx as he is offer'd in the gospel to be the only Sutable Saviour, to rely upon him for what he has done—to ^be^ in xJ, is to have the Image of Jx reinstampt in us and to have his Spirit in us, Yea to be in Christ is to have Christ Dwelling in us, and we in him—
2 They yt are in Christ Jesus are new Creatures they are Created anew in Christ Jesus, they dont only have Names but have new Dispositions—

[DCA Vault; herb recipe written on back page: "2 ou Consome of Roses, 1 ou of [word illegible] Balsam, 1/1 an ou of [word illegible]—all pounded in a Mass—take a piece as big as a Nut Meg every Mg and Night fasting." Courtesy of Dartmouth College Library.]

6 ❧   "SAYING WHAT THINK YE OF CHRIST" (II),
MATTHEW 22:42 (1766–1768)

Matthew 22:42
Saying What think ye of Christ

It Looks to me Some like a Dareing Presumtion, that I Shou'd Stand before you this Day as a Teacher, What Can I Say to you, you that are highly Priviledg'd of the Lord of Hosts, to Whom God has done great and Marvelous things, you tha[t] are Lifted Within Sight of Heaven, as it were, in Point of Gospel Blessings, and you that are refin'd with Literature and kinds of Sciences Who am I Shoud that I Stand Stand before this Great Congregation this Day, I [that] am but ^a^ Babe in Religion that begun to think of it, as it were but Yesteday, ~~and~~ imperfect every way, I shall but Betray my Profound Ignorance in Speaking ~~to~~ before you— ~~And what Shall do,~~ for I have not the Wisdom of the Wise nor Knowledg of the Learned nor Eloquence of ~~the~~ an Oratour—but I Wish Coud with Propriety Say to any one Poor Impotent Soul in this great Congregation, as Peter Said to a Poor Criple, Silver and Gold have I none But Such as I have give thee In the Name of Jesus Christ of Nazareth, Rise up and Walk[24]

Indeed Sirs, When I thus Consider with my Self I am ready to wish my self in the Meanest Corner of the House of God, if there is any Such Place, to attend with Silence and Proud humiliation, and Sh^o^u'd Esteeme it an Inestimable Privilege to Join with the People of God in his Divine Worship

Yet Since, God in ^his^ Misterious, yea almost Meraculous Providence, has taken me from the Dung Hill, and from Heathenish Darkness and Gross Idolatry,— to this Sacred Desk,[25] in this very before you, and before the Eternal Jehovah,—if it may be for Gods Glory and Honor, I think I am ~~to~~ ready to Stand before you all,

24. *Silver and Gold have I none:* Acts 3:2–10.
25. *Sacred Desk:* Pulpit.

if it is only as a Spectical and a Gazing Stock,[26] But by the Importunity of Some Friends—I am willg Willing to gratify you all, and Presuming the Candor of ~~the Whole~~ this Assembly, I Will ^now^ freely begin with the Text, with out any further Apology,—

And here I have Chosen an inexhaustable Text ^no Doubt you have heard^ which represents the ^very^ Life and Marrow of the Christian Religion, the Very Centre of the Whole Bible

John V.39

our Text Contains the ^greatest^ Question in the Christian Religion—Life Everlasting is the reward to them that Answeres it right but Eternal Death to them that won't Answere it right

But to make a way for the Text let us Consider the ocation of this Important Question—You may Remember, that Several Crafty Questions were Proposed to our Blessed by Different Sorts of People, to Intangle him, but they were taken in their own Traps and were Confounded, & While the Pharasees were gathered together, Jesus took an oppertunity to Propose unto them this one great and most Important Question, Which was Contain'd in their Religion, Saying What think ye of Christ Whose Son is he, they Said the Son of David, &c

Hear we may Plainly See, ~~how~~ what a Restless thing Mans mind is—how Busy were these thoughts of these Men about Christ,—Mans thoughts are always upon a go, In Some object or other, it is Like a Living Spring that runs Continually; and Indeed it is this that Distinguishes him from the Beasts of the Field;—But all the objects of thought Christ Shou'd be the only object of ^our^ Meditation

But man is far Degenerated that his thoughts are Continually runing other objects, upon Creature, more than upon the Creator,—how apt are men ^in^ ~~to~~ our Day, to Inquire after News and if any ^remarkable^ thing is done by our Fellow Men, how ready are we to Aplaud and Admire Such a one, as in our Day, Christ has greatly Honord, the King of Prussia in Rising him, to Humble his Enemies, how is he admird every where,[27] but it is ^to^ be feard Christ is forgot by many, he Shoud be our admiration and give him the Praise for it is he yt has done ~~this~~ all these these things by his Servant, indeed Sirs Caesar ought to have his Due

All that I Shall have to do with this Text is, to See What Different opinions there has been about Christ in all Ages, Both under the old and New Testament, and in doing of Which I Shall give you Short Acount of X According to Scripture

1 as he was the Promised Missiah,
2 as he was Actually Conceived and Born into the World

---

26. *Spectical and a Gazing Stock:* Occom here describes his experience touring England as a fundraiser for Moor's Indian Charity School. In a letter to Eleazar Wheelock dated July 24, 1771, Occom remembered the tour in almost identical terms: "I was quite Willing to become a Gazing Stock, Yea Even a Laughing Stock, in Strange Countries to Promote your Cause."

27. *King of Prussia:* Frederick II (1712–1786) ruled Prussia from 1740 to 1786. A renowned military genius, he led English-allied Prussian forces to victory in the Seven Years' War (1756–1763).

3 his Puplick Appearance and Ministration
   1 his Miracles 2 his Doctrine
4 his Death, Burial and resurrection, and Appearance to his Disciples
5 his Assention and Exaltation at the Right Hand of god the Father
6 his Intercession,
7 his Second Coming to Judge the World at the last Day

1 first then let us See how was Christ represented to the World under the old Covenant, and What Treatment he met with in the World, we find Acording to Scriptures that was Represented by various Name, Titles, and Shadows and Figures

he was Calld the Seed of the Woman the Seed of Abraham Isaac and Jacob, his Name was Shilo, Missias Emanuel a Servant the Branch a tryed Stone the Chief Corner Stone the Lord our Righteousness the Root and the Rod of Jesse the Morning Star, the Prophet Priest and King the Wonderful Counseller the mighty God the Everlasting Father the Prince of Peace,[28] besides these he was Represented by various Figures, Sacrifices, and Ceremonies, and his Servants the Prophets did many signs and wonders by his opperati[on] yet most all the World were against them Except a few, as the Jews were the Peculiar People of god all the World was against them, and there there were but few true Godly People even among the Jews, the and they were hated by there own ^[word illegible]^ Brethren, and were Slain Chiefly by their own Brethren

2ly When Christ was Born they Rose up against him and woud have Slew him as soon as he was born—And there were but few yt Rejoicd at his Birth Such as the Shepherds, and the [word illegible] and Anna the Prophetes[29] and wise men from the East &c

3l his Publick appearance and Ministration, 1 his Mira and Secondly his Doctrine we find his first appearance in the Temple of God, Sitting in midst of the Doctors, Both hearing and Asking them Questions[30] and after this we have an Account of his Miracles & and now was the Time for Man to think of him, but what did they think of him? and his Preaching was now also Publick to every mans Consideration, but what did they Say of him, there was Indeed Different Judgments a bout him Some &c

[DCA Vault; marriage vows handwritten into back of sermon booklet. Courtesy of Dartmouth College Library.]

7 ◦∾   A SERMON, PREACHED AT THE EXECUTION OF
MOSES PAUL, AN INDIAN (1772)

A SERMON, Preached at the EXECUTION of *Moses Paul*, AN INDIAN; Who was executed at *New-Haven*, on the Second of September, 1772; for the murder of Mr. *Moses Cook*, late of *Waterbury*, on the 7th of December, 1771. Preached at the Desire

28. *Wonderful Counseller . . . . :* See Isaiah 9:6.
29. *Anna the Prophetes[s]:* See Luke 2:36–38.
30. See Luke 2: 42–52.

of said PAUL. By SAMSON OCCOM, *Minister of the Gospel, and Missionary to the* Indians. NEW-HAVEN, *Printed and sold by* T. Green.

The Preface

THE world is already full of books; and the people of GOD are abundantly furnished with excellent books upon divine subjects; and it seems that every subject has been written upon over and over again: And the people in very deed have had precept upon precept, line upon line, here a little and there a little; so in the whole, they have much, yea very much, they have enough and more than enough.

And when I come to consider these things, I am ready to say with my self, what folly and madness is it in me to suffer any thing of mine to appear in print, to expose my ignorance to the world? It seems altogether unlikely that my performance will do any manner of service in the world, since the most excellent writings of worthy and learned men are disregarded. — But there are two or three considerations, that have induced me to be willing to suffer my broken hints to appear in the world: one, is, that the books that are in the world are written in very high and refined language, and the sermons that are delivered every Sabbath, in general, are in a very high and lofty stile, so that the common people understand but little of them. But I think they can't help understanding my talk; it is common, plain, every-day talk— little children may understand it; and poor Negroes may plainly and fully understand my meaning; and it may be of service to them. Again, it may in a particular manner be serviceable to my poor kindred the Indians—Further, as it comes from an uncommon quarter, it may induce people to read it, because it is from an Indian.

Lastly, God works where and when he pleases, and by what instruments he sees fit, and he can and has used weak and unlikely instruments to bring about his great work.

It was a stormy and very uncomfortable day when the following discourse was delivered, and about one half of it was not delivered as it was written, and now it is a little altered and enlarged in some places.

Introduction

BY the melancholy providence of God, and at the earnest desire and invitation of the poor condemned Criminal, I am here before this great concourse of people at this time, to give the last discourse to the poor miserable object who is to be executed this day before your eyes, for the due reward of his folly and madness, and enormous wickedness. It is an unwelcome task to me to speak upon such an occasion; but since it is the desire of the poor man himself, who is to die a shameful death this day, in conscience I cannot deny him; I must endeavor to do the great work the dying man requests.

I conclude that this great concourse of people have come together to see the execution of justice upon this poor Indian; and I suppose the bigest part of you look upon yourselves christians, and as such, I hope you will demean yourselves; and that you will have suitable commiseration towards this poor object. Tho' you can't in justice pray for his life to be continued in this world, yet you can pray earnestly for the salvation of his poor soul, consistently with the mind of God. Let this be therefore, the fervent exercise of our souls: for this is the last day we have to pray for him. As for you that don't regard religion, it cannot be expected, that you will put up one petition for this miserable creature: yet I would entreat you seriously to consider the frailty of corrupt nature, and behave yourselves as becomes rational creatures.

And in a word, Let us all be suitably affected with the melancholy occasion of the day; knowing that we are all dying creatures, and accountable unto God. Though this poor condemned creature will in a few minutes know more than all of us, either in unutterable joy, or in inconceivable wo, yet we shall certainly know as much as he in a few days.

The sacred words that I have chosen to speak from, upon this undesirable occasion, are found written in the Epistle of St. Paul to the

Romans VI. 23

For the wages of sin is death, but the gift of God is eternal life through Jesus Christ our Lord.

DEATH is called the king of terrors, and it ought to be the subject of every man and woman's thoughts daily; because it is that unto which they are liable every moment of their lives: And therefore it cannot be unseasonable to think, speak and hear of it at any time, and especially on this mournful occasion; for we must all come to it, how soon we cannot tell; whether we are prepared or not prepared, ready or not ready, whether death is welcome or not welcome, we must feel the force of it: whether we concern ourselves with death or not, it will concern itself with us. Seeing that this is the case with every one of us, what manner of persons ought we to be in all holy conversation and godliness; how ought men to exert themselves in preparation for death continually; for they know not what a day or an hour may bring forth, with respect to them. But, alas! according to the appearance of mankind in general, death is the least thought of. They go on from day to day, as if they were to live here forever, as if this was the only life. They contrive, rack their inventions, disturb their rest, and even hazard their lives in all manner of dangers, both by sea and land; yea, they leave no stone unturn'd that they may live in the world, and at the same time have little or no contrivance to die well. God and their souls are neglected, and heaven and eternal happiness are disregarded; Christ and his religion are despised—yet most of these very men intend to be happy when they come to die, not considering that there must be great preparation in order to die well. Yea there is none so fit to live as those that are fit to die; those that are not fit to die are not fit to live. Life & death are nearly connected; we generally own that it is a great and solemn thing to die. If this be true, then it is a great and solemn thing to live; for as we live so we shall die. But I say again, how do mankind realize these things? They are busy about the things of this world as if there was no death before them. Dr. *Watts* pictures them out to the life in his psalms:

> *See the vain race of mortals move,*
> *Like shadows o'er the plain,*

They rage and strive, desire and love,
But all the noise is vain.
Some walk in honour's gaudy show,
Some dig for golden ore,
They toil for heirs they know not who,
And strait are seen no more.[31]

But on the other hand, life is the most precious thing, and ought to be the most desired by all rational creatures. It ought to be prized above all things; yet there is nothing so abused and despised as life, and nothing so neglected: I mean eternal life is shamefully disregarded by men in general, and eternal death is chosen rather than life. This is the general complaint of the bible from the beginning to the end. As long as Christ is neglected, life is refused, as long as sin is cherished, death is chosen. And this seems to be the woful case of mankind of all nations, according to their appearance in these days; for it is too plain to be denied, that vice and immorality, and floods of iniquity are abounding every where amongst all nations, and all orders and ranks of men, and in every sect of people. Yea there is a great agreement and harmony among all nations, and from the highest to the lowest to practise sin and iniquity; and the pure religion of Jesus Christ is turned out of doors, and is dying without; or, in other words, the Lord Jesus Christ is turned out of doors by men in general, and even by his professed people. "He came to his own, and his own received him not."[32] But the devil is admitted, he has free access to the houses and hearts of the children of men: Thus life is refused and death is chosen.

But in further speaking upon our text, by divine assistance, I shall consider these two general propositions:

I. That sin is the cause of all the miseries that befal the children of men, both as to their bodies and souls, for time and eternity.
II. That eternal life and happiness is the free gift of God, thro' Jesus Christ our Lord.

In speaking to the first proposition I shall first consider the nature of sin; and secondly shall consider the consequences of sin, or the wages of sin, which is death. First then, we are to describe the nature of sin.

Sin is the transgression of the law:—This is the scripture definition of sin. Now the law of God being holy, just and good; sin must be altogether unholy, unjust and evil. If I was to define sin, I should call it a contrariety to God; and as such it must be the vilest thing in the world; it is full of all evil; it is the evil of evils; the only evil, in which dwells no good thing; and is most destructive to God's creation, where ever it takes effect. It was sin that transformed the very angels in heaven, into devils; and it was sin that caused hell to be made. If it had not been for sin, there never would have been such a thing as hell or devil, death or misery.

31. These are verses 3 and 4 of Psalm 39, "Teach Me the Measure of My Days," by English hymnodist Isaac Watts (1674–1748).
32. *He came to his own:* John 1:11.

And if sin is such a thing as we have just described; it must be worse than the devils in hell itself.—Sin is full of deadly poison; it is full of malignity and hatred against God, against all his divine perfections and atributes, against his wisdom, against his power, against his holiness and goodness, against his mercy and justice, against his written law and gospel; yea against his very being and existence. Were it in the power of sin, it would even dethrone God, and set itself on the throne.

When Christ the Son of the Most High came down from the glorious world above, into this wretched world of sin and sorrow, to seek and to save that which was lost, sin, or sinners rose up against him, as soon as he entered our world, and pursued him with hellish malice, night and day, for above thirty years together, till they kill'd him.

Further, sin is against the Holy Ghost; it opposes all his good and holy operations upon the children of men. When, and wherever there is the out-pouring of the Spirit of God, upon the children of men, in a way of conviction and conversion; sin will immediately prompt the devil and his children to rise up against it, and they will oppose the work with all their power, and in every shape. And if open opposition will not do, the devil will mimick the work and thus prevent the good effect.

Thus we find by the scripture accounts, that whenever God raises up men, and uses them as instruments of conviction and conversion, the devil and his instruments will rise up to destroy both the reformers and the reformed. Thus it has been from the early days of Christianity to this day. We have found it so in our day. In the time of the outpouring of the Spirit of God in these colonies, to the conviction and reformation of many; immediately sin and the devil influenced numbers to rise up against the good work of God, calling it delusion, and work of the devil.[33] And thus sin also opposes every motion of the Spirit of God, in the heart of every Christian; this makes a warfare in the soul.

2. I shall endeavor to show the sad consequences or effects of sin upon the children of men.

Sin has poison'd them, & made them distracted or fools. The Psalmist says, The fool hath said in his heart, there is no God. And Solomon, through his proverbs, calls ungodly sinners fools; and their sin he calls their folly and foolishness. The apostle James says, But the tongue can no man tame, it is an unruly evil, full of deadly poison. It is the heart that is in the first place full of deadly poison. The tongue is only an interpreter of the heart. Sin has vitiated the whole man, both soul and body; all the powers are corrupted; it has turned the minds of men against all good, towards all evil. So poisoned are they according to the prophet, Isaiah v. ch. 20 ver. "Wo unto them that call evil good, and good evil; that put darkness for light, and light for darkness; that put bitter for sweet, and sweet for bitter." And Christ Jesus saith in John iii.19,20. "And this is the condemnation, that light has come into the world, and men have loved darkness rather than light, because their deeds were evil. For

33. Occom here describes the transatlantic evangelical revivals of the 1740s now remembered as the Great Awakening. His own conversion came by the preaching of the infamous "New Light" itinerant John Davenport, brother-in-law to Eleazar Wheelock. Wheelock himself was punished for his itinerant preaching by "Old Light" clergy who opposed the revivals.

every one that doeth evil hateth the light, neither cometh to the light, lest his deeds should be reproved." Sin hath stupified mankind, they are now ignorant of God their maker; neither do they enquire after him. And they are ignorant of themselves, they know not what is good for them, neither do they understand their danger; and they have no fear of God before their eyes.

Further, sin hath blinded their eyes, so that they can't discern spiritual things; neither do they see the way that they should go, and they are as deaf as adders, so that they cannot hear the joyful sound of the gospel that brings glad tidings of peace and pardon to the sinners of mankind. Neither do they regard the Charmer charming never so wisely.—Not only so, but sin has made man proud, tho' he has nothing to be proud of; for he has lost his excellency, his beauty and happiness; he is a bankrupt and is excommunicated from God; he was turned out of paradise by God himself, and become a vagabond in God's world, and as such he has no right or title to the least crumb of mercy, in the world: yet he is proud, he is haughty, and exalts himself above God, tho' he is wretched and miserable, and poor, and blind and naked. He glories in his shame. Sin has made him beastly and devilish; yea, he is sunk beneath the beasts, and is worse than the ravenous beasts of the wilderness. He is become ill-natur'd, cruel and murderous; he is contentious and quarrelsome. I said he is worse than the ravenous beasts, for wolves and bears don't devour their own kind, but man does; yea, we have numberless instances of women killing their own children; such women I think are worse than she tygers.

Sin has made men dishonest and deceitful, so that he goes about cheating and defrauding and deceiving his fellow men in the world: yea, he is become a cheat himself, he goes about in a vain shew; we do not know where to find man.—Sometimes we find as an angel of God; and at other times we find as a devil, even one and the same man. Sin has made a man a liar even from the womb; so there is no believing nor trusting him. The royal psalmist says, "The wicked are estranged from the womb, they go astray as soon as they are born, speaking lies."[34] His language is also corrupted. Whereas he had a pure and holy language, in his innocency, to adore and praise God his maker, he now curses, swears, and profanes, the holy name of God, and curses and damns his fellow-creatures. In a word, man is a most unruly and ungovernable creature, and is become as the wild ass's colt,[35] and is harder to tame than any of God's creatures in this world. In short, man is worse than all the creatures in this lower world, his propensity is to evil and that continually; he is more like the devil than any creature we can think of: And I think it is not going beyond the word of God, to say, man is the most devilish creature in the world. Christ said to his disciples, One of you is a devil; to the Jews he said, Ye are of your father the devil, and the lusts of your father ye will do. Thus every unconverted soul is a child of the devil, sin has made them so.

We have given some few hints of the nature of sin, and the effects of sin on mankind.

34. *The wicked are estranged:* Psalm 58:3.
35. *wild ass's colt:* Job 11:12.

We shall in the next place consider the wages or the reward of sin, which is death.

Sin is the cause of all the miseries that attend poor sinful man, which will finally bring him to death, death temporal and eternal. I shall first consider his temporal death.

His temporal death then begins as soon as he is born. Tho' it seems to us that he is just beginning to live, yet in fact he is just entered into a state of death; St. Paul says "w[h]erefore, as by one man sin entered into the world, and death by sin; and so death passed upon all men, for that all have sinned."[36] Man is surrounded with ten thousand instruments of death, and is liable to death every moment of his life; a thousand diseases await him on every side continually; the sentence of death has pass'd upon them as soon as they are born: yea they are struck with death as soon as they breathe. And it seems all the enjoyments of men in this world are also poisoned with sin; for GOD said to Adam after he had sinned, "Cursed is the ground for thy sake, in sorrow shall thou eat of it all the days of thy life."[37] By this we plainly see that every thing that grows out of the ground is cursed, and all creatures that God hath made for man are cursed also; and whatever God curses is a cursed thing indeed. Thus death and destruction is in all the enjoyments of men in this life, every enjoyment in this world is liable to misfortune in a thousand ways, both by sea and land.

How many ships, that have been loaded with the choicest treasures of the earth, have been swallowed up in the ocean, many times just before they enter their desired haven. And vast treasures have been consumed by fire on the land, &c. And the fruits of the earth are liable to many judgments. And the dearest and nearest enjoyments of men are generally balanced with equal sorrow and grief. A man and his wife who have liv'd together in happiness for many years; that have comforted each other in various changes of life, must at last be seperated; one or the other must be taken away first by death, and then the poor survivor is drowned in tears, in sorrow, mourning and grief. And when a child or children are taken away by death, the bereaved parents are bowed down with sorrow and deep mourning. When Joseph was sold by his brethren unto the Ishmaelites, they took his coat and rolled it in blood, and carried it to their father, and the good old patriarch knew it to be Joseph's coat, and he concluded that his dear Joseph was devoured by evil beasts, and he was plunged all over in sorrow and bitter mourning, and he refused to be comforted.[38] And so when tender parents are taken away by death, the children are left comfortless.—All this is the sad effect of sin.—These are the wages of sin.

And secondly, we are to consider man's spiritual death, while he is here in this world. We find it thus written in the word of God. "And the Lord God commanded the man, saying, of every tree of the garden thou mayst freely eat: but of the tree of knowledge of good and evil, thou shalt not eat of it, for in the day thou eatest thereof thou shalt surely die."[39] And yet he did eat of it, and so he and all his posterity, are

36. *Wherefore, as by one man sin entered into the world:* Romans 5:12.

37. *Cursed is the ground:* Genesis 3:17.

38. See Genesis 37.

39. *And the Lord God commanded . . . :* Genesis 2:16–17.

but dead men. And St. Paul to the Ephesians saith, "You hath he quickened who were dead in trespasses and sins.["]⁴⁰— The great Mr. Henry⁴¹ says in this place, that unregenerate souls are dead in trespasses and sins. All those who are in their sins, are dead in sins; yea, in trespasses and sins; and which may signify all sorts of sins, habitual and actual; sins of heart and life. Sin is the death of the soul. Wherever that prevails, there is a privation of all spiritual life. Sinners are dead in state, being destitute of the principles and powers of spiritual life; and cut off from God, the fountain of life: and they are dead in law, as a condemned malefactor is said to be a dead man. Now a dead man, in a natural sense, is unactive, and is of no service to the living; there is no correspondence between the dead and the living: There is no agreement or union between them, no fellowship at all between the dead and the living. A dead man is altogether ignorant of the intercourse among the living:—just so it is with men that are spiritually dead; they have no agreeable activity. Their activity in sin, is their deadness, and inactivity towards God. They are of no service to God; and they have no correspondence with heaven; and there is no agreement or fellowship between them and the living God; and they are totally ignorant of the agreeable and sweet intercourse there is between God and his children here below: and they are ignorant, and know nothing of that blessed fellowship and union there is among the saints here below. They are ready to say indeed, behold how they love one another! But they know nothing of that love, that the children of God enjoy. As sin is in opposition to God; so sinners are at enmity against God; there is no manner of agreement between them.

Let us consider further. God is a living God, he is all life, the fountain of life; and a sinner is a dead soul; there is nothing but death in him. And now judge ye, what agreement can there be between them? God is a holy and pure God, and a sinner is an unholy and filthy creature;—God is a righteous Being, and a sinner is an unrighteous creature; God is light, and a sinner is darkness itself, &c. Further, what agreement can there be between God and a lyar, a thief, a drunkard, a swearer, a profane creature, a whoremonger, an adulterer, and idolater, &c. No one that has any sense, dare say, that there is any agreement. Further, as sinners are dead to God, as such, they have no delight in God, and godliness; they have no taste for the religion of Jesus Christ; they have no pleasure in the holy exercises of religion. Prayer is no pleasant work with them; or if they have any pleasure in it, it is not out of love to God, but out of self-love, like the Pharisees of old; they loved to pray in open view of men, that they might have praise from them. And perhaps, they were not careful to pray in secret. These were dead souls, they were unholy, rotten hypocrites, and so all their prayers and religious exercises were cold, dead, and abominable services to God. Indeed they are dead to all the duties that God requires of them; they are dead to the holy bible; to all the laws, commands, and precepts thereof; and to the ordinances of the gospel of the Lord Jesus Christ. When they read the book of God, it is like an old almanack to them, a dead book. But it is because they are dead, and

---

40. *You hath he quickened:* Ephesians 2:1.
41. *Mr. Henry:* Matthew Henry (1662–1714), renowned biblical commentator and author of *The Exposition of the Old and New Testaments* (1710).

as such, all their services are against God, even their best services are an abomination unto God; yea, sinners are so dead in sin, that the threatnings of God don't move them. All the thunderings and lightnings of Mount-Sinai don't stir them. All the curses of the law are out against them; yea, every time they read these curses in the bible, they are cursing them to their faces, and to their very eyes; yet they are unconcern'd, and go on in sin without fear. And lastly here, sin has so stupify'd the sinner, that he will not believe his own senses; he won't believe his own eyes, nor his own ears; he reads the book of God, but he does not believe what he reads. And he hears of God, and heaven, and eternal happiness, and of hell and eternal misery; but he believes none of those things; he goes on, as if there were no God, nor heaven and happiness; neither has he any fear of hell and eternal torments;—and he sees his fellow-men dropping away daily on every side, yet he goes on carelessly in sin, as if he never was to die. And if he at any time thinks of dying, he hardly believes his own thoughts. Death is at a great distance, so far off, that he don't concern himself about it, so as to prepare for it. God mournfully complains of his people, that they don't consider; O that they were wise, that they understood this, that they would consider their latter end.

The next thing I shall consider, is the actual death of the body, or separation between soul and body. At the cessation of natural life, there is no more joy nor sorrow; no more hope nor fear, as to the body; no more contrivance and carrying on of business; no more merchandizing and trading; no more farming; no more buying and selling; no more building of any kind, no more contrivance at all to live in the world; no more honor nor reproach; no more praise; no more good report, nor evil report; no more learning of any trades, arts or sciences in the world; no more sinful pleasures, they are all at an end; recreations, visiting, tavern haunting, music and dancing, chambering and carousing, playing at dice and cards, or any game whatsoever; cursing and swearing, and profaning the holy name of God, drunkenness, fighting, debauchery, lying and cheating, in this world must cease forever. Not only so, but they must bid an eternal farewel to all the world; bid farewel to all their beloved sins and pleasures; and the places and possessions that knew them once, shall know them no more forever. And further, they must bid adieu to all sacred and divine things. They are obliged to leave the bible, and all the ordinances thereof; and to bid farewell to preachers, and all sermons, and all christian people, and christian conversation; they must bid a long farewel to sabbaths and seasons, and opportunities of worship; yea, an eternal farewel to all mercy, and all hope; an eternal farewel to God the Father, Son and Holy Ghost, and adieu to heaven and all happiness, to saints and all the inhabitants of the upper world. At your leisure please to read the destruction of Babylon; you will find it written in the 18th of the Revelation.[42]

On the other hand, the poor departed soul must take up its lodging in sorrow, wo and misery, in the lake that burns with fire and brimstone, where the worm dieth not and the fire is not quenched; where a multitude of frightful deformed devils dwell, and the damned ghosts of Adam's race; where darkness, horror and despair reigns, or where hope never comes, and where poor guilty naked souls will be tor-

42. See Revelation 18:1–24.

mented with exquisite torments, even the wrath of the Almighty poured out upon the damned souls; the smoke of their torments ascending up forever and ever; their mouths and nostrils streaming forth with living fire; and hellish groans, howlings, cries and shrieks all around them; and merciless devils upbraiding them for their folly and madness, and tormenting them incessantly. And there they must endure the most unsatiable, fruitless desire, and the most overwhelming shame and confusion, and the most horrible fear, and the most doleful sorrow, and the most racking despair. When they cast their flaming eyes to heaven, with Dives in torments,[43] they behold an angry and frowning GOD, whose eyes are as a flaming fire, and they are struck with ten thousand darts of pain; and the sight of the happiness of the saints above, adds to their pains and aggravates their misery. And when they reflect upon their past folly and madness in neglecting the great salvation in their day, it will pierce them with ten thousand inconceivable torments; it will as it were enkindle their hell afresh; and it will cause them to curse themselves bitterly, and curse the day in which they were born, and curse their parents that were the instruments of their being in the world; yea, they will curse, bitterly curse and wish that very GOD that gave them their being, to be in the same condition with them in hell torments. This is what is called the second death, and it is the last death, and eternal death to a guilty soul.

And O eternity, eternity, eternity! Who can measure it? Who can count the years thereof? Arithmetic must fail, the thoughts of men and angels are drowned in it; how shall we describe eternity? To what shall we compare it? Were it possible to employ a fly to carry off this globe by the small particles thereof, and to carry them to such a distance that it would return once in ten thousand years for another particle, and so continue till it has carried off all this globe, and framed them together in some unknown space, till it has made just such a world as this is: After all, eternity would remain the same unexhausted duration. This must be the unavoidable portion of all impenitent sinners, let them be who they will, great or small, honorable or ignoble, rich or poor, bond or free. Negroes, Indians, English, or of what nations soever; all that die in their sins must go to hell together, for the wages of sin is death.

The next thing that I was to consider is this:

That eternal life and happiness is the free gift of God, thro' Jesus Christ our Lord.

Under this proposition I shall now endeavour to show what this life and happiness is.

The life that is mentioned in our text is a spiritual life: it is the life of the soul, a restoration of soul from sin to holiness, from darkness to light, a translation from the kingdom and dominion of satan, to the kingdom of God's grace. In other words, it is being restored to the image of God, and delivered from the image of satan. And this life consists in union of the soul to God, and communion with God; a real participation of the divine nature, or in the Apostle's words, it is Christ formed within us; I live says he, yet not I, but Christ liveth in me.[44] And the Apostle John saith,

43. *Dives in torments:* In Luke 16:19–31, a rich man named Dives who despises the poverty and suffering of the beggar Lazarus suffers "torments" in hell.
44. *I live says he:* Galatians 2:20.

God is love, and he that dwelleth in love, dwelleth in God, and God in him.[45] This is the life of the soul. It is called emphatically life, because it is a life that shall never have a period, a stable, permanent, and unchangeable life, called in the scriptures, everlasting life, or life eternal. And the happiness of this life consists in communion with God, or in the spiritual enjoyment of God. As much as a soul enjoys of God in this life, just so much of life and happiness he enjoys or possesses; yea, just so much of heaven he enjoys. A true christian, desires no other heaven but the enjoyment of God, a full and perfect enjoyment of God, is a full and perfect heaven and happiness to a gracious soul.—Further, this life is called eternal life because God has planted a living principle in the soul; and whereas he was dead before, now he is made alive unto God; there is an active principle within him towards God, he now moves towards God in his religious devotions and exercises; is daily comfortably and sweetly walking with God, in all his ordinances and commands; his delight is in the ways of God; he breathes towards God, a living breath, in praises, prayers, adorations and thanksgivings; his prayers are now heard in the heavens, and his praises delight the ears of the Almighty, and his thanksgiving are accepted. So alive is he now to God, that it is his meat and drink, yea more than his meat and drink, to do the will of his heavenly Father. It is his delight, his happiness and pleasure to serve God. He does not drag himself to his duties now, but he does them out of choice, and with alacrity of soul. Yea, so alive is he to God, that he gives up himself and all that he has entirely to God, to be for him and none other; his whole aim is to glorify God, in all things, whether by life or death, all the same to him.

We have a bright example of this in St. Paul. After he was converted, he was all alive to God; he regarded not his life but was willing to spend, and be spent in the service of his God; he was hated, revil'd, despised, laughed at, and called all manner of evil names; was scourged, stoned and imprisoned;—and all cou'd not stop his activity towards God. He would boldly and couragiously go on in preaching the gospel of the Lord Jesus Christ, to poor, lost, and undone sinners; he would do the work God set him about, in spite of all opposition he met with, either from men or devils, earth or hell; come death or come life, none of these things moved him, because he was alive unto God: Tho' he suffered hunger and thirst, cold and heat, poverty & nakedness by day & by night, by sea, and by land, & was in danger all ways; yet he would serve God amidst all these dangers. Read his amazing account in 2 Cor. 11.23 and on.[46]

Another instance of marvellous love towards God, we have in Daniel. When there was a proclamation of prohibition, sent by the king, to all his subjects forbidding them to call upon their gods for 30 days; which was done by envious men, that they might find occasion against Daniel the servant of the Most High God; yet he having the life of God in his soul, regarded not the king's decree, but made his petitions to his God, as often as he used to do tho' death was threatened to the disobedient. But he feared not the hell they had prepared; for it seems, the den resembled hell, and

---

45. *God is love:* 1 John 4:16.

46. In 2 Corinthians 11:23–33, Paul recounts the various imprisonments, assaults, and trials he suffered in his missionary travels.

the lions represented the devils. And when he was actually cast into the lion's den, the ravenous beasts became meek and innocent as lambs, before the prophet, because he was alive unto God; the spirit of the Most High was in him, and the lions were afraid before him. Thus it was with Daniel and Paul; they went thro' fire and water, as the common saying is, because they had eternal life in their souls in eminent manner; and they regarded not this life, for the cause and glory of God. And thus it has been in all ages with true Christians. Many of the fore-fathers of the English, in this country, had this life and are gone the same way, that the holy prophets and apostles went. Many of them went thro' all manner of sufferings for God; and a great number of them are gone home to heaven, in chariots of fire. I have seen the place in London, called Smithfield, where numbers were burnt to death for the religion of Jesus Christ.[47] And there is the same life in true christians now in these days; and if there should persecutions arise in our day, I verily believe, true christians would suffer with the same spirit and temper of mind, as those did, who suffered in days past.—This is the life which our texts speaks of.

We proceed in the next place to shew, that this life, which we have describ'd, is the free gift of God, thro' Jesus Christ our Lord.

Sinners have forfeited all mercy into the hands of divine justice and have merited hell and damnation to themselves; for the wages of sin is everlasting death, but heaven and happiness is a free gift; it comes by favour; and all merit is excluded: and especially if we consider that we are fallen sinful creatures, and there is nothing in us that can recommend us to the favour of God; and we can do nothing that is agreeable and acceptable to God; and the mercies we enjoy in this life are altogether from the pure mercy of God; we are unequal to them. Good old Jacob cried out, under the sense of his unworthiness, "I am less than the least of all thy mercies,"[48] and we have nothing to give unto God, if we essay to give all the service that we are capable of, we should give him nothing but what was his own, and when we give up ourselves unto God, both soul and body, we give him nothing; for we were his before; he had a right to do with us as he pleased, either to throw us into hell, or to save us.—There is nothing that we can call our own, but our sins; and who is he that dares to say, I expect to have heaven for my sins? for our text says, that the wages of sin is death. If we are thus unequal and unworthy of the least mercy in this life, how much more are we unworthy of eternal life? yet God can find it in his heart to give it. And it is altogether unmerited; it is a free gift to undeserving and hell deserving sinners of mankind: it is altogether of God's sovereign good pleasure to give it. It is of free grace & sovereign mercy, and from the unbounded goodness of God; he was self-moved to it. And it is said that this life is given in and through our Lord Jesus Christ. It could not be given in any other way, but in and through the death and sufferings of the Lord Jesus Christ; Christ himself is the gift, and he is the christian's life. "For God so loved the world that he gave his only begotten Son, that whosoever believed in him should not perish but have everlasting life."[49] The word says further, "For by

---

47. Protestants were executed at Smithfield, London, during the reign of Queen Mary I (1553–1558).

48. *I am less than:* Genesis 32:10.

49. *For God so loved the world:* John 3:16.

grace ye are saved, thro' faith, and that not of yourselves it is the gift of God."[50] This is given thro' Jesus Christ our Lord; it is Christ that purchased it with his own blood; he prepared it with his divine and almighty power; and by the same power, and by the influence of his spirit, he prepares us for it; and by his divine grace preserve us to it. In a word, he is all in all in our eternal salvation; all this is the free gift of God.

I have now gone thro' what I proposed from my text. And I shall now make some application of the whole.

First to the criminal in particular; and then to the auditory in general.

My poor unhappy Brother MOSES;

As it was your own desire that I should preach to you this last discourse, so I shall speak plainly to you.—You are the bone of my bone, and flesh of my flesh. You are an Indian, a despised creature; but you have despised yourself; yea you have despised God more; you have trodden under foot his authority; you have despised his commands and precepts; And now, as God says, be sure your sins will find you out. And now, poor Moses, your sins have found you out, and they have overtaken you this day; the day of your death is now come; the king of terrors is at hand; you have but a very few moments to breathe in this world.—The just law of man, and the holy law of Jehovah, call aloud for the destruction of your mortal life; God says, "Whoso sheddeth man's blood, by man shall his blood be shed."[51] This is the antient decree of heaven, and it is to be executed by man; nor have you the least gleam of hope of escape, for the unalterable sentence is past; the terrible day of execution is come; the unwelcome guard is about you; and the fatal instruments of death are now made ready; your coffin and your grave, your last lodging, are open ready to receive you.

Alas! poor Moses, now you know by sad, by woful experience, the living truth of our text, that the wages of sin is death. You have been already dead; yea twice dead: by nature spiritually dead. And since the awful sentence of death has been past upon you, you have been dead to all the pleasures of this life; or all the pleasures, lawful or unlawful, have been dead to you: And death, which is the wages of sin, is standing even on this side of your grave ready to put a final period to your mortal life; and just beyond the grave, eternal death awaits your poor soul, and devils are ready to drag your miserable soul down to their bottomless den, where everlasting wo and horror reigns; the place is filled with doleful shrieks, howls and groans of the damned. Oh! to what a miserable, forlorn, and wretched condition has your extravagance folly and wickedness brought you! i.e. if you die in your sins. And O! what manner of repentance ought you to manifest! How ought your heart to bleed for what you have done! How ought you to prostrate your soul before a bleeding God! And under self-condemnation, cry out, Ah Lord, ah Lord, what have I done!— Whatever partiality, injustice and error there may be among the judges of the earth, remember that you have deserved a thousand deaths, and a thousand hells, by reason of your sins, at the hands of a holy God. Should God come out against you in

---

50. *For by grace ye are saved:* Ephesians 2:8.
51. *Whoso sheddeth man's blood:* Genesis 9:6.

strict justice, alas! what could you say for yourself? for you have been brought up under the bright sun-shine, and plain, and loud sound of the gospel; and you have had a good education; you can read and write well; and God has given you a good natural understanding: And therefore your sins are so much more aggravated. You have not sinned in such an ignorant manner as others have done; but you have sinned with both your eyes open as it were, under the light even the glorious light of the gospel of the Lord Jesus Christ.—You have sinned against the light of your own conscience, against your knowledge and understanding; you have sinned against the pure and holy laws of God, the just laws of men; you have sinned against heaven and earth; you have sinned against all the mercies and goodness of God; you have sinned against the whole bible, against the old and new-testament; you have sinned against the blood of Christ, which is the blood of the everlasting covenant. O poor Moses, see what you have done! And now repent, repent, I say again repent; see how the blood you shed cries against you, and the Avenger of Blood is at your heels. O fly, fly, to the blood of the Lamb of God for the pardon of all your aggravated sins.

But let us now turn to a more pleasant theme.—Though you have been a great sinner, a heaven daring sinner; yet hark and hear the joyful sound from heaven, even from the King of kings, and Lord of lords; that the gift of God is eternal life, thro' Jesus Christ our Lord. It is a free gift, and offered to the greatest sinners, and upon their true repentance towards God and faith in the Lord Jesus Christ, they shall be welcome to the life they have spoken of; it is offered upon free terms. He that hath no money may come; he that hath no righteousness, no goodness, may come, the call is to poor undone sinners; the call is not to the righteous, but sinners calling them to repentance. Hear the voice of the Son of the most high God, Come unto me, all [ye] that labour and are heavy laden, and I will give you rest.[52] This is a call, a gracious call to you, poor Moses, under your present burden and distresses. And Christ alone has a right to call sinners to himself. It would be presumption for a mighty angel to call a poor sinner in this manner; and were it possible for you to apply to all God's creatures, they would with one voice tell you, that it was not in them to help you. Go to all the means of grace, they would prove miserable helps, without Christ himself. Yea, apply to all the ministers of the gospel in the world, they would all say, that it was not in them, but would only prove as indexes, to point out to you, the Lord Jesus Christ, the only saviour of sinners of mankind. Yea, go to all the angels in heaven they would do the same. Yea, go to God the Father himself, without Christ, he cou'd not help you, to speak after the manner of men, he would also point to the Lord Jesus Christ, & say this is my beloved Son, in whom I am well pleased, hear ye him.[53] Thus you see, poor Moses, that there is none in heaven, or on the earth, that can help you, but Christ; he alone has power to save, and to give life.—God the eternal Father appointed him, chose him, authorized, and fully commissioned him to save sinners. He came down from heaven into this lower world, and became as one of us, and stood in our room. He was the second Adam. And as God demanded perfect obedience of the first Adam; the second fulfil'd it; and as the

52. *Come unto me:* Matthew 11:28.
53. *This is my beloved Son:* Matthew 17:5.

first sinned, and incurred the wrath and anger of God, the second endur'd it; he suffered in our room. As he became sin for us, he was a man of sorrows, and acquainted with grief; all our stripes were laid upon him; yea, he was finally condemned, because we were under condemnation; and at last was executed and put to death, for our sins; was lifted up between the heavens and the earth, and was crucified on the accursed tree; his blessed hands and feet were fastened there;—there he died a shameful and ignominious death: there he finished the great work of our redemption: there his hearts blood was shed for our cleansing: there he fully satisfied the divine justice of God, for penitent, believing sinners, though they have been the chief of sinners.—O Moses! this is good news to you in this last day of your life; here is a crucified Saviour at hand for your sins; his blessed hands are out-stretched, all in a gore of blood for you. This is the only Saviour, an Almighty Saviour, just such as you stand in infinite and perishing need of. O, poor Moses! hear the dying prayer of a gracious Saviour on the accursed tree,—Father forgive them for they know not what they do. This was a prayer for his enemies and murderers; and it is for you, if you will now only repent and believe in him. O why will you die eternally, poor Moses, since Christ has died for sinners? Why will you go to hell from beneath the bleeding Saviour as it were? This is the day of your execution, yet it is the accepted time, it is the day of salvation if you will now believe in the Lord Jesus Christ. Must Christ follow you into the prison by his servants, and there intreat you to accept of eternal life, and will you refuse it? and must he follow you even to the gallows, and there beseech of you to accept him, and will you refuse him? Shall he be crucified hard by your gallows, as it were, and will you regard him not? O, poor Moses, now believe on the Lord Jesus Christ with all your heart, and thou shalt be saved eternally. Come just as you are, with all your sins and abominations, with all your filthiness, with all your blood-guiltiness, with all your condemnation, and lay hold of the hope set before you this day. This is the last day of salvation with your soul; you will be beyond the bounds of mercy in a few minutes more. O what a joyful day would it be if you would now openly believe in and receive the Lord Jesus Christ; it would be the beginning of heavenly days with your poor soul; instead of a melancholy day, it would be a wedding day to your soul: It would cause the very angels in heaven to rejoice, and the saints on earth to be glad; it would cause the angels to come down from the realms above, and wait hovering about your gallows, ready to convey your soul to the heavenly mansions, there to take the possession of eternal glory and happiness, and join the heavenly choirs in singing the songs of Moses and the Lamb: There to set down forever with Abraham, Isaac and Jacob in the kingdom of God's glory; and your shame and guilt shall be forever banished from the place, and all sorrow and fear forever fly away, and tears be wiped from your face; and there shall you forever admire the astonishing and amazing and infinite mercy of God in Christ Jesus, in pardoning such a monstrous sinner as you have been; there you will claim the highest note of praise, for the riches of free grace in Christ Jesus. But if you will not accept of a Saviour so freely offered to you this last day of your life, you must this very day bid a farewell to God the Father, Son and Holy Ghost, to heaven and all the saints and angels that are there; and you must bid all the saints in this lower world an eternal farewel, and even the whole world. And so I must leave you in the hands of God; and I must turn to the whole auditory.

Sirs, We may plainly see, from what we have heard, and from the miserable object before us, into what a doleful condition sin has brought mankind, even into a state of death and misery. We are by nature as certainly under the sentence of death from God, as this miserable man is by the just determination of man; and we are all dying creatures, and we are, or ought to be sensible of it: and this is the dreadful fruit of sin. O! let us then fly from all appearance of sin; let us fight against it with all our might; let us repent and turn to our God, and believe on the Lord Jesus Christ, that we may live forever; let us all prepare for death, for we know not how soon, nor how suddenly we may be called out of the world.

Permit me in particular, reverend Gentlemen and fathers in Israel, to speak a few words to you, tho' I am well sensible that I need to be taught the first principles of the oracles of God, by the least of you. But since the providence of God has so ordered it, that I must speak here on this occasion, I beg that you would not be offended nor be angry with me.

God has raised you up, from among your brethren, and has qualified and authorized you to do his great work; and you are the servants of the Most High GOD, and ministers of the Lord Jesus the Son of the Living God: you are Christ's ambassadors; you are called Shepherds, watchmen, overseers, or bishops, and you are rulers of the temples of God, or of the assemblies of God's people; you are God's angels, and as such you have nothing to do but to wait on God, and to do the work the Lord Jesus Christ your blessed Lord and Master has set you about, not fearing the face of any man, nor seeking to please men, but your Master. You are to declare the whole counsel of God, and to give a portion to every soul in due season; as a physician gives a potion to his patients, according to their diseases, so you are to give a portion to every soul in due season, according to their spiritual maladies; whether it be agreeable or disagreeable to them, you must give it to them; whether they will love you or hate you for it, you must do your work. Your work is to encounter sin and satan; this was the very end of the coming of Christ into the world, and the end of his death and sufferings; it was to make an end of sin and to destroy the works of the devil. And this is your work still, you are to fight the battles of the Lord. Therefore combine together, and be as terrible as an army with banners; attack this monster sin in all its shapes and windings, and lift up your voices as trumpets and not spare, call aloud, call your people to arms against this common enemy of mankind, that sin may not be their ruin. Call upon all orders ranks and degrees of people, to rise up against sin and satan. Arm yourselves with fervent prayer continually, this is a terrible weapon against the kingdom of satan. And preach the death and sufferings, and the resurrection of Jesus Christ; for nothing is so destructive to the kingdom of the devil, as this is. But what need I speak any more? Let us all attend, and hear the great Apostle of the Gentiles speak unto us in Eph. 6 ch. from the 10th verse and onward. Finally my brethren, be strong in the Lord, and in the power of his might; put on the whole armour of God, that ye may be able to stand against the wiles of the devil. For we wrestle not against flesh and blood, but against principalities, against powers, against the rulers of darkness of this world, against spiritual wickedness in high places. Wherefore take unto you the whole armour of God, that ye may be able to stand in the evil day, and having done all to stand. Stand therefore, having your loins girt about with truth, and having on the breast-plate of right-eousness; and your feet shod with the preparation of the gospel of peace: above all, taking the shield of faith, wherewith ye shall be able to quench all the firy darts of the wicked; and take the helmet of salvation, and the sword of the spirit, which is the word of God: Praying always with all prayer and supplication in the spirit, and watching thereunto with all perserverance, and supplication for all saints.[54]

I shall now address myself to the Indians, my bretheren and kindred according to the flesh.

My poor kindred,

You see the woful consequences of sin, by seeing this our poor miserable country-man now before us, who is to die this day for his sins and great wickedness. And it was the sin of drunkenness that has brought this destruction and untimely death upon him. There is a dreadful wo denounced from the Almighty against drunkards; and it is this sin, this abominable, this beastly and accursed sin of drunkenness, that has stript us of every desirable comfort in this life; by this we are poor, miserable and wretched; by this sin we have no name nor credit in the world among polite nations; for this sin we are despised in the world, and it is all right and just, for we despised ourselves more; and if we don't regard ourselves, who will regard us? And it is for our sins, and especially for that accursed, that most develish sin of drunk-enness that we suffer every day. For the love of strong drink we spend all that we have, and everything we can get. By this sin we can't have comfortable houses, nor any thing comfortable in our houses; neither food nor raiment, nor decent utensils. We are obliged to put up any sort of shelter just to screen us from the severity of the weather, and we go about with very mean, ragged and dirty clothes, almost naked. And we are half-starved, for the most of the time obliged to pick up any thing to eat.— And our poor children are suffering every day for want of the necessaries of life; they are very often crying for want of food, and we have nothing to give them; and in the cold weather they are shivering and crying, being pinched with cold.— All this is for the love of strong drink. And this is not all the misery and evil we bring on ourselves in this world; but when we are intoxicated with strong drink we drown our rational powers, by which we are distinguished from the brutal creation; we unman ourselves, and bring ourselves not only level with the beasts of the field, but seven degrees beneath them; yea we bring ourselves level with the devils; I don't know but we make ourselves worse than devils, for I never heard of drunken devils.

My poor kindred, do consider what a dreadful abominable sin drunkenness is. God made us men, and we chuse to be beast and devils; God made us rational crea-tures, and we chuse to be fools. Do consider further, and behold a drunkard and see how he looks, when he has drowned his reason; how deformed and shameful does he appear? He disfigures every part of him, both soul and body, which was made after the image of God. He appears with awful deformity, and his whole visage is disfigured; if he attempts to speak he cannot bring out his words distinct, so as to

54. See Ephesians 6:10–18.

be understood; if he walks he reels and staggers to and fro, and tumbles down. And see how he behaves, he is now laughing, and then he is crying; he is singing and the next minute he is mourning; and is all love to every one, and anon he is raging, & for fighting, & killing all before him, even the nearest and dearest relations and friends: Yea nothing is too bad for a drunken man to do. He will do that which he would not do for the world, in his right mind; he may lie with his own sister or daughter as Lot did.

Further, when a person is drunk, he is just good for nothing in the world; he is of no service to himself, to his family, to his neighbours, or his country; and how much more unfit is he to serve God: yet he is just fit for the service of the devil.

Again, a man in drunkenness is in all manner of dangers, he may be kill'd by his fellow-men, by wild beasts, and tame beasts; he may fall into the fire, into the water, or into a ditch; or he may fall down as he walks along, and break his bones or his neck; and he may cut himself with edge-tools. Further, if he has any money or any thing valuable, he may loose it all, or may be robb'd, or he may make a foolish bargain, and be cheated out of all he has.

I believe you know the truth of what I have just now said, many of you, by sad experience; yet you will go on still in your drunkenness. Though you have been cheated over and over again, and you have lost your substance by drunkenness, yet you will venture to go on in this most destructive sin. O fools when will ye be wise?—We all know the truth of what I have been saying, by what we have seen and heard of drunken deaths. How many have been drowned in our rivers, and how many frozen to death in the winter season! yet drunkards go on without fear and consideration: alas, alas! What will become of all such drunkards? Without doubt they must all go to hell, except they truly repent and turn to God. Drunkenness is so common amongst us, that even our young men and young women are not ashamed to get drunk. Our young men will get drunk as soon as they will eat when they are hungry.—It is generally esteemed among men, more abominable for a woman to be drunk, than a man; and yet there is nothing more common amongst us than female drunkards. Women ought to be more modest than men; the holy scriptures recommend modesty to women in particular:—but drunken women have no modesty at all. It is more intolerable for a woman to get drunk, if we consider further, that she is in great danger of falling into the hands of the sons of Belial, or wicked men, and being shamefully treated by them.

And here I cannot but observe, we find in sacred writ, a wo denounced against men, who put their bottles to their neighbors mouth to make them drunk, that they may see their nakedness:[55] And no doubt there are such develish men now in our days, as there were in the days of old.

And to conclude, consider my poor kindred, you that are drunkards, into what a miserable condition you have brought yourselves. There is a dreadful wo thundering against you every day, and the Lord says, That drunkards shall not inherit the kingdom of God.

And now let me exhort you all to break off from your drunkenness, by a gospel

55. *Wo . . . put their bottles:* Habbakuk 2:15.

repentance, and believe on the Lord Jesus and you shall be saved. Take warning by this doleful sight before us, and by all the dreadful judgments that have befallen poor drunkards. O let us reform our lives, and live as becomes dying creatures, in time to come. Let us be persuaded that we are accountable creatures to God, and we must be called to an account in a few days. You that have been careless all your days, now awake to righteousness, and be concerned for your poor and never dying souls. Fight against all sins, and especially the sin that easily besets you, and behave in time to come as becomes rational creatures; and above all things, receive and believe on the Lord Jesus Christ, and you shall have eternal life; and when you come to die, your souls will be received into heaven, there to be with the Lord Jesus in eternal happiness, with all the saints in glory; which, God of his infinite mercy grant, thro' Jesus Christ our Lord.—AMEN.

As it is expected that the inquisitive Public will be desirous to know some Particulars of Moses Paul, the following Sketches of his Life and Character, were collected chiefly from his own Mouth.[56]

MOSES PAUL, was born in the town of *Barnstable,* and Province of the *Massachusetts-Bay,* about the year 1742.

His Father, (as he has been told) died at the Siege of Louisbourg, in the year 1745.—He remembers but little of his Mother, only that she was a constant Attendant on Divine Worship, in the Presbyterian Meeting House in Barnstable.[57]

When about 5 Years old, he was bound an Apprentice to Mr. JOHN MANNING, of Windham, in this Government, with whom he lived 14 or 15 years, and in whose Family he learnt to read and write, and where he was instructed in many important articles of the Christian Religion.

After he left Mr. Manning's family, he inlisted in the Provincial Army, in Col. Putnam's Company, and Regiment. He says, that he contracted many sinful habits in the Army, which before his Inlistment he was a Stranger to the Practice of.[58]

Soon after the campaign was over, he engaged in the Seafaring Business, which he followed for several Years, as well in ships of war, as in Merchants service, where he got confirmed in those evil Habits which he too easily imbibed in the Army, which almost entirely eradicated from his Mind, those good principles in which he had been instructed, while he liv'd in Mr. Manning's Family.

---

56. Ava Chamberlain draws from colonial newspapers and church and court records to compose a fuller and more detailed account of Moses Paul's life, crime, trial, and execution in "The Execution of Moses Paul."

57. Jacob Paul married Mercy Richards in 1740. Both were probably Wampanoags from Cape Cod, Martha's Vineyard, or Nantucket. The Cape Cod community of Barnstable was historically home to a significant population of Christian Indians. Jacob Paul enlisted in the Seventh Massachusetts Regiment, which fought at the Siege of Louisbourg under Colonel Shubael Gorham (Chamberlain 418n14, 15). The Siege of Louisbourg took place during the War of Austrian Succession, when English army and naval forces attacked this French military and commercial outpost on Cape Breton Island in northern Nova Scotia.

58. Moses Paul served under Colonel Israel Putnam in the Connecticut Regiment from April to December 1764 (Chamberlain 419n17). During this time, Putnam's company was deployed to fight Pontiac's Rebellion in the Detroit area.

For these three or four Years, (since he has left the Sea) he has resided in this Government, living but a little while in a Place.——In the month of September last, he went to New-Haven, and living in a very unsteady Way, often getting intoxicated with strong Drink, and following other dissolute practices, till on the 7th of December last, in the evening, at Mr. Clark's Tavern, in the Parish of Bethany, he wounded Mr. Moses Cook of Waterbury, (who had put up at Mr. Clark's as a lodger) with a Club, and of which wound he died on the Thursday night following.——The Murderer was the same evening pursued and taken, and the next day he was committed to Goal in New-Haven.[59]

On the 20th of the same Month, his trial came on in this county before the Hon. Superior Court, when after a fair and impartial hearing, which lasted a whole Day, he was found guilty of the Murder of said Cook, and sentenced to be hanged.[60]

He has been accused of committing other Murders; particularly of killing a Sailor in the West-Indies, of which Charges, as a dying Person, he declares his Innocency, and that he has been guilty of no Murder, but that for which he is condemned to die.

He gratefully acknowledges the Kindness of the Ministers in the Town, for their unwearied attendance on him, during his imprisonment, and hopes that their Endeavors to promote his spiritual and eternal Welfare, has been attended with some good effect.

[Sermon text from first edition, published in New Haven, Connecticut, by Thomas and Samuel Green, October 31, 1772. Moses Paul biographical sketch text originally published as a broadside in New Haven on the day of the execution, September 2, 1772, and reprinted in third edition, published in New London, Connecticut, by Timothy Green, December 4, 1772. Courtesy of Dartmouth College Library.]

59. Moses Cook died from severe head wounds on December 12, 1771. Local newspaper accounts and court records relate that the already intoxicated Moses Paul became angry when the tavernkeeper's wife refused to serve him, was turned out of the Clark tavern, loitered outside, and assaulted Cook, the next man to leave, with a flat iron. By his own account, however, Moses Paul alleged that Cook verbally assaulted him, tied him up, beat him, threw him into a snowbank, and whipped him, "telling him to get up and Calling him a Drunken Dogg." After this assault, Paul reentered the tavern to reclaim a piece of clothing and was further threatened by Cook, who promised to "Still the Dogg" with a cane. Paul picked up a stick or club to defend himself. In his appeals, Paul accused Cook of "barbaric" behavior like "tribes of Northern Savages" (Chamberlain 421–422, 440–441).

60. At his trial by jury, on December 20, 1772, Moses Paul pleaded not guilty. The jury sentenced him to death by hanging, the first capital sentence issued in New Haven in more than twenty years. The execution was initially scheduled for June 17, 1772, but was delayed by appeals. Paul was represented on appeal by William Samuel Johnson, a prominent politician and lawyer who later served as president of Columbia College. In his appeals to the Connecticut General Assembly and the superior court, Johnson argued that racial bias and friendship with Moses Cook ruined the impartiality of the jurors in Paul's trial (Chamberlain 423–437).

8 ∽   "TO ALL THE INDIANS IN THIS
                BOUNDLESS CONTINENT" (1784)

To all the Indians in this Boundless Continent,[61]—I am an Indian also, your Brother
and you are my Brethren the Bone of my Bone and Flesh of my Flesh, I live at Mohegan or M^m^oyanhegunnuck, I have had a great Desire to Write to you a long
While, but I have put it off from Time to Time, to This Time, I am ^now^ Sixty one
years of Age—Now my Brethren lend me both your Ears and listen with great attention, and ^let^ nothing Croud into your Ears whilest I am Speaking, and prepare
your hearts. Let there be Room for my words & keep them there Choice and loose
them not, awake your Understanding and Call home all your Roving Thoughts, and
attend Diligently, and I Will Speak

     There is but one, Great ^good^ Supream and Indepantant Spirit above, he is the
only Living and True God,—and he has all Power, all Wisdom, all Knowledge and
Understanding, and he all Glorious and Excellent, and he is Infinitely happy and
Blessed in and of himself, and he is full of goodness, Mercy, Righteousness, Justice
and Truth,—And this God made Heaven and Earth and all things and all Creatures
therein— He made the Sun, Moon and the Stars, and fixt them in their Places, and
order'd them their Courses and they Continue their Races Steady to this age of the
World,—O how Wonderful and great is the Power and Wisdom of God,—and he
made this World and all Sorts of Creatures in it, and every thing that grows out of
the Earth, in Six Days he Made all things and all Creatures, and on the Six^th^ Day,
on the last Day of the Creation, he made one man, and after wards he Caused ~~woman~~
a Deep Sleep to fall upon the man, and God took out one of his Ribs and made a
woman for him, and they were Beautiful, Excellent and Glorious above all Creatures
in this World they were made in the Image & Likeness of their Creator, made little
Lower the Angels of Heaven and God Deliverd all this World and every Creature
every thing herein to the Man he freely gave it to him to ^be^ his own Inheritance
for ever, more over God made a garden for him, Where was everything that was
pleasant to the Eye and pleasant to the Smell, and Sweet to the Tast and good for
food and there was one Tree planted in the midst of the Garden, that was Gods Tree,
and the man and woman were forbid to meddle with it, and it was Call'd the Tree of
Kno^w^ledge of good and Evel, and god told them in the Day they eat of the Fruit
of the Tree they should surely die and this was all he had to do but to keep his hands
from this Tree and as long as he obeyed God, he was perfectly Hapy, he was indeed
the Richest man that ever was in the World, he had all this world, and everything
and Creature in it, and he was pure and Holy, he had no Sin, and his Happiness consisted in the full & uninterrupted Enjoyment of God his maker Which was his Superlative or highest Happiness—But it was not long before the bad Spirit which is
called the Devil and Serpent, Came to the woman, and Said, to God Say that in the
Day that ye ^eat^ of the Tree that is in the midst of the garden, ye shall Surely die?

61. The trope of America as a "boundless continent" also appears in petitions coauthored by Occom
     and the Montaukett and Brotherton tribes in 1785. It invokes a powerful sense of North Amer-
     ica as indivisibly and inalienably indigenous territory.

Yes Says the woman, god did strictly forbid us,—But the Lying Spirit Said, ye Shall not Surely die for god doth know, that in the Day ye eat thereof, then your Eyes shall be opened: and ye be as Gods knowing good and Evil and She was perswaded by the Lying Devil and She took of the Fruit and eat it and She gave it to her Husband also and he did eat of the Same,—Thus they both stold the Fruit of the Tree of God, and Broke the Command of God, by Disobedience. Now their Eyes were opened only to See their Misery, to know good and Evil to their Sorrow, and they now see and know, that they have lost all, they have lost the Blessed Image and Likeness of God, they have lost their Beauty, Excellence, Holiness, and glory, they have lost the Sweet Fellowship, Communion and Enjoyment of God, and Contracted the Image of the Devil and all his Likeness,—^and in Stead of being Gods they are Devils^—and have lost all this World, and the fullness thereof, they have lost the garden that god made for them Yea they are broke and become Bankrupts, and are fugitives and Vagabonds in the Earth, and are now liable to all maner of Miseries in this Life, liable to every Disease, Sicknesses, and Accidents, and is now Danger and Fear on every Side, and is liable to Death Continually, and as God told him that in the Day thou eatest thereof thou Shall Surely Die, and he is now Spiritually Dead, Dead in Trespasses and in Sins thus they have ruined themselves and all their Posterity with them—Now Whilest they they waiting and expecting Sin twice of Death from God, walking in the garden, in the Cool of the Day, and Adam and his hid themselves from the presence of the Lord God, amongst the Trees of the Garden, and the Lord God Called unto Adam, and said unto him, where art thou, and he said I heard thy Voice in the garden, and I was afraid because I was Naked; and I hid my self, What Change there was in Adam and Eve, to be afraid of God, that god in whom was their whole Delight a While ago, and now they try to hide themselves from God, O What Ignorance have they got into and he said Who told thee, that thou wast Naked? Hast thou eaten of the Tree, Whereof I Commanded thee, that thou Shouldst not eat? and the Man Said, the Woman that thou gavest to be with me, She gave me of the Tree and I did eat,—

And the Lord God said unto the Woman, What is this that thou hast done? And the woman said, the Serpent beguiled me and I did eat; and the Lord God said unto the Serpent because thou has done this, thou art Cursed above all Cattle, and above every Beast of the Field—And I will put enimity between thee and the Woman, and between thy Seed and her Seed, and it shall Bruise thy Head, and thou Shall Bruise his Heel,—Now in these last words the great and Merciful god, Discoverd his Love and Designs of mercy to Adam & to his Children, this Seed of the Woman is the Son of God, his name is Jesus Christ, he is the only Saviour of Sinners that believe in him; this promise was made to Adam and his wife in the Garden, and then he was turned out of the garden with his Wife—Now this one man and Woman, is the Father and Mother of all Nations of the Whole World.[62]

[CHS folder 1.25; CHS-M 403–407. Samson Occom Papers, Connecticut Historical Society, Hartford, Connecticut.]

62. See Genesis 1–3.

9 ∽ "MENE, MENE, TEKEL, UPHARSIN," DANIEL 5:25
(1785–1787?)

Daniel v:25:
& This is the writing that was writen—Mene Mene, Tekel Upharsin—

These Words, I dreamt of and Preachd from in my Dream Some Time ago, and they have followed me a great deal by turn ever Since, and last Spring I deliverd a Short Discourse from them, but I can not get rid of them yet, they Will follow Some Times Night and Day, and I am at last drove to write a Discourse from them for myself and others that may hear them—This is the most remarkable Text in all the Bible, and it was first sent to a great and Haughty King, and in a remarkable manner and the effect was remarkable, it was sent to Belshazzar while he was Feasting with a Thou of his Lords, with his Wives and Concubines, and Whilest they were Eating and Drinking, and Praising their Gods of Gold, of Silver, of Brass of Iron of Wood and of Stone; In the midst of their Rejoicing, the King discoverd Fingers of a Mans Hand and wrote over against Kindle-Sticks upon the Plaster of the Wall of the Kings Palace, and the King saw the part of the Hand that Wrote, Then the Kings Countenance was Changed and his Thoughts Troubled him so that the Joints of his Loyns were loosed, and his Knees Smote one against another and we may Safely Conclude that the Whole Company was Struck ^with^ Horror and Amazement, every Face was Changed, and the Whole Company was Seased with Trembling, Tears Gushing out of the Eyes of the Women—and all their Joy and rejoicing is turned into Death, at once,—The Writing was left upon Plaister of the Wall, but no one of the Company Could read it or understand it and the King hastily Call'd in all his Wise and Learned Men, Such as Astrologers, C^h^aldeans, and the Soothsayers, but they were not able to read or understand the Writing, and Kings Fear was still increased greatly, and his Lords his Princes and all his Mighty men were Terrified, and filld with Fear,—Now all their meriment is turned into Morning, Their Songs into Weeping, their Laughter into Sighing, and Lamentation, their Joy and Rejoicing into Bitterness itself, and there was nothing but Death and Dispare before them—Now the Queen by reason of the Words of the King and his Lords; Came in to the Banquet House: and the Queen Spake and Said, O King Live forever

Now we Shall Consider the Words and their Meaning and Interpretation—Mene, Thy Kingdom is numbered & finished—

Tekel, thou art Weighed in the Balances, and art found wanting

Peres thy Kingdom is divided and is given to meads and Persians

The Words of the Text were Writen by God, and in unknown Characters and Language none could read or understand them, but Daniel the Servant of the most High;—So it is now, ^none^ Can rightly understd the Book of God but them who are of the Family of God ^for the Name, the Life of God^ They have the Holy Ghost to Interpret the Holy Scriptures to their Understandings—But the World of Mankind as they are the offspring of fallen Adam, understand not the things of God, because they are Spiritually [deceived?] and they are Spiritually Blind, Yea they are Dead in Trespases and in Sins,—

From the Words we learn these great and important Lessons

I. Mene, ^God hath Numbered^ Thy Kindom and finished it,—All that we have in the World, both our Time and Substance, God Will Number, and will finish it

II. Tekel, thou art weighed in the Bailences, and art found Wanting—That every one of are Weighed in God's Bailence and are found either Substantial or Wanting

III. Peres thy Kingdom is divided and given to Meeds and Persians,—When we are taken out of this World, our Possions will be divided and given to others.

In the first Lesson we may learn, that every one of us is placed in the world according to gods pleasure, every one has some thing to do in place and relation in which god has Placed him—The gre^at^ Kings of the Earth, have their work in that high station, Kings are highest Rulers and they ought to rule for god and not for themselves, they ought to be Tender Fathers and Nursing Fathers to their Subjects, not Tyrants.—So all from the Highest of mankind to the lowest have Something to do for god in the World, & every one of us know Something of the Work or Duty he requires of us,—

[CHS folder I.25; CHS-M 435–438. Samson Occom Papers, Connecticut Historical Society, Hartford, Connecticut. Occom's diary records that he preached from Daniel 5:25 on October 16, 1785; November 30, 1786; January 2, 1787; and April 15, 1787.]

IO ∾ "THOU SHALT LOVE THY NEIGHBOR AS THYSELF," LUKE 10:26–27 (MAY 13, 1787?)

he loves his fellow Christian as his Brother in both Adams, and when he has the Spirit and Temper of Jx he loves all mankind as himself, he is Willing, all men in the World Shoud be happy as himself, Yea he does not begrouth[63] any man his happiness, and he is willing and desires men might have and enjoy the Same happiness in god as he enjoys & longs to have all men to be happy, in this World and Eternally in the World to come, Yea he rejoices in the happiness of his fellow men, and Morns at the Misery of of men and hates the Cause of misery of mankind and that is Sin, and they would not help their Neighbour in Sin any more than they would allow themselves in Sin, a true Neighbour will be very tender to his Neighbours Welfare as his own [words faded] and Character. When he Sees his Neighbour in distress, he is as ready to help him as he is willing to be helpt when in the Same Circumstance, he is ready to feed the hungry as he is willing to be fed when hungry himself, and he is just as willing to Sell to his Neighbour that is needy as he woud desire to have things sold to him when he Needs Some of his Neighbours things, and he is just as willing to Lend as to borrow,—Now to Nail and to Clinch all this ^we^ will bring the fore sited pasage Concerning the poor man who fell among Thieves, and the Samaritan, and we Shall mention other pasages of Scripture also—The Samaritan

63. *begrouth:* begrudge.

Saw the poor wretched man lying in the midst of the highway half Dead, panting for Breath and wallowing in the gore of his Blood, which has Spouled from his Dreadful Gaping Wounds, and he was Struck with Pity and Moved with Compassion to him and took a tender Care of him, bound up his Wounds, and caried to a Tavern and got him to take good care of him, and left money with him, and told him if he spent more than what he left, he woud pay him well when he returnd again,[64] here was that Lovd his Neighbour as himself, according to Christs own Doctrine—We Shall now go on to See What Christ have Said to his People Concerning Love, in Matt 5.43.^44^ is thus writen Ye have heard that it hath been Said, thou Shalt love thy Neighbour and hate thine Enimy; But I Say unto you, Love your Enemies, Bless them that Curse you, and do good to them that hate you, and pray for them which despitefully use you and persecute you—this ^is^ all contrary to Currupt Nature, Yet it is quite agreeable to grace; By this they Discover themselves to be the Children of God, as you may See it in 45 V in the 46:V: you have it thus, For if ye Love them which Love you, What Reward have ye? do not the Publicans the Same? in the next, and if ye Salute your Brethren only, What do you more than others? do not even the Publicans so? to Love our Neighbours and Enemies so as to Bless, to do good, and to pray for them Sincerely is Loving them as ourselves, and doing more than others— Christ Saith in John 15:12–13 This is my Commandment, That ye love one another as I have loved you, Greater Love hath no man than this that a man Lay down his Life for his Friends—Jesus Christ is a great Friend of poor Sinners, he is a Friend of publicans and Sinners not a friend of their Sins, and Wickedness, but a Compassionate Friend of their poor Condemned Souls and he Lay down his Life for them. this ^is^ in^deed^ a great Neighbour from Heaven, to poor Rebels and Enimies to God,— It is thus Writen in 1 John 3:16, Hereby perceive we the Love of God, because he laid down his Life for us; and he taught to lay down our lives for the Brethren—This is loving our Brethren as ourselves,—I Need not Say any^thing^ more upon this I think I have said quite enough,—Now I either understand this Text or I do not, I have either given Some thing of the Sense of our ^text^ or I am in a mistate about ^it^—But let ^yt^ be as it will. I have given my opinion upon the Text and it is either a false Doctrine, or it is a true one,—and as I have given my opinion upon it, So I Shall ^now^ draw Some Infrences from it—

Now let us listen to the Text.—Thou Shalt Love thy Neighbour as thy Self,— Harke ye! Who is this, that Speakes? It is he, it is the Same that Said unto Moses I am, that I am, It is the Eternal Jehovah, that Speekes. But who, does he Speak to, is there anyone in this gt [65] Congregation, that he is Speaking to? has he any business with any of us? has he any Power or Authority so to speak to us? take notice of that Word, Thou: it is in the Singular Number, it is to every individual of us, to one as much as nother, It is our God that Speaks, he made us, he Preserves us, it is in him, that we live, move, and have our Beings, and Therefore he has absolute right to command us,—and this Commandment ^is^ to us all,—Thou Shalt Love thy Neighbour; thou old man, thou old woman, thou middle Aged man, thou middle aged Woman,

---

64. See Luke 10:25–37.
65. *gt:* great.

thou Young man, thou Young Woman, thou Boy, thou Girl; thou Shalt Love thy Neigh-bour as thy Self, it is a possitive Command, from the Authority of Jehovah, and who dares to Say? that this Command does not include me, I am out of the Question, he is not my God, I do not own him, and therefore he has no Business with me; but I take it for granted, that every one, who is grown to Years of Some understanding, will readyly own, that this Command is to them, from their God, and will approve it as most Reasonable Command, Well let us See, Whether we comply with it, With all our Hearts, Whether we practice it Daily, it is one thing to Say, but another thing to do the Command, or to practice it,—do we Daily find a Love in our Hearts to our Neighbours, to have a Degree of Love to them, So as to have a Tender Concern for their Wellfare, have you a fellow feeling with them, do you find Pity and Compas-sion to the poor and needy, and do you help them out of their distresses according to your ability, and if it is not in your Power to help them, do you try to Exite others to help them; I have Seen many in Great Britain that was poor the^m^selves and had not withal to help their fellow poor, yet they woud go and beg for them, that Cant go about to beg for themselves, in Short do we find such Compassion on the miser-able and Distrest, as the Samaritan found in his tender Breast towards the poor man, Which he found in the High Way half Dead, and took tender Care of him, do we feel the same Love and pity to the miserable, and do we follow his example in releving the Distrest, and do we ^find^ their Commiseration to all Without respect of Persons, for this Love Which is required of us is without respect of Persons, and this Love the Samaritan Showd to a Stranger and to a man Who was quite of another Nation, Yea ^of^ a Nation Who dispisd him. There many who pretend to Love their Neighbours, but their Neighbours are either of their own nation or party, either in their Spiritual or Temporal Concerns but there is no party in this Love, and if we are true Neigh-bours, we are so to all; tho it is very natural for every Nation to have a National Love, and I believe it is not forbid in our Text, but then we Should have the Same Love to other Nations as we have to our Nation; and if this took place, there woud be an End of Wicked Wars and Blood Shed among the Nations, O How happy the Nations of the World live if they were all Neighbourly to one another but alas it is not so, Na-tions are pulling down one another, and Distroying each other,—but let us apply What we heard Closely to ourselves in our Daily Concerns with ^each^ other, in our Commerce.—Do we deal with one another as Neighbour, are we willing that our Neighbour shoud live as well as we, if we have anything to Sell, are Willg to Sell it Reasonably so as our Neighbour may live as well as we, indeed do we consult our own Wellfare, yes we do, every one does that, well this the very rule we are go by, we are to Consult the Wellfare of our Neighbour by Self Love, that that is not to Con-sult the Injury of our Neighbours in our Dealings, and if every one did but Consult the happiness of his Neighbour as well as his own, there woud be happy and Peace-able Living in the World,—But is there not a number here before God, Who Con-trives to Gratify nothing but Carnal, Beastly, yea Devilish Self if they can get all, tho themselves they dont care what is become of their fellow men,—Such Certainly dont regard, this great and glorious Command of god—tho it is most Rational and just,—the Lord Says thou Shalt Love they Neighbour as thy Self, You Say I will not Love him, I will have no regard for him I will do just as I please, this is the Language of the Practice of all oppressors, over reachers, Defrauders, Extortioners with holders of Corn and other Necessaries that they have to Sell, from their Necessitous fellow men, them that keep their Commodities horded up and will not ^Sell^ at present in hopes of Selling, much more in a few Days, are the very People, that will not regard god, these Say unto the Almighty, depart from us for we desire not knowledge of thy ways, and is there and Such now in this asembly, What a daring Creature you must be, What? not to regard God; and perhaps you prefer to be a Christian to, What a Christian and go directly Contrary to Christianity—But on the other hand I Woud hope, that there is a number here Who truely Love their Neighbours as themselves, according to our Text,—You know and you can appeal to Heaven, you have a Concern for your fellow men, you Pity the miserable, and you are free to help them; you have a fellow feeling with them; and You rejoice at the prosperity of your fellow men, Yea let them be of different Nations, if they Prosper in a Lawful way, You rejoice with them—but further you Love your Neighbor as yourself in a Spiritual Sense you desire his eternal happiness, you are Heartily willing he shoud have the Saviour with you, the Same Heaven and happiness with You, your desire for the Happiness of mankind extend to all Nations, yea you Love your Enemy in Sense as Yourself, you Desire his Conversion to God that he may be Happy you know, you can pray for your Personal enemies sincerely at Times,—and you are Conscious, you Love your Christian Brethren So, You ^can^ live and die with them, This is the Company you have Chosen in the World, they are the Excellent in the Earth in Whom is all your Delight; their Life, is ^yr^ Life, their Happiness, your Happiness, their Joy, your Joy, their Burden, your Burden, their Sorrow, your Sorrow, their Work, your Work, their Kingdom, your Kingdom, their People, your People, and their God, your God,— These you Love with a Love of Delight and Complacency, and you Love all men with a Love of Pity and Compassion—And in fact if you Love your Neighbour as yourself according to our text, it is an Evidence ^that^ you Love God, for this is the very fruit of it, if you Love God, it will naturally lead you to Love your Neighbour, the Beloved Apostle John Says, we know that we have passed from Death to Life, because we Love the Brethren, or our Neighbours as ourselves,—on the Contrary it is in vain for any ^of^ you to think that you Love God When you know, you ^have^ no regard for happiness of your Neighbour, you have no pity and Compassion upon the Poor and distrest—This is a black Evidence against you, it is a Sign that you do not Love God, if you think you Love god, you are deceiving yourselves See that passage of Scripture in 1 John 4:20, if a man Say I Love God, and hateth his Brother, he is a Liyar, if he does not regard the Happiness of his Neighbour he does not Love him, in reality he hates him, also, 1 John 3:17: But whoso hath this Worlds good, and Seeth his Brother have need, and Shutteth up his Bowels of Compassion from him, how dwelleth the Love of God in him, from this we plainly see, he that has no Love.

These are a Covetous People, They Covet every thing that their Neighbours have, Yea This Sort of People I think are Monopolizers; dont you think so? For these ^gen^ Men will Buy up evry Necessary of Life in the Town or State, even of the Whole World, were it in their Power especially in the Time of great Want and Distress, and When they have Horded up What they can then they will set an Extravagant Price upon their Commodities at once; They will sell you their ^goods^ today,

Yea this Morning, for Some of their goods for So much, and if another Comes at Noon or before, he must give a Little more for the Same Commodity, and if another Comes towards Night, he must ^give^ more ^Still^, and so they go on and that which did not cost the^m^ more than a Shilling, Yesterday, they will Sell for for twenty Shillings ^today^, and are not ashamd of it when they done Yea many Times they will brag of it, And if the Times like to grow harde^r^ and Distresses increase in the Land, these People will Shut up their Stores, and will tell you a thousand Genteel Lies, they'll tell you they [page torn—word missing] nothing now,—When they are only waiting for Worse Times,—I was going to Say, The [page torn] Praying for Worst Times, ^for Such Times Suits them,^ but I cant [page torn] Such People are Praying People, [page torn] they Pray to the Devil, for I am Sure that the Lord will not hear Such People with Pleasure he hears them with the greatest abhorence, their prayers are an abomination unto him, he will cast all their Prayers in their Faces as Dung, In my humble opinion, these are Devilish Lovers of themselves, I think these cant be calld, with any Propriety, to be godly Lovers of themselves Whats your Judgement, Concern Such People? am I wrong, or am I right in opinion?—But perhaps Some poor People or middling Sort of People may ready to excuse themselves ^& say^ I ant Such a Creature, but if they have the Disposision or Temper of Heart they are the Very People : & in every Station, Relation, and Standing of People in the World, if they have this Temper of mind, they are the very People, that Love themselves Contrary to God,—I think every Body may ^plainly^ See that is not the Self Love, mentiond in our Text—I might go on in this Topic, but Time woud fail me—

Therefore I woud proceed in the next place to Show that there is a Human Self Love, which which is noble and Commendable, I gather this from the Man Spoke ^of^ in our Text, I think [page torn] was ^not^ a Believer or a god man, yet he was [page torn]ted to the great Commandment,— I think it is [page torn] [p]lain that there is a Rational Self Love, we [page torn] Should have great Regard to our Life, as we [page torn] workmanship of Great God, so we Love ourselves, and Life Shoud be very Dear to us, and we Shoud take all proper means to preserve our Life and make ourselves Comfortable as we can, as long as we Live in this World,—let us remember this that we all Love to be lovd by our Neighbor we love to be taken notice of and Esteemd, and this Shoud be the Rule of our Conduct towards our fellow men, they Love to be esteemd as well as we, they are as much men and Gods Creatures as we are, and they Have the Same feelings and Sensations we have,—Now let us ^take^ a View of this in Scripture Light, The Samaritan that found the man that was half killd by Cruel Thieves, was not a Christian, yet he Shewd Self Love to the poor man, or he Lov'd him as himself, he treated and Used him, just as he woud have others treat him were he in the Same Condition, and this man Love this his poor N^r66 as himself—He-^This^ is very Remarkable among the Indian Heathen in this great Continent They Discover this Noble Human Self Love, they are very Compassionate one to another, very Liberal among themselves, and also to Strangers, When there is Scarsity of Food amongst them, they ^will^ yet Divide what little they have if

66. *N^r*: neighbor.

there is but a mouth full a Piece, and When any of kills any Creature, they will equally divide it amongst them all and when they have Plenty especially in what they got in Hunting & Fishing,—and when anyone is destitude of a Blanket, he that has two, will freely give him one, and they are very kind to one another in Sickness, and they Weep with them that Weep—This I take to be a Human Love or Being Neighbourly, according to our Text.

III There is a Christian Self Love, a Christian ought to Love himself as he is a Creature of God he is the most Noble and Excellent Work of God, The infinite Power, Wisdom, and Divine Skill of God is to be Seen ^in^ the formation of Man, and he ought to Love himself as he is the [Care] of Heaven, he is Wonderfully preservd in the World, all the Powers of Soul and Body are maintain^d^ by the Power of God every moment, and therefore he ought thankfully to Love himself; The Psalmest says I will Praise thee, for I am fearfully and Wonderfully made[67] and further, a Christian ought to Love himself as he is the redeemed of the Love, the Dear Purchase of the Precious Blood of the Lord Jesus Christ, the only Son of the Eternal God, he ought to Love himself in God he ought to be very tender of his Life, and be very Care[ful] of his Character and very Careful ^in^ his Temporal intrust and Wellfare, Especially for his Spiritual Life and Wellfare, and all out of Love and obedience to God—This ought to be the foundation of his Love to to his Neighbour, and indeed, he does Love his Neighbour as himself, When he is in his Christian Temper he Loves his fellow man as his Brother in the first Adam. [page or pages missing]

it is to every one that hears this Command it is Commanded to all men equally alike it is to the great and Small, to the Rich and poor, to Bond and free, to the Rulers and the Ruled, to the Honorable and Ignoble, to Merchants, and farmers, to buyers and Sellers, to old and Young, to the Jew and Christian, to English, Indians and Negroes and so forth—to the Professors of Religion *and non Professors,*—Yea to all that have any Love to themselves—I Shall now proceed to Show, Who our Neighbour is,—Every man ^& woman^ that we have any Knowledge of, is our Neighbour, yea them that we never had any acquaintance with are our Neighbours, and we are their Neighbours or ought to be Neighbours Now it is generally understood, that Neigh are those who Live Near together, take it in that Sense, then these that ^Live^ next ^to^ us [and] our Nearest Neighbours, that is, in their Situation, and he that Lives a little further is a Neighbour Still, and if he that lives nex to us, is not kind and obliging, we generally Say he is not Neighbourly and if he that lives further of, is kind and obliging, we Say such a one is Neighbourly, Well ^then^ he that is Neighbourly, is a Nei^r^ and from What we have Said amounts to this People that are Loving, Kind, obliging, and Tender to one another are Neighbours let them live together, or at a Distance, of one & Same Nation or not, it makes no odds—and let their Circumstances ^be^ never so different from each other, that makes no odds—The Rich has a poor Neighbour, and the Poor has a Rich Neigh^r^ and the Poor has his poor Neighbour, and the Rich has his Rich Neighbour—but let us hear Christ in his Word concerning a Neigh^r^ or Who a Neighbour is—You have ^it^ written in the 10 Chap^r^ of St Lukes Gospel, ~~and~~ you may read at your Leisure from 25 verse, but I shall read from

---

67. *I will Praise thee:* Psalms 139:14.

^the^ 29th Verse, (remember here is a Conference between our Blessed Saviour and an Old Lawer)—But he willing to Justify himself, Said unto Jesus, And Who is my Neighbour? and Jesus Answering Said, A certain Man went down from Jerusalem to Jericho and fell among Thieves, Which Stripped him of his Raiment, and Wounded him, and departed, leaving him half Dead, and by Chance there Came down a Certain Priest that way; and when he saw him he passed by on the other Side, And like wise a Levite, When he was at the Place, came and looked on him, and passed by on the other Side. But a Certain Samaritan, as he Journied, Came where he was, and when he saw him, he had compassion ^on^ him, and went to him, and bound up his Wounds, pouring in oil and Wine, and set him on his own Beast, and Brought him to an Inn, and took care of him and on the morrow, when he departed, he took out two pence, and gave them to the Host, and said unto him, Take care of him; and Whatsoever thou Spendest more, when I come again, I will repay thee. Which now of these three thinkest thou was Neighbour unto him that fell among the Thieves? And he said, he that shewed mercy on him, Then said Jesus unto him, Go and do thou Likewise.[68]—We see then from this holy Passage, all men in the world ought to be Neighbours one to another; The man who fell among Thieves was a Jew no Doubt, and the Priest was a Jew most certain, and the Levite also, but they were no Neighbours to their Brother Jew who fell among Thieves, ^no more^ than the Thieves were or the Devils are—But he that was a Neighbour in Deed, was a Stranger he was a Samaritan, one that had ^no^ manner of Connection with the Jews, Yea one that was Dispised and Set at Nought by the Jews yet this was a Neighbour, in God's account to the poor Jew who was almost Dead,—I think we need not Say more to know who ~~is~~ a Neighbour is—We Shall now Proceed in the next place, to show, What that Self Love is, by wh [page torn] we are to measure, or manifest our Love to our Neighbour ^in deed there is three fold self Love^—here I Shall Show both negatively and positively, I shall go on upon the Negatives—There is a Self Love that is Corrup^t^ a Narrow Contracted Self Love it may properly be Calld a Sordid Love—or rather a Devilish Self Love ^They^ that are Possest with this Love, Care not, What is become of their fellow Creatures if they can but obtain what they Desire it is all well, if thousands are Perishing ^all^ around them for want of the things they enjoy themselves, they don't Care—Such People will take methods to take advantage of their poor Neigbours, to get what they can of them, a Rich Self Love will let his Neighbour, who has little in the world have anything, till he get all his poor Neigh^r^ has, yea will Trust him freely & Seem to have a great Love for him, but by and by, he begins to enquire Strictly, how much ^his^ Neighbor is worth, is been Trusting, and having found out that he has Trusted him already as much as he is worth, and then directly Calls upon him for Payment, and the poor man is little delaying the Crediter with forth will Send an Officer, and poor man ^must^ be cast into jail, or give up everything he has, and when he has given up all, he and his ^wife^ and Children ^are Stript all they had also^ may Die and go to the Devil, for all their rich Neighbour—This Sort of People, if they can get Riches to themselves they don't car who is poor, if they can just have their Bellies ful, they dont care who

---

68. See Luke 10:25–37.

starves, as long as they have good Cloaths and enough, their Neighbours may go Ragged and Naked too for anything they care.—

[page or pages missing]

to his Neighbour, has none to God,—What Shall we think of those who take almanner of ways to hurt their Neighbours, either names or estates, Certainly these dont Love God, and consequently they have Religion, they are no Christians, let their pretentions be what they will in Religion,—they are worse than the Heathen, Heathen in general manifest more Humanity, than such degenerate Christians. The Savage Indians, as they are so calld, are very kind to one another, and they are kind to Strangers;—But I find amongst those who are Calld Christians, Void of Natural affection, according to their Conduct in the World,—and what Shall we say of you or think of you, or what do you think of yourselves; You that are Slavekeepers, do you Love God, and do you Love your Neighbour, your Neighbour Negroe as Yourself, are you willing to be Slaves yourselves, and your Children to be Slaves too, I think I have made out by the Bible, that the poor Negroes are your Neighbours, and if you can prove it from the Bible that Negroes are not the Race of Adam, then you may keep them as Slaves, Otherwise you have no more right to keep them as slaves as they have to keep you as Slaves; and at this age ^and understanding^ of the World I must Conclude, that Slavekeepers must keep Slaves against their own Light and understanding and they that will keep Slaves and plead for it, are not Neighbours to anyone, and Consequently they are not Lovers of God, They are no Christians, they are unbelievers, yea they are ungenteel, and inhumane, I believe many Christians, at the Time, have and do keep Slaves, but at this Time of the Day of the Gospel, they are much Troubled in their Confidence about, and great many have freed their Negroes already in these United States Since these Troubles began,[69] and it is a good work, them People show them Selves to be True Sons and Daughters of Liberty there are many who are mighty for Liberty, they will take all Liberty, but will give none,—There a set of men or ^a^ Certain order of men who have good [word illegible] my mind at this Day of Trouble, perhaps they woud be offended with me, if I shoud tell who they are, and if I shoud not tell who they are, maker will be offended with, and rather than to offend God, I will tell who they are, they are the Preachers or mi^ni^sters of the gospel of Jesus Christ it has been very fashionable for them to keep Negroe Slaves, Which I think is Inconsistant with their Character and Function, if I understand the gospel a wright, I think it is a Dispention of Freedom and Liberty, both Temporal and Spiritual, and the Preachers of the Holy Gospel of Jesus do preach it according to the Mind of God, they Preach True Lt[70] and how Can Such

69. Many New England slaveholders, impelled by a variety of moral, political, and economic reasons, emancipated their slaves during the Revolutionary War era. African-American slaves also pursued their own manumissions through the courts and through self-purchase. However, the abolition of slavery by northern states was a protracted and uneven process. Occom's home state of Connecticut passed a law banning importation of slaves in 1774 and a *post nati* emancipation statute in 1784, which dictated that individuals born into slavery during or after 1784 must be emancipated by the time they turned twenty-five years old. See Melish, Greene, Menschel.

70. *Lt:* light.

Keep Negroes in Slavery and if Ministers are True Liberty men, let them preach
Liberty for poor Negroes fervently with great Zeal, and them Ministers Who have
Negroes set an Example before their People, by Freeing their Negroes, let them show
their Faith by their Works, I heard not Long Since, that there is a Certain Minister
Westward, who preachd a Liberty Sermon for the Poor Negroes, and there were five
sot at Liberty immediately, the People had not many Negroes, and I hope that
Church and Congregation will Soon Liberate all their Negroes, I know of a Baptist
Church not far from this Place who have agreed and I think they have made it a term
of Communion, that they will not Commune with any one that will keep Negroe
Slaves[71]—A good Resolution this, the Lord that made all mankind alike in freedom
Bless them, I believe the mind of God, in their Resolution

[CHS folder I.26; CHS-M 464–476. Samson Occom Papers, Connecticut Historical Society, Hartford,
Connecticut. According to his diary, Occom preached from Luke 10:26 on May 13, 1787, near New
London, Connecticut.]

II ᥫ   "AND, BEHOLD, I COME QUICKLY,"
         REVELATION 22:12 (AUGUST 19, 1787?)

Revel 22:12

And behold I Come Quickly, and my Reward is with me to give every man According as his Works Shall be

We have many things in this Book of Revelation very misterious and Dark [to]
us, Yet they will be all made plain to God's People either in this World or in the
World to Come, and So far as these Misteries ^Concern^ the Church of God Miletant
have been made plain, and many of them have been fulfild in their proper Periods,
and others are yet to fulfill, Which will be fulfilld in their proper Seasons,—But
amongst these Misteries, there were many things Which are very Plain and they
Concern all men or every Man and Woman Concernd in them, As we find our Text,

71. Occom's reference here to a local Baptist congregation's refusal to commune with slaveholders
   suggests a heretofore undocumented eighteenth-century history of Baptist antislavery activity
   in New England. It is well known that in 1773 the Society of Friends became the first religious
   society in America to establish a policy requiring members to free their slaves. Congregational
   ministers such as Levi Hart, Ezra Stiles, and Jonathan Edwards, Jr., also voiced opposition to
   slavery as early as 1774; Edwards became a founding member of the Rhode Island Anti-Slavery
   Society in 1789, and in 1790 Stiles became founding president of the Connecticut Anti-Slavery
   Society. In 1790, a Baptist elder named John Leland unsuccessfully proposed a resolution that
   the general committee of the Baptist associations call for the abolition of slavery; Baptist leader
   Isaac Backus also quietly maintained antislavery opinions but did not encourage the church to
   join the debate (McLoughlin, 206). Occom here may refer to an independent action taken by one
   of the flourishing Baptist or Separate Baptist congregations in nearby Stonington and Groton,
   Connecticut, and Westerly, Rhode Island, congregations that attracted both African-American
   and Native American members; however, a search of the minutes of the Stonington Baptist Association between 1772 and 1795 yields no reference to noncommunion with slaveholders. Alternately, Occom may be describing an action taken by the Rogerenes of New London, Connecticut, a Quaker- and Baptist-influenced dissenting religious group that maintained antislavery
   opinions from the 1750s.

Behold I Come Q&—this Shoud Put every Soul in mind of their Accountableness unto god for all their Deeds, and they Shou'd be Exited to approve themselves to god in Jesus Christ by faith, and we Shou'd follow the Plain ^rules^ which god has given to us to approve ourselves to god by,—

But it is time for us to take notice of the text itself,—

And all that we Shall have to do at this Time, is to Consider the words as they are put down for us,—and then we Shall make Some Improvement,

The first word that we find in this, Behold, it is a word of Excitation, a word of awakening, a word of Admiration and wonder, a word to excite all the attention in the Soul, behold, Something is very great to be taken notice of, Behold I Come Quickly, here, the next word is I and it is a great I, and who is ^this^ I, it is the Lord Jx the eternal Son of god, this is that great I that is only worthy to be taken Notice of by Men and Angels with Wonder and admaration, dont we hear him Say, I am he, that Came Down from Heaven to visit your World to Seek and to Save that which was Lost I am he that was born among^st^ you &c

The Next Words are, I Come Quickly, Christ is a Coming into this World once once more, let us Consider the manner He will Come with the Sound of a Trumpet, the Arch Angel Shall give an Allarm ^to^ the Worlds and the Eternal I Shall defend, Behold the Lord Cometh with Ten Thousand of his Saints to execute Judgment upon all. and behold he cometh with Clouds, and every Eye Shall See him &c Rev 1:7: and the Son of Man Shall Come in his Glory and all the holy Angels with him &c Matth 25:31 and on—and he will will Come Quickly, it but a Little while before he will a thousand years is as one Day with him &c

And my reward is with me—to give every man according as his works Shall be, his reward is with him Proper and Just rewards for every one,—he has a perticular reward for every perticular work. Yet he has but two Essencial rewards Heaven and Hell,—Yet he

To give every man ^according^ as his work Shall be, he will exactly reward every one according to his Work, he will not, Shall I Say, Cheat any one a farthing, he wont wrong one Soul a might^te^———

Now let us apply wht we have advansd,

first then is it So as ^we^ have heard that Jx is a Coming, and will be here Quickly either by Death or at the Last Day, and does he Come with a reward for every one of you, and What reward do you Expect to receive from him, You need not mistake, You know What you have bee^n^ doing, you know your own Works, and So you must expect your rewards accordingly, Let us see then what is it, that you have been doing all this Time, have you been working the works of god, or the works of the Devil, have you believed on the Lord Jx, or have you not do you delight in the exercises of religion, or in the exercises of Sin, well according as your work is so Shall your reward be—you Shall be rewarded every Days work Since you have been Capable of acting, not one Day shall be forgoten, yea every Different work in a Day Shall be remember'd, and be reward, Yea every omission of Duty and every Commission of Sin Shall be rewarded, therefore Consider with your Selves, &c.

Han't you been Breaking the holy Commands of god, han't you been guilty of innumerable omissions—

[CHS folder 1.25; CHS-M 460–463. Samson Occom Papers, Connecticut Historical Society, Hartford, Connecticut. According to his diary, Occom preached from Revelation 22:12 on August 19, 1787.]

I2 ◌ "WHITHER SHALL I GO FROM THY SPIRIT?," PSALMS 139:7 (N.D.)

Psalms 139:7 Whither Shall I go from my Spirit &c—

Infidelity and Athiesim Seem to be a Sin, we are born with by Nature, David says, the fool Saith in his Heart there is no God, and when they own the being of God, they think he is altogether Such a one as themselves &c

David in his holy Psalms gives us a relation of his observation of men and his knowledge of god, by his Experience—

Sometimes he represents one of gods attributes Some anothere—as in the Psalm where in our text is &c—

From the words I shall take Notice

1 That there is no Such thing as runing a way from ~~the~~ God—
2 There is no hiding from him—

1 That there is no &c

This the holy Psalmest ~~by~~ knew by his experimantal knowledge and a lively Since he had of God when he Pen'd this Psalm, as the Psalm shows the Psalmest was Surpriz'd to find himself Surround with the omnipresence of god and his omniscience—

2 There is no hiding from him &c

1 We Can't hide our Selves from God who is a Spirit let us try to hide our Selvs where we will, he will find us out, &c— — —

2 We Can't hide our works from him, knows all things, &c— — —

Improvement

Is it to us we have heard that God is a Spirit and he is every where and knows and sees all things, that there is no Such thing as runing a way and hiding from, I Say if these things be true; Then, what manner of Persons ought we to be, in all holy Conversation and godliness—how Careful ought we to be in our Conduct in the world, how watchful over our thoughts words and Actions, how Careful ought we to be in obeying god in his word &c — — —

But alas how many there are in the world that hear of the Name of this glorious and dreadful ^god^, and yet regard him not

and is ^there^ not a great number in this great Congregation that are thus regardless of god and godliness; if not, what means all this distraction, and abomination, that is manifested in &c— —

know ye not that god hath Seen and knows you all and is acquainted with all your works, tho you may have forgot many of your own works, but god remembers them— —

And do you know that god Sees you now, and all your thoughts &c— —

and Where do you intend to run from his Presence or Where do you intend to hide &c— —

but in the last Place not to Leave you here—

I will give you a direction Where to run, run to god himself with a true Repentence, and faith toward our Lord Jesus x—in Jx you hide your Selves from the wrath of god, then you may hide your Sins, and they will be Seen and remembd by god no more— — —

[DCA Vault. Courtesy of Dartmouth College Library.]

13 ～ "I SAT UNDER HIS SHADOW WITH GREAT DELIGHT," CANTICLES 2:3 (N.D.)

Cant 2:3:
I Sat under his Shadow with Great Delight, and his Fruit was Sweet to my tast——

The Spouse, or the Church, is here relating her Sweet Experiences or Communion with Christ, and this she does by Comparing him to an Aple Tree, Which Yields Both a Pleasent Shadow and Fruit, and She Seting under it, with great delight and Satisfaction of Soul—

Since the Spirit of God compares Heavenly, with Temporal things, we will first Consider a Temporal Shadow,—

A Shadow Espicially a Shadow of an Aple Tree, that is full of Fruit, must be very Pleasent to a Weary Hungry and Thirsty traveller &c

So is Jx a Pleasent Shadow to a Weary Sinner—

[CHS folder I.15; CHS-M 439–440. Samson Occom Papers, Connecticut Historical Society, Hartford, Connecticut.]

14 ～ "CRY ALOUD, SPARE NOT" (I), ISAIAH 58:1 (N.D.)

Isaiah LVIII:1
Cry aloud, Spare not, lift up thy voice like a Trumpet; and Shew my People their Transgressions, and the House of Jacob their Sins—

The Religion of God is an Active Principle it is ^not^ a dead and inactive thing it is generally ownd by all sorts of People that the Religion of Jesus Christ, ought to be the greatest Concern in the World and if that be true, then there ought to be ^the^ greatest engagedness in Religious matters,—We have it set forth in Strongest terms in the Book of God, to rouse & engage the Hearts of the Children of men, in their Religious Concerns,—Those that are seeking and are under Spiritual Concerns, are calld upon with Such Language as this, strive to enter in at the Straight Gate, for many I Say unto you, will Seek to enter in and Shall [not] be able,[72] and the Religious are Commanded, to Run, to Wrestle, to Fight, &c &c—

And the Preachers of the Gospel are Commanded to be earnest, diligent, and

---

72. *Strive to enter:* Luke 13:24.

Faithful in their great and arduous work, they have an Auful Charge layd upon them by the eternal God, you may find it written in Eze. 3:7–22 and in many places besides—and in our Text we have a remarkable passage; The Lord Calling upon his Servant Isaiah to great engagedness and giving him direction, the First word we have in our Text is, Cry aloud, this denotes, the Compassion of God to his Careless People, a Sleepy People, a Stuped People, who are Stupified with Sin, they were greatly Degenerated,—Cry aloud, be in earnest, dont trifle with my mesage, be faithful, and then know you are delivering Realities and not Idle Tales, go with my Authority and with my Power, dont whisper nor be half asleep when you are delivering my Word,—Next words are, Spare not, don you spare your self, nor Spare the People, be willing to Spend and be Spent in Cause, dont Spare your Strength, nor your Voice nor your Time, nor your Substance nor your Name, be willing to be hated reproachd, and even to be killd for my Name—Spare not the People, let the great or Small, old or Young, Rich or Poor, Bond or free, Honorable or Ignoble—Next Words, lift up thy Voice like a Trumpet, Exert your Voice and Speak as loud as you can Speak as one in an Agony, Speak as one Seeing his Fellow Creatures in greatest Danger, next words are, Shew my People their Transgression, and the House of Jacob their Sins, This was indeed the message, and the matter of his Cry to tell the People their great Sins and Wickedness, Shew my People the Heinous Nature of their Sins as it is against me and as it is against their own ~~Destruction~~ Happiness yea as it is for their own Distruction—I have undertaken to Say Some thing from the Text we have Chosen at This Time, and by Divine assistance, I Shall endeavour to Show the Sins of the People, and the Conseq Consequences of Sin.

I. I am to Show of the People, and here I know not where to begin, the Command and the Charge is, Shew my People their Transgression and their Sins,—Here I see a large Field before me at once I dont know where to begin, and shan't know where to end,—I Shall begin with unbelieve, For this is the very Source and Fountain of all Sins, This is the most growing in our Day, the People do not believe the word of God and so consequently the dont God as he has revealed himself unto the Children of men, This is Horrible Sin of this Age of the World; From hence arises omissions in Duty, both to God and to their fellow men—Omission in the great Duty of Prayer, is a growing Sin, Family Prayer is I believe is neglected by People in general; even by too many Professors yea it is become Fashionable by many to have no family Prayer, Especially among the great ones of the Earth it is ungentiel to have family Religion, Asking a Blessing and returning Thanks at meal, is also much neglected by so many Professors; and I am ready to Conclude, that Secret Prayer is Shamefully Neglected by the greater part of mankind old and young, and Christian Conversation is layd aside, yea it is become loathsome and ungenteel to talk about Spiritual concerns; Publick Worship is greatly—yea abominably Neglected by too many in the Christian Land,—Reading of the Word of God is most Shamefully Neglected, Christian Visitations are much layd aside, and Visiting the Sick is Neglected, the poor are Neglected, the Fatherless and the Widow are Neglected,—Family government and Instruction I believe is greatly omitted,—In one Word, the Neglect of God, and the Soul, are the great omissions of this Age of the World, by all Sorts of People,—I might Said farther that Relitive Duties are greatly omitted, Children neglect their their Duty to their Parents, Parents neglect their Duty to their Children, Husbands and Wives omitt their Duty to each other, the Rulers and Ruled neg their Duty to one another, Master & Servants neglect their Duty to each other, Ministers and People, dont attend upon their to one another—We might Still go in this Strain but we will go on to enumerate the Sins of Commission,—Pride is a growing and abounding Sin every where among it all Sorts of People in all Nations, they are aspiring after greatness even to be gods, People are proud of everything, Some are proud of their Birth, because they descended from Such a Nation, or from Such a Family, they may be a Disgrace both to their Nation and Family, there may be Some indeed, that are ashamd of their Nation and Parentage, and from Whence is this Shame, why it is from Pride, Some are very proud of their Beauty, Such People take much Pains to [Deck] their Bodies with all manner of Finery to ad to their Beauty, that they may be admired by Foolish People and perhaps these people deform themselves, unman themselves, yea make the^m^selves Seven Times Worse than the Beasts of the Field, by their Daily Sins and all manner of abominations; Such Beauty is not Skin deep, Such Beauty is Deformity itself, There ^is^ Such a thing as True Beauty, and that Consists in the mind, and Vertuous Conduct, that is a Beautyful Person who bears the Image of God, and wa^l^kes agreable to the Gospel of Jesus Christ, such are Beautiful in the Sight of God, and the others are deformed and bear the Image of the Devil, and they are abominable in the Sight of God, The Lord hateth the proud Look[73] and the Lord Curseth the Proud;—Some are proud of their Strength, and will Strut about and Challenging his fellow man either to fight or wrestle run a race or fight, Such people forget God the giver of all our Powers both of Soul and Body, thier great Sin lies in miss using their Strength in abusing their fellow Creatures with Strength, and in not being thankful, to their maker, What hast thou, that thou hast not receivd, and if thou hast recivd thy great Strength why does thou Boast, O Strong man, and remember God will regaine thy Strength of thee in a little Time—Some Pride themselves in their Wit and Learning, and they ^will^ bend all their Wit and Learning to deceive their fellow mortals, and this is their great Sin, and they ^make^ themselv worse fools, than the Ignorant and the unlearned, Cursed be the Deceiver, the Lord Curses them, they look upon others with Scornful Eye,—The Wit and understanding a man has, the more good he ought to do among his fellow men especially among the poor Ignora^n^t—

I have no Patience to represent Pride in all its Shapes and Windings, Some are proud of their Cloaths, others are proud of their Riches, and Some are proud of their Children, Some are proud of their Priveledges, others are proud of their Religion, and this is the worse Sort of Pride, I have heard of a Certain Minister, who was Sensible of the Workings of his Pride he Said, If I preach, and find the People are well pleased, I am also pleas'd, and from Whence this pleasure, Why I find it Sprung from Pride, and if I dont preach Well, I am asham'd, and from Whence is this Shame, Why find it from Pride—and if I pray in Company, and if I think I prayd poorly, I am asham'd again, and this Springs from Pride, and if I happend to pray well in my

---

73. *The Lord hateth:* Proverbs 6:16–17.

own Nation, or others, then I am well pleasd, and this is from Pride also, yea Says he, I am proud of every thing—and this is ^the^ very Case of all men by Nature, they are proud of eve^ry^ thing, they are proud of that, which Shoud bring them to Shame and Confusion of Face—and this ^is^ a great Sin in this age of the World—Another grt Sin in the World is Loving the World above god, or making the World our greatest pe^r^suit, to the neglect of God and our own Souls,—Acording to appearence of mankind in general, their Hearts are ful of the Love of the World, and they Courting of it in all manner of Ways, it is thus Writen Concerning Such, James 4:4: Whosoever therefore will be a Friend of the World, is the Enemy of God, What a Devilish Sin this? to be at Enmity against god, our maker, Preserver and only Benefactor. There are men Discrib'd by the Word of God by these Terms, Lovers of Pleasure more than Lovers of God, and I believe our World is fild with Such Creatures in these degenerat Times, for there are Ten Thousand Sinful Pleasures Contrived and enjoyd to the Neglect of god, yea to the Contempt of God and Godliness, This is the great Sin of the Children of men in these goings Down of the Sun, and I believe every where in this degenerate age of the World; and is visiting the World with Sore Judgements for these Sins, and ^if^ the People will go on in their Complycated Sins the Lord will multiply his Sore Judgements, till the People return to God by evangelical Repentance—There is an Insatiable Thirst among the Children of men after great Power, Authority, and High Posts, that they may have ^great^ Honor in the World, from hence arises Tyrany which is abominable Sin in our Day, and this Tyranical Spirit Produces oppression, this is the most accursed Sin in our Day, Thousands and Tens of Thousands are growning and Crying under Oppressions Day and Night, the Faces of the poor are ground to the Bond in these oppressive Days—Contentions, Quarrilings, and Divisions amongst all sorts of ~~the~~ People, are Sins abounding in this Day, Divisions in State and in Church, Divisions among the Nations, Contentions in Kingdoms and remarkable Division in the English Kingdom, and there has been Remarkable Divisions in the English Nation in their Religious Concerns, and it Continues to be so there are as many Parties among them as any Nation in the World and there are Contentions in every Sect and Denomination ^among^ them, ^hence arises many Doctrines,^ this Certainly is a great Sin in the Sight of God, these Contentions are directly Contrary to his Holy Commandmen^ts^ and where there is Contention, there is every evil work, ^there is back biting^ and where there is Evil Works, there is or will be Distruction, if ^ready^ Repentance and reformation dont prevent,—Another prevallent and most abominable Sin in our Day is, Whoredom, this is too plain to be denyed, Whoredom, I suppose includes Fornication, and Adultery, O to what Degeneracy man has plungd himself into, ^he^ that was little lower than the Angels,[74] in Image and Likeness of god himself Shoud fall beneath the Beasts of the Field, for there is no Such thing as W^h^ordom Adultery or fornication among the Beasts; it is mor^e^ astonishing to See People, who have the Word of God amongst them and have had there Ministers to preach to them all their Days and yet be guilty of this foul and most abominable Sin, whi^ch^ the very Heathen in general abominate; Can these Such People be calld Christians with any propriety, What? Whoring

---

74. *Little lower than the Angels:* Psalms 8:5, Hebrews 2:7.

Christia^ns^ how does that Sound,—Lying is another Sin, that is growing plenti-
fully every where and they grow very large; this ^is^ indeed a Devilish Sin, the Devil
is a lyar, and all that are given to lying, Bear the Image of the old Devil, and I think
all people who are to lying may properly be calld Devilish People, their portion is
Specified in Revel 21:8 all Lyars Shall have their part in the Lake which burneth with
fire and Brimstone.

[CHS folder 1.25; CHS-M 419–426. Samson Occom Papers, Connecticut Historical Society, Hartford,
Connecticut.]

15 ∽   "CRY ALOUD, SPARE NOT" (II), ISAIAH 58:1 (N.D.)

Isaiah LVIII:1
Cry aloud, Spare not, lift up thy Voice like a trumpet, and Shew my People their
Transgression, and House of Jacob their Sins

The Religion of God is an active Principle, it is not a Dead and inactive Thing, it is
generally ownd by all Sorts of Professers of the Religion of Jesus Christ, that the
Religion of the Bible, ought to be the greatest Concern in the World and if that be
true, then there ought to be the greatest engagedness in Religious Matters.—We
have it Set forth in the Strongest Terms in the Book of God, to rouse and engage the
Hearts of the Children of Men, in their Religious Concerns.—Those that are Seeking, and are under Some Concern about their immortal Souls; are Call'd upon with
Such Language as this, Strive to enter at the Straight Gate, for many I say unto you,
will Seek to enter in, and Shall not be able, Escape for they Life, ^the^ Kingdom of
Heaven Suffereth Violence and the Violent take it by force, &c—And the Godly are
commanded to Run, to Fight, to Wrestle, and to Pray without Ceasing[75]—and the
Preachers of the Gospel are Commanded, to be earnest, Diligent, and Faithful in their
great and arduous Work. They have an Auful Charge lay'd upon them by the Eternal God, you may find it written in Eze 3:7–22, and in
  [page or pages missing]
  Sleep—The next Words are, Shew my People their Transgression & the House
of Jacob their Sins,—
  My People, the Lord [Claims] them as his People, they were the Choosen People
of God, they Were the Peculiar People of God, they were the only Covenant People
with god in the Whole World, tho' now they have abominably and most wickedly
Departed from God yet he Claims them as his People altho they have Denyed him by
their Wicked Works, and he Still Leads his Servant to them,—Shew my People their
Transgressions, they have Transgressed all my Laws repeatedly and a long While, and
the Whole House of Jacob have Sinned against me with all manner of Sins and their
Sins are much agrivated, they have all Sinned against me from the least to the to the
greatest, from the Highest to the lowest, From the Throne to the foot Stool, the great
Kings of Israel have grievously Sinned against me, they that ought to be the greatest Terror to Evil doer^s^ are the greatest Evil Doers themselves and encouragers of

75. *Pray without ceasing:* 1 Thessalonians 5:17.

Evil doers by their Wicked Examples and Terrors to the Godly and good Doers, and all the Magistrates under them, are like unto themselves, for the Wicked are set up, and they [word illegible] Rule,—and the Priests themselves are become Hirelings & the Prophets are become Lovers of Money, for they Divine for Money Micah 3:11. If the Hearts of the Peo are thus Currupt, no wonder if the members of every Society are So—Thus we have Seen the Jews were the first People of God, but they have wore out the Patience and Long Sufferings of their God, and Sinned away their Blessings and Inesteemable Priviledges and have been long Since un Peopled and un Churchd, and they are now [Scaterd] over the Whole World,—Has God no Covenent People then in the World Since the rejections of the Jews, Yet Blessed be God, where ever the Gospel of Jesus Christ is receivd by any People, they are the People of God,— and the English People are the Covenent People of god, they have enjoyd the Gospel Priviledges for a long Time, and they are now greatly Degenerated from the Purity and Simplicity of the Gospel and ^therefore^ they are the Very People that the Eternal Jehovah is Speaking of Speaking to in Text,—Some may query and say, Why may not this Text be more Sutable to the Roman Catholics than the English Why, I believe, Roman Catholics are left to themselves to themselves already they are unchurchd the Lord dont own them as his People they are in fact become only Christians—But the Lord is yet Sending his True Servants the Ministers of the Gospel of Jx the True Doctrines of the Bible are yet Preachd and Shine in English Israel,[76] So the Mesage is to them in particular—

Almighty God, Father, Son and Holy Ghost, I thy most ^weak & most^ unworthy Servant have undertaken to Speak from this thy Holy Word, Lord give me Light and understanding open to my understanding the Holy Scriptures by thy Spirit, and give me Gospel Courage and Boldness, and Sutable meekness and deliver me from fear of man

All that I shall do at this Time in Speaking upon our Text, will be to show the Sins of People of God in this age of the World—

I shall set down Unbelief to be the Root of all Sins or a fountain from which Streams all Wickedness, Unbelief is the Mother of all abominations in the World, it was Unbelief, that first enterd into our first Mothers Heart, I Shall Represent and prove Unbelief to be the first and greatest of all Sins—And I shall also Show the Dreadful Conseqences of Sin upon the Children of men

I. First then I am to show and represent the great Sin of unbelief—Unbelief is that, which Denys the Being of God, and ^if^ Unbelief alows of a God, Yet it does not alow him to be Such a Being as he is, unbelief makes God to be very Small and insignicant Being, so Small unbelief will not regard what he Says, Hence unbelievers will not believ what God says, unbelievers ^dont beli[eve]^ the mighty works of

---

76. The description of England as Israel can be traced back to the Reformation-era writings of Andrew Marvell and John Milton. The modern belief system known as British Israelism emerged most powerfully in the nineteenth century in texts such as John Wilson's *Our Israelitish Origin* (1840), which argued that remnants of the house of Israel took refuge in the British Isles and that Great Britain itself is Zion.

God, either in Nature or grace. They dont belive his miracles, many Sinners are worse than the Devils in their unbelief, The Deists[77] are worse than the Devils, Devils believe the holy Trinity, many dont believe Jesus Christ to be God as well as man, the Devils believe him to the holy one of God, believe to be the Son of God, many do not believe the Bible to be the [Book?] of God, the Devils firmly believe it to be the Book of God, unbelievers don't believe, Heaven or Hell, or future Rewards and Punishme^nts^ and if they have any Notion of these things they ^dont^ affect their Hearts anyway, yea Unbelief renders the Benefets of Christ Death and Sufferings ineffectual, and all the Promises and Threatening of God are ineffectual—From this Unbelief, Proceeds all manner of Sins, that are Committed in the World,—The Heart of man is the Seat of unbelief, Which is like an inexhaustable Fountain of all Wickedness—The great Saviour of the World Saith in Mark 7:21:22. For from within, out of the Heart of men, Proceed evil thoughts, Thoughts, first, then, Adulteries, Fornications, Murders, Thefts, Covetousness, Wickedness, lasciviousness, an Evil Eye, Blasphemy, Pride, Foolishness; St Paul also enumerate the Forms of unbelief in Rom. 1:29 :30 :31: Being filled with all unrighteousness, Fornication, Wickedness, Covetousness, Maliciousness, full of Envy, murder, debate, deceit, malignity; Whisperers, Backbiters, Haters of God, despiteful, Proud, Bo^a^sters, inventors of evil things, disobedient to Parents, without understanding, Covenant Breakers, without Natural affection, Implacable, unmerciful,—Again he repeats some of these Sins, and adds to them in his Epist. to the Gala, 5:19: Now the Words of the Flesh are manifest (or the Works of unbelief,) which are these: Adultery, Fornication, uncleanness, lasciviousness, Idolatry, Witchcraft, hatred, variance, emulations, wrath, Strife, Seditions, heresies, envyings, murders, Drunkenness, revellings, and such like— and having given a small touch Concerning, Unbelief, and having also gatherd some Fruits of Unbelief out of Scripture, and layd them as a foundation to build upon, I shall now begin to Show the Sins of the People of God—

I. Evil thoughts these are the first that are mentiond by the Great Saviour; and if ever the Hearts of the Children ^of men^ were filld brim full with all manner of evil thoughts, it is Now,—It is writen Concerning Antediluvians, or the People before the Flood, in Gene 6:5 And god saw that the Wickedness of Man was great in the Earth, and that every Imagination of the Thoughts of his was only Evil, Continually; and I think, without misapplying this Pasage of Scripture; You See now that the Wickedness of the Professors of the Religion of Jx is very great and that every Imagination of the ^thoughts of^ their Hearts are only evil, and that Continually Night and Day; it Seems unbelieving hearts are full of Evil Contrivances, as the Psalmist oft expresses it, The Wicked Deviseth Mischief on his Bed,[78] and amidst all their Contrivances, God and their Souls are left out, it is writen, God is not in all their thoughts;[79] I Judge by the Fruits, it Seems by the Conduct of Mankind in general that men of all Sorts have their Hearts full of Evil Thoughts; I hope there is a

---

77. *Deism:* Belief in a universe governed by rational principles and natural laws discernible through reason rather than scripture or revelation.

78. *The Wicked Deviseth:* Psalms 36:4.

79. *God is not in all:* Psalms 10:4.

Little number that have the Fear and Love of God, in their Hearts, but they are so few we can scarsly find them, by their works of Love and Faith,—Having Said Some thing of the Sin of the Heart, I Shall now proceed in Tracing Actual Sins, The next Sins to Thoughts, are Adulteries, fornications, Paul puts uncleanness with these, these sins seem to be near akin to each other, so I shall Consider ^them^ in their order, first the Sin of Adultery, this Sin is much Complained of in the Book of God and forbiden every where in Scriptures, and Certainly then is always abounding, in a degenerate Age, and this is a most abominable Sin in the World, the Heathen Abominate this Sin, and they punish it most Ignominious Punishment, The man, Whose Wife has Playd the Whore, will bite off her Nose, that She may bear the Shamful mark all the rest of her Days, Wherever She goes,—yet this Sin is Committed by Christians. What abominable this must be in the Sight of God and ^Christian^ man What? to have the light of the Bible, and Committ this ^Beastly^ Sin What? a Christian man, leaves his wife take another mans wife or no mans Wife; and a Christian Woman leave her Husband and take another Womans Husband, What a Cursed Sin this must be in the Sight of God, this Sin upon Baptized Persons, may be Seven times Worse than the He^a^then,—Fornication is a Sin every Where Condemned, in in the Bible, and this Sin is abominated by the better Sort of Heathen, Yet this Sin is abounding in Christendom and it is a prevailing Sin in this Country, amongst the White People, Who have all means of Instruction, have had the Whole Bible, and the Ministers of the Word of God, Yet this foul Beastly Sin is abounding amongst them; What pity it is that the Young People, that look so Beautiful and Comely in the Eyes of the World, Shoud make themselves viler than the Beasts that perish, they need not be guilty of ^this^ if they Sin, as long as there is a Lawful and Gospel allowance to marry, Yea, it is Said in the New Testament, Marriage is Honorable in all, and the Bed undefiled; but Whoremongers and Adulterers God will Judge.[80]—This Sin of Fornication, has been abominable and Shameful among Some Heathen Indians; that if Some Young Man and Woman have been too familiar, and like to be found out in this Sin, th^e^y woud voluntarily Banish themselves from their own Country and never to Seen there again—and is it ^so^ abominated by those that are Calld Christian People? no it is hardly esteem'd as Sin by too many— Uncleanness is also frequently mention'd and Condem^nd^ in Scripture, this Sin, I have been inford, is Practicd by those that ^are^ Calld Christian People, but I need not Say upon this I have Said Somthing upon the other two, this Sin is a kin to the other and so I Shall Say no more,—Now the punishment of these is Exclution of Happiness and infliction of Eternal Damnation—We ^have^ also Murder ^mentiond^ in the Catalogue of Sins, Murder is Such a Sin that is abhord by all Nations, it is most unnatural Sin, Yet this Sin is very Common in Christian Land, So Call'd, this is ^one^ of the greatest und^er^ which the Earth groans, tho open murther is not ^so^ frequent as it has been in days past, yet Privet murders Continue perhaps Some ^may^ ask, What is open murther? Persecution is open murther, Cain killd his Brother Abel for his Religion, & it was persecution, and it was murther There is one Sort of open murder is now Caried on & allowed by those who are Calld Christian People and here

---

80. *Marriage is Honorable:* Hebrews 13:4.

some may query again and say What is that, Why, it is encouraging and Carying on Negroe Slave Trade, this is a Murderous Trade, it is the most Complicated Wickedness to Cary on this Trade, it is the Most acursed and most Devilish Practice that ever was found among the Children of men, and yet this Trade is practic'd the who have the Word of God before them, I Cant Conceive how they read the Word of God, in Carying ^on^ the inhuman Trade a Lake of Negroe Blood has bee^n^ Shed, Thousands and T of poor Negroes have been Slain by Baptized People, there has been first, second, and Third hand Murder in Carying on Slave Trade, the gr^eat^ Men Imploy others to go to Affraca, and they imploy aga^in^ others to take the poor Negros

[CHS folder I.25; CHS-M 449–456. Samson Occom Papers, Connecticut Historical Society, Hartford, Connecticut.]

16 ᘇ   "WO UNTO HIM THAT GIVEST HIS NEIGHBOUR DRINK," HABAKKUK 2:15 AND ISAIAH 5:11, 22 (N.D.)

[Habakuk 2:15]
Wo unto him that give[th his] Neighbour Drink that [put] thy Bottle to him, and makest him Drunken also, that thou mayest look on their Nakedness.

Isai.V.11 Wo unto them, that rise up early in the Morning, that they may follow Strong Drink, that Continue untill Night, till Wine inflaim them.—Verse 22 Wo unto them that are mighty to drink wine, and men of strength to mingle Strong Drink.—

God, the Eternal Benefacent Father of all—Saw fit to Create this World, and he fill'd it with Variety of every thing, both Animate and Inanimate Creature The moving Creatures upon the Face of the earth are innumerable and various, both great and Small,—And the feather'd are without Number, and of all sort and the productions of the earth are amazing in their variety, both to [page torn] the Tast, [page torn] defferent Vertues [page torn] in the things to grow on [the] Earth—And Variety of Fruits upon the Face of the Earth.—And the Lord, made a garden also, and we must Conclude that it Contains the very Choice and the most excellent things in the World,—And the Sea the Lakes and all Streems were all full of every kind of Fish, great and Small.—and the Lumanaries also Were fixt in the Heavens like Lanthorns,[81] The Sun the Moon and the Stars Were made to give Light to this World.—and When the Lord God, had Bountifully and Richly furnishd, this World, with every necessary of Life—Then last of all, he made man for Whom he made this World,—he was the Crown, the Glory, and the Excellency and the Beauty of the Whole Creation. For God made him in his own Image and Likeness, Breathed into him the Breatt of Life and he became a living and Imortal Soul,—and the Lord formed Wo[m]an also out of the m[an] [an]d they two were the [page torn] that ever was, they we[re] little lower the Angels,—and the Lord ^gave the Whole World—^ placed in the Garden and freely gave it to them, and ever in it except one Tree which was in the midst of the garden, and they were not to eat of that, for in the Day that they Shou'd of it they Shoud die and we must Conclude, that Whilst they Stood in their Inocency,

81. *Lanthorns:* Lanterns.

they they use every Creature Comfort agreable to gods mind, they Glorified god in all things—and they fully Enjoyd God, & that was their Supream Happiness,—and had they Continued in that State of holyness, they might have been happy to end-less ages—But alas We find a malancholy account, of them; When the Tempter Came to our Mother with a lie, She put forth her hand Stold the forbiden Fruit and eat of it, and gave unto her Husband also, and he eat of it [after] which they lost all. They [lost the] Blessed Enjoyment of God, they Lost the Image of God, and all their Holi-ness and Inocency, all Light and Comfort,—They plungd themselves and all their Posterity into Sin and Darkness, and all manner ^of^ Misery, To Death Temporal Spiritual and Eternal—

This is the Miserable Situation of mankind, he is now prone to all manner of Sin,—alas, Where is man and What is man? The most Noble Creature is become the most Ignoble Creature, from being almost an Angel, is become a Divil.—He is now practicing all manner of Sins,—and amongst the various commited, Drunkeness is one of the Worst, yet it is growing amongst all Nations.— — —

I Shall now Say Something from the Texts I have read;—Some may think it Strange, that I Shoud take So many Texts to make one Discour^se^ upon; I aim to Speak to two Sorts of People in particular—

I Shall now take notice of the first—

Wo unto him that giveth his Neighbour Drink &c—There is a [law]ful use of [all?] Creature Comforts, they were made for our Support and Comfort in Life—but when we use them beyound the bounds of Temperance We Use them unlawfully, and Sin against God the giver of all these Comforts—and there is Sin, both in Com-municating and receiving these Comforts, as we See in our Text.—A dreadful is De-nounced, against him that gives Drink to his Neighbour, a bad intention—

[DCA Vault; booklet torn and worm eaten at top edge. Courtesy of Dartmouth College Library.]

17 ∾ ## "SAYING WHAT THINK YE OF CHRIST" (III), MATTHEW 22:42 (N.D.)

Math 22.42
Saying What think ye of Christ

Man is a Rational Creature he is Capable of thinking & Reflecting; the Mind of man is a restless thing it is always upon a go, diving into may things Daily. it is very in-quisitive, and there are inumberable objects of thought Continually

But Christ is only worthy object ^of^ our thoughts

But alas in our fallen State, our minds are ^runing^ upon rong objects

We find in this Chap Several Questions, Put to our Blessed Savi—by Several Sorts of People, and he Answered them all, to their Shame and Confusion, for they Brought their Questions to him to Intangle him they did not Come to for Inlight-enment or Knowledge, for they had Knowledge and Wisdom Enough in their own Conceit—

But they were Shamefully Intangld in their own Net, Now they had nothing to

Say for themselves and they darst nt Ask him any more Questions, Now Christ had wated Patiently &c

It was Now a good time for him, While they were together to Put forth unto them ^but^ one Q that was most material in the their Religion, Which they ^had^ forgot this he did out of Pity and Compassion to them, to Inlighten them not to Intangle them as they Intended to him in their Qs

Saying—

This Question is the very Centre of our holy Religion it is the Centre of the Bible our Life depends upon it, if we Answere it right we Shall live, if not we Shall Die— the method I Shall take is only to give a Short History of Christ According to Scripture Account, and See What ^opinions^ there has been among men about x,

and What opinions there is Now

and then Ask our selves the Question, and Answere it before god

And here first

What think of X as he was the Promised Missiah—under the Mosaic Dispen.

2ly   What think ye of X at his Birth. God man

3ly   What think ye of X in his Publick appearance and Ministrations—Prophet.

4   What think ye of X in his Acusation Condem and Death

5   of his Resurection

6   of the Ministration of word

6̶ 7 of his Asention

7̶ 8 of Intercession

9   What think ye of X as a Judge at the Last Day

[CHS folder I.25; CHS-M 457–459. Samson Occom Papers, Connecticut Historical Society, Hartford, Connecticut.]

18 ∽   "GIVING THANKS ALWAYS FOR ALL THINGS
              UNTO GOD," EPHESIANS 5:20 (N.D.)

Ephe V.20

Giving thanks always for all things unto God,

Perhaps there is no Duty incumbent upon Intellagent Creatures, more frequently Calld for, in the Providence of God, than this Duty of giving thanks to god, there is nothing so Reasonable and becoming in Dependent ^Creat^ as this giving of thanks, to their great Preserver—Yea all the Creation, even the Inanimate Creation Seems to manifest this Duty, to the great Creator—

We may at once Perceive Something very great and weighty in these few Words, if we doe but listen and attend to them, and Shou'd find work enough all days and a Glorious work too

In the first Place, upon Reflection we find the Work it Self or the Duty [page corner torn] Giving thanks, Seconly, upon inquiry to Whom we are to give thanks, we may find object, unto GOD; Thirdly we find, the Time When, this Duty, of giving Thanks is to be Done it is Always Fourthly we find the Matter, or for what we are to give Thanks; for all Things

These four Particulars I Shall endeavour to represent in the following Discourse

I. First then, I will endeavour Represent to you the Duty it Self, to Give Thanks,

This I Conclude is well understood by all, that are grown to Years of under-standing, It is to have a grateful Since and Right apprehention of the Benefits Con-ferr'd upon us and an Acknowledgment & Confession of our Obligations to our Benefactors with Glad Gladness of Heart, attended with Humility, and a Careful and Right Use of the Benefets we Receive, even agreable to the Mind and Pleasure of our Benefactors for which they bestow^d^ their Bounty upon us ~~The Work~~ Among Men, the work of the giver is one, and the work of the Receiver is a nother, We are dependent Creatures ~~upon~~ one to another, the greatest of men Can't ^well^ live with-out the vulger Sort, and we, as Sotiable and Fellow Creatures, give and receive Bene-fets, one from another, The giver has one Precept from God the great Benefactor, as we find the Duty in 2 to the Corin 9 6.7 and many other Places in the Word of god— and the Receiver has another Command or Precept from God the Great Benefactor, their work is to Receive Right, and to be [page corner torn] be truely Thankful, in the first Place to God the only giver of all good things, and next to god we are to be thankful to the Instruments by Whom we have Received Benefits,—let the Second givers or Instrumental Benefactors give as they Please Whether out aright [word il-legible] or not, that is none of the Receivers Business, they ought to See to it, to do the work that is lay'd upon them, by their Benefactors, to be Truely Sincerely and Heartly thankful, both to god and to his People by ~~his~~ whom they have received benefactions—But man is such a Creature, many of them when they Receive a Kind-ness from their ^fellow^ Men, they are Ready to query and wou'd know Whether the giver, gave freely and Cheerfully or Grudgingly and of Necessity, and if they Suspect the Sincerity of the Donor, they are Ready to dispise the Benefit and the Benefactor, and are ^Ready^ to fling the gifts back in the Face of the giver With ^a^ Surly Countenance—this Plainly Argues the Horrid and Hellish Ingratitude, in the unworthy Wretch, Such cannot be thankful to God, for they don't Consider that all these good things are from god, for it is he that opens the Hands, if not the Hearts of his People, to give to the Needy, and therefor Thanks and Praise is his Due Chiefly; ~~and~~ But if the Receiver Cant be thankful to their fellow Creatures that have Shown kindness to them, how Can they be Truely thankful to god—Isai. 1.2

But those that are truely Thankful are melted Down with the Benefets they have Receiv'd, it excites true humiliation and Self Loathing in them. As we find holy Pa-triarch Jacob Confessing his unworthiness of the Least of gods Mercies Gene. 32 [10] again an ungrateful wretch Sets Price upon the Benefits he rece^s^, or has a Scale as it were, So he wou'd Put the Donations in the one and Propotionable thanks in the other or rather his Black Ingratitude—the ungrateful Pharasee thought he did enough in Religion—

But the Grateful Man Sets no Price upon the Benefits he receiv^es^ nor limits to his thankfulness, he thinks he Can never be thankful enough for Favours receiv'd—

Thus we find the ^truely^ thankful King of Israel, the Psalmest, Psal 116.12 What Shall ^I^ render unto the Ld for all his Benefits towards me? it Seems by these words, that the holy Psal^st^ found himself unable ^to^ make Sutable Returns to God

for all the Kindness he had receivd ~~from god~~ from him, and it was his Diligent Search
or Study to find a way to manifest his gratitude by unto god, as his holy thanksgiving Psaˢ abundantly Show,—if we oservᵉ David in his great work of giving
Thanks, According to his Psalms, we may Easily ^find^ his experimental Notice and
his Wise Consideration of the Benefits of God towards him and this begets a grateful Sence of the Favours of God, and that breaks forth into Publick Praises and
thanksgiving—Yea upon finding himself unable to give suficient thanks to god for
all his goodness, he Calls all Creatures both in Heaven and Earth to Join with him
in his gr^e^at work of giving thanks and Praise unto God; and indeed it Reasonable
and Right that Dependent Creatures Shou'd be truely thankful to their upholder and
only Benefactor,—

This Seems to be inate in the very Dumb Beasts of the Field, they Manifest a
kind of Gratitude to their Benefactors or Masters, by a Certain Noise, or the Motion
of their Bodies,—the Fowls of the Air Mount up towards heaven and Sing forth their
Artless to God,—Toads and Frogs and all the Venomous Kind, have their way of giving thanks to their Ma[ster] [page corner torn], Yea the very Insects of the Earth Sing
their Various Notes of Praise to god, if all these Creatures give thanks and Praise to
God, how ought Man ^who is Endow'd^ to give thanks ^for whose sake^ thanks and
Praise to the God of Heaven, it is Mans Beauty and Glory as well as Duty, to give
thanks and Praise to Heaven, and it is his happiness So to do—

2 Secondly let us Consider the object, or to whom we are or ought to give
thanks, it is unto God, the great Creator of Heaven and Earth, and the upholder and
governor of the Same, and the only Benefactor, unto him we are to give thanks, Even

To him we are to give thanks that Curiously and wonderfully Fraim'd our Bodies
out of the Dust of the Earth—

To him, that Breathed into our Bodies the Breath of Life, yt Caused us ^to^ become Living Souls we are to give thanks

To him we are under Infinite obligations, Who Confers, not few and Small Incon-
siderable Benefits upon us, but ~~very~~ all good things not at times only, but Continually

To him we are to give thanks who hath Created ~~ye Light for our Eye~~ the Whole
World for our Sakes—

To him we are under greatest obligations, ^he^ that hath made the Pleasent
^Light^ for our Eye, ^he^ that hath Made the Herb of the Field, and all the Fruits of
the Earth for the Use of Man, He that hath made all manner of Four footed Beasts and
Creeping things and the Fowls of the Air, and the Fishes of the Seas, He that hath
given and Deliver'd all these Creatures unto us, to him we are to unfeigned thanks

To him we are to give most humble thanks, into whose Justice we have forfited
all Mercies, yet Continues his Mercies to us thru the Mediator

To him, in Whom Live Move and have our Beings, we owe all Possible Thanks—

To him, who hath given his only begoten Son into the World, to Save us Vile Sinners from everlast Ruin, to Eternal Happiness, I Say to him we are Bound to give most
Sincere and humble, yet Joyful Thanks—

3 Thirdly let us Consider the Time, when, this Duty of giving thanks is to be
done, it is allways there is no Limited Time, or a Certain T. ^in^ of our Life to give
thanks, but at all Times; this is altogether Reasonable, for we always Receive bene-

fits and Mercies of various Kinds from God, we live and Move and have our beings in him Continualy—all the Faculties and Powers Both of Soul and Body are Maintain'd in us by god Continualy, the food and Drink Which We Continualy Use is the Lord's, the Earth upon which we have Always Liv'd is the [page corner torn] [Lor]ds, the Air in Which we always Breathe in is the Lords; and So in return, as we always live upon goodness of God, So Shou'd our thanks be always to God—further this giving of thanks always may Suppose or require a thankful Fraim of Heart to God always to have grateful Sence of the goodness of God Always, and to have [word illegible] resolution to go on in giving thanks to god always, as David abundantly Shows in his holy Psalms his resolution was to Praise God all His Time; so shoud all rational Creatures resove,—again we Shou'd ^always^ be very Strict in attending to Certain Seasons or Perticural Times of giving Thanks to God; Whether Publik, Privet or Secret; yea as there is no Minute of our lives empty of Mercies from god, So Shoud we fill every Minute of our lives with thanks to god, ~~Im~~ David Says I will Praise god Seven Times a Day, or give thanks Seven Times a Day,—So Shou'd we give thanks to god, not only Seven Times a Day but Seventy Times Seven I mean to have a T^h^ankful Fraim of Heart all the Day Long—

We dont mean in all this that we ^are^ obliged to Manifest our thankfulness always in ^one^ Continued Act either by Word of Mouth or by the Posture of the Body for this is Impossible in the ^Present^ [situation?] of our Life, we are Necessarily Calld to other ~~emmediate~~ Acts of Duty from Day to Day, we Necessarily ^Spend^ our Time in Sleep, But this need not, yea Can't Break off our thankfulness, if we are true thankful—As a Wise Man, is a Wise Man—always whether he Sleeps or wakes Whether a broad or at home, he is Still the Same Wise Man—So a thankful Man is always So—

4 Fourthly and lastly let us Consider the Matter of our thankfulness, It is for all things for Everything that we have Receiv^d^ and any thing that we now Possess and Enjoy, and for all things yt we ^hope^ ~~for~~ to Receive hereafter—

Here we may be Naturaly Lead to Consider three Particulars, for which we are to give thanks to God

1 First for Creation
2 Secondly for Preservation
3 Thirdly for Redemption

First then we are to give thanks for ~~our~~ Creation ~~of our~~

[DCA Vault; lower right corner of booklet worm eaten. Courtesy of Dartmouth College Library.]

19 ⌀   "STAND FAST THEREFORE IN LIBERTY,"
                  GALATIANS 5:1 (N.D.)

Gala V:1: Stand fast therefore in the Liberty wherewith Christ has made us Free— —

There is nothing more Sweet and more Desirable, than Liberty and Freedom in [. . .] World, Yea it is Sweet to Dumb Creation, and thre is nothing more Disagreeable and Urksome than Servitude or Confinement—Liberty is a precious gift of Heaven, and it is the highest Happiness of a rational Creature either in this World or in the Worlds above to enjoy freedom Adam in his Innocency had perfect freedom and Liberty This was his perfect Happiness, he had free Liberty from his God to injoy the garden of Paradise or Eden, his gracious god free^ly^ gave him every thing that grew in the garden, except one Tree in the midst of the garden that god reservd for himself, to ^let^ Adam know that God was his Sovereign and he ^had^ right to put him under restriction and Law, ^& god forbad him to eat it^ God more over gave him the Whole World besides and ^all^ Creatures and things therein and he had uninterrupted injoyment of God with all his Creature injoyments, this was his Superlative Glory and Happiness—But alas he must needs take greater Liberty and freedom, than God gave him, he Stretched forth his Disobedient Hand to the Tree of God & Stole a Fruit from it and eat it,—By Which Wickedness, he lost all his Liberty freedom and happiness, for by this great Disobedience he lost his garden and the Whole Wo^r^ld, and lost the knowledge of god, and Consequently lost Communion with God, and forfeted every mercy at the hands of God, and was turn'd out of Paradice, for he had justly renderd himself unworthy of it, he is now broak, is become a Bankrupt, a vacaband, is become poor, extreamly poor to a Nakedness, nakedness indeed, ~~to a~~ ^with a^ Witness for he is Script of all, he is Script of ~~his glory~~ the Image and likeness of god ~~he has lost, the injoyments of god~~ the injoyment of god is now fled from him yea he Dreads the presence of God as Death, his Life is become Death, his Light is turned into Darkness, his Happiness into misery, he has turn'd the Love of God into Burning Anger, and every thing into Poison, yea he has Plungd himself into all manner of misery both Temporal Spiritual and Eternal, and all his future Posterity with him yea he has brought himself with all his posterity, into Captivity, Slavery, and Bon^d^age to Sin and Satan, and god in Strict Justice might left him there to perish in his Chosen Misery—But behold Instead of Casting him into eternal Misery, with the Rebel Angels,[82] to whom he had joind in Rebelion against God, which Misery he had justly merited to himself at the hands of a just God, I Say, instead of this The Lord Breathed forth from his Infinite Mercy and Love, a great Promise of a Saviour to him and to his Posterity, as many as will gladly receive the Promise, the great Saviour, was rapt up in these few words, God speaking to the Serpent the deseiver, not directly to Adam & Eve,—I will put enmity between thee and the Woman, and between thy Seed and her Seed: It shall bruise they Head, and thou Shalt bruise his heel,[83] this Womans Seed is Christ, & from that Time, the Lord revealed or point out the Lord Jx to the Children in various ways and Methods Christ was Exhibited to the People of God of old, by various figures modes, Types, and Shadows, and even by Dreams, Visions and Voices as well as by Revelations, and this Dawn of the Heavenly Day that Visited the Children of fallen man increaced unto the perfect Day, that is, this great Promise of the Mesiahs Coming, to visit this Dark World, grew from age to age Clearer and brighter; till he ^actually & personally^ appeard in the World—This is the Saviour of the World, the great Redeemer, and mediator, between the offended Jehovah and guilty man, This Jx is the Restorer

82. See Revelation 12:4–13.
83. *I will put enmity:* Genesis 3:15.

of all things that were lost at the Fall of Adam; He regain'd Paradise and eternal Happiness,—

In further Speaking upon our Text I Shall by Divine assistance, Endeavour to Show Several Propositions

I. That Jesus Christ is the only Redeemer of Lost Sinners of mankind, and the Regainer of all the forfited Mercies and Blessings, both of a Temporal and Spiritual Nature.

II. Shall Speak in a particular manner of the glorious Liberty that Jesus Christ hath purchasd for the Children of fallen Adam.—

III. Shall Show, that is it the great Duty of Christian People both to God and to themselves, to Stand fast in the LIBERTY where with Christ hath made them Free—

And then lastly Shall make application of the Whole.—

I. Then I am to Show, that Jx is the only Redeemer of lost Sinners of Mankind, and the Regainer of all the forfited Mercies and Blessings, both of a Temporal & Spiritual Nature.—

Jesus Christ is the Chosen of God the Father; to be the Mediator Redeemer and Saviour of Sinners God filed and prepared him, gave Power and Authority to fulfil the great work, and as Such, there is none that Can Stand in Competition with him,— let us take a Short View of his Qualifications, in order to be a Compleat Saviour; He was God equal with the Father and took upon ^him^ our Natures, and became as one of us, and Claimd kindred with us, —as we find it writen, and the Word was made Flesh and dwelt among us,[84]—For verily he took not on him the Nature of Angels; but he took on him the Seed of Abraham, Wherefore in all things it behoved him to be made like unto his Brethren: that he might be a merciful and faithful High Priest in things partaining to god, to make Reconcilliation for the Sins of the People,—He became man that he may obey god as a man and as he was an Holy man, without Sin of his own, he perfectly obeyd God, and he Stood in the room of a Sinner, yea he ~~was made~~ ^became^ Sin that is he took our Sins upon him and was the greatest Sinner that ever was in the World, Imputely so, and as Such, he Suferd in the room of a Sinner, and he was God, that he may rise again and that he may make eternal Satisfaction to the justice of God it woud be needless to Say much upon his godhead & his manhood

This misterious Doctrine has been Preachd a great deal,—

But I Shall proceed to Show the manner or way ~~the Lord Jx~~ [two words illegible], ^in order^ to redeem Sinners, and to procure Liberty or freedom for ~~Sinners~~ them,

———

Doctrine 1

Our Text plainly implys that man in his fallen State is in Bondage or Slavery—

~~I. Man by his Disobedience to God,~~ Man by his listening to Satan and Yielding to his temptations, Sold his himself ~~to~~ Turned his Posterity to Sin and Satan, By Which he Rebeld against his Sovereign and became Disobedient to his maker

84. *and the Word was made Flesh:* John 1:14.

[CHS folder I.25; CHS-M 429–434. First page faded at upper left. Samson Occom Papers, Connecticut Historical Society, Hartford, Connecticut.]

20 ❧   "WHEN HE DROWNED HIS REASON" (N.D.)

When he drowned his Reason he loses all that Time and he is fit for no Service at all, either for him Self, for his Family, for his Country, and how much more is he unfit to Serve God,—And yet, (to astonishment) he is just fit to Se^r^ve the Devil, Yea Drunk itself is the Service of the Devil, and This fits him for all manner of Service to the old Greedy, and ma^n^y has undone themselves, and their families by Drunkenness,—and this Practice is Condemn'd by all Considered People, and it is in the Power of mankind to break off from this accursed Sin if they Will, and they know it, it is in Vain to Say I Cant Help it, and it is a folly to blame the Devil does the Devil Carry the Man to Tavern and there call for the Liquor for him, and does ^take^ the Cup, and pour down in his Throat, and does the Devil pay ~~pay~~ for the Liquor, and does he repeatedly Call for Drink and keep pouring of in his Thrt till he has made him Drunk; if this is the Case then the man is Clear of Sin and Blaim, and the Devil is Guilty of ^that^ Sin,—But let us See a little further does not the Drunkard Use that natural Power & and understanding Which god has given him in his persute after Strong Drink? Dont he think and Consider Where he can get Liquor; and When he has found a Place in his Mind, he Will use them Legs, Which ^God has^ given him, and direct his Course to the Place Where he expects to get Liquor, and When he is got there, he will that Tongue and Speech, Which God ^has^ given him, and Call for Liquor, and When it is granted; he takes the Cup with his own Hands, and he pours it down in his own Throat and he Uses the power of Swallowing and Swallows down his Liquor and he will repeatedly Call, and pour down the Liquor till he has Transformed himself, from a Rational Man to Worse than a Natural fool—Now is it not in the Power of this Man to break off from this Course of Life— I am perswaded he Can,—Such a man that will Contrive and follow allways, to get Strong Drink, and take Pleasure in it, is properly a Drunkard,—a man may be overtaken Some Times, but if he is a Sham'd of it, and Repent of it, is not a Drunkard,— Let us Trace another Practice, Which is Universal, among the People Called Civilized Nations; That Cursing Swearing and Profaining the Name of God; it is so Common amongst all Sorts of People, that it is become Innecent and inofensive, but let it be never so Common, it is of the Same Nature as it ever was, it is the most ^Heaven^ daring ^& god Provoking^ Sin that man is Capable of Commiting, and it is the most ^un^profitable Sin, it neither Cloaths the Body nor feeds it, Why is a rational man so in Love with Such Language is it ^So^ Comely, is it decent, is it graceful, is it Credible, is it manly, is it genteel, is it Godly, and Christian Like, Why no, I think every Considerate Person must Say no, ^by^ no ^means^,—well, then it must be, uncomely, indecent, disgraceful, uncredible, inhumane, ungenteel, ungodly, unchristian, unholy, Yea ^in^ truth, it is ^earthly, sensual,^ Devilish, and Hellish Language, it is from the Bottomless Pit and it is fit for ^no^ Creature but Devils, and I Verily believe the Devils dont Cu[r]se and Sware and Profane the Name of God, as mankind does; It is Amazing to hear, how expert the White People are in Swaring, Men Women and

Children, of all ages Ranks and Degrees, it Seems to be a mother Tongue with them, or are there Schools Where they go to Learn this Language? Now, is it in the Power of Man to leave of Swaring, or is it not? I am glad there is no Such Language among the Indians, it is not because, that it ^is^ inca[pa]ble of it, ^but^ it is Horred, they will not Use Such Language,—I will tell ^you^ amazing Truth among them, they have Very great Veneration for the Name of the great God, in their perfect Heathenism they Calld God, Cauhtuntooct, Which Signifies Supream Independent Power, and they had Such Regard for this Name, they woud not Suffer their Children to mention that Name, they say it was too great for Children to Mention—and in the Evening When it is Time to go to Bed, an old man, (Who is apoited for that purpose), will go round the Town, with a loud Voice, Calling upon the young People and Children to disist making Noise and go to Sleep and not to Disturbe God, Now how is it amongst those that are Call'd Christians; ^dont ye hear yr [Children?]^ Don't you think these Heathen Indians will rise up against ^you^ at the last Day not only for this Sin but for many others also—Yea, don't they Testify against you now in this Life,—But you will reply and Say; are they so Clear of Sin as to rise up against us; no by no means; but you have learnt them many of the Sins they are Guilty of, and they are Ignorant Heathens, and You are Christians, and have ~~have~~ all Learning, and great knowledge, and ^therefore^ you ought to go before them in all Holy Conversation and Godliness—But in Stead of that, I am afraid you Lead them in the Downward Road in all maner of abominations; and ^many^ Diseases, ~~that~~ Europians Brought into this Country, that the Natives were intirely Ignorant before; Such as what they Call in Genteel Language, Venerial Disease, in Common Language French Pox. Captain Cook in his Voige Round the World, Says that there was a Vesel in a ^Place^ Called Otaheite, about fifteen ^months^ before him, and had left that a Cursed ~~disease~~ Common among the poor Indians, Which they were utterly Ignorant of before; The Captain was so Honest ^as^ to Say if he Could have learnt their Specific for the Venereal Disease, if ^Such^ they have ~~any~~ it would have been of great advantage to us, for when he left the Island it ^had^ been Contracted by more than half the People on Board the Ship, but he was not quite so Honest as to Say whether he had it himself—Vol 1:146:p.[85] This was only returning the Compliment, and they ^had^ no Room to Complain, and it was only giving back what they had receivd from the Europians and I suppose there ^was^ no difficulty in returning of it,—But Since, We have begun ^upon^ this Practice Which is Called, Whoredom, let us take notice of ^it^ a little, I Suppose it is Universal among all Nations, and it is Universally Condemned by Rational People, it is abo[mi]nable, inhuman and Beastly Practice, and it is more abominable When it is Supported and Countenanced by polite, Learned, and Christian People, but Some Will Say or Ask, who allows Such Practice, The Eng How many Boudy or Whore Houses are there in that Nation, and I Suppose it is just so among

85. This account of the *Endeavour*'s traffic in venereal disease at Tahiti appears in John Hawkesworth, James Cook, and Joseph Banks, *A New Voyage Round the World, in the years 1768, 1769, 1770, and 1771; undertaken by order of his present Majesty, performed by Captain James Cook, in the Ship Endeavour, drawn up from his own journal, and from the papers of Joseph Banks . . . and published by the special direction of the Right Honourable the Lords of the Admiralty*, volume 1 (New York: Printed by James Rivington, 1774), 146.

the French, these are Calld Christian Nations, and the most Learned Nations in the World at this Age of the World; and I never heard of any Such House amongst the Indians in this ^great^ Continent; Certainly Common Sense condemns Such Practices and the Heavenly Artilery is leaveld against it and the Thunders of Mount Sinai are Roaring against it, Yet Man will persist in it,—The grand Question occurs again, is man, a Rational Man, unable to turn from this detestable, Filthy, Shameful, and Beastly Practice? or Can he desist, and become a Chaste Creature? I immagine to hear an Answere Universaly from all Rational Men, Saying, O! Yes O! Yes, We[ll] Why don't he run then, it is because he will not he Chuses to go to Hell in his own Way,—and if he Will, Who can he Blame?—Mariage is Lawful, and Honorable, but God will Judge Whore Mongers and all Adulterors.

Another Practice which is very previlent every where amongst all Nations and all Sorts of People Contention, Quarriling, and Fighting, there is Scarcely any else, but Whispering, Backbiting, and Defaming one another—this Breeds Quarriling, & Wars Certainly this is unbecoming Rational Creatures, it Condemnd by the Light of Nature, and it is utterly Condemned by Scripture, and it is What we don't like from our fellow men, and if we dont like it, Why Shoud we give it to our fellow men, and if we dont like Such Treatment, and Can blame others for it, then we must believe, it is in their Power, to treat us and their fellow men better, Well, if they Can, then Certainly we Can too; and ^Why^ don't we do it; I have took a particular ^notice^ of the words Speaking against one another; Speaking against another must mean, belying ~~him~~ ^one another^, If I speak the Truth about my Neighbour, I don't Speak against him but for him, to make this plain let us take two Neighbours; one, is every way agreable to his Neighbours, he is kind, benevolent, loving, obliging, just and Honest in all his dealings with his Neighbours, he is a man of Truth, and uses no bad Language, he do not defame his Neighbours,—now if I should tell of his real Character ~~is this~~ woud that be Speaking against him, why no by no means, it is Speaking for him, but if I shoud give him Contrary Characters, that is Speaking against him, because I dont ~~give~~ give him his True Character,—But the other Neighbour is right to the reverse, he is every way disagreable to his Neighbours, he is Moross and Cross, unkind, Turbulent, he Cheats in his Dealings all he Can he Curses and Swares, Defames his Neighbours and Sets his Neighbours by the Ears, Sows the Seed of Discords, and he will lie for a Copper or for nothing,—now upon Ocation, If I Should tell his true Character, will that ^be^ Speaking against him? I think not, but if I shoud Say that he is a Clever, kind, just and Honest man, I Shoud say that of him, Which he is not, and therefore I Shoud Speake against him in so saying, Dont you think so?—There is another Way of Speaking against my Neighbour, that is, When I see my fellow Creature take a miss Step, and directly I ^take the^ ocation, to blaze it abroad, and exaggerate the matter, and make it Seven Times worse than it really is; this ^is^ Speaking against my Neighbour, in a Very bad Sense; it is discovering his Nakedness to the World, Ham like concerning his Father; for which he was Severely Cursd by his Father[86]—Now is it not in the Power of men to Treat one another better? I think they Can, and if they dont, they they ^are^ under blame,—

---

86. See Genesis 9:18–27.

Love is every where Commend and Command [by] the Holy Scriptures, and it is Certainly Beutiful and agreable amongst Rational Creatures, and it is more Power naturally to Love and to be kind to one another; and it is the Strength of a Kingdom and Nation to live in Peace and in Love, it is the Beauty of a State, City, Town or Family to dwell together in Love, Peace, and Unity,—The Scripture commands People to Provoke one another to Love and to good Works[87]—But I think in these Days, People in general are Provoking one another to Hatred & to Evil Works, if it is in our Power to hate one another, then there is equal Power to Love one another & if dont Love one another, then we are Self Condemn'd it is very Natural for mankind Love to be lovd, and used ~~well well~~ well well let us Practice that Rule upon our fellow men,— I might go on mentioning ^many^ Practices among the Children of men, but what has been Said is quite sufficient to Lead the minds of men, to Consider the Conduct of their fellow men, and also their own Conduct,—It is very Common amongst all Nations, and amongst all orders, Ranks and Degrees of men; and amongst all Ages, both men ~~and~~ Women and Children to find Fault with each other ^yea it is a Law of Nt[88] to find fault with one another,^—and it is very well that we can See so far, [this] must lay a foundation for us to See our own Conduct; and this makes it very plain, that we all [. . .] Power to do Well, and if our Conduct has been bad; we believe, it is in our Natural [. . .] to do better,—it is a Universal Doctrine, and it is the Preaching of all, that have any understanding to their fellow men, to do well, or to do better, this is the Universal Creed of all mankind; From hence [page torn] this Dayly Preaching,—The Kings of the Earth woud have their Subjects do well or better, [the] People woud have their Kings do well, all that have any Power and Authority over the People woud have them do well, the People find fault with their Rulers; and woud have do better, the Ministers of the gospel exhort their People to do better, and the People would have their Ministers [. . .] do better, Husbands woud have their [page torn]

[CHS folder I.26; CHS-M 398–402. Samson Occom Papers, Connecticut Historical Society, Hartford, Connecticut.]

---

87. *Provoke one another:* Hebrews 10:24.
88. *Nt:* nature.

HYMNS

Samson Occom maintained a lifelong interest in hymnody. Song had long been an important element of community life and ritual among Occom's Mohegan and other southern New England tribes. However, forces of dispersal including war, territorial infringement, indentured servitude, and boarding schools removed young people from their families, clans, and tribes, reducing their exposure to traditional languages, songs, and stories, and threatening the continuity of tribal song traditions. After the Great Awakening, many tribal communities in New England adopted hymn singing as a ritual of community reconciliation, consolation, and celebration. Samson Occom helped foster these new song traditions by composing original hymns and publishing *A Choice Collection of Hymns and Spiritual Songs* in 1774.

Occom's hymnal contributed to a tremendous shift in American religious music. During the eighteenth century, evangelical Protestants abandoned traditional psalmody in favor of new hymns written by British evangelists Isaac Watts and Charles Wesley. Some revivalists scandalized conservative clergy by pairing American-composed hymn-texts with folk tunes. In 1742, the Separate Congregationalist James Davenport caused a controversy when he wrote his own hymns and led hymn-singing processions through the streets of New London, Connecticut, near Mohegan territory. Davenport's brother-in-law Eleazar Wheelock taught hymnody to Occom, Joseph Johnson (Mohegan), Jacob Fowler (Montauk), David Fowler (Montauk), and other young Native men at Moor's Indian Charity School. In turn, these Native missionaries promoted hymn singing among tribes from the Oneida of upstate New York to the Montauk of Long Island. Occom further developed his interest in hymnody during his travels in England from 1766 to 1768. There, he met leading hymn writers and composers, including John Newton, author of "Amazing Grace." Occom also collected a number of English hymnals for distribution to Christian Indian congregations back home. In some Native communities, the demand for hymnals and tune books was so great that ministers like Joseph Johnson devoted long hours to the painstaking hand-production of songbooks.

After his return from England, Occom began to write and collect hymns for *A Choice Collection of Hymns and Spiritual Songs*, which was published in New London, Connecticut, in April 1774. Most of the hymns in the *Collection* came from famous authors like Watts, Wesley, Martin Madan, and John Mason. Occom also included twenty-nine never-before-published hymns, some of which may have been written by Native authors Joseph Johnson, David Fowler, and Jacob Fowler. Indeed, Occom suggested that he designed portions of the *Collection* with a Native American audience in mind, as he explains in the preface that he included some songs of "uncommon Measures, for new Tunes and new Singers." As one of the first American interdenominational hymnals, the *Collection* also appealed to a broad audience of Native and non-Native Christians. It was reprinted in 1785, 1787, and 1792 and served as a template for some of the most popular hymnals of the early nineteenth century.

Occom himself wrote and published at least six original hymns. "The Sufferings of Christ," or, "Throughout the Saviour's Life We Trace" was included in the 1774 *Collection*. "The Slow Traveller," or, "O Happy Souls How Fast You Go"; "A Morning Hymn," or, "Now the Shades of Night are Gone"; "A Son's Farewell," or, "I Hear the Gospel's Joyful Sound"; "Conversion Song," or, "Wak'd by the Gospel's Pow'rful Sound"; and "Come All My Young Companions, Come" began to appear in American hymnals around the time of Occom's death in 1792. Both the "Sufferings of Christ" and "A Morning Hymn" became standards of American hymnody, appearing in dozens of nineteenth- and twentieth-century hymnals.[1]

Although Occom's hymns resonated with a broad audience, they speak directly to the experience of Christian Indian communities in New England. "I Hear the Gospel's Joyful Sound" comforts converts who leave traditional tribal communities—their "parents and their house"—to join Christian settlements, such as Brotherton, in the "wilderness." "Throughout the Savior's Life We Trace" encourages Native singers to identify with the physical and spiritual sufferings of an embodied Jesus Christ. His being "push'd" "here and there" on the path to Calvary parallels the path of displacement and resettlement walked by emigrants to Brotherton. The image of the trail or the "beautiful path" carried tremendous spiritual value within Mohegan culture, where it appears in traditional carvings and embroideries (Tantaquidgeon Zobel). It also appears in the Occom hymn "O Happy Souls How Fast You Go," which honors ancestors as predecessors on a "journey" to "worlds above." Its chorus reads as follows:

> There all together we shall be,
> Together we will Sing,
> Together we will praise our god,
> And everlasting King.

These lines suggest that Occom and other Christian Indians understood sacred song as a way to build and renew the relationship between the individual and the community, the dead and the living, the past and the present.

---

1. Brooks, "Six Hymns," provides complete attribution and publication information for Occom's original hymn-texts.

I   ∾   PREFACE TO *A Choice Collection of Hymns and*
            Spiritual Songs; Intended for the Edification of
            Sincere Christians, of all Denominations (1774)

There is great Engagedness in these Colonies, to cultivate PSALMODY; and I believe it
to be the Duty of Christians to learn the Songs of Zion, according to good Method
or Rule; but the People ought not to be contented with the outward Form of Singing,
but should seek after the *inward* Part:—There are two Parts of Singing as St. Paul
informs us, in 1 COR. 14.15. (*I will sing with the* Spirit, *and I will sing with the* Understanding *also.*) To sing without the Spirit, (though with good Method) is like the
Sound of a musical Instrument without Life. To sing with the Spirit, I understand
Paul further to mean, to sing with spiritual Matter: And thus when we sing with the
Understanding or Method, and with spiritual Matter, by the Influence of God's
Spirit, we sing agreeable to God's Mind. St. Paul exhorts, in Col. 3.16. *Let the Word
of Christ dwell in you richly in all Wisdom, teaching and admonishing one another in
Psalms and Hymns, and spiritual Songs, singing with Grace in your Hearts to the Lord.*
The Songs of Zion, when they are sung with the Spirit of the Gospel, are very comforting, refreshing, and edifying to the Children of God—convincing to a carnal
World—well-pleasing to God, and destructive to the Kingdom of Satan. And it
being a good Work, I am willing to contribute something towards promoting it. For
this End I have taken no small Pains to collect a Number of choice Hymns, Psalms,
and spiritual Songs, from a Number of Authors of different Denominations of Christians, that every Christian may be suited. I have, in the first Place, chose out some
awakening and most alarming Hymns, next to them penitential, then inviting, and
then consolating Hymns, and the last Part contains Hymns of the Birth, Death, Resurrection, and Ascension of Christ, and his Appearance in the last Great Day. These
Hymns are in various Metres, and especially the last Part are of uncommon Measures,
for new Tunes and new Singers.

Here I present you, O Christians of what Denomination soever, with cordial
Hymns, to comfort you in your weary Pilgrimage; I hope they will assist and
strengthen you through the various Changes of this Life, till you shall all safely arrive to the general Assembly Above, and Church of the First-Born, where you shall
have no more need of these imperfect Hymns; but shall perfectly join the Songs of
Moses and the Lamb; where all your imperfect Services shall forever be at an End;
and you shall have open and full Vision and Fruition of GOD and the LAMB; where
you shall sit down in perfect Harmony with Abraham, Isaac and Jacob, and with all
the Saints and Angels in the New-Jerusalem; where all Sorrow, Grief, Trouble and
Pain shall forever cease, and all Tears wiped away from your Eyes.

[Source: *CC*]

2 ✎   ## "THE SUFFERINGS OF CHRIST," OR,
   ## "THROUGHOUT THE SAVIOUR'S LIFE WE TRACE"

1   *Throughout the Saviour's Life we trace,*
     Nothing but Shame and deep Disgrace,
     No period else is seen;
     Till he a spotless Victim fell,
     Tasting in Soul a painful Hell,
     Caus'd by the Creature's Sin.

2   *On the cold Ground methinks I see*
     My Jesus kneel, and pray for me;
     For this I him adore;
     Siez'd with a chilly sweat throughout,
     Blood-drops did force their Passage out
     Through ev'ry open'd Pore.

3   *A pricking Thorn his Temples bore;*
     His Back with Lashes all was tore,
     Till one the Bones might see;
     Mocking, they push'd him here and there,
     Marking his Way with Blood and Tear,
     Press'd by the heavy Tree.

4   *Thus up the Hill he painful came,*
     Round him they mock, and make their Game,
     At length his Cross they rear;
     And can you see the mighty God,
     Cry out beneath sin's heavy Load,
     Without one thankful Tear?

5   *Thus vailed in Humanity,*
     He dies in Anguish on the Tree;
     What Tongue his Grief can tell?
     The shudd'ring Rocks their Heads recline,
     The mourning Sun refuse to shine,
     When the Creator fell.

6   *Shout, Brethren, shout in songs divine,*
     He drank the Gall, to give us Wine,
     To quench our parching Thirst;
     Seraphs advance your Voices higher;
     Bride of the Lamb, unite the Choir,
     And Laud thy precious Christ.

[Source: *CC*]

3 ∾

"THE SLOW TRAVELLER," OR,
"O HAPPY SOULS HOW FAST YOU GO"

1   *O happy Souls how fast you go,*
    And leave me here behind,
    Don't Stop for me for now See,
    The Lord is just and kind.

2   *Go on, go on, my Soul Says go,*
    And I'll Come after you,
    Tho' I'm behind, yet I Can find,
    I'll Sing Hosanna too.

3   *Lord give you Strength, that you may run,*
    And keep your footsteps right,
    Tho' fast you go, and I So slow,
    You are not out of Sight.

4   *When you get to the Worlds above,*
    And all his Glory See,
    When you get home, Your Journey's done,
    Then look you out for me.

5   *For I Will come fast as I Can,*
    A long that way I Stear
    Lord give me Strength, I Shall at length
    Be one amongst You there.

[CHORUS]

There all together we Shall be,
Together we will Sing,
Together we will praise our god,
And everlasting King.

[Source: Rauner 000194 (1773). Courtesy of Dartmouth College Library.]

4 ∾

"A MORNING HYMN," OR, "NOW THE SHADES
OF NIGHT ARE GONE"

1   *Now the shades of night are gone,*
    Now the morning light is come:
    Lord, we would be thine to-day,
    Drive the shades of sin away.

2   *Make our souls as noon-day clear,*
    Banish every doubt and fear;
    In thy vineyard, Lord, to-day
    We would labor, we would pray.

3   *Keep our haughty passions bound,*
    Rising up and sitting down,

Going out and coming in,
Keep us safe from every sin.

4   *When our work of life is past,*
O receive us then at last;
Labor then will all be o'er,
Night of sin will be no more.

[Source: *DHSS*]

5 ∾   ## "A SON'S FAREWELL," OR, "I HEAR THE GOSPEL'S JOYFUL SOUND"

1   *I hear the gospel's joyful sound,*
An organ I shall be,
For to sound forth redeeming love,
And sinner's misery.

2   *Honor'd parents fare you well,*
My Jesus doth me call,
I leave you here with God until
I meet you once for all.

3   *My due affections I'll forsake,*
My parents and their house,
And to the wilderness betake,
To pay the Lord my vows.

4   *Then I'll forsake my chiefest mates,*
That nature could afford,
And wear the shield into the field,
To wait upon the Lord.

5   *Then thro' the wilderness I'll run,*
Preaching the gospel free;
O be not anxious for your son,
The Lord will comfort me.

6   *And if thro' preaching I shall gain*
True subjects to my Lord,
'Twill more than recompence my pain,
To see them love the Lord.

7   *My soul doth wish mount Zion well,*
Whate'er becomes of me;
There my best friends and kindred dwell,
And there I long to be.

[Source: *DHSS*]

6 ∾

"CONVERSION SONG," OR, "WAK'D BY THE GOSPEL'S JOYFUL SOUND"

1 *Wak'd by the gospel's joyful sound*
   My soul in guilt and thrall I found,
   Expos'd to endless woe;
   Eternal truth a loud proclaim'd,
   The sinner must be born again,
   Or down to ruin go.

2 *Surpris'd I was, but could not tell,*
   Which way to shun the gates of hell,
   For they were drawing near:
   I strove indeed, but all in vain—
   The sinner must be born again,
   Still sounded in my ear.

3 *Then to the law I flew for help;*
   But still the weight of guilt I felt,
   And no relief I found;
   While death eternal gave me pain,
   The sinner must be born again,
   Did loud as thunder sound.

4 *God's justice now I did behold,*
   And guilt lay heavy on my soul—
   It was a heavy load!
   I read my bible; it was plain
   The sinner must be born again,
   Or feel the wrath of God.

5 *I heard some tell how Christ did give*
   His life, to let the sinner live;
   But him I could not see:
   This solemn truth did still remain—
   The sinner must be born again,
   Or dwell in misery.

6 *But as my soul, with dying breath,*
   Was gasping in eternal death,
   Christ Jesus I did spy:
   Free grace and pardon he proclaim'd;
   The sinner then was born again,
   With raptures I did cry.

7 *The angels in the world above,*
   And saints can witness to the love,
   Which then my soul enjoy'd;
   My soul did mount on faith, its wing,
   And glory, glory, I did sing
   To Jesus Christ my Lord.

8   *Come, needy sinners, hear me tell,*
     What boundless love in Jesus dwell,
          How mercy doth abound:
     Let none of mercy doubting stand,
     Since I the chief of sinners am,
          Yet I have mercy found.

[Source: *DHSS*]

7 ∾   ## "COME ALL MY YOUNG COMPANIONS, COME"

1   *Come all my Young Companions Come,*
     And hear me boldly tell,
     The wonders of Redeeming Love,
     That Sav'd my Soul from Hell,
2   *It was but a few Days ago,*
     I Saw my awful Case,
     Nothing but hell and dark Dispare,
     Lay plain before my face.
3   *O then I Viewd the Damned Crew,*
     Of all the numerous race,
     And I of all that went to hell
     Deserved the lowest place.
4   *Justice of God So on me lay,*
     I Could no Comfort find
     Till I was Willing to forsake,
     And leave all my Sins behind.
5   *The Lord was Strong he bowd my Will,*
     And made me this to See,
     Nothing but Jesus Crusified,
     Could Save a wretch like me.
6   *O then I Viewd mount Calvery,*
     With gods eternal Son,
     Who on the Cursed Tree did Die,
     For Sins that I had done
7   *O how Rejoicd I Was to think,*
     A Saviour I had found,
     It turnd my Sorrows into Joy,
     To hear the Blessed Sound.
8   *Salvation from my God on high,*
     So pleasantly did Ring,
     It Sot my Soul at Liberty,
     To praise my heavenly King,
9   *And while I dwell on Earth below*
     I'll praise my Jesus here,

And then go to Yonder World
And praise my Jesus there.
10 *And there thro' all Eternity,*
In the Sweet Realms above
There I Shall Sing that blessed Song
Free grace and Dying Love

[Source: Rauner 000194 (1773). Courtesy of Dartmouth College Library.]

JOURNALS

For more than forty-five years of his life, Samson Occom faithfully recorded his activities and travels in small booklets he himself crafted from letter paper bound with sewing thread or small nails. His twenty-four surviving journal booklets comprise the most extensive body of autobiographical writing by a Native American in the colonial and early national eras. Beginning with his arrival at the doorstep of Eleazar Wheelock's home in Lebanon, Connecticut, on December 6, 1743, the journals document Occom's education, his early ministry and ordination, his travels and ministrations among the Native communities of Long Island and New England, his tour of England, Scotland, and Ireland as a fund-raising emissary for Moor's Indian Charity School, his involvement in the administration of tribal affairs, his almost constant itinerancy among communities in western New England and central New York, and his joyful participation in the organizational beginnings of Brotherton and New Stockbridge. Most of his surviving journals concentrate on the years after the American War of Independence when migration to Brotherton and Stockbridge began in earnest; Occom offers a unique firsthand account of this historic pantribal movement. In his journals, it is also possible to glimpse aspects of his personality: his love of hunting and fishing, his affectionate temper as a father, his strong sense of duty in the ministry, his friendships, his humility, his sorrows, and the spirituality that sustained him through the inevitable hardships and disappointments of his remarkable life.

The journals give us glimpses, but not sustained views, into Occom's interior world and family life. There is no mention of his courtship with Mary Fowler and little insight into their forty-year marriage. There is little discussion of his relationships with his eleven children. There is no overt ethnographic description of Mohegan daily life. Contemporary readers seeking these intimate details may be disappointed. But in our disappointment we confront significant differences in the way journal writing has been conceived over time and across cultures. How was journal writing conceived in eighteenth-century America? How was it conceived by early Native writers? As Malea Powell has argued, it is important to ask how Native writers have historically *used* writing, how they have theorized the value, purpose, dangers, and limitations of text-based literacy. What did it mean to Samson Occom—as a Mohegan, an ordained Presbyterian minister, an itinerant, a Native spiritual and political leader, an eighteenth-century writer—to keep a written account of his daily activities?

Comparing the journals of Samson Occom to those kept by his contemporaries gives us a clarifying contextual sense of how journal writing was conceived in early America. The best known early American journals served as a space for documenting daily events, personal, familial, and professional, as a way of contemplating broader patterns of significance. For example, the fifty-five-year diary of Boston judge and landowner Samuel Sewall (1652–1730) describes historical episodes such as King Philip's War and the Salem witch trials from the perspective of an established member of the Puritan elite. Sewell also chronicles the deaths of his wife and children and the transformation of Puritan society at the end of the seventeenth and beginning of the eighteenth centuries. The voluminous literary diaries of Yale University President Ezra Stiles (1729–1795) extend this habit of contemplation to Stiles's far-reaching intellectual and theological inquiries. Stiles used his journals as a space to document and correlate his correspondence with scholars of the scientific, ephemeral, and apocryphal on subjects from meteorology and the origins of American Indian tribes to dispensationalist history and silkworms. His diaries give us a sense of the ambitious and imaginative expansiveness of American intellectual life before the professionalization and disciplining of knowledge at the close of the eighteenth century.

The genre of professional missionary diary took shape after the Great Awakening, when missionary work and itinerancy constituted a greater portion of ministerial life. Religious societies charged the preachers they sponsored to keep an account of their travels, places they visited, churches, meetings, or small gatherings where they preached, scripture texts they preached from, and monies they collected and spent. Examples of this genre include the journal of David Brainerd (1744–1747) and the diaries of Moravian missionary David Zeisberger (1772–1795). Brainerd preached among the Lenape people of New York and New Jersey, while Zeisberger traveled among the Lenape in Pennsylvania, Ohio, and Michigan. Samuel Kirkland, a white graduate of Moor's Indian Charity School, also kept an account of his decades of missionary labors among the Iroquois. When he transcribed it for Harvard College in 1806, Kirkland characterized his own journal as "barren & uninteresting." "A man cannot travel forty years over the same ground & every year say something new of it," he explained.[1] Obligation rather than self-expression motivated this genre of life-writing.

For early African-American and Native American writers, however, the professional missionary journal could also serve unanticipated extraprofessional purposes. Beyond their fulfillment of responsibility to sponsoring white religious societies, journals kept by black and Native preachers document the lives and struggles of communities of color and the unique theologies and worship traditions they developed. The American-born free black evangelist John Marrant compiled and published a missionary journal (1790) of his itinerancy in Nova Scotia and his ministry at the black Loyalist refuge of Birchtown to discharge his professional responsibility to his sponsoring Huntington Connexion, the English Calvinist missionary network headed by Selina, Countess of Huntington, and personified by the transatlantic

1. Kirkland, 470.

celebrity George Whitefield. However, his diary also gives us dramatic narrations of physical, political, and spiritual struggles among competing parties of Birchtowners seeking self-determination and survival amidst the poverty, racial hostility, epidemic smallpox, dire winters, malnutrition, and starvation that characterized black life in Nova Scotia. Through the scripture references embedded in the text, it is also possible to glean from Marrant's journal a sense of the distinctively prophetic black Zionist theology he preached.

The journal of Samson Occom's son-in-law Joseph Johnson (Mohegan) also gives us a rich sense of the daily lives of Native people in southern New England, especially the lives and practices of the region's networked Christian Indian communities where Johnson lived. Unlike Marrant, who compiled his journal with publication in mind, Johnson utilized his manuscript diaries as a space for spiritual introspection. In his first diary, spanning October 1771 to March 1772, Johnson records his coming home from a life at sea to Mohegan and his subsequent spiritual reconciliation. His writing is impassioned and searching: "O my Soul forget not your Resolution how you have resolved as before God and the Lord Jesus, and the holy Spirit, and before the whole host of heaven, that you will by the Grace of God continue to work out your Salvation with fear and Trembling" (123). Johnson's second diary records his stay as a schoolteacher and minister from November 1772 to February 1773 among the Farmington Indian community. Here again, Johnson fully and poetically voices his interior struggles, especially his loneliness in separation from his own tribal community. "O mohegan O Mohegan . . . in you is lodged my father & mother Dear," he writes. "Keep them in thy womb O Mohegan, till thou dost hear the Voice of God" (160).

Samson Occom began to keep his own professional missionary journals at the instruction of Eleazar Wheelock. His diaries carefully track his frequent ministerial travels: places he stayed, families, churches, and communities he visited, individuals he baptized or married, scriptures he preached from, and the reactions of his audiences. Surviving documents suggest that Occom kept brief notes on his daily activities in account books, then sat down at semiweekly or weekly intervals to compose full journal entries. Occom maintained this writing discipline long after he severed ties with Wheelock and all other white sponsors and missionary societies. In fact, most of Occom's surviving journals represent the years 1785 to 1790, a period in his life when he experienced almost complete autonomy from white supervision. These were the founding years of Brotherton and New Stockbridge, years when Occom experienced a renewed sense of personal, spiritual, and professional purpose as a leader of these intertribal settlements. In these last years of his life, Occom resumed the habits of professional writing he first learned from Wheelock, not out of duty to a patron, but out of his own sense of divine calling and historic responsibility.

Highlights from Occom's early journals include his account of his own ordination on August 29, 1759; his horrified reaction to the "Cursing, Prophaning" "English Heathen" of New York City, on his first visit there on June 14, 1761; the intrigue and controversy surrounding his departure for England in December 1765; and his impressions of King George III, Queen Charlotte, Lord Dartmouth, George Whitefield,

and the "confusion" of urban London in 1766. Journals compiled after his 1768 return to America document Occom's growing renown as a preacher, especially after
the 1772 delivery and publication of his execution sermon for Moses Paul. For example, when Occom visited a white congregation at New Milford, Connecticut, on
February 6, 1775, he wrote that the people "were very urgent to have me Stay an[d]
have a meeting. They Pl[ea]d So hard it was very hard for [me] to pass by them, there
was one young Convert in particular Intreated with Tears in her Eyes to have me
Stay, they pulld very hard upon my Heart Strings." Preparing to preach on Sunday,
October 9, 1785, near Stillwater, New York, Occom also encountered once again white
audiences' preoccupation with his race. Seeking a horse to carry him to his preaching appointment, Occom was asked, "Whether I was going to hear the Strange
Mi[ni]ster. I told [the man] I suppose I should hear him, and then told him, the People
Could not See that Strange Creature till I get there." In this exchange, Occom dis-
armed white expectations with a dry sense of humor.

The most moving passages in Occom's journals document his participation in
the early years of the Brotherton and New Stockbridge settlements. Occom first saw
Brotherton on October 24, 1785. After a day of rainy, muddy travel, emerging from
a forest "dark" with hemlock trees, Occom records, "I heard a Melodious Singing,
a number were together Singing Psalms hymns and Spiritual Songs, we went in
amongst them, and they all took hold of my Hand one by one with Joy and Gladness from the Greatest to the least . . . the Lord be praised for his great goodness to
us." Further entries from October and November 1785 record the settlement's first
wedding, the celebration of traditional harvest festivals, and the formal organization
of Brotherton on November 7, 1785. During Occom's fall 1786 visit, he witnessed the
arrival of new emigrants, conducted baptisms and vibrant worship meetings, and
participated in land negotiations with the Oneida. Brotherton and New Stockbridge
residents joined forces in August 1787 to clear a lot for Occom's home. "I never did
receivd anything from my Indian Brethren before," Occom wrote on August 16.
"Now I do it out of Principle. It is high Time that we Shoud begin to maintain ourselves." Happiness also shines through journal entries from August 4–6, 1788, which
document a fishing trip he took near Brotherton with his sons Benoni and Andrew
Gifford Occom and his son-in-law Anthony Paul:

> We went [to the lake] to Fishing, got there Some Time before Night, and there was
> a great Number of Oniedas and Some Stockbr at Colo Luweys, to receive a pres-
> ent of Corn and Some Pork Sent to them, by a French Merchant, but I and my
> Sons went to the Lake . . . & it was Just Night, and we Fishd, and we Catchd a
> fine parsel of Fish presently, & made up a Fire by the Creek and had fine Supper
> of F and afterwards Prayd, & then we went to Sleep by our Fire quietly—

As such entries reveal, Occom experienced a tremendous sense of joy and pride in
these moments of Native healthfulness, autonomy, and self-sufficiency, the hard-
won historical moments that have sustained Native communities through centuries
of colonial imposition.

Moments of despair and spiritual searching also interrupt the affective restraint
that generally characterizes Occom's journals. Especially difficult for Occom was the

death of his daughter Tabitha, which he recorded on June 26, 1785: "My poor Tabitha is Dead & Buried, the Lord the Sovereign of the Universe Sanctify this Dispensation to me and to all my Family." Comfort came to Occom in dreams. He recorded a remarkable nighttime visitation from George Whitefield on Saturday night, April 1, 1786. "[Whitefield] came to me," Occom wrote, "and took hold of my wright Hand and he put his face to my face, and rub'd his face to mine and Said,—I am glad that you preach the Excellency of Jesus Christ yet, and Said, go on and the Lord be with thee, we Shall now Soon done . . . this Dream has put me much upon thinking of the end of my Journey." Occom did not choose to elaborate on these reflections in his journal. Indeed, the journals rarely mention the seasons of sadness that Occom experienced throughout his adult life. Only on January 10, 1790, after some weeks' lapse in writing, does Occom confess, "I have been to no meetings four Sabbaths . . . my Mind has been filld with Trouble So that I have had no peace, but Sorrow, grief, and Confusion of Heart—and I am yet in great Trouble—." If he did keep up his journal writing after 1790, during the final years of his life, these diaries do not survive.

Despite what some may consider their shortcomings as an intimate record of Occom's interior life, these journals are an incomparable source of information for understanding Occom's world and for contextualizing his other writings. Like the diaries of Joseph Johnson and John Marrant, Occom's journals offer a thick descriptive sense of the everyday workings of community life in places like Mohegan and Brotherton, the daily textures of visiting, meeting, preaching, and eating that knit together tribes and kin. We see weddings and funerals, fishing trips and ginseng-digging expeditions, hymn singing and harvests. The journals also provide an incomparable sense of Occom's daily life. We get a visceral sense of the cold, damp, and discomfort he experienced throughout his seemingly endless travels, the pain of his lame hip, the unreliability of his mare, the fleas he fought for his bed. We discover Occom's deep sense of responsibility to answer countless requests for extemporaneous preaching, his delight in the Dutch New Yorkers who received him with warmth and generosity, his enjoyment of fireside spiritual conversations, random moments of spiritual intimacy he shared with those he met along the way. Only the journals tell us that Occom was an avid fisherman and a skilled hunter, like his father. Only in the journals do we witness his frequent happy visits with his son-in-law Anthony Paul and his daughter Christiana Occom Paul, his judgment of the "unseemly" behavior of the Oneidas, and his coolness to the preaching of John Sergeant, Jr.

After so much scholarship has concentrated on Occom as a cultural intermediary or imputed to him some confusion or internal conflict about his own identity, it is refreshing to find few traces of this self-conscious "betweenness" in his own journals. We never sense that Occom is striving to reproduce for his white audiences an ethnographically familiar Indianness, although he does engage and defuse with dry wit their racial fascinations. It seems clear that Occom understands himself first as a Mohegan man with responsibilities to his family and his home communities in Connecticut and at Brotherton, then as an ordained minister with responsibilities to preach and administer saving ordinances to the worthy and deserving, whoever or wherever they might be. His patterns of self-accounting remind us that identity can be understood as an exercise of responsibility, rather than primarily as the product of self-expression, performance, or affective manifestation. The moments when Occom does reveal his internal states of feeling are the moments when he feels he has fallen short in his responsibilities as a husband and father, minister, or community leader.

Occom's journals also give us an unmatched sense of his personality as a preacher and his concerns as a theologian. They offer a steady record of the scriptures from which he preached to Native and non-Native communities over the course of almost fifty years. His patterns of scripture selection suggest that in itinerant preaching contexts Occom espoused a practical theology that prioritized the necessity of a saving change of heart and a rejection of worldly ways including alcohol use, promiscuity, profanity, usury, and slaveholding. When he preached specifically to the Brotherton and New Stockbridge communities, Occom continued to emphasize the necessity of individual regeneration in Christ and the necessity of brotherly love to the spiritual welfare of the community. He also paralleled the intertribal gathering and reconciliation of the Brotherton tribes to the experience of Old Testament Israel. At the founding of Brotherton, on November 6, 1785, Occom preached in the morning from Joshua 24:22, in which the people of Israel affirm their covenant with God, declaring "We are witnesses," after their arrival in the land of Canaan. That evening, he chose as his text Esther 7:2, which marks the moment when King Ahasueras recognizes Esther and hears her request to save Israel from the genocide planned by Haman.

More than any of his other writings, these journals give us a profound sense of the way Occom understood, imagined, inhabited, and moved through the geopolitical space he called "this Indian world." Beginning with his leaving home to put himself under Wheelock's tutelage, the journals chronicle his movement and his travels, not his quiet days at home. Consequently, we glean from them an understanding of the historic and evolving networks of travel and exchange that economically, socially, and politically linked Native communities in early America. Except for his fund-raising mission to England in the 1760s and a brief preaching tour of New England in the 1770s, Occom traveled almost always in the service of Native communities. Following his footsteps on visits to "Indian towns" and "Indian places" from Groton, Connecticut, to Oneida Castle, New York, helps us glimpse a distinctive Native demographic topography, a mental mapping of an "Indian world" unrecognizable to white inhabitants of the same places. Contemporary Native scholars like Lisa Brooks have used historical and contemporary Native writings to reconstruct this powerful, alternate Native sense of space.[2]

Some readers will be surprised by the extent of the travels Occom chronicles.

---

2. In preparing these journals for publication, I have encountered and struggled with the limits of my firsthand knowledge of the places where Occom lived, preached, and traveled. To complicate matters, many of the small towns he identifies have disappeared from modern maps, or have been renamed in the succeeding centuries. Readers more intimately acquainted with the Native and non-Native places of New England will be able to read these diaries with a far better sense of space than I have.

Especially in the last ten years of his life, Occom was almost constantly on the move between tribal communities at Brotherton, New Stockbridge, and Mohegan. One of the express aims of colonial Native education experiments like Moor's Indian Charity School was to domesticate Native peoples, transforming them from wanderers and hunters—as they were perceived by white colonists—into farmers attached to particular homesteads. Occom's constant motion reveals a profound failure of this aspect of the colonial educational mission. Occom himself roamed and traveled almost his entire adult life, leaving care of the family and household to his wife, Mary. In her study of the Natick Indian community, Jean O'Brien has noted the frequent absences of men from their families and homes. Even as these absences disadvantaged Native families in their efforts to attain economic self-sufficiency on the New England agricultural-patriarchal household model, according to O'Brien, they also suggest that Native men to some extent "resist[ed] English notions about men's work, and at least in the case of military participation and seafaring, [reformulated] Indian ideas about mobile male economic roles" (144). Occom traveled for both political and ministerial purposes. He traveled to renew old kinship networks and to build new intertribal relationships and new political futures for Native peoples of New England. In one of his hymn compositions, Occom expressed the joy and autonomy he experienced in his travels: "Thro' the wilderness I'll run, / Preaching the gospel free; / O be not anxious for your son, / The Lord will comfort me." The travels documented in Occom's journals—his own itinerancy, as well as the movements of the Brotherton and New Stockbridge settlers—hearken back to the oral traditions of the Mohegan, stories that trace the origins of the people to ancient migrations from the Great Lakes and New York to present-day Connecticut. Did Occom and other Mohegans consider the Brotherton movement a kind of homecoming? Perhaps this is one of the meanings of the elm bark box carved with the traditional pattern of the "beautiful trail" or "beautiful path" that Samson Occom sent from Brotherton to his sister Lucy Occom Tantaquidgeon, who remained at Mohegan.

Reading the journals of Samson Occom, finally, gives us some sense of how Occom conceived the value and purpose of life writing. Certainly, his approach to journal keeping was shaped by traditional Mohegan notions of appropriate self-expression, by the professional discipline instilled in him by his teachers and sponsors in the ministry, and by his own personality and disposition. Given the fact that both Occom and Joseph Johnson grew up Mohegan and were trained by Eleazar Wheelock, the difference between the affective restraint of Occom's journals and the poetic expressiveness of Johnson's is especially suggestive and striking. Johnson felt more at home in his autobiographical writing than did Occom; Occom, it appears, preferred genres like petitions, letters, and sermons, shaped by discrete purposes and particular relationships or responsibilities. It is perhaps most revelatory that Occom begins his journals when he enters the world of Eleazar Wheelock and goes quiet whenever his travels return him to his Mohegan home.

ꙮ JOURNAL I

December 6, 1743–November 29, 1748

> *Occom arrives at Eleazar Wheelock's school to begin his studies. He frequently takes leave from school to visit Native kin and friends at Mohegan and Niantic. Occom attends Yale Commencement in September 1744 and meets the young child Joseph Johnson, Jr., his future son-in-law, in April 1745. In September 1745, he partici- pates in a visiting party to Native communities on Long Island, and he visits the praying Indian town of Natick, Massachusetts, in November 1748. Visiting Native communities in the region to establish and maintain friendly and kinship relation- ships and political ties may have been one of Occom's duties as a tribal councillor.*

December the 6th 1743 I went to the Revd Mr Wheelock^s of Lebanon Crank to Learn Someting of the Latin tongue, and was there about a Week, and was obliged to Come away from there again to Mohegan, and Stayd a bout Fortnight at mohgn and then I return'd up to Mr Whee^s again and Some time towards Spring again I went home to Mohegan, and Stayed near three Weeks before I return'd to Mr Wheelocks again, and August the 7th A.D. 1744 I went away from Lebanon to Moheg^n^ and I got So far as M^r Bs at Norwitch that Night, & In the Morning I Sot out from thence, and I got home to Mohegan just before Noon

August the 13th I went from Mohegan to Nahantuck, and visited all the Indians, and I Return'd Home again to Mohegn in the 16th of D Instant, and so imedeatly up to Mr Wheelocks. And September the 7th we Sot out from Lebanon for New-Haven, and we got there in the 10th of September, and there we had the ^plan^ of Seeing the Scholar's Comminst,[3] and We Return'd homeward again in the 12th of Sepr and we Got home again in the 20th of D Instant—

Novr the 7th AD 1744 Da-O was taken Sick and I went Down to see him in the 12 of D Instant, and I Return[']d again in the 17th of D Instant to the Revd Mr Wheelock's—

January the 11th AD 1744 [1745] I S[o]t out from Lebanon for Mohegan and I got there about Sun Set and the next Day to Mothers at bozrah[4]—and in the 14th of D inst I return'd again ^to^ the Revd Mr Wheelocks

Febry the 23^d 1744 [1745] mater mea et Duo Libri Ejus Venierunt ad Dominum Wheelock manere ibi Tempori[5]

March 20th 1745 I went from Leba to Mohegan and I there [yt] Night, and in the 4th of April AD 1745 Joseph Johnson and I went over to Groton—and there we Saw

---

3. Occom here refers to the Yale commencement ceremonies, traditionally held to celebrate the be- ginning of study each fall.

4. Bozrah, Connecticut.

5. *mater mea . . . .*: It appears that Occom began his course of study in Latin as soon as he arrived at Wheelock's home: like the white students already under Wheelock's tutelage, Occom was given a college preparatory education. This sentence loosely translates as "My mother sold two books to Mr. Wheelock to stay there for a time," suggesting that Sarah Occom supported her son's ed- ucation by selling books to Wheelock. A second translation rests on the possibility that Occom may have misspelled the noun *liberi* as *libri* and the verb *venerunt* as *venerunt*: "My mother and her two children came to visit Mr. Wheelock for a while."

Joseph [was?] the first time that ever I saw him,[6] and we Return'd home a gain in the 6th of D Instant and in the 11th of April I re[d] home again up to Lebanon and June 24th AD 1745 I went Down to Mohgean and got there that Day[,] ^and was sick there,^ and I ret[d] again in the 14[th] of July to Leb

August the 20[th] 1745 I went away from Leb- to Mohegan, and I return['|d to Leb[n] again in 23 of D Instant—

August the 26[th] AD 1745 I sot out from Leb[n] for Norwich and from thence to Plainfield and So next from there to Canterbury and Wed[s]day I got to Windham, and third day I got home to Leb[n]

Sepr the 7[th] AD 1745 I Sot out from Leb[n] for Mohegan and ^got^ there Some time before Night And in the 10[th] of Sep[r] we we Sot out from Mohegan for Nahantuck, and in the 12[th] of D Instant we turn'd again to Mohegan, and in the 13th of Sep[r] Many of us Sot out from Mohegan for Long Island and we got so far as New London that Night, & in the Morning we Sot Sail from there, and we got to the place of our De- sire in the Evening, and Some of us Lodg'd at [Queen's] Wigwaum that Night, and there we were very kindly Entertained by all of 'em, We had Several Meetings to- gether, and there was Some Stir among 'em—And in the 18th Sep[r] we all Return'd home again to Mohegan, and to Several Places where we belong'd, and we didnt get home till the 19th of Sep[r] Some tim in the Evening, And I went to Leb[n] 23[d] of Sep[r]—

Dec[r] ye 16th 1745 we Sot out from Lebanon Crank for Windham, and we got there at night, and I Lodg[d] at Deacon Wheelocks yt Night and the Next day at Windham, and in ye 18th of Dece[r] between 2 & 3 o'clock in the after Noon the Poor Girl was Executed,[7] and I went right home to Lebanon that Day—

May the 2[d] AD 1746 I Sot out from Crank for Mohegan[,] and I arrived there about 3 o'Clock in the after Noon and I Return'd in 16th of may.

August the [1[t]] AD 1746 I Sot out from Lebanon for Mohe- and I got there before Night—and Return'd again in the 8th of August

August the 26th AD 1746 I went from Lebanon to Mohe- and got there the Same day—And I Returned to L- again the 27th of D Inst—

April y[e] 6th 1747 went from Leba- to Mohegan and got at Night—

April the 25th AD 1747 I retur to Lebanon—

June ye 7th AD 1747 Sot out from Lebanon for Moheg[s] and got about 4 oC in the after Noon—

June ye 25th we sot out from Mohegs for Nahantuck, and return'd from thence again to Mohegs the 28th of D inst—and I Return'd to Lebanon ye 30th of June—July ye 7th I went to Infield, and the next Morning to L. Meadow and from thence Right Back to Infield and So Right thro to Windsor, and then to Hartford, and then from thence to L. Crank again—

---

6. Occom here meets the young Joseph Johnson, Jr., for the first time, at the family home in Groton. New London First Church records indicate that Joseph Johnson, Jr., was baptized on June 3, 1751. For fuller biographical information, see the list of individuals named in Occom's writings.

7. Elizabeth Shaw was executed in Windham, Connecticut, for infanticide on December 18, 1745. She is alleged to have abandoned an infant child among some rocks in the woods after secretly giving birth. Hers was the first public execution in the county.

July ye 16th I went from L to Mohe and got there the Same Day—

Tuesday August ye 26th I Return'd to Lebanon—

From Last Spring to this Time I have Lost 11 weeks

Novr ye 2d went from L. to Mohegan—and Return'd to L. again, the 9th of [D] Inst

Novr ye 10th I Left Leba- C and went Down to Some parts of New London, and kep School there at ye Winter—

March the 12 AD 1748 I went up to Lebanon C & and got there about 3 o C in the after Noon,—& March the 14th Sir Maltby and I Sot very early in the Morning from L C for Hebron, and got there about 8 o C—And March the 16th I Sot out from Hebron for Mohegs and got there ^at^ ~~before~~ Night—and Came up again to Hebron the 18th of [word illegible]

May the 22d I went from Hen Down to Mohegan—and ret to Hebron again in the 2d of June—June 17th went from Hebron to Mohegan—and Returned again in the 22d of [D] Inst—

August the 6th Samuel Lee and I went from Hebron to Lyme—

August the 10th I Sot out from Naha for Mohegan and got there before Night, and in the 11th of [Sd] Inst I retur[n]'d Back to Hebron, and in the 13 [Sd] inst I was at Mr Wheelocks—

September 2 AD 1748 I went Down to mohegan and got there before Night—

Sept ye 15th we Sot out from mohegan for Nahantuck and we got there Some time before Night—

Sept the 21d I returnd Back to Mohegan—

Octr the 3d AD 1748 I return'd to Hebron,

Octr the 6th I went Down to Norwich and returnd back to Hebron the Same Day

Monday Novr ye 14th I went to Mr Wheelocks and went to Hebron same Day—

Novr the 17th 1748 I Sot out from Mr. Pomroy's to Lebanon, Intending to Set out from thence to Boston; But I was Disappointed, and So turn'd my Course to Mr Wheelocks; and Fryday Novemr ye 18 I Sot out from Mr Wheelock's for Boston, and got so far Mr Bingham's in Windham and Lodg'd there and was very kindly Entertain'd and Saturd— Novemr the 19th Sot out from thence on my Journey, and Stop't at Mr Mosleys in Scotland, about one hour, and then went on and ^got^ so far as Mr Williams in Pomfret, and there taried over the Sabbath, and was Exceedingly Well Treated all the While I Stay'd there—

Novr the 21 Monday Morning I Sot out from Pomfret on my Journey [S]till and got So far as Hills's which is 30 miles this Side Boston—

Tuesday Nover the 22d as soon as it was Day we Sot out from thence onward, and I Left my Company by ye way, and I got to Rachsbury b[y] 2 & 3 O'C in the after Noon, so Strait to Boston; and Returnd to Roxbury in the Evening and Lodg'd at Capt Williamss & was Entertain'd With all kindness &c

Saturday Novr the 26th, I Left Roxbury, and Returned Homeward, and So far as Natick at Night, and Lodg'd at Dean Ephraims, and [was] kindly Receiv[e]d and Entertaind, & Next Day I Went to their Publick Worship, and found too much Levity as I thought and Monday I to Visiting amongst them and found all very kind to a Stranger,

Tuesday Novr the 29th I Sot out from Natick, and Jacob Chalkcom and Isaac Ephraim accompanied me 3 or 4 miles—and so we parted—

[Courtesy of Dartmouth College Library]

❧ JOURNAL 2

June 21, 1750–February 9, 1751

After arriving at Montauk, Long Island, in November 1749, with a commission to keep school, Occom developed his relationships with ministers and Native communities on Long Island. In June 1751, he visited the Presbyterian minister Samuel Buell, who would deliver the sermon at Occom's ordination five years later and who was to Occom a lifelong friend. That October, Occom participated in the green corn or harvest festivals of the Montaukett and Shinnecock. He married Mary Fowler (Montaukett) sometime in 1751.

Thirdsday June ye 21st 1750 I Sot out from Montauk for Easthampton and got there Some time before Night, and taried at Revd Mr Buel's that Night, *Fryday June ^ye 22^ 25th* John Ashpo Came to me from Montauk about 10 in the morng and we Emediately Sot out from thence for South Hampton, and got there About 4 in the after N and taried at Dea. Tu[b]s, and we Stayd there amongst our Country Men till Monday June ye 25, and then we Return'd from thence to wards Montauk, and We got there Some time before Night Safe & Sound—

Saturday August ye 4 AD 1750 I Sot out from Mont^k for East and got there before Night and Lodged at Mr. W. Hedges' that—and Monday Just at Night I Came away from East and got to Mont^k Just after Sun Set—

Monday Sepr ye 10 AD 1750 I Left my School and to Napeeg,[8] and got there Just after Sun Set, and we went further in the Night.

Saturday Sepr ye 15 we Sot out Sail from Long Island for main, and got over a bout 1 o'Clock in the after Noon, and I was Landed at Stoneing Town[9] and I Sot out from thence for mohegan & got there Some time in the Night and found Most of my Relations Well

Thirdsday Sepr ye 20 AD 1750 I sot out from Mohegan, for Lebanon, and Got to Mr Williams Just before Sun Set and Lodg'd there and was kindly entaind and *Fryday Sepr ye 21* Early in the Morning, I sot out from thence to Crank and go to M^r W^s before Noon and found madam and Theodora[10] very Sick, and I Stay'd there till after Noon—and then I Sot out from thence for Hebron and got there Just after Sun Set and found most of 'em Well, and Monday Sepr the 24th I Sot out from Hebron for Mohegan, and got there Some time in the Night, -and

Fryday Sepr ye 28th I Sot out from Mohegan for [Nawyyuk?] and got there Just before Sun Set and tary'd with one Lemuel Burrows & Satur Day morning Sot out

---

8. *Napeeg:* Napeak, Long Island.

9. *Stoneing Town:* Stonington, Connecticut.

10. *madam and Theodora:* Eleazar's wife, Sarah Davenport Wheelock, and his daughter, Theodora.

from thence for Naroganset and got there Some time in the Night & Lodg'd with one James Simon, & was kindly Entertain by my Friend, &c &c—

Thursday Octr ye 4th AD 1750 I Sot out from Naroganset for [Nawaunyounk] and got there Some time in the Night and Lodg'd at [Toowis's] Wigwam and Fryday morning sot from thence for New London, and got there about 9 in ye morning, and from thence Strait up to Mohegan—and Monday Oc^r ye 8 Wen Down to New London in order to go over to Long Island &c &C and Tuesday Octr the 9th was at New London all the Day and at Night about 1 or 2 o'C we Set sail from New London for Montauk, and got a Shore Just before Sun rise at [word illegible] and I Sot from there Directly for the Indian Towns, and went among the People to get Some Sweet Corn,[11] and then I went to Neapeek, and back again to Indian Town and got there in the Evening &c—

Saturday Octr ye 13 I went from Montauk for East & taried there Sabbath and Monday Oc^r ye 15th I returned to Montauk again—

Thursday Oc^r ye 18 We Sot out from Montauk for East and taried that Night and Friday Morning we Set away from thence for the Shenecock and we got there at about 9 about 11, we went to the Indian Town, there we heard Mr White Preach a thanksgiving Sermon to the indians, & we taried there till Monday following Octr ye 22 then we returnd to Montauk again and we got there about 7 at Night &c

*Wedensday November ye 14 ^1750^* I Sot out from Montauk for East to thanksgiving and Fryday Novr ye 16 I returnd again to Montauk and got there just before Sun Sit and so forth

Saturday December ye 1 1750 I Sot out from Montauk for Sagg[12] to See Mr Maltby and I got there Just before Sun Sit and Lodg'd at M^r [Russils] was kindly Entertaind, and Next Day I heard Mr Maltby preach, and was with him in the after Noon, at M^r [Gulson's], and Taryd at Night with Mr Maltby, And Monday I part with him at M^r [Gulson's] and Came away ~~home~~ towards home to Montauk & got there at Night, &c

Saturday February ye 9 175[1] I went to E. Ham and participate with 'em [the] Sacrament of the Ld's S and Tuesday February ye 12 I returnd to Montauk

[Courtesy of Dartmouth College Library]

∾ JOURNAL 3

June 28, 1757–September 25, 1760

Occom is examined for the ministry at the home of Solomon Williams in Windham, Connecticut, on July 13, 1757. He is examined and ordained by the Long Island

---

11. For many New England and Long Island tribes, the fall harvest festival is the central event of the ceremonial year. The Mohegan celebrate this event as a "Wigwam Festival," during which tribal members participate in the ritual grinding of corn or *yokeag*. Yokeag, too, was a central element of Mohegan life. See [Tantaquidgeon Zobel], *Medicine Trail*, 47–59. It is worth noting that Occom continues to observe ceremonial cycles as he is intent on getting his own supply of corn during the festival season. He also celebrates the festival by traveling with a delegation of Montaukett to attend a thanksgiving sermon at Shinnecock on October 18.

12. *Sagg:* Sag Harbor, Long Island.

Presbytery on August 29–30, 1757. In April 1760, Occom, his father-in-law, James Fowler, and his wife, Mary Fowler Occom, cross the Long Island Sound in a whale-boat to deliver Samson and Mary's oldest son, Aaron, then seven years old, to Moor's Indian Charity School. Occom continues to visit Native communities in southern Connecticut and on Long Island. In September 1760, Occom accompanies his brother-in-law David Fowler, who had also studied under Wheelock, on his first missionary visit, to the Tunxis-Mohegan-Pequot-Niantic community at Farming-ton, Connecticut.

Tuesday June ye 28 AD. *1757* I set out from Montauk for N. England, in order to Pass an Examination there &c—And Wednesday Morning I Sot out from Easthampton, with the Revd Mr Pomroy and Woodbrige and others, Down to Northwest, & about 12 o C. we went aboard of Mr Dayton, and emediately weighted Anchor; and Spread sail to the Winds, and ^a^ way toward New-England Shores, and we got to the Mouth of Seabrook Harber[13] about 9 at Night, and for Fear of the Flats, we Dropt Anchor at a Distance from shore and there taried all Night, and in the Morning of the [30 June] we Arose, and weighted Anchor, and Put to Shore, and Mr Pomroy and the two young Women went a Shore, and I Shifted aboard of another Boat whose owner was one M^r [H]orton who Came Down the River from up Country, and was removing With his Family to Stoningtown—And he sot me a Shore at Black-Point[14]—and I went to Indian Town—and found my Friends generaly well—and taried at my Aunt Justice's that Night—

Fryday morning July ye 1st I set out from Nahantuck, for Mohegan and got there at Night to Mothers, and found all my Relitives in good Health &c—and there kept the Sabbath—and Monday July ye 4, I went from Mohegan for Lebanon and got ~~there~~ to Mr Wheelocks Just before Sun Set, and was very kindly Receiv'd, and found them all in good Health—and after a little Conversation, Mr Wheelock Concluded, and appointed the 12th Inst to be the Day of my Examination, at his House—and Emediately Sent and gave Notice, and Desired the assistance in the Examination, of 5 Neighbouring Ministers, viz Mr Solo. Williams of Lebanon, old Society ~~and~~ Mr Benjn Pomroy of Hebron ~~and~~ Mr Nathan Strong of New Coventry, ~~and~~ Mr Stephen White of Wi^n^dham, and Mr Saml Mosley of Canada—

Tuesday July ye 12 Expected the Gentlemen to attend the Examination, But we were Disapointed ^The Voice of [one] Crying^[15] there ^was^ none Come, But the Revd Mr Pomroy,—we Judg'd the Weather Hinder'd them, it being wet Day,—and Mr Wheelock and Mr Pomroy Consider'd the Matter, and Concluded to Send to the Ministers that Day—to Come together on the next Day, which was the 13 of July, at the House of the Revd Mr Williams, and accordinly they Come together about one

---

13. *Seabrook Harber:* Seabrook Harbor, Long Island.

14. *Black Point:* Black Point, Connecticut.

15. *The Voice of [one] Crying:* Occom here refers to the New Testament description of John the Bap-tist as "The voice of one crying in the wilderness, Prepare ye the way of the Lord, make his paths straight" (Matthew 3:3; Luke 3:4; Mark 1:3; John 1:23). It is not clear whether this was the text for his examination or a figurative allusion to the fact that his examiners did not appear at the appointed time and place.

o'C P.M.—and there I Pass'd an Examination before the Revd Messrs Solomon Williams Eleazar Wheelock Bejamin Pomroy Nathan Strong and Stephen White,—and they ^were so far^ Satisfied, as to Conclude to proceed to an ordination here-after &c—And Just before Sun Set I went Down towards Mohegan, and got so far as Norwich farms, and taried at the House of one Deacon Huntington, a Tavern keeper,—

Thirdsday July ye 14th 1757 I went on my Journey and got to Mohegan about 11 o'C A.M. and found my Relitives well in general, July ye 15th my Brother and I went Down to N London in a Conoo,[16]—and I taried there that night,—Saturday July the 16th I went aboard of one [word illegible] Williams of Stoning Town and we got to Masons Island[17] Some time in the after Noon, and there I Stay'd over the Sabbath,—

Monday July ye 18th about 1 in the after Noon we went aboard again, and Sot Sail, for Fishers Island[18] and got there some time after Sun Set, and Tuesday July ye 19th we Sot Sail very Early for Long Island and we sailed all the Day in the Sound, and Some time in ye Night we got Near by Gardener's Island,[19] and there we Dropt Anchor, and Taried all Night—

Wednesday Morning July ye 20th weighed Anchor and Hoisted Sail and Steered toward Napeeg Harber, and Reachd there about 10 in the Morning, there I went a Shore and then I went by Land to Montauk, and I got home about 2 P.M., and found my Poor Family in Comfortable Circumstances,—Praise be to god for his Tender Mercies to us heard—

May ye 7th AD 1759—I Sot out from montauk for Easthampton, In order to go over to New England with some Expectation of Passing an ordernation there, and Lodg'd at Mr Hedges that Night—

Tuesday Morning May ye 8 we went Down to Northwest, and I taried there at the House of one Mr Ebenezer Hedges, that Night and Wednesday May ye 9 we went aboard of Mr Dayton, and Crosst the Sound, and got over about 9 at Night, and we Lodg'd at my Aunt Justice's house

Thirdsday May the 10th we Set out very Early in the morning for Mohegan and got there before Sun Set at my Mother's, Fryday May the 11 I went from Mohegan for Lebanon, got there Some Time before Sun Set, found Mr Wheelocks Family very Poorly with the Measels Especially our David[20]—

May the [15] the Revd Association Sot at Mr Wheelocks House, & Consulted my Case, and, Concluded ^and to^ to Refer my ordernation to the Revd Prespetery on Long-Island and Accordingly Wrote, and Refer'd me to the Revd Prespetery on Long Island,—[21]

16. Jonathan and Samson Occom traveled on the Thames River, which links Mohegan territory to the seaport town of New London.

17. *Mason's Island:* Near Mystic, Connecticut.

18. *Fisher's Island:* Located in the Block Island Sound, south of Groton, Connecticut.

19. *Gardener's Island:* Gardiners Island, located in Gardiners Bay at the eastern end of Long Island.

20. *our David:* David Fowler.

21. The Windham Association of Congregationalist Ministers in eastern Connecticut referred Occom's ordination to the Long Island Presbytery because prominent Presbyterians including

Thirdsday May ye 17^(th) Return'd to the Island, and Stopt at Mohegan and kept the Sabath there with Indians—

Monday May ye 21 we went Down to New London, and taried there that Night— and Tuesday May ye 22 we went a Board of Mr Gardeners Boat, of Isle of White, got to the Island after Sun Set, and we Taried there Two Nights—

Thirdsday May ye 17 we went over to the Fire Place, got there about 1 O'C in the after Noon, from thence I went to Town, got there about 3 in the after Noon & I Deliver Revd Association's Letter to Mr Buell

Fryday May ye 18 I went home to Montauk, Got there about Noon, and found my Poor Family Well, and Most of Neighbours Praise be to god therefore—after this I heard the Revd Prespetery on Long Island Receiv'd the Letter,—and Apointed the 29 of August 1759 for my ordernation—and they Sent a Text to me out of 72 Psalm the 9 verse & they yt Dwell in the Wilderness shall bow before him—and also an Exegesis in these Words—An [Ethnicus] qui Evangelium Nunquam Audiat, Eterneum Salutem Obtinene—Posit[22]—And the Apointed Time Being Come I appear'd before the Revd Prespetry at Easthampton, and Pass'd an Examination, and Thirdsday Augt ye 30^(th) in the after Noon the Revd Prespetery Proceeded in Solemnity of my ordernation, the Revd Mr Buell of Easthampton, made the first Prayer, and Preach'd from Gal. I.16, and the Revd Mr Brown of Bridghampton Demanded my Publick Assent to the Christian Doctrines and the Articles of Faith, which I did—then Emediately Proceeded to ye Imposition of the Hands[23]—the Revered Mr Brown Presided, made the ordernation Prayer; the Revd Mr Barker of South Hole Gave the Right Hand of Fellowship; and the Revd Mr Prime of Huntington gave the Charge and made the last Prayer; thus the Solemnity Ended. Laus te Deum—[24]

Montauk Oc^r ye 8 AD 1759 I Sot out from Montauk for the old Mans where the

Samuel Davies and members of the New York Correspondents of the Society in Scotland for Propagating the Gospel had recruited Occom to undertake a mission among the Cherokees. Although Occom had been trained as a Congregationalist, it was determined that the denomination that sponsored his mission should also handle his ordination. Occom was deterred from his Cherokee mission by reports of violence in the area and instead undertook a mission among the Oneida in 1761 (Peyer, *Tutor'd*, 69; Love, *Occom*, 50–51; see also DCA 758221, 75867.1, 759307). As Lisa Brooks observes, this mission proved crucial in his development as a political leader because it afforded him a clarifying Iroquoian perspective on colonial relations, intertribal alliances, and tribal politics.

22. Although Occom's transcription of the Latin query is imperfect, it appears that he was asked, "Can a gentile who never heard the gospel obtain eternal salvation?"

23. *The imposition of hands:* In this central ritual of his ordination, the assembled ministers conferred authority upon Occom by placing their hands upon his head and pronouncing a prayer or blessing.

24. The two-day ordination of Samson Occom included examination in Latin and other ancient languages, as well as theology. The assembled ministers also queried Occom as to his own conversion experience and his views of pastoral responsibility. Samuel Buell's sermon on August 29, 1759, was later published as *The Excellence and Importance of the Saving Knowledge of the Lord Jesus Christ in the Gospel-Preacher [. . .] A Sermon, preached at East-Hampton, August 29, 1759; at the Ordination of Mr. Samson Occum, A Missionary Among the Indians* (New York: James Parker, 1761). For a fuller description of the ordination, see Love, *Occom*, 51–53.

Presbytery was to Set and Mr Reeves was to be ordained, and got so far as Se-baunuck and Preach'd there and taried all Night among the Indians Tuesday Oc^r ye 9 I Sot out very Early on my Journey and got to the old mans about O'C P.M. and went directly to meeting, Mr Brown of Bridge Hampn Preach'd from Prov. II.30, and Taried [one] Mr Miller's where the Presbytery Sot—

Thirsday Morning the Presby brock up, the Ministers Dispersd about 11 in the Morning, and I went down to South, and got to Mastick[25] about 4 PM found the Indians very Sickly, Preach'd to them at Evening, They Seem'd to give very good atention—Fryday Oc^r ye 12 I Sot out from Mastick very Early in the Morning, home-ward, and got so far as Mr Browns at BridgHampn and Tarried there all Night,—and Saturday Oc^r ye 13 about 9 I Sot out from thence onward and got Home little after Sun Set, and found my Poor Family in Health Praise be to God-

April ye 1 AD 1760 Went to Smith town where the Presbytery was to Set, and got so far as Connoo. Place that Night, and Tuesday April the 2 Sot out early in the mornig, and got to Smith Town about 4 O.C P M and Wednesday the Pres. Sot at Esqr Philip's and Thursday about 3 O.C. in the the Presbytery Broke up and I imediately Sot out from thence to Mr Reeve's at South and got there Just about Day light in, and was kindly Receiv'd by Mr Reeve, and Fryday April the 4 I away from thence home ward and got So far as Mr Brown's at Night and there I met with Mr Horton and we taryed there all Night and Saturday April the [5] about 9 O.C in the morng we took Leave of one another and I Home about Son Set and all Well at Home—

April ye 26 AD 1760 A Number of us went from Montauk in our Whale Boat for New England, and got over to N. London about 3 PM and Stopt there til' Just before Son Set and then we Sot out from thence for Mohegan and got there about 9 at Night found my Relatives all well

Sabath April ye 27 kept the Sabbath at Mohegan with the Indians I Preach'd Both Parts of the Day found nothing Special among them—

Monday April ye 28 my Wife and Father Fowler and I and my Little Son Aaron Went to Lebanon to See Mr Wheelock, and we got there before Night found all well, and Deliver up my Little Son Aaron to the Revd Mr Eleazer Wheelock to be Brought up by him—

Tuesday April ye 29 we Returnd to Mohegan again and got there before Night and Stay'd at Mothers yt Night Wednesday April ye 30 about 9 in the morning we Sot out from thence towards home and got So far as N London and there Stay'd at Capt Shaw's yt Night

Thursday May ye 1 we Sot away from N London for Home and got no further than Harbers Mouth and Stay'd all Night at one Mr Harris's Coopper House,

Fryday May ye 2 we Sot Sail very Early in the morng from thence and got upon Montauk Shore about 10 in the Morning and found all Well &c—

~~June the 25~~ *May ye 18 ad 1760* I Preach'd at Easthampton.[26]

Saturday May ye 24 I went from Montauk for Westward, and got so far as M^r

---

25. *Mastick:* Mystic, Connecticut.

26. Sermon notes in the Connecticut Historical Society archives indicate that Occom preached in the morning from Ephesians 3.5 and in the afternoon from Canticles 5.16 (CHS folder I.21).

Brown's, and there kept the Sabbath with Mr Brown and received the Sacred Supper of the Lord with the People of Bridgehampton—

Monday May ye 25 Mr Brown & I went together westward, and we got to Quaugg and Lodg'd at one Mr Howell's that Night, and Tuesday May ye 26 we Sot out from thence on ward and got to Smithtown at Night and Lodg'd with one Justice Phillips over the River, Wednesday may ye 27 we Sot away from them about 9 in the morning, and got to Huntington about 1 in the after Noon, and the People had gone to meeting, and we went directly to meeting and heard Mr Reeve of South—after meeting we Return'd to Mr Prime's where the Presbytery Sat and Examined two young men in order to ordination—Nex day finish'd the examinations with them, and then emediately went to the House of god and Proceeded to in the Prelimminaries of the ordernation, Mr Brown Preach'd the ordernation Sermon, M^r [Prime] made the ordernation Prayer Dureing the Imposition of hands upon Mr Barrat and Mr Brown made the Prayer dureing the Imposition of Hands upon Mr Smith, and Mr Prime gave ye Right hand of Fellowship and ye Charge and Mr Occom made the Concluding Prayer

Fryday may ye 30 the Presbytery Brok up about 10 in the morn and the Ministers Dispersd emmediately, I Preach'd at Huntington in the after Noon and towards Night I went to Oister Bay ~~Saturday May~~ and Taried at Widow Wicks, and Saturday May the 31 I Preach'd at oister Bay, from 16 13.[27]

Sabbath June ye 1 I preach'd there again all Day from Eph 5:14 and Cant 5 16.

Monday ye 2 I return'd from oister Bay, got to Huntington about 11 A.M. and about 1 in the after N I Sot out from thence Homeward got to Smith town Just before Sun Sot and Taried at Justice Phillips Wm Phillip's that Night, and Tuesday June ye 3 Preach'd at Smithtown began about 10 A M from Rev 22:12 and after meeting I went Down to Seetauket and Preach'd there that after Noon from Matt. 22 42 Taried at Mr Tallmedge's that Night

Wednesday June ye 4 Sott out from Mr Tallmadge's about 9 AM and went Down to South, and got to Mr Hedge's about 12 O.C. and Taried there about one Hour and half, and then Sot away from thence Eastward and got the Indian Place just before Sun Set, and had a Short Discourse with them in the Evening.

Thursday June ye 5 I gave a word of exhortation to the Indians, very Early in the morning and then took Leave of them, and journied Eastward and got so far as South Hampton, and thence Taried all Night with one Mr Stephen Foster, and was very kindly Entertaind,—Fryday Morning June 6 was very Stormy Weather and it was [word illegible] Fast Day with the Southhamptoners, and I went to meeting with the People in the fore Noon, and heard Mr White Preach from Levit 26.40.41.42. In the after Noon the Storm moderated, and went on my Journey home ward, went to See M^r [Pane?] and Mr Brown by the way, and So Pass on and I got to Easthampton Just

27. Oyster Bay, Long Island, was the birthplace and home of the African-American poet Jupiter Hammon (1711–1806?). Hammon wrote his first poem, *An Evening Thought: Salvation by Christ with Penitential Cries*, on December 25, 1760, seven months after Occom preached in Oyster Bay. Sermon notes in the Connecticut Historical Society archives indicate that Occom preached this day from Matthew 22:42 at Huntington and from John 16:13 at Oyster Bay (CHS folder I.21).

before Sun Set met with Mr Buell who had just got home from the Main, Brought a Tragical News Concerning a Young Woman—I Lodg'd at Mr Buell's. Saturday June ye 7 Sot away from Easthampton for home, and got to Montauk about 3 O.C. in the After Noon, and found all well at Home, &c—

Monday Sepr ye 1 1760 I Sot out from Montauk with John Harris of N. London, for New England, and we got a Shore at N. London Harbers Mouth Tuesday morning— and from thence I sot out by Land for Mohegan and got there Just after Sun Set, and found all my Relations well in general at Mohegan, and Stayed there two Days, Fryday Sepr ye 5 Sot out from Mohegan for Lebanon got there Just before Sun Set, found all well as Common at Mr Wheelock's, and Saturday Sepr ye 6 David Fowler accompand me to Farming-Town, and we got there about Just after Sun Set and there we found our Friends Some from Mohegan Some from Nahantuck, and Some from Groton and we held a meeting at one Solomon's House, I Deliver'd a Short discourse to them, Sabath Day Sepr ye 7 we met together again at the Same House, I Preach'd to them again, Monday Sepr ye 8 we Set out from thence Homeward, and I got to Mr Pomroy's at Night and I taried there but David went to Mr Wheclock's[28]

Tuesday Sepr ye 9 I left Mr Pomroys—^New London Sepr ye [9] I went to see the Revd Mr Graves, and he gave me 9 books and one Dollar [ ]^[29] and went to Mr Wheelocks, and about 10 o.C. the Indian Scholars and I went Down to Mohegan, and got there at Night

Wednesday Sepr ye 10th we Taried at Mohegan Thursday we went to New London, and Fryday we Stay'd at N. London Saturday we went to Nahantick and Stayd there the Sabbath over, and Monday Sepr ye 15 we Spent the Day there. Tuesday we Sot out for Mohegan again, and got there about 2 in the after Noon, and Wednesday and Thursday we spent at Mohegan, and Fryday Sepr ye 19 about 10 o.c. we went aBoard of Mr Culver, and Sail'd Down to N. London and a Number of us Lodg'd at Cap Shaw's and many that Came with us were Bewitchd with Strong Drink.

Saturday Sepr ye 20 a few of us went over to Nahantick again and got there about Noon, to the Surprize of my Friends, being unexpected there—found them all well—&c

Sabbath Day Sepr 21 we kept the Sabbath there, Monday we went Back to New London got the there about 8 in the morning and Spent the Day there, and saw the exercises of Joy in New London on account of the Victory gain'd in Canada over the French,[30] Taried at Capt Shaw's that Night again

Tuesday Sepr ye 23 we sot out from N L for Long-Island and Sail'd most all that Day and Night Towards morning we got to Qister Pond, and Some of us went a Shore

---

28. Occom's brother-in-law David Fowler (Montaukett) entered Moor's Indian Charity School on April 12, 1759. Wheelock considered him one of his most promising students. His accompaniment of Occom on this visit to the Tunxis-Pequot-Niantic community at Farmington, Connecticut, is the first missionary travel of Fowler's long career.

29. This interlineation appears as a footnote in the manuscript diary.

30. On September 8, 1760, French governor Vaudreuil surrendered Montreal and New France to the English led by General Jeffrey Amherst, concluding the last major military campaign of the Seven Years' War.

~~about~~ went a Board again and Saild for Shelter Island being Wind Bound we Saild in to Shelter Island Harber, at Night went to House found nothing but negroes and Indians in it but they were very kind to us. the Indians in ye hearing I was on the Island, a number Cam together to hear the word of god, I gave a Short Discourse—

Th[ird]sday September ye 25 we got up very Early in the Morning and a Board and Sot Sail for Montauk Arriv'd there Some time in ye ~~time before~~ Night, found all our Friends well,—

[Courtesy of Dartmouth College Library]

∾ JOURNAL 4

May 30, 1761–July 7, 1761

Occom and David Fowler undertake a mission to the Oneida, sponsored by the New York Correspondents of the Society in Scotland for Propagating the Gospel. On their way upstate, they visit New York City, where they are warmly received as well as personally astounded by the "English Heathen" of that city. Occom receives a letter of endorsement from General Jeffrey Amherst and meets Sir William Johnson in July 1761. Johnson, in turn, introduces Occom to the Oneidas and Tuscaroras and sends three students, including the young Joseph Brant, to Moor's Indian Charity School in August. The Oneida and Tuscarora build a church to support Occom's labors, and he baptizes five or six people.

Montauk May ye 30. 1761 After repeated invitations from the Revd David Bostwick of New-York, to go and make a Visit to the Onoyda Indians This Day took leave of my Poor Family, and Friends with tender Affection, about 12 Sot out for Easthampton Got there after Sun Set, Lodg'd at the Revd Samuel Buell's—

Sabbath May ye 31 Spent the Day at Easthampton, Mr Buell Preacht in the fore part of the Day, in the after Noon I Preach'd from Eph 5:20

Monday June ye 1 taried at Mr Buell's on account of his only Son's Dangerous Sickness

Tuesday June ye 2 As the Day Appear'd, the Child Dyed, and was Buried Wednesday Just before Sun Set,[31]

Thirdsday Morning June 4 took leave of my Good Friends at Easthampton, and went Down to Northwest, and a bout 12 went aboard of Mr Dayton at Cedar Point, we had Favourable Wind, we Sail'd Strait to Sea Brook—Landed a Capt Harris's about 9 at Night and Lodg'd there,

Fryday June ye 5 Sot out Early in the Morning for Mohegan, Stopt at Nahan[32] about two Hours, then Sot off again, got to Mothers about 9 at Night found my Relations and Friends well in general here I taried the Sabbath over

Monday June 8 took leave of my Relations and Friends at Mohegan, Sot out for

---

31. Peter Buell (1753–1761) was Samuel Buell's only son by his first wife, Jerusha Meacham. He probably died from smallpox.

32. *Nahan:* Niantic.

Lebanon, abou 9 in morning, got there before Sun Set, found them all well as usual at Mr Wheelock But it was very Sickly and dying Times in the Parish[33]

Wednesday June ye 10 about 3 P M, Brother David and I took Leave of Mr Wheelock and his Family and Sot out on our Journey for Onoyda by way of New York—Reach'd Heartford about 9 at Night; Lodg'd [Capt] Daniel Bulls, and were very kindly Treated—the Man seemed to be Truely Religious keep very good order in his House—

Thirdsday June y 11 about 9 in the Morning we Sot out on our Journey[,] and got about 6 miles westward of N. Haven and Lodg'd at one Woodroffs—

Fryday June y 12 Sot Early in the Morning, got to Stanford at night Lodgd at a Certain Tavern—

Saturday June y 13 wen on our way, got within 5 miles of the City of New York, and turn'd to in one Mr Goldsmiths—

Sabbath June ye 14 taried at Goldsmiths, we did not go to the City to Publick Worship for fear of the Small Pox, being Informed very Brief there—But I never Saw a Sabbath Spent So by any Cristian People in my Life as Some Spent it here. Some were Riding in Chairs[34] Some upon Horse Back orthers traveling foot, Passing and Repassing all Day long, and all Sorts of Evil Noises Caried on by our Drunkards were Realing and Stagaring in the Streets, others tumbling off their Horses, there were others at work in their farms, and ever any People under the Heavens Spoke Hell's Language, these People did, for their Mouths were full of Cursing, Prophaning Gods Holy Holy Name—I greatly Mistake if these are not the sons and Daughters of Belial.[35] O thou God of Heaven, thou y^t Hast all the Hearts of the Children of men in thine Hands, Leave me not to Practice the Works of these People, but help me, O Lord[,] to take warning and to take heed to my self according to thy Holy Word, and have mercy upon the wicked. Convince and Convert them to thy self, for thine own glory. I have thought there was no Heathen but the wild Indians, but I think now there is some English Heathen, where they Enjoy the Gospel of Jesus Christ too, Yea I believe they are worse than ye Savage Heathens of the wilderness,—I have thought that I had rather go with the meanest and most Dispis'd creature on Earth to Heaven, than to Go with the greatest monarch Down to Hell, after a Short Enjoyment of Sinful Pleasures with them in this World—I am glad there is one defect in the Indian language, and I believe in all their Languages i.e. they Can't Curse or sware or take god's Name in Vain in their own Toungue—

Monday June ye 15 to the City, and were Conducted to Mr Wells at freshwater and were Very Kindly receiv'd by him and by all his family[,] I believe the Fear of God in their House and this was our Home as long as we Stay'd in the place.—The People of the City were Extreamly kind to us, there was not a Day Scarsly, but that I was Invited to Dine with one Gentleman or another, The Ministers of all Sects and

---

33. A smallpox epidemic ravaged New England in 1760–1761.

34. *Riding in Chairs:* Riding chairs were two-wheeled, horse-drawn carriages popular in the eighteenth century.

35. *the sons and Daughters of Belial:* In Old Testament usage, Belial is a noun signifying destruction or wickedness, and the children of Belial are the ungodly.

Denominations were uncommonly kind to me—my Friends Increased Daily while I Stayd at New York.[36]

Thirdsday June y[e] *25* we left New York and went on our Journey, Reach'd Peekskills at Night—

Fryday June 26 Sot out very Early in the Morning and we made it Night [five words crossed out] at Rynbeck—

Saturday June y 27 Sot out very Early, and made it Night between Claverack and Kinderhook,—

Sabbath, June y[e] *28.* Went to Kinderhook about five Miles, and there Stopt all Day,—but did not go to Publick Worship, Because the People were Barbarians to us and we to them, in our [Toungs], they were Dutch.

Monday June y 29 left the Place very Early, and got to Albany about 12 o'c and were Conducted to one M[r] [Staats] Unsantvoord & taried there, and the People in Albany were very kind to us, I went to wait upon his Excellency Gen.[ll] Amherst the After Noon after We got to Albany, but he was busy and I Coud not see him, one of his waiters Came out to me, and told me I should have the Generals Assistance and I should make my appearance about 10 in the Morning, Tuesday June y 30 I made my Appearance before his Excellency at the Time Apointed according to orders, his Excellence Met me at the Door and told me he had wrote a Pass for me, and he unfolded it and Read it to me, and when he had Read it, he Delivered it to me, and gave me good Advice and Counsel and Wish'd me Success in my undertaking & I return[d] unfeigned Thanks to him and then took my leave of him &c—The Pass which he gave me was very good ^one^ indeed, which I will Coppy Down here—

By his Excellency
Jeffery Amherst & Esq[r]:
Major General, and Commander in Chief of all His Majesty's
Forces in North America &c &c &c—

To All Whom it may Concern

Whereas the Correspondents of the Society in Scotland for Propagating Christian Knowledge, have Acquainted me that the Bearer hereof, the Revd M[r] Occom, is sent by them, as a Missionary to Reside Amongst the Indians about the Onoyda Lake, These are to order and direct the officers Commanding at the Several Posts, to give him any Aid or Assistance he may Stand in need of to forward him on his Journey, and on his Arival at y[e] Onoyda Lake, the Officer Commanding there will Grant him all the Protection and Countenance he may want, in the Execution of his Duty &c

Given under my Hand & Seal at HeadQuarters in Albany, this 29th Day of June 1761 by his Excellency's Command

Jeff Amherst
Arthur Muir

36. Occom further describes the hospitality of his New York patrons in his June 24, 1761, letter to Eleazar Wheelock.

Wednesday July ye 1 left Albany about 10 in the Morning, got to Scenectady about 3 in the after Noon, Stayed there one Night,—

Thirdsday July 2 Went from Senectady, In Company with Colo Whiting and Dr Rodman, they Seem^ed^ to be Quite Friendly Gentlemen to us, we got about seven miles westward of Sir William Johnson's—

Fryday July ye 3 went to See Sir William at his ^Farm^ Seven Miles out off the Road, in the Wilderness, got there about 9 in the Morning, and were very Kindly Entertaind by his Honor, I Showed him my Recommendatory Letters, and a Pass from Genl Amherst, he Promised me his Assistance as Need Should Require, he was exceeding free with me in conversation—But we Stayd ^there^ but about two Hours, for he was geting in Readines to go on our way on the Next Day towards Detroit with five [Battows] Laden with Presents for the Indians, he [S]aid he wou'd overtake us on the Morrow before Night—We took Leave of his Honor and went our way, after we had got to the Main Road, we Call'd in at Certain House—and there we were Detaind one Night, by a Storm—[37]

Saturday July ye 4 Went on our Journey and Reach'd the German flats at Night, and we Turn'd in at one Mr Frank's a Tavern Keeper—

Sabbath July ye 5 we stay'd at Mr Franks, but did not go to Publick Worship with the People, because they Spoke unknown Tongue to us, But it did Seem like Sabbath by the appearance of the People—

July the 6—Sir William came to us at Mr Franks—

Tuesday July ye 7 Sir William and the Chiefs of the Onoyda Indians Met at this Place, to make up a Breach, which one of the Indians made lately, by killing a Dutchman, they talk^d about an Hour at this Time, and then Brok up Towards Night they Met together again, and talk'd together about 3 quarters of an Hour, then finaly Brock up, without being fully Satisfied on both sides for the Indians Insisted upon an old agreement that was Settled between them and the English formerly, that if any Such Acident Shou'd ever happen between them in Peaceable Times, they Shou'd make it up in an Amicable manner without Sheding of Blood But Sir William told them it was the Comand of General Amherst, that the murderer sho^d be delivered up to Justice— but the Indians said [that] murderer was gone off no body knows where &c.[38]

[Courtesy of Dartmouth College Library]

37. Occom here encounters Sir William Johnson, North American superintendent of Indian affairs, preparing to carry gifts to the Wyandot, Ottawa, Ojibwe, and Pottawattomie peoples of the Detroit area; gift giving and the cultivation of personal alliances were important implements of Johnson's diplomacy (Flexner, Mullin). As Lisa Brooks notes, the Mohegan had already established their own historical-political alliances with the Mohawks and other Iroquois tribes; still, Johnson's diplomatic standing within Iroquoia, his membership in Mohawk kinship networks through marriage, and his ability as a translator advantageously positioned him to introduce Occom to the Six Nations. This renewed relationship with the Six Nations proved strategically valuable to the Mohegan: Occom and his fellow Mohegan Samuel Ashpo gained through their acquaintance with the Six Nations a new perspective on New England Indian affairs, as Lisa Brooks observes, and Occom later solicited advice from Johnson concerning Mohegan-colonial conflicts. See L. Brooks, 147–151.

38. On July 11, 1761, General Jeffrey Amherst wrote to William Johnson concerning this case and expressing his intention that the accused murderer be punished (WJM 5:108).

ᴏ Journal 5

September 15, 1761–October 22, 1761

The Oneida and Tuscarora mark the end of Occom's first visit among them by of-
fering him a belt of wampum to confirm their relationship. Occom reaches his Mon-
tauk home on October 22. He brings with him a young Oneida man, who will stay
through the winter to learn the Mohegan-Pequot-Montaukett language.

Sep[r] ye 15 I Set out from Connistooknah by way of Tuscarora and took my leave of
them about 10 O'C Several of the Indians went with me to Onoyda got there about 1
in the after Noon—Was kindly Receivd by the on[o]ydas

Sabbath Sep[r] ye 20 Preachd at onoyda [to] a great Number of the Indians Came
together from all the Castle to hear the word of God, Baptizd 3 [Persons] at Night
Several made a Public Confession three of the heads of ye castle made a [2 words
illegible] and returnd thanks by a Belt of Wampum &c[39]

Monday Sep[r] ye 21 I Left Onoyda and several a Companyd me to fort Herkermer
[my mare] got away from me at Night, and did not find me [there] till Fryday Just
Night, Saturday Sep[r] ye 26 we Sot away from Fort Herkermer—got about 4 miles
below Sir William Johnsons—

Sabath Sep[r] ye 27 Sot out very Early and got to Schenectady about 10. Went
Meeting with the People—heard M[r] Vroman Preach but I Cou'd not undersd went
to See the Preast in the Evening and the Next morning, he treated very Kindly gave
me a Mohaque Book—Sot out about 9 got to Albany at 12 and Several Insisted upon
s[t]aying at Albany the Week out, and to Preach on the Sabbath, and at Length I
Complyd with their Disire—

Sabath Octo ye 4 I Preachd in the morning in the City Hall to Presbyterian Congregation, and in the after Noon I Preachd in the English Church Monday—Married
a Cupple in Albany, had 3 Dolars Marrying. —Sot out in the after Noon towards
Home, got so far as [Quemuns.]

Tuesday Oct[r] ye 6, Sot out very Early in the morning, and Reachd to Kings Bridge
at Night

October ye 7 we Sot out from the Kings Bridge very Early in the Morning and
about the Midle of the after Noon my mare was about [shirking her fold?] and we
were obliged to Put up at [words missing] Sot out very Early in the morning for
[word illegible] and [we] Stop at Poughkeepsie to Mr. Preach in the Evening, and
about Candle Light we began our Exercises in the State House and there was a great

39. The fullest account of this important meeting is preserved in a November 25, 1761, letter from
Eleazar Wheelock to George Whitefield. According to Wheelock, Oneida and Tuscarora leaders
welcomed Occom as a religious instructor, requested English help in establishing a school, asked
for the prohibition of alcohol, and expressly requested to be "protected on our Lands, that none
may molest or encroach upon us" (DCA 761625.1). See also Wheelock's account of the event in
his 1767 Moor's Indian Charity School *Narrative* (1767), 27. Tribal leaders also presented Occom
with a wampum belt to affirm and commemorate their relationship. The wampum belt was later
taken from Occom to be sent to Scotland as evidence of the activities of the New York Scotch
Society (Love, *Occom,* 93n14). It is noteworthy that Occom did not record the council's speeches
in his diary, but instead took care to memorize them.

Number of People to attend, and attended very Seriously,—and they gathered £1.7.0 for me—and they were very solisitous to have me stay the Sabbath over but I cou'd not to be my Duty to Comply—

Fryday Oct^r *ye 9* we Sot out from Poughkeepsie Towards York, and got so far as Rogers at and so far as Rogers at Night, and there turn'd in.

Saturday Oct ye 10 We Sot out very Early in the Morning on our journey, and got so far as Browns', by [Dobs's] ferry, and there turnd in, but met with very Disagreeable Company—

Sabbath Oct^r *ye 11* about 2 o'C in the after we Sot out for N. York and by way of White Ferry and Lodg'd by the Ferry—

Monday Oct^r *ye 12* about 9 we got over upon Long Island, and from there sot away for N. York and got into the City about Sun Set went to Mr. Wells and were very kindly Receiv'd, found them all well &c—Next Day went to visiting my Friends, was kindly Receivd by all—

Fryday October ye 16 to wards Night we went over to Long Island and to Jamaica at Night, and Saturday Octr ye 17 Sot Early in the Morning, and got to Huntington at Night and kept Sabbath there

Monday ye [18] we Sot away homeward got so far as Mulfords at Night

Tuesday Oc^r *19* Sot out very Early in the Morning and got Shenecock at Night, found the Indians well, they were very glad to See me once more,—

Wednesday Oc^r *20* We went off very Early in the Morn^g got to Bridgehampton before Night Lodg'd at Mr Brown's, my Friends were Exceeding glad to See me—

Thirdsday Oc^r *21* we went on our Journey, got to Mr Buells at Eastham—some Time in the after Noon, We were very Kindly receiv'd by all my Friends—

Fryday Oc^r *22* went on towards home, visited my Friends, and Neighbours al the way, got were Extreamly well receiv'd by them all, got home at Night found my Poor Family well except our youngest Child,[40] it had been very Sick, but it was geting well,—thanks be to Almighty god for goodness to us

[Courtesy of Dartmouth College Library]

∞ JOURNAL 6

November 21, 1765–July 22, 1766

Wheelock recruits Occom to undertake a fund-raising mission for Moor's Indian Charity School in England, Scotland, and Ireland. Despite some controversy concerning the visit among his sponsoring missionary societies, Occom embarks from Boston on December 23 with Nathaniel Whitaker, a minister of Norwich, Connecticut. In England, Occom is received warmly by George Whitefield, who introduces him to William Legge, Lord Dartmouth; prominent ministers including the archbishop of Canterbury and John Newton; and other potential supporters of the school, such as Lady Selina Hastings, the Countess of Huntington. Occom preaches from

---

40. *our youngest Child:* It is unclear whether this child is Christiana Occom (born in 1757) or Talitha Occom (born in 1761).

the pulpits of George Whitefield and John Wesley and in smaller chapels through-out England, Ireland, and Scotland. He also visits Parliament, Westminster Abbey, Bedlam, the Tower of London, and the king's robing room. During his visit, he is inoculated against smallpox. Occom's fame as a preacher grows so that he becomes an object of impersonation on the London stage. This section of his journal concludes in July 1766, when Occom and Whitaker leave London to tour rural England, Scot-land, and Ireland. By the time they departed England in spring 1768, Occom and Whitaker had raised about 12,000 pounds for Moor's Indian Charity School.

Mohegan Nov: 21, 1765 The Honorable Commissioners In Connecticut New England for propigating Christian Knowledge & Litterature among the Indians having Ma-turely Consulted the Expeediancy of Sending Some fit Person to Europe to calicet Assistance from Gods People at Home in this Heavy and good Work and appointed the Revd Nathaniel Whetaker to go—and thought it good to Send me to accompany him—and Acordingly, not Doubting the Call of god, and my Duty to go, on Thirds-day the 21 of Nov as above; in obediance to the Strange Call of Providence, having Commited my Self Family and Friends to the Care of Almighty God, took Lieve of them about 11. A. M: and went on my Journey towards Boston in order to take a Voige from thence to Europe—

Saturday Novr 23 ariv'd at Boston about 3 in the after noon, and put up at Mr Moses Peck's and was very kindly receiv'd by him—on Wednesday following Mr Whetaker ^with^ whome I was to travel return'd to Boston from Portsmouth, met with good incouragement by Friends Eastward, he Brought with him, almost Enough for our ~~voige~~ Pasage,—Here we Stay^d in Boston near 5 Weeks,—Friends in this place to the affair We are upon appear as near and Sincere as ever and increase Daily—The Adversaries Stand at a Distance Like Shemei,[41] But they don't Speak a Loud as they did, they now Contrive their Projects in Secret, and it is Supposed they are prepar-ing Whips for us (Letters) [word illegible/crossed out] to Send to Europe by the Same Ship, we are to go in—[42]

Monday Decr 23 about 9 in the Morning went a Board in Boston Packet a Ship,

41. In 2 Samuel 16:5–13, Shimei curses and throws stones at King David and his entourage as they travel. He repents and is forgiven by David in 2 Samuel 19:26–23.

42. On October 2, 1765, Andrew Oliver (1706–1774), then secretary of the Boston Board of Commis-sioners of the Society for the Propagation of the Gospel in New England (SPG), wrote a letter to Jasper Mauduit, head of the London Society, accusing Wheelock and Occom of failing to credit the SPG for its supporting role in Occom's education and of misrepresenting Occom's conver-sion and early career. Oliver's letter insinuated that Occom was incorrectly represented as "a mohawk, very lately bro't out of gross paganism & in a very little time fitted by M Wheelock to be what he is" in order to "procure large contributions" for Wheelock (DCA 766367.2). The circulation of the letter among missionary societies in England and the opposition of the SPG became a source of ongoing difficulty for Wheelock, Occom, and Nathaniel Whitaker. For his part, Whitaker believed that Oliver's letter reflected the SPG's "fear of being eclipsed" by Whee-lock in their efforts to evangelize American Indians (DCA 766315.2). From 1751 to 1764, the SPG sent Occom a total of £225 (Richardson, 129). This amount was grossly insufficient to support Occom's family let alone to justly compensate his work as a schoolmaster and missionary, as Occom himself argued in his 1768 autobiography. On the controversy, see also Peyer, *Tutor'd*, 74–75, Love, *Occom*, 133–136.

John Marshall Capt, and at 9 and half we Spread Sail to Wind—Trusting in ^y^e^ Living god—There was four Pasanger of us, Mr John Williams and Mr Thomas Bromfield of Boston, Mr Whetaker and I—We had very agreeable Company. The Worship of god was Caried on Daily, and had a Sermon every Sabbath, the goodness of god is very great to us,—We had favourable Winds except 3 Short Spells of hard Gail, we lay low, and When we got Within 200 Leagues of Lands End, Moderate Easterly Winds met us And Stopt us 20 days and remarkable Warm Weather we had most of the Time—and then we had Some favourable Winds,—and Sabbath the 2^d day of Feruary 1766 about 10 in the morning we discover'd the land of England,—and the Wind headed us again, and the next Day which was ye 3 of Feb^r we went a Shore on great Briton in a Fish Boat, and Land at a Place Call'd Bricksham, ^in Tar Bay 200 Miles from Lond^ Just after Sun Set, and put at one Widow Womans House—Blessed be thiy great Name O god for thy goodness to us over the Waters, and hast Brought us upon the Land, Lord wright a Law of thankful'ness in our Hearts, and preserve me on the Land as thou hast done on the Seas, and deliver me from all Evil, especially from the Evil of Sin—

Feb^r 4 Went on our Journey Early in the Morning on Horse Back, got to Exon about 4 PM 30 M from Bricksham—We were Call'd up half after 10 in the Night, & Went off in a ^Coach of Six Horses^ at 11, from Exon pretty Large City and reachd to a City Call'd Salsbury about 10 in the eveng we went a 100 miles this Day But we had very Cold Day—Thanks be to god for his goodness to us heatherto—

Thirdsday Fe^r 6 we were Call'd up again Just before 2 and at 2 in the Morning We Went on our Journey—and by the goodness of God, ^we^ ariv'd to London about 7 in the Evening, and we Call'd upon Mr Debert[43] and were kindly receiv'd, and Lodg'd there, in ye Morning Mr Smith of Boston Came to See us, and Conducted us to Mr Whitfields, and were Extreemly well receiv'd by him, O how marvillous is gods goodness to us thus far—Mr Whitfield & other Friends here advise not to be open as yet,[44]—We rode with Mr Whitfield ^in his Chaise^ to a good Friends, ^and Din'd there^ but We Were Private about it, Lodg'd at Mr Whitefields—

Saturday Febru^r 8: Was at Mr Whitefield's, Conceil'd—and on Sabbath 9th Feb^r was Still Conceil'd

Monday, Febru^r ye 10th Mr Whitefield took Mr Whetaker and I in his Coach and Introduc'd us to my Lord Dartmouth,[45] and apear'd like a worthy Lord indeed, Mr Whitefield Says he is a Christian Lord and an uncommon one—after We Pay'd our Compliments to my Lord—Mr Whitefield Caried us to my Lady Hotham's, and She receiv'd us with all Kindness, She is an aged Woman, and a Mother in Israel, and we rode about Both in the City and out,—the Land about the City & in the Country is like one Continued Garden.—last Sabbath Evening I walk'd with Mr Wright to Cary a letter to my Lord Dartmouth and Saw Such Confusion as I never Dreamt of—there

---

43. *Mr Debert:* Denys DeBerdt.

44. Whitefield encouraged Whitaker and Occom to maintain a low profile until the controversy surrounding Occom's identity and his relationship to the various missionary societies abated or resolved.

45. *Lord Dartmouth:* William Legge, Earl of Dartmouth.

was Some at Churches Singing & Preaching, in the Streets some Cursing, Swaring & Damning one another, others was hollowing, Whestling, talking gigling, & Laughing, & Coaches and footmen passing and repassing, Crossing and Cross-Crossing, and the poor Begars Praying, Crying, and Beging upon their knees,—Tuesday Din'd with Mr Savage, and in the eveng Mr Whitefield and his people had Love Feast at the Chappel.[46] Mr Whitaker and I Join'd with them.

Wednesday Feb^r 12 rode out again

Thirdsday Feb^r 13 Mr Whitefield Caried us to the Parlament House—there we Saw many Curiosities, from thence went over Westminster Bridge a Cross the River Thames made all of Stone—thence went to Greenwich, and ^had^ a glance of Hospital there,[47] But a Tedious Cold rainy Day ^it^ was—[w]e were Introduc'd by Mr Whitefiled to Mr Faudagel[48] a Quaker—got home again in the Evening—

Fryday Feb^r 14 Early in the morning Mr Whitefield Carried us to Mr Romains and Introduc'd us to him and to Mr Madin,—and to Mr Singenhagan and old Apostolec German Minister,—and return'd Home again—Mr Whitefield takes unwearied Pains to Introduce us to the religious Nobility and others, and to the best of men in the City of London—Yea he ^is^ a tender father to us, he provide everything for us, he has ^got^ a House for us,—ye Lord reward him a thousand a Thousand fold—He is indeed ^a father^ in God, he has made him a Spiritual Father to thousands and thousands, and god has made him a Temporal father to the poor,—His House is Surrounded with the poor, the Blind, the Lame, the Halt and the mamed, the Widow, & the Fatherless, from Day to Day, God Continue his useful Life.[49]

Sabbath I Preach'd in Mr Whitefield's Tabernacle to a great Multitude of People; I felt . . . . .[50]

Monday Febr^y 17 Mr Whitefield presented us to Dr Gifford a famous Baptist Minister and were receiv'd Extreamly Well—and Dined with him—

Tuesday we Stayd Home—

Wednesday, Feb^r 19 we were Conducted to See the Kings Horses Carriages, and Horsemen &c—and then went to the Pt House[51] and went in the Robing Room and saw the Crown first, and Saw the King,[52] had ye Pleasure of Seeing him put on his

46. *Love Feast:* Although its name refers to communal meals shared among early Christians, eighteenth-century love feasts were not meals but worship services held among Methodists and related Protestant groups.

47. *Greenwich Hospital:* A palace building at Greenwich, England, designed and built by Sir Christopher Wren from 1696 to 1715.

48. *Mr Faudagel:* John Fothergill.

49. Whitefield was celebrated for his philanthropy, especially for his Bethesda orphanage near Savannah, Georgia, which he established in 1740.

50. Whitefield's original tabernacle was a wooden shed built in Upper Moorfields in 1741. A second chapel was built on Tottenham Court Road in London in 1756. Occom inserts ellipses here to indicate the indescribability of his feelings in preaching from the pulpit of the century's most famous transatlantic evangelist.

51. *Pt House:* Parliament House.

52. *the King:* King George III.

Royal Robes and Crown,—He is quite a Comly[53] man—his Crown is Richly adorn'd with Diamonds, how grand and Dazling is it to our Eyes,—if an Earthly Crown is So grand—How great and glorious must the Crown of the glorious Redeemer be, at the right ^hand^ of the majesty on High—tho' he was once Crown'd with Thorns—The Atendence of King George is Very Surprizing, as he went to the House of Parlament ^he &^ his glorious Coach was was atended with footmen Just before and behind were all round, and the Horseman Just behind and before the footmen, and the Bells & all Sorts of Musickal Instru Instruments Playing, and the Cannon Firing, and Multitudes of all Sorts of People Throning all Round—if an Earth King With his atend[c] is So great, How grand, how Dreadful and glorious must the appearing of the Son of god be—when he Shall Desend from Heaven, to Judge the World, He will Desend with Cherubem[s] and Serephems with Angels and Archangels and with Sound of the Trumpet and with great Power and glory, with Thunder & Lightning,—and the Family of Heaven, and Earth, and Hell Shall appear before him, and the Eliments Shall melt with fervent Heat—Lor Jesus prepare me for thy Second Coming—

We went Emediately from Seing The King to Dine with a Nobleman My Lord Dartmouth a most religious Noble-man and his Lady also, the most Singular Cupple amongst Nobility in London [Dinners?]—This Day also went to Westminster Abey, and had a fuler Vew of the Moniments—in the Eveng ^saw Bedlem also^ we return'd again to M[r] Whitefield's——

Thursday Feb[r] 20—This is the Queen Chalottes Birth Day, was Conducted to St James's[54] where the Royal Family and the Nobility were to be together to keep a Joyful Day—but we were too late, however we ^Saw^ some of the Nobility In their Shining Robes and a throng of People all around,—the Sight of the Nobility put me in mind of Dives and the Rich Gluton, and the poor reminded me of Lazarus—What great Difference there is Between the Rich and the Poor—and What Diference there ^will^ is and will be, Between Gods poor and the Devils Rich, &c—[55]

O Lord God Amighty let not my Eyes be Dazled with the glitering Toys of this World, but let m be fixt and my Soul Long after Jx[56] Who is the only Pearl of great Price—This evening Went into our House which M[r] Whitefield Provided for us and all the Furniture also—and a Made to Wait on us—Blessed be god, that he has Sent he Dear Servant before us—

Fryday Feb[r] 21: was Conducted to the Tower, saw the Kings Lions Tygers Wolf and Leopards &c—Saw the Kings guns and the monuments of antient Kings on Horse Back and their Soldiers on foot with their Antient Armour of Brass and Tin—Dind with M[r] Keen, and then went to a funeral, M[r] Whitefield gave an Exhortation to the People and then Pray'd—

Saturday Feb[r] 22 Went to See Doc[r] Burton a Minister of the Church of England, was Introduced by M[r] Smith of Boston, and the Doc[r] Was Very Kind, he wou'd have

---

53. *Comly:* Comely, or handsome.

54. *St. James's:* St. James's Palace, a royal residence that until 1837 was the primary home of the King and Queen.

55. Occom here refers to the parable of Lazarus and Dives; see Luke 16:19–31.

56. *Jx:* Jesus Christ.

feign perswaded me to Holier Orders and I modestly told him, I had no Such vew when I came from Home, and added, I had been Ordained Six Years in a Dissenting Way.—This after Noon Mr Whitaker & I went to wait upon Doc^r Chandler, an old Disenting Minister, found him Very Careful in his own way Gave us Advice not to own Mr Whitefield a Friend either to Desenters, or to the old Standards of the Church of England[57]—Promis'd his Countenance to the Affair we are upon—

Sabbath Feb^r 23 in the morng I heard Mr Davis in the Tabernacle in the afternoon I heard Dr Gifford in the Evening I Preachd at Dr Giffords—and Lodg'd at his H this Night—

Monday Feb^r 24 went home Early in the morning—

Tuesday F 25 Din'd with Mr Savage—

Wednesday Feb^r 26: this afternoon went to See Dr Gibbons an Independent Minister, receivd us kindly and promisd to assist us according to his Influance, in our Great Business—

Thursday Feb^r 27 Preach'd at Doc^r Conder's Meeting House, Went from the meeting to Sup with Mr Randal,—

I have kept House now above a Week by reason of a Cold I have—

March 11 1766 on Wednesday about a Quater after 3 P M—I was Inoculated by the Revd Mr Whitaker near M^r G Whitefields Tabernacle in London[58]

Wednesday March 13: I was violently Shoikd with the working of Phisicks was very full of Pain all Day—was kindly visited by Gen^n and Ladies Constantly—and had two Do^rs to do for me—on the 20th of March I began to Break out—and had it but light—and was attended like a Child by my Friends—I Cou'd'n't be taken Care of better by my own Relations, I had a very tender and Carefull Nurse a Young Woman—and by the first Day of April I Was Intirely Well, all my Pock Dried up, and Scabs Dropt off—O how great is gods goodness and mercy to me—O that god wou'd enable me to live Answerable to the mercies and favours I injoy—and that he wou'd cure my Soul of all Spiritual Diseases, by the Blood of Jx which Cleanseth from all Polution—and that he ^wou'd^ fit and prepare me for himself—

April 5 Went to Some Distance from our House—

Sabbath April 6: took my last Physick after my Pox—Just at Night My Lady Huntington came to Mr Whitefields, and we were Introduc'd to her by Mr Whitefield, and She is most Heavenly ^woman^ I believe in the World, She appears like a Mother in Israel indeed—a woman of great Faith—

Monday April 7 I went about the City good Deal—I am ^now^ Continually invited by ~~my~~ our good Friends,—

---

57. Dissenters like Chandler distrusted Whitefield because he affiliated with Methodists and reformers while remaining a member of the Church of England.

58. The practice of inoculation consisted of the purposeful insertion of smallpox scabs into an incision in the patient's skin, causing the patient to suffer a mild case of smallpox and obtain immunity to the disease. Originally practiced in Africa and Western Asia, inoculation was adopted into Western European and Anglo-American medical repertoires in the early eighteenth century. A slave named Onesimus taught Cotton Mather about inoculation, and Mather subsequently became a major American advocate of the controversial practice. See Occom's letter to Wheelock, March 11, 1756.

Thursday April 10 Went ^over^ Thames with Mrs Webber to a Private Meeting—
Fryday April 11 Went with Mr Weekes to Meeting at the Lock[59]—
Sabath April 13: Preach'd at Dr Chandler's—and was very ill amidst my Discourse—
Wednesday April 16: we Din'd with Doc^r^ Stennet a Baptist Minister, a very Worthy Man—and hearty Friend to the Business we are upon—
~~Tuesday~~ ^Wednesday^ *April 23* we Breakfasted with Dr Stennet—
Thursday April 24: I went to See Dr Condor, a Very Worthy Minister and a Hearty Friend to the Business we are upon, and went from the D^rs^ to Mr Brewers, and was very kindly recivd—he is a warm Servt of Jx—
~~Wednesday~~, *April 2[?]:* Preach'd in the Evening at Mr Whitefield's Capel, to a great Multitude, ~~and~~ the L^d^ was present with us I hope
Sabbath April 27: ~~In the~~ Preach'd at Little St. Hellens and Devenshare Square[60]— and I something of a freedom in the after Noon,—
Monday April 28 Went to See Several Gent^n^—Mr Dilly gave me 4 Books for my own Use—Din'd with Mr Barber a good Disenting Minister—then went with Mr Whitaker to Mr Baileys, and Mr Whitaker Baptiz'd a Child for him,—and then went home,
Wednesday April 30 We went to wait upon his grace the Arch Bishop of Canterbury[61] and he apear'd quite agreable and Friendly—In the evening I Preach'd at Mr Whitefield's Tabernacle to a Crouded Audience and I believe the L^d^ was with us of a trouth—
Thursday ~~April~~ May 1st Dr Stennet Introduc'd us to the Arch Bishop of York,[62] and we found him a greable Gentleman, and and Friendly Dispos'd to our Cause, and Promis'd to do Something towards it—and then went from there to Mr Onslow an old Genttleman from Speaker in the House of Commons—he apear'd very Friendly to us & was Well pleas'd to hear the Indians in America were Inclin'd to receiv'd the Gospel—
Sabbath May 4 Preach'd at Mr Barber's meeting and had Some Freedom in Speaking—and in the after noon I Preach'd at Mr Britton's meeting, a Worthy Baptist—to a Crouded Audience and the L^d^ was with us in a measure—
Monday May 5 we went out with Dr Stennet, but we were Disapointed in our Visets—and we went to Dr Charles Hotham to return thanks to him for generous Donation to our Business—found him full of god, his talk was nothing but about Jesus X—
Wednesday May 7 We Din'd with a Number of Ministers and other Gentlemen at Barbers Hall, and found many gentlemen well Disposd towards our Business—
Thursday May 8: We went to Clapham, found Some Friends and opposition—
Sabbath May 11: Preach'd at Mr Brewer's to a Crouded Audience, and the L^d^ gave

59. *The Lock:* Lock Hospital, Hyde Park Corner, London, was founded in 1746. Martin Madan served as hospital chaplain.
60. The court of Little St. Hellens and Devonshire Squire both stood on Bishopsgate Street in London.
61. Thomas Secker (1693–1768) was archbishop of Canterbury from 1758 to 1768.
62. Robert Hay Drummond (1711–1776) was archbishop of York from 1761 to 1776.

me freedom to Speak, and the People attended with great affection—Praise be to god—In the evening I Preachd at Mr Shillon's to a throng'd Congregation, and there was a Solemn appearance of the People, the was with us, Glory be to his great Name forever & ever—

Monday May 12 We went to wait upon Mr Onslow and he appear'd very Friendly to our Business highly aproved of it—

Tuesday We din'd with Mr Savage—

Wednesday I Din'd with Mr Morison—

Thursday We Din'd with Thornton at Clapham a Sincere Christian Gent^n and a Hearty Friend to our afaire, and Will use his Influence—We have Seen much of the goodness of God this week thanks be to his holy N—

Fryday may 16: in the Ev^g Preach'd at Mr Clarke's & the gave me Some Strenght to Preach—and the People were very attentive—

Saturday may 17 we went to wait on Mr Jackson the Second time Met some What cold reception,—

Sabbath May 18: Preach'd at Doc^r Gifford's AM: with some freedom, in the after Preach'd at Dr Stennets with Strength, blessed be god for his Assistance—

Wednesday may 21: I went to See Mr Romain was kindly receiv'd by him, he is freer man to talk about religion at Heart than Mr Whitfield we came into the Town together in a Coach—and then Mr Bulkley Conducted me to a Baptist Meeting Where there was a Number of Baptist Ministers about 20 of them, after meeting I Dined with them, and they were very civil to me—and then I returnd home—

Thursday may 22: went to Mr Skinner's then Home, and from thence to a Meeting with Mr Fold and his Family Mr Fold Preach'd,—returning home we heard a Man and Woman kill'd By the Coach's over Setting, and a Cart runing over them—this Evening I was taken with a Violent Purging—[63]

Fryday May 23 was very Sick with a Sort of Bloody[64] and Kept me down a Week before I was able to go out—

Sabbath June 1 I was able to go out to Preach [in]—Preachd at Mr Bulkley's a Baptist Mi^r and had but few hearers In the after Noon Preachd for Mr Winter to a great Congregation found my Self but week in Body—This weak I was Busy geting ready to Send Some things to my Children,—

Saturday June 7 I went to North Hampton, got there Just before Night, and was receivd with all kindness—

Sabbath June 8, Preach'd to at Mr Riland's[65] Meeting Hs to a throngd Congregation, & the L^d gave me Some Strenght and the People attended with great Solemnity and affection and was told afterwards one young Man was Converted and hopefully Convected—in the after Noon Preach'd in Riland's Yard to about 3000 recken'd,—

Monday June 9: Mr Newton of Olney about 15 miles off Came to fetch me to his Place after Breakfast we Sot off, ~~got~~ rode in a Post Chace there a little after 12: this Mr Newton is a Minister of the Church of England, he was a Sailor, and god

63. *Violent Purging:* severe diarrhea.
64. *Bloody:* bloody flux, or dysentery.
65. *Mr Riland:* John Ryland.

marvellously turn'd him and he is a flaming Preacher of the Gospel,—at Evening I Preach'd at one of the meetings in the Place, to a Croud of People,—Lodgd at Mr Newton's,—a Number of good ^people^ live in this place but very ^poor^ in this World—

Tuesday June 10 Mr Newton and I took a walk towards Northampton about miles—and [there] Breakfasted—and there we parted he went Back a foot, and I went on Horse to Northamp^n, got there about 12: Din'd with Mr Hextal one of the Desenting Ministers of the place,—at 6 in the Eveng I Preachd the Meeting House where great Doc^r Doddrege was Minister, and there was a great Concourse of people and attended with great Solemnity—Lodg'd at Mr Riland's—there ^is^ a number of Warm Christians in this Town—

Wednesday June 11 got up a little after 3 and was in a coach before 4: and returnd to London—Got there a little after 6:—found my friends well. Thanks be to god for ^his^ goodness—

Sabbath June 15: Preachd in the morning at Mr Burford's Meeting had some freedom—in the after Noon I preachd at Mr Pitts, with Since of Divine things in the Evening Preachd at Shakespears walk[66]—and Sup'd with M^r [Wares] this Evening—

*Monday ^June 16^* Went to Mr Thorntons at Clapham and was Entertaind with all Kindness. he is a gen^n of emence fortune, and he is the right Sort^s of Christian^s and a very Charitable man—Lodgd with him this Night—

Tuesday Morning Mr Thornton took me in his Chariot and Caried me to my Lodgings—

Wednesday June 18: I went in the Morning to See Mr Guinap, a Baptist Minister of Saffron Walden, Breakfasted with him—

Thursday June 19 Preach'd in Mr John Wesley's Foundry[67] to a Crouded Audience, begun at 7 in the Evening—

Saturday June 21: Mr Whitaker and I went to Saffron Walden got there before Night Lodg'd at Mrs Fuller's—

Sabbath June 22: Went to Meeting Mr Whitaker P and in the after Noon I Preachd to a Crouded Congregation, and I was Very Poorly, but I belive the L^d was with us of a truth and in the evening Preachd again to great Assembly and I had Some Strength, and the People made a Collection

Monday June 23 we return'd to London, got there some time before night—the L^d be Prais'd for all his goodness to us—this Evening I heard, the Stage Players, had been Mimicking of me in their Plays, lately—I never thought I Shou'd ever come that Honor,—O god wou'd give me greater Courage—

Thursday June 26 Din'd with Savage, in the Evening was visited by Mr Furly a Minister from Yorkshare, one who truely Loves the L^d Jx I believe—

Fryday June 27. Preach'd Early in the Morning at Mr Richardson's Meeting,

Sabbath June 29: Preach'd at Mr Brewers in the latter Part of the Day to a Crouded

---

66. A dissenter's meeting and school was held at Shakespeare's Walk in the Shadwell district, London.

67. Wesley opened a church in a converted cannon factory or foundry in Moorfields in 1740. Until 1778, the foundry served as the headquarters of Wesleyan Methodism.

Congregation, and they made a Collection for us to the amount of 100:30 the L^d reward them a many fold in this life and in the World to Come Life everlasting—

Monday June 30 Mr Smith of Boston in America, and I Went Down the River
Thames to Shearness by the Sea Side near Sixty miles from London we went by
water So far as Gravesend, a fine Prospect we had each Side of the River, flat Land,
and very Fruitful, indeed it is like one Continued garden—But the Maloncholy
Sight was to See So many Malefactors Hung up in Irons by the River[68]—We took
Coach at Gravesend to Chatham—and then went by water again, and we Sail'd
through a great Number of Man of War all the Way to Shareness. Got there between
and eleven,—

Tuesday July 1 We went all about Shearness, vewing every thing we Cou'd see,
towards night we went to Bathing in Salt Water,—

Wednesday July 2: we return'd went by Water So far as Chatham, and it Rain'd
and Thunder'd very hard—While we were on the water got to Chatham about 9
and there took Post chaise and went on to London, got there about 6, found my
friends well, and receiv'd Some Letters from America and by them my family was
Well the 29 of April last—Blessed be god for his tender Mercies to me and to mine,
O that the L^d wou'd teach us to be thankful at all times—

Sabbath July 6: Preachd at Mr Webb's meeting to a Small Congregation—in the
afternoon I heard Mr Preach,—

Monday July 7 I went to Clapham to See Esqr Thornton, and was very kindly re-
cev'd, after Dinner Mr Thornton and I went in Chace to and rode all the after Noon
and had very agreeable wride—and we had agreable Conversation about religion of
Jx—Just at Night we went to See his Sister ^Willber^ at Winbleton, and they were
very urgent to have me Stay there that Night, and Lodgd there—

Tuesday July 8: Mrs Willberforce Caried me in her Coach to London—She is a
Sound Christian—in the after Noon I Din'd with M^iss Gideon a Jewis by Birt but a
true Christian, had a Sweet Conversation with her—from there went to see Sr James
Jay of New York in America and then went ^to^ See Mr Wintworth of Portsmouth
in America and then went home—

Wednesday July 9 went to viseting again but found none that I wanted to see—

Thurdsday July 10 Went with Mr Whitaker to Several Places, and then went to
Stepney and Din'd with a Number of Ministers and were very kindly receivd by
them—from thence I went home—

Fryday July 11 Went to ^wait^ upon Mr Penn but he was not at Home, and it
Thundred and rain'd very hard in the morng and returnd home again—

Sabbath July the 13 Went in the morning to Dedford and at Mr Oldings Meeting,
a good Puritanical Independent, and we had a very Crouded Audience, and they
made a Collection for us—Went Direcly to London and Preachd at Mr Stafford's meet
But it was not very Crouded—after Meeting Went with one M^r Co[o]ks to Drink Tea
and While we were at Tea I Seriously ^ask'd^ Mr Cooks who was to Preach at M^r

68. Pocahontas died and was buried in Gravesend, England, on March 21, 1617. As a key passenger port, Gravesend was also a site of detention and transfer for English convicts awaiting
deportation.

Whitefield's? he with all gravity Said Mr Occom, Mr Occom? Says I, yes, Says he, I know nothing of it says I again, it is So Concluded says he—so I emediately went and Preachd to a Multitude of People, and the L^d gave me Some Strength Blesseded be his great Name

   Tuesday July 15 Went to Din'd with Doc^r Gifford, after Dinner went with Sir James Jay to wait on one Mr Person, and Saw many of his Curiosities—and then went home—

   Wednesday July 16: in the Evening Preach'd at Dr Gifford's Meeting—to a Small number of People—

   Thirdsday July 17: Mr W. and I Went to Hitchin in a Stage Coach, about forty Miles from London, got there Jut about 12 and were receiv'd with all kindness by our Friends—I Lodg'd at Mr Thomas' and Mr Whitaker Lodg'd at Mr Wellshare's—

   Fryday July 18 We Visited all Day at Hitchin—

   Saturday July 19: We went to Southwell I Preach'd to a Small number of People— the People made a Collection for us they a Collected about £15— return'd again in the Evening to Hitchin—

   Sabbath July 20: I Preach'd in the Morning at Mr Hickman's Meeting, a very worthy Minister of Jx,—and in the after Noon Preach'd at Mr James's, a Baptist Min—and a very Worthy Man—the Meeting very Much Crowded and as Soon as the Meeting was done—a Post Chaise[69] was ready for me at the Door and I went Emediatly to Luton about 9 Miles from Hitchin, and in Mr Hall's Meeting, to a great Multitude and as Soon as the was done I Went Back to Hitchin, got there about 10— the Lord gave me Some Since of Divine Things this Day, and gave me Some Strength— Glory be to his great name for his Condesention—

   Monday July 21 Went Back to London—got there about 5 P.M.

   Tuesday July 22, Went about to leave of my good Friends and Wednesday and thursday to leave of my good Friends Heitherto the L^d helped us and glory be to his great and holy Name—

[Courtesy of Dartmouth College Library]

ᑯ JOURNAL 7

July 8, 1774–August 14, 1774

Occom returns from England in 1768 and resides with his family at Mohegan. After Wheelock relocates Moor's Indian Charity School to Hanover, New Hampshire, and phases out its Native educational programs, Occom ends his relationship with his former teacher in 1771. He turns down subsequent invitations from white missionary societies to proselyte among other tribes and turns his attention to resolving factionalism within his own Mohegan community. Occom's stature as a Native political leader grows, as does his fame as a preacher after his delivery and publication of the best-selling Sermon, Preached at the Execution of Moses Paul *in 1772. On March 13, 1773, Occom and his son-in-law Joseph Johnson invite to Mohegan*

---

69. *Post Chaise:* Horse-drawn, four-wheeled passenger carriage.

Native peoples from Stonington, Lyme, Long Island, Groton, Charlestown, and Farmington to organize the intertribal Brotherton movement. In this segment of his diaries, Occom and David Fowler travel to upstate New York to affirm the relationship between the Brotherton tribes and the Oneida, who in January 1774 had promised them lands for resettlement. Along the way, Occom and Fowler visit "Indian towns" and "Indian places" in Connecticut, western Massachusetts, and New York.

July 8 1774: David Fowler and I Sot out about 3 O'C in the afternoon from Mohegan on a Journey towards Onoyda to Visit our Brethern; reachd So far as to Colchester; Lodgd at Mr Gansefoot's, and were very kindly entertaind. Saturday, July 9: Very early in the morning went on our Jour; rode about 8 or 9 miles were kindly invited in by one Mr Luther I believe a ChrN man and brake our fast with him, after Breakfast went our Way, Stopt at Mr Frothinghams, a Separate Minister in Midletown, and Din'd with him, after Dinner went on again reached the Borders of Farmton in the evening and We put up at a Tavern.—

Sabbath July 10: got up very early in the Morning and went on to Indian Town, arrivd there about 7 O'C in the morn put at Friend Elijah Wympi's Preachd twice this Day and in the evening.—

Monday, July 11: we were at the Indian place all Day visited amongst them, found them well in general and Well Disposed towards [R]eligion.

Tuesday, July 12: about 9 we left the Place and went on to New Hartford about 8 miles where 2 or 3 Families of Indians Live, there preachd in the after Noon; in the evening went to an English House and Lodged there, and was very kindly entertained—

Wednesday, July 13: attended ordination at the place called [ ] one M^r [ ] ordaind, went to the Indian Place again and Preachd Just before Night, after ordination after meeting went 2 or 3 miles to one Changum's and Lodgd there he is an Indian from Block Island and has a White woman for his wife.

Thirdsday, July 14: Went over the River and Breakfasted with Duncan—; after Break fast went to New Hartford to Mr Marsh's and to meeting at 10 O'C, after meeting went Back to Mr Marsh's to Dine with him after Dinner went on to Norfolk with our [ ] and got to the Place Just before Sun-Set, Lodgd With the Same gentleman that conducted us here.—

Fryday, July 15: had a Meeting about 9 O:C this morning, after meeting went on our way to Stockbridge reachd to the Place Some Time before Night, we calld on Mrs Kirkland and found her and hers well, good Mr Sergeant came to see us, and in the Evening went home with him and Lodgd there.—

Saturday July 16: was at the Place all Day, visited Some Indians, towards evening met at [Honise's] to converse with the Indians, but with we had no Interpreter, how ever we had Some Conversation about Spirituals and Temporals—Lodgd again at Mr Sergents.

Sabbath July 17: in the morning heard Mr Periham Preach. In the after Noon I Preached Twice, first to the English, and Just before Night to the Indians—There was a great Number of the White People.—Lodgd at one Capt Joness this Night—

Monday July 18: met the Indians in the morning at Honise's; had Some Conversation with them Concerning Temporal and Spiritual Concerns.—Dined at Capt Jones['s] and emediately after Dinner Went our way towards Richmunt Deac^n Willson and Capt Jones and others went with us, got there Some Time in the after noon, here met with my old acquaintance from Long Island, good Doctor Tarbell, Mr Jeremiah Miller, Mr Lewis Hedges, and Mr Reuben Hedges. I Preachd at the Place this after Noon to a Crowded Auditory; after meeting went to Doc^t Tarbell's and Lodgd there and was very kindly entertaind.

Tuesday July 19: Soon after Breakfast went ^over^ on to New Canaan, Preachd there this morning, as soon as meetig was over went with Mr Johnson to New Lebanon and Preac^hed^ there this after Noon, Soon after this meeting we had governor Franklin and a gentleman from the west Indies and others and Some Ladies, Soon after meeting we Set off on our Journey and we Travelld till about 10 O'C in the Night, we could not find a Tavern, and as obligd to put up at a poor privet House—

Wednesday, July 20: got up very early in the morning and went on our way; got to Albany about 8 O'C in the forenoon. Stopt a little while there, and past on to Schenectady, got there Some Time in the after Noon, put up at Mr Post's, our old Friend's, and they were very glad to See us and we were glad to See them also.

Thirdsday, July 21: in the morning Preachd at this place in Mr Miller's Meetg House, Dind at Mr Millers Lodgings, Soon after meeting left the place and Proceeded on our Journey, arrivd to Colo. Guy Johnsons Just before Sun Set; Sat a little while with him, found him very Solitary on the account of the Death of Sir William [Johnson]. Last Fryday was the first of our hearing of his Death, which Dampt our Spirits much, about Sun Set we left Colo. Guy Johnson, and we went on and travell 5 or 6 miles and put up at one Mr Bourne's.[70]

Fryday, July 22: went off very early in the Morning, towards night reachd the upper Mohawk Castle Called Fort Hindreck;[71] put up at Joseph Brant's but he was not at Home. Saw but few of the Indians.

Saturday July 23: left the place early in the morn and went on our way, Still went no further than one Mr Thomson's

Sabbath, July the 24: we thought it best to travil, being a fine Clear Day, arrived at old Onoyda about 4 O'C in the afternoon, found our Friends well in general, and they were very glad to See us and we were as Glad. Stopt about an Hour and a half and so pusht on to Cannoharohare, got there just in Dusk of the evening, a great number of them essued out of their Houses and were overjoyed to see us, and we were very glad to see them, after Salutations went to Mr Kirkland's, and he was Surprizd to See us, and we embracd each other for Joy, and a Number of the Indians

---

70. William Johnson died on July 11, 1774.

71. *Fort Hindreck:* Fort Hendrick, also known as Fort Canajohare, was located at the Upper Castle of the Mohawk, near the town of Danube, in Herkimer County, New York. Named for the Mohawk king Hendrick (d. 1755) and constructed under the direction of William Johnson, it served as a British outpost during the Seven Years' War. It was also the home of Joseph Brant.

came in and they Sung Psalms [Sweetly?] before they went out[72]—The good Lord be Praised, that he has Safely brought to the place of our Desire and that we have found our poor Brethren So Well—about 10 took rest for the Night—Spent the Week with a agreeable vew of the Situation and hopeful Prospect of the Indians future Happiness—Great alteration has been made among these Indians both as to their Temporal and Spiritual Concerns ^since I was here 12 years ago^ the Lord bless them more abundantly—Yet I find the Devil is very is very busy at this time to obstruct the pure Doctrines of the Gospel of Jesus Christ. the Leaven of the Pope, which has been planted among these poor Indians long Since [page torn: word missing] Now fe^r^ments among them and the leaven of the apostatis[d] Protestant Christians which is worse than the Heathen, with the Heathen Superstions are all fermenting together at this Time, to oppose the True Religion of Jesus Christ, which Consists in the Power, as well as in form, and produces Love to God and Man and Holiness of Life—[73]

July 31: M[r] Kirkland Preachd in the Morning, and I in the after Noon.—These Indians have got a good large meeting house almost compleated outside, with a Neat Belfray to it—This week on Wednesday had a Conference with Indians concerning the True Doctrines of being all ways offensive to a Carnal mind.

Saturday, August 6: was able to ride to Fort Stanix with M[r] Kirkland, expecting to meet a Great Numr of Indians there as they were all going to Salmon fishing but we did not with So many as we Expected, tho there be considerable Number of them.

Sabbath, Aug[t] 7, 1774: I preach'd all Day to the Whites, in the evening a Numr of the Indians Came in to M[r] Proofs to Sing, and and a Numr of the Whites came to hear—Last night Night and this morn a French man, a Roman Cath and an English Woman Presst us very hard to Baptize their Children, but understanding their Immorality we Declin'd to Baptize them—

Monday, Aug[t] 8: was [not?] well enough to Proceed to the Fishing Place, and So I returnd to Cannoharohary with M[r] Kirkld [and] got to the place before Night, Spent the week peacably I went a Fishing almost every Day and we had Small fish [enough] every Day—

Sabbath Aug[t] 14: M[r] Kirkland preachd, and toward evening I put a Questn to them, which was this,—what is it that makes a Christian or who is a Christian a Number of them Answered & they answerd well[74]—This week and last week We have heard very Bad News the Shawanese have had a [word illegible] engagements

72. Hymn singing was an important element of Christian Native practice in both New England and upstate New York. Occom compiled and published *A Collection of Hymns and Spiritual Songs,* which included several of his own compositions, in April 1774. See Brooks, *American Lazarus,* 51–86.

73. Samuel Kirkland took his place as a missionary among the Oneidas in 1766. A strict Calvinist, Kirkland criticized the tremendous syncretism of the Oneida community at Canowarohare and the mixed Oneida-Tuscarora-Mohawk community at Onaquaga, New York. See Graymont, "The Tuscarora"; Valone; Pilkington.

74. Notice Occom's pedagogy here: rather than simply preaching to his Native audience, he posed a question to them and engaged their answers. It appears that he developed this pedagogy in his school at Montauk, where as his 1768 narrative records, he "Proposd Questions of my own, and in my own Tonugue," to his Native students.

with the Virginians and many were Slain on both Sides and Shawanese have Sent belts of Wampum all around among the Tribes of Indians for assistance, but we cant know how Tribes have Joind [them]. [Page Torn] about a week ago the [page torn] Chief Wariors Came to Onoyda from the Shawanese Country, with Ten Belts of Wampum and Three Scalps, two Indian and English Scalps, they with a cry to the five Nations for help—The 2 Indian Scalps Signify that the English were too ^many^ for the[m] and killd off em, the one Scalp that Indians have killd but few English,—the Six Nations have been Called to assemble at Onondaga, there the grand Council was to Sit, but most of the Six Nations are at This Time Dispers'd every where for Provisions, and nothing is Done yet; ~~they will this week~~ ^are about to^ [send] the Runners the Second Time. [page torn] Supposed the Six Nations Join the Shawanese— [page torn] determine to abide by their [agreement?] and Covenant with [the] English, enter at the End [of] the last wars with ^the^ French [page torn].—[75]

[Courtesy of Dartmouth College Library]

JOURNAL 8

December 22, 1774–February 9, 1775

Occom tours Connecticut and southeastern New York, visiting Congregationalists, Separates, Baptists, Presbyterians, and Anglicans. He receives many invitations to preach, and large crowds attend several of his sermons. The popularity of his now frequently reprinted Sermon, Preached at the Execution of Moses Paul *undoubtedly prepares the way for his success.*

Thirdsday, Decr 22: it Snowd Still yet a great Number of People came together at the appointed Time, after meeting went home with one Mr West, Seven Day Baptist Preacher a godly man I believe, a very meek and humble man and well reported by his Neighbours, his wife is a Moravian Woman by Profession a Pious woman, [page torn] them this Night.

Fryday, Decem 23: Was with Mr West all Day, Lodgd with them again.—

Saturday, Decem^r 24: as this is their Sabbath, so the People got together for meeting at their usual Hour and I preach'd to them, as soon as I had done Mr Green Preachd, a Short Discourse, and after meeting, I went back to Mr Wiard's and Lodgd there.

~~Monday~~ *Sabbath Decem 25:* People got together about 11: a great Number and I preached to them twice, in the evening went to Mr Mechams my good old Friend, he Came from Westerly and Lodgd there. I was very Poorly this Night. I was Troubled with a Disorder in my Bowels very much—

75. Armed conflicts between encroaching white settlers and the Shawnee of the Ohio River Valley escalated during spring 1774, as settlers (with the support of colonial governments) breached the terms of the Proclamation of 1763 by moving into Native territory beyond the Allegheny Mountains. In "Lord Dunmore's War" of summer 1774, Virginia governor John Murray Dunmore sent troops to put down Native resistance and support colonial expansion. See Kerby, Brand.

Monday Decem 26: was very Comfortable this morning; my Disorder was gone. About 10 went to Herington[76] Meeting House, Called on one [ ] from there went to Mʳ Wooddruff, and there put up my Horse, and went to meeting. Preachd to a large assembly, and the People attended with great Solemnity.—In the evening Went to See Mʳ Bartholomew, the old minister of the Place, he has laid down Preaching by reason of Infirmities, he Seemed to be a good sort of a man—Lodgd with Mʳ Wooddruff.

Tuesday, Decʳ 27: after Breakfast went on my Journey; Stopt at Litchfield a few minutes Just to [eat] at a Tarvern, and then Set off again, and directed my Course towards New Milford, reachd the Place Just before night. Calld on one Mʳ Baldwin and Tarried there all night, and appointed a meeting 10 O'C for the next Day, this Night we had a Terrible Storm of Snow.—

Wednesday, Decemʳ 28: Storm Continued very Hard, yet we went to meeting and there was a Considerable Number of People, Went to [Mʳ Taylor's], the minister of the Place, and was very kindly and tenderly entertaind—

Thirdsday, Decʳ. 29: went with Mʳ Tallor to attend upon a Lecture which he had appointed some Days before about 7 miles South from the Town. I preachd, and there was a Number of People got together, Considering the Deep Snow, after Service, the people were very urgent to have another meeting in the evening, and I Consented, and So preachd again; and we had a very Solemn meeting, the people in general were greatly affected—after meeting Went home With one Mʳ Hitchcock and Lodgd there. I believe the man and his Wife were true Christians. Sat up till late and then went to Bed quietly. Mʳ Tallor went home this evening and I desird ^him^ to Send word to New Presten, that I woud be there on the next Day and give them a Short Discourse towards evening

Fryday Dec.ʳ 30: after Breakfast returnd to Milford, got about 12 and found Mʳ Taylor had not sent word to Presten, and I Past by as soon as coud; one Deacon Hogekins accompanyd me; and we got there a little before Sun-Set, and they gave notice to the People, and began our Meeting in the evening, and there was a great Number of People, and they attended Well. As soon as the meeting was done, we went back again to New Milford this Night Lodged with one Mʳ Campbell, a Seperate Minister and a very ^godly^ man I believe.—

Saturday, Decʳ 31: had a meeting at one Deacon Baldwin's, among the Seperates, had a Comfortable meeting; after meeting went into Town, Lodged at Mʳ Taylor's.

Sabb ~~Decemʳ~~ ^Janr^; Preach at the Place all Day to an amazing Number of People. Lodged at Mʳ Hynd's whose wife is a very good woman; was very kindly entertaind, this evening two young women came to me under great Concern of Soul and I gave them a word of advice and Counsel.

Monday Janʳ 2: left New Milford early in the morning and went on to New Fairfield; got there about 10 OC Call in at Mʳ Sill's, the Minister of the Place, a few minutes, and then went to meeting; Preachd to a large Number of People; after meeting went to Mʳ Sills and Dind and Soon after Dinner, left the Place and went on towards Kent. Mʳ Sill went with me, went thro [Presenttomook]; Stopt a few Minutes at the Indian Place but there was no Indians at home Scarsely, and so we past on, got to Mʳ

76. *Herington:* Harwinton, Connecticut.

Bodwell's about 7 in the evng and they sent word all around that Night to have a meeting next Day about 10 in the morning.

Tuesday Jan^r 3: went to meetg about 10 and had a great Number of People to Preach to, and the People attended with great Solemnity and affection. After Meeting went to Mr Bodwell's and Dind there, and Soon after Dinner went on my towards 9 Partners, and got to Esqr Hopkinss about 7 in the evening and Lodgd there.—

Wednesday, Jan^r 4: Preachd at the red Meeting House,—

Thirdsday, Jan· 5: Preachd at a private House, in the Place—

Fryday, Jan^r 6: Went to Mr Knibloes in Esq Hopkins's Slay; got there before noon; about 1 Went to meeting and it was extreamely Cold; I Delivered a Short Discourse; after meeting Went to Mr Plat's and Dind there, and then went on our way Home to Esqr. Hopkins; got there just after Sun Set—

Saturday, Jan^r 7: was at Esqr Hopkins all Day—

Sabb. Jan^r 8: Preachd here all Day; just at night left the Place and Went over the Mountain to Mr Woods' Meeting House, and Preachd there, and it was extreamly Cold, went home with Mr Fowler in his Sleig[h] and Lodgd there.—

Monday, Jan^r 9: left Mr Fowler's early in the morning and went on towards Pleasant Valley; got to Mr Case's before Night. Mr Case was not at Home; in the evening he came Home, and we had a Joyful meeting: he and his Family were very Well and his People. Lodgd there—

Tuesday, Jan^r 10: Towards evening went to the Hollow and Mr Case went with me, I Preachd at the House of one M^r [Struit?], a young Dutchman, who is under great Conviction of Soul, we had a great Number of People and a very Solemn Meeting we had—

Wednesday, Jan. 11: we went 8 or 9 miles Northwest ward and to one Mr Sam Smiths and preachd there in the evening to a Crowd of People, and they attended exceeding well—Lodgd in the Same House. One Mr Ward brough hether in his Sleig from Mr Case's.

Thirdsday, Jan^r 12: went off very early in the morning towards Statesbourough, got there about 10 in the Morning; put up at M^r [Struits]. Young M^r [Struit] brought ^us^ here, Mr Ham Came With us in the after noon about 1 began a meeting, there was not a great Number of People at this Time, they Came by mistake the meeting was appointed at evening,—In the evening a great Number came together, and I gave them another Discourse, the People here are Chiefly Dutch, and I found Some excellent Christians amongst Lodgd at M^r [Struits].

Fryday, Jan^r 13: Sot off very early in the morning towards Pleasent Valley for we had appointed meeting there at 1 O'C this Day, got there just bout meeting Time, and there was a great Number of People. I preachd, after meeting I went with one Mr Newcomb, a Baptist Brother, a man of great Riches, was very kindly entertaind; Lodgd here, with much Satisfaction.—

Saturday Jan^r 14: this morning I made use of my Printed Notes or Christian Cards,[77] [word illegible] about 11 I Walked Down to Mr Case's; Mr Newcom went with me. Spent the rest of the Day with Mr Case; he is quite a Clever Sort of a man—

---

77. Occom used "Christian Cards" printed with Bible verses to educate and entertain during his preaching travels. Subsequent entries in his diary suggest that Occom invited individuals to

Sab: Jan' 15: Preachd at the place again to a vast Crowd of People, and we had a Very Solemn meeting, many were brought to Floods of Tears. [2 words crossed out] It was a Sacrament with the People, and I Join the People, it was a Comfortable Season—As soon as the Service was over we went to a Place Called Oswago, about 6 miles off; got there in the Dusk of the evening, found a prodigious Number of People, Preachd to them, Mr Case made the last Prayer. I Lodgd with one Mr Plat.

Monday, Jan' 16: Went to another part of Oswago about 7 miles off, to a Baptist meeting House, meeting began abot 1 in the afternoon, and there was a great multitude of People of all Sorts and Denominations, the greater part of the People Coud not get in to the House, and we had a Solemn meeting—as soon as the meeting was done, we went towards Poughkeepsy, and had a meeting in the evening at one Capt Hagmans and had a prodigious great Number of People and the People attended with much affection—

~~Monday~~ Tuesday, Jan' 17: early in the morning went on to Poughkeepsy and Stopt a Little While at a publick House, and So past by and went on towards the Ferry about four miles Down the River. Mr Case and Mr Ward went with me about a mile out the Town and there we took leave of ~~me~~ each other in Friendship;—and I went to the Ferry, there met with ~~maj~~ major Durgee of Norwich in his return Home from Susquehannah, got over before Sun Set & went down to Mr Debois's and Lodgd there. Found them all well except his wife, they were very glad to See me, and receivd with all kindness—

Wednesday, Jan' 18: after Breakfast went Down to New Windsor, Calld on Mr Saml Concling and also one Mr Clark, my old Friends, and acquaintances; they were extreamly glad to See me I stopt no more till I got Butter Hill,[78] where one Mr Joseph Wood Lives; he is an old Disciple indeed, We had a joyful meeting, We had not Seen each other in Ten Years. I felt as if I was in my Father's House. Sat up till good bed Time, and then took our Repose for the Night.

Thirdsday, Jan' 19: Was at Mr Woods till towards Night, then went to meeting at Mr Clark's; there were so many People they could not all get in, and we had a Comfortable meeting: after meeting returnd Home with Mr Wood again and Sat up Some Time after we got Home

Fryday, Jan' 20: Was at Mr Woods again till towards Night again and went to New Windsor for Meeting, had a meeting in one of Elder's Houses Returnd home again with Mr Wood.

Saturday, Jan. 21: left Mr Wood's early in the morning and on towards Malborough, Stopt at New Windsor, Breakfasted with Mr Close, after Breakfast went on my way got to Malborough before Night Stopt at Mr Clark's. Mr Case, the general Post master, Brought me here in his Sleig from Newborough: he is one of my good old Friends here. I ~~lodgd~~ [3 words crossed out] ^went^ home, and Lodgd with him—

Sab. Jan' 22: about 10 went to the meeting House and a Multitude of People

---

draw cards from his deck fortune-teller style and interpret the scriptures' significance to their present or future spiritual state.

78. *Butter Hill:* Now Storm King, New York.

came to meeting, and we had a Solemn meeting: in the evening went to Mr Debois's House and had a meeting there and a great Number of People were together again. I Baptized two Children. We had the power of God with us; many were brought to floods of Tears—I Lodgd here.

Monday, Jan^r 23: in the morning went back agin to Newborough and preachd there in the Church of England to a great Number of People; as Soon as the meeting was over I went up to Malborough & Preachd in the School House to a Crouded People and they attended with affection,—after meetg went back to Mr Clark's and Lodgd there.—

Tuesday, Jan^r 24: Went away early in the morning: Mr Clark went with me and Mr Dayton also went towards [Wall Hill], got to Mr Tolton's about 11, Where we were to have a meeting. About 12 we began meeting & there was a Multitude of People. I had Some freedom in Speaking this Night. Stayd with Mr Tolten.

Wednesday, Jan^r 25: Held a meeting not far from Mr Tolten's in a Dutchman's H, a great number of People came together again.—In the evening had another meeting not far the Place, where had a meeting in the Day, and I believe the Lord was with us of a Truth, there was great Trembling in the Congregation. This night Lodgd with one Mr Norton; had a long Conversation with them, they were Baptists—

Thirdsday, Jan^r 26: in the morning went away to another place a bout 6 miles off, where we had appointed a meeting at a Dutchman's House; we got there about 11 about 12 went to meeting in a Barn, the People Crouded like Bees and we had a Solemn meeting; after meeting I went with a gentleman 2 or 3 miles Norward; in the evening a Numr of Neighbours Came in to meeting, tho we did not mention any meeting, and I gave a Word of Exhortation. Lodg'd here—

Fryday, Jan. 27: Set off in the morning and rode to Blooming grove, about 20 miles off; got there about 3 in the after Noon; was kindly entertained by one Mr Brewster; Lodged there.

Saturday, Jan^r 28: was at Mr Brewster's all Day; in the evening one Hoseah came to See me; he is a multoe man Reckend a Christian man, we had Some Conversation together in Religious matters—

Sab: Jan^r 29: Preachd at the Place to a vast Crowd of People and I had but little Sense of Divine things, howeve however, the People attended with great attention—towards Night went [Oxford?] about 4 miles off there we had an evening meeting to a Crouded Audience, and I had Some Sense of Divine things, & the People were much affected. I believe the Lord was with us of a Truth.—Lodgd at Deacon Little's.

Monday, Jan^r 30: in the morning quite early I set off for Smith's Clove. Deacon Little accompanied me, got the there about 10, about 12 We began Divine Service and there was a great multitude of People, and I had much freedom in Mind and Speech, and many People were melted into floods of Tears. As soon as the Meeting was done I went Down to Murtherer's Creek, got there befor night, went to Mr Woods, found them all well, in the evening went meeting towards the Creek, and had Some What Solemn meeting, after meeting went to the Creek and Lodgd there.

Tuesday, Febru Jan^r 31: went off early in the morning in order to get over the River; Stopt a little while with Mr Close at New Windsor, there was no passing there, and so I went to Newborough, Breakfasted at M^r [ ], and then went to the ferry, about

11 went over to Fishkill Side, and went on to the Center of the Place, got to the Presbyterian Meeting House about 3 in the after Noon, the People Stopt me to have a meetg on the next Day, and I went to one [ ] and Lodgd there, and was Very kindly treated and entertaind.

Wednesday: Feb^r 1: 1775:—About 11 O'C went to meeting and there was a great multitude of People, and we had a Solemn meeting. As soon as the meeting was over, I went on towards the mountains, Lodgd with one [word crossed out] Judge [ ] and was very kindly entertaind, and he sayd, if ever I Shoud come there again, I Shoud make his House my Home.

Thirdsday, Feb^r 2: Went off very early in the morning to a Place Calld the Mills; there I had a meeting, began about 12: Preachd in a Barn to a vast great Concorse of People, and the Power of God was manifest amongst us. There was great trembling among the People. After meeting Went with one Mr Lawrence a Baptist minister, he lives in the mountains, and I Lodgd at his House—

Fryday, Feb^r 3: about 12 went to meeting, Preachd to Amazing Number of People in the Woods, and we ^had^ very good meeting, the Spirit of God moved upon the People, after meeting went Home with Mr Lawrence, in the Evening Mr Lawrence and I went to Capt. Champlin and we had *long* and Friendly Conversation together in Religious Matters, Lodgd here this Night, and was extreamly well used and entertaind.

Saturday Morning. Feb^r 4: left the Place and went over to Dover, Mr Miller went with me. we got to Mr Waldo's about 10: he is a Baptist Minister of the Place, and he receivd me with Brotherly kindness, and Love. Lodgd here.

Sabb Feb^r 5: about 10 went to meeting, and there was great Number of People Got together, and I Preachd with much freedom the People were affected many of 'em, after meeting, went Down to New Fairfield, got to Mr Sills before Night, the meeting was appointed at his House, and the People came in So thick there was not half Room ^enough^ for them, and just as we were about to begin Divine Service a Messenger Came from the meeting House, which ^is^ a mile off, and Said there was great Number of People got together there, and we were obligd to remove to the ^meetg^ House and when we got there we found a great Number of People—the meetg House was Crouded, and the Lord gave me freedome in Speaking, after meeting went back with Mr Sill and Lodged there—

Monday: Feb^r 6: in the morning went down to a Town House of Fairfield and there Preachd began about 12 and there was a great Number of People got together and we had a Comfortable meeting; as soon as the meetg was over I went towards New Milford; got there towards Night, Stopt at Mr Hindss: and there were very urgent to have me Stay and have a meeting. They Pl[ea]d So hard it was very hard for [me] to pass by the them, there was one young Convert in particular Intreated with Tears in her Eyes to have me Stay, they pulld very hard upon my very Heart Strings and it Hard Work to get away from them, however I did get a way, and went on towards New Preston, got there Some Time in the eveng put up at Mr Cogwells, a Tarvern, and he gave me my Entertainment—

Tuesday: Feb^r 7: Sot very early in the morning, and reachd to Farmington Some Time in the Evening, put up at Elijah Wympy's found them all well—

Wednesday, Feb^r 8: went off very early in the morning and got So far as M^r

Cornwells, East Side of Connecticut River about 10 miles, I intended to have gone further, but the Land Lord Cornwell u^r^gd to have me Stay, and I Consented at last, and presently it was Noised about, I was there, and they had a Notion of haveing a meeting and at last Consented, this was about half an hour after Sun Set; and in a [hour more?] the House was Crouded with People and I preachd and I had Some Freedom—and after meeting went to Rest quietly,—

Thirdsday, Feb. 9: Set out very early in the morning, and on my way, made but little Stops by the way, arriv'd to my House just before Night, and found all my Family in good State of Health.—Blessed be the Lord God of Heaven & Earth for his goodness to me and to my Family, that he has carried me out and brought [me back in safety.]

[Courtesy of Dartmouth College Library]

∞ JOURNAL 9

September 13, 1777–September 26, 1777

> *Occom tours southeastern Connecticut, Rhode Island, and Massachusetts, preaching mostly among Separates and Baptists and visiting "Indian places." High demand for his preaching reflects Occom's renown after the publication of his* Sermon, Preached at the Execution of Moses Paul.

Saturday, Sepr 13 1777: Left home and reachd Voluntown Lodgd with Mr John Gordon. Preachd at the place all Day

15: Monday went a little way east and preachd, after meeting went on Eastward, arrivd to Scituate, put up at one Mr Samuel Angells, a Preacher presentaly after I got there a number of People Came together and I gave them a word of Exhor^n

16: Tuesday had another meeting

17: Wednesday went to Gloucester ^8 miles^ and preachd in Elder Winser's meeting House, after meeting went House with Deacon Brown and Lodged there—

18: Thirdsday went back to scituate and there met Mr Killey, S+R Ashpo at one Mr Modburys and had meeting there, S. Ashpo Spoke,—had another meeting in the Same House in the evening, I went home with Mr Ab^m Angell and there Lodged—

19: Fryday went to Johnson M^r S Angel went with me, preachd in the meeting House, in the Eveng preachd again, in a privat H Lodgd at Esqr Belknaps, my old Friend—

20: Saturday morning went on my way towards the East Esqr Belknap went with me, we stopt at one Esqr Martans and we took our Breakfast, after Break went on and Calld on Widow Pain from Long Island, the Esqr left me at Providence, I kep on Eastward, got to Mr John Allens about 2 in the afternoon in Rehoboth, Dind there. Soon after dinner went to Mr Pecks [a separate] Minister of the Place, and there Lodged.

21: Sabbath Preachd in Mr Pecks meeting H all Day,—went home with Deacon Blanding, had meeting there, and Lodgd.

22: Monday went towards Bridgewater Deacon B: went with me about 3 miles and Saw Kelley [and] As^h^pos again after Dinner, went on my way towards Bridge-water: got to Tanton and there Stopt at Mr Hoskins a Seperate Preacher, and Lodgd there.—

23: Tuesday went to meeting at the place heard one Mr Willis, a Baptist preacher after he had Spoke, I gave a word of Exhortation, and then went home with Mr Hoskins and Tarried there all Day, and in the Evening had a meeting at the Same House; Lodged there again

24: Wednesday went off early in the morning and Stopt Mr Dean's and a meeting there, in the afternoon went into Town & had another meeting there in the House; abot Sun Set took Tea with M^{rs} Mc[Water], Lodged [ ] where Mr Jones Boarded, a young Preacher—

25: Thirdsday got up very early and went on towards Freetown, Stopt at Mr Toby's in Berkley & took Breakfast there, Soon after went on, arrivd to Freetown about 11: Calld on Mr Walcut a young Preacher, was there a little while and went on again. Mr Walcut went with me to the Indian Place, got there Some Time before Sun Set I Lodgd at Daniel Wards, the principle Indian in the Place

26: Fryday about 10 in the Morn had a meeting and there was a

[Courtesy of Dartmouth College Library]

✑ JOURNAL 10

May 8, 1784–April 26, 1785

> *Emigration to Brotherton, New York, commences after the end of the American War of Independence. On May 8, 1784, Occom and an early party of emigrants including his brother-in-law Jacob Fowler, his daughter Christiana Occom Paul, and their families embarks for Brotherton by boat up the Hudson River. Leaving the emigrants at Saratoga, Occom returns to Mohegan in early June. (For another account of this trip, see Occom's letter to Solomon Welles, September 26, 1784.) Occom resumes his diary in January 1785, recording that he "made a Public Confession of my miss Conduct" to his Mohegan faith community. A revival season follows during the unseasonably cold spring of 1785, as Occom preaches to receptive and tearful gatherings in the Mohegan–Norwich–New London area. He also attends tribal business matters in April 1785.*

Saturday, May 8, 1784; We Saild very early in the Morning from New London for Albany in Capt. Hayleys Sloop Called Victory, there was a number of English and Indian Families, and we had very Small wind, till towards night, the the Wind sprung up about South West, and we directed our Co^u^rse to Long-Island, & Dropt Anchor near the Shore Some Time in the evening—

Sabbath May 9: Was very Calm, and the People desired me to give a Discourse; and I Complied, I expounded Some part of 25 Chap^r of Matth: and the People attended with good attention.—In the after Noon the Wind Sprung ^up^ about South and we pushd on on way and Some Time in the evening we Anchored again—

Monday May 10: it was very Calm again but the wind rose early, and we went on, and about 6:O:C in the after noon we got to N-York—

Tuesday May 11: about 9:O:C we hoised Sail again and went into North River, & about 12: Jacob and I went a Shore to wait upon Some gen^n and we calld upon Doc^r Livingston and Doc^r Rodgers, the principle Ministers in the City—and they gave us encouragement that they woud try to get Some thing for the Indian Families that were going up to Onoyda Country to Settle, We Lodged in the City this Night.—

Wednesday May 12: We went aboard of a Certain Sloop belonging to Albany, one Mr Waters Master of her, and there ^was^ a number of Very agreable gentlemen, there were four Colonels, and Esq^{rs} and two young agreable gentlemen, these Colonels and Esqs were members of New York Asembly and they were greatly Pleasd with our Indians moving up to onoyda Country to Settle; and all these gentlemen were very Friend to us. I eat and Drank with them every Day While we were together—We got up a little way up in the North River and Dropt Anchor—

Thursday, May 13 Went on again a little way the wind was Very Small and Contrary.

Fryday May 14: moved very Slowly again Wind Small and Contrary,—

Saturday May 15 Sailed Very Slowly yet,

[Sabbath] ^*May 16*^ about 2 in the afternoon went a Shore a number of us and had a meeting in a Dutchmans H, and I gave them a Short Discou^r^se and they made me a Collection gatherd about 3 Dollars, after meeting we went a board again in the evening Saild in a little way the Wind was Contrary and hard

Monday May 17: had good wind and Went up the River fast & got to Albany before night,—Capt Hayley and Capt Billings Just got up there, and we found them all well—And we made applications to the Chief men of the City for assistance, and there was no Provisions to be had for Indians, which Use to be allowd, in Times past;—however, our Folks were allowd to put up in the Hospital,[79] and the People of the City were very kind to us and were very much taken with our Indians,—

Wednesday May 19: I was invited to preach to the Prisoners, and I Complied,—

Thirdsday I preachd in Mr Westerlo's Church and the People made a Collection for our People,—We got about 9 pounds.—

Saturday May 22 our Folks left Albany and they went on towards Schenactedy, and I Taried Still at Albany,—

Sabbath May 23: I preachd twice in the Prisbiteryan Meeting House, and they a Collection for our Folks, they Collected 8: pounds,—

Monday May 24: John Paul went after our Folks, and Caried the Collection to our People,—

Tuesday May 25. in the Morning Anthony Paul and his Family and his Mother and I Went up together in a Waggon to the New City,[80] in the afternoon I preach in the Place to a large Congregation, and they made a Small Collection, in the evening I returnd Back 3 mile towards Albany on the other Side of the River, Where I left my Daughter Christiana and her Family and her Mother in Law. From this Place An-

79. *Hospital:* Hostel, or lodge.
80. *New City:* Troy, New York.

thony went up to Seratoga for a Horse to help up his Family there, where my Daughter and Children intend to Stay this Summer and in the Fall they will proceed to Onoyda.—

Wednesday May 26 Early in the Morning, I went into a Waggon to Albany; got there about 9:O:C: and found the Vesel, that I Was to go in to New York was just gone, & Luckily I found another that is to Sail the next Day,—

Thirdsday May 27: about 12 I went off a ^in a^ Sloop, Capt Bogat and a number of gentlemen also went in the Same Vesel, and they were very agreable & great Doc^r Young was one of the Company, and he went down the River about 20: Miles & Dropt Anchor,—Fryday we had very Small wind, and Slow way down, yet we down Some distance that Day and the Night following,

Saturday May 29: We had a find Wind as as much as we wanted and we got down to new York about 6:O: C: in the after noon and I immediately went a Shore and went home with Mr John Haggerman, a good Friend, we found, when we Stopt there the other Day going up. I Set down but few minutes, and then went to see Doc^r Livingston and Doc^r Rodgers, Doc^r Livingston was at home but Collected no thing for us; and Doc^r Rodgers was not at Home, and his People had Collected nothing, and I was good Deal disappointed, for I had given my Note of Hand for 36 Dollars for the Pasage of our People from New London to Albany,—

Sabbath May 29 Was at N: York and Went to hear Mr Gano in the morning and at noon he invited me to go home with [h]im to take dinner—and Desired me to preach to his People on Monday eveng, in the afternoon I went to hear Mr Mason the Seceder,[81] of the Church of Scotland but he did not Preach So I went to my Lodgings. I was fatigued walking, and went to no meeting in the afternoon,—

Monday M:30 was in the City, in the evening about Seven, I preached at Mr Gano's Meeting House: he is a Baptist Minister; the meeting House was very full and they made a Collection, of five pounds one Shilling just in York currency,—So I continued in the City till Fryday, ~~Ma~~ June 4: in the evening at eight o:c. I preach in a Methodist meeting and it midling ful and they Collected 3 Dollars and Seven Shillings in York currency,—

June 5 Saturday, in the after noon went a Board of a little Mast Boat, Capt Harris of New London Harber's Mouth.

Monday June 7: just after Sun rise we got to Capt Harris's House, and ~~went~~ took Breakfast with him, after Breakt I Bought a mare of him, and So I went on directly homeward,—I got Home about 11 & found all my Family in good State of Health, But Taby;[82] She had been very Sick with Swelling in her Throat, but thro' Mercy She was now much better. Blessed be God for his goodness to us Since I have been gone from home.—

Mohegan, Jan^r 23: 1785 Made a Public Confession of my miss Conduct, and was receivd universally by the People, and immediately preachd to the People and there was great and affectionate attention among the People and in the Evening we had a meeting in my House, and we felt Some love.

81. *Mr Mason the Seceder:* John Mitchell Mason.
82. *Taby:* Tabitha Occom.

Jan^r 28. Preached in our School House and there were many People both Indians and English and there was good attention.—

Jan^r 30 Preachd at Mohegan in Deac^n Henrys[83] House to a Crouded Assembly, and I had Som freedom to Speak and many of the People heard with ^a^ flow of Tears from their Eyes,—in the Evening we met at Henry's and we gave encouragements to one another and I believe the Lord was present with us—

Feb^r 6: 1785. Sabbath preachd at Mr John Heart Adgates and there was abundence of People, both English and Indians, and I believe I had Some help from above to Speak to the People and there was great Solemnity, and Some affection among the People, in the Evening we had a meeting in Deacon Henrys and our Hearts were melted down before the Lord in Some measure, Glory be to God.—

Feb^r 10: 1785. At Mr Josiah Maples ^in eveng^ and there was a great many People and attention becoming Rational Creatures, till I had done Speaking, and then was Some Levity among the Young People but Mr John Maples was so good as to give them a reprof and they Soon desisted;—and I lodgd at the House that night by the Desire of Mr Maples and his Wife, and we had a very agreable Evening; they were very free of their own accord to relate to me, their Spiritual exercises, and I believe the Ld will manifest himself to them more and more,—

Feb^r 11 in the evng gave a word of exhortation to a few People,—

Feb^r 13: on Sab—was at Mr John Brown's and there was a great number of People tho' it was uncomfortable walking, and I think I had Some Sense of Divine things, there was great Solemnity among the People,—

Feb^r 20 on Sab Preach at Mohegan in Deac^n House, to a large number of People, the House was Crouded Chiefly White People and I believe there was a moving of the Spirit of God in the Assembly for I took notice of many Tears,—

Feb^r 24: had an Evening meeting at Mrs Fitches and it was amazing to See how many People Collected together, and we had a Solemn Meeting; I believe the Lord assisted both the Speaker and the Hearer and we parted in Peace and Love for I think I felt Calmness and Love—

Feb^r 27: Sab. Preachd at Mr Darts to a Crouded Audiance and well behav'd People, and Some were effected with the Word,—

March 4: 1785. Preachd at Doc^r Alpheus Rogers in the Parish, to a great many People, and many were much affected, with the Word,—

Feb^r 6, on Sab Was at Mohegan in Deacon Henry's, and there was many People and I believe the Lord was present with us by his Divine Spirit—D. Henry [two words illegible] and went

March 12: Evening had an unexpected meeting at one Sherrys House a Negro man, there was not more than an Hours Notice give^n of the meeting, and the People Crouded in Directly and I preachd to the Word of god to them and they attended with great Eagerness and affection they Seemed to have a Taste for the Word of god— and when the People were dispersing one Capt Troope invited me to go Home with him, but I did not love to go out after Exercise—Lodged at Sherrys

March 13: on Sab—Robert Ashpo and I went to Mr Downer's about a mile and

83. *Deac^n Henrys:* Henry Quaquaquid.

half, before Breakfast and were received with all kindness and Brotherly affection and took Breakfast with them—and it was a Snowy uncomfortable Day Yet the People began to flock together presently and there was great Multitude of People got together more than the House coud Contain, they Crouded in every Corner even up in the Chambers—and I preachd to them the Word of the Lord, and it fell heavy upon the People it produced many Tears and deep Sighs tho' there was one man manifested a Displeasure at my Saying Some thing about Universal Scheem[84] he Spoke out in the meeting, but he did not Say much neither did he Disturb the People any—in the after Noon we removed the meeting to another House a few Rods off, Which was very large, and the People increasd and they Crouded that House also, and they attended with uncommon Solemnity and affection Tears flowed Down from many Eyes freely; I Cant help thinking, that god is about to work amongst this People, in the Evening. We had a meeting again in Brother Downers and there ^was^ a great number of People again and I preach again, and we had a Comfortable meeting the Lord refreshed the Children, and they manifested Love to one another; I Lodgd here this Night, went to bed late in the Evening. the Lord be praised for his goodness to us thus far—

March 14: Monday I preachd at one Mr Vesters began about 11 o c & there was good many People tho' it was a Snowy Day and extreamly bad riding or walking, and there ^was^ great attention, and I believe Some felt the Power of god, the man of the House gave ^me^ a Text and I Spoke from it, Which I never Spoke from before, it is Writen in the first Epistle of John 5:5: after meeting we Stayd Some Time, took Dinner with them, and we Sot off for Home, ^about 3: o:c^ We got home just in the Dusk of the Evening, found my Fam^l in Health. Thanks be to god for his goodness to me—

March 20 on Sabb—Preach'd at Mrs Fitch's in the North Parish of New London and there was a large Congregation of People, and they attended with great Solemnity and Affection the Lord was present with his Word, I believe in Some measure— Took Dinner with them after meeting, and ^then^ I went Home—The Week past has been very remarkable for Cold and Snow deep and Crusty & it has layn Steady almost all Winter except 3 Days in Jan^r it went off then and Come on again, directly, and it ^has^ not been off Since and it has been very Steady Cold all Winter, Very Spending for Creatures of all kinds, but the Lord takes care of the World, and he does all things well, if we dont See it, it must be all right—

March 23. It was very Cold, Windy and blustring last Night, and it Continues all this Day, it is remarkable Windy Cold Day and a Crusty hard Snow is now above a foot Deep in many Places—

March 26: 1785 on Saturday Went from Home about noon towards one Mr Avery's about 5 miles northwest from the City of New London Snow continues to ly upon the ground and it is hard Crusty, and it has been Cold all this Week, Stopt at M^r

---

84. *Universal Scheem:* Universalism is the belief that all people are saved in Jesus Christ. American universalism originated as a theological controversy within New England Congregationalism, and the first American Universalist Church was founded by the English-born John Murray (1741–1815; second husband of Judith Sargent Murray) at Gloucester, Massachusetts, in 1779.

Darts, and the old Folks were not at Home, and So I went to Mr Amess and was very kindly entertaind, took Supper with them, after Sun Set went back to Mr Darts and Lodged there, and was most kindly and Friendly treated, Sabbath ^M 27^ Mr Dart and his Wife and Daugh^r Sot out with me to meeting, about three miles, got there before 11 and the People began to come to meeting, and there was a vast Concourse of People, there were near as many out Doors as in and Preachd to them the Word of the Lord, and the People behavd Decently, and heard with great Solemnity a many with affection in the afternoon Preachd again and Sufferd greatly with Cold was much Chil'd before I had done the People attended with great Solemnity—after meeting took Dinner with Mr Duglas he lived one end of the House,—just before Sun Set, took leave of the People of the House and went to Mr Robert Duglas's about half a mile eastward, found him very ill with a bad Cough and Shortness of Breath, he Set up in a great Chair most all the Time, Night and Day, he is very old near ninety, and I believe an old Disciple his Wife is not so old, very agreable old People the, were very kind to me, Lodged there, March 28: got up in the morning Prayd with the Family, had free & ^agreable^ Conversation with them last Night and this morning about the great Concerns, after Breakfast, took my leave of them in Peace and Friendship and Sot off for New London, got to the City about 10: Call upon Mrs Shaw, found her little Complaining of her Health, being troubled with Cold,—Sot awhile, then went to the Ferry, Calld at Mr Baileys a Tavern, and Sot down to Write, and While I was Writing, Mr Rathbond came in I suppose to See me he was put in Jail Some Time back, it is Said for Deffamition in his Preaching, he is one of those that ^are^ stiled Shaking Quakers;[85] and We had a long discourse together—He is a young man of good Sense, but in my Opinion he is altogether Caried away with very Strong Enthusiasm and I am afraid a bad one there is good Enthusiasm and there ^is^ a bad one, he Says they go by immediate opperation of the Spirit of God, their Bodies are greatly agitated very often when they are in Divine Exercise in various ways, their arms are Stretched Strait Some Times which they Call a Sign, they must go that way that their hands point to,—and they Say they have new Tongue given many Times, tho I perceive they dont retain them, and he Says they have gifts of Healing but I cant find out, that they have done any remarkable mericle, and they dont allow their Brethren and Sisters that were married before they came into this Way, to use the means for Propagation of their Species, and the unmaried not to mary yet he Says he forbid none to marry[86]—he calls this way that he is in a New Dispensation, which will defuse thro the World;—and he has a Notion too, they atain to Sinless Perfection in this Life—in the whole I believe he has got into another gospel if it is right to Call it gospel I can not See it to be the gospel of Jesus Christ,

---

85. The Shakers, or Shaking Quakers, so called for the bodily tremors that believers experienced as a manifestation of the Spirit, emerged in Manchester, England, in the 1740s as a splinter group of the Society of Friends. "Mother" Ann Lee led a small group of Shaker emigrants to upstate New York in 1774, and the group gained adherents across the Northeast during the "New Light Stir" of the late 1770s and 1780s. A visionary-millenarian religious group, Shakers committed to lives of celibacy, simplicity, and communitarianism. See Stein, Humez.

86. *forbid none to marry:* In 1 Timothy 4:1–3, Paul descries the prohibition of marriage as a form of apostasy.

which his Apostles preachd, and the Lord have mercy upon them and bring them to the Knowledge of the Truth as it is in Jesus—Towards Night, went out of the City, Stopt a while at Capt Wheelers, and then went to old Mister Jonathan Smith's and Lodged there, and was kindly receivd; he is troubled with many Infirmities besides old age—

Tuesday March 29: took leave of them early and Sot off for Home and it was prodigious bad riding noth Side of the Hills glased with Ice, and South Sides horse break thro' the Ice, I was obliged to go a foot Some Times, and being lame I made Slow progress, I got home near noon, found my Family well thro' the goodness of a mercyful god—The Night following provd very Stormy of Snow Hail and Rain, and it froze as it fell, and it Continued very severe next Day like a Winter Storm.—This Winter past and the Spring thus far, is Judged by the oldest men we have, to be the Hardest in their memory, the most spending, for no Creature that is kept by man Can get nothing to eat only What ^is^ given them—

April 1: 1785 on Fryday went from my House a foot down to Mr J. H. Adgates, and got his Mare Sot off from there for New London Stopt a While at Capt Wheelers

Sab. April 3: 1785 went from my House to one Mr John Brown's about 3 miles and it was very uncomfortable riding I ever known for the Time of the Year, Snow is now above foot Deep and Very hard, the roads are bare on the Suny Side of the Hills and very mirely,—got ^to^ the House, before 10: the People had not began to Collect, but presently after they did, and large Company got together presently, tho it was very bad Traviling, and between 11 and 12 I began the Divine Exercise and I not not much Light and freedom, yet the People were greatly attentive—after meeting Sot in the House with Mr Wm Comstock a Preacher and the man of the House, had friendly Conversation took a Comfortable Dinner with them, just at Night Night I Sot off for Home, and as I was going out Mr Brown gave me a pair of Shoes, and I excepted of them thankfully, in the Dusk of the Evening I got Home

April 7: 1785 Got up very early, and a little after Sun rise I Sot off from my House afoot to Mr J. H. Adgates, got his mare and took breakfast with them, and then went down to New London, got to the City about 10: O:C: and went over to Groton, and to [to] Mr Jabez Smiths about 1 in the after noon, to Dinner there, and about half after 2: went back towards the Ferry, and I turnd to the Northward from the meeting House, to one Capt Robert Latham got there Some Time before Sun Set,—and had a meeting in this House, and there was a great Number People, Considering the extreem bad traviling both on Foot and Horseback, and I preachd to them the Word of god, and I had Some Sense of Divine things, and the People attend with Solemnity and Some afection, I believe the Lord was present with us in Some measure Thanks be to his name—After meeting, took Comfortable Supper with the Capt, his Wife looks quite young, and they are very agreable Discreet Couple,—after Supper we had little exercise, with my Printed, Versified Notes or Christian Cards, and it was very a greable Exercise, I hope it may do them Some Benefit,—Went to bed I believe near 12: took Comfortable,—got up very early & they all got up took breakfast with them; and soon after eating took Friendly leave of them, & the Capt Sent as a Present of Tea to my Wife, Went to the Ferry and so over to the City of New London went to see alderman Thomas Shaw but he was not at Home, and I sot off for Home, Stopt a while at Capt Wheelers, and then went to Mr J. Smith's Calld for Dinner there, and after I had eat, I sot off again, and it began to rain and it was a Terrable Storm, Stop a good while at Mr Haughtons—Dried me, and after awhile went on again, and it raind very hard and it was windy & Cold. got Home Some Time before Night, and I was much wet, and Cold, found my Family Well thro the goodness of god—

April 10: 1785 on Sab: Preach'd at Henry's[87] in Mohegan there was Considerable number of People chiefly Young People and White People mostly, and they behaved well in the Room but Noise was out off Doors, and I felt Some Strenght in delivering The word and I ^believe^ Some had movings in their Minds—

Saturday April 16: 1785 Sot off from my House for Preston, got there at Deacon Averys about Sun Set, and found them well, and was affectionately recivd by them, lodgd there.—

Sabbath April 17: went to meeting with them Represented Some thing of my past Tryals and Troubles, and also my miss steps and askd their forgiveness, and was accepted, and I preachd all Day, and I believe had some assistance, and the People attended with great Solemnity and with many Tears,—and When I had done Mr Park the Minister of the Church administered the Sacred Ordernance of the Lord's Supper, and it was a Solemn Season, and it reviving and refreshing Time with my Lord after participation of the Holy Supper, Several Christians broke out in Praises and adorations to god with floods of Tears of Joy, and having Sung two or three Times in Divine Love and Fellowship we parted in Peace and Love.—Went to the Deacon's, took Dinner wh them, after Dinner took my leave of them, and parted in Love.—I went to one Mr Winter, an old Disciple, and was kindly entertained in the Evening, had agreable exercise with my Christian Cards, with the Whole Family,— about 9 O C went to bed with thankfull Heart in Some measure, the Lord be Praised for the Mercies, Favours and the Privilledges of the Day past,—

Monday ~~March~~ ^April^ *18:* got up very early, Prayd with the family, and then went of for Home, got Home about 10: found my Family well, and I went on directly to Mr Houghtons to meet our Honorable overseers,[88] and did our Tribe business before Night, and got back to my H little after Sun Set.—

Wednesday, April 20: 1785 It was general Fast[89] in Connecticut, I preachd at Widow Fitchs and there was a goodly number of People, tho it was very bad riding, and going Foot, by reason of the Dreadful Storm the Day before, both of Rain and Hail, Hail was two or three Inches Deep this Morning, and it was Cold, the People attended with great attention,—after meeting I Sot a while in the House took Dinner,— and then went to Mr Josiah Maples and Preachd there to Considerable Number of well behaved People—about Sun Set Went Home, Thus far hath the Lord lead me on, and thanks be to his Holy Name—

---

87. *Henry's:* Henry Quaquaquid.

88. *overseers:* Beginning in 1720, the Connecticut General Assembly appointed "overseers" to supervise the affairs of local American Indian tribes (St. Jean). Pequot intellectual William Apess later capitalized on the slaverylike connotations of the term "overseer" in his pro–tribal-sovereignty political writings of the 1830s.

89. *general Fast:* New England colonies (and later states) traditionally appointed a spring weekday for public fasting and worship. See Love, *Fast and Thanksgiving Days.*

Thirdsday April 21: about 12 Sot off for Lebanon, went via Norwich Landing, got to Capt Troop's about Sun Set and a meeting there, and there was Considerable number of People and they attended well,—Lodged at the Same House, and was kindly entertaind.

Fryday April 22: got up very early and took Breakfast and then went to see Colon^l Wm Williams, found him at Home and did Business with him in an Instant— and went back to Capt Troop's, and in the after Noon about 3 O: C: we had a nother meeting and a Number of People and they Heard with great attention and Solemnity. I Lodged there again.

Saturday April 23: got up very early but I did not Set out Till a bout 8 O: C: got down to Norwich Landing about 12 and so went on my way, went by my House down to Mr Houghtons, got there about 2: and was there a Little While & then went back to my House got Home Some Time before Night

April 24: on Sabbath morning got up very early, and went Long Society, and Preachd there at one Mr Nathan Standishs, and there was a great number of People and there was great attention, the Word fell with great Weight, and there was flow of Tears from many Faces, the Lord gave me Some Sense of Divine Things and freedom of Speech,—Soon after meeting had Dinner, and then Sot off for Home, Calld at a Certain House near Norwich Landing, and were five or Six women, and an old woman of the House desired to have a meeting there as Soon as I Coud, and I told her I woud. We had a little Exercise with my Christian Cards, and there was Solemnity and affection amongst Especially two young women—were much affected,— and about Sun down left them and went on my way, got home about Day Light in— found my Home almost emty; my Folks were all gone to fishing, and I went to bed soon, the Lord be thanked for his goodness to us thus far.

Tuesday April 26: 1785 We met our Hon^l Overseers at Mr Houghtons, Upon aplication of a Number of Merchants of the City of Norwich, to purchace a Pice of Land near our River to make a Landing Place,[90] but none Came from Norwich but Mr Howland in behalf of the rest,—but we coud not agree at this Time, and So We parted.

[Courtesy of Dartmouth College Library]

∞ JOURNAL 11

May 1, 1785–October 3, 1785

During a summer season at home, Occom preaches and visits Indian towns in Connecticut and Rhode Island. In June, Occom reports the death of his daughter Tabitha, widow of Joseph Johnson, Jr; his aunt Hannah Justice Samson dies at Niantic in September. On September 22, Occom embarks from Mohegan to visit the growing Brotherton settlement in Oneida territory, stopping along the way at New England Indian towns like Farmington and Stockbridge that have been depleted by the emigration.

90. Mohegan territory encompassed the west side of the Thames River, which linked Norwich to New London, Connecticut, and the Long Island Sound.

May 1: 1785: Sabbath Preachd at Mrs Fitchs and there was a large number of well behavd People, and the Word of god fell among the People with Some Weight and
Some were much afected especially in the fore part of the Day, after meeting, took
Dinner with the Family and after that went Home felt Some what Spent, and went
to Bed Soon—

May 10: a number of us went to Seabrook to fishing, a Storm met us the next
Day, and we Stopt at New London.

May 13: Went on our Way & got to the Fishing, near night and we Stayed there
till 24 and we had pretty good Luck

the 28: We got home and found our folks well,

Sabbath may 29: had meetg at Harrys,[91] and we had a Penitant meetig, I Sayd a
few Words from the Brasen Serpent,[92] and we felt the Power of god I think.

June 5: had a meeting at Harrys and I spoke from Rom 4:7

June 12: Sab: Henry and I went to Pawquonk and I preachd in Mr Reuben
Palmers Meeting House and there was Considerable number of People, and they
attended with great Solemnity, both parts of the Day, & Spoke from 1 Sam 22:2: and
Rom 4:7 and after meeting went to Mr Carters, and took Dinner there and after eating we Sot away for Home, and got a little after Sun Set,—

June 18: Henry and went from Mohegan for Charles Town[93] and we got a little
before Night, we put up at James Niles^s, and were kindly receivd by them—

Sab: June 19: in the morng went to See old Samuel Niles, and found him very
low, and I believe he never will get up again, went back to James, and then to the
meeting House, and was a Number of People, but not large, they had but a Short
Notice of my Comig and I preachd from Rom 4 in the after Noon we went to Sam
Niles and I preachd from Daniel 5:25 in the evening met at another House and John
Cooper was there he Spoke, and he deliverd a party Spirit,[94] afterwards I rehearsed
the History of Joseph[95] and then returnd to James Niless, and Lodged there once
more,

Monday June the 20: Sun about 2 Hours high Deacon Henry Quaquaquid and
I left Charles Town and went on Homeward, and we go Home Some Time in the
evening, found our Families Well—

Sab: 26: Went to New Concord, and Preachd in Mr Troops meeting House—from
Mat 4:10: in the after Noon from 1 Corin 16:22 and was a large number people and
they attended with great Solemnity, after meeting went to See Mr Troop and found
him in low State of Health, Supped with them and Soon after Supper took leave of
them and return'd homeward, Calld at Mr Jabaz Crokers and found in him in hard

---

91. *Harrys:* Henry Quaquaquid.
92. *Brasen Serpent:* See Numbers 21:7–9.
93. *Charles Town, Rhode Island:* Home to a large Narragansett Indian community.
94. *party spirit:* Occom probably refers here to political factionalism within the Narragansett community.
95. *History of Joseph:* In response to the factionalism articulated by John Cooper, Occom preaches
the Old Testament story of Joseph as a parable for the costs of tribal disunity, probably recounting Genesis 37, when Joseph is sold by his brothers into slavery in Egypt.

Sickness, full of Pain & distress prayd with him, and after Prayer went on, and I Stopt at Mrs Fitches and Taried there all Night, next Morning after Breakfast went on and got home about 9 found my Well three Days ago I heard a heard heavy News, my poor Tabitha is Dead & Buried, the Lord the Sovereign of the Universe Sanctify this Dispensation to me and to all my Family—

Tuesday, June 28: a Young man came to me from lower part of Groton in greatest distress of Soul I ever Saw any one this long while and he wanted I shoud go with him to groton rite away, and I told him I woud be there on the next Day—

June 29: Rode down to new London, and So over to Groton & a meeting at Mr Burringtons and there was a goodly number of People and they attended the word with great Solemn attention, and the young man that came to Mohegan for me was greatly afected, broke out in bitterness of Soul, and Cryed for Mercy, Several gave him a word of Exhortation—I Lodged in the Same House

Thirdsday June 30: about 11 Capt Lathem came to the H where I was, and I went Home with his directly, Dined With him and his Wife they have no Children; near about 3 went to Mr Giddion Saunderss and there ^was^ a Number of People got together & we began the Worship of god Directly, and I preachd to there was an Effectionate attention, and after I had done Speaking Mr Avery gave a Word of Exhortation, and then he prayd and when he had done the People Sot Still and Wou'd not go away, it Seem'd, they Wanted to hear more, they were hungry after the Word, and so we gave out more Exhortations, and after a While they went a way with heavy hearts, and Some of em Wanted I Should preach to them again on the next Day, but I told them I wanted to get home to attend upon other People, Where I had engagd,—Lodgd at Mr Saunderss, and was very kindly entertaind,—

Fryday July 1: 1785 after breakfast took my leave of the Family in Peace and good Friendship; Calld at Capt Robert Lathems but was not at Home, only his wife, Sot there a while, and then went to the Ferry and went over to the City of New London, and So on home ward, got home about 3 O: C: and found no one at Home—

July 3: 1785: on Sabb Sot out Early in the morning for Pauquonk Mr Eliphalet Lister went with me, we got to the Place Some Time before meet meeting Call on Elder Palmer and there took Breakfast, & then we went to meeting and was Considerable Number of People, Mr Lister Preachd, And in the after Noon I preach, and towards night we went about 3 miles further towards Colchester Town and there I preach again to a large number of People and both Elder Palmers were there the Father and the Son and there was Solemn attention—after meeting went back with Mr Abel Palmer and I Stopt at Mr Carter's and Lodged there, and had very agreeable Conversation with Mrs Carter and one of their Daughters, in Religious Concerns, Went to bed late,

Monday July 4: got up very early and took my Horse and went Home.—got Home about 10: and found my geting ready to go to Pauquanunk a fishing, and I ^went^ with Directly, got to the Place before night—

July 9: Saturday Went to New Concord, got to Deacon Huntingtons about Sun Set, and was kindly recevd and entertain'd Lodged there

Sab: July 10, Deacon Huntington and I Went to meeting, and there was a great Number People Collected together, and I preachd from Luke 12:21: in the after Noon from John 12:21: and the made me a Collection,—towards Evening preachd at Deacon Huntington's,—and Soon after meeting I went to bed, but did feel well, and was restless all Night.—

July 11: got up early and they would have me Stay Breakfast and I Consented & after eating Sot off for Home got Home about 10: and found all my Family Well,—

July 16 Sot off from Home for Preston, got to Deacon John Avery Just after Sun Set, and kindly receivd by them Lodged there

Sab. July 17: Went to meeting with the Deacon, and Mr Park Preachd in the Morning,—in the afternoon I preach'd from [ ] after I had Mr Park admisd the Sacrament of the Lord Supper and I partook With them, and it was a Comfortable Season to the Children of God. Some old Christians broke forth in Praises and adorations to god and they encouraged one another to on in their Christian Course. after meeting I went directly Home. Went With Mr Story of Norwich Stopt at his House, and took Supper with him, and was kindly treated, Soon after Supper I Went on my way got Home Some Time in the Evening, and went to bed quietly. Thanks be to god for his goodness to me and Family hitherto—

July 24: Sab: early in the Morning got up and got ready and went down to Gales Ferry and went over to Groton, to Mr Sanderss and got there about 9: and was tenderly receivd by the Whole Family about 10 the People begun to gather and there was a Number of People Collected together, and I preachd to from Luke 2:11: and in the afternoon from John 21:22 and I think had Some assistance especially in the afternoon—and the People attended with great Solemnity and affection I believe many felt the Power of the Word,—I Stayd at Mr Sanders^s and had Some Exercise with Several, in the evening with my Christian Cards and after that went to bed quietly—

Monday after breakfast went off after taking affectionate Leave of them and Stopt at one Mr John Shoolers to See a Sick Woman, found her very ^much^ Distrest both Body and Mind, I gave her Some Councill and prest to believe on the Lord Jesus Christ, and prayd with her and then went on my way, got near noon, and rested a few minutes and took Horse again and down to New London, to buy Corn and got home again Some Time in the Evening—

Sabbath July 31: Went to M^rs and preachd there twice from 1 Corin 7:29:30 and 1 Corin 4:7 and there was not great many People and they attended well towards night I went to Mr Chapels and preachd there to a few People and as soon as the meeting was done, I went Home, and got H- about Daylight in—

Sabbath Augt 7: Sot of from Home and went to upper part of Long Society, got to Mr Mosss near 10 and from thence we went to Mr Woodworths, and there was a great Multitude of People and preach'd to them from Daniel, 5:25 and John 8:47 Toward Night I preachd at Mr Mosss ^from 1 Cor 7:29^ and there was great attention, and many were Deeply affected, and Some broke forth in Praises, especially in the Evening,—I Lodged at Mr Mosss and Brother London a Negroe preacher was with us all this Day and this evening and he and [Several?] of the young Christians Lodged at Mr Mosss—Monday Morning we got up early in the morning, and London and I were Seting off, but Brother woud have us stay to Breakfast and we Consented, and after Breakfast we Sung and Prayed and the Power of god Came down amongst us and the Young Christians were filld with Love to god and to one another,

and one of Brother Mosss Daughters who met with Consolation last Night was greatly
filld with Divine Love and we had a Blessed meeting—and we parted in Love Peace
and Fellowship—and I got Home about 12: and found my Family well the Lord be
Praised—

Sab: Augt 14: Went from Home early in the Morning for Long Society, got there
before 10 call on Mr Jonathan Smith and took Breakfast with them and then went to
meeting and there was a great number of people and I preachd to them from Heb:
4:2: & 2: Cor 17 Some Time after meeting I went Home Stopt a while at Mr Ephraim
Storys in the Landing, and there I Saw Brother London a Negro preacher and they
was to a meeting in the evening and they woud have me Stay to meeting, but I did
not, I got Home Some Time in the evening—

Thirdsday Augt 18: Went to Mr Posts at Weems Hill ^& Sister Betty with me^[96]
and preach to a Number of People and they attended Well with great Sobriety—
after meeting Drank Tea with them and then we Sot off for Home, got Home Some
Time in the Evening, Thanks be to god—

Sab Augt 21: Went from Home very Early in the morning for Pauquonk, got there
some Time before meeting, Calld upon Mr Carter, and was kindly receivd, by the
Family, and took Breakfast, and after that went to meeting, and there was a goodly
number of People and I preachd to them from Acts 2:37 and the People attended
with gravity and Sobriety, Especially the Young People—Soon after meeting I went
Home, and got H in the Dusk of the Evening—

Sab. Augt 28: Sot off from my House before Sun rise and went on towards north
part of Preston, got to Mr Daniel Mosses before meeting, and we went on to Mr
Woodworths and found a great Number of People Collected together, I preachd to
them, from Luke 16:5 and Matt 11:28: and there was great Solemnity and affection,
Soon after meeting, I went to Brother Mosss and preachd there, before Night and
there was a Croud of People, from Luke 7:23. Mr Heart was there, I Lodgd at the
Same House, Monday Augt 29: after Breakfast Br Moss and I went to see Mr Heart
found him very kind and friendly, Went from there to Mr John Putnams and there
I preachd to a Small Number of People but there was great Solemnity among the
People, took D^r there and after Dinner went to one Mr Fitch's 3 or 4 miles and there
I preach'd to a great Number of People and the Word of god fell with Weight upon
the People, and I believe they will not forget it Soon—after meeting I Went Home
with old Mr Fitch, about a mile and an Half East of Long Society Meeting House and
there I Lodged, and was very kindly Treated—

Tuesday morning after Breakfast took leave of the Family and went on home
ward, got Home Just before Noon and found no Body at Home

Sepr 3: Saturday towards night left Home, and went to lower part of Groton, was
detain'd Some Time at Gales Ferry, but got over a bout Sun Set, and reachd to M^r

---

96. Sister Betty may be a sibling of Mary Fowler Occom. Her presence as Occom's preaching companion indicates the important ministerial role Native women played in the separatist Christian Indian communities of southern New England. In his diary, Joseph Johnson frequently
mentions Native women who host household prayer and singing meetings or who make home
pastoral visits. See L. Murray, *To Do Good.*

Saunders before Day Light in and was receivd by the whole Fa with all Kindness, Lodged there

Sepr 4: Sab about 10: a great Number of people collected together and I preachd to them from John 11:28: in the after noon from 1 C[h]roni 29:5: and there was very deep, Solemn, and Silent attention the People lookd as if they were araind before the Judgement Seat of God, I believe they felt the Power of the Truth of the Word of God,—Soon after meeting I Din'd with the People of the House—and then I went to one Mr Jabez Smiths about 3 miles Southward I got there about Sun Set, I had no thoughts of having a meeting but presently after I got there 2 or 3 Neighbours were there and they whisperd among themselves & presently they askd me whether I woud preach if Neighbours woud Come in, and I told them I woud I woud, and they ^Sent^ out to give notice, and in about half an Hour a number of People came in so as to fill a large Room or almost, and I Spoke to them from [1 John?] 4:10: and the People attended Well,—Lodged here this Night and was kindly entertaind—

Monday Sepr 5 very in the morning I got up and had my horse Catch'd, and I Sot off and directed my Course to Capt Robert Lathems got there Just as they were geting Breakfast ready, Sot down with them, after eating I went to Mr William Sheffields I had a little Temporal Business with him, but I found him not he was just gone from Home,—and so I Went back to Capt R. Lathems, took dinner with them, and after Dinner took leave of em and went to went to Mr Sheffields again and he was at Home, I did my Business with him; and directly went to the Ferry, meet my good Friend Mr Saunders, and he gave me a piece of money & I was very loth to take it but he woud make me take it and so I was obligd to it, and the good Lord reward him and his family a Thousand Fold,—went over to the City of New London met Mr Smith, and we did our Business, and so we parted in good Friendship—I went on my way, and Stopt at Capt Wheelers and Lodged there—

Tuesday M Sot off very early, and got home once more, Well, and my Famy was much Scatterd What was at H were well, the Lord be Praised for his goodness to us thus far—

Sabbath Sepr 11 Got up very early in the morning and Sot of from Home and went to Long Society, got there Some Time before the people Collect Stopt at Mr John Smith, was kindly recivd, near 11: went to the House of Worship and there a great Number of People and attended with great and Solemn attention,—Preachd from Isaa 3:4 & 1 Peter 1:24 Directly after meeting I with Mr Fitch and eat with them, and after eating, went to Mr Downs, & preachd there to Considerable number of People and they behaved Well I was much paind in Left Sholders Spoke from Lamen 3:40 Lodgd at the Same House, and was kindly entertaind,—Monday very early got up and got my mare and went on, Stopt at Mr Fitchs and took Breakfast with them, and Soon after I went on Homeward, and I got about 11: found my Family was as Common, Thus far the Lord has led me on and glory be to his Holy Name—Rested a while & a bout 3: in the afternoon, took up my Mare again, and went to Nahantick in Lyme, to see the Sick, got to Rope Ferry just after Sun Sit, and heard, my Aunt widow Hannah Justice was Dead and Buried. She died Satur Night and Buried on Sabbath got to the Indian Town in the Dusk of the Evening, ~~after Br~~ found my Cousin Isaac with wife and all his Children consisting four were all very Sick[97]—Prayed with them and then home with Cousin Joseph, and Lodged there, Tuesday, found Isaacs Family little easy, Saw Some other Sick—about 12 I preachd in Cousin Josephs House to few People—about 3: Sot off for Home, got there just after Daylight in—

Saturday Sep[r] 17: Some Time in the after noon left Home and went to Preston, got to Deacon Averys in the Dusk of the eveng and was affectionately receivd by him and Lodged there

Sab. 18: about 10 went to M and there was a Considerable number of People— M[r] Park preachd in the morning and in the after I preachd from Luke concerning the Prodacal Son[98]—Directly after Sermon M[r] Park administer'd the ordernance of the Lords Supper and I partook with them once more; and Directly after I went the Indian Town of Groton with Jo: Sunsummon, and had a meeting there, and I believe the Lord was present with us the Christians were much movd, Some Time in the evening we broke the meetg and after a While I Went to bed Quietly—the Lord be praised—

Monday Sep[r] 19 Sot of for Home Early in the Morning after I took good leave of the Family got home about noon, found my F well,—

Thirsday about 9 in the morning Sot of from Home, for Onoyda, and went up to lower part of Canterbury got to M[r] Clarks about 3 in the after noon, and the people had got together, and M[r] Clarke had begun the meetg he was at Prayer,—and I preachd and there was great Solemnity & affection, and many Tears flow down freely—Soon after meeting went with Mr Clark to his House and took Dinner with them—and the People Collected together again the in the Evening, in M[r] Clarkes House, and we had a Comfortable meeting, many were melted down with Love, and they broke out in adoration & Praise, and Some Time in the evening we parted in Love, Peace, and I believe in Divine Fellowship and then went to bed peaceably the Lord be Praised—

Fryday Sep[r] 23 had a little Exercise with my Cards with the Family, and it was Comfortable Season with us, and after Breakfast I took Brotherly leave of them, and went on my way and got to M[r] Post's ^in Crank^ about 1 and took Dinner, and about 3 I Sot of again, just Call on M[rs] Pomroy and so past on, and got to one M[r] Posts a little of Galiad Meeting House, and I was very kindly entertaind,—Saturday morning we Sot off very early in the Morning, and went on our way got to Esq[r] Welless about 10 Sot a while, and Esq[r] was very urgent to have me Stay over the Sabbath, But I Coud not, and So we went on, and it was rainey kind of the Weather, Just before Night we got to Indian Place in Farmington and put up at Daniel Mossucks, & the Indians were well, there were but eight Families of Indians,—

Sabbath Sep[r] 25: Preachd 3 Times many white People were together and they attended well—here I met with George Pharoah and his Fami from Long Island, they were moving up to Onoyda Country,—

---

97. It appears that the Niantic community was suffering an outbreak of smallpox, which was epidemic in North America in the 1770s and 1780s.

98. *Prodacal Son:* The parable of the prodigal son is given in Luke 15:11–32.

Monday Sepr 26: We Sot of about 9: and got to Brother Phineas about 2: and here I had the doleful account of the Death of my Daughter Tabitha, a mornful and heavy addition to all Troubles and Sorrows, Went to See my poor Daughters Youngest Child, and it was a Sorrowful and very affecting Sight—~~went bac~~ had a meeting with the People on the next Day twice, and the People were very Solemn—This Night Lodged at one Mr Safford's the woman is extraordinary in Christianity of great understanding, and Experiance

Wednesday Sepr 28 Sot of early having taken leave of the Fam and I went on my way, Sot at Brother Phins took Breakfast with them, Mr Willson was with me a Son in Law to old uncle Chauccum, Soon after eating took leave of the Family and we went on our way, Stop at Mr Chaucums—and here Mr Woodbridge the Preacher among this People overtook me, and was extreamly urgent to have me Stop to preach once more but I denyd him, and we past on, he went with us a little way and then parted in Peace and we went on, and got to Canaan Just Night and we went to Mr Joseph Marshals a minister of the gospel and Lodged there found his wife very poorly with Lameness—

Thirday Sepr 29 got up very early and Sot of and got Stockbridge about 3 in the after noon, and Call'd at Capt Yoke's but he was not at Home, and most all the Indians were Scaterd, what were left of those that are gone up to Onoyda,—about two thirds of them are gone up to Onoyda—Just before Sun Sit went to see Mrs Kirkland, and was a little while and then returnd, Call on Mrs Serjant and Lodged there, Mr Serjant was not at Home—

Fryd Sepr after Breakfast went back to Capt Yokes, and was there Some Time, and then Sot off,—Stopt a while at a Tarvern, and here I met with one Capt Baldwin of New Canaan and he urgd to have me Stop at his place to have a meeting in the evening, and I Consented, and went on to Richmond, and got there before noon Stopt at Mr Millers an old aquaintaince of mine, found them all well, din'd with them, and Soon after Dinner went on our Way, and got to New Canaan Just before Sun Set, Calld on Colo Whiting he we was Busy, and so I past on reachd Capt Baldwins, in the Evening the People began to gather and there was a great Number of People Collected, and I preachd to them from Exod the words go forward &c[99] and I had but little Sense of Divine things, yet the People attended with gravity—Lodged at the Same House,—

Saturday, Octr 1: 1785 Sot of early, and Stopt at Mr Camps and took Breakfast with him and Sent of James before me—after awhile I Sot of, and about 11 o c Calld at a public House the mans Name was Robbinson and he knew me and Some others, and another Came in, and they began to impertune and urge very hard to have me Stop to keep Sabbath them, was a man desired me before to go so far as to green Bush and Mr Camp desired me also to Stop there and keep Sabbath at one Esqr Woodworths,—

---

99. Occom here preaches from Exodus 14:15, "And the Lord said unto Moses, Wherefore criest thou unto me? speak unto the children of Israel, that they go forward." In Exodus 14, the Red Sea is parted and Israel escapes the Egyptians. His selection is especially significant in the context of his recent transit through Stockbridge, where almost two-thirds of the Native population had left for Brotherton.

and finily Concluded to Stop at Mr Robinsons to preach there in the Morning, and so go to gree^n^ Bush in the after noon and so lodged in Mr Robinson's—The Place is Call'd Phillips Town—

Sabbath Octr 2: The People Collected together, and there was a great Assembly, and I preachd to them from 1 Epist V:10: and soon after meeting took dinner and then went of to Esqr Woodworth's in green Bush, Mr Robinson and another gentlen went with me, and we got there about 4:P:M: and there was Number of People got together and I began the Service Directly, and there a Solemn attention,—The People Collected Something for me, Lodgd in here this Night and was kindly entertaind,—here I met Mr Hally from Norwich he is preaching in a Place Calld New Betheleham—in the evening a Number of us had agreeable Exercise with my Christian Cards and after that went to bed Quietly—

Monday Octr 3: was at Esqr till 12 then went to New Beth Stopt at Mr Townsends and there took dinner, and then kep on, Got to the Place about 2: and a great Number of People had got together, and began the meeting directly, and after went back to Esqr

[Courtesy of Dartmouth College Library]

∾ JOURNAL 12

October 4, 1785–December 4, 1785

Occom continues his travels toward Oneida territory and Brotherton, stopping along the way to preach to large and curious crowds and to visit his daughter Christiana Occom Paul at her home near Saratoga, New York. When he reaches Brotherton on October 24, 1785, he is greeted by a gathering of hymn singers at the home of David Fowler. Occom participates in the town's harvest celebrations, conducts the first wedding at Brotherton, and witnesses the formal organization of Eeyawquittoowauconnuck, or Brotherton, on November 7 and 8, 1785. The land at Brotherton, Occom reports, is rich and fruitful: "the best land I ever did see in all my Travils." He also visits the New Stockbridge settlement before embarking homeward.

Tuesday Octr 4 After Breakfast, took leave of the Famy and went on towards Albany got there about 11: I turnd to Mr John McKinnys a Tervern keeper, and it Raind extream hard, the Rain Catcht us just as we got over the Ferry,—when the Rain abated I went to See Some Friends, but most of my particular Friends were gone out of the City, went to our good Friend Hollenbacks inquired of him of my Daugh Christiana but he coud not tell anything about them, he desird me to Baptise his Child, that was born the Sabath Day ~~Day~~ before which was the Second Day of the Month, and I Examend them Concerning their Knowledge of the Nature of Baptism and their Duty to bring up their Children in the Fear of god and nor to do it only out of Custom and Fashon, and they promise to do their Duty,—and indeed it was a great Trial to me, and finally I Consented and Some Time in the evening I Baptised the Child by the

Name of Jenney, with the great Name of the ever Blssed Trinity—Lodgd at the Same House, and was kindly intertaind,—[100]

Wednesday Octr 5 was in the City till after noon, Dined at Mr Hollenbecks, and Soon after Dr Sot of from Albany, and got to Landnd Ferry and We coud not get over, and Lodgd at Mr Fundys, and they were very agreeable Folks,—

Thirdsday Octo^r 6: Went of very early in the morning and went up to the North-ward because we coud not get at this Place, and we went so far as to Mr Whitneys in [Nessavania?] and we wander about backwards and forwards all Day,—got over the River lower part of [Nessavania?], and Lodgd at poor Tervern one Mr John Smiths,—

Fryday Octr 17: got up very early in the morning and Sot of for Saratoga and we Stopt at [Several?] places by the Way, and we found no friends ^in the^ Road—got to Still Waters about 12 Stop M^r [ ] at a Tervern and Several knew me, and they offerd us Dinner and we acepted of it kindly,—and here found out the People had con-cluded to have me keep Sabbath with them, good old Mr Campell is a Minister of this Place, and he was Sent for he Came Directly to see me and Concluded further to be with them on the Sabbath, and two went on but the Bridges were So gone and Shat-terd by the Flood, that we Coud not go a long by the River; and turned right off from the River and inquried after Mr Kalley, and found him in the Dusk of the evening, and was kindly recevd his Wife was not Well; and I Went to another Family to Lodge one old Mr Concling Lodged with me,—

Saturday Octr 8: Soon after breakfast Sot of and went to the River, got to the River ab 12: Call in at M^r McCartys and the offer us Dinner and we Sot down to eat,—and here we understood my Daughter was east Side of the River Close by the River, Soon after Din^r we Sot of again I went afoot and left my Horse with M^r McCarty, got over the River about 2: in the after noon and went to the place where I heard my Daughter was, ^got^ to where Sister Dina lives, and there was no body at home bout old mother Margery after a while Isaac Tattleton Came home, and I got his mare to go to Where my Daughter lives, a bout 7 miles further, and we got to the Place Some Time in the evening, and not Well but better than She had been for She has been very Sick, the rest were Well, Thanks be to the great god for his mercy to me in the preservation of me and my Daughter and her Family Lodged here—

Sabbath Octo^r 9 got up very early and Sot of to go Still Waters to preach in Mr Campels got to the River about 9, and Sent the mare back by James Waucus for he Came down with me; got over Soon and I on a foot and tryed to get a Horse at the first House, But I Coud not and went on foot, and two or three Places and all in Vain, a wagon came by me goining to meeting ~~and~~ I Desired him to help me a long, but he woud not, at last I gave up, and Sent Word forward to have Horse Sent me and I went into a House, told the man of the House of my difficulties, and he asked me Whether I was going to hear the Strange Mister. I told I Suppose I Should hear him, and then told him, the People Could not See that Strange Creature till I get there, and then he asked me whether it was I that they expected I told him Yes,—and he was Surprised,

---

100. Occom's hesitation to baptize Hollenback's child probably stems from his sense of pastoral re-sponsibility for the Christian education of the child, which he as an itinerant cannot promise to supervise.

and there were then Several People going by, he Calld to them and told them I was in the House and wanted help, and one of the men got down and offerd me his Horse to ride to meeting, and I took it and went on, got there at half after 11, and there was a prodigious large Congregation the bigest that ever was See in the Place, and I went in, gave them a Short Discourse, from Jona [illegible] verse in the after noon from another the ~~go~~ People attended with great and Solemn attention and with many Tears—as Soon as the meeting was done, a gentleman took me in his wagon, and Caried me to Mʳ Powerss, the good man recevd me With tenderness and Friendship, at Candle lighting we went to meeting in a Small Log meeting House and it was crowded like a Bee Hive, and the attended like Criminals at the Bar, I belve they felt the Power of the word tho I was much Spent—Lodgd at Elder Powerss—

Monday Octʳ 10 Was at Mʳ Powers till near meeting Time, Elder Powers let me have his Horse to ride to Mʳ Kalleys meeting got there near 12 Stopt a While at a House near the meeting H- and Mʳ Kalley came to me & we went to another House, and there we took Dinner—and Soon after eating we went to meetg and there was a Multitude of People, and I preachd to them from [ ] and there was an affectionate attention the Christians were some what Elivated, and the Sinners were alarmed, and I believe the Hypocrites were Surprised, and we had a little intermission, and went to meetting again at Candle Lighting, and there was a great number of People again and they attended Solmnly; after meeting I Went home with with one Mʳ John ~~Smith~~ Carpenter about one Hundred Rods[101] from the meeting House, and was extra well entertaind, we had very agreable Conversation with the man and Woman, after Conversation, I Went to bed quietly,—

Tuesday Octʳ 11: about 9: in the morning, Mʳ Kalley and I went towards the North River, Call'd on Mʳ Powers, and he was geting ready to go with us, and so we went on; got to Mʳ Bacon's about 11: and the People began to Collect together, and about half after one we began the meeting, and the people Seemed to be tied to the Word, and I believe they felt the Power of the Word, Soon after meeting we went to Mʳ MᶜCartys where I had left my mare, and the man charged me nothing for keeping my mare, and went on presently and Calld on Mʳ John Smith and took Tea with them, and directly went on to the Ferry—got over about Sun Sit, and went to Mʳ Matt Van burans and the People Collected together, and we had a meeting and there was Considerable Number of People, and they behaved well, Stayd at the Same House,—

Wednesday Octʳ 12: Isaac Tattleton and I went to my Daughters & we got there about 12: and I rested a little at my Daughters and then we went to meeting to Mʳ [ ] and the People behaved well generally but not So Solemn as at other [ ] after meeting, went back to my Daughters, and rested a little, and in the evening, the People Collected at Mʳ Begle's and we had a little meeting after meeting went to my D's again, and went to bed very Soon

Thirdsday Octʳ 13: after Bre left my folks and went on to Mʳ Jonathan Thomsons, got there before noon, and took Dinner with them,—at 2 we went to, Mʳ Tomsons Son's a few Rods, and there we had meeting, and there was Considerable number of People and they attended well,—as Soon as the meeting was done, they desired me

101. *Rod:* five and one-half yards, or sixteen and one-half feet.

to preach to them again in the evening, and I Complied, and I begun a gain in about half an H and there was greater attention Still, the People were much affected, Lodged at Mr Tomson's,

Fryday Oct 14: Some Time after Breakfast, Mr Tomson and I took our Horses and we went to Still Waters,—got there Some Time before meeting, about 1 we went to meeting, and there was a great number of People, and they attended with great affection, after meeting went to Mr Campell's and, near Sun Sit we went to Mr Butners and had an evening there, and there was a great Number of People a gain, and they attended with all gravity, and after the People were dismist, a number Stay'd, and I gave out out my Cards to the People and we had agreeable Exercise, and Some Time in the evening the People disperst and I went to bed Quietly once more Thanks be to god The People in this Place are exceeding Friendly and kind to me, Mr Campel is as a Father to me

Saturday Oct 15 Some Time after Breakfast went on my way, Stopt at Mr Campels a few minutes, and then took leave of them, and went on my way towards Ball Town got to Capt Dunnings about 12: Dined with them, in the evening we had a meeting in Mr Gregorys House, and there was a goodly number of People—and it was a Solemn meeting—after meetg Went home with Capt Dunning again and Lodged there, the Capt and his whole Family are exceeding agreable Folks—

Sabbath Oct 16: Went to meeting with the People and it was as a bad Way as ever I was at in all my Travils Mirery the bigest of the way went we got to the Place the People had got together a great Number—they have a new meeting Ho^u^se very large for a new Settlement I preach to them from Daniel Mene &c[102] in the after noon from John ye are my Friends &c[103]—Soon after meeting, Went to the old meeting House West Side of the Lake, and preachd in the evening, and there was a Considerable number of People, here I Met my old acquaintance Mr Dake,[104] I lodgd at one Mr Weeds, and his Son in Law Mr Cable with his wife Desird me to Baptise their Chile, and ^when^ I had Examined them about the Nature of Baptism and finding them well ground in the gospel Faith I Baptised their Child, and after I had performd my ofice, one Mr Bright made an Objection, and we talke upon the matter awhile and I Coud not be Convincd that I was wrong, and we dissisted, ~~and~~ they went a way, and I went to bed quietly once more—

Monday Oct 17: after Breakfast I went to 5000 Acres, before I had got to the Place, I met Mr Dake, and he Went back, with me, and I Went with him to his House, about from the meeting House, and took Dinner with him, and Soon after dinner Mr Dake and I Went to meeting & there was a Considerable number of People, their meeting House is made of Logs, and I preachd to them from Matt thou Shalt worship the Lord &c:[105] and there was an Auful Solemnity in the Asembly,—after meeting I Went Home with one Mr Holms, and I was very kindly entertain'd the old People apper'd very Religious, Some Time in the evening I had Some Exercise with the

---

102. See Daniel 5:25. This sermon appears in this volume.
103. See John 15:14.
104. *Mr Dake:* Charles Deake.
105. See Matthew 4:10.

Children of the House, they were all grown up but one, and they appear'd very Solemn in the exercise, and then we prayd together, and after that I went to Bed Quietly once more—

Tuesday Octr 18: Soon after Breakfast took good and Friendly leave of the Family, and I went on to Galaway, and I mist my way, lost about 3 q^{rs} of a miles and it was very disagreable, to my mind, I was obligd to go right back, and it put me in mind of missing a way to heaven it must be dreadful beyound all Expression to miss Heaven finaly at last: I got to Galaway, before 12: and Calld in at Good Mr Otis's one that went from New London North near by where I live, and he & his wife receiv'd me with all kindness,—about 2 O:C we went to meeting a few Rods from Mr Otiss House—and there was a good Number of People, I preach'd to them from the Words—we will go Three Days Journey &c ^gen 8.27^[106] in the evening I preachd again in the Same House and there was a good number People of again I Spoke from Ruth—What is thy Petition &c[107]—Sot Some Time after meeting had Some conversation with Some Friends and it was agreable, and then went home with Mr Otis, and I went to bed Peacably once more thanks be to Heaven—

Wednesday Octr 19: after Breakft about 9: I took Friendly leave of Mr Otis and his Family, and one Mr Dean went with me 6 or 7 miles, to direct me in the way—got to Mohauk River near 12: and So I went on got to [Cankunnawaha?] in the evening, and I put at one Vuders a Dutch Tavern—

Thirdsday Octr 20: Sot of very early in the Morning, and Went over to Southside of the River a little above the Nose and kep on till I got to one Mr Mabee's and I took Breakfast, and Soon after Breakfast Went on, and about 11 it began to Rain hard, and I Stopt at one Esqr Henry Wauruth, agreable gentleman; Stayd here all Night,—

Fryday Octr 21: got up very early even before break of Day a great while, and the Esqr got up too Soon after—at broad Day light, I got up on my Horse, and pushd on my way, reach'd at Widow Tygers[108] about 9: and took breakfast there, and after eating Went on again, here I heard our Antony[109] and James Waucus slept, and one Mr Prince with them, and I never over took them till I got to the turn of the New Road to our Peoples Settlements, Just as I was going to one of the Houses Antony Calld me, and I looked back and there was Antony Smiling, and we went in to House together, and Concluded to Stop here,—and he Calld Mr Prince and Jamy, and they came back,—and to one Mr Folts and Lodged there.—

Saturday Octr 22, we got up quite Early and got ready to go on our way, just as we were going off, Elijah Wympi Came to our Lodgings, and he told us David and Jacob Fowler and most all our men were in another House just by and I Sent James, and they Soon Came to me, and it was a Joyful meeting—and then I went to Where the rest of them were and they all rejoice to See me and was with them a little while and then went back to Mr Folts and Concluded not to go thro the woods this Day,

---

106. See Exodus 8:27.
107. See Esther 9:12.
108. *Widow Tyger:* Madaline Dygert.
109. *our Antony:* Anthony Paul.

because it was a misty kind of weather, Some went thro, but I Stayd and Some others, I taried at Mr Fols—

Sabbath Octr 23: This Morning was a Snowy Morning, and it Raind all last Night,—and I taried at Mr Conorand Fols all day, they were quite agreable Family, Stayd here again this Night—

Monday Octr 24: Some Time after Breakfast Brother David Fowler and I Sot of to go thro the Woods to our Indians new Settlements and presently after we Sot out it began to Rain and it Rain'd all the way not very hard,—and it was extreemly bad muddy riding, and the Creeks were very high, and some Places very Mirely, and we were over taken with Night before we got in, and Some places were very Dark where Hamlock Trees were our Eyes did us but ^little^ good, we travild a bout a mile in the Dark, and then we arrivd at Davids House as we approach'd the House I heard a Melodious Sin[g]ing, a number were together Sin[g]ing Psalms hymns and Spiritual Songs, we went in amongst them, and they all took hold of my Hand ^one by one^ with Joy and Gladness from the Greatest to the least, and we Sot down a While, and then they began to Sing again, and Some Time after, I gave them a few words of Exhortation, and then Conclude with Prayer,—and then went to Sleep Quietly, the Lord be praised for his great goodness to us—[110]

Tuesday Octr 25 Was a Snowy Day was very uncomfortable Weather I kep Still all Day at Davids House and it was Crouded all Day, Some of Onoydas Came in—In the evening Singers came in again, and they Sang till near ten O:C: and then I gave them a word of Exhortation and Conclude with prayer, so we ended another Day—

Wendesday Octr 26: Snow is about is about ancle Deed this morng and all [word illegible] under the Snow and the Land is foul of water every where, and the Brooks are very high—it is not Clear Wheather yet—in the evening we had a little Singing again—This morning I rench'd my Back, only puting on my Stockings, and ^was^ put to some diffeculty to go out all Day—

Thirdsday Octo^r 27: Cloudy but moderate, my back Continues as it was yesterday,—

Fryday Octo^r 28: it was warm and pleasent Day but Cloudy the begest part of the Day—in the evening they Sung ~~in Abra^m Simons House, a mile from David Fowlers~~

Fryday Octo^r 29 David intended to gather his Corn but it lookd very much like for Rain, and So defer it to another Day,—the Young Folks went in the evening to Abraham Simons a mile of from David Fowlers to Sing, but I did not go my back Continued out of order,—

Saturday Octr 29: David gatherd his Corn he had a number of Hands tho it was Cloudy in the morning and little Rain, and in the after noon he husked his Corn, and the Huskers Sung Hymns Psalms and Spiritual Songs the bigest part of the Time, finished in the evening,—and after Supper the Singers Sung a while, and then dispe^r^sed—[111]

---

110. On hymn singing at Brotherton, see J. Brooks, *American Lazarus,* 63–70, 84.

111. Fall festivals centered on the harvesting of corn such as the Wigwam or Green Corn Festival are traditionally the pivotal event of the ceremonial year for Native New England communities like the Mohegan; see Tantaquidgeon-Zobel, *Medicine Trail,* 53–59.

Sabbath Oct' 30: Had a meeting in Davids House and a Number of Stockbridgers Came to meeting to the distance of Six miles, they had eleven Horses and there was a number of foot People, and there was a Solemn Assembly, the People attended the word with affection many of them—I Spoke from Mathew IV.10: in the after Noon from XXXII:1: in the evening we had Singing a long while and then gave them a word of Exhortation and Concluded with Prayer—

Monday Tuesday and Wednesday nothing hapen'd remarkable only Rainy and Snowy Weather and I was much confind with my Wren^t^ch Back—

Thirdsday Nov' 3:1785 Towards Night we attended upon the antient ordernance of Marrage the first that ever was Selebrated by our People in their New Settlement in that this Wilderness The Cupple to be married and the Young People, formed in a Neighbouring House and Came to the House of Weding in a Regular Procession according to their age and were Seated accordingly—and the old People also Seated themselves Regularly, and A great Number of Stocbridgers Came from their Town to attend the Weding, but many of them were too late—When I got up, I Spoke to them Some Time upon the nature of Marrage, the Honourableness and Lawfulness of it Where by we are distinguished from the Brutal Creation: Said Some of the first marrage in Eden ^&^ of the Marrage Where Christ and his Disciples were invited and the Honour he did to it by working ^the^ first mericle he wrought in the World by turning Water into Wine and then we prayed, after Prayer I orderd them to take each other by the Right Hand alternately and then I declared them in the Face of the Asembly to be a Lawful Husband and Wife, according to the Law of god—and then prayd, ^& Prayer being ended Marriage Salutations went round regularly^ & again, and Concluded ~~with~~ by Singing a Marriage Hymn,—and then the People Sat down,—and Jacob Fowler Who was appointed Master of Serimonies at this Marriage, gave out Some Drink[s] a Round the Company and then Supper was brought Sot in order on a long Board, and we Sot down to eat, and had Totty well Sweeten'd with Wild Sugar, made of Sugar Trees in the Wilderness; and after Supper, we Spent the Evening in Singing Psalms Hymns and Spiritual Songs,—and after that every Went home Peaceably with any Carousing or Frollicing[112]

Fryday Nov' 4: The Young People put on their best Cloaths and Went to a Neighbours House, all on Horse back, and they appeard agreeable and Decent, and they had no Carousing, they had Some Pleasent Chat and agreable Conduct, Some Singing ^of^ Psalms Hymns and Spiritual Songs, Some Time in the after Noon they dined together, and after Dinner every one went Home Quietly,—So the Weding ended, and

---

112. A marriage ceremony is inscribed on the back of one of Occom's sermons—"Saying what think ye of Christ" (II), Matthew 22:42 (1766–1768)—archived at the Dartmouth College Library: "You do take this woman to be your Married Wife and do in the Presence of God and before these witnesses Promise and covenant to be a loving and faithful Husband unto her until God shall separate you by death. You do in like manner take this man to be your Married husband and do in the Presence of God and before these Witnesses Promise to be a loving, faithful and obedient wife unto him till God shall separate you by Death. I do then before God and these witnesses Declare you to be Husband and Wife. Therefore what God has joined together let not man put asunder." See also Love, *Occom*, 251n2.

it was Conducted, Caried on, and finished with Honour and great Decency—and the Lord help this People to go on Regularly in all their Concerns,—

Sab: Novr 6: Brother Jacob Fowler and I went of early in the Mor^g for Stockbridge Indians that lately Settled at old Onoyda,[113] got there Some Time before meeting went to Sir Peter Pauquunnuppeets House, he is a Collegian brought up and Educated at Dartmuth College, and he receiv'd With all kindness Friendship,—about 11 went to meeting, and many of our People from our new Settlements Came to meeting, to the distance of Six miles,—I Spoke to them from Joshua 24:22: and Esther [7]:2: in the Evening we had another meeting, and we had Solemn Day and evening the People attended with great attention and Solemnity, after I had done Speaking; we Sot down and the Singer rose up and they Sang Some Time, and then dispersed, every one to his quarters and Sister Hannah[114] and Sister Esther[115] and I Lodgd at Widow Quinnys Where the meeting was—

Monday Novr 7: Some Time after ~~Breakfast~~ ^Sun Rise^ I Sot of with Brother Roger[116] and his wife to our Place; and Stopt at [Roger's] and I took Breakfast with them, they live near three miles from the rest of the People and after eating I went on to the Town, got there about 12 and found them all well,—in the Evening we met on our Temporal and Religious Concerns—We met once before but we did not come to proceed any business—But ^now^ we proceeded to form in^to^ a Body Politick—We Named our Town by the Name of Brotherton, in Indian Eeyawquittoowauconnuck[117]—^J. Fowler was chosen Clarke for this Town^ Roger Waupieh, David Fowler, Elijah Wympy, John Tuhy, and Abraham Simon were Chosen a Committee or Trustees for the Town, for a Year and for the future the Committee is to be Chosen Annually,—and Andrew Acorrocomb and Thomas Putchauker Were Chosen to be Fence Vewers to Continue a Year. Concluded to have a Centre near David Fowlers House the main Street is to run North and South & East and West, to Cross at the Centre[118] Concluded to live in Peace, and in Friendship and to go on in all their

---

113. During the American War of Independence, about forty-five Brotherton Indians took refuge at Stockbridge (Ottery and Ottery, 45; see also L. Murray, *To Do Good,* 264–265). After the war, in response to the occupation of Stockbridge territory by white squatters, Stockbridge tribal members initiated a plan to migrate to Oneida territory with their friends from Brotherton. The Stockbridge migration to Oneida began in earnest in spring 1785. The Oneida granted the Stockbridge a six-mile-square tract of land to be called "New Stockbridge," located about six miles west of Brotherton. Love estimates the 1785 population of New Stockbridge at 420 (*Occom,* 245). See also Wyss, 81–122; Mandell.

114. *Sister Hannah:* Hannah Garrett Fowler.

115. *Sister Esther:* Esther Poquiantup Fowler.

116. *Brother Roger:* Roger Wauby or Waupieh.

117. On the Mohegan-Pequot-Montauk word "Eeyawquittoowauconuck," see note 28 in the introduction.

118. Brotherton town founders adapted some spatial-organizational features of New England towns in order to facilitate the intertribal cohabitation of their new territory. Examples here include the appointment of fence-viewers—officials responsible for resolving property boundary disputes—and the town's spatial orientation around centering cross-streets. In October 1786, Brotherton elders insisted that the Oneida allot them a bounded tract of land, even though the Oneida desired the settlers to live "at large" with them on their territory. (See Occom's diary

^Public^ Concerns in Harmony both in their Religious and Temporal Concerns, and every one to bear his ~~Public~~ part of Public Charges in the Town,—They desired me to be a Teacher amongst them, I Consented to Spend Some of my remaining with them, and make this Town my Home and Center—[119]

Tuesday Novr 8: got up early and Sot of for Stockbridge Indians got there Some Time before meeting, This is a Day of fasting and Prayer, with the People here and they desired me to assist them the Design of this fast is to Confess their Sins before god, and to repent and beg the Pardon of all their Sins and desire the Blessing of god up on them, and to Prosper them in their New Settlement, and also bless them in their Religious Life—and I preach to them, in the fore Noon from Jonah 3:8: in the after noon from Prover 23:26 and it was a Solemn Fast Day many were deeply afected, all attended like Criminals before the Barr; in the Evening they met again, and they advisd and gave Councel to one another to Conduct Well and be Careful in all their Conduct the ensuing Winter as they were about to disperse for the Winter, that they may get together in the Spring in Love and Peace,—and after advice, they Spent Some Time in Singing of Spiritual Songs, and when they had done, I gave them a Word of Exhortation, ad^v^ising them to Use their Natural Powers and Conduct as becomes Rational Creatures, and to break off from all out breakings of Sin, and Especially to break off from that abominable Sin of Drunkenness and give themselves to watching and Prayer, and so Conclude with Prayer,—and the People dispersed in Peace—I Lodged at Sir Peter Pauquunuppeets

Wednesday Novr 9: Breakfasted with Capt Hindreck & Soon after Eating, I Sot off for Home, got to our Place about 12 and found our Folks Well—

Thirdsday Fryday and Saturd look[d] about a little to See the land and it is the best land I ever did see in all my Travils. John Tuhy Planted Just about one acre of ground, which he Cleared last may, and this Fall he took of 20 Bushels of good Corn 56 Bushels of Potatoes about 200 Heads of Cabage, and about 3 Bushels of Beans, and about 2 Bushels of [Parsnips?] and Beats together; besides Cucumbers and Watermelons; of the Same ground, and it was not Plowd nor dug up With a Hoe, only leaves and Small Busheses were burnt on it and great many Logs ly on it now[120]—and I was told last week among the Stockbridge Indians, that in their clearing Some Spots of land where it has been improvd in years past, they Plowed up, and dug up good many Potatoes, where they had been Planted perhaps 10 or 12 years ago, one man got 3 skipples,[121] and he planted them, and he has raised a fine passel of them, and

---

for October 16–18, 1786.) Love suggests that early Brotherton settlers originally modeled their town government on Connecticut General Assembly statutes; in 1796, the New York General Assembly passed its own act to appoint town superintendents, apportion land into assigned lots, and supervise town governance at Brotherton, while Native-organized governmental agencies such as a town council and peacemakers' court continued (*Occom*, 299–300).

119. Samson and Mary Occom moved their permanent home from Mohegan to Brotherton in May 1789.

120. Occom's description of planting lands being burned rather than plowed accords with more traditional modes of Native Northeastern agriculture. See Cronon, 128.

121. *skipple:* a unit of dry measurement equivalent to about 3 pecks; the term was adapted from the Dutch schepel and was used in colonial New York.

Brother David Fowler told me and his Wife and others Confirmd it that he ^had^ one Cabage Stomp Stood three Summers and it headed every year, the last it Stood, it three Heads—

Sab, Novr 13: Preachd at David Fowlers and many of the Stockbridgers Came to meeting, and there was good attention, and I believe Some felt the Power of the Word,—in the Evening we had Some Singing,—

Monday Novr 14 was geting ready to return homward,—

Tuesday Novr 15: got up very early in the morning, and we were fitting to go off, and little after sun rise We Sot off, Brother David and his Wife Daughter and James Waucus went together Elijah Wympys, two Daughters[122] and others—Some Stockbridgers there were Eight Horses of amongst us and many foot men and we got thro the woods Just as the Sun was going down I put up at Mr Fols's—

Wednesday Novr 16: We Sot of very early in the morning and I got to Esqu^r [Wanfrets?] in the Evening, and Lodged there, and three Stocbridgers were there also—

Thirdsday 17: I Sot off very early, and about 11: I got to Capt Roof's and there I Stopt and finished writing for our Folks, Just Night David Came in—and here we Lodged—

Fryday Novr 18: I went to Bomens Creek and got there about 1: put up at Esqr Kimbets and they were very glad to See me and I was as glad, and Lodged there, had a meeting there this Evening, and there was a Considerable of People, and they attended well,—

Saturday Novr 19: I left the Family, Doc^r White went with me about four miles and so we parted, and I to Esqr Manbee's about 3 O: C: and here I put up, & was receivd with kindness—here I overtook my Son Anthony Paul,—

Sabb Novr 20 Preachd here to Considerable Number People, and they attended with all Seriousness they were most all Dutch; Spoke in morning from Acts 9 Lord What Wilt thou[123]—in the afternoon from Luke So is he that layeth &c[124] Elijah Wympeh and his Son, and 3 Stockbridge girls, were here also—I Lodged here again,

Monday Novr 21: Some in the morning it was about 8: I sot off, and got So far to Mr Peter Van Wormer, about a mile from Mohawk River in the Woods North Side— This Day I Saw the Revd Mr Romine a Dutch Minister in Cacananweeku by Mohawk River, I met with him at a public House, and he apear'd quite Friendly at once, he desired me ^me^ that if I Shoud Come a long this way again at any Time, to call upon him, and have a Discourse with his People, and I told I wou'd—

Tuesday Novr 22: got up very early and it was very cold morning, and did not Sit out so early as I intended, took Breakfast before I Sot out, about 8: I went on my way thro the Woods and it was Very Riding it was not froze hard enough to bear a Horse in Muddy holes; I got to Mr Otis's in Gallaway a little after 12 and found them all well, and put up here, and took Dinner with them, Concluded to have a meeting

122. According to Love (*Occom*), Elijah Wympy had six daughters: Eunice (d. 1767), Eunice, Sarah, Hannah, Esther, and Jerusha.

123. See Acts 9:6.

124. See Luke 12:21.

this Evening about Daylight in I went M[r] Dean's to meeting and there was a Considerable of People, and I Spoke from Joshua, 24:19: and the People attended with Seriousness,—after meeting went back to M[r] Otis's and Lodged there—

Wednesday Nov[r] 23: Some after Breakfast Sot of to go to a Place Called Smith Field, about 6 miles of, M[r] Messenger went with me and it was thro a Desert a[ll] the way,— got there Just before 12 went into M[r] Smith's House where the meeting is to be, about 2: we began the meeting and there was Considerable Number of People Collected together, for they had but Short Notice and it is a New Settlement, and the People attended with all gravity and Solemnity, I believe Some felt the Power of the Word, Soon after Meeting, one M[r] Coffin, a Universalist Preacher desired to have some Conversation with me, and we had Conversation a little while together without much Debate, for we disagreed altogether,[125]—and the People disperst, and I Stayd at the House all Night, and M[r] Mesanger went home; and M[r] S^m^ith and his wife and I had very agreable Conversation and their Son in Law his Name was Alexander, Scotchman by Nation, was very much biggoted to their Version of Psalms, We had some debate about them, and upon Some of their Points[126]—Sot up late, and was Extreamly well Treated by the Head of the Family and all the Young People; Slept very comfortably,-

Thids Nov[r] 24 got up quite early, Stayd till after Breakfast, and then Sot of M[r] Hughwee Alexander went with me, and we to Gallaway about 10, call'd at M[r] Messengers and Dined with them, and had agreable Conversation Soon after Dinner went to M[r] Otiss & from there to meeting about a mile where was a Sick woman, we soon got there M[r] Otis went with me and another man, had some conversation with the Sick Woman and found her resigned to the Will of god, & was Comfortable in her mind; and then we began the Worship of god, there was but few People and they attended with great Seriousness and Some Affection—I Spoke from Matt 6:10: after meeting M[r] Culloch invited me to go home with him to Stay all Night and was Treated very kindly & Tenderly,—

Fryday Nov[r] 25: got up early and Stayd till after Breakfast and then went back, Calld at Mr Mesengers and Dinner with him, and afterwards went to M[r] Otiss,—and in the evening went to meeting again in M[r] Deans House and there was Considerable Number of People and there was great Solemnity among the People. I spoke from James 4:17: after meeting went back to M[r] Otis's and Lodged there, had a number Friends to viset me this Evening, Some Scotch People and we had quite agreable interview—

Saturday Nov[r] 26 did not preach this Day, just at Night went to Warran's a little distance and was Wellcomd, and treated very kindly, he is a Baptist man by Denomination, Sot up Some Time for had Some Company, M[r] M[c]Larran a Scotchman was With us and very agreable Conversation, and good bed Time I went to Bed quietly once more—

Sab. Nov[r] 27: about half after ten we went to meeting, a few Rods in a Barn, and

---

125. On universalism, see note 84.

126. In 1650, the General Assembly of the Church of Scotland approved a metrical psalter developed by Francis Rous for use in its churches. Church of Scotland members considered the Scottish Psalter the most faithful to the original Hebrew of the biblical Psalms.

there was a great Number of People, for a new Settlement, and I Spoke from 1 Samuel 15:14 in the after noon from John 11:28 and there was great and Sober attention through the Assembly, and I believe Some felt the presence of god—after meeting went home with Mr Warran and took Dinner with them,—and in the eveng went to Mr William Kalley a Scotchman, and had a meeting there and there was a good number of People, and I preachd to them from Joh: 11:26 and I believe we had Some assestance both in Preaching and in hearing—Lodgd at the Same House, and was kindly entertaind—

Monday Novr 28 was at Mr Kalley's till after Breakfast, then went to Mr Otiss and was there till about 2 in the after, and then Mr Otis his & Mr Messenger and his and went to a weding, and there was a number of People, but great many, and I married the Cupple, their names were Mr Jonathan Bunyan Cotes and Polley Doulin,—and the People behaved exceeding well,—we good Cake and Cheese to eat & Totty to Drink—just before Sun Sit we that came together went back again, I Calld in at Mr Messengers and was there till the young Wedendners came home, and then I went to Mr Otis and Lodged once more, and his Brother Lodged there also,—

Tuesday Novr 29: Took my leave of Mr Otis and his Family 9: O'C and I directed my Course towards Scenactady Mr Messenger went with me, and we parted before We got to the Place, and I went on to the Town, got there Some Time before Night: Calld at Mr Shooter's, and Sot a While and then went to see Mr Post my old Friend, and found them all well and was there a While, and his Son Came in, and he invited us to go home with him, and there I Lodged, and kindly Treated, & Slept very Comfortable,—

Wednesday Novr 30: got up early took Breakfast with Mrs Post, Mr Post was gone out,—after eating I went to see Several Friends payd my visited the Revd Mr Romine, the Dutch Minister of the Place, and he appeard very Friendly, but I Stayd not Long about 10 o:c: I Went over the Ferry again to go to the 5000 Acres; Mr Messenger went with me again, we traviled together about 7 miles, and then we parted in Friendship—I Went on, Calld at one Mr Sharewoods to warm my feet, and I had sot but few minutes before the woman asked me whether I woud Stay till she Can make Some Tea I told her I woud, and she got it ready Quick, and I eat very Hearty, and just as I had done the man of the House came in and appeard very agreeable and as I Was going away, he desired me to Come See him again before I left the Place, & I told him I woud, then went on to Mr Holmss Soon got there and found them all well, and was kindly receivd by the Family, and I put up there,—

Thirdsday Decem^r 1 1785 Was at Mr Holmss till near Noon, and I went to Mr Woods a little distance and Dined there, and just before Sun Set, I went to one Mr Rogers, and Lodged there, I found ^him^ and his wife very understanding in the Scriptures and I believe they were Experienced Christians they are Ireish Folks, we had very agreable conversation & Sot up Some What late, I saw the man was not well pleasd with Doc^r Watts Psalms, and we had a long talk upon them, we did not agree about them, but we did ^not^ Contend about them,[127] after conversation, we Sung

---

127. Until the late eighteenth century, many conservative Congregationalists opposed the adoption of hymns and psalms by Isaac Watts into their repertoires of sacred music. For his part, Occom

a Psalm and read a C^h^apter, and Prayd together and then went to Peaceable and I had a Comfortable Sleep—

Fryday Decr 2: Got early and took Breakfast with them after eating we Sung and Read, and then I had Some Exercise in the Family with my Christian Cards and it was very Solemn and agreable;—about 10 I took my good leave of the Family, and returned to Mr Holmss,—and in the after noon about 1: O C: I went to Mr Clarkes and there was a goodly number of People and I preachd to them from Acts 2:37: and there was great Solemnity and Some affection I believe they felt Some thing of the Power of the Word after meeting a Number of the People Stayd, and in the Evening had Exercise a long While with Family, with my Christian Cards and it was very agreable and Some Time in the Evening we went to Bed quietly,—

Saturday Decr 3: about 10 went to Mr Holmss and sot a While and I went to Mr Sharewoods about half mile of, and him Very kind to me, and Conversable & he is an understand Man took Dinner with him, and was there till Tea was got, and took with them, and Just night returnd to Mr Holmss again, and Lodged there,—

Sabb: Decr 4: Mr Holms went to meeting with an Ox Slead, and his whole Family went and I went with them, the meeting was again in Mr Clarks H and there was a Vast Number of People tho' it was Stormy Day, I Spoke from Isaiah 5:[128] and was uncommon attention and Flow of Tears, from old and young, and I am perswaded the Power of the was felt by many Souls, I preachd only once—after meeting, I took Dinner with Mr Clark, and after eating we Sot Some Religious Conversation—about Sun Set we went to good old Mr Northrop and the we had a ^comfortable^ meeting, and it was very Comfortable meeting, and was great many Peo I Spoke from Matt 5:13 Mr Northrop gave me the Text and after the meeting was over a Number Stayd, and we had agreable Religious Conversation Lodgd at the same House

[Courtesy of Dartmouth College Library]

꙾ JOURNAL 13

December 5, 1785–December 14, 1785

> *Embarking for Mohegan from Brotherton, Occom spends a month in and around Saratoga Springs, New York, preaching, baptizing, and performing weddings. At night, after his sermons, he often uses a set of "Christian Cards" or "Notes" printed with Bible verses to instruct and entertain.*

MondDay Decr 5: 1785 got up very early, and Prayd together & Soon after Prayer I went to Mr Clarks and from there to Mr Holmss, I rid Mr Clarks mare and Came directly back, for Mr Dake was waiting for me to carry me in his Slay to Ball Town; about 9: we Sot off, & to Balls about 12: and I put up in Mr Weeds House, and he receivd me kindly; ~~about 2~~ went to meeting and there was a little Number of People

---

selected twenty-eight Watts hymns for inclusion in his own *Choice Collection of Hymns and Spiritual Songs* (1774).

128. Occom does not record a verse.

and I preachd to them from Acts, XIII.30: and there was great Seriousness in the asembly. after meeting went to Mr Weeds and took Some Victuals and ~~Lodged~~ Some Time in the evening, a man came to the House and desired me to go to See a man that was very Sick, and I went directly and Soon got there, about eight O:C and found the man very Sick his Name is Mr Theophilus Hide, and was greatly Desirous to be Baptisd and I Examind and found him much Distrest about his Soul, and I endeavourd to Explain to him the Nature of Baptism, and finding him to understand Some thing of the Nature of Baptism & he earnestly Desiring it, so at last I Concented and I Baptised him—and his Wife was also greatly Exercised about her Soul, and they wanted to have their Child Baptised also, but I declined—and I lodgd there and Doc^r Jerviss was there all Night.—

Tuesday Decem^r 6: after Breakfast went to Mr Weeds in a Slay Mr Hide Carried me, got to Mr Weed Some Time before noon about 1 went into the meeting House, and there but few People from the Smallest Congregation I have had in these parts, and I Spoke from Acts VIII:30: the People attended Well,—Went with one Mr Hollister and in the evening, there a Number of Neighbours Came in and my good old Friends Mr Larkins[129] and his wife Came in also, I was well acquainted with them on Long Island, and we were very glad to See one another, and 2 of their Children Came in also a Son and Daughter, a likely young Folks,—and we had Very agreable Exercise with my Cards and we Sung and Prayd together and then I went hom with Mr Larkins and Lodged there and was extreamly well receivd & Treated, went to bed late and Slept Comfortablely—

Wednesday Decr 7: after Breakfast, Mr Hollister came to Mr Larkins with a Slay to carry to meeting Mrs Larkins and her Daughter Bettsey went with us in the Slay; we got the meeting about 10: and the people had not got together but few, and we Stayd till about 12 and went in to a School House and there was pretty good number of People & I Spoke from 1 Peter 1:24—and there was great Solemnity in the Asembly, Soon after I went to one Mr Jeremiah Bettys House and a number of People went also, and the man desired me to Baptise his Child, the woman was of Baptist Persuasion, Yet she gave her ful concent, and after Examination, I got up to Show the Nature of offering a Child unto god in Baptism & the woman was much afected and I Proceeded to Baptise the Child,—after that I Sot down to eat with them, Soon after, I went to Mr Palmers and in the Evening, we again had Exercise with my Cards there was a Number of Young People and they behaved Well,—late in the evening I Went to Bed quietly once more, the Lord ~~the~~ be Praised—

Thirdsday Decr 8: got up very early, and Mrs Palmmer got Breakfast early and Soon after eating I went of to a meeting North part of Balls Town, to Preach got to ~~the~~ Mr Weeds Some Time in the morning, and Stayd Some Time, and one Mr Sprague Come with a Slay for me, and we went off Directly, and got to Mr Spragues about 12: and took Dinner with them, and then directly went to meeting, and there was a great number of People, and I Spoke from John XVII.3: and there was a great and most Solemn attention there were many Tears—Soon after meeting I went directly back with Mr Spragues Folks; and went directly to Mr Turners, and had a meeting there

---

129. *Mr Larkin:* Joshua Larkin.

in the Evening, and there was a Number of People again they Crouded the House and I preachd from Hebre- 2:3: and I belive the Lord was present, I had some Sense of Divine things, and the People were greatly affected, there was a flood of Tears,— I Lodgd at the Same House—

Fryday, Decr 9: Some Time after Breakfast, I Went of a Young man went with me I Call on Colo^l Gordon, and he Treated me very kindly woud had me Stay to Dine with him, but I Coud not Stay, and So went on Soon, Calld on [ ] but Stay but a few mintes and So went on, got to Mr Weeds before Noon, and was there till about Sun Sit; and then Mr Hollester Came with his Slay for me, and went with him directly, and got to his House and got there Some Time in the Evening—and when, we ^got there^ found a number of Friends together waiting for us; and I Sot a little While, and I began with them with my Cards and we had Very agreable Exercise, and we Sot up late and finally we broke up, and I went to bed quietely once more. Blessed be the name of the Lord for his goodness to me

Saturday Decr 10, Some Time after Breakfast went to Mr Larkins and took Dinner with them, and Soon after Dinner I went back to Mr Hollesters Call, on Mr Bettys and Sot only few minutes, and went on,—and Some Time in the afternoon, Mr Hollester got his Slay ready and we went on, Mr Amos Larkin, Mr Ely and a Woman went with us, and we got to Mr Rogers just before Sun Sit, and we Stopt there a while, took Tea with them,—and Soon after Tea we went on, and Calld on Mr Clarke, a few minutes and then we went on to good old Mr Northrops and there I Lodgd, We had Some agreable Exercise with my Cards only With the old People and one young man, I read a great Number of the Cards after they had Chosen each of them a Text—

Sabb: Decr 11 After Breakfast went to Mr Clarkes and about 11 the People began to Collect fast, and a Prodigious number of People gathered,—and I began the Exercise about 1 and I Spoke from Cant 2 ^16^ and I think the Lord was present, the People attended with all attention, and there was great Solemnity and many Tears were Shed, and I believe the People will not forget this Sabbath Soon, especially some after meeting took Dinner with Mr Clark—and in the evening, I went to one Mr Brown, to attend ^upon^ the young with my Cards, and there was a Prodigious number of People old and young, and we had had very agreable Exercise it was a Solemn Night, and the People, old and young I believe will not forget it all their Days, and I hope & pray that it may be a Night to be rememberd to the Glory of god—Choice Portions of Scriptures were Sown this Night among the People as they never had;—We broke up near midnight, and I went to Mr Benjamins, and it was Rainy,—and went to bed late

Monday Decr 12: Some Time in the morning I Went to Mr Clarkes, and from thence to Mr Holm'ss, and was there till about 2 in the after noon and there was a young man Came to fetch me from Gallaway, and I went off with him directly, and we got to Mr Anderson's near night where I am to marry a Cupple of Scotch Folks and they receivd me with all kindness and Friendship, Lodged there and had a Comfortable rest,—

Tuesday Decr 13: We all got up very early, and they got Breakfast soon,—and we waited for Weddeners, and about 1 O.C. they Came, and a Young man went out with a bottle to meet them and treated them round before they Came into the House, and soon after they got into the House, we proceeded in Celebrating the ordernance of Marriage,—and as Soon as it was over we Sat down to Dinner, and when that was over, the Weddeners Sot of to the North end of Gallaway,—and I returnd to 5000 Acres, and got to Mr Holms just before Sun Sit, and in the evening a number of People came in and we had exercise with my notes, and it was quite agreable, and went bed late,—

Wednesday, Dec. 14: This morning Conversation, with Mr Coffin, the Universalist Preacher, the Same I had Conversation with the other Day, he is a very bold Creature[130] about 10:I Went of to go to one Mr Wakemans, and had a meeting there, and there was a goodly number of People, after meeting went home with Mr Seeley and in the evening a number of People came in to Exercise with my notes and it was very agreable Meeting, Lodged here,—

[Courtesy of Dartmouth College Library]

∾ JOURNAL 14

December 15, 1785–January 22, 1786

> *Occom continues his homeward journey through Bennington, Vermont; Pittsfield, Massachusetts; and Stockbridge, Massachusetts. At Stockbridge, he finds that "most of the Indians" have been "Scatered."*

Thirdsday Decr 15: about 10 O: C Sot of for another meeting about 2 miles to Mr Coles and there was a Small number of People and I Spoke to them from [ ] just before meeting I was Calld by a man from 5000 Acres to marry a Cupple this evening,—and So as Soon as the meeting was over I Sot of, and I got there after Sun Sit and I Sot a lettle while at Mr Northrops and then ^went^ to the House of Wedding, and married a Cupple and Soon after marriage I went with home with Mr Benjamin and his wife and there I Lodged—

Fryday Decr 16 Soon after Breakfast, I went of to [word illegible] got there about 12: and in about an Hour we began the meeting, and there was a Considerable Number of People chiefly Scotch People and I Spoke from Isaiah [^16^ 5?] and the People were greatly bowd before the Word, and the Lord, I believe, gave me Some Sense of his Word, as Soon as the meeting was over I went of to Ball Town got to Mr Leroys about Sun down, and it was Rainy, yet a Number of People Came together, and we had agreable Exercise with my Notes, Sot up late, and Lodge at the Same House, and was kindly entertain'd—

Saturday Decr 17: in the morning went to Mr Jeremiah Sealeys and took breakfast with them, and soon after eating I Went of, Calld a while at Mr Benjamins, and from there went to Mr Cundys a Dutchman, and was extreamly well received, Stayd the rest of the Day and the night ensuing,—and we had very agreable Exercise with my Notes—

Sabb Decr 18 Soon after Breakfast Mr Cundy and I went to Gallaway to meeting

130. See Occom's diary for November 23, 1785.

with the Scotch People we got there about 12: and there was a great Number of People, Chiefly Scotch People, and I began the meeting Soon after I got there,—I Spoke from Eph V:14 and I much freedom: and there was very deep and Solemn attention, many were greatly affected, after Service, I took Dinner with the Family where the meeting, the mans name was M^r McKinsley Soon after dinner, I returnd to 5000 Acres, I went alone, I got to Mr Moorhouses before Sun Sit, and Stopt there for the night and was affectionately receivd—in the Evening a number of young People and Some others came together, to have Exercises with my Notes, and it was a it was a Comfortable meeting, the Company broke up about 10, and after that we Sot up Some Time, and we went to Bed quietly—

Monday Decr 19: got very Early, and got my Mare Shod and after Breakfast, I took good leave of the Family, and Sot of to take leave of my other Friends as soon as Coud, for a young Came for me this morning, to go to North part of Balls Town 8 or 9 miles from this Place, got a way from my Friends about 12 and so went on as fast as I Coud, Calld at Mr Seeley's and took Dinner there, and so went directly on again got to the Place a 2, and married a Cupple of English their Names were Sanford White & Hannah Hide—I the evening I went to another House one Mr Smith's and there we had a meeting, and there was a goodly Number of People, and it was a refreshing meeting, many I believe felt the Power of the Word, I Spoke from Luke VIII 41 after I had dismist them, a number Stay'd, and desired to have Exercise with my Notes, and there was great Solemnity amongst them, many were Deeply affected, there was a flow Tears from many Eyes it was late before we broak up, and I went to bed once more in Peace, thanks be to god—

Tuesday Decr 20: got up very Early and had my Horse got for me, and went one Mr Unisteads a few Rods[131] and there took Breakfast, after Breakfast took my Notes, handed out to 3 or 4 Children, and then I Sot of of for Eastward, got to Mr Weeds about 12: took dinner with them, and Soon after Dinner Went on again one Mr Nash Conducted me over the North End of the Lake and Mr Nash desired me to go home with him and to have a meeting in the eveng at his House or Some other and I Consented, and We had a meeting, and there was great Number of People & I Spoke from, Hebr 11:3 To what purpose &c[132]—Lodgd at Mr Nash

Wednesday Decr 21: was up early, and got ready to go a way, And Mr Nash had a notion of Exchanging mares with me, and I Considered of it a little while and Concluded to Swap with him, and he took off my Saddle put it the other, I gave him 2 Dollars and an half, and I so I went on to Mr Beldens, and took Brea[k] and Soon after Breakfast I Went on again; I Just now heard Brother David, had good Luck in Selling his Roots,[133] & had Success with the Honoble Congress, in his Memorial for

---

131. *Rod:* see note 101.

132. Hebrews 11:3 reads "Through faith we understand that the worlds were framed by the word of God, so that things which are seen were not made of things which do appear." The scripture Occom cites is found in Isaiah 1:11. See also his diary entry for December 21, 1785.

133. David Fowler developed an enterprise harvesting and selling American ginseng, which grew wild in the forests of the Hudson River Valley. See Occom's diary entry for August 30, 1786. Imperial trade with China first encouraged European demand for ginseng in the seventeenth

help;[134]—I got to Capt Deardens a little while before Night, found them all well and was kindly recivd by them,—took Dinner at Mr Gregorys,—In the Evening I went to Mr Gregorys to meeting and there was a large number of People, tho it was exceding bad Traviling both on horse back and foot,—I Spoke from Isaiah 1:[11] to what purpose and I think I had some Sense of Divine things the [Sowd?] by the Word,—Lodgd at Mr Gregorys—

Thirdsday Decr 22: after Breakfast Some Time I went to Capt Dunnings Stay till after Dinner and then took leave of the Family, and Sot of for New-Town, Capt Dunning went with me about 2: and half miles, and and then a kind Dutch man Conducted me, till he got me to a plain Way, and I got to Mr Taillar, and was enquiring Where the People meet together to Worship and he Said they had no meeting and he found me out at last that I Was a Preacher and desired me to light, and I did, he was very kind to me and to my mare, and Lodgd there,—Rested Very Comfortably—

Fryday Decr 23: got me up Some Time before Day and made me up a fire & Sot down by it,—and here I Stayd till Some Time in the after noon, and then I went to Still Waters, got to Mr Bakers before Sun Sit and in the Evening a number of People Came in, and Mr Marsh a Preacher amongst this People Came in also, and we had Conversation Some was not So agreable before we broke up we had Some Exercise with my notes and it was late before we had done, Lodgd here,—

Saturday Decr 24: Towards noon, I went to see Mr Campel and took dinner with them, Soon after Dinner, I went of to go back to New-Town, Calld at Mr Andruss, but he was not at Home, and I went on, Stopt at old Mr Miller and there I Taried all night and was kindly entertaind went to bed prety early—

Sabb. Decr 25: got up some Time before Break of Day and the Family got up too and they got Breakfast soon and a little after Sun rise we were getting ready to go to meeting,—and Mr Tayler and I went of Soon, and to his Suns good While before meeting, about 11: the People began to flock in fast, and about 12 we began the Exercise, and there was a prodigious Number of People Collected together, and I spoke from Lucke [ii]:10: and there was very great attention—and in the Evening we had another meeting, and there was a large number of People, tho it was a Dreadful Storm of Snow and Wind blew very high, and the Snow flew and it was Cold,—I Spoke from the Words –but one thing &c Luke and then was very good attention again,—went to Bed soon this evening and had a Comfortable rest,—

Monday Decr 26 Did not get up Soon—Some Time after Breakfast I Sot of for Still Waters, and it was very Cold, got there before noon Call at Mr Andrusss and Sot a

century. In 1718, the Jesuit missionary Joseph Francois Lafitau announced in his published *Memoire* that he had identified an American variety of ginseng growing in Iroquois territory, and American botanist William Bartram also identified ginseng growing along the Susquehannah River in 1738. For most of the eighteenth century, international trade in American ginseng flourished with high exports to Europe as well as to China. Native peoples of New York may have been introduced to the trade by Sir William Johnson, who sent a shipment of ginseng to England in 1759. See Appleby.

134. For David Fowler's successful "memorial" to "Congress," see "Brotherton Tribe to United States Congress, [1785]," in the petitions part of this collection.

little While, and went of and Calld at Mr Bakers, and they all insisted I Shoud and preach, and finally I Concented, Dind with Mrs Norton and her Daughter Lois Directly after Dinner went to Mr Campels and Preachd there to a Small Number of People—Spoke from XV 1 King and 14 and there was good attendence Soon after meeting, I went of in order to go over the River; two men went with me, but I Coud not get over, there was too much Ice and So I turnd my Course & went up to Mr Powerss a baptist minister, got there a little after Sun Sit and put up there, he and his wife receivd me very kindly—

Tuesday Decr 27 Was at Mr Powerss all Day and it was extreem Cold; in the evening, went to meeting amongst Mr Powerss People & there was quite great many People for the Cold Season I Spoke from Psalms 125.1 and the People Seem to be in deferent in their attention, their Bodies were Cold and I believe Hearts too,—after meeting went back with Elder Powers and Lodged there again,—

Wednesday Decr 28: Some Time after Breakfast, I went to Mr Kalleys[135] meeting House to preach, got there about 12 Mr Powers Went with me Went into an House Just by the meeting, was there a few minutes and Mr Kalley Came in with his Wife, and it was So cold they Concluded to meet in a Dwelling House, and we went directly, and there was not great many People I Spoke from 1 Croni 29: and there was good attention Some were affected, Soon after meeting I went to about 2 m further to preach amongst Mr Powerss People; one Mrs Ireish Caried me in her Slay, got to the House just before Sun Sit about Candle Lighting went to meeting in a School House Just by, and there was a Crowd of People, and I Spoke from Luke Lord teach us to pray[136] Lodgd this night at Mr Ireshs and Sot up late, Mrs Ireish & I had very agreable Conversation after the rest went to bed, after a while I Went to bed Quietly, and had a Comfortable rest—

Thirdsday Decr 29 got up very early, and went of Stopt a few minutes at Mr Chatcham's and So past on, and Stopt at Mr Kalleys and took Breakfast there and soon after Mr Chatcham Came along, and I got upon Horse, and went along with him and we Stopt at Mr Powers and got my things, and took my good leave of him and his wife and went on again, and Mr Chatcham and parted near the River, I Went up the river a little ways, and Crost the River and went on, and came to an House of one Capt Wright[137], and he desired to go into his House & I did, and took Dinner with him and he deisred me to have meeting at his House, the Sabbath following, and I Concented,—and so I past on Seeking after my Daughter,[138] Went to old Mr Begles and there they told me they were gone towards the River, and So I turnd right about, and went on and I Calld at Hawkins and there I was told, they livd about a mile & a Quarter, got there about Sun Sit, and found them all well; thanks be to Heaven for his goodness to me and to my Daughter, Lodgd here, once more—

Fryday Decr 30: it was a Snowy Day and very Cold Stayd till about 11: and then

135. *Mr Kalley:* Beriah Kelly.

136. See Luke 11:1.

137. *Capt Wright:* Job Wright.

138. Probably Christiana Occom Paul, who settled with her husband, Anthony Paul, near Saratoga, New York.

I went of to go to meeting, but I could not get Hor^s^e to ride to Mr Hawkinss for my mare was there, and I so I got a young man to go for my Horse and he Came back Soon, and so I went of, and Calld on Mr Hawkins, and it Snowd very hard, and they Sayd it was most Night, and they perswaded me to Stopt and not to go on and I Complyd, and Stay there all Night and they treated me with all kindness the woman I had knowledge of when She was a little girl, they have Six Children four Boys and two girls, and they agreable, Spent the evening with them very agreable had Some Exercises With my Notes after a while went to bed—

Saturday Decr 31: Some Time after Breakfast, I took leave of the Family, and went on to the River got over on the Ice about 11, Call on Mr Williams, and took Dinner there, after Dinner took leave of them and went down the River, Calld on M^r McEarly, a few minutes & So past on, and Calld on Mr Bacon and there I Stopt for the Night and was kindly entertaind—

Sabb Jan^r 1, 1786 got me up Some What Early, and took Breakfast, and Soon after Eating, had my Mare got up, and I took leave of the Family, and went over the River to Capt Write's,[139] and about 11 the People Came fast and at 12 We began the Meeting, and there was Considerable Number of People, and I Spoke from Gene [ ] How old &c[140] after meeting was at Capt Writes and intended to Stay all Night but presently after Sun Sit a Cupple of Young Came to Capt Writes and Desired me to go with them, and I went, and Exercises with my Notes With the Family and sat up late but at last I went to bed,—

Monday, Jan^r 2: got up early and went back to Capt Writes Mr Lewis Williams Carried me part of the way to the Cap^ts and I got there about 8 and was geting to go on my way towards Pitts Town,—and I was Saying if any one to help towards upper part of Saratoga, I would go and Capt Wright Said he woud Contrive to Carry me, and I Concluded to go, and about 10. o. c. one of Cap^ts Sons got up a Slay and we Sot of, and We got to good old Deacon Hewits about 1: and there I Stopt, and they concluded to have a meeting in the Evening, and Mr Write Went back—Deacon Hewet was not at Home, but his Son was at Home with whom he lives—in the evening a number of People got together, and I spoke to them from Jerem [XX]III 39:40 and the People were exceedingly attentive and Solemn—went to bed Soon, and had a quiet Sleep once more the Lord be Praised,—Lord enable me to live this year as if I knew it was the last, that I may live to thee in all things, that I may Consecret my all unto Thee—

Tuesday Jan^r 3: got up very early, and took Breakfast with Mr Richard Hewet and about 10 Mr Hewet took me in his Slay, and we went on towards the North River, got to the River about half after 11 and we were afraid to go over the Slay on the Ice, and I Went over a foot, went to one Mr Riders and tryed to hire Horse, but I Coud not get any, and So Mr Hewet went back over the River, to fetch his Horses, and he Soon got back and I got on upon one of them and we went on to Boughten Kill, and we Stopt at a House, to enquire of the way, and there we met with one Mr Lake, he had a Slay going directly to the place where I was going and he was so kind as to take

139. *Capt Write:* Job Wright.
140. See Genesis 47:8.

me in his Slay, and Mr Hewet went back, and I went on, and we got to Mr Tanners past middle of the after noon, but there was no Body at Home, and we went to old Mr Fosters, and there I Stayd, there I took Dinner, Mrs Tanner was there, Mr Foster and his Wife are old People, about Sun Sit I Went back to Mr Tanners, and meeting was appointed here, and the People began to Come in Soon, and Mr Tanner got home after Sun Set, and We soon began the Exercise, ther was but few People, and I Spoke to them from John 9: Soon after meeting I went to bed——

Wednesday Jan^r 4: got up early and was at the House till near 9 then Mr Tanners Son Thomas Carried me in a Slay to meeting, at the House of Mr Forster Mrs Tanner and old Mrs Foster were in the Slay also, got to the House about 10 and there was a great gathering of People I began ab 1 in the after noon, and there was a Solemn attention, many were greatly affected,——Soon after I went with Mr Rose and his Wife in his Slay, and took Some Victuals with them and Soon after eating we went to meeting again, we met at Mr Kinnion's, and there was a goodly number of People, and I believe the Lord was present with us and I believe the Night will not be forgot Soon, after my I went back with Mr Rose in his Slay, this Mr Rose Came from Block Island, I was well acquainted with his Brother William,——I lodged here——

Thirdsday Jan^r 5: got up very early, and they got Breakfast directly, and about 9 Mr Kinnion Came to Mr Roses to go with us & we Sot of Soon, in a Slay and went back to Saratoga got to Generals Seat about 11: and we past on to Fish Creek got to Mr Hewets about 12: & we Stayd a little while, and we returnd back to General Schilers Seat, got there about 2: The men that brought Stayd a While, and then went of and I Stayd at Mr Tomsons in one of general Schiliers Houses, and had a meeting there in the evening, but there was a Small Company, and they attended Well They were Chiefly Dutch People, and they attended well,——after meeting Some Time I had Exercises with my Notes, in the Family and it was a Solemn Time, the poor Negroes were Surprizd With the Texts they Chose,[141] Some Time in the Evening I went to bed quietly and had a Comfortable rest——

Fryday Jan^r 6 we got up very early, got Break Soon, and a little after Sun rise, a Slay and Horses were ready to Carry me down towards the Still Water, and, the generls Boss order'd one of the genls Negroes to Carry me, Boss in English is Overseers,[142] We had a fine Span of Horses We got to Mr Williams, in about an Hour, 6 miles & half, the Negroe return right back, and I Stayd a little While, and I took my [word illegible] mare, and Sot of after taking good leave of Mr Williams and his Family, and went on towards Pitts Town, Stopt a while at Capt Wrights,[143] and Mrs Wright Woud get me Dinner, and as Soon as I had done eating, I Went on again, traveld thro Woods the bigest part of the way, towards Night, I mist my way, and was obliged to go back, about half a mile and Call at an House, the man was a Black Smith his Name is [ ] and they were quite willing to let me Stay, and the man and I lodgd together, and I had quite a comfortable Nights Rest Saturday morning got up very early, and my mare was got up and I went on before Sun rise, and I got to one Colo^l Tomsons

141. On Occom's use of Christian Cards in a mode of Christian fortune telling, see note 77.

142. The English word "boss" derives from the Dutch "baas," or master.

143. *Capt Wright:* Job Wright.

about 8; and he knew me and received kindly, and took B there, and was there Some Time after eating, I took my old mare, and went to Mr John Lambs and was kindly received, and there I Stayd and Lodged there and found the Cupple very agreable, both of them are Christians, I believe in Truth they are youngerly Cupple they are of the Baptists—

Sabb Jan^r 8 Some Time about 10 we went to meeting at the House of one M^r [ ] about 11: we went to meetg and the People began to gather thick about 12 we began the Divine exercise and there was a great Num^r of People, one half Could not come into the House, and I was obligd to Stand at the Door; and it was Cold, and I spoke from Eph V 14: and the People attended with great attention, and many were deeply affected and there were flow of Tears, and I believe they will not forget the Day very Soon,—Soon after meeting I went home with Colo Tomson in his Slay. Mr Holsted and his Wife went with us he is an old Bap elder, took Dinner with them, in the evening we had a Meeting again and there was a great Number of People again, many [word illegible] of People were obligd to go back because there no Room for them in the House, and it was Cold, & there was great attention again,—Lodged at the Colo and was extreamly kindly entertaind, the Colo and his Lady are very agreable Cupple—

Monday Jan^r 9: after Break I Sot of and Went to see a young man that was Sick and found him quite poorly was under deep Concern for his poor Soul, gave him Some Concel and prayd with him and then went towards the East, Betsy Hinkly a young Woman went with me, and we got to Mr Bigalos about 12: where the meeting was to be—People began to Collect Soon, and there was not a great many People, and I Spoke to them from Luke VII 23: and the People were very much affected many of them Just before the Exercise was over a Cupple of young men Came on purpose to invit to go with them, to the distance of 7 miles, and I was at a Stand Some Time what to Say to them, finally Concluded to go with them, & took Dinner and Soon after went with them in their Slay and one of them Rode my Mare, and it was about Sun Sit when we Sot of and was extreemly [word illegible] and it Cold, We got to the Place Calld Hoosuck, put up in the House of one Mr Porter, and there Lodged and was well receivd—

Tuesday Jan^r 10: about 12 the People Collected fast, and we began the Worship & there was a great number of People, and I Spoke to them from Matt IV:10 and I believe many felt the Power of the Word Soon after meeting, I went of with Mr Reed, and his wife his wife ^in their Slay^ was from New London North parish where I was brought up took Dinner ^with^ them and directly after Dinner we went to meeting again, about 2 miles off, and there was a great number of People again it was at the House one Mr Price, and I Preach to them from Matt XI:28, and there was an affectionate attention there was a Shower Tears, the meeting was apointed here on account of a Woman that was going to meeting Yesterday to hear me, and She was Taken with a Fit of Apoplexy[144] about half a mile from her House and was taken up Speechless but She is now better, Can Speak but not very plain and She is Numb one Side but She Can Walk Some—Soon after meeting I went with Mr Reed in their Slay and Lodgd at their House, and was affectionately entertaind—

144. *Apoplexy:* stroke.

Wednesday Jan^r 11 got up early and took Breakfast and a While after my Mare was brought, and I took leave of the Family and Sot of and had not gone more than 60 rods before I met a Slay from St [word illegible] to fetch me and I got of my mare in and in the Slay and went on fast, it was about 8 m We had to go, and got to the Place about 12 I put up Mr Lathems, and about 1 in the afternoon we went to meeting,—and there was a Prodigious number of People and I Spoke from Isaiah [LX or IX] 6: and there was a very great and Solemn attention many were much afffected,—after meeting went back to Mr Lathems in the Evening went [home]— again and there was a Number of People, and I Spoke to them from Prov 5 10 and there was great atten^n again, after meeting I went with M^r [ ] Stopt at Doc^r to see his Wife, She was Sick and they desired me to Stay and concluded to Stay, Sot up very late, and went to Bed about 11: had uncomfortable Night it was very cold [word illegible] Cold,

Thirdsday Jan^r 12 got up Some Time before Day and Sot up by the fire, and the Doc^rs Wife got up and sot up and Desired me to Sit by her and I did, and She gave me a Relation of her Experiences, and they were Some What weak but apeared like the gospel, and I think had good affect upon her, Soon after Day, I went away Stopt at the House where we meets, and Soon after I got in a man Came in, and desird me to go back a little way to See a woman that was put to bed last Night in Child Birth, and I went, they were Dutch Folks, I prayd with them, and then went back to Mr Lathems, and there a little, and then I expected a Company, but they did not come, so I Sot of for Little White Creek, got to the Place about 12: went into an old Dutch man's House and he appeard very friendly and took care of my Mare and the People began to gather presently, and about 1 I went to ^the^ meeting House, it is a Log meeting House, where one Elder Wait[145] Preaches, and there was a Multitude of People, I began the meeting Soon after I got in, the People Coud not all get in I Spoke from Rom VIII:13: and I believe the People felt the Power of the Word of god, for there was a flood of Tears—Soon after meeting, I got up on my Mare and went on to Wards, Mr Cross, Mr Downer[146] a Baptist Preacher went with me, and we Stopt at Mr Dakes, Mr Edward Dakes, Brother formerly a Schoolmaster at Charles Town among the Indians here we took Dinner, Soon after Eating we went on again got to Mr Crosss about Sun Set and the People began to gather directly, and we began the meeting, and there was a vast Number of People & I Spoke to them from James IV:17 and the People we greatly bowd with the Word,—Lodgd here, Mr Cross is believe a Sincere Christian, he gave me an account of his Experiences and Exercises, Some in the Evening I Went to bed once more quietly, and had Comfortable Rest,—

Fryday Jan^r 13: Rose early and, and we had Prayers and after that Breakfast Came on, and Soon after Eating I Sot of for Shursbury M^r [ ] ^and his wife^ went with me, we Stopt at Esqr. [ ] from thence we went to see Mrs Burnham She was lately taken with a fit, and she is very Sick—I prayd with her, and then went on to the meeting H got there about 12 Stopt a while at a Tarvern, about 1 we went to the House of god and it was Extreem Cold, there was not a great many People and I Spoke from

---

145. *Elder Wait:* William Wait.
146. *Mr Downer:* Cyprian Downer.

Psal 32:1 after Service went to the Same House Where I Stopt took din^r and direclty after Dinner I went on towards Benington Mr Amos Burroughs went with me a little ways and we parted, I got to Mr Swifts[147] a little after Sun Sit, and was very kindly Receivd & he insisted upon it that Shoud keep Sabbath with him, and Concluded to Stay, Lodged here,—

Sabb Jan^r 14: Was at the Place all Day, towards Night went to the Printers and Coming back I calld on Mrs Robbinson an old Mother in Isreal, and had agreeable Conversation, about Sun down went back to Mr Swifts and Lodged there again—

Sabb Jan^r 15: about half after 10 went into the House and there was a great Multitude of People, it is a large House and it was well filled,—I Spoke from Luke XII:2: and there was a Serious attention—in the after noon Spoke from 1 Corin XVI:22: and I believe the Power of god accompanied the Word there was a great Shower of Tears, and I think they will not Soon for get the Day,—after Service went to Mr Swifts, took Din^r and Directly after eating went on to Pownal, Mr Potter took me in his Slay, this Potter went from Rhoad Island State Some years back and I have been in his House before when he livd West of Sea brook got to his House about Sun Sit, and was kindly enterta^d Slept Quietly.—

Monday Jan^r 16: got up very Early, and about 12 the People began to Collect & there was a large Congregation, and I Spoke to them from Rom VIII and there was a good attention of People and they attend Well, but I had not much freedom—as Soon as the meeting was over, I Went in a Slay to Esqr Jewets, and preachd there in the evening, and there was a great Number of People, and I Spoke to them from 1 John V:10 and I had but a little Sense of the Word, yet there was good attention,— Lodged there,—

Tuesday Jan^r 17: went on my way Soon after Breakfast. went thro Williams Town & Lainsbourgh—got to Pitts Field in the Evening and Lodged at Mr Ingasols a Publik House, and found him & his Wife very agreable—

Wednesday Jan^r 18: Sot of after Breakfast, and it was Extream Cold, Stopt a little at Brother David Fowlers in Richmond[148] they were all well in the after Noon Some Time I past on, got to Mr Sajants[149] after Sun Sit and Lodged there,—

Thirdsday Jan^r 19, it was Some What pleasent Day went about 10: Call on Capt Yoke, and they were well, but most of the Indians were much Scatered, Sot ~~but~~ a little while and So past on,—got to Mr Heccocks in Sheffield a Tarvern, and Lodged there—

Fryday Jan^r 20: I concluded to go with a Cupple of men to Hills Deals in Nobbe Town and they had to go a mile a two to Iron Works, and they were gone all Day, about Candle Lighting, they returnd back to Mr Hecocks and I went there in their Slay and left my mare at Mr Hecocks, and it was about 18 miles we had to go, and

---

147. *Mr Swift:* Job Swift.

148. David Fowler probably established a household in Richmond, Massachusetts, during the American War of Independence, when many Brotherton settlers fleeing violence in upstate New York took refuge in the Stockbridge area.

149. *Mr Sajants:* John Sergeant, Jr.

Stopt Twice and we got to the Place at Mr Jordans and it was about midnight, and I was much Fateagued, and went to Sleep Soon, and had a Comfortable rest—

Saturday Jan^r 21: Was at Mr Jordans all Day, Some Time after Sun Sit Mr Jordan Carried me in a Slay to Mr Latins about a mile, and there I Lodged, and was kindly entertaind, he is a Rich man, and it was a pleasent evening, and it thawd all Night,—

Sabb. Jan^r 22: about 9 the People Came prety thick and there was a great number of people Collected together and I Spoke from Rom IV 17: and the People attended Solemnly, Soon after meeting Mr Philip Lott took me in his Slay and Carried to a Dutch Meeting House about 5 miles of We got there about Sun Sit and present after we went in to the House of god, and there was a large Number of People, and Spoke from Acts 9—Soon after Mr Lott took me again in his Slay and Went home with him, and it was very bad Slaying by this Time, and there I Lodgd and was Extreamly Well receivd, and rested quietly once more

[Courtesy of Dartmouth College Library]

∾ JOURNAL 15

January 23, 1786–April 26, 1786

Much to the relief of his family, Occom reaches his Mohegan home in early February, disproving rumors that he had been killed. He spends the rest of the month setting his finances in order and visiting local congregations. In March, he attends a local Quaker funeral with Jemima Wilkinson, the visionary founder of the Society of Universal Friends, and he witnesses an "uncommon" manifestation of the Northern Lights. On April 1, Occom is visited in his dreams by the late George Whitefield, who embraces him affectionately and encourages him to continue in his ministerial labors. Occom concludes the month visiting and ministering to Indian communities at Groton and Pauquawnunk.

Monday Jan^r 23: was a Very bad Storm of Snow and it Thawd all last Night & it was now extreamly bad Travilling on foot, Slaying or Riding, and I Taried all Day at Mr Lott's, I was to hav^e^ gone 7 or 8 miles to meeting but it was so bad weather I did not go,—in the evening a good Number of People Collected together for meeting and I preachd to them. Spoke from Luke VIII, 30: and there was very good attention: and after meeting, a number Stayd, and we had Exercise with my Notes, and it was very agreable, and Solemn Some Time after the Exercise the Remainder of the People went home Peaceably, and presently after I went to bed

Tuesday Jan^r 24: Got up quite early, and Breakfast was got Soon, and after eating, the Slay was got ready directly, and Mr Lott took me in his Slay once more, and Carried me to South east part of Noble Town, and it was poor Slaying we got to Mr Briants about 7: miles, at 10: and was there but few minutes, here was a remarkable Sight four Cripples of us happend to be together, one never could ~~Wa~~ Walk, another was much Troubled with the Rheumitism and he cant walk, and the other was lame in one of his Legs as I am—from this House, one Mr Shaw took me in his Slay to his House, a little better than a mile, and there I Stayd the rest of the Day. In the Evening we went to meeting a little Distance at Mr Zekeus Covels and there was a Considerable of People, and I Spoke from Jonah III:5 and I believe the Some Sense of the Truth of god, and there was a great Solemnity and Some affection, I believe they will not [word illegible] the Night very soon after meeting: Mr Drusdel car'd me to his Home in his Slay they are a young Cupple and very agreable Cupple, was kindly entertaind Some late I went to bed & Slept quietly once more

~~Tuesday~~ Wednesday Jan^r 25. Got up early and it was Dull kind of the Day it was warm about 11 we went to meeting Mr Drusdel caried me in his Slay to a [word illegible] distance at one Mr Ephraim Ri^t^lys Barn and there was a great Number People and I Spoke from Acts ^26^ 11 Soon after meeting I went with one Mr Hentrek Decker a Dutch man, about 2 miles South ward, and got there a little before Sun Sit, and took Dinner there, in the evening went to another House a little distance to meetg and there was a Considerable Number of People Chiefly Dutch. and I Spoke from James IV:17: and the People were very attentive,—after meeting went back with Mr Decker, and there I Lodgd and Treated very Friendly, and Sot up quite late, and so at last went to Bed, and Slept Comfortably once more—

Thirdsday Jan^r 26 got up early and we had Exercise with my Notes, and they were much taken with them. Soon after Breakfast Mr Decker got his Wagon and we went back to the meeting House about 4 miles of, We got there before any People got together, about 1 in the after the People got together and I went to the House of god, and there was Considerable Number of People Colleted, and I Spoke from Song V. 16 and there was an Afectionate attention and it was very cold, after meetg Mr Robert McGonegall took me in his Slay, and helpd me to one M^r [ ] and I took Dinner there, & Just before Sun Set, he tooke me in his Slay to M^r McGonegal and there we had another mg and a great Number Collected and I Spoke from Ruth ^[number illegible] 2^ and I believe the Lord gave me some Sense of Divine things the People were much affected—Lodged at the Same House,—and Slept Comfortably—

Fryday Jan^r 27: got up very early, and took Breakfast, and Soon after Eating, M^r McGonegall let me have one of his old Horses to ride Down to Sheffie and he accompanied me, we Stopt a little while at Mr Lomiss, and he urgd very hard to have me Stay and preach in the Evening or in the morning; and I coud not Consent Consistant with my View of Duty, and so we past on, We got to Mr Heecock's about 12: and my good Friend went back and I took my mare & went on to Mr Mashall's got there about Sun Sit and found them as well as Common, and they receivd me with all kindness; and the young People had a Sing meeting here this evening and they Conducted with great Decency—and after Some Time, the Singers went a went away, and we Sot a while, and then we had Exercise with my Notes and it was very agreable and Solemn; about mid Night we went to bed, peaceably once more—

Saturday Jan^r 28: was at Brother Mashall's all Day and we had very agreable Conversation and he has a Charming ^2^ young Daughters very Discreet and Courteous & understanding Especially the Eldest her Name Abagail—

Sabb. Jan^r 29. Went to meeting a bout 9. to one Mr How and there was a great gathering of People, about half afr ten we begun the meeting and I Spoke from 1 Croni 29:5 and the attention was very great and Solemn many were affected.—In the after noon I Spoke from [ ] and the attention was greater and I believe they will [word illegible] the nor forget the Day. Soon, after meeting took Dinner with Mr How, and Mr Marshall was with us also;—in the evening we had a meeting in Mr Marshalls and there was a great number of People again, and I Spoke from the Words The night cometh[150] and the People were very attintive again and Solemn Lodgd at Mr Marshalls once more,—

Monday Jan^r 30: it was a Stormy Day,—and was very warm,—towards night I went to Mr Babcock's a little way of, he and his wife are old,—In the evening a little Number of People came together, and we had Exercises with my Notes. and it was very agreable and Solemn Lodgd at the Same House—

Tuesday Jan^r 31: Some time in the morning, I went to Mr Mashal and got ready and took leave of the Family and went on towards home and it was very cold got to Mr Tobeys a little after noon, and Calld in, and Mrs Tobey was very poorly and had been so Some Time in a very week State of Body and She desired me to Stop and I Conclude—towards Night Mr Tobey got Home, we had Concluded to have a meeting in the evening, and good many Came together, and Spoke from John IV:10: and it was a Comfortable Season with us—after meeting Some Stayd behind, on purpose to have Some Exercise with my Notes and it was very agreable and we Sot up very late and at last we went to bed beds were brought by the Fire and we Lodgd quite Comfortable Mr Mashal Lodgd with me—

Wednesday ^Febru^ 1 1786 Some Time after Breakfast I took leave of the Family and Mr Mashal, and went on once more, Stopt a little while at Mr Phelps and then went on, got to Mr Bacons about 2 in after. it was altogether Providential that I Saw Mr Bacon,—and he desired to Stopt to have a meeting in the Evening and got to Mr Knoss in the evg a Tavern and Lodgd there

Thirdsday Feb^r 2: got up very early, and sot of got to Mr Bacons a little past Noon, and he urg'd to Stay to have meeting in the Evenig and I Consented, and there was a considerable number of People, and I Spoke from Matt IV: and the People were very attentive, Lodged at the Same House—

Fryday Feb^r 3 Was at Mr Bacons till about 12 his wife is in a Maloriosly Situation She is having Distraction[151]—I went to M^r [ ] to Dine, Soon after Dinner I went to Mr Willcocks about 2 miles East, and there I had a meeting, and there was a good Number of People, and I Spoke from [ ] in the evening preached again. Spoke from [ ] and there was a great number of People and they attended well, Lodgd at the Same House, and was very kindly entertaind.—

Saturday Feb^r 4: took Breakfast very early, and Soon after I went of, and got Willtenbury about 11: and a Certain young man Desired to go with him to his House, he had been to our Place and to my House, in the Time a Militia encamped at our Place a little while, and I went with him and his father and Mother were very kind, they earnestly desird me to Stay over the Sabb— to preach, but I thought it was not my Duty to Stay, and so I passd on, went thro Winsor, enquird after my Daughter Olive[152] but I coud not hear of her, and so pasd along. I Came a Cross one Mr Darbe

150. See John 9:4.
151. *Distraction:* dementia, derangement.
152. *my Daughter Olive:* Olive Occom Adams.

at the River and we went together to Mr Hill's in 5 mile Hartford and there Mr Hill
Desired me to Stop and keep Sab— with them on the next Day and I Consented, and
Lodgd there that Night—

Sabb Feb^r 5 Before meeting, I went to see Mr Phelps the Minister of the place,
and he receivd me very kindly would have me preach all Day, I desired him to
preach part of the Day but he woud not, and I was obligd to preach all Day, and it
was a Snowy Day, and there was but few People and they attended with gravity and
Seriousness, after meeting went to Mr Phelpss again and Dined there, after eating
Sot a while and then went to Capt Hill's again Meeting was appointed ther^e^ this
Evening; Soon after Sun Sit the People began to come, and there was a large Number of People Collected together, and they heard with greater Solemnity than in the
Day, I Spoke from 1 Croni XXIX 5: P.M. Acts XI:26 Eveng,—Lodgd here again.—

Monday Feb^r 6: got up very early and got ready sot of about Sun rise and went
on, Stopt at Mr Abr Averys and there took my Breakfast, there were very glad to see
me & I was as glad, he came from our Place, they were all well but the woman ^one
of^ her Shoulders has been out Soon after eating I Sot of again; got to Mrs Pomroys
in the Hebron, before 12: Sot there a few minutes, and so went on, got to Mr Benjamin Darbe's about 1: and there I Stopt we expected to a meeting here this evening
about Sun Set, the People began to Collect, and there was Considerable Number got
together, and I Spoke to them from Luke XII.21 and there great attention Lodged
there and was kindly entertaind—

Tuesday Feb^r 7 got up quite early and took my leave of them, and so went on
Stopt at Lieu^t Joness & there took Breakfast, and Soon after eating went on again,
Calld in at Widow Coffs and Sot down a few minutes and sot of, Stopt also at M^r
Tucks an English man married to an Indian woman, from Naroganset, they have a
Notion to move up to Onoyda and after a while went on again; Call at a certain House
where I was aquainted in Times past, but the Family was gone, and another came in,
however I was well receivd, the woman that receivd me was a Widow Woman her
Name is Mrs Leads, took Dinner with her, and after Dinner Sot of again, Stopt at
Mr Carters, he was not at home but the Woman was very glad to see me and I was
too, Sun about one Hour high at Night, I went of again, Stopt nowhere till I got to
Neighbour Church's and sot there a while, and past on and got home about Day light
in, and found my Family all well, Blessed be the great and glorious Name of the
Lord,—they had heard that I was killd, but they coud not believe it, and now all the
World can't make them believe it—

Wednesday Morning Febru^r 8 an officer came to my House and attachd my oxen
for a Small Debt I owed, and Thirdsday I went down to N London to see whether
the Law, in the New Revised Law Book was yet in favour of the Indians, and I found
it Strong in favour of us,—and I sent a line to one of the Men, and the next he came
and Promisd to withdraw his action, and they did withdraw[153]

153. Laws concerning private debt underwent revision during the 1780s, and the U. S. Constitution, Article I, section 8 specifically called for Congress to effect bankruptcy laws. Some of the
   new laws effected by states in the early republican era instituted terms of debt repayment favor-
   able to debtors, for example, by requiring creditors to accept paper money for debt repayment.
   On the debt law climate of the 1780s, see Mann, 169–182.

Sabb. Febru^r 12: Preachd att Deacon Henrys,[154] and there was but few People they had not sufficient Notice—in the evening Preachd there again, and there was some moving amonst the poor Indians, and two of em made Confession of their back Slidings and Ask'd forgiveness & they forgave one another.—[155]

Saturday Feb^r 18: Some in the morning, I went down to the City of New London, and so over to Groton; Met Capt Rob Lathem Ju't by his House, he was going to the Ferry & I went to his House got there about 2 o: c: found Mrs Lathem well, she got me dinner directly, and taried there,—

Sabb: Fbr 19, about 9: we went to meeting to Mr Gidion Saunders's We Stopt at Capt Edward Lathems Mrs Lathem and her Daughter an only child were poorly, they had been so Some Days, She desird me to pray with them, and so we prayd, and then went to Mr Saunders, and they were Extreemly Glad to see me & I was as glad, near 12 we began the Divine Exercise and there ^was^ a great Number of Peop I Spoke from 2 Cor V. 14. in the Evening had a meeting at Mr Lathems ^from^ Just by, ^&help me^ and there was a large Number of People, and the People attended with great Seriousness this Day, and Especially in the Evening, just before Night went to See a woman that has been ailing a long while and she is in Some Concern of mind, and I believe is Some What Troubled with hypo,[156]—Lodged at Mr Lathems where the meeting was this Evening and was most kindly and tenderly treated and entertaind went to bed Some What late & Slept Comfortably—

Monday Feb^r 20: got up very early and found it very Stormy of Snow, was hear till after Dinner, Mrs Lathem gave me as a present a Pair of Silk Stockings never wore more than two or three Times, the Lord reward her a thousand fold in this Life and in the World to Come—a School mistress Lodgd here also, a very Curtious, understanding and Sociable Discreet woman never was married yet, She is about fourty two years of age we had very agreable & Friendly Conversation together Some Time in the after noon I went to Capt Robert Lathems in the Evening we had a meeting here and it was a Tarable Storm of Rain yet there was a great Number of People, explaind a little upon the 2 to Timo III 10:17 and then we exercised with my Christian Cards, and it was a Solemn Exercise, the minds of many were much Bowed down and a Night I believe they cannot forget Soon, I believe Some of the Texts were fastend in their Minds, after meeting sot up a while, and then I went to bed once more quietly the Lord be Praised for his great goodness to me—

Tuesday Feb^r 21: intend to go home this morning but two men importuned me last Night to have meeting in two Places, where one ^aged^ Woman was very poorly had been So some Time, in the other house an aged man is blind and finally I Concented, about 9: I went of and Stopt a little while at one Mr Lathem^s^ and from there to the House where the meeting is to be the Womans name is Dayball Call took Dinner with them, had Some Conversation With old Lady and she was very ready to

---

154. *Deacon Henry:* Henry Quaquaquid.

155. William Simmons notes that rituals of confession and reconciliation for backsliders were a distinctive practice of some separatist Christian Indian congregations in New England ("Red Yankees," 263).

156. *Hypo:* depression.

give me something of her Experiences and present Exercises, found her a woman of good Experience but She Complains of being in Dar^k^ness—about 12 the People began to get together and the was a Considerable Number of People got together for, a by Place, about about 2 we began the Exercise, and there was Deep attention: I Spoke from Matt VI:10—good Mr Park Avery was with us; directly after meeting I went with one M^r [ ] got to his House near night took Tea with them, and soon after eating, we went to Mr Street and when we got there the People had begun to Collect and there was a great assembly; and Spoke from Rom. VIII.13: and the People attended Seriously many I believe felt the Power of the Word; the People gave Some thing, as they have done in other meetings, but it is Scarce Times for money—Lodgd here, and the People of the Family were exceeding kind and Friendly old and young, went to bed Some What late, Lodged comfortably—

Wednesday Feb^r 22 got up very early, and the Family got up Soon, and we prayd together and tooke Breakfast with the Family, and they were writing out the Cards they had Chosen, about 9 I went of, and just as I was geting Capt Robert Lathem meet me and he turnd right abou^t^ I Stopt Some Time at his House, and then got ready to go of, and the Capt sent Some Tea to my wife, the good Lord Bless this man and his wife, for their kindness to me and mine tooke good leave of them and the woman Mother and the good School Mistress before mentiond, went to the ferry, and went over to the City, and So on home ward got home before Sun Sit—found my Family well as Usual—

Saturday Feb^r 25 about 9 Deacon Henry and I sot off from Home, and went Groton Indian Town, got there Some Time before Sun Sit, just at Widow Pauquinnups, found them all well, and they were very to See us, and we were as glad,—

Sab. Feb^r 26: about 10 the People began to gather, and near 12 we began the Divine Exercise, and there was a large Company of People: I Spoke to them from Matt 17:5 and there was great and Serious among the People, in the Evening we had another meeting and there was greater Solemnity among the People, many were afected I Spoke from XIX.9.—

Monday Feb^r 17: we sot of Soon after Breakfast. We made some Stops, I got home Some Time before Night,—

Sab. March 5: preachd at Mohegan Spoke from Matt VI:6 in the evening from fight the good fight &c[157]

Monday March 6: about 12 sot of from home and went down to New London and so over to groton, went to Capt Robert Lathems he was not at home only his wife, and I Sot there a little while, and then went to Mr Street's and was there Some Time in the Evening and then went back to the Cap^ts and there was a number of People they heard there was to be meeting—Lodgd there—

Tuesday March 7: went towards Mistick Ferry, Calld on Mr Keene the minister of the Place, but he was not and so past on Stopt at Mr Park Averys, a separate minister, and was very kindly receivd, was there but few minutes, Mr Avery was going to Burying and Mr Benjamin Browns, he had lost a Child four Days ago, and is to be buried this Day,—and Mr Avery and I went together we got there just after the meet-

157. Occom's evening preaching selection is from 1 Timothy 6:12.

ing began, Jamima Wilkinson was Speaking; and I coud not get near so as to See her, the People Crouded so, after awhile I got so as to see her, but She did not Speake long She sat down, and there was another and another one after another, I saw and heard ten six Women and four men, Some spoke repeatedly, Jamima got up 3 Times and I spoke & others did so,—after a long Time, they Shook Hands which was a token of conclution of the Exercises of the meetings,[158]—and the Head of the Coffin was opend, and the morners came round the Dead, and ther^e^ was great Lamentation,—and after a While the Corps was Carried out to be Buried a grave was Dug, not more thirty Rods[159] from the House, they Caried a Table to the gra^ve^ and they put the Coffin upon the Table, and the face of the Corps was measured again and it was there Some Time and the Survivers of the deceasd made a Doleful Lamentation again, after a while Judge Potter orderd a Cupple of Stics to be layd a cross the grave and the Coffin was Carefully layd upon it, and they took a long Cords, and run them the strings that were fixt at each of the Coffin, and then they let down the Coffin into the grave, and then 2 or 3 men were orderd by the Judge, to throw the finest Dirt first, and after that the Coarse, and the [word illegible] was to last, and they formd the grave as neatly as a mole,—before they had [got?] done I went a way; got to the Ferry Sun about 2 Hours high, but I coud not hear of my Bear Skin, and I turnd right about, and Stopt a while at Mr John Packers, and was kindly receivd, took dinner with them, soon after eating I went on, got to Mr Avery's in the Dusk of the eveng and Lodged there,

Wednesday March 8: abou^t^ 10: Sot of and went down in the neck to see James Niles but there was no Body at Home,—and I turnd about and went towards the North Calld on Mrs Dayball, and found her better than she had been,—was there a little whi^le^ and went on, Call on good old Mr Adams, from there went Mr Lathems, Two [for?] and at Mr Goodmans, and then went Mr Woods where the meeting is to be this eveng got there near Sun Sit & the People began to Collect Soon, and there was a gr Number of People, and Spoke to them from Exod. 14:13, and there was very good attention,—Lodgd at the Same House, and was kindly entertain'd, Sot up Some Time had agreable Exercise with my Christian Cards with the Family—

Thirdsday March 9: Sot of about 10: Call on Mr Street, was there a while and then went to Capt R. Lathem's, and he was not at Home, and so took leave of the woman, and went down to the Ferry, got over about 12: and so homeward got home a little while before night—

Sab March 12: Went to Capt Kiblers to meeting, and there was a great Number of People, about 12 I began the Divine Exercise, and there a Solemn attention in gener^al^ I Spoke from I Peter IV:7: took Dinner with the Capt, and Soon after Dinner

158. Occom here attends a funeral for a child whose family was affiliated with the Society of Universal Friends, the religious movement begun by visionary Jemima Wilkinson in 1776. The Society of Universal Friends combined elements of New Light Baptist and Quaker belief and practice. During the 1770s and 1780s, the movement was based primarily in Rhode Island and Connecticut, although Wilkinson and some of her followers removed to utopian communities in New York in 1790.

159. *Rod:* see note 101.

I retur^n'd^ home,—in the Evening we had a meeting at Deacon Henrys[160] and there was a Number of White Young People and I Spoke from the Words. Lord teach us to pray[161] and they attended with Seriousness, and there was but very few Indians, Soon after meeting I went Home——-

Tuesday March 14: Went Some Time in the afteroon to Doc^r Jewets,[162] but he was not at Home, and there I Saw Mr Cook, the minester of the Parish, and repremanded me in Sundry things, I did not think he used me as I ought used, by a young minister, I am an old man and looked upon by many as Minister too in the evening went to hear Elder Abel Palmer he Preachd in Mr Josia Mapless, and I was well entertain'd, and there was a great Number of People, Soon after meeting I went Home,—

Saturday March 18: Near 12 went of from Home to Lower part of Canterbury Stopt at Doc^r Marsh's a while, took Dinner them? after eating went on I got to Mr Nathaniel Clark's before Sun Sit and was kindly receivd by the whole family, they were all well but one of his Daughters She was Sick with a Canck^er^,[163] and Sore Throat,—Lodged there—

Sabb: March 19 abou^t^ 9 the People began to Collect Swift, and about 10 we began the Exercise and there was a Prodigious Number of People: I Spoke from Exodo XX:8: in the after noon from Eclesi 1:15 and the People attended with great Solemnity and much afection, especially in the after Noon the assembly was greatly bowed down here I found Brother Sun Summan amongst the multitude,—Dind with Mr Clark in the Evening we went to Mr Jedediah Brewsters & to have a Conference meeting, but there was Such a multitude of People Mr Clark I must preach, and I was obliged to preach I Spoke from Cant V.16: and there was good attention but not so Solemn as in the Day, I Lodgd at the Same House, a Pious Family I believe, they about middle aged Couple—

Monday March 20: was at the House till about 9: then went to Mr Allens, and from there to Mr Winchesters & went with Mrs Winchester She Came to Mr Allens to See me, and was there Some Time and had very agreeable Conversation with the woman especially, Just before I went a way, we exercised with my Notes, & it was agreable—about 12: I went of, went to Mr Smiths, and there we had meeting, and there was a great Number of People and Spoke to them from John 11:28: and there was Seriousness and good attention took Some Victuals after Dinner, and Several Stayd after meeting, & in the Evening we had Note Exercise and it was very afecting to Several, in deed it was a good Evening to us, a Night to be rememberd, I Lodgd at the Same House and kindly entertaind, rested Comfortably

Tuesday March 21: Early in the morning to Mr Smiths to see a woman that has been greatly Troubled with a Cancer, a long while, and Such a Sight as I never did See, one of her arms is Swelled to a Prodigious bigness, they Say it measures 19 inches round some par^t^s of it,—took Breakfast with them, Prayed with them, and then wen^t^ back to Mr Smith's and from thence to Mr Clarks and from thence we went

---

160. *Deacon Henry:* Henry Quaquaquid.
161. See Luke 11:1.
162. *Doc^r Jewets:* David Hibbert Jewett.
163. *Cancker:* cancer, ulcer, or tumor.

[to] Scotland, got to Mr Podin^es^ Just about meeting Time 2 o:c: in the after noon—and we went into the meeting House. and there was not a great Number of People, I Spoke from 1 Peter IV:7 and there was good attention among the People—Soon after meeting we went back to one Mr Joseph Allen and there we had meeting I Spoke from [ ] after Sermon a Number of Young People Stayd to have exercise with Texts of Scripture and it was very Solemn many were deeply affected, and I believe they cant forget the Night, the most careless of them will remember it as long as they live and long ~~le live and longef~~ even to eternity they must carry it,—it was late before we broke up—I Lodgd at the Same House, and Mr Clark went Home—

Wednesday March 22 Some Time in the morning I went of Mr Allen went with me to Mr Clarks, we got there about 10: and I was there a little while and then Mr Clark and I went of to Newent got to Mr Luiss about 12: & the People were Just began to collect, about 1 we began the Exercise & there was a large number of People, I Spoke from 2 Corin V:14 and the People attended with great Seriousness, and I think I had som Sense of Divine things.—took some Victuals Soon after meeting; and then we went to Mr Reeds and there we had an Evening meeting, and there was a considerable Number of People, and I had but a little Sense of things Mr Chace was there a yound Preacher; and the People were in Surprise by an uncommon Northern Lights, there were Streeks of Red and white, most all round and the Points met where the Sun is when it is noon and it frighted Some young People, and after I had done Speaking, a Number Stayd to Exercised with my Tickets[164] and there was a great Solemnity among the People, many were much moved with Solemn affection, and I believe the Night wont be forgot very Soon, and it was late before we left off, and finally we went to Bed Quietly once more

Thirdsday March 23: Some Time after Breakfast, we went down to Norwich Landing, we got there Some Time abou^t^ 12: and I took leave of Mr Clark, and so we par^ted^ in Love, and I went on home ward ~~ward~~ got about 3 in the after Noon and found my family not well Some of them—

Sab, March 26, after Break fast, went to Doc^r Jeremiah Rogers's, to have a meeting I got there a little past 9 and there was but a little Number of People, I began the Service, near 12 and Spoke from 2 Corin V:10 took Dinner with Mrs Rogers for the Doc^r was not at Home and Some Time after Dinner I went home, got Home Some Time before Sun Set, and in the Evening we had meeting at Deacon Henrys and there was but very few People.—

Tuesday March 28: Some Time in the morning sot of from, and went to Mr Griswolds in Northeast par^t^ of Norwich, Mr Lebens Houghton went with me & we got there a bout 12: and I was very kindly receiv'd took Dinner with them and the People Soon began to gether, and about 2 we began the Divine Exercise was a good number of Peop^le^ and I Spoke from Dani [illegible], 19: in the evening 22: verse—and there was good attention; especially in the evening, there was great Solemnity, and flow of Tears—Lodgd at the Same House,—

Wednesday March 29 abou^t^ 9 I went of, and Call on Mr Yelomebester but he was not at Home, was there but few minutes, and past on and Stopt at Brother Downers

---

164. *Tickets:* Occom's "Christian Cards" or "Notes," preprinted with biblical verses.

and he was not at and sot a little while and so past on towards Crank got to Mr Jonathan Treadwa^ys^ and did Business with him, and took dinner with them, and towards I went back, got to Mr Troops about Sun Sit Stopt but a few minutes, and went to Brother Sherrys and he was not at Home and I past on to Brother Downers and was at home I Lodgd there—

Thirdsday March 30: Stay^d^ there till meeting Time and that was about 3 and there was but few People and they attened with much affection, it was a Comfortable meeting—in the evg went Sherrys and Lodged there,—

Fryday March 31: got up very early, and went of and I got home about half after 9.—

Sab: April 2: I was to have gone Yesterday to lower part of Groton, to preach at Mr Gidi Saunderss, but a Sevier Storm came on about 10.0:c and it Continued till about 10 this Day very Seveer with a Tarable hard wind, and Snow flew extreamly, and very uncomfortable; and so contented myself quietly at Hom,—last Night I had a remarkable Dream about Mr Whitefield, I thought he was preaching as he use to, when he was alive, I thought he was at a certain place where there was a great Number of Indians and Some White People—and I had been Preaching, and he came to me, and took hold of my wright Hand and he put his face to my face, and rub'd his face to mine and Said,—I am glad that you preach the Excellency of Jesus Christ yet, and Said, go on and the Lord be with thee, we Shall now Soon done. and then he Stretchd himself upon the ground flat on his face and reachd his hands forward, and mad a mark with his Hand, and Said I will out doe and over reach all Sinners, and I thought he Barked like a Dog, with a Thundering Voice—and I thought Some People Laughd Some were pleased, and some were frighted,. and after that he got up, Said to me I am going to Mr Potters to preach and Said will you go, and I Said yes Sir—and as we were about to Sit out I awoke, and behold it was a Dream—and this Drea^m^ has put me much upon thinking of the End of my Journey.

Sab April 9: Preachd at Deacon Henrys[165] and there was a great Company of White Young People, and some old, and but few Indians. I Spoke from 1 Croni 16:34 and there was much affection amongst the Christians—I in the evening we had another meeting in Henry again, and it was a Comfortable Time, I did not preach, only gave a word of Exhortation—

April 12: Wednesday I went towards Lyme where widow Mercy Uncas had lost a Child, it died Tuesday, got there about 4 o:c in the after Noon, and they got ready to go to Mohegan with the Corps Sun about a Hour high at Night, and I sot of for Home, got Home about 10—

Saturday April 15: Went from Home to Groton Indian Town, got there towards night put up Widow Samsons & them all well, and in the Evening we had a meeting Robert Ashpo was there and there was a considerable Number of People, and we had a Comfortable meeting I Said but little, I was poorly Sot up late, and went to bed at last quietly—

Sabb: April 16, Soon after Breakfast went to one Mr Barns, about 3 miles Sou^th^ from the Indian Town, got there Some Time before 10: & a great Number of People

---

165. *Deacon Henry:* Henry Quaquaquid.

collected together, and I Spoke from Hebr 11:6: and there was very Serious attention and many Indians were there, directly after meeting took Dinner, and as Soon as I rose from Table, I went to another Mr Barnss near Lanthron Hill, and there was a great congregation, both Indians and English, and I Spoke from Eccle: 1:15 and I believe power of the Word fell heavy upon the People there was flow of Tears, the People attended, like Criminals under Sentance. Soon after meeting, I went with a number of Indians, to Groton Indian Town, and in the Evening had a meeting, I Spoke from Jerem 8:6

Monday April 17: in the morning went to See a molato girl, and found her very Sick, and she was very Stuped, and there was a number of Indians, we sung and prayd, and then went back, Call at a House where John Coopper was, he Signified to groton Indians he wanted to [meet] up with them, and they appointed a Time when they meet—then went to Susanna Charles—took Dinner there and then we went to Mr Isaac Stanton's and had a meeting there, and there was a great Number of People for a Week day, good many Indians were there,—I Spoke from Luke XIII, 6–9 and it was a Solemn Season, after I had done the People, the People woud not go, they Seem to want to hear more one Mr Brown Spoke Some yet after he had done, they Sot Still, and we Sung a again, and after a while the People moved out, and I returnd to the Ind Town again, it was too near Night for me to go home, and I did not feel well, Lodged at Widow Samson again, and we Sot up Some Time,—

Tuesday April 18: got up very early, and went on homeward, got home about 10: and found all my Family in Comfortable State of Health Thanks be to god—

Wednesday April 19: was a fast Day I went to Mrs Fitch, and preachd there and there was a great Nr of People, I Spoke from II Chron XV:12 13 and it was a Solemn Day with us, the People attended with great attention—in the after Noon went to Mr Post's at Weems Hill, and preachd there, and there was many People, I Spoke from Jerem VIII 6 and the Peop attended Well; Soon after meeting took Dinner with them, and after that I went homward, Calld at Widow Fitchs Sot a little while, and then went on got hom in the Dusk of the Evening—

Fryday April 21: about 12 left home and went down to New London, from thence to Groton, got over the ferry about Sun Set, and went on to Capt Robert Lathem's, found them well, Sot a few minutes and went to Mr Streets, found them all well also,—and was kindly receiv'd, and Lodged there—

Saturday April 22 Some Time after Breakfast I sat of to go to Pauquawnunk to See James Niles; Call'd at Mr Goodman's—Stayd a While, Prayd with M^rs goodman She was put to bed by 2 or 3 Days back,—and then went on,—Calld also at Mrs Dayballs, about 10. I got to Jamess and he was not at Home, and Some Time in the after noon he came home, they were all well, & towards Night I went of again and went to Mr Saund^ers^ got there Just at night, and found them well, but the old gentleman, he had sadly Cut three of his Toes, one Just off hangs on a Skin—Lodgd there, was very kindly Treatd

Sabb. April 23: about 9 the People began to Collect, and it was Some What Dull weather yet there was a great Number of People, and I spoke to them from 2 Kings 20.1: and the People attended Solemnly, in the after noon Spoke from 2 Cron. XV.012 13 and there was greater attention in the afternoon,—in the evening Preach^d^ at

Mr Woods House, and there was a prodigious Number of People, and I Spoke from Psal 37:34, and the People attended with all gravity, Lodgd at the Same House, and was extreamly well entertaind—

Monday: April 24: after Breakfast Sot a while, and it Rainy Still, about 8: went to Mr Streets and presently the People began to gather and about 10 we began the Divine exercise and there was Considerable Number of People, and Preachd from Heb 3:19 and there was a remarkable Solemnity, and flow of afection among the People, I believe they will not forget the meeting very Soon—after meeting took Dinner, and then took good leave of the Family, and parted in Peace Love and Friendship. Calld at Capt R. Lathems but he was not at Home, Sot a few minutes & then took good leave of Mrs Lathem, and went on to the Ferry Soon got Over, and so on, got home near Sun Set, found my poor Family in good Health, Thanks be to god for his goodness to us—

Tuesday April 25 was abou^t^ my Domistic affairs, Just before Night, I went over to one Mr Babcocks over the River in Norwich, Jamime and Unice Occom went over with me, and there we had a very melting and Comfortable meeting, there was a Considerable Number of People for a Wet and Dark Night—We Lodgd at the Same House Spoke from Psalm CL:6, We sot up very late—

Wednesday April 26. got up very early, and went over Mr Benjamin Story Sot us over; and I got Home Sot about and Hour and half high Thanks be to Heaven—

[Courtesy of the New London County Historical Society]

∾ JOURNAL 16

June 26, 1786–December 10, 1786

Occom returns to Oneida territory, reaching Brotherton on July 7. For five months, he visits, ministers, and counsels with the people of Brotherton and New Stockbridge, as emigration from Mohegan, Montaukett, Narragansett, and Farmington continues. Occom doctors injured residents; conducts funeral services, baptisms, and religious meetings; and, despite a crippling back injury, hunts, fishes, and harvests ginseng with the people. Traditional Oneida attend some of his services; their appearance, Occom records, reminds him of "the old Britains in their Heathenism." From October 16 to 18, Occom, David Fowler, and fourteen other town elders meet in council with the Oneida to discuss the allotment of a bounded plot for Brotherton within Oneida territory; the Oneidas encourage the New England tribes to live at large on their lands rather than claim a bounded township. Occom departs for Mohegan on November 9, visiting Albany and several Dutch settlements on his way home. The Dutch, he observes, have been unjustly judged by both the English and by Native peoples as "Careless" and "profane," but are in fact "really hungry after the Word of God."

Monday June 26: Some Time in the morning I went over the River, and rid down the River, Call'd at Mr Cragues, and he was not at Home, but M^rs was at Home, and She knew me and was glad to See me, and I was glad to See her after She told me whose

Daughter She was, for I had been to her Fathers House in Blooming grove, many yrs back, When she was a little girl, and She Showd me a Book, Which I gave her, at her Fathers House. She is a prety little, handsome discreet Woman and talkd very Sensible; Sot there a While, and then went on got to Mr Vedders Some Time about 12 and there I took Din^r with them, old Mrs Vedder & her Daughter Molley Came to me at her Sons Soon after I got there, and after a while the old gentleman Came, and we Sot together all the after noon, Just at Night I went with the old Lady to her House and there I Lodged and was kindly entertaind they are Dutch, and exceeding agreable Family, old and Young a Christian Like Family—

Tuesday June 27: It began to rain about Break of Day it rain'd till near Noon and as Soon as it [Slutchd?], I went on to Esqr Harper's at Hunter, got there about 12 and about 2: We Went to ^meet^ at fort Huntter and there was but few People; and I Spoke from John 12:[ ] and after meeting went with Esqr Harper and Lodged there again—

Wednesday June 28: Some Time after Breakfast, Went to the River, and Went over at Mr Wasaps, and the River was ~~quite low~~ ^higher^, rid over very well for all Went down on the North Side; ~~Capt Craye~~ ^not^ Calld at the Door of Mr Young Vedder and So past on, and Stopt at a Tavern and while I was there I discover'd my Son Anthony[166] and his Family John Tuhy with them in a Connoo goining up the River and so went down to the R and they Stopt a few minutes and past on, and I went back to the House, and got up my mare and went back and Stopt a While at Mr Vedder and they past on, Just at at Night I Went over the River and directd my Course Southw and it was Just Night, and a lit way, I calld a Certain House to enquire the Way to one Esqr Mr Masters and desired ^me^ to Stay and I eccepted his kind offer, his name was M^r [ ] and was kindly treated found them very agreeable People Went to Bed Soon—

Thirdsday June 29: got up very Early, and it was very Lowerry[167] and it began to rain Soon, and after Breakfast, I Sot out, and got almost to the House where I was to preach, and I was informd that they had not heard of any meeting appointed, and I turnd right about, and went back to the northward,—Call on Capt Crague, and he was at home and I Dind with them, the Capt is very agreable man, this is the man that was killd at Fort Standwix in the last war,[168] he was Shott, by an Indian, thro the back Tomy Hawked on the Head, and Scalp'd. Yet is a live and well, and is as likely to live to the Common age of man as any man.—Soon after Dinner I went on again, and I over took my Folks Just before Sun Set near Major Fundee's and I went over the River there, and went on to Esqr Maybees and there I lodgd, and they were

166. *my Son Anthony:* Anthony Paul.

167. *lowery:* gloomy, cloudy.

168. During the Seven Years' War, the British built Fort Stanwix at the Oneida Carrying Place, a centuries-old site of political and commercial exchange and treaty-making crucial to the Iroquois Confederacy. Fort Stanwix was renamed Fort Schuyler during the American War of Independence. Oneida and American militia defended the fort during a British siege led by St. Leger in 1777. In October 1784, Fort Stanwix was the site of an important treaty negotiation between the Six Nations and the United States that affirmed the rights of the Oneida and Tuscarora to inhabit their traditional territories.

glad to See me and I took Supper with them & after Supper Went to bed once more quiely—

Fryday June 30 Was at Esqʳ MayBe, till after Dinner and then I went of to go to B mans Creek, got to Esqʳ Kembel, Some Time before N. and was kindly receivd by them, and Lodged there—

*Saturday ^July 1^* was at the Esqʳˢ till about 10 and then I went to see a Remarkable Spring about 3 miles of got there Soon, tho it was a very bad way, and it was amazing Sight to me, it is Sulferous it Boils right out at a bottom of a mountain, Close by a little Creek, the hole is near as big as a Barel's head, and it makes all the Stones are White with Brim Stone, I drank of the Water & it has very ugly taste and it is Cold as Ice, all the poor Toads that come to the water dies—I Scraped Some of the Brimstone of the Stone, and put in Paper, and I Carried it to Esqʳ Kimbels I put on a cold of Fire and it Burnt and Smelt like B, after a while I returnd to the Place, and this Night I Lodgd at one Mʳ John Whites and was kindly treated—

Sabb July 2, about 9 went to meeting at Mʳ [ ] Barn and there was a great Numb of People, I Spoke from [ ] and the People attended with great Solemnity and affection—Soon after meeting I took Dinner, and then went of Springfield got there Sun about two hours high, the People had been waiting for me, and had just dispersd, and they gave out word directly that I woud preach, and they immediately Collected, in a Certain Dutch M House, and there was a large Number of People, and I Spoke from Eclesi 1.15 and there was a deep attention among the People, after meeting I went home with two Mʳ Winters, two Brothers Youngerly folks, all have a hope of Expermental Religion,[169] and they talk and appear as Such—

Monday July 3, took Breakfast early, and Soon after went to meeting, to a Certain House in the Woods and there was a large Collection of People, we began the Exercise a little after nine I Spoke from the Words What think ye of Christ[170]—and there was an affectionate melting attention amongst the People & Soon after meeting, I Baptised three Children, one by the Name of Joseph ~~and the~~ ^Mʳ Nahapas Piohits son^ the Children Mʳ Griffen Hanna ^~~and Mr. Miller~~^ I [word illegible] Isaac then I went home with Mʳ Griffen (and Baptised another for Mʳ Griffin), took Dinner with them, and soon after eating, I Sot of for the German flats. Got to Mʳ Conrad Fols after Sun Sun Sit Some Time, and there I Lodged & had Comfortable rest—

Tuesday July 4 Went to see my folks at Mʳ Tygut's and Wednesday was there yet.—

Thirdsday July 6 in the morning Some Time We Sot of to go thro the Woods, near 12 We reached at [word illegible] we turnd out our Horses and my Mare run away and we were obligd to Stay there all Night, we Coud not find her,—*Fryday July 7:* We went of pretty early, and got to our Settlement Some Time in the afternoon, and we were glad to See one another, but many of our People were gone a way ^to^ Seek after provisions, for food is very Scarce—

---

169. *experimental religion:* denotes the New Light belief that experience, or the heart, rather than intellection, or the mind, is the proper theater of conversion.
170. See Matthew 22:42. Occom preached frequently from this scripture throughout his career. Three sermons on this scripture appear in this volume.

Saturday July 8: Anthony[171] and James Fowler Waucus went after my mare—

Sabb. July 9: we met together at Abraham Simon's There was but few of our folks and good many Stocbridgers were with us. I spoke from Cron Rom viii and there was good attention amongst the People—

Monday July 10: In the evening Anthony and James Came back without my mare, They found her in a mire, Dead, Sunk almost all over, there is the end of her.—

Fryday July 14 Andrew Corricomb had a Son Born[172]

Sabb July 16, Preachd at Brother David Fowler's. Spoke from Matt, Jesus Cried[173] and from Romans, if god be for us &c[174] most of our People were there and a great number of Stocbridgers, and there was great and Solemn attention—

Sabb July 23 went from Roger Wauby's to the Town of Stockbridgers, and many of our People went and we had a large Assembly. Mr Dean and four with him Came to meeting they live about Six miles of, and I spoke from Matt vi:9: and Psalm 133:1, and the People attended Well. We had a Shower just as meeting was Concluded and we Sot till it was over and that was Soon, and then we pusht on homeward, I got Jacob Fowler's about Sun Set, and I was Some What woried—

Sabb July the 30 About 9 I went to Brother Davids & there I preachd, and many of the Stockbridgers were there and four young Onoyda men were there, and were drest Compleat in Indian way they Shind with Silver, they had large Clasps about their arms, one had two Jewels in his Nose, and had a large Silver half moon on his Breast; and Bells about their Legs, & their heads were powderd up quite Stiff with red paint, and one of them was White as any white man and gray Eyes, his appearance made me think of the old Britains in their Heatheism.—I spoke from Hosea xiii:9: & [two words crossed out] Eclesi xii.1 and there was great attention among the people, after meeting the Singers sung some Time and then we all dispersd—

Monday July 31 a number of us Went to the Flats, we got there before night, and I put up at Mr Conrod Fols, Tuesday was at the place all Day—

Wednesday, Augst 2 Sun about two hours high we Sot again for hom, and got home Just about Sun down, all well, and found our Folks well. Thanks be to god.—

Sabb ^Augt^ 6. Preach'd at Jacob Fowlers in fore Noon, and there was but few People it was rainy morning.—In the after Noon we went to David Fowlers, and there was a large number of People. Several of the Stockbridgers Came, I Spoke from Rom II.28.29: & Luke xvi.13—and the People attended well. in the evening I returned again to Brother Jacob—

Tuesday, Augt 8: Some Time in the morning I went to Fishing at Orisco Creak, and I catchd 5 Doz^n and five Salmon Trouts,—and Just at Night I removd to Brother David Fowlers to Stay a While,—

Saturday Augt 12 In the after Noon I Sot out for Stockbridgers, Stopt awhile at Roger Waubys took Dinner there, and after eating, went on, got to the Place Some Time before Night, Lodgd at Sir Peter Paukquunnppeats—

171. *Anthony:* Anthony Paul.

172. According to Love (*Occom*), this is Thomas Corricomb (340).

173. See Matthew 27:46.

174. See Romans 8:31.

Sabb Augt 13: About 10 we began the holy Exercise at the House of Jacob Cunk-cuppot,[175] and there a large Collection of People, Some White people,—I spoke from Jerem [XXXV?] 14 in the after noon from Luke X.42 and the People attended with great Solemnity, and with Some affection; and it ^it^ was a Rainy after noon, I Lodgd again at Sir Peters—

Monday Augt 14: got up very early, and Sot of for Brotherton,—Stopt at Roger Waubys, and took Breakfast and Soon after eatg I went on again: got at Brother Davids abot 10 & found them all well—

Wednesday Augt 16: Towards Night, the Young People came together at Jacob Fowlers to receive Instruction; and I gave them a Short Discourse from Proverbs IV 13: and they attended exceeding Well, they behaved becomingly, and were Solemn, and there was Some affection, with Tears, after I had Spoke and Prayd I orderd them to Sing, and they Sung three Times, with great Decency and Solemnity, and as they were going out, Elyjah Wimpy ^first^ gave me thanks, and all manifested thankful-ness; The Lord Bless them, and give them teachable Hearts, that they be Wise unto eternal Salva

Sabb Augt 20: Went to David Fowlers Some What early, and about 10 began the Holy Service, and there was a large Number of People many Stockbridgers came and there were four out of Mr Deans Family, and [one] more what man,—I Spoke from Luke ii:10:11 and Psalm XXXI:1 and there was great and Solemn attention in the As-sembly; after meeting our People Stay'd Some and Psalms—near Sun Set I went down to Brother Jacobs, and to bed Soon and rested quietly once more—

Wednesday Augt 23 Towards Night the Young People came to Jacob Fowlers, to receive instruction; and I Spoke to them from Prover^b [ ] a little Whi and then we Prayd, and after Prayer, I Exercised with my Christian Cards with them, and they were agreable to them, and they were Awd with the Various Texts of Scripture, and I believe they will not forget the evening Very Soon, there was one Stockbridge Girl Came on purpose, and there was one English Girl, and they also Chose each of em a Text; and they Concluded with singing Several Tunes, and the whole was Caried on with Decency, & Solemnity—

Sabb. Augt 27 Had a meeting at Abraham Simons on acount of his Wife's Sick-ness; he was not at Home, he has been gone five weeks tomorrow,—There was a great Number of People, a number of Stockbridgers was there, and two white Men from the New Town. I spoke from Gene. xxii.12 and in the after Noon from John iii.16 & I believe we had the Presence of God with us, there was uncommon attention, and great Solemnity and many Tears flowd down the Cheeks of many; after meeting a Number of Singers went to Jacob Fowlers and Sung a While, and then we Prayd & so every one ^went^ Home Soberly & quietly—

Wednesday Augt 30 Soon after Breakfast thirteen of us Sot out into the Woods, they went after Ginshang Roots,[176] and I was going to Mr James Dean's, we travild together about 3 Miles, and there they incamped made up great Fire, and soon after

---

175. *Jacob Cunkcuppot:* Jacob Konkapot.
176. On ginseng, see note 133.

I went on, Sister Hannah Fowler went with me, and then we went thro' a Hedious Wilderness for three or four miles. we had only markd Trees to go by, and there was but very poor Trac We arrivd to Mr Deans Some Time in the after noon, found them all Well, and we were receivd with all kindness, and that ~~Evening~~ at Sundown Brother David Came runing in pufing and Blowing and all of a fome with Sweat, he had treed a couple of Racoons and he for a gun, ^and one young man^ and went right back; and Some Time in the [word missing] he Came in with one Racoon—

Thirsday Augt 31 about 11, we took leave of the Fa and went to New Stock-bridge—got there Some Time in the after noon, we Calld on Sir Peter Paukquunnu-peat & I put up there,—

Fryday Sepr 1: Som Time in the after noon, we had a meeting, and I spoke from Psalm 32:9 and there was very good attention—I the evening they got together to Sing, and after Singing, we had exercise with Christian Cards, and it was new them and very agreeable, they attended with great solemnity, but all did not draw that intended to draw. it grew late, and so we broak up.—

Saturday Sepr 2: I was at the Place all Day long. I Visited Some Families, as I did yesterday, in the evening we met together again to go thro' the Exercise we began the last Night, with my Christian Cards, and it was very agreeable, Some were much affected, We Concluded with Singing a Psalm—

Sabb: Sepr 3. About 10 we began the Divine worship of god and there was a great number of People for this wilderness, Some White People—I spoke from Matt xi.12 and I Kings XIX.13 and I be the Lord was present with us, I Some sense of the great things I delivering, and I believe many felt the Power of the Word, for there was great Solemnity, and Auful Atention thro the Asembly, many Tears flowd from many Eyes,—as soon as the meeting was done I went Home with our People, we got Home Just before Sun Sit; and our Singers got together and they Sung some Time, we had some new Comers at the singing meeting,—Last Saturday 13 of our People came to our Place to Settle, a Family from Mohegan & a Family from Montauk and some from Narganset and one from Farmington—

Wednesday Sepr 6: towards Night I attended upon our Young People, and ten Stockbridgers Came to the meeting old and Young, and many of our old People Came too. We begun with Singing, and then Prayd, after Prayer the Young People rehearsed the Texts and Verses they had Chosen at our Second Meeting, and they Were Very Solemn, and when they had done, I began a Discourse with them, from I Timothy, VI.19 and it was a solemn Time with the People, many were much affected. Concluded with Prayer and Singing.—

Sabb Sepr 10 In the morning we went Abraham Simons to meeting, began about 10 and there was a great number of People, many from Stockbridge, and we had to White men at the meeting, they were going to Niegara from Johns Town, and there was a Solemn attention thro' the Asembly. I spoke from Matt IX. In the after noon we went to David Fowlers, and I Spoke from Job XXI.14, 15 and there was greater attention many affected deeply, after meeting the Singrs Stopt and Sung Some Time and concluded with Prayer and so we parted—

Monday Sepr 11. I went down to the German Flats. Young Elijah Wympy & I went together, we got thro Just before Sun Sit, and I put up at my good Friends Mr Conrod

Fols, was Some Waried and went to bed soon but had uncomfortable Nt of it there were so many Vir^n177

Tuesday Sepr 12. got up Very early, and it was very Lowery and so did not Sot out So Soon as I intended, took Breakfast, and about 10 I Sot out for Springfield, and just before I got to the Place I mist my way, got to South West of the Place good ways and towards Night it began to be Lowerry, and just at Night, I calld at a Certain House, to of the way, and it began to rain, and askd me Whether I Might Stay there and I thankd him told I Woud and so I Stayd; took Supper with them,—and Went to bed Soon, and had Comfortable rest,—

Wednesday Sepr 13 Got up very early and got ready and they woud had me Stayd to take Breakfast with them but I told them I wou'd take it another Time.—The man's Name is Mr Nicholas Lowe they were very kind to me the man had heard me at New York about 20 years back. So tooke good leave of them and went on my way. got to the Place about 9 and Calld on Mr Winters but they were not at Home, the Women were at Home, and they got me Breakfast, they were exceeding kind,—and from thence I went to Mr Griffins, and was there till near Sun Sit, and then I went to Mr Stansels where a meeting was apointed, and there was a large Number of People Collected together, and I Spoke from Rom. ii. 28–29: and the People attended with all gravity and believe Some felt the Power and Love of God,—I Stayd at the Same House, it is a Dutch Family and there is one young man in this House, Very Remarkable in Religion. he is a living Christian I believe is not ashamed of his Lord and Master, he was Converted last Winter, and he is much oppos'd by the most of the Family, Yet he keeps on—he and I Lodg'd together this night, after we had a long Conversation in the Family; I was Treated well by the whole Family, Rested Comfortably—

Thirdsday Sepr 14 and Fry^d was at the place Went to See Some Families, Lodg'd once at Mr Dicks and once at Mr Crippins—

Saturday Sepr 16 Just after Dinner we went to one Mr Nicholas Pickards where the Christian People were to have a Conference meeting, the People collected Some Time in the after Noon, and they began by Prayer and Sung, and they began to relate their Experiences, and there were 12 men and three women, that related the work of god on their Souls and it took them till near Mid Night, and it was the most agreable meeting that ever I was at, there were several Nations and Denominations & yet all harmonious, there was no Jar amongst them, but Peace and Love, there experiences were acording to the Doctrines of the gospel,—I Lodg'd at the same House & was very kindly entertaining the man is a Dutchman & his is Ireish woman, and both I believe were Sincere Christians—

Sabb Sepr 17: Near 10 we went to meeting, at old Mr Pickards in his New House only Coverd over head, and there was a Prodigious Number of People and I spoke from Acts XI.26. in the after Noon from the last Psa and the last Verse^178—after meetg went to Deacon Childs, and in the Evening a number of young People came to the House to receive Instruction, and I spoke to them from some passage of Scrip-

177. *Vir^n:* Vermin; probably bedbugs or fleas.
178. See Psalms 150:6.

ture, and after that we had Exercise with my Notes, and there was great Solemnity amongst them, they were most all Dutch People they Stayd late—

Monday Sepr 18: It was a Rainy Day, and I did not Sit out, towards Night I went to Mr Pickards from Mr Crippens. Mr Nicholas Pickard went with me, the old gentleman and his wife received me with all kindness—and in the evenig the Young People Came together again for Instruction, and I spoke to them the words Remember thy Creator &c[179] and after that we had Exercise With my Cards again, and the People were much solemnised, We Sot up somewhat late again, I rested Comfortably once more—

Tusday Sepr 19: got up early, and got Breakfast and then sot off, and got to Mr Fols just after Sun Set, Went to Bed Soon—

Wednesday Sepr 20 Sot of Some What early, old Wimpy went with me and we got thro before Night we overtook a num of Stockbridgers just Come from there old settlement, found our Folks well—

Sabb Sepr 24 Had a meeting in David Fowlers Barn, and there was a large number of People Collected. great many from old Town,—the bigest Assembly we have had Since I Came to this Place. I Spoke from I Corin VII 29.30.31: & Acts xvi.28, and I believe we had the presence of god with us many were deeply affected there was flow of Tears from many Eyes,—in the evening the Singers went to Jacob Fowlers to Sing, and I went there too, and they Sung near two Hours and then gave them a word of Exhortation and prayd, and things were done decently and in order, and so we parted once more in Peace and Love, I Went back to Brother Davids and Soon went to bed quietly once more. The Lord be Praised—

Monday Sepr 25 Sot of about mid Day for old Town. David went with me in order to the Lake to Fishing,—Lodgd at Widow Quinnys,—

Tuesday Sepr 26, I did not feel well, and it looked like for Storm, and so we returnd back got home Some time before noon—

Fryday Sepr 28: in the morning went to Stockbridgers, and toward Night Preachd a Discourse to them I Spoke from Gala VI 15 and there was great Solemnity in the Congregation—Lodgd at Sir Peters—

Sabath, Octo^r 1: Had our meeting in Jacob Concoppots[180] and there was a Prodigious large Congregation for this Wilderness, Some White People—I spoke from Psalm 58:[5?]: in the afternoon from Ezek xxxii:11 and we had an Awfull solemnity in the asembly, there was a Shower Tears, I felt Bowels of Compassion towards my poor Brethren; in the Evening the Stockbridgers met at Sir Peters, and they rehearsed what they heard in the Day, and they were Very Solemn; at the end of their rehearsal, Sir Peter Pohquunnuppeet made a Confession of his Wanderings from God, and Askd the Peoples forgiveness, and he was very Solemn, and the People received him in their Charity—

Wednesday Octr 4: had a meeting with our Young People, and there was many old People also,—I Spoke from Prover XXII.1 and there was uncommon attention amongst the People, Especially the Young People—

179. See Ecclesiastes 12:1.
180. *Jacob Concoppot:* Jacob Konkapot

Saturd morning Sep^r [October] 6: after the reading a Chap^r I took notice of Some Passages and Spoke to the Family, and there was a Solemn attention, and then I attempted to Pray and I had an awful Sense of ~~our~~ ^the^ Miserable Situation of mankind, and the goodness of God Which melted down my Soul before God, and there was much affection in the Family,—

Sabb Octo^r 7: Had a meeting in Brother Davids & there was but a little number of People by reason of the Uncommon Floods in all the Creeks, and on the Land, most of the Bridges were Carried off, for it had been Raining Several Days last week; and it Rains yet; Some Stockbridgers Came to meeting for all ~~all~~ the dreadful Traviling. there five women and four men. I spoke from I [word missing] XL 22. and I think I had an Auful Sense of the Deplorable State of Sinful race of Adam, and Some Sense of the greatness and goodness of God, and there was an Auful attention and flow of Tears—in the afternoon I Spoke from Gene XXIV.58: and there was again a moving among the People: I hope they will not soon forget the Day.—In the evening they sung at Davids, and after Singing I spoke to the young People in particular, and they were greatly bowed down before the word. Some were deeply affected; and it was some before we broak up the meeting, and they went home with Solemnity,—

Wednesday Octr 11: towards Night had a meeting with the Young People, and we had Exercise with Christian Cards out of the old Testam^t and there was an uncommon affection amongst them, I believe there was Scarcely one but what was Some What moved, and old People were moved too,—We Sung a little after the Exercise— and So parted—

Sabb Octr 15 Had a meeting in Brother David Fowlers and there was a great Number of People, and we had a Solemn Meeting, I Spoke from Matt 5 and

Monday Octo^r 16: a number of us, I think Sixteen, all men, went to New-Town to have a Treaty with the Onieda we had Calld them to our Town but they to ^chuse^ to have us Come to their Town, and we drove one Creature to them to kill we got there after Sun Sit went directly to the Councell House, David and I Lodgd there, and there rest were ordered elsewhere. I had but poor rest all Night, they have too many Vermine for me—

Tuesday Octo^r 17: Some Time in the after noon, were Calld to appear before the Councell, and we were permitted to speak for our Selves,—and we related the Whole of our transactions with them about the Land they gave us—for they had a notion to take it back again last Summer, and only allow one mile Square which we utterly refusd, and ~~when~~ we ~~had~~ [word illegible] not got thro that Day, and we were dismist in the evening, we all went together in a Certain House to Sing and Pray together, & after prayers ^B^ David and I Back to the Councell House to Lodge—

Wednesday Octo^r 18 Near mid Day we were Calld again to the Councell, and we resumed our relation and soon finishd and then we went out, and were Calld again Soon, and they began to rehearse we had deliverd, and they Said it was all good and True, and then they made a New offer to us, to live in the Same Spot of Ground, but to be bound by any Bounds, but live at large with them on their Land, Which we refusd, and we told them we Chuse to bounded, and they had bound us allread, all most all round, and we wanted only to be bound alround where we were, and they took it under Consideration,—[181]

Thirdsday Oct' 19: We wer Calld again We received the News of the Death of our oldest man in our Town, old uncle Cornelius, Dead the evening before, and so we were obligd to Drop our Business, and went homeward; I stopd at old T Lodged at Sir Peter Pohqun—

Fryday Oct' 20. I went off early, to our Town about 10: Towards Night we all to the House of mourning and I deliver a short Discourse from [word missing] xxxix.4.5. and from thence went to the grave, and we finished Buriing after Sun Sit and I went home—

Saturday Oct' 21: Soon after Breakfast, Sot of for old Town Sally Skeesuck and I went together got there before Noon, I Sot a while in Widow Quinnee and then went to Sir Peters— and was there a While, and there Came a man, and brought a Maloncholy word; Concerning Sally, as she was returning and had Just got out of the Town the Mare got a fit of kicking up her heels, and Crouded up against a fence, and She fell Backward, and broak her right Arm; I went directly to See her and found her in great Misery, we Splinted up her arm and So left in the evening, went again to See her, and She was in great Pains, and I tryd to bleed her but I Coud not make out

Sabb Oct' 22, at Usual Time went to meeting and our Folks had Just Come and most of them Went back to try to Carry home Salley, the assemble was not so large as Usual by reason of the above mentiond accident. And I spoke from 1 Corn X.21 in the after noon from Matt III:11 and there was most solid attention thro the Day, I Baptized Sir Peters Wife and Child,—In the evening a Number of em met at Sir Peters, and there were 9: or 10 Manifested their Exercises of Mind. they never were so awake^n^d about their Souls affairs as they are now, there never was So many men brought to Such Consideration as they are now, they Confest they have been are Vile Sinners, and determine by the help of god, to turn from their evel ways and Seek God, They say, they it is by hearing me Preach to them; one old Woman Said, She had Some thoughts about Religion, and was Baptizd Some time ago, and She thought it was well enough with her, till she heard me, She thinks now, She never has met with any thing, and she thinks it is a gone Case with her; I gave her encouragement to press forward if at eleven Hour with her, She may yet Come in—We Sot up a long while at last we broke up, and I went to bed Soon,—

181. On October 4, 1774, the Oneida granted a bounded plot of about six square miles to the Brotherton tribes. The grant, which identified specific geographical boundaries to the Brotherton allotment, was recorded by Guy Johnson, superintendent of North American Indian affairs. (Its full text appears in L. Murray, *To Do Good,* 242–243.) After the American War of Independence brought tremendous upheaval and destruction to Oneida, the tribe was besieged by new pressures from the state of New York and white settlers to obtain their territory. Oneida clans resolved to stop selling their lands after the Treaty of Fort Stanwix, in 1784. Still, encroachment and land loss continued at a staggering rate, due to aggressive actions by the State of New York—which flouted the new federal government's assertion that only Congress had the power to treat with tribes—at the Treaty of Fort Herkimer (1785) and the Treaty of Fort Schuyler (1788). Crucial land cessions were encouraged by the Rev. Samuel Kirkland, a Presbyterian missionary among the Oneida.

Monday Oct' 23 A little past Noon four of our men Came to old Town on their way to New Town, and I sot of with them directly, and we got there Just before Sun Sit, and the Councell was then sitting, and were orderd to a certain House, and in the Dusk of the evening of the evening we were Calld, and after we Sot there good While they read their Speech and Conclusion, and it was if did not accept of their offer they would take the Land back again, and we woud not accept of their offer, it was take the Land at large without any bounds.—[182]

Tuesday Oct' 24 our men went to [Caunserake?] to Fishing, and I Sot of for home, Stopt at the old Town, and intended to pass along, but they desired me to Stay to have a meeting in the Evening, and I consented; in the evening they Collected together I believe most all the old People, and many Young P. I Expound upon II Corin.xiii:[11] and there was deep attention with flow of Tears, after I had done two or three spoke in their own Tongue[183] reharsing what I had deliverd, and their Chief man askd me as I was about to leave them, how they Shoud go on in their religious Concerns, and I told them as they were not formed into Church State, they Shoud enter into Christian Fellowship and put themselves under Watch care of one another, and Cary on the public Worship of god in Singing Praying and reading of the word of God, and some Exhortation, and some Explination of the Word of God and maintain family Worship Constantly—

Wednesday Oct' 25. Some Time in the morning I left old Town and went to our Town, got there a little before noon, and found Davids[184] Family well, but one Child was unwell, but not very sick—

Saturday Oct' 28: Our People pretended to have a converence meeting, but one man who was most Concernd in the meeting did not Come, and so they did nothing,

182. This 1786 meeting between the Oneida and the Brotherton tribes reflects Oneida efforts to consolidate and protect their territory in a context of extreme instability, encroachment, and land loss. Their request that Brotherton people relinquish specifically bounded plots and "live at large" on Oneida territory may indicate that the Oneida believed that bounded lands such as those allotted to Brotherton residents were particularly vulnerable to white purchase, leasing, squatting, seizure for debt repayment, seizure for fine repayment, and the whole range of paralegal and extralegal techniques employed by white settlers to take Indian lands. Additionally, Oneida historian Anthony Wonderley suggests that the Oneida may have renegotiated their land allotments to Brotherton as a consequence of the Brotherton settlers' retreat from Oneida territory during the war and their failure to stand with and fight alongside the Oneida (Wonderley, "Brothertown," 475-476). See also Love, *Occom*, 285–287. On Oneida land controversies and treaties, see Lehman; Wonderley, "Brothertown"; Hauptman, *Conspiracy*; Campisi and Hauptman; Hauptman and McLester. The Brotherton rejection of the Oneida proposal to "live at large" on their territory demonstrates that different tribes developed different strategies for protecting land holdings against white encroachment. As veterans of protracted legal land battles such as the Mohegan-Mason case, Brotherton tribal members probably viewed written titles to specifically bounded lands as key legal instruments in maintaining territory, while the Oneida developed a different strategy of land consolidation in the context of white encroachment and aggressive treaty making following the American War of Independence. Brotherton founders also viewed individually allotted and bounded lands as a tool for facilitating intertribal cooperation and cohabitation.

183. *their own tongue:* Oneida.

184. *David:* David Fowler.

they Concluded to Cut the Road thro to the Flats Just at Night two white men came to our Town from Spring Field, about forty miles from here, they Came on purpose to give us a Christian Visit, we expected them and acording they Came, and we were Glad to See each other. In the Evening we had a meeting, and there were Some Stockbridge Brethren with us, and there was great moving and Some making, and there was Some Crying out, held the meeting late,—

Sabb. Octo^r 29: Many Stockbridgers Came to meeting, about ten we began the Exercise, and there was great Asembly. I Spoke from Matt xxiv:14: and we had a Solemn meeting[,] many were affected—in the evening we had another meeting, and there was great moving and some Making up, and many were affected, but I believe there was more Natural affection than ~~Gracious~~ Gracious,[185] an there was Considerable Noise we were late before we left the Place,—

Wednesday Novr 1, I had a meeting with the Young Peop at David Fowler's, and they repeated the Verses upon the Texts they Chose, the last Time they met, and it was a Solemn Time with us, many Tears were Shed, Several indeed are Deep Convictions, and been So for Some Time—

Saturday Novr 4: near noon I Sot of for New Stockbridge Stopt a While at Brother Roger Waubys and took dinner there, and after eating past on got to the Place towards Night, put up at Capt Hind in the Evening we had a meetg I dropt a few Words, and many discoverd their Spiritual Exercise and it was a Solemn Time, many Confest and lamented their past Conduct, and determind to live a Regular life in Time to Come &c—

Sabb. Novr 5: People began to Collected together, and there was a great Number of P, we began the Exercise about ten. I Spoke Joshua XXIV:15, and I believe the Lord acompanied his word by his Divine Spirit, the People were Bowd before the word,— after speaking I Baptized [ ] in the Eving we met again I did not Say much, and there was a number again that discoverd their Concern and resolutions, and it was a Solemn Season, and we held the mg late, Lodgd at Capt Hindricks again—

Monday Novr 6: We had another meeting quite early, and there was much affection, I Spoke to them about the Nature of Baptism very Close, and I Baptized [ ] Some Time towards noon I left New Stockbridge, Stopt a little while at Roger Waubys and so past on, got to Brother Davids Some Time in the after Noon,—in the eving we had a meeting, and it was a Comfortable meeting;—

Tuesday Novr 7 Was geting ready to return homward, Visited some Families—

Wednesday Novr 8. Visted again and was busy geting ready—

Thirdsday, Novr 9: sot of early Sir Peter Pohquennuppeet, Cat[h]y Quinney, Betsy Fowler and Elizy Corricomb went with me, and we were obligd to Lodge in the Woods we coud not get thro and it rain'd Some we found a good Hutt, and made out to make fire and we lodged quite Comfortable I had good rest—

Fryday Novr 10: got up Some Time before Day, and as Soon as it was break a Day

---

185. In judging his audiences' affective responses to his preaching, Occom utilizes a theological distinction between natural affections, behaviors arising from human inclinations or volition, and gracious affections, the evidences of the saving operations of the Spirit. The most famous exposition of this distinction is Jonathan Edwards, *Treatise Concerning Religious Affections* (1746).

we tacled our Horses and went on. we got to M[r] Folss. Just after Sun rise, took breakfast at Mr. Fols[s]: and about 8: we Sot off again, Stopt a little at Esq[r] Franks, and near
12 we went on again, got to Spring-Field, Some Time in the Evening, we put up at
Brother Crippens and we were Gladly receivd and we were glad to See them—

Saturday Nov[r] 11. We were at the Place all Day, in the Evening, we had a meeting
in M[r] Crippins House, and we had a Comfortable Time, the Christians were much refreshd, and there was one Boy Spoke, he was much Exercisd in his mind, John Tuhy
Came here just before meeting began, We of my Company Lodgd at M[r] Crippins—

Sabb Nov[r] 12: About 9: We Went to M[r] Pickards where the meeting is to be. about
11: We began the Exercise, and there was a great Number of People, and I Spoke from
John XII:36 and the People attend with great Solemnity and many were much
affected,—in the Evening we had another meeting in the Same House, and the People were greatly movd, Several Cried out, the Christians were much Strengthen'd—
I Lodged at M[r] Pickard's—

Monday Nov[r] 13: Betsey Fow and Eliza Corricomb Came to me very early, they
were going home, and I got up, and went directly to M[r] Crippins and As soon as
they got breakfast they went of, poor girls they were all in Tears, When we parted,
and I went back to M[r] Pickards and from thence I went to Brother Nicholas Pickards,
and after a while Brother Tuhy and Peter Came to me, and Sot there a while, and then
took leave of Sister Pickard, and we went on to M[r] Ways where meeting is to be, he
lives in Cherry Valley we got there before Night, we were receivd with all kindness
and Brotherly affection,—took Dinner there,—in the evening a few People Came
together, I Spoke to them from the words what will ye that I Shall do[186]—unto you,
and we had a good meeting—

Tuesday Nov[r] 14 Some Time after Breakfast we Sot of and our Course to Bowmans
Creek we got to Esq[r] Kimbels about 12: and took dinner there, and soon after Dinner, we went on again and we got Esq[r] Maybee's in the Dusk of the Evening and I
lodgd there, and John[187] and Peter[188] went over the River—

Wednesday Nov[r] 15, Got Break early and Soon after I went over and got to Major
Fundees Soon, there I found my Company and was there Some Time; and then Peter
[Pohquonnoppeet] and I Sot of and Went down, we Calld on Cap[t] Grig, and was there
a few minutes, and went on again, and I Stopt at M[r] Albert Vedders, and was kindly
receivd, Peter past on,—

Thirdsday Nov[r] 16, Some Time after Breakfast, I went over to M[r] Bartlets, and
was kindly receid, and Concluded to have a meeting on the next Day at M[r] Keenes:
towards Night, I went back to M[r] Vedder's and Loded there again and had Comfortable rest—

Fryday Nov[r] 17, about 12 we went over to meeting, got to there about 2: and Soon
began the Meeting, and there was a Considerable number of People, I Spoke from
Mark V.4: and many were affected, it was a Solemn Time.—after Sermon we attended
upon the ordernance of Baptism I Baptised two White Children and one Negro Child,

186. See Matthew 20:32.
187. *John:* John Tuhy.
188. *Peter:* Peter Pauquunnuppeet.

one for Mr David Wright by the name of Sarah, one for Mr John Robbinson by the Name of Martin, one Cato Quash by the name Simon after meeting I went home with Mr Eliot, and there I Lodgd, and was very kindly treated,—

Saturday 18, Some Time in the morning a number of Neighbors came together, and had an Exercise with my Cards, and it was very agreable, and Solemn towards night I went to Mr Bartlets and there I lodged and Lodged Comfortably once more—

Sabb Novr 19. About 9 we went over the River and so we went down to M^r [Ahasuerus Mericlus?], and there was a great Number of People and we begun the Service about 12: I Spoke from Rom II. 28.29 and the People attended exceeding well, and was affection, after meeting took dinner at the Same House, and there was one Mr John Connoot Dine there also, he is a Reader of Divine Service, on Sabbaths, among the Dutch, he is filing and Preparing, to be a Preacher, he is a Zealous Young man,—after Dinner I went back to Mr Vedders and Lodged there once more was very kindly entertaind—

Monday Novr 20: Sot of early in the morning, and we found it hard to get over the River, there good deal of ice came down the River, I went down the river and got Mr John Hageboom's about 12: and there I had a meeting, there was Considerable number of People, I Spoke from Mark VIII.36:37, and the People were much affected, they were Chiefly Dutch, and Mr John Connoot was here again I Lodgd at the Same House and was very kindly Treated—

Tuesday Novr 21: Some Time after Breakfast, I took leave of the Family, and went on to Schenactada, Call'd on one Mr Elias [Quistey?], but was not at Home, there was only Mr Vedders Daughter at Home, and I soon past on, and got Mr John Post's about 12: and there I put up—

Wednesday Novr 22: Was at the Place, got Some Cloa[t]h for a [word illegible] and a Jacket, and got them made up, and had a Shirt made also—

Thirdsday Novr 23: Was about to Set of, but the English Peop Desired to Stay over the Sabb and I Consented,—

Sabb Novr 26: about 10 went to meeting, and it was extream Cold, and was but few People, I Spoke from Mark 6 6 in the after noon from Jonah 3: 5 and there was great Number of People, and they attended with great Solemnity,—

Monday Novr 27: Some Time in the morning, I took leave of my Friends and went on to Nesquney, got there about 12: and about 1 went into the meeting and there was great Number of People, and I Spoke from Hebrew XI:6 and the People were much moved many of them, it was indeed a Solemn Time, they made a Some Collection,— Soon after meeting, I went with one Mr Fordt about a mile & Eastward from the meeting and there I Lodged, and was very kindly treated, we Sot up Some what late, and went to bed at last, and had Comfortable rest—

Tusday Novr 28. It was very Cold, and Some Time after Breakfast, I took leave of the Family, and went on to [word illegible], I Calld on my old Friend Mr Sanford, and took Dinner with him; and Soon after Dinner, I went on and call'd on Mr Cornelius Vandenburgh, and Stayd there Some Time took tea there, Just at Night, I went to Mr David Feros, and kindly receivd, ~~and lodged there~~ about Sun Set we went meeting at the House one Major Fondee and there was a large number of People, and I Spoke from 1 Epis of John V.10. and the People attended with great Solemnity, and

Shed Tears, Soon after meeting I went back with Mr Feros Family in a Slay, and there I Lodged,—

Wednesday Novr 29: Some Time after Breakfast, Mr Henry Fero and I Went to See the Falls,[189] and it is a grand Sight, the Power of god is to be seen in it, after a while we went back, and I took Dinner with him; and towards night, I went to Mr Jacob Lawnsons; and I had no thought of a meeting, but Soon after Dark, the People began to come in and there was large number of People, and I preached to them from Mark V:4: and and there was great Solemnity and affection among the People and I believe they will Soon forget the Evening—I Lodgd at the Same House, and was exceedingly well treated, Went to bed Some what late, and had comfortable rest-

Thirdsday Novr 30: was at Mr Lawnsons, till about 10 then I went to meeting, I Stopt a little While at Mr Levinus Lawnson, and about 11 we went to the meeting House, and there was a large numbr of People, and I Spoke to them from Diniel: V.25[190] and there was great Solemnity and may were I believe felt the Power of the Word, after meeting, went to Mr Levinus Leighsons again and took Dinner with them and Some Time towards night I went to Mr David Feros and the People Collected together again for a meeting, and there was a large Number got together, and I Spoke from Rom.II.28–29 and the People attended with much affection, I believe they will not forget the Night, Very soon—Lodged at the Same House and rested Comfortable—

Fryday Decr 1 Got up very early and we were geting ready to go to Albany, one of Mr Faros Sons one Daughters and a Daughter in Law; we sot of in a wagon before Sun rise, & we got to Albany near 10, it is about 9 miles. I Calld at a Certain House, from thence I went into the City, one Mr Blackney went with me, and as I was going along I cast my Eyes down Street and and saw my good Brother Peter Pohquonnuppeet, and another man with him they were returning to Oneida, and we spent Some Time together in a Certain Tavern and there I Saw Mr Kirkland a minute or two, about 12 Sir Peter and I parted, I went to See M^r McDonal[191] a Minister of the Presbeterian Congregation, found him very Sociable, and a lively gentleman took Dinner with him, and Soon after Dinner, went of so took my Company, and went to the Same House, that I went into first, & was there but few minutes, and had an opportunity to return to Debought in another wagon and we to M^r [ ] and presently after 9 we got there there was a number of Neighbours Came in to hear Something from the Word of god, and I dropt a few Words to them, and I Lodge there and was exceedingly well Treated, and the People of the House appeard and talked like Christians, and there was one old gentleman helpless has been so for some Time.

Saturday. Nov^r [Dec^r] 2 Soon after Breakfast the man of the House got his Horses & Wagon ready and he carried me to Mr Fero's, and I was there a While, and then took leave of the Family, and left the Place & went to half Moon, & Stopt at Mr Leighson's and took Dinner with him, and Soon after Dinner I went on, and Stopt at Mr Fundees he keeps a Ferry, and he was not at home, and presently after Mr Leighson

189. Probably Plotter Kill Falls, New York.

190. A sermon by Occom on Daniel 5:25 appears in the sermons part of this volume.

191. *M^r McDonal:* John McDonald.

came to me, and So We went on together to half Moon he went afoot, and we got to Mr Clutes Some Time before night and I was kindly receivd; and in the Evening we Went to Colo^l [ ] and there was a Number of men, and we had very agreable Conversation, took Super there, and Some after I returnd with Mr Clute, and there I Lodgd and a Comfortable rest—

Sabb ~~Nov^r~~ *Decr 3:* about 10: went to meeting, about a mile, and there was a large Number of People, tho' it was a Cold Day, I Spoke from Marke VIII.36.37: and the People were greatly bowd before the Word many were deeply afected,—after meeting I with one Mr Comstock, and took dinner there he is an Englishman, after Dr we had Exercise with my Christian Cards with a few People, and it was agreable to them;—In the Evening, went to meeting to a Certain House, but there were So many People, we were obligd to go to Meeting House again and there was near as many this evening as there was in the Day Time, and I Spoke from 1 Kings XIX:13 and there was greater Solemnity than in the Day Time. it was a Night to be remember'd,—after meeting went home with Mr Clute, went to bed Some What Early, and had a Comfortable Sleep—

Monday Decr 4: After Breakfast, a Number of People Came in, and we had Exercise with my Christian Cards and it was very agreable to them—Some Time towards Noon I took leave of the Family, and of & went to the Point, inteded to go over the River there, I went to Mr John ~~Venkar~~ R. Vender^war^ken and they had a great Mind to have me Stay so as to have a meeting in eving, and Finally I Concluded to Stopt and so in the evening I went to meeting So in the evening we went to the City and had a meeting in a large uper Room, very elegant and there was a Considerable of People and I Spoke from John XII and the People attended with great and Solemn attention; and after exercise I Sot down a while by the Fire, and Capt Morgan the man of the House began to ask me Some Questions, in favour of universal Salvation,[192] and we had a mile Conversation, and many People heard us, and they may Judge between us—and So after a while I returnd home with Mr John R. Venderwarken and it Snowd quite fast, and we Sot a long while after we got home, and we had very agreable Conversation, and at length I went to Bed quietly once more—

Tuesday ~~Nov^r~~ ^*Dec^r*^ 6 ^5^: We found Considerable depth of Snow this morning and it Continued to Snow,—This morning I Baptized a Child for one Mr Stephen Picket by the Name Stephen Gregory, I Stayd here all Day. it was Cold Day, and it Snowd till about 12 in the Evening. We had exercise with my Cards, and it was very agreable to the Company and was much Pleasd; we Sot up Some what late, and it was very Cold all Night—

Wednesday ~~Nov^r~~ ^*Dec^r*^6. It was extream Cold, and I Continued to be here all Day again; in the Evening a few Neighbours Came in, and we exercise with my Cards and we had quite agreable evening, the Company was much gratified, and Well Pleasd.—

Thirdsday ~~Nov^r~~ ^*Dec^r*^ 7: Soon after eating, Mr Venderwarken Got his Slay ready, and took me and Carried me to Mr Fundees ferry I calld at Mr Fundees, and took Dinner there, Soon after Dinner, Mr Funde took me in his Slay, and we went to Mr Fero's,

192. On universalism, see note 84.

we Calld at Mr Lenghsens and he went with us, and we Came back Soon, and we Stopt at Mr John Lenghsens, and there we took Tea; Soon after Tea, we went along; and I Stopt at Mr R. Lenghsen, where meeting is to be this evening. Just at Dusk, the People began to Come together, and there was a large number of Pople, and I Spoke from III Heb two last verses, and it was a Solemn Time, the People attended with great affection—I Lodged at the Same House and was Treated with great Tenderness and Friendship, Went to bed in good Season and Comfortable rest—

Fryday Decr 8: I got up a great while before Day, and a young Woman, a House keeper got up too, and as I was going down Stares, She took hold of me and helpd me down;[193] & the old gentleman got up too Soon after, and we had very agreable Conversation upon Religious Concerns; and before Day we had our Breakfast; after that we had Exercise with my Cards, there were only one white person, and Several Negroes and after that we prayd and it was broad Day light and my Horse was got up, and before Sun rise Some Time I was on Horse back, and I Just Calld on Mr John Lenghsen, and so past on, Call'd at [ ] a few minutes, and so past on my way to Albany; got there a little after 9: put up at a Tavern went to See Some Friends—about 2 I left Albany, and went over the River, got to Esqr Woodworths just after Sun Sit and found them well but one girl, and there Lodgd—it is remarkable, that Since I left Onoida, I have been with Dutch People almost altogether I have lodgd in English Familys but twice, and I never was treated better by any People nor So Well,—and I have preachd amongst Chifely, and there is a remarkable attention amongst them, as ever was Seen amongst hereabouts, indeed there is great moving among them in Several Places, especial at Debaught, I preachd there Six Times. Yea, they woud get together, Where ever I am to get instruction, they Seem to be really hungry after the Word of god. at half Moon, the Dutch People are the forwardest for meetings there are a great Number of English Families, but not half so forward for meetings as the Dutch are,—I believe the Ld is about to Call them by his Divine opperations in a more Remarkable manner than they have had yet in this Country, they have been lookd upon in general both by Christian People and Heathen Indians, as a Careless profane People, as any that pretends to Christianity, or those that are Calld Christian People

Saturday Decr 9 was at Esqr Woodworths all Day, and it Snowd all Day, and it was quite Cold—

Sabath Decr 10: It Snowd Still & there was a great Body of Snow on the ground, it was about 3: feet and 3 inches Deep upon a level and it was exceeding Cold, about 10 the People began to Come together, and there was a few got together yet as many again could be expeted for the Weather and Snow, and about 12: we began the Service, and I Spoke from 2 Corin XI.17.18 and the People attended Well,—Lodgd at the Same House again, and it was extream Cold Night, I was

[Courtesy of Dartmouth College Library]

193. Occom was crippled in one hip by a fall on ice in 1780.

ॐ JOURNAL 17

December 11, 1786–April 7, 1787

Occom continues his homeward journey from Brotherton, preaching to large crowds and visiting Stockbridge along his way. Met in Lebanon, Connecticut, with news that his son Benoni is awaiting execution for murder near Boston, he reaches home on January 4, 1787, where he learns much to his relief that the rumor is unfounded. He spends late winter and early spring 1787 visiting friends, preaching to local congregations, and attending to tribal business.

Monday Decr 11 About 12 I took leave of Esqr Woodworths Family, and went on to Stephen Town, got to Mr Tobiass Just before Sun Sit and Taried there, and was very kindly intertaind, by the Family Lodged there.—

Tuesday Decr 12: about 11 the People began to Collect and there was Company of People, for the Season, it was very Cold, and much Snow on the Ground, and it is a Scaterd Place,—We began the meeting, a little after 12 I Spoke from Matt, VI.10 and the People attened with great and Solemn attention, many were much affected,—I Lodgd here again, and had a Comfortable rest.—

Wednesday Decr 13: Got up early, and Sot of Soon, Stopt at Mr Robinsons a While took there, and Soon after Breakfast I went on ^a^gain, got to Esqr Shermehorns about 11: and took Dinner with them Soon after Dinner, went on to Mr Dimons, and found them well, and was kindly receivd, Especially by Mrs. Dimon, She is an old acquaintance and Frie^n^d of mine, She came from Rhode Island State, Lodged there, and was very tenderly intertaind, Lodged Comfortably by the Fire accordg to my desire,—

Thirdsday Decr 14: About 10 we went to Esqr Shermehorns to meeting, the People got together at 11, and I went into a Store House, where the People collected, and there was a Prodigious Concourse of People. I Spoke from the Revel. of John 1: Chap [numbers illegible] and there was a melting attention amongst the People many tears were Shed, and presently after meeting I went home again with Mr Dimond and his Family in their Slay, and there I Lodgd again.—

Fryday Decr 15. got up very early, and the whole Family got up, also, and Breakfast was got ready Soon, and we ate and Soon after eating Mr Dimond and his Wife, and I went to Stephen Town in his Slay, it is about 10 miles distant We Stopt at Mr Jabez Spencers a little While, and So past on, and about 10 O.C. We got to Mr Nathan Brockways and there we put up, he was not at Home, and towards Night, he got home and in the Evening, the People Collected together for meeting, and there was a large Asembly, and I Spoke from XXV. Matt.43: and the People attended with great Solemnity, many were affected much, and after meeting, many Spoke to me with tenderness, after the People were gone we Sung Several Hymns, and had agreable Conversation, Sot up very late, at last went to bed quietely—

Saturday Decr 16: got up early and had Exercise in the Family with my Cards, and the Young P attend with gravity and Decincy and Some Time after Breakfast we Sot of again, to return to Philips Town. got to Mr Dimonds House about 1: and there Stayd again.—

Sabb Decr 17. about 10 we went to meeting at Esqr John Scharmarhorn's and there was the bigest number of People, that ever was Seen in one meeting in this Wilderness Settlement, it was thought there was about 500 People, We met in a large Barn,—I Spoke from Amos III.4, and I think I had Some Sense of Divine things, and there was an affectionate attention thro the Asembly, the People were bowd under the Word, they Sat like Criminals under a Sentance of Death—Soon after meeting I returnd with Mr Dimond and his Family in a Slay;—In the evening a Company Came together, at Mr Dimonds for meeting, there was but few People, it was a Tedious Snowy and Rainey evening, I Spoke from John IX: and the People attended with great Solemnity Some were affected.—

Monday Decr 18. Soon after Breakfast Mr Dimond got his Slay ready and went Mr Samuel Wheeler's to meeting about 5 miles, we go there about 11, and the People Just began to Collect, and there Considerable of People got together, I Spoke from Matt V.5 and it was a Solemn meeting, Soon after meeting, we went went back, got home before Sun Sit, and Lodgd there—

Tuesday Decr 19: Got up very early, and they got Breakfast directly, before Sun rise I took leave of the Family and went on my to Stephen Town; Calld at Mr Spencers, at Mr Joness, and So on to Mr Joshua Gardners and there was a prodigious Number of People Collected together, and I begun the Exercise directly, I Spoke from Ecles 1:15: and there was very deep and Solemn attention thro the Asembly, many Tears were Shed;—Soon after took Dinner and then went with one Mr Ezekiel Shelden, and had an Evening meeting there and there was a Considerable of People I Spoke from Matt V.5 the People Seemed to attend with some feeling of the Word after I had done two or three Spoke with Some affection, I was Tenderly treated. Lodgd at the Same House, and rested comfortably. ~~about~~

Wednesday Decr 20. About 10 we went to one Hammond to meeting, and there was a large number of People, and I Spoke from John VII.37 and there good attention Soon after meeting, I We Went back with Mr Shelden again in his Slay took Dinner with them, and directly after eating, we went to one Mr Haywards and there we had another meeting, I Spoke from Mark V:4 and the People attended well, one or two Spoke after I had, here I Lodgd.—

Thirdsdsay Decr 21: After Bt[194] Mr Rufus Price and I went to Mr Brockway's and Mr Price went back, and Mr Brockway took me in his Slay, with his Family, to a meeting about 3 miles nothward got there a 12: and a large Number of People had Collected together, and I began the exercise directly, I Spoke from John VI 36: and there was uncommon attention amongst the People, there was a flow of Tears, I believe the Lord was present with his word,—as Soon as ever the meeting was done, I went back with Mr Brockway,—and in the evening we had meeting again and there was Considerable number of People & I Spoke from 1 Peter and the People attended with great Solemnity, Lodgd at the Same House—

Fryday Decr 22, Soon after Breakfast, I leave of the F and went on to one Mr Gardners, upon the border of Handcock,[195] and there was a meeting to be, the People

---

194. *Bt:* Breakfast.
195. Hancock, Massachusetts.

began to Collect when I got there, and there was large Number of People—I began about half after 11: I Spoke from Acts VIII and the P were greatly attentive and Some manifested affection Soon after meeting I went Home with Mrs Goodrich and her Son[196] in a Slay, got there Some Time before night the Place Where they live is Calld Jaricho; tooke Dinner with them, the Man of the House is helpless as a Child, he is troubled with a Num Palsey,[197] in the Evening, we went in the Slay again to meeting at the House of one Mr Hammond, and there was great many People, I Spoke from [ ] and the People appeared very Serious and Some were affected—Soon after meeting went back with Mr Goodrich and there I Lodgd, and was kindly Treated,—

Saturday Decr 23: Soon after eating, took leave of the Family, and went on towards New Lebanon;[198] Stopt a while at Mr Patchins his Wife has been Sick a long While, I had Some Conversation with her, She Complains of much Darkness but I believe she is a real Christian; about 11: I went on, a man went with me, and he Conducted to the Pool and it is a remarkable Spring, and a Clump of House are on and round was there but few minutes and I went on to the meeting House, and I put up at Capt Joness Close by the meeting House, and he and his wife were not at Home,—in the evening they Came home and they are agreable Couple—Lodged there and was kindly entertaind.—

Sabb. Decr 24: It was a Very Cold Day, I went into the meeting House, about 11: and there was a Considerable number of People for the Cold Season, I Spoke from the words there is at Jerusa^m a Pool, &c[199]—and there was a good attention, after meeting went to Capt Joness again. in the evening went to one Mr Abots and there we had a meeting and there was a great Numb^r of People, and I Spoke from 1 Corin VII: and there was a Solemn attention many I believe were much affected—after meeting I went back to Capt Joness and Lodgd there again,—

Monday Decr 25: got up very early, and took Break^t and Sot away, and got to Richmound,[200] about 9: Calld on Mr Berg a minister of the Place, and he and another man, were very urgent to have me Stop and preach in the evening, and I Consented and I went to Mr Millers, and there I put up, in the evening we went to meeting to Mr Collin and there was a Considerable number of People, and I Spoke from 1 Kings XIX: and the People attend well, I Lodgd at the Same House and they were exceed kind to me.—

Tuesday Decr 26, got up ^v^ery early, and they got Breakfast Soon, and we had Exercise with my Cards, and it was very agreeable to them, about 9 I set off, a young Carried me in a Slay to Mr Millers, and about 10, I Sot away again got to Stockbridge, before 12: took Dinner with Mr Sargant, and then went Capt Youks and he was not at Home, and so I went back to one [word illegible], and in the evening went back to Capt Yokes: and Lodged there, they were very glad to See me,—

196. *her son:* Daniel Goodrich.
197. *numb palsy:* paralysis resulting from stroke.
198. New Lebanon, New York.
199. See John 5:2.
200. Richmond, Massachusetts.

Wednesday Decr 27: got up very early, and a little after Sun rise I went on my way, got to Mr Babcocks in Canaan, and Lodgd there,—

Thirdsday Decr 28. got up quite early Sot away, and Stopt at Several Houses; got to Mr Enos before Sun Set, and put up there—

Fryday Decr 29: got up very early and got Breakfast and Sot of Soon, got to Mr Wallins before noon and they desired me to Stay over the Sabbath, and I Concented, and Lodgd there—

Sabb. Decr 31: about 10 the People began to Collect, and there was Considerable number of People, and I began about 11: Spoke from Amos 3:3 and the People attended very well, but not so Solemn as I have Seen in other Places.—took Dinner after meeting; and Some Time in the after noon, I sot of and got to Esqr Robertss in the evening, and he desired me to tary all night with em and I accepted of his kind offer and I went to bed Soon and rested Comfortably—

Thus I have Ended one year more, and have experienced much of the goodness of god to me in many respects, tho, I have been greatly and Shamefully wanting in Duty to myself, to my fellow Creatures, and to my Maker,—O god Almighty freely parden all my Sins

Wittenbury Jan^r 1: 1787 In the morning we had Exercise, in the Family and it was very agreable to them, they were very Solemn and I prayd in the Family. Some Time in the Morning Mr Walcut Came, to the House where I was, invited to his House, he is the Minister of the Place, and the People had Concluded to have me Preach on the next Day; and Some Time past Noon I left Esqr Roberts's and went to See Mr Samuel Eno I Calld by the way at Mr Felleys they were exceeding glad to See me, and they Sent for Deacon Manley and he Soon Came he is an old Disciple, appears to be an Isrealte[201] indeed, and we had agreable interview after a while, I went on and Saw Mr Eno, he and his Wife were glad to See me,—Just at Night I went to Mr Wolcotts and was kindly receivd ~~receivd~~ Thus I began a New Year The Lord enable me to Live a New Life more than ever I did, that I might Live as a Dying and accountable Creature unto god. The Lord enable me to do what ever work I have before me; and that I might resign myself into the Hands of God—

Tuesday Jan^r 2: Near 11 Mr Wolcott and I went to meeting, and we found but few People at the meeting H Sot a While in a House, and a little past 11: went into the meeting House and there was Considerable Number of People got together, and I Spoke from Daniel V:25[202] and there was deep attention many were much affected, Soon after meeting, I went into an House and took Dinner, and then I Went on and Call on Mr Rowland at old Windsor, Sot but few minutes and past on, got over the River well, and went to my Daughter Olives, got there in the Dusk of the evening and found them all well. Lodged there, Sot up late—

Wednesday Jan^r 3: got up early, and took few mouthfulls of Victuals, and so went on my way; Call on Mr Colton at Bolton, a Minister of the Place, and he was exceeding Glad to hear of the Work of god in the wilderness amongst the Indians, took

---

201. *an Israelite:* a true believer, one of the faithful.

202. See Occom's manuscript sermon on Daniel 5:25 in the sermons part of this collection.

Dinner, and Soon after eating, I past on again, & I got so far as Mr Lomiss in Lebanon, a Tavern keeper went to Bed prety Soon, and rested Comfortably—

Thirsday Jan^r 4: got up early, and Sot of directly and it was very bad rideing, it had been thawing ever Since last Saturday Stopt at Capt Hide's, and there took Breakfast, and Soon after eating I went on my way, Stopt a little while at Mr Champions and there I heard a Surprizing News, that one of my Sons had been guilty of murder near Boston, and was Sentencd to be hang'd, and my Wife was Seen thereabout three Weeks ago, and was mourning and weeping herself almost to Death, and I was Some What Surprizd & began to think many things but When I got in Town, I found there was nothing in it; about 2 in the after noon, I got home, and found my poor Family all in good State of Health Blessed be the Name of the Lord

Sabb Jan^r 7: Went to meeting to Deacon Henry Quaguaquids but there was but very few People, and I only gave them the relation of my Journey, and Prayed,—

Thirsday Jan^r 11: my Wife was robd by a Molatto—

Fryday Jan^r 19 The above mentiond Mollato was tried before two Justices, and was found guilty—

Saturday Jan^r 20: went to lower part of Groton, went over the River at New London got to Capt Robert Latham's a little before Sun Sit, and found them all well, and was kindly receivd, and Lodged there, and went to bed Soon and Rested Comfortably—

Sabb Jan^r 21: It was a Stormy Day and was all last Night about 10 went Meeting at Mr Gidion Sanderss, and there was but a little number of People, and I Spoke to them from James II.26 in the evening went to Mr Abel Babcocks and had a meeting there, and there was a large Number of P and I Spoke from James IV:4 and the People attended with great attention; I Lodgd at the Same House,—

Monday Jan^r 22: Soon after Breakfast, went back to Mr Saunderss: and was there but a little while, and then went to See Mrs Latham, Sot a little while, and so Went on to Mr Streets, Calld at Mr Woods was there a While & then Went to Mr Streets, and was kindly receivd by the Family, about 1 began the Mg and there was Considerable Number of People, tho it was a Snowy Day, and I Spoke from Rom 11.28:29 and the People attended well after meeting took dinner at the Same House,—and in the Evening went to Mr Lesters and had another meeting, and there was a great number of People tho the Storm Continued, & I Spoke from James IV.7 and the People attended with great Seriousness,— I Lodgd at the Same House—

Tuesday Jan^r 23: Some Time after Breakfast, I took Leave of the Family; and went to Capt Robert Lathams & took leave of them, and then went down to the Ferry, and went over to New London and was there Some Hours and So past on, and got Home Some Time before Night, and found all my Family well, thro the goodness of god.—

Saturd Jan^r 27: About 10 Sot of from Home, and went to a Place Calld Jewet City got there Some Time before Sun Sit, put up at Mr Elea Jewet and was kindly re^d Sot up Some What late and rested Comfortably—

Sabb Jan^r 28, A little past 11 went into the meeting, and there was a great Number of People, and I Spoke from Rom II:28:29 and there was a Solemn attention in the Asembly, after Service went to Mr Jewet and took Dinner there, and Soon after Dinner took leave of the Family, and went to Deacon Tracy's, and there had a meeting again and there was a great Number of People, I Spoke from 1 Sam XII.24 and there was a Solemn attention, many Shed Tears,—Lodgd at the Same House, and rested Comfortably—

Monday Jan^r 29: got up early; and had my horse got ready Soon, and went on my way, Stopt at one Mr Reeds and took Breakfast there, and after eating had Some Conversation with an old woman, 92 years of age or near, and had a little exercise with a ^Card in the^ Family and another Family Came to the House,—and then went on, got Home about 2 o.c: and found my Fa well as Common—

Sabb. Febru^r 4: About 11 Sot of from Home, and to Mrs Fitchs and it was extreem Cold, wind Blew very hard at North West, and Snow flew like fog,—got ^to^ the P Soon, and there were Some People, more than Coud be expected for the Severity of the Weather. I began the Exercise about 12 or past I Spoke from Eclesi III.2 and there was a Solemn attention—after Service took Dinner and and towards went home and Soon got Home.—

Wednesday Febru^r 7: 1787 Left home early in the Morning, and to one Mr Smith in Newent, Stopt a while at Doc^r Mask's in Norwich and took Breakfast there and Soon after went on, and to Mr Smith's about 10 and they were glad to See me. the old gentleman is quite helpless with Num Palsy[203] and about half after 1: o.c I began the meeting and there was but few People. I Spoke from Job: XXXV.10 and the People attended with great Solemnity: Soon after meeting I went back, and got home in the Dusk of the eveng and was Some what tired and went to Bed soon—

Saturday Febru^r 10: About 12 Sot off from my House and to Groton Indian Town—got there about Sun Sit, and put at Widow Paukquunnup's found them all well, and we were glad to See each other again once more this Side of the grave, went to bed in good Season, and had a Comfortable rest,—

Sabb Feb^r 11: We began the meeting near 12: and there was Considerable Number of People, and I Spoke from, 1 Peter IV.8: and the People attended well,—in the evening we had another meeting, and Considerable number of People for it was a Rainy evening, and I Spoke from 1 Kings XXI.29 and I had but a little Sense of Divine things, Yet the People attend well,—We Sot up a long while and Sung, Mr Silas Spicer Lodgd there, and many of the Indians, went to bed at last & I rested well,—

Monday Febru^r 12: got up and attended on Family Pray and then Sot of Soon, Stopt a While at Mr John Williams, and took Breakfast here, and Soon after eating went on my way, got home a little past Noon and found my Family all well as usual—

Fryday, Feb^r 16: Towards N went to Mr Chappel's and a Mg there, but few People got together and I Spoke to them from Psalm 146:5: and the People attended Soberly, Stayd at the House all Night, we Sot up late yet had Comfortable Rest by Sleep in the Silent Watches—[204]

Monday Feb^r 17: got up early, and they Breakfast Soon, and I eat with them and Soon after Went Home and Stopt a while at Mr T. Averys, got home about 11—

---

203. *numb palsy:* paralysis resulting from stroke.

204. Occom here leads an all-night "watch night" service, a type of service originated and promoted by John Wesley as a means to encourage individual believers to reflect on and renew their relationship to God. Watch night services are customarily held on New Year's Eve.

Saturday Febr.y 24 Sun a bout an Hour high, Sot of from home, and went to Canterbury Calld on Doc.r Marsh, and Sot a While and past on, and got Brother Clarkes Some Time in the afternoon, and found them all well and was kindly receivd, and Lodgd there,—

Sabb. Febur.r 25: Soon after Breakfast, Went to meeting, in Scotland, M.r Palmers meeting House,—and there was but a little number of People,—I Spoke to them from Prov: IV:13 and in the afternoon from Psalm 146:5 Directly after meeting I went back to M.r Isaac W.ms and had a meeting there in the evening and there was a large Number of People, and I Spoke from Luke XXIII:40 and there was good attention, and so there in the Day,—Lodgd at the Same House, and kindly entertain'd, Went to bed Some what late and had Comfortable rest—

Monday Feb.r 26: Sot of very early, Stopt a few minutes at M.r Lions and so past on, Stopt at M.r Joseph Smiths, and there took Breakfast, and Soon after eating went on and got home about 12: and found my Family Well Thanks to the Father of all mercies—

Sabb March 4: Some Time in the Morning sot of from Home and Went over to Groton, and it was very bad riding, Snow was Some What deep, and drifted, and it Snowd again got to M.r Chapman, about 11, and the People began to gather, and there was Considerable number of People and we began the meeting about 12: and I Spoke from James IV.14: and there was Solemn attention,—after M- took Dinner with the Family and Soon after eating, Sot of for Home, got home before Sun Down—

Sabb March 11. Got up Some Time before Daybrake and was geting to go up to Canterbury, Sot of a little after Sun rise, Stopt a few minutes at Doc.r Marshes and So past on, Calld at M.r Smith's also, and took Some Victuals, and so on got to Elder Lyon's near 12: and he directly Sent out among the Neighbours to give notice of my being in the Place, and the People Collected Soon and about 1: We began the Service of god,—and I Spoke from Matt V.5. and the People attended with great Solemnity—after meeting took Dinner with Brother Lyon, Just before Night, We Went to M.r Dyer Brewsters and there we had another meeting, and there was Considerable number of People; and I Spoke from Matt VI:9: and the Lord I believe was present with us; the Hearts of Some Christians were Warmd with the Fire of Love. Some deliverd few Words after I had done I Lodgd at the Same House and was entertaind with Brotherly kindness, rested Comfortably,—

Monday March 12: after Breakfast, I went to see Brother Sunsummon, found all Well, about 10 went back, and soon to M.r Clarks took Dinner with them, from thence we went to Brother Lyon's to meeting about 2 began the meeting and there was a great Num.r of People; and I Spoke from 1 Corin VII 29.30 and I believe the Lord was present with his Word, many of the People were mov'd Some rejoiced and others were bowd under the Word many Tears were Shed. Brother Lyon was so full he quite Boild over, and he kiss'd us all with a kiss of Charity not with his mouth, but with his Heart,[205]—Stayd at the Same House all Night,—

Tuesday March 13: It was a Stormy Morning it Raind very hard, and So Stayd quietly had agreable entertainment both with Victuals and Drink and Conversation.

205. See 1 Peter 5:14.

took Dinner with them, and the rain Slacked, and so I Sot of for home, Stopt a while at Mʳ Joseph Smith's, Prayd with them, and went on again, got home just after Sun Set.—

Fryday March 16: Went to New London on the Tribes Business to See the Deeds of Mʳ John Raymond, and Mʳ Ebenezer Smith Juʳ I found Smithˢ, but Coud not find Ray got home again Some Time in the evening.—

Sabb March 18: Went to Mʳ John Browns, Calld on Docʳ Rogers, and Sot there a while and then Went on,—got to the Place about 10. and we began the meeting near 12: and there was Considerable numʳ of People, for a Wet Day and I Spoke from Hosea IX.1 and the People were very attentive—after meeting took Dinner with the Family, and Soon after went homeward got home Just before Sun Sit, found my wife quite poorly.—

Sabb March 25 Went over to Esqʳ Asa Averys and there was a large Nʳ of People, and I Spoke from Mark VI.6: and the People attended well took Dinner with the Family, after meeting—in the evening went home again—

Thirsday and Fryday March 29: 30 March attended on Tribe affairs with out Overseers, Went on our Business without much Difficulty—

Fryday April 6: got up very early and Sot of for New-London got there about 8 o.c. and found a pasage going directly to Sag harb about 10 we Sot Sail the vesel is Calld Starling Packet, William Booth and we had Contrary w and Small and contrary Tide also and we were obligd to return back to New London, got a Shore again before Sun Sit, and I went over to Groton and Lodgd at Mʳ Lesters and was kindly receivd.—had a Comfortable rest—

Saturday April 7: got up very early and went down to the Fery, Calld on Esqʳ Leadyard and he desired me to take Breakfast there, but I was in hast and the woman gave me a good lunch of Bread and meat and went directly over, and about 8 we sot Sail again and had Small and Contrary, and we were obliged to run into Sea Brook & there we Spent the Night and I lodged aboard—

[Courtesy of Dartmouth College Library]

∾ JOURNAL 18

April 6, 1787–July 4, 1787

Occom travels to Long Island to attend a meeting of the Long Island Presbytery and to visit with the Montaukett and Shinnecock tribes. Upon his return to Mohegan, he is met with the news of the deaths of two women in his community: the Mohegan elder Widow Peguun and his niece Eunice Occom. Occom preaches at their joint funeral on April 24. He embarks again for Oneida territory on May 26. At Torrington, Connecticut, he visits renowned African American Congregationalist minister Lemuel Haynes. Occom continues through western Connecticut on to the Schenectady-Albany area, stopping in with old friends and preaching to gathered crowds. Occom arrives at the home of his daughter Christiana Occom Paul on July 4.

April 6. 1787 on Fryday got up very early, and Sot of for New London, got there about 8. o:c, and found a Pasage going directly to Sea Harber; about 10 We Sot Sail the vesel I went in is Called Starling Packet, William Booth master: and we had Contrary Wind and Small, and Contrary Tide also, and we were obliged to return to N. London got a shore again before Sun Sit and I Went over to Groton and Lodgd at Mr Lesters, and was very ^kindly^ receivd—had Comfortable rest.—

Saturday April 7: got up very early, and went down to the Ferry. Calld on Esqr Leadyard, and was receivd Friendly, and he desired me to take Breakfast with them, but I was in hast, and M^rs L gave me a good lunch of meat and bread, enough to last me a Whole Day, and went directly over, and went a Board about 8, and Sot Sail again, and had Small and Contrary Wind, and we were obliged to run into Sea Brooks and there we Spent the Night, I Lodged aboard.—^206

Sabb April 8 Got up very early and we Soon ^got^ under Sail, and we had Very Small Wind and not fair and we went on Slowly, and got north part of Starlling, and there I went a Shore about 3:o:c: & I Travild, to South part & Calld at a Certain House, and the Woman of the House knew me, the Name of the man of the House is Mr Wm Albertson it was now towards Night the man was not at Home, and the woman desired to tary all Night, and I accepted of her offer, Just at Night the man Came home from meeting and appeard very agreable, and was well treated, took Supper with them, and went to Bed prety Soon, and had Comfortable rest.—

Monday April 9: got up early and it was very Foggy morning and I Stayd to take Breakfast, and after that I went to the Ferry, and was detain'd a long While, and about 9 I was Carried over, on Shelter-Island, and there I tried at Several House to hire a Horse but I coud get none, and so went on a foot, till got to Sag Harber, which was about 7 miles, and I was very much beat out when I got there, I never Travil so far on foot Since I have been lame,^207—and I tried there to get a Horse, and I Coud not, and there ^was^ one good Capt Person meet with me, and he tried to get me Horse and he Coud not, and So he and I rode together on his Horse, and ^got^ to his House Some Time before Night and there I lodged; and was extreamly kindly treated, and he got me Horse that Night to go to Southhampton on the morrow,—

Tuesday April 10: Got up early and took Breakfast with them, and about 9 I went on, and to the Place about 11: Calld on Mr Williams, and was there a little while, and understood, that the Presbytery did not meet till next Day and so past on to Cold Spring where the Indians live, and happend to Call at one Saml Peters, he was not at Home but the Woman was, and she appeard very agreable, & Soon found out she was a professor, and Some Time towards night the man Came home, I took Dinner here, after a While Brother Saml Waucus Came to me, and we Soon Concluded to have a meeting in the Evening, and so in the evening the Indians Came together at the House and there was a Considerable N^r and I spoke to them from 1 Kings XIX:13: and there was very good attention, I Lodgd at the Same House, and rested well,—

Wednesday April 11: rose early and after Prayers, Brother Peter and I went to Brother S. Waucus and there took Breakfast, and Soon after Breakfast, I went to see

206. Occom concluded his previous journal booklet with entries for April 6 and 7, 1787; he begins this journal booklet with similar entries documenting the same dates.

207. Occom was crippled in one hip by a slip on the ice in 1780.

old Widow Waucus, and there but few minutes and I went to the Town, got there past 8 and the Presbutery had got together about 10 we went to meeting and the Revd Mr Buell opened the Presbutery by Prayer and then a Sermon Sutable to the ocation, from 2 Corin V:20: and Soon after meeting We returnd to Mr Williamss and Dined together and after Dinner we proceeded in Business, and Several things were in agitation and went on in Business Harmoniously, in the Evening I went to Shenecock, and I preached to the Indians, at the house of one Simeon [Simons], and the Audience was very attentive and the Christians were Some what enlivend, I spoke from 1 John V.10 after meeting we Sot up Some What late, and ~~Sot up~~ lodged at the Same House—

~~Wednesday April~~

Thirdsday April 12: got up early and took Breakfast and Soon after Went to Town got there after the Ministers had got together and we went on in our Business, and there was preaching again and the People Wanted I shoud preach,—but I Chose to attend upon the Presbytery, and Mr Bradford P—

Fryday April 13: We met early, and went on Business; and about 2 I was obliged to go to Bridgehampton to Preach got there there about half after 3 and went right into the meeting House, for the P had been waiting a while I Spoke from Mark V:5: and there was great attention Soon after meeting I went ~~to~~ with Mr Woolworth to Colo Hulbert's and Mr Buell went with us, and there we took Tea and Soon after Tea I went to Mr Personss and had another meeting there and there was a great Number of People and I ~~Skop~~ Spoke to them Rom: 2:28.29 and there was a Solemn attention among the People—I Lodgd at the Same House and went to Bed Soon and had Comfortable rest—

Saturday April 14: got up early and took Breakfast with Family and Soon after eating Mr Persons and I went Down to Sag-Harber; got there about 9: and was till about 12: took Dinner with one M^r [ ] and Soon after Dinner I went a Board of one Mr Case from South H on a Neck of Land Calld Hog Neck Just about Sun Set, and I went a Shore, and went to one Capt Horton's, and Lodgd and was very kindly entertaind the man of the House was very Sick, very like to Die; went to Bed Soon, and had Comfortable Sleep—

Sabb April 15: got up very early, and they got me Horse and went on to the Town, Stopt at one M^r [ ] and he got his Chair ready Soon and he Carried to the Town, Got to Mr Stores about 8: found them Well, and I took Breakfast with them, and about 10 we went to meeting, & there was a great Number of People, and I Spoke from 1 Cor XVI:22 and there was a Solemn attention In the after Noon I went to the Western meeting House about 5 miles Mr Horton Carried me in his Chair and there was a large Congregation, and I Spoke from Dan V.25,[208] and the People attended with great attention and Solemnity, as soon as the meeting was over, we went back to the old Town, Stopt a while at Mr Greens and took Tea there, and went on got to the Town Some Time before Sun Set, Stopt at Mr Storess, and Candle Lighting we went to meeting, and there was a large asembly again, and I Spoke from Jonah III:5

---

208. Occom preached frequently from Daniel 5:25. See his manuscript sermon on this scripture in the sermons part of this collection.

and the People attended Well after meeting went to Mr Hortons and there I Lodged, and was most kindly treated—

Monday April 16: got up before Day Break and Calld up Mr Bradford Who was then Preaching in the Town, he was to go with me to Oister Point and we got ready Soon, and were on Horse Back before Sun rise, and went on, Stopt a While at one Deacon Tuttle's and there took Breakfast, and as Soon as we had done, we past on, and got to the Point, about 10 and Call'd at Mr Tuttles & I Waited there for a Boat that was to Take me in at this Place took Dinner here, and just as we had done the Boat Came and I went to the Shore and Mr Bradford and Mr Tuttle went with, and I took leave of them at the Shore and I went a Board, and we had a fair Wind, and just before Sun Set we arrivd at the City of New London; and I Lodgd at Mr Muxsles, and had Comfortable Sleep—

Tuesday April 17 got up very early, and was about the City till afternoon and then I had an opportunity to go with Mr Nathan Champlin of Lyme up to Mr Houghtons Cove, we got there Some Time before Sun Set, and I got Horse and went home got there about Sun down, and found my Family in good Health all but my Wife, She Complains Some Pains yet, but not so bad as I left her, She is better Thanks be to god for his goodness to us—

Saba April 22 Went to Mr Elijah Browns at Massuppeek Point, and Preached there, I Spoke from Isai:1:2: in the after Noon from Zech VIII.21: and there was a large Asembly for a by Place and the People attended Well,—Soon after meeting took Tea, and after eating went Home—

Tuesday April 24 We had a mornful Day, we attend upon two Funerals at one House, Widow Peguuns Corps was Brought to Widow Eunice Occoms, where there was another Corps, Eunices Daughter Eunice was Dead, these Died the Day before, within an Hour an half of each other, and there was most all our Indians together, and I deliverd a Discourse to them from John IX.4 and the Word fell with Power among the People, and Soon as I had done we marchd to the Burying Place, and we buryed the oldest first and as Soon as we had done we returnd Severally to our Houses—

Saturday April 28: just before Noon I Sot of from Home and went to Stonington, Stopt a while at Mr Chriesies in the Landing, and took Dinner there, and Soon after eating went on, and got to John Quinnip's just before Sun Sit, and there I Lodgd and was much out of order had very bad Cold, rested Some What Comfortable—

Sabb April 29: it was Lowry[209] and raind Some, near about 10 Went to meeting and People Collected and there was a large number of People, and I Spoke from Acts II:17 and 2 Corin V.20 and there was very great attention many Tears were Shed, the Christians Comforted Soon after meeting left the Indian Town, and went to Groton Indian Town, Stopt at Telex Deshon's and there took Dinner, Just at night went to Widow Samsons, and there we had meeting again I Spoke from Rom III:18: and the People were greatly bowd under the Word, the young People were much afected, and after meeting we Sot up a great While had agreable Conversation, and it was past mid Night when we went to Bed and I rested Well—

209. *Lowery:* gloomy, cloudy.

Monday April 30 Got up early and we prayd together, and took Breakfast together, and I Spoke to them about Gospel Rules and the Discipline of the House of god; and about 8 I took leave of them: Calld at Mr John Williamss and presently past on took my Book at Esqr Gene's Stopt a While at Norwich Landing, and got Home about 2 in the after Noon and found my Family as Well as I left them—

Fryday May 4: Went to Groton Stopt at Mr Elijah Browns, and there took Dinner, and Soon after Dinner, went over the River, Some of Mr Daniel and Elijah Brown's Families went over with me, in a large Conoeu—and went to Capt Wylliss, and there was a Considerable of People Collected together, and I Spoke to them from Rom: VIII.38.39 and there was a Solemn attention, many were much affected; Soon after meeting I went over with the Same People that came with me Stopt a few minutes at M^r E Browns, and past on homward, got home near Sun Sit—

Saturday May 5: Some Time in the after noon, went down to Gails Ferry and went over there, and got and got to Mr Gidion Saunderss about Sun Sit, and found them all Well and was kindly recievd by the Family and Lodged there,—

Sabb: May 6, near 10 we went Esqr William Averys Funery he was of the Principle men in the Place, and there was a vast Concouse of People, and Mr Keene Preachd, from John XI:25: Soon after Sermon the Carried the Corps to the Burying ground, about 4 miles off and I went to Mr Saunderss, and from went to Capt Edward Lathems and there took Dinner, and toward Night, People Collected together and I preachd to them from [word missing] VIII.2: and there was very good attention and Just as I Concluded it began to Rain, I Lodged at the Same House, and was very kindly entertaind, went to Bed Soon, and was well refreshd with Sleep—

Monday May 7: Went to Mr Saunderss to break my fast with them, Soon after he took Leave of them, and then went back to Mrs Lathems and took leave of them, and so took of Several Families, and then went down to the Ferry and went over to New London and so on to Mr Saml Roger's and there had a meeting and there was a large Collection of People, and I spoke from Job XXI:14.15 and there was great Solemnity, Soon after meeting took Tea with them, and went on my way homward, got home Some Time in the evening and went to Bed Soon—

Saturday May 12 about 2 in the after noon left home and went to one Capt Waterhouse, and it was Rainey Stopt a While at Doc^r Rogerss took Dinner there and I bled the Doc^r and just at Night went to Mr John Browns and I Lodgd, and was kindly entertaind—

Sabb: May 13: got up early and had my Horse up and went on, and it was Rainey Still, I got to Mr Ebenezer Darts about 8 and took Breakfast there, near to we went to meeting at Capt Waterhouse's and there was not many People and I Spoke from Luke X.26 and there was good attention in the after noon, I Spoke from John XII.36 and there was a great ma^n^y People and they attended with great Solemnity and affection, Soon after meeting took Dinner, and after eating went a way intending to go to Mr John Brown's to preach; but it Rain'd Still and it was Cold, and I Stopt at Mr Darts and I did not feel Well, and there Lodgd and went to Bed Soon.—

Monday May 14: rose very early and went down to New London, and it was Rainey Still and Chilley, Soon got to the City, and Calld on Mr Muxley, and there took Breakfast; and was in the City till Noon, and then went homeward, and got home about 3:—

Sabb. May 20: Some Time in the morning left home, and went to Mr Posts in Weems Hill. Got there Some before meeting and there was but a Small Collection of People We began the Service a little past 10 and I Spoke from Habk III:17 18: and the after noon from Psalm 119:105; and the People attended Well,—after meeting to Victuals and Soon after eating went home Stopt at Jo Ashpo's and bled his Daug^r Mercy She was very Sick,—got about Sun Sit—

Saturday May 26 About 3 in the after noon, I took leave of my Family, and Sot off for Onoyda, went by the way of Windsor, got there Some after Sun Sit, put up at Mr Lothrops a Seperat Preacher and was very kindly reciv'd Lodged there,—

Saturday May 27, got me up very early and went to Mansfie^l^d, got to the Place before 9 and near 11 went to meeting and Mr Gurley Preachd; he Spoke from John, Broad is &c²¹⁰ in the after noon I Spoke from 1 Peter IV:17. the People attended Well,—and towards Night went on to Mr Weltch and there I Lodged and was kindly treated,—

Monday May 28. got me up very, and took Breakfast and Went on my way Stopt a little while at Mr Strongs and So past on and got to my Daughters about 2 in the after noon and there I stayd, found them all well as Common—²¹¹

Tuesday May 29: got up very early, and Went on, Stopt at Mr Maccluers in old Windsor took Breakfast with them, and Soon after went over the River; And on to Westtonbury Calld on Mr Woolcut the Minister of the Place, but he was not at Home, took Dinner there, and Soon after past on, Calld on Esqr Roberts, and was kindly receivd, Bated my Horse and about 2: went on, Calld on Mr Stebbins in Symsbury, and was there a little While, and so past on got to Mr Cases and Lodged had Comfortable rest—

Wednesday May 30 Stay'd to take Breakfast, and Soon after took leave of them & went on my Way, and it Clouded ^up^ Soon, and it began to wet, Near 12 I reachd Torringford, and Stopt at Mr Mills's a Minister of the Place, but was not at Home and the Rain and wind came on very hard; and it was a Tarible Storm and so Stayd all Day and Lodgd there,—

Thirdsday May 31 got up not very early, and it was very Foggey, but it soon Cleard off took Breakfast with the Family, and Soon after went on to Torrington, got Mr Hainess²¹² about 10 he is a Preacher among the People, he is mustee,²¹³ half white

---

210. Occom probably preached this day not from John but from Matthew 7:13, "Enter ye in at the strait gate: for wide is the gate, and broad is the way, that leadeth to destruction, and many there be which go in thereat."

211. This daughter is Olive Occom Adams.

212. *Mr Haines:* Lemuel Haynes. This is the only visit with Haynes recorded in Occom's journals, but it is likely that it is not the only time Occom stopped in with Haynes during his frequent transits between Mohegan and Brotherton. During one of their visits, Haynes purchased from Occom this book: Thomas Horton, *Forty-Six Sermons upon the Whole Eighth Chapter of the Epistle of the Apostle Paul to the Romans* (London: A Maxwell for Tho. Parkhurst, 1674) ("List of Books Owned by Lemuel Haynes," Rauner Library Vertical File).

213. *mustee:* a mixed-race person; derived from the Spanish *mestizo.* Here, Occom uses the term to describe Haynes's black and white ancestry. The term was also used to denote an individual of mixed black and Native descent.

and half Negro an Extraordinary man in understanding, & a great Preacher I was there Some Time, took Dinner there, and Some in the after Noon, I went on my Way again; Stopt at Capt Baldwins in Goshen, and they urgd to Tary all Night, and I Consented, and was kindly entertaind, Took Supper Soon, and went to Bed early and rested Comfortably,—

Friday June 1: got up very early, and Sot of on my way; Calld on Mr Farring at Caanan; but he was not at Hom, took Breakfast there; and Soon after went on again, Stopt Capt [word illegible] in Salbury, and there I Saw Peter Shadock, and Elijah Wympe Ju^r of Brotherton he Just Come from there, and they were then all well, when he Came away; Took Dinner here, and Soon after I went on my way; and Calld on Mr Dakins at ~~little Nine Partners~~ Dover and was there a little While and past on, and got on the Mountain Some Time before Sun Sit and Calld at Deacon Bulkleys and was going further, but they urg'd me to Stay there, and a young woman Said, you Shant go from this House To Night, and so I Stopt and was exceeding well treated—and Went to Bed as Soon as the Night came on—

Saturday June 2 was all Day at Deacon Bulkleys and Lodgd there again and rested Well—

Sabb June 3: Went to meeting with the People, and I Preachd to them from Luke [ ] and there was affection attention among the People all Day,—Directly after meeting I went with Mr Winchel to his House & took Dinner with them and as Soon as we had Din'd, Mr Winchel got his Waggon ready and he took me into his wag^n and he and his Wife went to Dover to meeting in Elder Dakinss meeting and I Preachd from 1 Peter IV.7: and there was a Solemn attention, many Tears were Shed, Soon after meeting Mr Rowe took me in his waggon and Caried me to his House, and there I Lodg'd, and was very tenderly treated,—

Monday June 4: Lay in Bed Some What late & When all the People got up, they got together & I exercised with my Notes in the Family, and it was a large Family it Contain'd near 30 & it was a very Solemn Season, many were much affected it took us Some Time to go thro', and then we Prayd,—About 2 in the after noon we began a meeting, and there was a great Number of People, and I Spoke from [ ] and there was good attention, Soon after meeting they got me a Horse, and I went on the Mountain, and Stopt at Mr Winchels and from there I went to Deacon Bulkley's and there took Tea, and Soon after took my Horse, and went to Esqr Buship's, and there had another meeting and there was a Considerable Number of People, and I Spoke from Mark VI.6: and there was ^a^ Solem^n^ attention,—Lodgd at the Same House, and rested Comfortably once more—

Tuesday June 5: got up very early, and would have gone of, but they woud have me Stay to take Breakfast, and Soon after went on my way, made no Stops, towards Night I Calld at a Certain Tavern, and was waried, and So Concluded to Stay all Night went to Bed quite early, and was well refresh'd with Sleep—

Wednesday June 6: got up early, and had my Horse got ready, and So went on, Stopt a little while at Mr Youngs in Kinderhook, and So past on arrivd to Esqr Woodworth's about 12, and found them all well, took Dinner there—Concluded to have a meeting here tomorrow about 3 in the after Noon, here I met with Mr Thirstin, and he urgd me to go to keep Sabbath with the People in his Place about 12 Miles, Lodgd here,—

Thirsday June 7 Stay here all Day, about 3 People got together, and we began the meeting, and a large number of People and I Spoke from Dutero: X.12.13 and the People attended well,—Taried here again—

Fryday June 8: After Brea^t Mr Thirstin and took leave of the Family, and went to North part of Phillips Town, got to the Place about 12: din^d with one M^r McGee, and after eating went on to Mr Thirstin's House, found his Family Well, Lodged there and it is a Christian Family—We had a meeting here in the evening, and there was a Considerable of P I Spoke from [ ] and the People attended with great Solemnity—

Saturday June 9 I had a meeting at one Mr Linton's he is Sick and there was quite a large number of People I Spoke from [ ] and there was a Solemn attention after meetin went back to Mr Thirstins, and from there to Mr Baileys Brother Thirstin went with me, and there we Lodged, Mr Bailey and his wife I believe are Sincere Christians they are much engaged—

Sabb. June 10 about 9 went to meeting and one Mr Adams and there was a prodigious Number of People, the bigest that ever was Seen at once in this New Sittlement, I Spoke from Gene [ ] Preachd three Times this Day Lodgd at the Same House, Sot up Some What late—

*Monday ^June 11^* got up very early & took leave of the Family and went to M^r McGee's and there took Breakfast, and Soon after, went to New Bethlehem and I preachd, and there was a large number of People I Spoke from Song VIII.5 directly after meeting went with Deacon Herrinton and Dined there; and Some Time in the after went a place where there was burying, and there was a great number of People, and after Burying I preach to the People, and there was good attention I Spo from Kings Set thy House &c[214] and Soon after meeting I went on to Esqr Woodworth's and I Lodged,—

Tuesday June 12 after Break Sot off and Stopt a While and M^r McDonal and Call on Some others and So past on to De Bought, got to Mr Onderkirk's about Sun Sit, and was exceedingly well receiv'd, and they were all well, but the old gentleman, he is quite helpless—Lodged there—

Wednesday June 13, Some Time in the morning after Breakfast, I Went on to Mr John Landsons, and in the evening we had a little meeting. Yet there was quite a Number of People, I Spoke from Psalm CXXXIII.1: and there was a Solemn attention and they were all glad to see me. Lodgd at the Same House—

Thirsday June 14, Towards Night had another meeting & there was a great Number of People, and I Spoke from Rom VI and there an affecting attention among the People many Tears were Shed. ~~Lodgd at the Same House~~ Soon after meeting went with Mr Fondee at the Ferry and there I Lodgd, was kindly treated, went to Bed Soon and had Comfortable rest—

Fryday June 15 got up early and went over the River Soon and went to the Point Calld Waterford, I mist my way and Calld at one Mr Devoo^s and he and his Wife, and old maid that was there were exceeding glad, and they never Saw me before, but the

214. See 2 Kings 20:1.

good old maid, they talkd very freely upon Religious Matters; and I Conversd with them a While and went on again, Stopt at M^r [ ] and took Breakfast there, they were extreamly glad to see me, Soon after eating went on to Mr Vanderwarkens and there I put up for the Day a meeting to begin 4 in the afternoon took Dinner here in the after Noon the People Collected, and there was not many, the Notice was too Short, I Spoke from 2 King 20 and there was very good attention; and Several Came too late, and after I Sot a while in the House, I had Exercise with my Christian Cards, with some young Women that Came late for the Sermon, and Some were Some What Startled, but Some began, they were all delighted, and behaved very decent, and Some old People Chose Texts also, and it was agreable exercise. I Lodged at the Same House and was Extreamly well treated by the Whole Family.—

Saturday June 16 got early and desird to be brought up, and I went of before Breakfast, Stopt at M^r [ ] and they urged me to eat, but I would not; and took leave of them and past on Stopt at Mr Fundee's and there took Breakfast. Soon after eating, I went on to Visit Some Friends and at Night Stayd at good old Mr Faro's.—

Sabb June 17: near 9 went to the Church, and there was a prodigious gathering of People the Church Coud not Contain them all, began the Service before 10, and it began to Rain Soon I Spoke from Isaiah V.2.3: & John IV: [illegible]:—and there was a Solemn and affectionate attention the Congregation was bowd before the Word of god; Soon after Service I went of to over to Half Moon, and English young man accompanied me, and We Stopt at Mr John Landson's and there I took Tea, and Soon after, went on, and before we reach'd the Place, it Rain'd very hard, and I was very wet that Time we got to the Place; Stopt a little While at Capt Comstock's and then went to the Church, and there was but a little Number of People and I Spoke from Dutero 10. and there was very good attention, and went back to Capt Comstock's and Lodg'd, and rested indeferently—

Monday June 18, after B took leave of the Family, and went on towards New-Town, got Mr Teachhouse's about 10, and took Dinner with them; and about 3: we began the Worship of god; we met in a large Barn, and there was large number of People, Spoke from Psalm CXXXVI.1. and there was a very deep attention, many were much affected. Soon after Service went towards Lowden's Stopt at Mr Clutes, and Just in the evening a Number of People Came in, Wanted I Shoud preach, and I was Some What Backward, but finally thought it my Duty to preach, though I was Some What Warried, and I Spoke from Matt VI.33 and there was greater Solemnity, than in the Day Time, there was flow of Tears and after I had Concluded, the People desired to have an Exercise with my Cards, and so gratified them, and it was a Comfortable Exercise; and we Sot up very late, at last the People went of and so I went to bed, and rested but poorly for a little Child Cryed much and I had but a little Sleep—

Tuesday June 19, got up early and got my Horse ready, and I went on to [word illegible], Stopt at the Ferry, and there I under Stood, there were 2 or 3 Families of Indians about half a mile of, and so I turn'd went to see them, and they were intire Strangers to me, and they are Miserable poor, and perfect Heathens, I asked them, whether they ever went to meeting, they Said no, and told them, I was going to Preach a little ways and askd them, Whether they woud go to meeting, they said nothing, and so I left them, I went with one Mr Fordt to the Ferry, went into his House, and he asked me, Whether I had broke my fast, and I told him, I had not, and so he order his negro to get me Victuals directly, and She hastend, his wife was not at Home, and so I Sot down and eat heartily. Soon after he Carried me over, and asked nothing, and went to Mr Simon Fordts and there Stopt, and took Dinner with them, and after Dinner I layd me down in Bed to rest, and I Slept a little & past one we went to meeting and there was a Multitude of People at Church, for Such Short Notice, and I spoke from Isaiah I:2:3 and the attended with great attention—after Sermon took Tea with one M^r [ ] and Soon I went on to Schenactida, and got there just before Sun Sit and put up at Mr John Posts and found them all well, went to bed prety Soon, and a Comfortable rest,—this Day saw Hindreck Pumham from Onoida and heard by him, that our People there were all well about a Fortnit ago—

Wednesday June 20: Was at Schenectida Lodgd at Mr Posts again—

Thirdsday June 21: got up early and went to Nescune,[215] got there 8 Stopt [ ] and there took Breakfast, about 9 we went to meeting, it is a fast Day with the Dutch People every where and there was a vast Concourse of People Collected together Most all Dutch; and about 10 we began the Service, the Church Coud not contain all the People I Spoke from Isaiah I.11 and Isaiah LVIII.5.6 between meetings went to Mr Bassets, and I felt much out of order and I layd me, and had a little dose. after meeting I went to Mr Miller's one of the Elders and was kindly entertain'd took Tea with them, and Soon after layd me down, felt quite poorly got up just before Sun Set, and went to bed Soon and rested Comfortably.—

Fryday June 22: Rose prety early, and took Breakfast, and Comfortable, and Soon after eating, took leave of the Family, and went of to Schena got there about 10: and Stayd in the Place till near Night and then took leave of my Friends and went of and rid about 7 miles and put up at a Certain Tavern, and went to Bed Soon, and was Some What disturbd by the Company that was there they made much Noise a long while—

Saturday June 23 got up early and orderd my Horse to be got ready, and I push'd on Soon, and went to Mr Howboom's and there took Breakfast, they were very Glad to See me, and Soon after Breakfast went on again, and Stopt at Mr Bartlet's and was kindly receivd, and they Soon put out my Horse, and Said I Shoud Tary there that Night took dinner with them, and present after, Mr Bartlet and I went over the River to See Mr Vedder, and they were exceeding Glad to See me old and young after a While I layd down and took Sleep, and Just a Night we took Tea with them, and then the Boys Carried us over back again, and went to ^B^ Soon & had a Comfortable rest,—

Sabbath June 24, about 8 I went down, the west Side of the River, and left my Horse at a Certain Tavern, and went over to [ ] and there we had a meeting, and there was a prodigious Number of People, we began the Service a little after 10: and I Spoke from Exod XX in the after Noon from 2 Corin V.20: and there an affectionate attention, may many were Bowd under the Word, Soon after meeting went Back over the River, and went with one M^r [ ] he is an English man, and was very kindly Treated,—

215. *Nescune:* Niskayuna, New York.

Monday June 25, got up quite early, and of to Mr Hocoboom's and presently after I got it began to Rain, and the People began to gather Soon, and it Raind hard yet there was large Number of People, and I begun the meeting about 10, and we had a little, Intermission, and Preachd again in after Noon and the People attended with great Solemnity many Tears were Shed. I Spoke from Acts [ ] and Proverbs [ ] Lodgd at the Same House and went Bed Soon and rested well—

Tuesday June 26, got up very early and took leave of them and went of to Mr George Eliots, got there about 8 and took Breakfast, and after eating went to See old Mr Eliot about a mile of, and took Dinner there and Soon after went back to meeting at Mr George Eliots and there was a larg numbr of People, I Spoke from Song VIII 5 and the People attended with great Solemnity, ^Baptisd one Child for a Scotchman—^after meetg went to the House, for we met under Trees, and I Stayd there all Night,—

Wednesday June 27 got up quite early, and Sot of to the westward, Calld on Several and got so far as Esqr Maybees and there I Lodgd there—

Thirdsday June 28: Stayd till after Breakefast, and then went of once more, Stopt at Several Houses, got to Esqr Harper's about 10 at Fort Hunter, and Stayd there till about 3: and then took leave of them, and went on my way, Reach'd to Esqr Maybees at Conajohary Just after Sun Sot and I Lodgd there, and was kindly treated; The Esqr was not at Home; went to bed soon and had Comfortable rest—

Thirdsday June 28, got up Early, and had my Horse got ready, and went on towards Bowman's Creek, got to Esqr Kemballs about 10: and there I put up for the Day, and Concluded to preach here on the Morrow, went to See Some Friends and Lodgd at Esqr Kimballs

Fryday June 29. was at the Place, went to fishing in the Creek Catch'd 60 Small fish took Dinner with the Esqr again and about 2 went to meeting & there was but [word missing] People, and I Spoke from 2 Kings XX.1 and it was a Solemn meeting many here much affected. as soon as the meeting was done I went on towards Springfield. Stopt at Mr Lucass and took Tea, and as Soon we had one I went on again; got so far as to Mr Wautrot's a Tavern and there I Lodgd—

Saturday June 30 got up very early and payd my reckening and went on my way, Stopt a While at Mr Millers, and past on; Stopt again at Mr Dike's and there I Broke my fast, was very kindly entertaind. Soon after Breakfast went on again, got to B^r Crippins about 10: and was kindly receivd. there I Stay'd in the after noon, went to See Some Friends was kindly receivd by all; towards night went back to Brother Crippin's and I Lodgd.—

Sabb July 1 about 9 went to meeting at one Mr Wautrots & there was a large number of People, I spoke from John what is that to thee? &c:[216] in the after noon from Rom VIII. and there was a melting attention, I believe many felt the Power of the Word there was a Flow of Tears. after meeting Stayd at the House, till near Night, then there was a word Sent me to go old Mr Pickards and a Number of us went, and he related a Strange Sight he had Seen, twice and Dreamt about it once; There has

216. See John 21:22–23.

been 9 Persons Baptized fornit ago, by way Immarshing or Plunging,[217] a few Days after this man was pasing by the Place, and he happened to Cast his Eyes to the Place where the Person were Baptized; he Says he ^Saw^ a man Strugling to rise out of the Water, and the water [blazd?] a round him, and it was gone in a moment, and it put his mind in great agitation, and Consternation—a few Days after he went again to the Place, and he Saw just Such Sight again, and it has put him to great amazement and a Night or two back, he Dreamt, he went to the Place again, and Saw just Such Sight again, and he was greatly Surprized, and he kept it to himself till this Day and he Says, he Coud not keep it any longer, and so told it to his family, and relate it to me and to a number of People and it took affect upon Some People, tho they don't know what to make of it,—in the evening we went back to Mr Wautrot's and there I lodgd and had good rest—

Monday July 2 after Breakfast Sot of once more Calld on Mr Creeppin, and took my things, and about 10 took leave of them, and went on, Calld on Mr Sprague near the Lake and was there a While, and went on again, and got to Andrews Field a little past 12: and there I Stopt Some Time turnd my Horse out to feed & took Dinner myself,—about 2 I went on again, and went a New Way, and got to the upper part of German Flats and as I Came out of the Woods and had a View of the Flats, I did not know it, I was quite Lost, I went to an House, that was hard by, and I did know the House, and it was a H that I well knew too, and I asked a Woman, where the Mohauk River was, She pointed to the Flats, and Said there—and I asked her Where Mr Fols[218] livd, She Said about 2 up, and then every thing Came right, and so went on, and got to Mr Fols in the Dusk of the Evening, & and they were glad to See me once more and there I put up, and went to Bed Soon and Comfortable Rest once more—

Tuesday July 3. Some Time after Breakfast, took my old Horse and went down the River and got about a mile, I met John Tuhy, one of our People from Brotherton, and he gave me an Intiligence of the State and Situation of our People, they were well in general, Several of them Died Since I left them, & I went on, and went with me, went so far as one Mr Smith's a merchent, and there but a little while, and we went back got to Mr Fols's near 12 and took Dinner there, and Stay the rest of the Day and Lodgd there again,—

Wednesday July 4: got up early and was geting ready to go thro' the Wilderness, and Just as we Sot down to Breakfast, Brother David Fowler, his wife their Daughter Phene and Sister Esther Brother Jacob Fowlers Widow Came in, and were glad to see one another once more; and after Breakfast we had Some Conversation together, and then they went off, and John Tuhy and I went on our way also, and we had a fine Day to go thro' the Woods, and we Stopt a while at [word illegible], and here lives a negro, he is all alone and has planted Some Corn & it is a fine Spot of ground, where he has pitched his Tent, we Sot here Some Time, bated my Horse

---

217. Baptism by immersion entails submerging the entire body of the baptismal candidate under water. In the eighteenth century, it was practiced by Baptists, as well as some New Light and Separate congregations.

218. *Mr Fols:* Conrad Folts.

and after a while we Sot off again; and we got thro the a little While before Sun Set Calld at John Tuhys and they were all Well, and took Dinner with John, here I found Widow Peter from long Island, an old acquaintance of mine, here was a number of young men working for John and Seemed to be glad [page torn—word missing] see me. and then I went to my Daughter Christiana Pauls and found them all well, and we Rejoicd to See each othere once more,—Blessed and adored be god for his infinite Goodness and mercy to my Children, my Daughter and her Husband, have a Comfortable Hope, that they have life in God thro' Jesus Christ Lodged at my Daughter.—

[Courtesy of Dartmouth College Library]

∾ JOURNAL 19

July 5, 1787–September 16, 1787

> *Even as he discovers that many Brotherton residents have been "Scatter'd on account of the Scarcity of Provisions," Occom leads a season of spiritual renewal at the Oneida territory settlements. At New Stockbridge, he preaches with translation assistance from Hendrick Aupaumut and ministers to Catherine Quinney as she suffers a bout of soul sickness. On August 15, 1787, Aupaumut and a number of New Stockbridge and Brotherton residents clear a plot of ground to build Samson Occom his own home. Their efforts touch Occom deeply: "I never did receivd anything from my Indian Brethren before," he writes. "Now I do it out of Principle. It is high Time that We shoud begin to maintain ourselves." Occom conducts the first ever baptismal ceremony at Brotherton on August 26, 1787, baptizing his son-in-law Anthony Paul and his four grandchildren Samson, James, Sarah, and Phebe. The next day, on August 27, Aupaumut, Peter Pauquunnuppeet, and five other Mahican-Stockbridge men draft a formal invitation to Occom "to Come and Settle with us, and to take the Charge over us, and to live and die with us," so that they may be led as a community in pursuit of their spiritual welfare "by one of our own Collour." Consequently, controversy ensues when the white missionary John Sergeant, Jr., arrives from Stockbridge, Massachusetts, in September to resume his pastorate over the Mahican-Stockbridge.*

Thirdsday Jul. 5 arrivd here Yesterday, this Day went no where but kept at Christiana all Day

Sabb July 8: about 9 went to Brother Davids and pretty many People Collected together Both Towns got together, and Some White People, from Clenton we began about 10: in Brother Davids Barn, I Spoke from Mathew [ ] in the after Noon from Deuto X: and the People attend with great Solemnity and Some affection, towards Night went back to Daughters and Lodged there—

Thirdsday July 12: Some Time before Noon I Sot of from our Town, and went to New Stockbrig Stopt a while at Brother Rogers[219] and took Dinner there, and soon

219. *Brother Roger:* Roger Wauby.

after went on again, got to the Place about 2. Put up at Cap[t] Hindricks[220] and Lodged [T]he People were exceeding glad to see me; but many of them were gone a fishing after Salmon.——

Fryday July 13: Some Time after Breakfast went to See a Woman that had been Some Sick, Peter Pohquunnuppeet went with me, and I had Some Conversation with her about her eternal Concerns She Seemed to be resignd, She said, she was willing God shoud dispose of her as he Pleases. Prayed with her, and then went back to Cap[t] Hindrecks, and towards Nig went to meeting and there was but few Collected, and I Spoke to them from XXXIII Psalm 12 verse and there was very good attention after I had done Speaking Cap[t] Hindreck rehersed what he coud remember in his own Tongue and he made the last Prayer and so the People were dismised, and I went home with Cap[t] Hin[k] and Lodged there again——

Saturday July 14: Some in the morning went to see Joseph Pye, alias Shauqueath-quat, and had very agreable Conversation with him his wife Sister & another old Woman, about their Heart Exercises, and they asked Some Questions and I answered them, and after a While I went back.——

Sabb July 15 about 10, we began the Divine Service, & there was a large number of People, many English were with us. I Spoke from 1 Corin 2:2: and Luke VII.48 and the People attended with great Solemnity, and Gravity, after meeting went back to my lodgings, and Just before Sun Set went to meeting again, and Cap[t] Hindreck and Peter Peet rearsed in the Indian Language,[221] the Discourses I Deliverd in the Day, because many of the People Coud not readly understand, What I deliverd in the English, and in the Evening went back to Cap[t] Hs and Sir Peter Jo Quiney and John Quinney Came to ~~came~~ ^my^ Lodgings and they asked many Questions, and we had very agreable Evenings Conversation and it was Rainey Night, went to Bed some what late and had Comfortable repose——

Monday, July 16, Went to See Several Families.——This Evening after we had got to Bed, Sot up quite late too, Widow Quenney knockd at the Door, and She just lookd in, and Spoke & She went back; and I askd what was the Matter, and Cap[t] Hindreck said, that Cathrine Quenney was taken very Strangely at once her Breath was most gone all of a Sudden, and Cap[t] Hindreck and his Wife, got up and went to See her, and I lay Still, and told them, if She Continued so, let me know, and the Cap[t] Came back directly, and desired me to go over, and I got up and Drest me and went over, and when I got into the House, I went right to her Bed Side, and Sot down, she lay very Still, only Breathe with Struggle, and Sigh'd once in a While; and I asked her Whether She was Sick; She Said no, What then is the matter with you, and She Said, with Tears, I want to Love god more, and Serve him better; and I Said to her, if She really Desired and Askd for it She Shud have her desire granted, for it was a good Desire, & gave her Some further advice and Councel, and She desird me to Pray with her, and I ask her, What we Shoud pray for, She Said, that She may have more Faith, that ^She^ might ~~she~~ serve with her Whole Heart, and so we prayd, and after

---

220. *Cap[t] Hindricks:* Hendrick Aupaumut.
221. *Indian Language:* Housatonic-Mohican.

that I went back, to my lodgings, and went to bed again quietly, and had Comfortable rest—

Tuesday, July 17: Soon after Prayers I went over to See Catey and She was yet a Bed and I asked how did She Said well and askd how her mind was She Said, She found more love and Peace, and She wanted to Serve god with all heart, Said, She Slept none or but little all Night, and her Body felt very weak, but her heart felt well; She desired me to pray with her I asked her, what She wanted to pray for, She Said for Wisdom and more Faith; and Soon after Prayer I went to my Quarters and about 10, my Son in Law, Anthony Paul Came to me and little Jo Wauby, and we went to the Lake, Stopt a little While at Mr Aucut's, and were well treated, he is from Connecticut,—and so we past on, got Colo¹ Lewee's just after Sun Set, and Lodged, but I had but Small Portions of Sleep, Flees Plagued me all Night.—

Wednesday, July 18: was at Lewees ~~all Day~~, we Cou'd not find a Connoo till just ~~Sun Down~~ ^till after noon,^ and then we went to the Lake, about 3 quaters of a mile, and We made up a Fire, ~~the~~ where the Black Creek runs into the New Town Creek, and there we Spent the Night, Some Time in the after, I went to Salmon Creek near 3 miles, where the Block House was once, I had been there 26 years ago,²²² there was then a number of Sodiers, but is is all grown up with Large Stadles,²²³ there I saw a Family over the Creek, I suppose moving to the West, but I did not go over to See them towards Night went back to our Fire, and we Catchd Some Fish—we made up great Fire, and after a while went to Sleep, but I was Cold,—

Thirdsday July 19 got up early and Pray'd and then got Some Victuals, and soon after, we Sot off to go the Salmon Creek, Soon got there, I rode and the Boys went by water in a little connoo, we went to fishing, but had no Luck, and so went back to our Fire, Soon got there and went to fishing in the Creek, and Catchd few fish Just at Night, we got ready to return home[;] Lodgd again at Colo¹ Lewees, but I had no Comfort, I had too many Bed Fellows—²²⁴

Fryday July 20 got up quite early, and went of Soon; Stopt a While at Mr Alcuts in New Town took Dinner there, Soon after we went on again got to New-Stockbridge Some in the after Noon, Sun about two hours high at Night, we had a meeting, there was not great many People, and I Spoke to them from [ ] and there was good attention, after mg went to my Lodgings, and went to Bed Soon and had a Comfortable rest— —

Saturday July 21 Lay a Bed Some What late, and Some Time before noon, I left the Place and went to Brotherton, Stopt a little while at Brother Roger Waubys and Soon past on, got to my Daughter Christianas Some Time before Night, and at Night went to Bed Soon and had good rest.—

Sabb July 22 about 9 went to Brother Davids²²⁵ to meeting, and about 10 began the Service, and there was a large Assembly, I spoke from 1 Corin III.11 & Matt

222. The Royal Blockhouse was built at the eastern end of Oneida Lake in 1759. Occom's very first visit to Oneida territory took place in 1761.
223. *Staddles:* trees.
224. *Bed Fellows:* fleas.
225. *Brother David:* David Fowler.

XXV.46 and there was uncommon attention among the People, many were melted Down to Tears, some were alarmd, I felt the Power of god's Word my self. After meeting went to Brother David's House, for we met in his Barn, Just at Night went to my Daughters.—

Thirsday July 26 towards Night I Went to Abraham Simons married him to Sarah Adams they did not make any widding yet there was good many People, Lodged there—

Saturday July 28 Some T in the Morning David Fowler and his Wife and I Sot of to go to Deans Ville, and we went by way of Clenton, got to Clenton Some Time in the after noon, and it was a Rainey Day, and very bad way, many Mirery holes, Stopt a few minutes at Capt Foots, and so past on got to Mr James Dean's about Sun Set, and I was kindly receivd, and I Lodgd there, Brother David and his Wife went to Mr Jonathan Deans and Lodged there—

Sabb July 29: about 9 went to Mr Felpss to meetg and there was Considerable Number of People, and I Spoke from the words, he that Soweth to the flesh &c[226]— and let the Word of Christ Dwell in you &c[227] and there was very good attention. after meeting went back to Mr James Deans, and Lodged there again—

Monday July 30: after Breakfast we sot of for Brotherton, got home about Noon, towards Night I went to my Daughters and found them Well—

Thirsday August 2: towards Night I went to Widow Esther Fowlers, and we had a mg there, and there was not a great Number of People our People are much Scatter'd on account of the Scarcity of Provisions,—I spoke from Luke IX.62 and the was an affectionate attention among the People I lodgd at the Same House—

Saturday. Augt 4: Went to New-Stockbridge, got there before Night,—I put up at Sir Peter Pohquenuppeets

Sabb, Augt 5 about 10 went to meeting, and there was a goodly number of People,—I spoke from Revl. 3:20 and the People attended well, the People met again toward Night and Capt Hindreck and Sir Peter Rehearsed What I had delivd in the Day, Baptised 2 Children one for Sir Peter by the Name Mary, and other was for Joseph Quiney by the Joseph.—

Monday Augt 6 was at the Place all Day—

Tuesday Augt 7 Some Time in towards noon I went to Brotherton Stopt a little while at Rogers and so past on got to Brother David abt 2: and was there a ltle While, and down the Hill got to my Daughters Some Time in the after Noon found them Well—

Thirsday Augt 9 Just at Night Went to meeting at Sister Esther Fowlers and there was but few People it was Raney, I Spoke from Matt XIII.2:&c. and there was great Solemnity amongst the People,—I Lodgd at the Same House—

Sabb Augt 12 went to Davids and about 10 we began the holy Service and there was a great Number of People of and I Spoke from Duet XXXIII.27 and the People attended well Lodgd at Brother Davids—Monday Morning went to my Daughters,—

Wednesday Augt 15: I had a Number of People Come to Clear a bed of ground for

226. See Galatians 6:8.
227. See Colossians 3:16.

me, from New Stockbridge, and from this Place,—the Name of the Stockbridgers, Capt Hindricks

Thirdsday Augt 16 they worked again, and they Laboured exceeding Well this ^is^ the first Labour I ever had from my Brethren according to the Flesh, and it was a Voluntary offer and I accepted of it thankfully, I never did receivd anything from my Indian Brethren before, Now I do it out of Principle. It is high Time that We shoud begin to maintain ~~of~~ ourselves, and to Support our Temporal & Religious Concerns, towards Night, we went up on the Hill and a meeting at Brother David's, there was a Considerable of People & I Spoke from Psalm CXIX:97 and the Word fell with great Power many were deeply Bowed down;—after I had done, the People Sung Some Time. I Lodged at Brother David's and many of the Stockbridgers Stayd here too and we went to rest soon—

Fryday Augt 17 many of the Stockbridgers took Breakfast at Davids, and then they went home, I Soon went after them,—I got to the Place before Noon, & put up at Capt Hindricks towards Night we had a meeting, and there was not many People, and I Spoke from John XV:1.2 and we had a Comfortable meeting, the Word was weighty in the minds of the People, Mr Kirkland was present and one Mr Olcut was there also,—

Saturday Augt 18 in the after noon towards Nt the People got together & Capt Hindrick Rehearsed what I deliverd the Day before, and there was a Solemnity among the People— —

Sabb Augt 19, about 10 we began the Service and there was a large N of People, and I spoke from Deut XXVI.16.17.18.19 and Reval XXII.12 and it was ^a^ Solemn Day with us, as Soon as the meeting was over, I had my Horse got up and I Sot a Way for Brotherton with our People; got home to Davids about Sun Sit and there Lodgd.—

Thirdsday Augt 23 I had 6 Stockbridgers to help me to Clear Land,—and Sun about an Hour high we had a meeting at Widow Fowler, and there was but a Small number of People and I Spoke from Hos VI:3 and there was very good attention.— I Lodged at the Same House

Sabb Augt 26 about 9 went to meeting upon the Hill at Brother Davids, and about 10 began the Divine Worship and there was a large number of People & I Spoke from Roms. [illegible]: and there was a solemn attention amongst the People.—at the end of the after noon Sermon, I baptized my Son in Law Anthony, and my Daughter Christiana owned her Baptism and renew her Covenant with God, and I Baptized their Children; their Names are, Samson, James, Sarah Phebe—these were the first that were Baptized in this New Settlement, and I hope and Pray that ^it^ may be only the bigining of multitudes in this Wilderness, till the whole Wilderness Shall Blossom as the Rose,—

Thirds Day Augt 30 Just at Night went Widow Fowler's and had a meeting, but there was but very few People I Spoke from the words O that my People woud Consider[228]—

Saturday ~~Aug^t~~ Sepr 1 I went to Deansville, one Dr Petre went with me he is a garman Doctor, we got there Some Time before Nig^t took ~~Dinner~~ Tea at Mr James Dean's,

228. Possibly Isaiah 1:3.

and before Sun Set I went to Mr Jonaⁿ Dean's, and there I Lodged and the Doctor Lodged there also,——

Sabb. Sepr 2 about 11 we began the Worship of god, and there was but a Small number of People and I Spoke from John XV 23 & XIV 23 and People attended with Solemnity all Day. Lodged at Mr James Deans where the meeting was, Esqr White and I Lodged together, and had a Comfortable rest——

Monday Sepr 3: I got up early and Went to Mr Phelpss and there I took Breakfast, Some Time in the Morning, went back to Mr James Deans, and leave and went home. got to Brotherton about 1 in the afternoon——

Thirday Sepr 6: towards Night went to Sister Esther Fowlers and had a meeting, and there was but few People, and I Spoke from ~~James~~ 1 Peter 1:15: and the People attended Solemnly to appearance, as Soon as the meeting was over I went back to my Daughters and it was very Dark, but had Torches to give us light thro' thick Woods——

Sabb Sepr 9: went to Brother Davids to meeting we began the Service about and there was Considerable number of People, and I Spoke from Acts XVII.28 & 30 and we had a Solemn meeting many were deeply affected, several Onoyda were there—— toward Night I went back to my Daughters and went to bed Soon——

Thirdsday Sepr 13 this Day we had appointed as a Day of fasting and prayer we met at David Fowler's and there was a Considerable number of People, and I spoke from [ ] Luke XV and it was a Solemn Day there were Some that made Confession of their Wanderings from God, many were bowd before the Majesty of Heaven and I believe Day will not be forgot Soon——

Sabb Sepr 16 had our meeting at Brother David Fowlers, and ther was a great Number of People 3 men Came from Stock—left Mr Serjan's[229] meeting and there were some White People, and the People attend with A[u]ful Solemnity I Spoke from Daniel and Psalm CXIX.1 after meeting went George Peters and took Supper there and after went back to Davids & Lodged there.

[Courtesy of the Connecticut Historical Society]

229. *Mr Serjan:* John Sergeant, Jr. Following in the footsteps of his famous father, the younger Sergeant became minister to the Mahican congregation at Stockbridge, Massachusetts, in 1775. When many Mahican emigrated to establish New Stockbridge in Oneida territory after the American War of Independence, Sergeant did not immediately follow. New Stockbridgers instead relied upon seasonal preaching and ministerial visits from Occom. Sergeant made the first of what would become regular visits to New Stockbridge in September 1787, one month after several New Stockbridgers formally invited Occom to serve as their resident minister. (See "Mahican-Stockbridge Tribe to Samson Occom: Brothers in the Lord," August 27, 1787, in the petitions part of this collection.) With the backing of a Massachusetts-based missionary society, Sergeant established his own church at New Stockbridge in 1788. Rivalry between Sergeant and Occom divided the New Stockbridge community. Conflict between the two ministers peaked with a public debate on July 26, 1788, as Occom's diary for that date records. See Love, *Occom,* 279–281.

◦❁ JOURNAL 20

September 20, 1787–December 5, 1787

> *The arrival of John Sergeant, Jr., at New Stockbridge opens a season of controversy. At the invitation of a group of Stockbridge men, Occom continues his ministry at New Stockbridge even after Sergeant's arrival; he also preaches at Brotherton and surrounding towns. A Native wedding at New Stockbridge on October 18, 1787, draws a "vast concourse." Notes Occom, "There were ten different Languages among the People." Disagreement and contention over the status of Brotherton land tenure flares up again, as ever-increasing numbers of white settlers encroach on Oneida territory. The factionalism resulting from disputes among Brotherton and Oneida tribal members manifests even in worship meeting, Occom observes ruefully. He baptizes six of his nieces and nephews—the children of David Fowler—on November 11, and leaves Brotherton on November 13. Occom preaches, ministers, consoles, baptizes, and conducts marriages along his way.*

Thirdsday Sepr 20, 1787 Just at Night had a meeting at Widow Fowlers, and there was not many People, and I gave them a few words of Exhortation, from Luke VI.8 and the People attended with great Solemnity, and Some affection—after meeting I went to Brother Davids & Lodged there—

Fryday Sepr 21 Some Time in the morning, went to New-Stockbridge, David Fowler Ju^r Went With me, we got there about 2, Call on Mr Sergant, and he appeared good Condition'd, and So to Sir Peters,[230] and directly from there we went to meeting and there was Considerable number of People, and I Spoke from Mark X.9 and there was very good attention. This meeting was Designd Chiefly for the Young People,—Soon after meeting went back to Sir Peter's, and took Some refreshment, and Soon after Sun Set, went to meeting again, and there was great Number of People and there was Several that related there exercises of mind; three men, three women relate their Exercises, a young man, and a maried woman, manifested their desire of Being Baptized, and Some Children, were to be Baptized all also,—Mr Serjant made Some objection, against two Being Baptizd, but the Professors gave their fellowship, to their Desire,[231]—& So we broke up our meeting Some late in the Evening, I to Peter's and their I Lodged and had good rest—

Saturday Sepr 22 Was all Day at the Place,—

Sabb Sepr 23: about 10 we went to meeting, and there was a large number of People, many of our People from Brotherton Came also, and Some White were there, and Mr Serjant, read a Discourse to the Indians, in their Tongue[232] and read it also in English, he read his Prayer also in Indian, and he prayed partly in English—In the after noon I tryed to Preach, I Spoke from Acts X.34.35 and there was very great

---

230. *Sir Peter:* Peter Pauquunnuppeet.

231. In objecting to these New Stockbridge baptisms, John Sergeant, Jr., asserted his continuing pastoral authority over the Stockbridge community (see note 229). It is not clear whether his objections here stem from some knowledge of the two candidates for baptism or from his rivalry with Samson Occom.

232. Mahican-Housatonic.

Solemnity, Some were much affected,—and I Baptized, at this Time Eight persons two adults & the rest Children; The Name of the young is Solomon and the Woman Soon after meeting I went to Sir Peters.—In the evening we had another meeting, one of the men reharsed, What had deliver'd in the Day, after meeting went back with Sir Peter and Lodged there again—

Monday Sepr 24, I took Breakfast with Mr Serjant and Soon after Breakfast I return'd to Brotherton, Betsy Fowler rid behind me and got to the Place near Noon Stopt but few minutes at Brother Davids and past on to my Daughters[233]—

Tuesday Sepr 25: eleven Stockbridgers Came to our Place to help and Some of our men came also.—

Wednesday. I had help a again till after Noon—

Thirdsday Sepr 27 in the Evening, had meeting at Widow Fowler's, there was but few People, and I Spoke from [ ] and there was a Solemn attention after I had done Speaking two of our People Spoke a word one after another & when they had done a White man got up and Spoke, and he Spoke with a feeling Sense of Divine concerns, he gave and account of a Remarkable reformation in Vergena[234]—He came from Stockbridge—after meeting, I went up to Brother David Fowler's & Lodged there.—

Saturday Sepr 29 about 1 in the after Noon, my Son in Law Anthony Paul and Daughter Christiana and Betsey Fowler, sot of for Whites Bourrow, but we were overtaken with Night at one Mr Blanchets and there we Lodged, and were exceedingly well entertaind, and we had a little Exercise with a Christian Cards, we went to Bed in good Season, and I had a Comfortable Rest—

Sabb Sepr 30 got up very Early and Prayd together and then We Sot of. We had near four Miles to go and it was extreamly Bad riding Dreadful miry,—We got to the Place just as Esqr White was about taking Breakfast, and we Sot down with them— and Soon after Breakfast, we went to meeting to another House and there was a large N^r of People, and I Spoke from Isaia 43:21: and there was great attention in the Assembly I believe they felt the weight of the Words, after meeting, I went home with Mr Wentmore, and took Dinner with them, in the after Noon meeting was removed to this House on account of a funeral that is to be attended in this House, for an Infant just Born Dyed in this House last Monday, it livd about two Hours after it was Born, and they have kept the Corps to this Day, for they expected me here this Day, this is the first Death that happend in this Place[235] Since it has been Settled it has been Settling three years, and it is now a large Settlement. This after Noon I Spoke from Isaia 38:1 and it was a Solemn Time indeed many were deeply affected there was a Shower of Tears, Soon after meeting we Carried the little Corps to the grave it was but a few Rods from the House, after Burying returnd to the House,—in the Evening went to Mr Livingworth's and Spent the evening there—about 10 went back to Mr Wentmores and Lodged there—

Monday Octo^r 1 got up early, took Breakfast with Family, after Breakfast went to

233. *my Daughter:* Christiana Occom Paul.

234. A wave of revivalism originating at Hampden-Sidney Presbyterian College swept Virginia during the summer of 1787. See Boles, 1–11; Gewehr, 172–173.

235. *this Place:* Whitesborough, New York.

Esqr Whites and got ready, and about 9 we Sot off for Home, Lieu^t White & Mr Leavett went to our Place,—as we past a long, took Notice of the Settlement, and it is a fine Spot of Land, and a very large Spot too, and the People has made a rapped Progress in Cultivating the Land, if the People were as ingagd in Religion as they ^are^ ~~were~~ in their Temporal Concerns this Settlement woud be very ^much^ like the garden of Eden, Which was the garden of god. the Lord be with them and Bless them that they may indeed be a Peculiar People unto god, that they may be Lights in this Wilderness—We Stopt a while at Clenton,—and we got Home just as the Sun was Setting.—

Thirdsday Octr 4: in the Evening had a meeting in Widow Fowlers and there was but few People, and I Spoke from [ ] and we had a Comfortable Season.—

Sabb Octr 7: had a meeting in Brother Davids and there was not many People, and I spoke from [ ] and we had a Solemn meeting,—Lodged at Brother Davids—

Tuesday Octr 9: about 1 in the after noon, I Sot of for Clenton, got there Some Time before Night Stopt a little while at Mr Joness to See his Wife had been Sick Some Time and She was very poorly, and went from there to Capt Foot's and in the Evening the People Collected together, and I Spoke to them from John XXI.22 and there was great Solemnity amongst the People. I believe Some felt the Weight of the Word,—the Begining of last March, there was no House in this Place, a perfect Wild Wilderness, Now there are 20 Family and there were Seventy odd Persons in the meeting this evening, and have made great apperance in their improvements. there are chiefly from New England and youngerly People—[236]

Wednesday Octr 10 Stayd here till after Dinner, and then went to a Certain House between this Place, and Whitesbourough about half way, the mans Name is Blanchet, I got there Some Time before Night, and had a meeting, and there was a Considerable Number of People, and I Spoke from Psalm CVII.31: and the People attended exceeding Well,—this was all a Wild Wilderness in the begining of last Spring & now the People are Settling all along from Whitesborough to Clenton—in few Years this will be Settled thick as any part of the globe the Land is so good, it draws all Sorts of People and Nations are flocking here Continually—

Thirdsday Octo^r 11 Some Time Breakfast I Sot of for home,—Stopt a while at Capt Foots in Clenton and took Dinner there. and Soon after Dinner went on again, got to my Daughters—and in the evening we had a meeting Sister Esthers,[237] and was not many People, and I Spoke from Psal CVII.31 [or CXII.31], and there was an uncommon attention, many were deeply affected.—

Fryday Octo^r 12 Some Time in the morning I sot of for N. Stockbridge and had a meeting there in the Evening, and I Spoke from [ ] and there was good atention. Lodgd at Sir Peters—

Saturday Octo^r 13: About 2 in the after noon I went to Deanville, ^got^ to the Place about Sun Set ^Peter went with me^ found Mrs Dean exceedingly distrest with

---

236. Treaties, leases, and purchases of Native territory engineered by the state of New York enabled massive white migration to central and western New York in the decades following the American War of Independence. A majority of the emigrants were from New England. See Darlington.

237. *Sister Esther:* Esther Poquiantup Fowler.

uncommon Difficulties in her Pregnancy, and Peter and I Went to Mr Jonat Deans and Lodged there, and 2.o.c. in the Night I was Calld up, to the other House, and Bleed Mrs Dean and I went directly, and found her much distrest and took Blood from her foot, and Bled exceeding Well,—and her distreses began to mitagate directly, and I Stayd the rest of the Night and She was Some What Comfortable—I was Calld up again before Day to write ^to Doc^r^ for them, for they were Sending to Albany for one, and were Sending for Mr Dean too for he had been gone Some Time to Spencertown—

Sabb Octo^r 14: about 10 the People got together, and there was a large number of People, many White People from other Places and many Indians from Both our Towns, I Spoke from Matt V.20: and there was a Solemn attention all Day. Soon after meeting Peter and I went to Clenton got there a little after Sun Set, We put up at Capt Foots and the People Collected directly and there was quite a large number, and I Spoke from [ ] lodgd at the Same House & had Comfortable rest—

Monday Octo^r 15: Soon after Breakfast went to mill, and was there Some Time, before we we Coud get grinding[238]—we got to our Place about 1: and Sir Peter past on to his Place—

Thirdsday Octo^r 18: ~~had a meeting at Widow Fowlers~~ Went to Stockbridge to a Wedding Just before Sun Set, attended upon Marriage the Young man was, one the Sachem's Son[239] and the Young Woman was of noted Family, and there was a Vast concourse of People of many Nations, it was Said, there were ten different Languages among the People and the People behaved decently, but the Oneydas began to behave unseamly and in the Night they had a tarable froleck even all Night[240]—

Fryday was all Day at the Place,—in the evening we Collected together at Capt Hindrecks[241] I Spoke from Matt 6:22.23 and there was a Solemn attention, after I had done Capt Hindreck rehearsed the Same, Lodgd at the Same House—

Saturday Octo^r 20: Some Time in the ~~morning~~ ^after noon^ I returnd to Brotherton, Mr Warmsly went with me, we Stopt at Roger Waubys and there took Dinner, Soon after Din^r I went on and Mr Warmsly went back, I got to Brother Davids before Night and I Lodgd at David's—

Sabb Octo^r 21 about 10 the People got together & was a large Number of People Some white People and I Spoke from John XIII 17 and the People were very Solemn and many were affected, Lodged at the Same House—

Monday Octo^r 22, in the evening had a meeting in Sister Fowlers, and there was not many People and I Spoke from [ ] and the People attended well Lodgd at the Same House

Tuesday Octo^r 23. People from Stockbridge came to help me. the were 5 of them and the Workd two Days

---

238. Brotherton settlers petitioned Congress for assistance in building their own sawmill and gristmill in about 1785. See "Brotherton Tribe to United States Congress" in the petitions section of this collection.

239. This is probably John Quinney, son of Stockbridge sachem Joseph Quinney.

240. *froleck:* frolic, celebration.

241. *Capt Hindreck:* Hendrick Aupaumut.

Thirdsday Octo^r 24: We were Calld Suddenly to appear before the Chiefs of the Onoyda, that had Just come to our Place,—and we eat our Breakfast in hast, and went direcly to Widow Fowlers and there the Chiefs meet with us, and it was about our Land But there was Such Confusion, I woud not Say a word about it, it was a party Scheam, Contrivd by a few of our People, they been agreing with the the Onoydas for a Piece of Land; Without the knowledge of the Head men of the Place, Some of the Contrivers of this mischief were much intoxicated and they drove on the Business with all fury in no order, it was like Whirlwind, Some Time towards Night we brok up and every one ^went^ his way: in great Confusion of mind,—I went to B^r Davids and there Lodgd with a Sorrowful mind.—²⁴²

Fryday Octo^r 25 was at our Places all Day

Saturday ~Octo^r 27~ *Octo^r 26* Towards Night Just as I was going a way to Clenton Brother Crippin and Br Swane came to my Son in Laws and we had a little Conversation, these Brethren are from a Place Calld Springfield, Going to Cherry valey; So I left them and Went on to Clenton got there a bout Sun Set, put up at Capt Foots, found them all Well.—

Sabb Octo^r 27 about half after 10 we began the exercise, and there was a large Number of People Some from other Places & Several Stockbridgers were with us. and there was very great attention, both before noon and after noon I Spoke from John, I know you that the Love of god is not in you,²⁴³ in the after noon from Mark VIII.36.37 as Soon as the meeting was done I went of to Brotherton, the Stockbridgers went with me, we got there a bout Sun Set, we eat a few mouthfulls and went to meeting at Sister esters and there was not much moving there Seemed to be Some party Spirit in the meeting.—

Sabb Novr 4 Preachd at New Stockbridge & Spoke from [ ] and there was very Serious attention all Day

Monday Novr 5: went back to Brotherton—

Sabb Novr 11: Preachd at Brotherton once more and Baptized Brother David Fowler's Children Six of them,²⁴⁴ and we had a Solemn Day of it, in the evening we had a nother meeting, and it was a Comfortable meeting—

Monday Novr 12 this Day intended to Set out for home but it began in the morning, and so Stopt for the Day—

Tuesday Novr 13: got up very early and got ready, and we Sot out Sun about an Hour and half ~half~ high, Betsy Fowler Jerusha Wympe and Henry Stensel a young Dutch man went with me we had exceeding *fine* Warm Day, got thro' the Woods be-

242. Aggressive appropriation of Native lands by the state of New York and massive white emigration to Oneida territory exacerbated ongoing disagreements over land allotment between the Oneida and Brotherton tribes. This incident represents a continuation of the discussions begun by Oneida tribal elders in October 1786. (See Occom's diary entries for October 16–18, 1786.) It also marks the political emergence of a contentious Brotherton faction headed by Elijah Wympy that would assert itself in tribal dealings over the next several years.

243. See John 5:42.

244. David Fowler had nine children: David (b. 1767), Hannah (b. 1768), Elizabeth (b. 1770), Benjamin Garrett (b. 1774), Lurheana (b. 1776), Mary (b. 1778), James (b. 1784), Jacob (b. 1788), and Rhodolphus (b. 1791). Occom probably baptized the oldest six.

fore Sun Sit I put up at Conrad Folss Jerusha and Betsey went to Mr Smiths about 2 miles further.—

Wednesday Novr 14 got up very early and went on Stopt a little While at Esqr Franks and So past on, and Stopt at Andrews Field and there we took Dinner, and past on, and we got to Mr Thomas Crippins Just before Sun Sit and we Lodged there, and we had a meeting this evening and there was a Consideral N^r of People, and it was a refreshing Time, I Spoke from these words Love is the fulfilling of the Law.[245]—

Thirds Day Novr 15: We were at the Place all day we went to see some Friends— Lodged at M^r [Wautrods]—

Fryday Novr 16: Some Time in the afternoon had a meeting in Mr Pickards and there was a large N^r of People, and I Spoke from Matt, he doeth the will of my Father, The Same is my Brother &c[246]—and the People attended well.—

Saturday Novr 17: was at the Place, Towards night went to Brother Nicholas Pickards, and in the evening a few People Came together to Sing, and we Lodged there.—

Sabb. Novr 18 had a meeting at Mr Dyks and there were So many People we were obligd to meet out in the Field, and it very warm, I Spoke from Psalm CXIX. O how Love I thy Law &c and it was a Solemn meting,—towards Night I married a Cupple, and it was a Solemn Weding, Conducted very agreable, Supped with them—and Soon after Supper, we went to old Mr Stensels, and there we had a meeting, and there was a large Collection of People, and I Spoke from [ ] and the attendd well We Lodged at the Same House.—

Monday Novr 19: took leave of Some of my Friends and So went out of the Place, the girls rode along with me a little ways & took leave of them, they went on with Tears, and I went on my way: Stopt at Brother Swans and took Breakfast with them, and Soon after eating, I went on, and was going on, but I was obligd to wait Some Time for a girl that was going with me, but they Coud not find the Horse that She was to ride, and so I tooke her behind me, and went a Little way, and a young man overtook us and I desired him to take her behind him, and he readily took her and we went on, and soon got to Bowmans Creek, Where I was to preach, and the People had been waiting Some Time and So I began the Worship of god directly, and there was but few People, I Spoke from [ ] I Lodged at Mr Whites,—

Tuesday Novr 20: got me up early, and Went to Esqr Kimbels and there took Breakfast,—Towards Night I went to Esqr Younglove's and just in the evening People began to Come in and there was a large N^r Collected, and I Spoke to them from, Matt 6:33: and there was a Solemn attention, I Lodgd at the Same House but lay uncomfortable all Night.—

Wednesday Novr 21: got up very early, and had my Horse brought, and I Went to Cherry Valley, and it was rainey, and I on fast and Soon got to the Place Calld on Colo^l Cambel & there took Breakfast, and about 10 went to meeting at one Mr Rechee's and there was a Considerable of People, and I Spoke from Psalm CXII and the People attended Well, and Soon after meeting went to Colo Cambels again and

245. See Romans 13:10.
246. See Matthew 12:50.

there Dined; and was detained by a Black Smith he was Shewing my Horse, and I Coud not get a way till the Sun was gong down and then I went to Bowman's Creek got there Some Time in the evening, it was very bad riding, and Some few People got together, at Mr Whites, and I Baptized a Child for one Mr Griswool by the Name of Joenna, and Lodge at the Same House and rest well.—

Thirdsday Novr 22 got up early, and went over to Eq^r Kimbel and took Breakfast, and Soon after eating, went of and got to Mr Romines Some Time in the after noon, and Stopt there a while and took some Victuals, and Soon after went on again, got to one M^r [ ] and Lodged there here I met with a woman that was much in exercise of mind and had some Conversation with her, and found under great Concern of Soul, and I gave her advice and Councel—

Fryday Novr 23: got up early in the morning, and went on, got to Capt Grigss about Breakfast Time and took Breakfast With him, and Soon after went on again, and got to Mr Vedders before 10: and went over the River, and Stopt at Mr Bartlets and there took Dinner and Soon after got up my Horse and Went to Yungey Hill, and Lodged at Mr Mudges the People got together directly, and I obligd to preach to them before I Went to Bed, and it was a Solemn Time, the Christians got quite warm Some Spoke.—

Saturday Novr 24: Rose very early, and I went to Esqr Harper's Mr Mudge went with me, Soon got there and found them all Well, there took Breakfast, and Stayd till after Dinner, and then went back to Mr Mudges and was there but few minutes & I past by and went to M^r [ ] and just in the evening People began to Come in & the House Soon filld, and I was obligd to preach to them, I Spoke from the words Let thy House &c[247] and there was great Solemnity, and affection amongst the People, I Lodgd at the Same House and rested Comfortably.—

Sabb Novr 25 about 9 to the Place of meeting & there was a prodigious Nr of People and I Spoke fr Job: XXIII.8. 1 Joh 1:6: and there was great Solemnity amongst Soon after meeting I took D^r with Mr Frank, and then went to Mr Bartlets by the River, and had nother Meeting there, and there was a large Number of People and attend well, but just as the last Singing was began, Mr Bartlets Daughter fainted, and we dissisted Singg and I Lodged ^not^ at the Same House, but I went over to Mr Vedder's east Side of the River, and rested well.—

Monday Novr 26: got up early, and after Breakfast, went over the other Side of the River, and Just Calld at Mr Bartlets and got my up and took leave of them Calld on Mr Keeny, a few Minutes, and past on,—in the evening had a meeting at Mr Andrew Eliots, and was great many People and I Spoke from [ ] Visited a Young Woman that was very Sick. pray with her,—

Tuesday Novr 27: got up early and to Vist the Young Woman again, and She was Some What better, and then took leave of them and other Families, and to one M^r [ ] and there was many People, and Lodged there—

Wednesday Novr 28: towards Night went over the River to one Mr Groot and Preachd there in the Evening, and there was great many Peop and Lodged there—

Thirdsday Novr 29: went back to West Side of the River, and got up my Horse at

247. See Ruth 4:12.

Mr Mertin Vanolendas and took leave of them, and Just as I got on my Horse, I ^heard^ Some one hallow and I lookd to the River, and behold I saw my Law my Son Anthony and his Family, and they went Down the River they a Connoo and I went on to Schenactada, I got there Some Time in the after Noon and put up at Mr John Posts Just before night Anthony got there, also: I Visited Some few Friends, Lodged at old Mr Post's my good old Friend.—

Fryday Novr 30 got up early and Mr John Posts and got up my Horse & went down the river a little and went over, and so on Downwards, to a Place Calld put at M^r [ ] here Lives Mr John Mudge a Baptist Preacher in the after Noon preachd, and there was great many Peop Spoke from what is thy Name[248] in the evening had another meeting there was a large N^r again. Lodge at the House where the meeting was,—

Saturday Decr 1: after Breakfast, Went on towas Nesquan Church, got to Mr Fishers early in the Day and took Dinner there, after Dinner went to See Mr Peters in the evening went back to Mr Fishers and Lodged there and went to bed soon—

Sabb: Decr 2: after Breakfast went with the Family in a large Connoo to Church over to Nesquana: and there was large gathering of P and I Spoke to them from [ ] and as Soon as the meeting was over, I went back to Mr Fisher's and took Dinner with them, and Soon after, Went to back in the woods, and Preachd Twice, and Lodgd at the last House I preachd in—

Monday Decr 3 Went to New Town and Preachd at M^r [ ] Spoke from [ ] and Soon after meeting went to the Southward, and Stopt at Mr Conells and took Dinner ~~There~~ there, and then went to another House and Preachd there, and Soon after meeting went back to M^r [Conells] and Lodged there—

Tuesday Decr 4: got up early and went to one old School-Masters and there took Breakfast, and Soon after went to half-Moon Church, Stopt at one Mr Clules in from thence to Colo [ ] and to Capt Compstocks was there a while, and Just as I was going away Brother Peter Pohquunnuppeet Came to me, and was glad to See him, and then Came also Mr John Venderwarken and we went with him to his House and Lodged there

Wednesday, ^Dec^r 5^: in the afternoon went to the Church and Preachd there, but there was not many People, I Spoke from [ ] Soon after meeting went back with Mr Vanderwarken and Lodged there—

[Courtesy of Dartmouth College Library]

∾ JOURNAL 21

December 11, 1787–August 10, 1788

> *Occom travels southward through New York and New Jersey. Along the way, he dines with Princeton College president John Witherspoon and visits the same Delaware Indian communities that sent Daniel Simon and Hezekiah Calvin to Moor's Indian Charity School more than twenty years before. From January 22 to*

248. See Mark 5:9, Luke 8:30, Genesis 32:27, Judges 13:17.

February 22, he joins Peter Pauquunnuppeet and David Fowler on a visit to Phila-delphia to solicit financial support for churches and schools at Brotherton and New Stockbridge. The trio also visits New York City in an unsuccessful attempt to raise more funds. Fowler and Pauquunnuppeet head homeward to Oneida territory on March 14, while Occom preaches in the area for a few more weeks before sailing for home. During early April, Samson and Mary Fowler Occom visit their family and tribal communities on Long Island. On May 26, Occom departs again for Oneida territory, arriving at Brotherton on July 8. Occom preaches in the new schoolhouse at Brotherton. At New Stockbridge, the rivalry between Occom and Sergeant cul-minates in a public doctrinal debate. Occom and his sons take a late summer hunt-ing and fishing trip, escaping for a few days the increasing pressures of religious and political factionalism. "We Catchd a fine parsel of Fish presently, & made up a Fire by the Creek and had a fine Supper of F and afterward Prayd, & then we went to Sleep by our Fire quietly," Occom writes. Two days later, he notes, "I killd a great gray Eagle and a Raven."

Monday Decr 10: Got up very early, and took leave of the family, and we went on to Albany, got there about 12 and we lodgd at one M^r [ ]

Tuesday Decr 11: We got up Some What early, and went over the River, and got to Esqr Woodworths before Night and we Lodged there, we were receivd with all kindness and Friendship

Wednesday Decr 12 Some Time in the Morning, went on to New Bethlehem and We Stopt at one M^r [ ] and I preachd in the evening, Spoke from the words But one thing is needful[249] and there was great many P and they attended well, and after meeting I went with one Mr Mofat a Baptist Preacher and there we Lodged.—

Thirdsday Decr 13 Preach'd here this Day, and there was a good Number of People. I Spoke from [ ] as Soon as the meeting was done, we went to another Place about 4 miles off, and there I preachd to a Considerable Number of People, and there Lodged,—

Fryday Decr 14 We went to Phillips Town, and got to Mr Cooks Some Time be-fore Noon, and there we put up, and in the Evening we had a meeting to another House, & it was extreem Cold yet there was a large Number of People and after meet-ing went back to old Mr Cooks and there we Lodgd and we Lodged Comfortably by the Fire—

Sabb Decr 16: Soon after Breakfast I went to meeting to one Mr Adamss, I went afoot thro the Woods, about [1?] began the Meeting, and there was a large Number of People, and I Spoke from [ ] The People expected Mr Perry from Richmount, but he faild them, and they desired me to administer the Ordernance[250] and I Complied & we had a Solemn Day of it—in the Evening we had another meeting in Young Mr Cooks House and there was a large number of People, I Spoke from [ ] and I Baptized Six Children for M^r [ ] their Names were [words missing] after meeting went back to old Mr Cooks again and there we Lodgd.—

---

249. See Luke 10:42.
250. *the Ordernance:* communion, or the Eucharist.

Monday Decr 17 got up very early and went New Bethlehem and there I had a meeting, and I Baptizd a Child for one Mr Bunce, Soon after meet went to green Bush and in the Evening we had a meeting at Esqr Woodworths and there was Considerable number of People, and they attended well. We Lodged at the Same House—

Tuesday Decr 18: got up early and took Breakfast, and Soon after took leave of the Family and went on our way and wrode about 30 miles and put up at a Tervern—

Wednesday Decr 19 got up very early and went on our way and got Stansborough Some Time in the after noon and We Calld in at one Mr Straights and there we had a meeting in the Evening, and there was a large number of People for a Short Notice, and the People attended with great Seriousness I Spoke from [ ] We Lodged at the Same House and were kindly entertaind by the Family—

Thirdsday Decr 20: got up early, and took Breakfast with the Family, and Soon after eating we went on again and got to Esqr Firmans Some Time before Noon and there we Stoptd, and in the Evening we had a meeting in a School House about one m²⁵¹ of and there was a great Number of People and there was great Solemnity among the People, after meeting went back to Esqr Firman and we Lodgd,—

Fryday Decr 21: Some Time after Breakfast we went into Nine Partners and Stopt at Mr Gasleys and in the Eving we had a Mg and there was a Prodigious number of People, and there was great Seriousness. I Lodged at the Same House this Family is a Christian Family indeed.—

Saturday Decr 22 We were here abouts all Day—

Sabb Decr 23 after Breakfast we went to meeting to a Place Calld the Hallow, I Went with Mrs Gasley in their Slay, and it was a Dreadful Storm of Snow, yet there was good many People, and they attended Well. Soon after Meeting, we went back, and we Stopt at [word illegible] and took Dinner there, and Soon after eating, we went on again, and got to Mr Gasley's before Night, and in the Evening the People Came together and I Spoke to them, and there was great Solemnity in the meeting, and after meetg we had Exercise with Christian Cards and it was late before the People Dispersd and we lodgd at the Same House—

Monday Decr 24: got up very early, and went to Pleasen Valley with Mrs Gasley and her Daughter in their Slay, got there before meeting, and about 11: we went to meeting and there was a large Number of People, and with great Solemnity the People attendd the word of god, directly after meeting we went to Mr Platts, and there we had another meeting, and there was a great many People Mr Case & Mr Grover were there and I Spoke from James IV.17 and as Soon as I had done Speaking Mr Grover began, and Spoke Some Time with great firvency, and when he had done, Mr Case got up and he Spoke Some Time with great earnestness, and the People the were greatly Solemnizd, and it was a Powerful meeting; the Lord has been Visiting the People about here with his Divine Power many have been Converted to God, and after meeting we took leave one of another and it was an affectionate parting, lodgd at the Same House and had quiet Sleep—

Tuesday Decr 25: Some Time in the Morning, we went on our way after we had took leave of the Family, & directed our Course to Poughkeepsie, and so down the

251. *m:* mile.

River about 4 miles and there we went over the River and we went into a House Where one Mr Havens lives and his Wife was upon point of Death, I askd her Some Que^ns found her Comfortable in her mind and was willing to lieve the World,[252] I pray with her & and then went on, got to Major Deboises before night and there we put up and were kindly receivd.—

Wednesday Decr 26, in the morning a Certain Man Came to the House, and gave information that Mrs Havens was Dead, and Mr Havens desired me to attend upon his Wife's Funeral and accordingly as Soon as the Breakfast was over I went, and there was a large Number of People Collecting and I preachd from the Words Set thy H— in order &c:[253] and as Soon as the meeting was over, we went back to Majors and from there just at Night to meeting House and there was a great Concource of People and I Spoke from Psalm CVII.31 and it was a Solemn Asembly, and as soon as the meeting was done I went with one [ ] about five miles of in a Slay, and there Lodged, & was kindly treated—

Thirdsday Decr 27: Some Time in the Day Peter[254] & Henry[255] Came to me, and towards Night, we went towards the South part of Newborough, and there we had a meeting and there was a great many People and I Spoke from [ ] and the People be-haved well,—here Brother David Fowler came to the meeting, Just over took us, after meeting we went with one M^r [ ] and there I Lodgd and was Friendly entertaind,—

Fryday Decr 28: took Breakfast and Soon after Sot off and went to New Windsor, just Calld on Mr Close and So to Mr Woods 4 or 5 miles out the Town, and we were very glad to See one another, and we Concluded to have a meeting in Esqr Clarks in the evening, and accordingly mett and there was a great N^t of People, and I Spoke from [ ] and the People attended with great Solemnity after meeting went back to Brother Woods, and there we Lodged.—

Saturday Decr 29 got up very early and took leave of the Family, and went of, Call in at Esqr Clark's and took Breakfast there and Soon after past on again Stopt a while at Mr Brewsters in Blooming Grove took Dinner there, after eating went on again, and Just in the evening, we got to Florada and put ^up^ at Mr Robinsons, a Tervern.—

Sabb: Decr 31 Had an Invitation to Preach, and I Concented, and about 11 the People got together, and I went into the meeting House and there was a great Num^r of People, and I Spoke from [ ] and the People attended with great attention—as Soon as the meeting was over we took Dinner, and then we went on Warwick, about 5 miles, and there I preachd in the Evening to a great multitude of People and I Spoke from Jonah III.5: and the P. were very Solemn, after meeting, I went to a Cer-tain House and there I Lodged and was kindly treated.—

Monday Decr 31. got up very early, and we Sot of, and Stopt at Colo Hathhorns and there we took Breakfast & Soon after eating we went on again, and Some Time in the afternoon at Mr Smiths a Publick House,—and the P desired me to Stopt and so have a meeting in the Evening and I Concented, and the People got together in

---

252. Being "willing to leave the world" was a measure of spiritual preparedness for death.

253. See 2 Kings 20:1, Isaiah 38:1.

254. *Peter:* Peter Pauquunnuppeet.

255. *Henry:* Henry Quaquaquid.

the evening and there was a large num^r for the Cold Season and Short notice—and I Spoke from [ ] and the People behaved well in the Room, but Some in the other Room made much Noise—we Lodgd at the Same House—

Tuesday Janu 1. 1788 got up quite Early and got ready Soon and went on our way again, and in the evening we got to Mill Stone, and Lodged at a Publick House.—

Wednesday Jan^r 2: took Breakfast early, and Soon after went on ^a^gain and got to Doc^r Weatherspoons[256] in Prince Town Just about 12: took Dinner with him & Soon after we past on, and got to a Certain Tavern and there we Lodged, and it was very Cold Night,—

Thirdsday Jan^r 3: we got up very early and went on Some Time in the after noon we got to ~~gepelak~~ Quakeson an Indian Place[257] we went into one House and was there a while found them Extreemly Poor.—and So we went to a Tavern and there we Lodgd.—

Fryday Jan^r 4 after Breakfast we went back to the Indian Place just Calld in the Same House we Calld in Yesterday and So past on and we got to Agepelack another Indian Place, Calld at one Mytops and I Stayd I was very poorly with a Cold and Lodgd here the Night following, and was kindly treated.—

Saturday Jan^r 5: was here again all Day, Continued much ill, and Lodgd here again—

Sabb: Jan^r 6: about 11 we went to meeting at the meeting House, and there was not many People and it was now pleasent Day and I Spoke from the Words that which is wanting Can not be numbered,[258] and after meeting Daniel Simon invited me to go home with him to his Mother in Laws Widow Calvin and there we were all this week and I was much troubled with Cold attended with Cough,—

Sabb Jan^r 13 Preachd here again, from the words Set thy House in order &c[259] preachd here 4 times in the Whole—

Monday Jan^r 14 left the Place and went on towards Philadelphia, got to the River east Side against Philadelphia & there We Lodged in a Tervern and rested Well—

Tuesday Jan^r 15[260]

Tuesdad Jan^r 1. 1788. We got up early and went on our Way, and get to the Revd Mr Baldwin of [ ] and in the evening we went to a Certain House to See a Sick man— and afterward went back to Mr Baldwins and there I Lodged—

Wednesday Jan^r 2 Some Time after Breakfast, we went to Pirsippann to Mr Grover's, & towards night went back to Mr Baldwin's, and so to another House a mile of two off and there we had a meeting and there was a number of People, and I Spoke to them from [ ] and I Lodgd at the Same House.—

---

256. *Doc^r Weatherspoon:* John Witherspoon

257. *Quakeson:* Also spelled Coaxen; township near Southhampton, New Jersey, home to a band of Lenape Indians once proselytized by David Brainerd.

258. See Ecclesiastes 1:15.

259. See 2 Kings 20:1, Isaiah 38:1.

260. A curious break in sequencing occurs here, as Occom appears to retrace his steps during the previous two weeks. Occom may have been correcting his own manuscript diary against a separate account book.

Thirdsday Jan^r 3: We went of early in the morning and gone but a little way & a Certain gentleman Calld us and desired us to go in and we did, and took Breakfast with him, and gave us Some m besides, Soon after eating we past on, and Just Stopt at Mr Baldwins and So past on, and and went to Mr Grovers, and towards noon we went to Mr Beaverrout's and in the evening we had a meeting, and there was a great Number of People and I Spoke from [ ] and there was great Seriousness among the People, and Lodgd at the Same House—

Frid^day^ Jan^r 4 after we broke our fast we Sot of again & Call at the Revd Mr Greens and was there a few minutes and So on, and we got to Mr Chapman's at Newark mountains[261] a little past 12 and we took Dinner there, and Soon after Dinner, we went to Crain Town and got there a little before Sun-Sit, and was word given out, for a meeting and I put up at Mr Crains, and in the eveng Went to meeting and there was a great number of People and I Spoke from 1 Joh V.10 and there was very great Solemnity. after meeting went back to Mr Crains and there I Lodged & rested well—

Saturdad Jan^r 5: Soon after Breakfast, we Sot of for Horse Neck and Soon got there, and it was extream Cold, and we put up at Esqr Crains—

Sabb day Jan^r 6: about 11 we went to meeting, and it was extreem Cold, yet there was a large Number of Peop and I Spoke from [ ] and the People attended well. Soon as the Service was over I went back to Esqr Crain and the we took Dinner, and as Soon as we had Swallowd our Dinner we went of to another Place, three or four miles, and there we had an Evening meeting and good many People and a well behaved People We Lodg at the Same House—

Monday Jan^r 7 went off Some What early, and directed our Course to Morris Town We Stopt a while at Mr Grovers and there we left Henry Stensel, We Calld also at Doc^r Darbes, and so on, we got Morris Town Just before Night, and we put up the Revd Mr Johnes's and in the Evening Went to the Meeting House, and I preachd to a Vast number of People and I Spoke from the Words thy Heart is not right &c[262]— and the People attended with great Solemnity—after meeting went back with Doc^r Johnes and Lodged,—

Tuesday Jan^r 8: after eating I Sot off and went to Basking Ridge, Stopt at Deacon [ ] where Peter and David Lodged and it began to rain, and we Sot of, and we got to the Place Some Time before noon and we Calld in to a Certain House and about 11 we went to attend upon a Funeral of one the Revd Canadas Daughters, and it was very uncomfortable Rainy Sloppy Day and yet there was a large number of People, and I Spoke from the words, But the End of all things is at H[263] and Soon after, we followd the Corps to the grave, and went directly to the House where we first put up and there we Lodgd,—

---

261. Jedediah Chapman was the master of the Orange Dale Academy of New Jersey. In 1790, Occom sent New Stockbridge resident John Quinney to the Academy. See Occom's June 1790 letter to Chapman in this collection.

262. See Acts 8:21.

263. See 1 Peter 4:7.

Wednesday Jan'' 9: after we Broke our fast, we Sot off again, and got So far as to Mill Stone and there we put up at a Tavern.—

Thirsday Jan'' 10: got up very early and took Breakfast and Soon after went on our Way, and about 12 we arrivd to Doc'' Whetherspoon's in Prince-Town, and took Dinner with him—and Soon after we went on again & in the evening we put up ^at^ Black Horse Tervern, and it was very Cold, Sot up Some What late,—

Fryday Jan'' 11: after eating we went on again, & got to Quakson towards Nig Where there three or 4 Families of Indians, we Calld in at one, and they appeard extreamly Poor, So we went to [ ] and put up at Tervern, and it was Cold yet we Sot up long and I was ill with a Cold & Cough'd—

Saturday Jan'' 12: after Breakfast we Sot off again and we arriv'd to Agepelack Some Time before Night, and we Stopt at Friend Mytop's and I was very poor with my Cold and Coughd much and So I Stayd here over Night and was kindly treated—

Sabb. Jan'' 13 I felt a little better, and about 11 went to meeting, and there was not many People they but little Notice, and it was now a Pleasent Day, I Spoke from the Words, that which is wanting &c[264] and the People attended well after Service I went home with Daniel Simon to his Mother in Laws House and Stay'd here all the Week Daniel Simon Lost an only Ch this week and I preach a Funr Discourse from the Words Set thy House &[265] and we had Singing meetings every Night[266] and prayd with them and gave them a word of Exhortation—

Sabb Jan'' 20 Preachd here again and it was very bad Traviling, and there was a Considerable number of People Collected, and I Spoke from [ ] and the People attended well, and after meeting went Back to Widow Calvin's and in the Evening People Came together and we had exercise with Christian Cards and we Sang and prayd, and it was a Solemn Time many were much affected, and the People were very loath to leave the Place & they Stayd late—

Monday Jan'' 21: We were up very early and got ready as Soon as we Cou'd, and we took leave of the Family, and others that Came to take leave of us, and So we directed our Course to Philadelphia and in the Evening We got to the River against the City and we put up in a Tervern one Friend Coopper,—

Tuesday Jan'' 22: We got up very early, and went over in a Boat upon the Ice, & a little after Sun Rise we were in the City, and we went to See Doc'' Duffield a Physition, and were kindly receivd, and from thence we to See Doc'' Sprout, and he receivd us kindly, and we went on to visit Ministers of all Denominations, and they were all very Friendly, and we Dind with gentlemen almost every Day—We Lodgd two or three Nights at M'' Bushels, and then we were invited by M'' Innes a brewer a Scotchman and a good man and the Whole Family is very agreable we were treated with all kindness—

Sabb Jan'' 27 in the afternoon Preachd in Doc'' Duffield's Meeting House, in the

---

264. See Ecclesiastes 1:15.

265. See 2 Kings 20:1, Isaiah 38:1.

266. Occom's report suggests that Lenape as well as Algonkian Christians sustained a strong culture of hymn singing.

Evening Preachd in Doc^r Sprouts Meeting, and they made Collections for me—This Week Visited all Week and found kindness by all Sorts of People—

Feb^r 3: on Sabb in the morning Preachd at Duffield's in the afternoon preach'd in a Baptist meeting and there was a large number of People—

Fryday Feb^r 8: this evening we were invited, with a number of gentlemen and Ladies to Drink Tea with a Dutch Captain in his Ship, his Name was DeHorse—and we had a genteel entertainment—and after Tea the Company Plaid the little man, which died very often—[267] Stayd till near 9 and then we Indians took good leave of the Company and returnd to our Quarters—

Sabb Feb^r 10 Preach'd in the morning in Doc^r Duffields Meeting, in the Evening preachd in Ewning's and they made me Collitions—This week went on in our Usual Visits amongst all Sorts of People and were kindly treated by all People—

Sabb Feb^r 17 I went in the morning to Doc^r Sprouts, and it was a Sacrament Day[268] Mr Green Preach'd, and I partook with them, and it was a Solemn Day with me, and I believe with others—In the after Noon I went to Baptist meeting, and heard Mr English one of the Baptist ministers in the City—and we were now geting ready to leave the City and it was hard work to take leave of the People that have been So kind to us Since we have been here—the Quakers in particular were exceeding kind to us and Freely Communicated their Substance to help our People in the Wilderness—Two Schools Communicated Some thing to our Children in the Wilderness—[269]

Fryday Feb^r 22 about 10 we left Philadelphia and it was bad Crosing the River, we went on Ice most all the Way over and it was Cold Day, and in the Evening we got Mores Town and Brother David[270] was Sick, & Peter[271] went [to] Agepelack, and D and Lodgd in a Tervern—

Saturday Feb^r 23: I went to Quakson ^& left David very Sick^ and got there before noon, and put up at a Public House in the after noon went to an Indian House, towards Night went a Public House—

Sabb. Feb^r 24: about 11 went to meeting to a meeting House wh Mr John Brainard Use to preach to a Number of Indians[272] and there was Considerable of People and I Spoke from Acts XI.26 and Some Time towards Night, we went to Mount Halley, got there near Sun Sit and we put up at Doc^r Rosss and David was very Sick, and here we Stayd Some Days, and I preachd four Times in this Place,—

FryDay Feb^r 29: I left Mount Halley and left David there he was not well enough to Sit out and it was very Cold, I got to Trinton in the evening. Calld at Revd Mr Armstrongs but he was not at Home So I Went to a Public House, and Lodged—

---

267. Probably an eighteenth-century folksong or game.

268. A day designated for the administration of the Eucharist, or communion.

269. See Occom's February 22, 1788, letter "To the Friends in Philadelphia" in this collection.

270. *Brother David:* David Fowler.

271. *Peter:* Peter Pauquunnuppeet.

272. John Brainerd, brother of famed missionary David Brainerd, served as a missionary to Native communities in New Jersey, New York, and Pennsylvania, before moving to Deerfield, Massachusetts, in 1777.

Saturday March 1: Went back to Burden Town got there Some Time before Night, and I Lodgd Mr Wilsons a Baptist ministers, House but was not at Home, but the Woman treated me with all kindness—

Sabb. March 2: and it was extreem Cold, I preachd in a large upper Room and there a large number of People for that Cold Season, and Some time in the after Noon I left the Place and went back to Trinton and got there before Night, and I was to preach here this evening, but the Season was so Severe, they Concluded defer it till the next Day at 10 of the Clock in the morning and So I Went to my old Lodgings and rested Comfortably—

Monday March 3: about 10 we went into the meeting House and there was Considerable N^r of People and I Spoke from Mark V.4: and there was good attention. after meeting went home with Mr Armstrong and Dinned with, and Some Time in the after noon I went back to Draw Bridge and there I had an Evening meeting and there was a Vast number of People, and I Spoke from Sol, Song VIII.5 and it was a Solemn Time.—I Lodgd at the Same House.—

Tuesday March 4: David & I Sot off prety early, and we got to [ ] and Lodgd at a Dutch Tevern,—

Wednesday March 5: We got up early and got Victuals & Soon after Sot of, and We got almost to New Brunswick and David out he had forgot his Bundle, and So he went back and I went on, got to N Brunswick before noon and I put up at a Public H and Soon went to See the Revd Mr Munteeth, and there I din'd with him, after Dinner we went to See Doc^r Scott, and I was recevd with all kindness and here I found Peter, who had been Stragling from us almost a fortnit, and presently after David Came up with us, and and in the evening there was a Society,[273] and we went to it, and I Spoke a few words by way of Exhortation and after meeting we returnd to Doc^r Scotts and there we Lodged,—

Thirdsday March 6: got up early and went to Several Houses, a Visiting, and we were treated kindly, Dined with a Dutch Minister; and was exceeding Friendly,—in the Evening we had a meeting in the Presbyterian meeting House and there was a large Number of People, and I Spoke from [ ] I Lodged at Dr Scotts again and David and Peter Lodged in another House—

Fryday March 7 We got up early and went to take Breakfast with a Certain gentleman and Soon after Breakfast we went back to Doc^r Scotts and got ready about 8: we took leave of Doc^r Scott and his Family and others and went on our way, and we Stopt at the Rev^d M^r [ ] in Woodbridge and took Dinner there, and Soon after eating we past on, and we got to Elisabeth Town Just before Sun Sit, and we Calld upon Esqr Woodroffs a few Minutes, and went on to N.ark, and we got there Some Time in the evening and we put at a Publick House I went to Doc^r McWartles, & but was not well and did not See him and So went back to the Tavern—

Saturday March 8: got up very early and got ready and went on our way to Newark Mountains, got there about 9: and Calld on Mr Chapman and took Breakfast there, and Mrs Chapman was very Sick and So we went to Crain Town and I put up

273. A meeting of the Methodist Society.

a Deacon Crains, and we were most kindly entertaind David and Peter Lodgd in another Mr Crain's House—

Sabb. March 9: about 9 went to Meeting got to the Place as the People began to
Collect, and there was a very large Numb^r of People and I preachd all Day from Mark
V.4: and the People attended with great Solemnity,—The Revd Mr Chapman Went to
Newark to preach,—and in the evening I had a meeting to attend upon in Newark
and there was a Vast Number of People and I Spoke I Corin XVI:22 and the People
were very Solemn and ~~we~~ I Went with Doc^r Burnet and Lodged there and P & D
Lodged in the Publick House I Went to Bed Soon—

Monday March 10 was at the Place all Day, and in the Evening, I preachd again to
a multitude of People and I Spoke from [ ] and the People attended with all gravity
after meeting I went home with Doctor Burnet again and there Lodgd—

Tuesday. March 11 Some in the morning we took leave of our Friends and went
on our way towards New York got over there Some Time in the afternoon and we put
up at the North part of the City with one M^r [ ] a Tavern keeper—

Wednesday March 12: Went to Waited on Doc^r Rodgers and other gentlemen
upon our Business but there was no prospect of doing much The good Friends or
Quakers Did more than any they gave David and Peter Six pounds to bear their Expences to Onieda and they gave Some other things to our People in the Woods—

Fryday March 14 Brother David Fowler and Peter Pohquunnuppeet left me at
New York and they returnd homeward to Onieda—

Saturday March 15: in the evening I preachd in Mr Gaines meeting House and
there was a large number of People and I Spoke from [ ] and the People attended well
Some with affection—

Sabb. March 16: in the morning went to hear Doc^r Rodgers but I was disappointed, I heard Mr Miller from Some part of the New Jersey—in the after noon I
went to hear the Methodists, and I heard a Young man but was not extraordinary in
the evening went to my Lodgings—

Wednesday March 19: Some about 12 took a pasage in a Boat to Elisabath Town,
got there Just Sun Sit, and I put up at a Publick House with one M^r [ ] a Religious
man and was kindly Treated by him & his Lady—

Thirdsday March 20: in the morning Some Time, M^r [ ] took me in his Carrage,
and we went to Newark, to See about my Money that was to be Sent Doc^r Rodgers
in New York for me; We got there Soon, but I Cou'd not hear about ^it^, I Calld on
Doc^r McWartler, in the evening Went back but I Stopt at one Mr Lyon, and Lodged
there we had a meeting this evening in a Baptist Meeting House, this Place is Calld
Lyons Farmes.—[274]

Saturday March 22: in the Evening I heard Mr Ogden in Elisabeth Town Church
and he is a good Preacher of the gospel of Jesus Christ.—Lodgd at my old Quarters—

Lords Day March 23 Preachd all Day in the Presbyterian meeting House and
there was a large number of People I Spoke from [ ] in the evening I attended a Society, gave a word of Exhortation—and Lodged at the Same House—

---

274. Lyons Farms Baptist Church in Newark, New Jersey, was founded in 1769. It was later renamed
the Elizabeth Avenue Baptist Church.

Monday 24: early in the morning went to a Certain Place 5 or 6 miles southward and preachd in a Certain M House, and the Revd Mr Ogden was present, and there was a great Number of People tho' it was Very Cold, and as Soon as I had done Speaking Mr Ogden gave a word of Exhortation, and there was great Solemnity amongst the People. I Spoke from Psalm CVII:31: Some Time after meeting I Went with a Lady in her Carriage to her House, and from thence to another House, and in the evening went to another and there I preachd to a large Congregation and I Spoke from [ ] and the People many of them were much affected. I Lodged at the Same House,—

Tuesday March 25 got up very early, and got ready and a Negro Carried me in a Carriage to Elisabeth Town, and from there Esqr Woodroff carried in his Carrage to the Point and had a passage directly. and I went aboard, and was at New York about 12: and went directly to Doc^r Rodgers to See Whether my Money had got there, but it was not, and So immediately went to Pownal Ferry and went over, and took Stage Waggon and was at Newark before Sun Set and there I found my money at Mr Ogden's, and So I went to Doc^r MacWartlers and he was not at Home, and I Went to bed Soon being much Waried the fatigues of the Day, and Some Time in the Evening the Doc^r Came Home, and he Came into the Room where I Lay and he was much Surprizd to See me a bed, he knew not I was in the House—

Wednesday March 26: got up very early and went to Mr Ogdens to Lay out my money, for it was Chiefly in Jersey Bills, and Coppers,[275] & I was to go in Stage Waggon again, but I was too late, and went to the Landing and happily found a Sloop going to New York, and I with Joy went a Board, and was at New York before Night, & went to my Lodging once more—

Thirdsday March 27, found a pasage to [New] London, and so was getting.—

Sabb: March 30: about 10 Sot Sail, and had good Wind

Monday March 31: had but Small Wind, till near noon & then we had a fine Wind & and Just at Night we got a ground on Oyster Bed, & it was near my Home, and So I went a Shore and the Capt also, and we got Horses, I had about a mile to go, and the Capt had about 5: miles to go, found my poor Family thro' the great goodness of god, in good Health, Bless be the Name of the Lord, that I Lodge in my own House once more after a long absence and had experiencd much of the goodness of god

April 1 went to the Bridge to fetch my things up,—

Wednesday April 9 My Wife and I Went to New London in order to go over to Long Island and we got to New London Just before Sun Set and we found a Boat going over to Plum Island we went a Board directly and was on the water all Night just about break of Day we got a Shore, and we went to a Hutt and turnd in till broad Day Light, and then we went into Mr Bebees House and there we took Breakfast, the Family was very kind to us,—and we were very Soon Call'd to go aboard again, and Saild on for Napeek and we arrivd there before noon, and we went to the Pines and

---

275. Although Congress established the United States dollar as the official national currency in 1785, paper currency issued by colonies continued to circulate. New Jersey and a handful of other states minted their own copper coins in the 1780s.

there we Saw Sister Phebe Pharaoh, and Young David Fowler—and So we all went together to east part of Hetherwoods, and there we found Mother Fowler,[276] here are three or four Families of Indians and one Family English,—

Fryday April 11 was at Mothers all Day, was much tired of Yesterdays Journey in the Evening we had a meeting in Mr Hands House, and there was a Considerable Nr of People Indians and English and they appeard Solemn—

Saturday April 12: about 10 I Set out for Easthampton got there a little before Night and put up the Revd Mr Buells and we were glad to Se one another once more—

Sabb: April 13: Went to meeting bout 10: Mr Buell began and I finishd the fore noon Service, in the after Noon I preachd from Jona III:5: and there was a great Asembly and they were exceeding Solemn—towards Night I went to Winscot and there I preachd; Spoke from [ ] and there was good attention. I Lodge at the Same House, the man name was Mr Conkling—

Monday April 14: Set off early Calld a few minutes at Colo Hubberts to See Mr Woolworth and he had not got up I just Saw him, and went on again Calld at the Revd Mr Williams in Southhampton, and to Victuals there, he was not at H[277] from there went to the Indians in Cold Spring, and there was a number of Indians Some from Westward, and Some from Montauk, and them that belong to the Place in the after noon I went to Shenecock, and it began to Rain just as got there, and here I Saw one Benjamin Townsend a New Exhorter one that came from New-England.—in the evening we had a meeting, and there was a Considerable Number of People tho it was very Stormy I Spoke from Psallm CVII and the People were much moved Some made Noise—after meeting the Spent Some in Singing Psalms and Hymns and Spiritual Songs—I lodgd at the Same House—

Tuesday April 15: I got up very early, and went on my way towards Montauk again Stopt at Mr Williams and took Breakfast with them, and Soon went on again, Stopt a few minutes at Mr Woolworth and So past on, Stopt at Mr Buells also, and ate my dinner there and kep on, Calld at two Houses in Ameganset and past on Stopt at Mr Benjamin Hedgess, and so on got to Mother Fowlers about Day light in and went to Bed Soon I was good tired and had a bad Cold—

Wednesday April 16: was at the Place all Day—

Thirdsday: April 17: about 1 took leave of our People and went to Napeek, got there about 10: and aboard of Mr Horton, and went Straite to New London, got there Some Time before N^t and we Stopt a little while and So went on to Pommechag and we went a Shore & my wife and I went home mother Fowler & Betty Stayd at Mr Adgates—[278]

---

276. *Mother Fowler:* Elizabeth (Betty) Pharoah Fowler.

277. *H:* home.

278. Samson and Mary Fowler Occom moved Elizabeth Fowler and her granddaughter Betty from Long Island to Mohegan in preparation for their own household move to Brotherton. Betty, the daughter of David and Hannah Garrett Fowler, apparently remained behind to care for her grandmother when the rest of the David Fowler family emigrated to Brotherton. At Brotherton, Elizabeth Fowler lived with her son David until her death in 1795.

Fryday April 18: in the morning went with the Cart to fetch our things The Lord be thanked for his goodness to us—

Monday May 26: 1788 about 11 I took leave of my Family once more & went on my way towards Onieda, and got so far as to one Mr Joness Just before Night, and there I Lodgd: I Just Calld on Mr Tuck as I Came along—

Tuesday May 27 got me up early and went on my way Calld on Mr Huntington in New Malborough, and took my Breakfast there with them, and Soon after went on. Calld at Mr Stevenss and at Mr Eelss and took Dinner there, and Soon after went on, and Calld on Mr Marsh in Weathersfield, and from thence went to Esqr Welless and was there Some Time about 4 o'c in the after Noon went on again, and got to Farmington Just after Sun Set, Calld on Mr Pitkin a few minutes, and so past on and got Solomon Mossucks in the Evening and found them all well, and there I Lodged—

Wednesday May 28: was at the Place all Day, and Searchd into my Olives affair, and Saw writings about it to my Satisfaction,—[279]

Thirdsday May 29: after Breakfast took leave of the Family, and went on my Way, Stopt a little while at Mr Wawdsworths and left Olive's affair with him,—and So went on my way again, Calld a while at Mr Wiridard, and he was much Sick and So went on again Soon, and Stopt at Mr Meechems in Herrington, and found him a Strange posture like a little Child,[280] took Dinner there, and Soon after went on again and in the evening got to a Place Calld Warren, and there I Lodgd in a Public H and there was a number of People, and they wanted to have me preach to them & I told them it was too late and they insisted, I Shoud, & I Sayd again it was too late but if they woud get together in the morning I woud gratify them, and so we left the matter—

FryDay May 30: Just after Six I went to Mr Stars the Minister of the Place, and the People got together a little after 8 and deliverd a Short Discourse to them & Soon after I went on my way again, I Stopt at Mr Bodwells and took Dinner there, and about 2 in the after, I went on again and got one Mr Canfields a Publick House and Lodgd there and went to rest Soon—

Saturday May 31: got up early and went on my way reachd to the Hallow about 8 and took Breakfast, and Soon after past on and Stopt a little at Esqr Newcoms & then went to Mr Case's and Stopt there a few minutes & on again, Calld at Mr Firmmonds and took Dinner there and Soon after left the Valley and went on to Mr Gasleys in Bethel, and it Raind Considerably, got there there Time in the after Noon, and we were glad to See each other and there I put up.—

Sabb: June 1. 1788. about 8 we went to meeting one of Mr Gasleys Daughters

---

279. Olive Occom married Solomon Adams (Farmington) in 1775. According to Love, Adams died in about 1783 and Olive Occom Adams afterward lived on his lot at Farmington. Samson Occom's diary entries place Olive and her three children near Windsor, Connecticut, in 1786 and 1787. Love reports that she later emigrated to Brotherton, and that the Adams children disposed of the family plot at Farmington in 1801 (*Occom,* 336). "Olive's affair" here negotiated by Samson Occom probably concerns the status of her husband's land at Farmington and her legal relationship to it.

280. Mr. Meechem may have suffered some stroke-related physical or mental disability.

Carry me in a Chair, and there was a great Number of Peop Collected together, and I Spoke from Jona III:5: Soon after Meeting we went to Colo Blooms and took Dinner there, and after eating I went home with Mr Elias Mulford of Long Island, he was one of Scholars formerly at Montauk[281] and he entertained me with all kindness, and there I found Widow Betty Peter from Long Island.—

Monday June 2: Preach at Mr Milfords and there was a great Number of People— Soon after meeting I went of with Some People to another Place and Stopt at Mr Sherrils and Lodged there.—

Tuesday June 3: Some Time before Noon I went on to one Esqr Ganseys, and ther I preachd began about 2 and there was a large Numb^r of People and I Spoke from the Words I have a mesage &c[282] and there was an affectionate attention amongst the People and Soon after meeting, I went home with one Mr Hunting. there I Lodged, and was exceedingly well entertaind—

Wednesday June 4: Went on my way early, and I So far to Kinderhook and Lodged at a Tervern—

ThirdsDay June 5: got up early and went on my way and got Esqr Woodworths at 10, and found them all well and was there till Some Time in the after Noon, and then went to eastwards, having heard, that Mr Macdanol had not got home from Philadilphia and I Wanted to See him, in the evening went so far as Mr Tobiass and there Lodged—

Fryday June 6 got up early and was going on, and one Mr Burdick Invited me to go into his House and take Breakfast with him, and I did, and Soon after I went on, and got to Mr Robbinson's about 10: and was there but a little While and Concluded to keep the Coming Sabbath in this House and so Went on ^to^ Mr Dymonds and got there Just before noon and there I Stayd found my good Friends in good Health and was glad to See them—

Saturday June 7: was at Mr Dymonds all Day—

Sabb. June 8. about 9 went to Mr Robinsons to meeting and there was a great Numb^r of People, and I Spoke from Jeremiah X:10: and Job XXIII.8 and the People attended with great Seriousness—and after meeting took Dinner, with Mr Robinson, and Soon after I went to Mr Tobias's Mr Robins went with me, and we found a vast Number of People of All Sorts and I preach to them from John XV:23: and the People were, many of them much affected—after meeting I went with my good old Friend Mr Phillip Lott, one who I was acquainted with in Noble Town, and now he has Just moved in these Parts, and we were exceeding glad to See one another, and there I Lodgd; and had a Comfortable rest once more—

Monday June 9 about 3 in the afternoon I preachd in Mr Lotts Barn and there was a large number of People and I Spoke from [ ] and the People attended Well, I Lodgd at the Same House again—

Tuesday June 10: asoon as we broke our Fast I went to a Certain House where there was a Woman Died Yesterday and I deliverd, a Discourse upon the Ocation, and

---

281. Elias Mulford was a white resident of Easthampton, Long Island. Occom's diary entry implies that he taught both white and Native pupils at his Montauk school.

282. See Judges 3:20.

there was a large number of People and I Spoke from James, the words were, for What is y^r Life[283] and there was a Solemn attention, and Soon after I went to New Bethlehem, and Preachd there in a Lg meeting H and was not a great N^r of People and they were Solemn—I Spoke from [ ] and the People behaved well Soon after meeting, I went with Mr Mofat, to his Lodgings at Mr Miress and there Lodgd and was much Tired.—

Wednesday June 11: got up early, and I went on to Esqr Woodworths, Soon got there and took Breakfast with them, and about 10 we went to meeting at the oake Tree, I preachd in a New Dutch Meeting House and there was a great many People, it was a Day of Fasting and Prayer amongst the Dutch Christians thro' New York and Jersey States, and I Spoke from Isaiah LVIII. & Acts Soon after the Service was over, I went on to Albany got to the City Some Time before Night, went to See M^r McDonal, a Presbutery minister, but I heard nothing by him Concerning my Letter I Sent to Doc^r Duffield[284] & I went to See Mr West too and he was glad to See me once more. from there went to my Lodgings at a Public House & Went to Bed Soon—

Thirdsday June 12: Went to See Some Friends again and about 10 I went out of the Place, and went on to Bought, and got the Place before Night Some Time, Calld on Several Friends, Lodgd at Mr Fero's my Friends were all very glad to See me once more and I was as Glad.—

Fryday June 13, I Went over to half Moon, and Lodgd at my old Friend John Vanderwarken—

Saturday, was there all Day, towards Night went to See the old People—

Sabb June 15: about 9 went to meeting to Half moon meeting House and there was a great Numb^r of People, and I Spoke from John XVII.3 & Titus I.16 Soon after meeting went to Bought, and preachd there and there was a Vast number of People I Spoke from [words illegible] one Mr Striker a young Dutch Preacher, preach'd here to Day as Soon as the meeting was done I went home with Major Fundee and Lodged there and was very kindly entertaind.—

Monday June 16 Visited all Day Just at Night went to Mr Clute's near the Mohawk River, and there Lodged,—

Tuesday June 17 Some Time after Breakfast I took leave of my Friends and went on to towards Neskeewney[285] got there Some Time before Noon, and Stopt at Mr Simon Fordts, and took Dinner there, and about 3 went meeting, and it began to rain, about 4 we began the Service, and there was a large Number of People & I Spoke from Lam. 3:40 and the People attended with great Solemnity. Soon after I went over the River, and I put up at Mr Fisher's and they were glad to See me and I was as Glad to See them—

Wednesday June 18: Some Time after Breakfast, I took leave of the Family, and went to Mr Peters—and took Dinner there, about 1 went to meeting at one Mr Smith's about 4 miles off and there was a large number of People and I Spoke from

283. See James 4:14.
284. This letter apparently does not survive.
285. *Neskeewney:* Niskayuna, New York.

Prvr[286] IV and there was a Solemn attention among the People, Soon after went towards Ball Town in quest of M[r] Gazley, and just before Night I found him, and we were excessively Glad to See each other, and was there a few Minutes, and a Company Came, to Stay all Night, and one M[r] Nash invited me to go home with him, and I went with him & Lodged there.—

Thirdsday June 19. after eating I return'd to M[r] Gazlays and taried there till Some Time after Dinner, and I went to Esq[r] Ganzys M[r] Gazlay went with me, and about 4 in the after noon, the People had Collected, and we began the Service, we met in M[r] Barnss Barn and there was a great Number of People and I spope from John XV.23 and the People attended well and Some were affected much Calld in Esq[r] Ganseys after meeting, and took Some Bread and Cheese, and directly after, weth home with M[r] Gazley, got there before Day Light in, and Sot up a while, and then went to Bed—

Fryday, June 20: Was poorly, yet Just at Night, went towards the Lake,[287] Calld at M[r] Scribners and Sot there a While, and then went back to M[r] Gilberts and there I Lodged and was kindly Treated went to Bed Soon—

Saturday June 21, after Break went to M[r] Gazleys and the Company that was at M[r] Gaz was geting ready to go home to Albany, M[r] Heart and M[r] Winess and their Wifes and their Children, and one Woman Composed the Company, and they Soon Sot off, and I was there till towards noon and M[r] Gazlay and I went to the Lake afishing, and we took Dinner at M[r] Kallocks and after Dinner went to the Lake and fishd, and we Catchd a fine Passel, and went back got home about 4 in the after noon—and Lodged there once more—

Sabb. June 22: about 9 went to the Meeting-House, and there was a large Asembly Collected, and I Spoke from [ ] and there was a Solemn attention Soon after meeting went back to M[r] Gazlays, Stopt at M[r] Gilberts and took Tea there, and Soon after went on, and the People Colleted thick at M[r] Gazlay's and I Spoke to them from [ ] and the People attended well I Lodgd at the Same House & was very tenderly Treated—

Monday June 23: Lay a bed late, took Breakfast with them, and after Breakfast I went of to go to Schenacatada M[r] Gazlay and his Sister Diadamia Went with me, got to the Place a little past Noon,—and I did my Business Soon, and about 5 we return back and directed our Course to Freehold got to the Place in the Dusk of the evening, I Lodgd at my Daughters,—

Tuesday June 24, about 3 I p[288] in the meeting House, and there Considerable Number of People and I Spoke from 2 Corin V:20 and the People were much affected, after meeting went back to M[r] Northrops, and there M[r] Gazlay and his Sister took leave of me with much affection—& in the Evening a Number of People Collected together at M[r] Wilson Northrops, and we had a Short Exercise—and I Lodged at the Same House.

~~Wednesday June 25. got up Some What late, and got re^a^dy and my Son in Law~~

---

286. *Prvr:* Proverbs.

287. Oneida Lake.

288. *p:* preached.

Anthony ~~and I went to Ball Town and did our Business and I went of to Schenac-~~
~~tada got there just after noon, I took Dinner at Mr John Glands~~

Wednesday June 25: Some Time before Noon, I went towards Gallaheny, to at-
tend upon a meeting, but they no notice, and so I went back to Freehold, got there
Some Time in the after Noon, and in the Evening we a meeting in Mr Wilson
Northrops, and the was Considerable Number of People I Spoke from the Word, thy
Kingdom Come,[289] and there was a Serious attention among the People, I Lodgd at
the Same House and it was late—

Thirdsday June 26: Some Time in the morning, I went to Ball Town, Anthony
Paul went with me, we soon got got there, and waited on M^r [ ] upon our L[290] afairs
and he gave us advice, and Soon after I went on to Schenactada, got there about 1:
and did my Business, and went back to Freehold, and got to Mr Rodgerss Just about
Sunt Set and they were very glad to see me and there I Lodged—

Fryday June 27 was at the Place all Day, and it was a Rainey Day, Just at Night I
went to Mr Holmss and there Lodgd,—

Saturday June 28 Some Time in the ~~morning~~ ^after Noon^, I Sot off, and went to
Gallaway, got to Mr Otis's Just before Sun Set and very kindly receveid.—

Sabb June 29: Went to meeting and we met in a Barn and it was a Rainey Day,
Yet there was a large Number of People and I Spoke from [ ] and the People behaved
well after meeting went back to Mr Otis's and in the evening had a meeting in M^r [ ]
House, and there was a Conside Number of People and I Spoke Words to them,—
and I Lodgd at the Same House, and rested Comfortably.—

Monday June 30: Went to Mr Callocks, and took Breakfast there, and Some Time
before N Sot off and went to Scotchbush got there Some Time before Noon and put
up at Mr Franklin about 2 went to Mr Mans and there we had a meeting and there a
large Number of People & I Spoke from [ ] and the People attended well & and I Baptized four Children Two For Mr Franklin, by the name Sophia and Elisabeth, two
for Mr Ephraim Potter by the Lucy & Lucinda, and Soon after Meeting, I went with
M^rs [ ] about 3 miles off and there & was well entaind, and rested Comfortably—

Tuesday July 1: got up early and took Breakfast and then went on my way, Stopt
a while at Mr Vedders by Mohawk River and took Dinner there, and soon after Dinner, went on again Call on Capt Crages a little While and So past on,—got So far as
to Domine Romine's and Lodged there, was kindly receive and Lodged there—

Wednesday July 2: Some T after Breakfast, took leave of em and went on again
got to Esqr Maybees before N and was there a little while and past on, and went Fort
Plain and did my Business there, and turnd about and towards Bowman's Creek & got
there Some Time before Night, and put up at Esqr Kimbels and kindly recevd and
Lodged there—

Thirdsday July 3 Some in the morning I to fishing and had got Suckcess, While I
was Busy, I was Calld in, and as I was going Mr Eliott met me he is from Warren Bush,
& we were glad to See each, and when I had got in, behold Elder Mudge was there,
and a nother man, and we had agreable Conversation.—about 3 in the afternoon we

289. See Matthew 6:10.
290. *L:* legal.

went to meeting, and there was Considerable number of People & I Spoke from John; Search the Scriptures &c[291] and the People attended well—Elder Mudge and I Lodgd at the Same House where the meeting was, which was M[r] John Whites, and we had a Cold night on it,—

Fryday July 4 Some Time before noon took leave of the People, and Went to Esq[r] Young Love's at ol oak hill, and there I had a meeting, and there was a Considerable number of People tho' it was a Rainey Time, I Spo from [ ] and Soon after meeting I went on to Cherry Vally and Calld at M[r] Ways he he not at Home but the woman was, and there I Taried all N and was tenderly treated—

Saturday July 5 after Breakfast went to M[r] Nicholas Pickards and there Stayd till Some Time in the after Noon then I went to told M[r] Pickards & there I Lodged—

Sabb July 6 about 10 began the meeting, and there was a great Number of People & I Spoke from [ ] and the People attended with great Solemnity,—towards Night went to M[r] Nicholas Pickards, and I Baptized 3 Children, one for him by the Name Jona, one for Adolf Pickard, by the Name ^Susana^ William, and one for M[r] Stokes by the Name ~~Susana~~ William—and Soon after I went back to Old M[r] Pickards and from there to M[r] Crepins and there was a meeting M[r] Frimman Preachd, and it Raind very hard before he had done, and many Lodgd at the Same House—

Monday July 7 Some Time after eating I took leave of the Family, and I Went on my way and got M[r] Fols Just after Sun Sit and there I Lodgd—

Tuesday July 8: about 10 Jeremiah Tuhy Came to me and I got me ready and went with him to go thro the Woods Elijah Wympy and Ben Garrett Fowler also went, and we got to Brotherton about Sun Set, and was glad and thankful to See our People once more: Thanks be to god for his goodness to us. Lodged at Brother David Fowlers—

Sabb July 13 about 10 we began the meeting at the School-House which was made for meeting House too, and there was not a great Number of People, being a Rainey Day, and I Spoke from CXVII Psalm and 1 Cron: XVI.9 10 and the People attended with great tenderness, many affected,—after meeting went back to Brother Davids—

Monday July 14, Some Time in the morning, I went to Clenton, & Came back in the evening.—

Wednesday July 16: in the evening we had a Singing Meeting and I gave a Word of Exhortation to the People from the Words, do thyself no harm[292]—and I Lodged at Sister Esther Fowler's, and as the People were returning, Elijah Wympy was attaced by by Peter and Jeremiah Tuhy & they abused him much, and it was difficult to part them, and fell upon Young David Fowler but David was too much for him and it was a Sad night with 'em and very shameful—[293]

Fryday 18. about 9 I went to New Stockbridge; Stopt at Rogger Wauby and took

---

291. See John 5:39.

292. See Acts 16:28.

293. This altercation may have been an expression of fierce factionalist tensions developing among younger men at Brotherton as they came into conflict over issues of town governance and land management. Elijah Wympy was leader of a group that sought to lease out Brotherton lands to white settlers.

Dinner there, and about 2 went on again, got to Stockbridge about 3, and towards evening there was a meeting, Mr Sergeant Preachd, and it was in Indian and it was no Edification to me—after meeting went to Sir Peters and took Supper there, and then went to Capt Hindreck's and there I Lodged.—

Saturday July 12: Was at the Place all Day—Yesterday the Oniedas a Number of them went to Brotherton run the Line—[294]

Sabb July 20. about 10 began the Service and there was a large Number of People, and I Spoke from Judges III.20 and the People attend with Seriousness, I Baptized two Children one for Capt Hindreck Aupanmut & the name it was Joshua, and the other Child was ~~Joseph Quinneys~~ and his Name is [ ] ~~and I Lodged at Capt Hindreck again~~ in the Evening I Went Home to Brotherton Lodged at B. Davids

Monday July 21 Sot of very early in the morning to go to Fort Schilyrs got there about 12: and there I found my Daughter Christiana & her Family, I Lodged at a Widow Dutch Womans House and they were unruly—

Tuesday July 22: Some Time in the morning Sot off again for Home, but we did not get any further than Clenton I Lodged at Mr Lovels—

Wednesday July 23: it was Some Time before our Team Came up to Where I Was, for had a hevy Load, and we unloaded, and Stayd till afternoon, and then we went on, left our Load, and got Home Some Time before Night, and I Went to meeting Just at Night, and after meeting went to Sister Esthers Fowlers, & Lodged there—[295]

Thirdsday July 24: Some Time in the morning I went back to my Daughter and towards Night our Team Came to my Daughters,—

Fryday July 25: towards Noon I went to N- Stockbridge got there about 3 near Night went to meetg Mr Sergeant Preachd, Lodgd at Mr Peter Peets.—

Saturday July 26: about 9 we met together to have a debate with Mr Sergeant but he Chuse not to Debate, I desired him to point out the Errors he had Charged us with, but he declin'd and finally Concluded, that everyone Shoud have full Liberty to Chuse and act in according to the Light and understanding he has in his Religious Concerns, and So we parted in Friendship, Concluded to agree and to disagree, and so we returnd to Brotherton, got to my Daughters before Night—[296]

Sabb July 27. about 9 I went to the meeting House, and about 11 we began the

294. *run the line:* Survey the boundaries of the Brotherton allotment. This survey takes place just two months before the historic Treaty of Fort Schuyler, September 22, 1788. Under the terms of a deceptively crafted "instrument of cession," which the Oneidas signed with an understanding that the state would protect their land against speculators, but which the state enforced as an outright relinquishment of Native lands, the treaty effected the loss of five million acres of Oneida territory, excluding an Oneida reservation tract and the Brotherton and New Stockbridge allotments (Hauptman and McLester, 10–11, 19–37; Campisi and Hauptman, 51–54).

295. Here, Occom receives the first load of his household goods at his new Brotherton home. He and Mary Occom completed their move to Brotherton in May 1789.

296. This doctrinal debate marked the apex of the rivalry between Samson Occom and John Sergeant, Jr. Sergeant first visited New Stockbridge in September 1787, one month after several New Stockbridgers formally invited Occom to serve as their resident minister. Sergeant established his own church at New Stockbridge in 1788. See also Occom's diary entries for September 16 and 21–24, 1787.

Holy Service & I Spoke from Luke XX.6: Prov X.5 and there was Some Seriousness among the People—after meeting Went back to my D^s—

Wednesday July 30: had an evening Singing, and I gave a word of advice and Councell to the Young People.—

Sabb. Augt 3 went to New Stockbridge, got there Just as the People were Collecting together and there was a large number of People, and I Spoke from Jerem [II?]:12.3: John I.12 and there great attention among the People, in the Evening went to meeting again, and Capt Hendrick and Sir Peter Peet rehearsed what was delivrd in the Day—I Lodgd at Capt Hendricks,—

Monday Augt 4: Anthony Paul Benoni[297] and Andrew Gifford[298] Acompanied me to the Lake we went there to Fishing, got there Some Time before Night, and there was a great Number of Oniedas and Some Stockbr at Colo Luweys, to receive a present of Corn and Some Pork Sent to them, by [ ] a French Merchant, but I and my Sons went to the Lake, which was but about half mile off & it was Just Night, and we Fishd, and we Catchd a fine parsel of Fish presently, & made up a Fire by the Creek and had fine Supper of F and afterwards Prayd, & then we went to Sleep by our Fire quietly—

Tuesday Augt 5: We Fishd by Spels all Day, but we got but few,—

Wednesday we tried again but we got but few, I killd a great gray Eagle, and a Raven this Day—

Thirdsday, Augt 7: We tryd to fish a little while, and but but 5:—and So We Sot off for home, we Stopt at Mr Olcuts but they were not at Home one of the Stockbridge women was there, and She Cookd a Dinner for us, and Soon after eating we went on again & I Stopt at N Stockbridge & my Sons went on—I Lodged at Sir Peter Peets—

Fryday Augt 8: I was at N. Stockbridge all Day, in the Evening we met and I gave a word of Exhortation from the W^s[299] and there was good attention Lodgd at Peters again—

Saturday Augt 9: Some Time before Noon I Sot off for Brotherton got to Brother Davids and found Young David[300] very Sick, to home before Noon—

Sabb Augt 10: Went to meeting about 9. and the People Just to the Lake and went to fishing and we Caught a fine parsel of Fish for the little we to fish, and we made up a fire by the Creek and there we Lodgd,—

[Courtesy of Dartmouth College Library]

---

297. *Benoni:* Benoni Occom. Although Benoni Occom is not known to have joined the Brotherton movement, he may have traveled to Brotherton in 1788 to help with his parents' household move.

298. *Andrew Gifford:* Andrew Gifford Occom.

299. *W^s:* words.

300. *Young David:* David Fowler, Jr.

∾ JOURNAL 22

May 11, 1789–October 9, 1789

> *Samson and Mary Fowler Occom finally move their household from Mohegan to Brotherton in May 1789. Occom preaches in the Brotherton area during June, and he attends a military training exercise in September. In mid-September, Occom and his son Andrew Gifford depart for Mohegan again.*

Monday May 11: 1789: We arrivd at Albany Just before Night, and I We Went to See about geting a Wagon to Cary us to Schenactida,—but got none,

Tuesday May 12: got a wagon early, and we Loaded about 10: and We Sot off, and we got to Schenactada Just before Sun Sit, and we were very wet for had Rain most the way and I was much beat out, and we put our things in Mr John Post Barn, and there we lodgd We went to Bed Soon—

Wednesday May 13: about 5: I attended upon a Lecture and there was not many People, because they had no Notice, I Spoke from, 1 Corin 7:29.30: and the People attended becomingly, and they made me a Collection, and it was good for the Times—

Thirdsday May 14: was at the Place all Day—

Fryday was at all Day again—

Saturday May 16: about 10 we put a Board of a Batoe our things, and we went over the River, and walkd up the River a bout 2 miles and there we Stopt Some at a Certain House and the man of the House gave us a Dinner and about 1: the Boat Came up, and Sot off. Some Time in the after Noon, and we got to [word illegible] Tavern, and there we Lodgd,—

Sabb May 17: Sot off early and we got to Warrans Bush, at Night, and my Wife I Lodgd at Mr Bartlets, my good old Friends—

Monday May 18: Wen on again early, and reached to Kaconawanka and my Wife I Lodgd at Mr Vaders—

Tuesday May 19: Sot off again early, and we were over with Rain at Major Fonda's and my Wife I went into the House, and we were kindly Treated had Dinner, and we [went] a little further and there Lodgd at Mr Hardys—

Wednesday May 20: got up early and got us Breakfast and then we passed on and we got up above fort Plain and we Made up a fire by the Side of the River and there we Spent the Night—

Thirdsday May 21 got up early and got Breakfast and as Soon as we had ate we went on again, and in the we got to Conajohare and we Lodgd a little above ^old^ Mohawk Castle, and we made up a fire near the River, nearby one Mr John Vantmeser.—

Fryday May 22: Soon after eating we went on again and in the Evening we got a little below Fort Hawkamer and we made up a Fire again by the River, and there we Slep—

Saturday May 23 in the morning we went on again we made a Halt at Mr Franks and after that we past on here a White Woman took our Little Salley,[301] and made

---

301. According to Love, Sally Occom is either the youngest child of Samson and Mary Fowler Occom or their grandchild (*Occom*, 354).

walk about 8 miles. She only four and half years old She was much Worried—in the Evening We got M[r] Tygurts, and there we Lodgd my wife and I in a Hovel the Rest Lodgd in the Boat—

Sabb May 24: got up early and I went over the River and went to Fort Denton and there I preachd, Twice to a large number of People, and I Spoke from Jonah III.5 and 1 Corin XVI.22 and the People attended with all gravity and Solemnity,—took my Dinner at M[r] Tolents—and as Soon as the meeting was done I went with D[r] Petre and there took Tea—and as Soon as we had done I had an Horse got up for me and a Young man with another Horse to accompany me towards Fort Schiler[302] and we Soon Sot off, and we got about 4 miles Short of the Fort, and there I got down and the Young man went back with Horses, and I Walkd along about a mile, and found Tired, and I went into a Certain House, and asked Whether I Coud not Stay there, and they Said I might, and so I Stayd—and the man of the House askd me wether I Cou'd not give them a Discourse, I told them I Coud and So they Sent out Word, & Neighbours Came in directly and there was a Considerable Number of People Collected and it is a New Settement and I Spoke from the Words he that believeth on the Son of god hath the witness in himself[303]—and the People attended with Solemnity— Soon after meeting I went to bed, and rested well.—

Monday may 25. got up early and Sot off, and I got to Weavers Town Soon, and went in old M[r] Weaver's House, and there took Breakfast, and Soon after went on again & got to my Family about 10 ^at Fort Schiler^ and found them all well, and there we Stayd all Day and the Boat that brought us went on to Niagara.—

Tuesday May 26: Was again at the Place all Day—towards Night, our Anthony Paul ~~came~~ and Brother David Fowler came to us, and Stayd all Nig with us—

Wednesday May 27: Soon after Breakfast, we Sot off for Brotherton, and we had Rain to travil in, and to our Place a little before Sun Sit, and were very much worried, and we went to Bed Soon.—

Sabb May 31: Preachd at Brother Town—to not a large Congregation, Spoke from, [ ] and the People were attentive, and were glad to See me once more.—

Monday June 1 &c: this week went to Warrins Bush,—

Sabb June 7: Preachd at Elder Mudges Meeting House in Yankey hill, Spoke from [ ] and there was a vast Number of People, and attended with great attention,—

Monday Towards Night Preachd at M

Tuesday June 9. Went to Albany Bush, and there I preachd at a Certain House, and there was not many People, and they attended with Seriousness—

Wednesday June 10, was at Philadelphia Bush, Came here last Night, and Lodgd at one M[r] Sharmans,—and about 9 the People Collected together at the Same House, and I preachd to them, Spoke from [ ] and the People attended well as soon as the meeting was over, I with one M[r] [ ] and I Dined there, and as soon as I had ate, I went on to John Town, and So on—

Fryday June 12 got to Fort Plain before Noon, put up at M[r] Jonathan Deans, one

---

302. *Fort Schiler:* Fort Schuyler.

303. See 1 John 5:10.

of my good old Friends, found them all Well;—Towards Night the People Collected, and there was but few;—and I Spoke from [ ] Lodgd at [at] the Same House

Saturday June 13: Some Time before Noon, Sot off again, and got to German Flats Some Time before N, and I put up at Esqr Franks,—

Sabb: June 14 after Breakfast went over to Fort Dayton and there preachd in a Dutch meeting House, and there was a large Number of People, and I Spoke from Isa V:

July 1 Sab Preachd at the German Flats—

Augst 1 Sab Sepr 1 and Sepr the last Sab, the Text I Spoke from by one man Sin entered into the World &c Jesus Christ the Same &c Understandest them what thou readest[304]—at Esqr Franks on Week Day thy heart is not right in the Sight of god So then every one of us Shall give an account of himself to god.[305]—

Sepr 1 Was Call by the Major Coldbreath to be with them in their Training at Clinton; about 2 in the after noon they were all Collected, and the major Came to Capt Tuttles Where I was and he acompanied me to the Company, and a fine appearence they made for the first Time there was upwards of a Hundred likely young men, the Place has been Settling only one ^2^ year and an half,—I gave them a few Words of Exhortation, and then Prayd, and then they exercisd a little while,—and then went to Dinner, they put me at the head of the Table, and a fine Dinner we had, in the evening I went to Capt Bullings and there Ld and was kindly entertaind.—[306]

Sepr 2: I went home—

Sepr 18: 1789 Fryday left home and Sot out for New England, my Son Andrew acompanied, We got to Fort Schiler before Night, and Stayd there all Night—

Sepr 19 We got up very early and Sot off, and we got to Fort Dayton near 12, Calld on Mr Talcutt, and took Dinner, and Soon after eating, my Boy went back,—And towards Night I went overt to Esqr Franks and there Lodgd,—

Sabb: Sepr 20: Preachd at Esqr Franks Barn, and there was a Vast Number of People, Lodgd at the Esq^{rs}—

Monday Sepr 21: Some Time in the Morning, I Went to Mr Rains and was there a While, and then went back, to Fort Harkumer,[307] took Dinner with M^r [ ]

^*Tuesday 22*^ Towards Night, Esqr Phelps Battoo[308] Came along, and I got a Both in it, and I went a Board, and we went down and got to the little Falls after Sun Set and there we Lodgd,—

Wednesday Sepr 23, got up very early, and had things caried below the Falls and so we went on down the River, and we got to Cohnewanku and we Lodgd at a Tavern we found the River exceeding low and very difficult in Some Places to get along, the men were obliged to get out of the Boat *very* often—

---

304. See Romans 5:12, Hebrews 13:8, Acts 8:30.

305. See Acts 8:21, Romans 14:12.

306. It was traditional for clergy to deliver a sermon on annual muster or training days for local militia. See Mook, Ahearn.

307. *Fort Harkumer:* Fort Herkimer.

308. *Battoo:* bateau, or light flat-bottomed boat.

Thirdsday ~~Sep⁻ 24~~ *Oct⁰ 1* Sot off very Early again, and got to Schenactada a little before Night and I Lodgd at M⁰ Posts—

Fryday Oct⁰ 2 got up early and went to a Certain House where I expected to have a Chance in a Wagon, but was disapointed and so I went on a foot, and Some in the after Noon a Friend over took me, and he took ^me^ in his Wagon and we got to Albany Just after Sun Sit, and I Lodgd at M⁰ Orrs and I Went to Bed Soon—

Saturday Oct⁰ 3 Some Time before Noon Sot off a foot again Went to [words illegible], and I met D⁰ Utter, and his Brother and they Said they woud be back Soon, and Woud take Me in their Wagon, and Just before Sun Set they over took and I Went with them, and we Calld at D⁰ Utters a little while and M⁰ Jesee Utter Caried to his House, and it was near mid N before we got there, and there I Lodged;—

Sabb 4: as Soon as we got our Breakfast, we went into a Wagan and to meeting at Do⁰ Utters about 4 miles & there I Preachd Spoke from Acts VIII.21 and the People attended well—In the after Noon, we went to M⁰ Conrod Tenikes Barn and there We had a meeting, and there was a large Number of People, and I Spoke from Jonah III:5 and the People attended with great Attention, and it was a Rainey Day,—in the evening Preachd in M⁰ Conrod Tenikes House, and there was a Considerable of People, and I Spoke from Matt 1:21: and the People behaved well—Lodgd at the House they are Dutch People, and they were very kind to me, and rest well—

Monday Oct⁰ 5: Some Time before Noon, I had an Horse brought me and I went to M⁰ Northrops and found them very Religious about 2. we began the meeting and there was a great Number of People.—Lodged at the Same House—

Tuesday Oct⁰ 6 As soon as I had done eating, we went to D⁰ Stantons—and we began the meeting about 11:1 and there was a great Number of People and I Spoke from—in the after Noon preachd again—and Spoke from [ ] in the Evening I Went to M⁰ Stantons and did not expect to have any People but there was a number came together & we a little meeting,—and I Lodgd at the Same House and rest well—

Wednesday Oct⁰ 7: Soon afr Beakfast we went to M⁰ Tenikes about 2 we began the mee the meeting, and there was a great Number of People and I Spoke from Marck V:4 and the People attended well—Logd at M⁰ Tenikes after meeting I we to M⁰ John Colvins, and there we had anothere meeting, unexpectedly, and there was a large number of People and I Spoke to them Matt Seek Ye first &c:[309] and the People were much movd, it was a Comfortable meeting, I Lodgd at the Same House,—

Thirdsday Oct⁰ 8: in the morn I went to See a woman that had been Sick Some Time and Said few word to her and Prayd with her,—and then went back, and took breakfast, and Soon after M⁰ Colvin went with me to the River, and We parted the River, and I over to [Seedock?], and from there went to M⁰ Lotts about 7 miles and I walkd about 2 m and half and then M⁰ Brown overtook me, and he Caried me to M⁰ Lotts, got there near Sun Set and we were very glad to see each other once more, Lodgd at the Same House—

*Fryday ^9^* Some Time in the morning I went to M⁰ Daniel Muchmullins, and to M⁰ Ephraim Bailys,—towards Night went back to M⁰ Lotts, and there we had a meeting in the evening and there a large Number of People I Spoke from Gal. IV.11 [words

---

309. See Matthew 6:33.

missing] gether to Meeting and I Spoke from Job I:9 and the People attended with great affection I Lodgd at the Same House—

∾ JOURNAL 23

October 13, 1789–January 10, 1790

Occom continues his progress toward Mohegan by boat, arriving at New London on October 25. His son Benoni, who has elected not to participate in the Brotherton movement, remains at Mohegan. Occom also visits his old Mohegan household, now occupied by new inhabitants, and holds a Sabbath meeting there on November 29. After a lapse in writing of some six weeks, Occom records on January 10 that he is suffering spiritual despair: "I have had no peace, but Sorrow, grief and Confusion of Heart—and I am yet in great Trouble." It is unclear whether he writes these lines from Mohegan or from Brotherton, where factional controversy over town governance and disposition of land continues to deepen.

Tuesday Octr 13: Mr Whitly came to Mr Lotts quite early to acompany me down to Seedock Landing, got there Soon, and Capt Allyn was not ready, & Mr Whitly went back,—

Wednesday, Octr 14: Was at the Schooner all Day—

Thirdsday Octr 15: Some Time in the after Noon we weigh Anker, and Spred Sail to the Wind, and went the River got but about 10:11: and there we Dropt Anker—

Fryday Octr 16 found the Wind a Head of us and so we lay Still till about 2 in the after Noon and the Wind Sprang about West Nor West and went down again

Saturday Octr 17 Some Time in the Day went on again but did not go but little ways—

Sabb: Octr 18: Went on again but did not go far—

Monday Octr 19, got but a little ways again—

Tuesday Octr 20 went on again not far.

Wednesday Octr 21 went on Still got near New York—

Thirdsday Octr 22 a little after Sun rise We were a Shore—went directly to find a Pasage to New London and found one Soon, a Sloop goin to N London Towards Night I put [page torn] my things, and Lodged a Board Capt Fellows is Master of her—

Fryday 23 Some Time before Noon we Sot Sail, and went on the Wind in our Favour and we Saild all Night,—

Saturday Octr 24. We went the Wind in our favour Considerable towards Night the wind began to Blow hard, and the Clouds gatherd thick and So we Sought for a Harbor, and Some Time before Sun Sit we made a Harber, against Brandford, and there Lay all Night, and it was a Stormy Night.—

Sabb. Octr 25 Some Time in the Morning we Sot Sail, the wind was right a Head as we were geting out of the Harbor But it was very fair when we got out, and the Sun was about an Hour and half high at Night when we got fast ^at a^ warf and I went to See Some Friends—Lodgd at Mr Perrys a public House,—and I Sot up late with two women, Conversing about Religious matters about 11 I went to Bed, and I was taken Strangely in the Night with an Uncommon Sweat but after a while went to Sleep but did not Sleep Well—

Monday Octr 26: Got up early and it was a Stormy Day it Raind very hard, and wind blew hard also—towards Night I went over to Groton, Calld on Capt Lathem a few minutes, and then went to Mr Streets, and there I took food, and they let me have a Horse and went to Mr Woodmancys and there I Lodgd, and was very kindly entertaind. went to Bed Some what late, and Soon after I got to Bed, I began to Sweat again very much and was uncomfortable Slept but poorly—

Tuesday Octr 27. got up early and after Breakfast, I had a Horse of Mr Woodmancy and I went to Mr Saunderss and I met Mr Saunders, and Mr Woodworth and they glad to See me, and So I past on, and when I got to the House, how glad they were, and there I Stayd all Day—I expected my mare, that I Left with Mr Culver but She was rid a way last Sabb: and was not returnd, and [and] So I stayed all Day and all Night—

Wednesday 28: After Breakfast took leave of the Family, and went to old Mr Culvers, and by the way I met Mr Culver bring my Mare to me, and so got up and went on my way, and soon got to Gails Ferry, and the Wind was very hard, and Coud not get over, and So Stayd all Day at evening the Wind was Still very Strong and [word illegible] and So Concluded to Stay all Night, and in the evening the People of the Family askd me, whether it woud be agreable to me to have a few Neighbours Come together, that I might Pray with them, I told them it was quite agreable,—

Thirdsday Octr 29 got up early, and took Breakfast and then went over—and got to Son Benonis Some Time before noon, and found him Sick & had been very Sick for about 6: weeks, and was now a little better—and I went on to my old House, and them that live in my House were well, except the woman and there I Stayd—and I was poorly with the uncommon Cold that is every where—

Sabb Novr 1: was very warm and I felt a little easy, and I went S Ashpos expecting, to [word illegible] meeting, but he had none and so went back—

Saturday Novr 7 was much poorly yet I went to groton Indian T got there after Sun Set, and was receivd with great Love in the evening we had a little meeting—

Sabb: ~~Octr 8~~ Novr 8 the People got together about 10, and a great number there was, and I Spoke from Mat 1.21: and Acts VIII.21 and the People attended with great attention and many were much affected—in the evening went to Mr Stantons, and there another meeting, and a great many People there was—I Spoke from Gala IV.11 and the People were very Serious—I Lodgd at the Same House—

Sabb 15 Went to Mr Whalley and preachd to a great Number of People. I Spoke from Gal IV.11 and the People gave very great attention,—as Soon as the meetg was over I went to Widow Fitches and there was Considerable Number of People, and they attended Well, and as soon as the meeting was done, I went home to my Old House—

Sabb Novr 22 was to go over to [Pawcuthunnuk?] but it was Very Stormy, and Stopt about 10 the Storm abated Some and I Sot off got there about 12 and we the Service about [3] and there was [page torn] People and I Spoke from Jerem. VIII.6 and the People attended with great Solemnity—and the People desired to have another meet in the evening and So we had another, and there was more People in the evening than in the Day-Time, and Spoke from 1: Corin VII.29.30, and there was greater attention than in the Day Time—I Lodgd at the House the Man's Name was Mr Herkules and was kindly Treated.—

Monday Novr 23 after Break I went to the River on Horse Back and the Wind blew very hard but I had a fine chance, in a Whale Boat, to get over the River got home about 10: and directly went to the People, that were surveying our Land.[310]—

Thursday Novr 26. Was to go over to Mr Babcocks at Groton but it was a very bad Storm

Saturday Novr 28: towards Night, I Went to Mr Posts at Weens Hill, in Norwich, got there after Sun Set, Calld at Mr John Posts, and took supper there, and after that Went to old Mr Posts, and found, him very poorly, and there I Lodgd, and he had Several fits in the Night—

Sabb: Novr 29 The People began to get together about 10: and there was a large Concourse of People we began the Exercise about 11. and Spoke from Isai 1:12. and the People attended with great Solemnity, and many were affected to Tears—Soon after meeting after Dinner, I returned home and had a meeting at my own House and there was a great many People, and I Spoke from II Timo. 3:—

Jan^r 10 I have been to no meetings four Sabbaths, we had one very bad Stormy Sabb and my Mind has been filld with Trouble So that I have had no peace, but Sorrow, grief and Confusion of Heart—and I am yet in great Trouble,—

[Courtesy of Dartmouth College Library]

☙ JOURNAL 24

February 21, 1790–March 6, 1790

> *The final surviving section of the diary follows the sixty-six-year-old Occom as he travels between Brotherton and Albany, visiting his daughters Christiana and Olive, and graciously answering invitations to preach along the way.*

[Sunday, Feb 21] and there was A large N^r of People, and I Spoke from [ ] and the People attended well—after meeting I went to Deacon's Swan[n]s and Lodged there—

Monday Feb^r 22 after B went on my way to Albany Stopt but a litle while; Dind with Mr John Andrews, in the after Noon, went on again, towards Bought got Eq^r Olcuts and there Lodgd, and was very kindly entertaind,—

Tuesday Feb^r 23: after B went on again, Calld on two or three Friends, and so past on to half-Moon Point Calld on old Mr Bogardus and there took Tea in the evening went to the Point, Calld on my good Friend Mr J. Vanderwariker, and had a meeting at a Widow Womans House and there was much People, and I Spoke from Eph 2: and the People behaved well—Lodgd at Mr Vanderwarikens,—

Wednesday Feb^r 24: Soon after eating I went back to Bought and in the Evening had a mt at old Mr Fero, and there was a large N^r of People, and I Spoke from [ ] and the People attended well Fero's Lodgd at the Same House—

---

310. It is unclear whether this is a survey of Occom family lands or Mohegan tribal territory.

Thirdsday Feb' 25: Soon after Breakfast, took lea of the Family and went on towards Balls Town got to Nescayouna[311] towards Night; I put up at one Mr Fishers,—and in the evening we had a meeting, and there was a large number of People and I Spoke from [ ] Lodgd at the Same House—

Fryday 26, after Breakfast I Went to Mr Gernsy's and there all Night—

Saturday Feb' 27 Some Time in the Morning, I went back to Mr Thomas Smiths and there in the evening we had a meeting, Chiefly for Singing Andrew,[312] John Quinny Solo^n and his Wife were at the meeting—Lodgd at the Same House and rested well—

Sabb Feb' 28 as Soon as eating was over, Mr Smith took me in his Slay and we went to meeting at one M^r [ ] and there was a great Number of People and I Spoke from Jesus Christ the Same &c and the People attended well, Soon after m I went with Mr Gernsy in his Slay,—and toward Night we had a meeting in his House, and the People Coud not all get in, I Spoke from the words Sin is the Transgression of the Law,[313]—Lodgd at the Same House—

Monday March 1 Stayd all Day at the Same House I had forgot my Bag—

Tuesday March 2; Soon after eating I went off, went to See my Daughter Christiana in Balls Town, got there Some in the after Noon, and was there a While, and then went on to Freehole,—got to Mr Northrops in the Evening and there Lodgd—

Wednesday March 3 went to See my Daughter Olive, and found them well, but Cinhia Wawcus,[314] She was poorly,—Soon went back and at about 11: we had a meeting, and there was a Considerable number of People, and I Spoke from Gala—I am afraid of you[315] and the People attended well Soon after meeting took Dinner, and then went off got to Mr Grotes and Lodged there and was well Treated—

Thirdsday March the 4: got up early, and took B: with them; Soon after went on my way, got to Capt Prooffs and Lodged there and was kindly receivd.—

Fryday March 5: after Breakfast, went on again Stopt a while at Mr Deans in Fort Plain, I heard Brother David and his Wife were about a Mile off, went on again, and got to Esqr Franks in the Evening he and his Wife were not at Home, and Lodged there

Saturday March 6: Some Time in the morning I over to Fort Dayton Calld on M^r [Talcut?], but he & his Wife were not at home and was there a while, and returnd back with a Certain man to Esqr Franks again

[Courtesy of Dartmouth College Library]

---

311. *Nescayouna:* Niscayuna, New York
312. *Andrew:* probably Andrew Gifford Occom.
313. See 1 John 3:4.
314. *Cinhia Wawcus:* Cynthia Waucus.
315. See Galatians 4:11.

Individuals Named in Occom's Writings

This biographical dictionary features individuals whose identities could be discovered and verified, especially clergy, Native Americans, and other persons of historical or political interest.

Acorrocomb, Andrew (Farmington; b. 1747): Member of a prominent family at Farmington, Connecticut; friend of Joseph Johnson, and a founder and early settler at Brotherton. Took refuge at Stockbridge during the American War of Independence.

Adams, Olive Occom (Mohegan; b. 1755): Daughter of Samson Occom. Married Solomon Adams (Farmington) in 1775, and resided near Windsor and then at Farmington, Connecticut, before removing to Brotherton.

Adgate, John Hart (1759–1809): Resident of Norwich, Connecticut.

Amherst, Jeffrey (1717–1797): British military commander during the Seven Years' War and governor-general of British North America until 1763. Amherst is often remembered as the deviser of a plan to distribute smallpox-infected blankets to American Indian tribes as a form of warfare.

Armstrong, James Francis (1750–1816): Princeton-educated Presbyterian minister, who served at Elizabethtown and Trenton, New Jersey.

Ashpo, John (Mohegan; b. 1740): Son of Samuel Ashpo and Hannah Mamnack.

Ashpo, Mercy (Mohegan): Daughter of John Ashpo.

Ashpo, Robert (Mohegan): Brother of Samuel Ashpo. Joseph Johnson mentions that he led a singing meeting at Farmington. His signature appears on a 1746 tribal petition. Did not migrate to Brotherton.

Ashpo, Samuel (Mohegan; 1718–1795): Member of prominent Mohegan family and influential preacher to several southern New England Indian communities. Ashpo converted during the Great Awakening and with Sarah Occom joined the church of David Jewett. He served as a schoolmaster in the Mashantucket Pequot Indian community (1753–1757; 1759–1762), and lived for many years thereafter at Groton. He is believed to have married Hannah Mamnack (Wangunk; d. 1801); the couple had at least six children. In preparation for a mission among the Onondaga, he entered Moor's Indian Charity School on September 25, 1762, and received a license to preach in 1763. He preached among the Six Nations and southern New England tribal communities, serving as an important conduit of political and ideological exchange between them. Ashpo, who died at Montville, Connecticut, did not migrate to Brotherton.

Aupaumut, Hendrick (Mahican; 1757–1830): Stockbridge-born and Moravian-educated, Aupaumut enlisted and was commissioned as an army captain during the American War of Independence. He was selected as a councillor to Stockbridge sachem Joseph

Quinney in about 1777. When the Stockbridge community moved to Oneida lands in the 1780s, Aupaumut served as a diplomat between United States government and the Shawnee, Delaware, and Tuscarora tribes. He wrote an account of his travels—"A Short Narration of My Last Journey to the Western Country"—in 1794. In 1829, Aupaumut again removed with the Stockbridge to Menominee lands in Wisconsin.

Aupaumut, Joshua: Son of Hendrick Aupaumut, baptized by Samson Occom.

Avery, Abraham (1744–1817): Resident of Montville, Connecticut. Avery grew up on Mohegan lands obtained by his grandfather Captain Thomas Avery (1651–1737), who served as an interpreter for the Mohegan tribe in a 1721 lawsuit.

Avery, Asa (1721–1789): Member of the prominent Avery family of Groton, Connecticut.

Avery, John (1732–1794): Clockmaker and silversmith in Preston, Connecticut.

Avery, Park (1710–1797): Minister, member of Connecticut Colonial Assembly, and member of the prominent Avery family of Groton, Connecticut.

Avery, William (1724–1787): Member of the prominent Avery family of Groton, Connecticut.

Baldwin, Theophilus (1728–1804): Separatist Congregationalist deacon of New Milford, Connecticut.

Barker, Nehemiah (1720–1772): Presbyterian minister of Southhold, Long Island, who participated in the ordination of Samson Occom.

Bartholomew, Andrew (1714–1776): Congregationalist minister of Harwinton, Connecticut.

Bostwick, David (1721–1763): Presbyterian minister, and president of New York Board of Correspondents for the Society in Scotland for Propagating Christian Knowledge (SPCK). Bostwick encouraged Occom's early mission activities among the Oneida.

Brainerd, John (1720–1781): Yale-educated Presbyterian minister and brother of the celebrated missionary David Brainerd (1718–1747). John Brainerd also served as a missionary to Native communities in New Jersey, New York, and Pennsylvania, before moving to Deerfield, Massachusetts, in 1777.

Brant, Joseph, or *Thayendanega* (Mohawk; 1742–1807): After his sister Molly Brant married Sir William Johnson in 1753, Joseph Brant became a student at Moor's Indian Charity School (1761–1763). He afterward served as secretary and interpreter for William Johnson and Guy Johnson. Brant soon assumed a diplomatic role for the Mohawk tribe, and he secured Mohawk loyalties to the British during the American War of Independence.

Breed, Gershom (1715–1777): Grocery merchant in Norwich, Connecticut.

Brimmer, John Baker (1746–1784): Boston merchant who sometimes acted as business agent for Joseph Johnson and Samson Occom.

Brown, Benjamin (1741–1822): Resident of Groton, Connecticut, follower of Jemima Wilkinson, and member of her Universal Friends society.

Browne, James: Yale-educated Presbyterian minister of Bridgehampton, Long Island; presided over the ordination of Samson Occom.

Buell, Samuel (1716–1798): Presbyterian minister of East Hampton, Long Island, who served as an itinerant preacher during the Great Awakening and preached the sermon at the ordination of Samson Occom, which was later published.

Bulkley, Charles (1719–1797): Connecticut Baptist minister and author.

Bulls, Daniel (1709–1776): Resident of Hartford, Connecticut.

Calvin, Widow (Lenape): Mother-in-law to Daniel Simon. Possibly the mother of Hezekiah Calvin (Lenape; b. about 1755), a Moor's Indian Charity School student and missionary.

Campbell, Robert (1709–1789): Separate Congregationalist minister of New Milford, Connecticut.

Chalkcom, Jacob (Natick): Acquaintance of Occom; appears in Middlesex, Massachusetts, court records for his marriage to Leah Thomas on March 31, 1730. The couple had nine children.

Chamberlain, Theophilus (1737–1824): Yale graduate, taken prisoner by Native American troops during Seven Years' War, who was subsequently appointed by Eleazar Wheelock to serve as schoolmaster among the Mohawk.

Champlin, Nathaniel (1766–1836): Resident of Lyme, Connecticut.

Chandler, Samuel (1693–1766): Presbyterian minister of London.

Changum (Niantic): Resident of New Hartford, Connecticut.

Chapman, Jedediah (1741–1813): Presbyterian minister and schoolmaster of Orange Dale Academy in Newark Mountains, New Jersey.

Charlotte, Queen (1744–1818): German-born wife of King George III.

Clark, Nathaniel (1720–1793): Resident of Canterbury, Connecticut.

Clelland, Robert: Scottish-born Presbyterian missionary, who served as schoolmaster at Mohegan (1752–1765), with the support of the Boston commissioners of the Society in Scotland for Propagating Christian Knowledge (SPCK). Clelland was rejected by Samson Occom and many other Mohegans for siding with the Connecticut colony during the Mason land case.

Colden, Cadwallader (1689–1776): Scottish-born New York colonial official, intellectual, and author of *The History of the Five Indian Nations* (1727); served as surveyor general and lieutenant governor of the colony of New York.

Colton, George (1736–1812): Yale-educated minister of Bolton, Connecticut.

Cook, Moses (?–1771): Son of Samuel Cook, of Wallingford, Connecticut; murdered by Moses Paul.

Cooper, John (Mohegan): Resident of Groton, Connecticut, signer of 1746 Mohegan tribal petition against the colony of Connecticut, and beloved lay preacher among southern New England tribal communities. Did not migrate to Brotherton.

Cornelius: See Hannibal, Cornelius.

Corricomb, Eliza (Farmington; b. 1768): Daughter of Andrew Accorocomb; Brotherton resident.

Crocker, Jabez (1725–1785): Resident of Norwich, Connecticut.

Cuish, Phillip (Niantic; 1716–1789): Baptist preacher. His son Joseph married Amy Johnson, sister to Mohegan missionary and Occom's son-in-law Joseph Johnson.

Dantuckquechen, John: see Tantaquidgeon, John.

Darbe, Benjamin (b. 1756): Resident of Hebron, Connecticut.

Dartmouth: See Legge, William.

Deake, Charles (1737–1803): Baptist resident of Rhode Island, who moved with other Baptists to White Creek Township, New York, in 1774 or 1775; settled Greenfield, New York, with his four sons, in 1786.

Deake, Edward (b. 1733): Schoolmaster to the Narragansett Indians at Charlestown, Rhode Island. He later moved to White Creek Township, New York, with his brother Charles Deake.

Deshon, Telex: Native American resident of Groton, Connecticut.

Devotion, John (1730–1802): Yale-educated Congregationalist minister at Westbrook, Connecticut (1757–1802).

Doddridge, Philip (1702–1751): Hymn writer and dissenting minister of London.

Downer, Cyprian (1741–1819): Baptist preacher of Shaftsbury, Vermont.

Duffield, John: Philadelphia physician; served at Valley Forge during the American War of Independence.

Duglas, Robert (1705–1786): Resident of New London, Connecticut.

Dygert, Madaline (Lana) Herkimer (b. 1728): Resident of Frankfort, New York, and sister to American War of Independence hero General Nicholas Herkimer.

Ephraim, Deacon Joseph (Natick; d. 1761): Prominent member of the Natick Indian community; husband to Judah and father to at least seven children, including Deborah, Ebenezer, John, Joseph, Judah, Sarah, and Simon. Joseph Ephraim signed petitions to establish a meetinghouse at Natick (1747/8) and to defend Natick fishing rights against English encroachment (1748). He also contributed to the community's efforts to recruit and maintain their own minister. By 1755, town records describe him as elderly.

Ephraim, Isaac (Natick; d. 1754): Acquaintance of Samson Occom and prominent member of the Natick Indian community. Isaac Ephraim signed petitions to raise a new meetinghouse at Natick (1747/8) and to defend Natick fishing rights against English encroachment (1748); he also advocated for the community's retention of a minister.

Ewing, John (1732–1802): Princeton-educated minister of the First Presbyterian Church of Philadelphia; provost of the University of Pennsylvania from 1779 until his death.

Fish, Joseph (1706–1782): Harvard-educated Congregationalist minister of North Stonington, Connecticut, and member of the Connecticut Board of the Society in Scotland for Propagating Christian Knowledge (SPCK). Fish kept a diary of his interactions with the southern New England Indian communities—Stonington Pequots, as well as Narragansetts at Charlestown, Rhode Island—he was charged to attend.

Folts, Conrad (1747–1793): Resident of Frankfort, New York, and veteran of American War of Independence.

Fothergill, John (1712–1780): Prominent member of the Society of Friends in London and friend of George Whitefield. A botanist and physician, Fothergill is credited with discovering the disease diphtheria.

Fowler, Benjamin Garrett (Brotherton; 1774–1848): Son of Hannah Garrett (Pequot) and David Fowler (Montuakett); became Brotherton leader, serving as town marshal and peacemaker. Benjamin Fowler removed with many Brotherton residents to Wisconsin.

Fowler, Betty Pharoah (Montaukett; 1707–1795): A member of the prominent Pharoah family of Montaukett and a descendent of the seventeenth-century chief Wyendanche, Betty Pharoah married James Fowler (Shinnecock). She was the mother of six children, including David, Jacob, and Mary Fowler, and was mother-in-law to Samson Occom. In 1787, Occom moved her from Long Island to Brotherton, New York.

Fowler, David (Montaukett; 1735–1807): Brother-in-law and friend to Samson Occom, David Fowler was the son of James and Betty Pharoah Fowler. He attended Moor's Indian Charity School (April 12, 1759–1761), accompanied Occom on a trip to Oneida in 1761, and served as a schoolmaster among the Oneida and Mohawk (1765–1767) and Montaukett (1767–1770). One of the founders of the Brotherton movement, Fowler himself settled at Brotherton in 1775, where he served as a town trustee and a peacemaker. He was married to Hannah Garrett; the couple had nine children.

Fowler, David, Jr. (Brotherton; 1767–1826): Son of Hannah Garrett (Pequot) and David Fowler; Brotherton resident and town clerk.

Fowler, Elizabeth (Brotherton; b. 1770): Daughter of Hannah Garrett (Pequot) and David Fowler (Montaukett); remained with her grandmother and the Montaukett community on Long Island until 1787, when she moved to Brotherton, New York.

Fowler, Esther Poquiantup (Pequot): Daughter of Samson Poquiantup (Pequot) and Esther (Mohegan; 1725–1822); married Jacob Fowler and moved to Brotherton, New York.

Fowler, Hannah Garrett (Pequot; 1747–1811): Daughter of a politically prominent Pequot family, Hannah Garrett entered Moor's Indian Charity School on December 17, 1763. Married David Fowler and had nine children. One of the founding settlers of Brotherton.

Fowler, Jacob (Montaukett; 1750–1787): Brother-in-law and friend to Samson Occom, Jacob Fowler was the son of James and Betty Pharoah Fowler. He attended Moor's Indian Charity School (November 27, 1762–1766) and served as a schoolmaster to the Oneida (1766–1770) and Mashantucket Pequot at Groton (1770–1774). He also taught one year at Moor's Indian Charity School in Hanover, New Hampshire (1774–1775), and served as Connecticut Governor Jonathan Trumbull's messenger to the Six Nations (1776). Like his brother David, Jacob Fowler was instrumental in the founding of Brotherton, where he served as a town clerk. He married Esther Poquiantup.

Fowler, James (Shinnecock; 1700–1774): Husband to Elizabeth Pharoah Fowler, father to six children, including David, Jacob, and Mary Fowler, and father-in-law to Samson Occom.

Fowler, Rhene (Brotherton; b. 1776): Daughter of David and Hannah Garrett Fowler; migrated to Brotherton, New York.

Franklin, William (1731–1813): Oldest son of Benjamin Franklin; appointed royal governor of New Jersey in 1763. A staunch Loyalist, Franklin met Samson Occom while being held as a prisoner of war in Connecticut for refusing to relinquish his office during the American War of Independence.

Frisbie, Levi (1748–1806): Student at Moor's Indian Charity School and member of first graduating class at Dartmouth (1771). Went as a missionary among the Oneida (1769) and Lenape (1772–1773). Became minister at First Congregationalist Church in Ipswich, Massachusetts, in 1776.

Frothingham, Ebenezer (d. 1798): Separate Congregationalist minister of Middletown, Connecticut.

Fundy, Major: Trader on the Mohawk River, New York.

Gano, John (1727–1804): A descendent of French Huguenots, Gano was pastor of the First Baptist Church in New York City (1762–1788).

Garrett, Benjamin (Pequot; b. 1725): Member of a prominent and politically active family; father of Hannah Garrett and father-in-law of David Fowler.

George III, King (1738–1820): King of England.

Gibbons, Thomas (1720–1785): Independent-Congregationalist minister at Haberdasher's Hall in London.

Gifford, Andrew (1700–1784): Baptist minister at Eagle Street Church in London, assistant librarian at the British Museum, and namesake for Samson Occom's youngest son.

Goodrich, Daniel (1765–1835): One of twelve sons of the proprietary Goodrich family of Hancock, Massachusetts; reared a Baptist; became a Shaker with most of his brothers in 1790; his farm became the site of a Shaker settlement.

Gordon, James (b. 1749): Resident, Ballstown, New York, and lieutenant colonel, Twelfth Regiment, Albany County Militia.

Hannibal, Cornelius (Montaukett; d. 1789): Brotherton town elder called "Old Uncle Cornelius" by Samson Occom.

Hannibal [Hannabal], Temperance (Montaukett): Member of politically prominent Hannibal family. Gave her spiritual confession to Samson Occom in 1754.

Haynes, Lemuel (1753–1833): First African-American ordained by a major Protestant denomination in the United States, and published sermon author. Haynes met Occom while serving as a Congregationalist minister at Torrington, Connecticut.

Hedges, William (1706–1775): Resident of Easthampton, Long Island; a friend and benefactor of Samson Occom's family during his years at Montauk.

Hickok, Jeremiah (1748–1809): Tavern owner of Sheffield, Massachusetts, and captain of the Berkshire Regiment in the American War of Independence.

Holstead, Mr.: Primitive Baptist minister at Fishkill, New York.

Horton, Azariah (1715–1777): Yale-educated Presbyterian missionary among Montaukett and Shinnecock communities on Long Island, supported by Society in Scotland for Propagating Christian Knowledge (SPCK). Horton left his Long Island mission after confrontations with New Light exhorters, and subsequently ministered in New York and Philadelphia.

Hotham, Lady Gertrude (d. 1767): Follower of George Whitefield and friend of Selina, Countess of Huntingdon.

Huntingdon, Lady Selina Hastings, Countess (1707–1791): Friend of John and Charles Wesley, patron of George Whitefield, and founder of the Huntingdon Connexion of evangelical Calvinist preachers.

Ide, Hannah (b. 1761): A native of Redding, Connecticut, Hannah Ide was married to Sanford White by Samson Occom at Ballstown, New York, on December 19, 1785.

Irish, David (1757–1815): Baptist elder at Stillwater, New York.

Irish, Mary Mercy Sweet (1760–1831): Wife of David Irish.

Jay, James (1732–1815): Physician and older brother of the statesman John Jay. He met Occom while visiting England on behalf of King's College (now Columbia College).

Jewett, David (1714–1783): Harvard-educated Congregationalist minister at Montville, Connecticut, and member of the Connecticut Board of Correspondents for the Society in Scotland for Propagating Christian Knowledge (SPCK). During the Great Awakening, Mohegans including Samuel Ashpo and Sarah Occom joined Jewett's church; however, many Mohegans left his church for Samson Occom's pastoral care when Jewett sided with the colony of Connecticut in the Mason land case.

Jewett, David Hibbert (1745–1814): Son of the Rev. David Jewett, and a Cambridge-educated physician.

Johnson, Guy (1740–1788): Nephew and son-in-law of Sir William Johnson and his successor as superintendent of Indian Affairs.

Johnson, Joseph, Jr. (Mohegan; 1751–1776): Friend and son-in-law to Samson Occom, and principal architect of the Brotherton settlement. Johnson attended Moor's Indian Charity School (1758–1765) and served as a missionary and schoolmaster to the Oneida (1766–1768) and Farmington communities (1772–1773). He married Samson Occom's daughter Tabitha in 1773; the couple had two children. Johnson's diaries, sermons, and letters constitute an important body of early American Indian literature.

Johnson, Joseph, Sr. (Mohegan; d. 1758): Father of missionary-schoolmaster Joseph Johnson. Served as a scout in the Seven Years' War, and was highly esteemed in southern New England Indian communities. Married Elisabeth, or Betty, Garrett (Pequot) and had at least two children, Joseph and Amy.

Johnson, William, Sir (1715–1774): British diplomatic emissary to the Six Nations and friend of Samson Occom. The Irish-born Johnson settled in the Mohawk Valley, New York, in 1738, was appointed superintendent of Indian affairs in 1746, and married

Mohawk Molly Brant in 1753. He served as as a major-general in the Seven Years' War and helped craft the Treaty of Fort Stanwix (1768).

Justice Samson, Hannah (Mohegan; 1705?–1785): Aunt of Samson Occom, sister to Sarah Samson Occom, and resident of the "Indian Town" near Black-Point, Connecticut. Justice married into the Poquiantup family (Niantic), creating kinship ties between Samson Occom and the Niantic community.

Keen, Robert (d. 1793): London wool merchant, friend of George Whitefield, and supporter of Moor's Indian Charity School. Keen served as secretary for the school's trust fund.

Kelley, Beriah: Baptist minister of Stillwater, New York.

Kirkland, Samuel (1741–1808): Congregational minister, founder of Hamilton College, and friend to Samson Occom and the Fowler family. Kirkland attended Moor's Indian Charity School and then the College of New Jersey (now Princeton University), before serving the Society in Scotland for Propagating Christian Knowledge as a missionary and colonial emissary to the Seneca and Oneida. A longtime resident among the Oneida, he is now remembered as a controversial figure who encouraged the Oneida to cede millions of acres of territory in treaties with the state of New York. Kirkland preached at Occom's funeral.

Kirkpatrick, William (d. 1769): Presbyterian minister of New Jersey. While serving as a chaplain during the Seven Years' War, Kirkpatrick came into contact with Oneida tribal members, and solicited a school at Oneida from Eleazar Wheelock.

Konkapot, Jacob (Mahican; d. 1835): Native of Stockbridge, Massachusetts; son of John Konkapot, Stockbridge tribal councillor and graduate of Dartmouth College. Jacob Konkapot had a long military career. During the American War of Independence, he served at the battles of Bunker Hill, White Plains, and Saratoga, and later served as lieutenant of a Stockbridge Indian company in the War of 1812. He eventually removed to Wisconsin.

Larkin, Amos (1761–1827): Son of Joshua Larkin, and resident of Ballstown, New York.

Larkin, Joshua (b. 1732): Resident first of Easthampton, Long Island, then Ballstown, New York. Samson Occom called Joshua Larkin and his wife Bethia "good old friends."

Lathem, Robert (b. 1756): Resident of Groton, Connecticut, and friend to Samson Occom.

Law, Richard (1732–1806): District judge of New London, Connecticut, and later chief justice of the Connecticut Superior Court.

Legge, William, Earl of Dartmouth (1731–1801): A follower of George Whitefield, William Legge, Earl of Dartmouth, became a key supporter of Moor's Indian Charity School. During the 1760s, he secured contributions from prominent Britons including King George III and presided over the school's trust fund. Moor's Indian Charity School was renamed Dartmouth College in his honor. Dartmouth was appointed British secretary of state to the colonies in 1772, but resigned his post on the eve of the War of American Independence in 1775.

Lester, Eliphalet (1729–1816): Resident of New London, Connecticut, and affiliate of the Society in Scotland for the Propagation of Christian Knowledge (SPCK).

Livingston, John Henry (1746–1825): Yale-educated pastor of the Fulton Street Dutch Reformed church in New York City; professor of theology and president of Queen's College, New Jersey (1807–1825).

Livingston, William (1723–1790): Member of the New York legislature, Continental Congress delegate, and governor of New Jersey; signed Occom's recommendation to Oneida.

Madin, Martin (1726–1790): Anglican priest converted by John Wesley, minister at Lock Hospital chapel, and associate of Countess Huntingdon.

Manning, John: Resident of Windham, Connecticut. Moses Paul was bound to his family from about 1747 to 1762.

Maples, John (1719–1798): Lifelong resident of Montville, Connecticut; father of Josiah Maples. He married Sarah Baker (1721–1797).

Maples, Josiah (1762–1847): Resident of Norwich, Connecticut.

Marsh, Jonathan (1714–1794): Congregationalist minister of New Hartford, Connecticut (1739–1794).

Mason, John Mitchell (1734–1792): Scottish-born Presbyterian minister and renowned preacher. A member of the dissenting "Secession" Church of Scotland, Mason emigrated to New York City in 1761 and established the Associate Reformed Presbyterian Church in 1782.

Mazeen, Moses (Mohegan): Counselor to Ben Uncas III; probably did not migrate to Brotherton, as he appears on a 1799 Mohegan census.

McClure, David (1748–1820): Yale graduate (1769), ordained at Dartmouth (1772), who subsequently conducted a mission among the Delaware with Levi Frisbie (1772–1773). McClure was also a Dartmouth trustee (1777–1800) and editor of the *Memoirs of the Rev. Eleazar Wheelock* (1810).

McDonald, John: Scottish-born Presbyterian minister of Albany, New York (1775–1795).

McWhorter, Alexander (1734–1807): Presbyterian minister of Newark, New Jersey.

Miller, Alexander: Presbyterian minister of Schenectady, New York (1770–1781).

Moorhead, John (d. 1773): Founding minister of the Boston Church of the Presbyterian Strangers (now the historic Federal Street Church). Moorhead was among the public figures who signed their names to an attestation to Phillis Wheatley's literacy that appeared in her *Poems* (1773). He was slave-master to Scipio Moorhead, a black painter praised in Wheatley's poems.

Mosely, Samuel (1708–1791): Minister of Windham, Connecticut; member of Connecticut Board of Correspondents for the Society in Scotland for Propagating Christian Knowledge (SPCK), and trustee of Moor's Indian Charity School.

Mossuck, Daniel (Farmington; d. 1782?): Son of Solomon and Eunice Mossuck. Entered Moor's Indian Charity School in July 1762 and stayed for a short season. Soldier in American War of Independence. Although he endorsed the Brotherton plan with his father, Daniel Mossuck apparently did not migrate to New York and died at Farmington.

Mossuck, Solomon (Farmington; 1723–1802): Member of the Farmington church; endorser and advocate of the Brotherton plan.

Newton, John (1725–1807): Former slave-ship captain who became an Anglican priest and hymn writer. Newton, coauthor with William Cowper of the *Olney Hymns* (1779), is best remembered for his hymn "Amazing Grace."

Niles, James (Narragansett): Nephew of Samuel Niles, and member of Charlestown, Rhode Island, Indian community. James Niles attended Moor's Indian Charity School, fought in the American War of Independence, married Barbara Poquiantup (Niantic), and had five children. The family removed to Brotherton about 1796.

Niles, Samuel (Charlestown-Narragansett; b. about 1706): Influential southern New England Indian leader, and resident of Charlestown, Rhode Island. After he was disciplined for exhorting in a Congregationalist Church at Westerly, Rhode Island, Niles and one hundred Native people founded their own Freewill Baptist Indian church.

Niles was ordained by three of his fellow Native congregants. He preached and pastored among Narragansett, Mohegan, and Pequot Indian communities. At Narragansett, Niles led a political faction opposing the tribal sachem Thomas Ninigret, who was selling away tribal lands. Niles and six Narragansett were among the first emigrants to Brotherton in 1775. Most of his congregation eventually removed to Brotherton.

Occom, Aaron (Mohegan; 1753–1771): Oldest son of Samson and Mary Fowler Occom. In 1760, Aaron Occom was delivered by his father to be "brought up" by Eleazar Wheelock, and he continued an intermittent student at Moor's Indian Charity School until 1767. Married Ann Robin (Wangunk-Farmington), and fathered one son.

Occom, Andrew Gifford (Mohegan; b. 1774): Youngest son of Samson and Mary Fowler Occom; participated in the Brotherton movement.

Occom, Benoni (Mohegan; 1763–1829): Son of Samson and Mary Fowler Occom; remained at Mohegan and did not participate in the Brotherton movement.

Occom, Eunice (Pequot; d. 1787): Daughter of Joshua Occom, Jr., and Eunice (Pequot); niece of Samson Occom.

Occom, Jonathan (Mohegan; 1725–?): Brother of Samson Occom. Fought in both the Seven Years' War and the American War of Independence.

Occom, Lemuel Fowler (Mohegan; 1771–1790): Son of Samson and Mary Fowler Occom, died at Mohegan by drowning.

Occom, Mary Fowler (Montaukett; b. about 1730, d. after 1792): Daughter of James and Elizabeth Pharoah Fowler; married Samson Occom in 1751; mother to ten or eleven children. Mary Occom single-handedly ran the Occom household during her husband's frequent travels. Anecdotal histories report that although Samson Occom used English at home, the English-literate Mary Occom insisted on speaking Montauk-Pequot-Mohegan at home and retained her Native dress style.

Occom, Sarah Samson (Groton Pequot; b. 1690–1705): Daughter of Sabientouset II, also known as General Samson; married Joshua Ockham (Mohegan; b. before 1700, d. before 1743); mother of Samson, Jonathan, and Lucy Occom.

Occom, Tabitha (Mohegan; 1754–?): Daughter of Samson and Mary Fowler Occom. Married Joseph Johnson, Jr., in December 1773. A 1782 Mohegan census identifies her as "Anna," says she has two sons named William (b. 1774) and Joseph (b. 1776), and has been "cast off for her incontinency." The diary of Samson Occom records the death of Tabitha in 1785; however, legal documents indicate that Tabitha Occom, daughter of Samson Occom, was alive in 1807. Tabitha entered into a second marriage with Joshua Cooper. The couple had two children, Betsy and Charles.

Occom, "Widow" Eunice (Pequot; d. 1809): Wife of Samson Occom's older brother Joshua. Did not migrate to Brotherton.

Ocus (Montaukett; b. 1712): Taught Samson Occom traditional Montaukett herbal lore. His name also appears on a 1760 muster list from Suffolk County, Long Island, New York.

Oliver, Andrew (1706–1774): Lieutenant governor of Massachusetts (1770–1774).

Onslow, Arthur (1691–1768): Speaker of the English House of Commons until 1761.

Packer, John (1753–1835): Resident of Groton, Connecticut.

Palmer, Reuben (1753–1822): Baptist minister of Scotland, Connecticut.

Paul, Anthony (Charlestown-Narragansett; b. 1758): Son-in-law to Samson Occom; married Christiana Occom about 1777. Anthony and Christiana Paul moved to Brotherton with his mother and brother John in 1784. Anthony and Christiana Paul had at least six children. Samson Occom baptized Anthony Paul and four of his children at

Brotherton in August 1787. Anthony Paul is believed to have inherited a portion of his father-in-law's papers. He and Christiana left Brotherton in about 1797 and lived the rest of their years near Lake George, New York.

Paul, Christiana Occom (Mohegan; b. 1757): Daughter of Samson Occom, probably named after character from John Bunyan's *Pilgrim's Progress*. Married Anthony Paul about 1777; mothered at least six children. Samson Occom often stayed with Christiana and Anthony Paul during his travels before his emigration to Brotherton.

Paul, John (Charlestown-Narragansett): Brother of Anthony Paul; emigrated to Brotherton in 1784.

Paul, Moses (Wampanoag?; 1742–1772): A native of Barnstable, Massachusetts, Paul was bound out as a child indentured servant and subsequently worked as a soldier and sailor, before being executed for the December 7, 1771, murder of Moses Cook at a tavern in Bethany, Connecticut. Samson Occom preached the execution sermon at Paul's request.

Pauquunnuppeet, Peter (Mahican): Native of Stockbridge, Massachusetts; attended Dartmouth College (1771–1780); selected councillor to Stockbridge sachem Joseph Quinney in 1777. Pauquunnuppeet (also Pauquaunnuppeet, Poquunnupeet, Pohquaunnuppeet) helped lead the Stockbridge removal to New Stockbridge, Oneida, New York. He was sometimes called "Sir Peter," after the Dartmouth College custom of calling seniors "Sir."

Peabody, Oliver (1725–1752): Harvard-educated missionary among Native communities at Natick, Massachusetts, and Groton, Connecticut.

Peguun, Widow (d. 1787): Resident of Groton Indian town. Possibly Elizabeth, the widow of Thomas Peegun, a Christian Indian from the "praying town" of Natick, Massachusetts, who went to preach at Mohegan in 1732.

Peters, Elizabeth (Montaukett; b. 1737): Emigrated to Brotherton with her children George, Oliver, Rhoda, and Frederick.

Peters, George (Montaukett; 1761–1801): Early Brotherton settler; married Elijah Wympy's daughter Eunice; fathered three children. George Peters was executed in 1801 for murdering his wife.

Pomeroy, Abigail Wheelock (1717–1797): Wife of Benjamin Pomeroy; sister of Eleazar Wheelock.

Pomeroy, Benjamin (1704–1784): New Light preacher and Separate Congregationalist minister of Hebron, Connecticut; brother-in-law to Eleazar Wheelock; trustee of Moor's Indian Charity School. Samson Occom studied Latin, Greek, and Hebrew with Pomeroy in 1748.

Post, John (1749–1830): Resident of Schenectady, New York; visited often and called an "old friend" by Samson Occom.

Potter, William (1723–1814): Resident of South Kingstown, Rhode Island; dedicated follower of Jemima Wilkinson's Universal Friends movement.

Powers, Lemuel (1756–?): Baptist minister of Stillwater, New York; father of Abigail Powers Fillmore, wife of United States president Millard Fillmore.

Prime, Ebenezer (1700–1779): Presbyterian minister of Huntington, Long Island; participated in the ordination of Samson Occom.

Putchauker, Thomas (Wampanoag; d. 1795): Early Brotherton settler, who served as a town official. Member of the Elijah Wympy faction.

Putnam, Israel (1718–1790): Colonel of Moses Paul's army regiment; celebrated Revolutionary War general.

Pye, Joseph: Legendary Native American traditional medicine practitioner of New England; namesake for the "Joe Pye" weed (*Eupatorium purpureum*), also known as Queen-of-the-Meadow or Trumpetweed, which he used to treat typhus. Migrated with his wife and sister to Brotherton.

Quaquaquid, Henry (Mohegan): Mohegan and Brotherton church deacon, and sometime preaching companion of Samson Occom. Quaquaquid opposed Ben Uncas III during the Mason case and visited Sir William Johnson as an emissary of the reconstituted Mohegan tribal government. He hosted worship meetings at his house. "Henry Quaquaquid's family" of two appears on 1799 Mohegan census.

Quinney, Catherine (Mahican-Stockbridge): Possibly the daughter of Joseph Quinney; migrated to New Stockbridge, New York; sometimes accompanied Occom on ministerial visits.

Quinney, John (Mahican-Stockbridge): Possibly the son of Joseph Quinney; migrated to New Stockbridge, New York; later went to study at Jedediah Chapman's Orange Dale Academy in New Jersey. Probably the father of John Wannauaucon Quinney (1797–1855), Stockbridge diplomat and leader.

Quinney, Joseph (Mahican): Also known as Joseph Quanaukaunt. Became Stockbridge community sachem in 1777; migrated to New Stockbridge, New York, where he served as a church deacon, schoolmaster, and singing-leader.

Rodgers, John (1727–1811): Presbyterian minister of New York City, and member of New York board of the Society in Scotland for the Propagation of Christian Knowledge (SPCK). Supportive of Occom, Joseph Johnson, and other Native ministers.

Rogers, Alpheus (1750–1833): Congregationalist minister of Montville, Connecticut.

Rogers, Jeremiah (b. 1752): Physician of Uncasville, Connecticut.

Romaine, William (1714–1795): Anglican minister and rector at St. Anne's Church in Blackfriars; follower of George Whitefield.

Ryland, John Collett (1733–1792): Schoolmaster and Baptist minister.

Samson, Widow (Charlestown-Narragansett): Resident of Groton Indian town; may be the wife of Little Samson, brother to Sarah Samson Occom and uncle to Samson Occom.

Saunders, Gideon (1726–): Resident of Gales Ferry–Groton, Connecticut, and friend of Samson Occom.

Sergeant, John (1710–1749): Yale-educated Congregationalist minister; missionary to the Mahican Indians; a founder of Stockbridge Indian town.

Sergeant, John, Jr. (1747–1824): Son of John Sergeant, who followed his father as a missionary and minister to the Mahican-Stockbridge Indians. He moved to New Stockbridge, New York, in 1788, where he established himself as a rival to Samson Occom.

Shaw, Nathaniel (1708–1778): Wealthy ship captain of New London, Connecticut; frequently lodged Samson Occom and his friends.

Shaw, Temperance Harris (b. 1709): Wife of Nathaniel Shaw.

Sill, Elijah (1724–1792): Congregationalist minister of New Fairfield, Connecticut.

Simon, Abraham (Charlestown-Narragansett; b. 1750): Son of Sarah Simon; entered Moor's Indian Charity School in 1768 or 1769; went as a missionary to Oneida (1772). Simon followed Jacob Fowler as a schoolmaster at Groton, until he enlisted in the American War of Independence. Removed from Charlestown, Rhode Island, to Brotherton and was appointed a town trustee. Married to Sarah Adams by Samson Occom in 1787.

Simon, Daniel (Charlestown-Narragansett): Son of Sarah Simon; entered Moor's Indian Charity School on March 17, 1770; graduate of Dartmouth College (1777); appointed as a Presbyterian minister in 1778. Daniel Simon preached among the Mahican tribe at Stockbridge and the Lenape tribe at Cranberry (now Cranbury), New Jersey. He married a sister to his classmate Hezekiah Calvin.

Simon, James (Charlestown-Narrangansett): Separatist Christian Indian preacher and resident of Charlestown, Rhode Island. In the 1740s, Simon was ordained to lead a Narragansett congregation which rivaled that of Samuel Niles. Possibly the husband of Sarah Simon.

Skeesuck, Sally or Sarah (Charlestown-Narragansett; b. 1776): Daughter of Daniel (1750–1828) and Elizabeth (b. 1750?) Skeesuck. Born at Charlestown, Rhode Island; emigrated to Brotherton.

Sprout, James (1721–1793): Yale-educated minister at the Second Presbyterian Church of Philadelphia (1768–1793).

Standish, Nathan (b. 1753): Resident of Norwich, Connecticut; descendent of Myles Standish.

Stanton, Isaac (b. 1743): Resident of Stonington, Connecticut.

Stennet, Samuel (1728–1795): Baptist minister at Little Wild Street Church in London.

Stiles, Ezra (1727–1795): Scholar, theologian, minister, diarist, and president of Yale University (1778–1795).

Stillman, Samuel (1737–1807): Minister of the First Baptist Church of Boston (1764–1807); a founder of Rhode Island College, now Brown University; friend and ally to Boston's African-American community.

Story, Ephraim (1722–1794): Resident of Norwich, Connecticut.

Sunsummon, Joseph (Pequot): Native of Groton Indian Town, who itinerated with Occom in 1785, and later removed to Brotherton.

Swift, Job (1743–1804): Resident of Bennington, Vermont.

Tantaquidgeon, John (Mohegan; b. 1727): Member of a prominent Mohegan family and ancestor to the contemporary Mohegan Tantaquidgeon family. John Tantaquidgeon served as a counselor to Ben Uncas III. He married Samson Occom's sister Lucy. The couple had three children.

Tantaquidgeon, Lucy Occom, or Tecomwas (1731–1830): Sister of Samson Occom; wife of John Tantaquidgeon. Lucy Occom Tantaquidgeon did not participate in the Brotherton movement, but instead emerged as a crucial cultural and political leader at Mohegan. She oversaw the founding of the Mohegan Church and maintained continuous tribal governance and cultural practice through the church-affiliated "Ladies Sewing Circle."

Taylor, Nathaniel (1722–1800): Yale-educated Congregationalist minister of New Milford, Connecticut; chaplain of Connecticut regiment in Seven Years' War; grandfather of theologian Nathaniel William Taylor (1786–1858).

Thornton, John (1720–1790): London merchant and philanthropist. Member with William Wilberforce, Hannah More, and Josiah Wedgewood of politically active "Clapham Sect" of evangelical Anglicans, which advocated abolition of the slave trade; English trustee of Moor's Indian Charity School. Close associate of John and Susannah Wheatley and steadfast friend and financial supporter of Samson Occom.

Tracy, Joseph (1682–1765): Resident of Norwich, Connecticut.

Treadway, Jonathan (1755–1843): Resident of Lebanon, Connecticut; served as a drummer boy in the American War of Independence.

Tuhy, Jeremiah (Charlestown-Narragansett; b. 1768): Son of John Tuhy; Brotherton resident.

Tuhy, John (Charlestown-Narragansett; 1744?–1811): Native of Charlestown, Rhode Island; Brotherton emigrant and town peacemaker.

Uncas, Ben, III (Mohegan; d. 1769): Controversial sachem installed and recognized by the colony of Connecticut, but opposed by many Mohegans, including Samson Occom, for his cooperation with colonial interests, especially in the Mason land case.

Uppuiquiyantup, Isaac (Niantic): Called "cousin" by Samson Occom; possibly the son of Samson Poquiantup and Samson Occom's aunt Hannah Justice.

Vedder, Albert H. (b. 1736?): Founder of Amsterdam, New York; gristmill owner on the Mohawk River.

Wait, William (1738–1811): Baptist preacher of Kingston, Rhode Island, then White Creek Township, New York; grandfather of Samuel Wait (1789–1867), president of Wake Forest College.

Waldo, Samuel (1731–1793): Baptist minister of Dover, New York.

Watts, Isaac (1674–1748): English nonconformist minister and celebrated hymnodist.

Wauby, Joseph (Pequot; b. 1776): Son of Roger Wauby; husband of Phebe Niles, the daughter of James Niles. Resident of Brotherton.

Wauby or Waupieh, Roger (Pequot; b. 1734): Friend of Samson Occom and Brotherton founder. Lived at Stonington and among the Narragansett before enlisting in the American War of Independence. It is believed that Samson Occom was related to the Wauby family by marriage on his mother's side.

Waucus, Cynthia (Farmington): Possibly the daughter of James and Rachel Waucus; Brotherton resident.

Waucus, James, Jr. (Farmington; b. 1768): Son of James and Rachel Waucus; student of Joseph Johnson at Farmington, Connecticut. Moved to Brotherton; married Philena Adams, granddaughter of Samson Occom, daughter of Solomon Adams and Olive Occom.

Waucus, Rachel (Farmington): Widow of James Waucus (1728–1778); removed to Brotherton with her son James.

Wesley, John (1703–1791): Anglican clergyman who with his brother Charles Wesley founded the Methodist Society.

West, Jacob (b. 1741): Seventh Day Baptist preacher of Tolland, Connecticut.

Westerlo, Eilandus (1737–1790): Dutch Reformed minister of Albany, New York.

Wheatley, Phillis (1756?–1784): Pioneering African-American poet; author of *Poems on Various Subjects, Religious and Moral* (1773); slave to Susannah and John Wheatley of Boston, Massachusetts.

Wheatley, Susannah Wheeler (b. 1709): Best remembered as the slave-mistress to poet Phillis Wheatley, Susannah Wheatley was a prominent figure in New Light religious circles in Boston, a friend of George Whitefield, and a supporter of Samson Occom.

Wheeler, Thomas (b. 1722): Resident of Stonington, Connecticut.

Wheelock, Eleazar (1711–1779): Yale-educated Congregationalist minister; Great Awakening New Light evangelist; friend of George Whitefield; Wheelock founded Moor's Indian Charity School in Lebanon Crank, Connecticut, in 1754; he moved the school to Hanover, New Hampshire, in 1769, where it became Dartmouth College.

Wheelock, John (1754–1817): Son of Eleazar and Sarah Davenport Wheelock; second president of Dartmouth College (1779–1815).

Wheelock, Ralph (1742–1817): Son of Eleazar and Sarah Davenport Wheelock; sent by his father on a failed mission to the Oneida (1766–1768).

Wheelock, Sarah Davenport (1702–1746): Sister of James Davenport; married Eleazar Wheelock in 1735.

Wheelock, Theodora (1738–): Daughter of Eleazar Wheelock and his wife, Sarah Davenport.

Whitaker, Nathaniel (1732–1795): Princeton-educated Presbyterian minister at Norwich, Connecticut. Assigned by Society in Scotland for the Propagation of Christian Knowledge (SPCK) to accompany Samson Occom to Great Britain to raise funds for Moor's Indian Charity School.

White, Sanford (b. 1757): Native of Redding, Connecticut; married to Hannah Ide, by Occom, on December 19, 1785.

White, Stephen (1718–1794): Presbyterian minister from New Coventry, Connecticut; examined Samson Occom for ordination.

Whitefield, George (1714–1770): Anglican evangelist; celebrity itinerant of the Great Awakening; chaplain to Selina Hastings, Countess of Huntingdon.

Wilkinson, Jemima (1752–1819): Religious visionary, who in 1776 founded the Society of Universal Friends, combining elements of Baptist belief and practice with Quaker tenets of pacifism. Wilkinson called herself the "Public Universal Friend."

Williams, Solomon (1700–1776): Moderate "New Light" Congregationalist minister of Lebanon, Connecticut. Grandson to Solomon Stoddard and cousin to Jonathan Edwards, Williams was recruited to tutor Occom in theology in 1748, but declined by reason of health. He later examined Occom for ordination.

Williams, William (1731–1811): Son of Solomon Williams; town clerk of Lebanon, Connecticut and town representative to Connecticut General Assembly. William Williams fought alongside Hendrick Aupaumut and under Sir William Johnson during the Seven Years' War. Married Mary Trumbull, daughter of Jonathan Trumbull.

Wilson, Peter (1716–1777): Baptist minister of Bordentown, New Jersey.

Witherspoon, John (1723–1794): Minister in the Church of Scotland and leader of the church's "Popular Party"; president of Princeton College; signer of the Declaration of Independence.

Woodbridge, Timothy (1709–1774): Successor to John Sergeant as schoolmaster among the Mahican tribe at Stockbridge.

Wright, Job: Resident of Stillwater, New York; served as company captain during the Revolutionary War.

Wympy, Elijah (Farmington; 1734–1802?): Member of the Farmington Indian community, veteran of the Seven Years' War, and participant in the organization of Brotherton. Among the early emigrants to Oneida territory in 1775. Married to Jerusha Wympy. In the 1790s, Elijah Wympy led a controversial faction at Brotherton that advocated the leasing of Brotherton lands to white settlers.

BIBLIOGRAPHY

MANUSCRIPT SOURCES

Connecticut Historical Society, Hartford, Connecticut. Samson Occom Papers.
Dartmouth College, Hanover, New Hampshire. Dartmouth College Archives.
Dartmouth College, Hanover, New Hampshire. Eleazar Wheelock Papers.
Dartmouth College, Hanover, New Hampshire. Rauner Special Collections.
East Hampton Public Library, Long Island. Long Island Collection.
The Huntington Library, San Marino, California.
Library of Congress, Washington, D.C.
Mashantucket Pequot Museum and Research Center, Mashantucket, Connecticut.
Newberry Library, Chicago, Illinois. Edward E. Ayer Collection.
University of Georgia, Hargrett Rare Book and Manuscript Library, Athens, Georgia.
New London County Historical Society, New London, Connecticut.
New York State Library, Albany, New York. Sir William Johnson Manuscripts, 26 volumes.

PUBLISHED SOURCES

Ahearn, Marie L. *The Rhetoric of War: Training Day, The Militia, and the Military Sermon.* Westport: Greenwood, 1989.
Ales, Marion Fisher. "A History of the Indians on Montauk, Long Island." In *The History and Archeology of the Montauk.* Vol. 3 of *Readings in Long Island Archeology and Ethnohistory.* Ed Gaynelle Stone. 2nd ed. Stony Brook, NY: Suffolk County Archeological Association, 1993. 5–66.
Allen, Clifton, et al., eds. *Encyclopedia of Southern Baptists.* 2 vols. Nashville, Tennessee: Broadman, 1958.
Allen, William. *Memoirs of Samson Occom, The Mohegan Indian Missionary, Including His Own Journal of Many Years, With Specimens of his Sermons, and various Notices Relating to the Indians of his Tribe.* N.p., 1859. Dartmouth College Archive.
Apess, William. *On Our Own Ground: The Complete Writings of William Apess, a Pequot.* Ed. Barry O'Connell. Amherst: U Massachusetts P, 1992.
Appleby, John. "Ginseng and the Royal Society." *Notes and Records of the Royal Society of London* 37.2 (March 1983): 121–145.
Axtell, James. *The Invasion Within: The Contest of Cultures in Colonial North America.* New York: Oxford UP, 1985.
Baker, Brenda. "Pilgrim's Progress and Praying Indians: The Biocultural Consequences of Contact in Southern New England." *In the Wake of Contact: Biological Responses to Conquest.* Ed. Clark Spenser Larsen and George R. Milner. New York: Wiley-Liss, 1994.

Balmer, Randall. *A Perfect Babel of Confusion: Dutch Religion and English Culture in the Middle Colonies.* New York: Oxford UP, 1989.

Bartram, John. *The Correspondence of John Bartram, 1734–1777.* Ed. Edmund Berkeley and Dorothy Smith Berkeley. Gainesville: UP of Florida, 1992.

Belknap, Jeremy, and Jedediah Morse. "Report on the Oneida, Stockbridge, and Brotherton Indians, 1796." *Indian Notes and Monographs* 54 (1955): 3–39.

"Bits from Book of Jeremiah Pharoah." *Sag Harbor Express,* July 31, 1924.

Blodgett, Harold. *Samson Occom.* Hanover, NH: Dartmouth College Publications, 1935.

Boles, John. *The Great Revival: The Beginnings of the Bible Belt.* Lexington: UP of Kentucky, 1996.

Boone, Elizabeth Hill. *Stories in Red and Black: Pictorial Writings of the Aztecs and Mixtecs.* U Texas P, 2000.

Boone, Elizabeth Hill, and Walter D. Mignolo, eds. *Writing Without Words: Alternative Literacies in Mesoamerica and the Andes.* Durham: Duke UP, 1994.

Bosco, Ronald. "Lectures at the Pillory: The Early American Execution Sermon." *American Quarterly* 30.2 (Summer 1978): 156–176.

———, ed. *Sermons for Days of Fast, Prayer, and Humiliation and Execution Sermons. The Puritan Sermon in America, 1630–1750.* Vol. 1. Delmar, NY: Scholars' Facsimiles & Reprints, 1978.

Bourne, Russell. *Gods of War, Gods of Peace.* New York: Harcourt, 2002.

Bragdon, Kathleen. *Native People of Southern New England, 1500–1650.* Norman: U Oklahoma P, 1996.

Brainerd, David. *Memoirs.* Ed. James Sherwood. New York: Funk & Wagnalls, 1884.

Brainerd, Thomas. *The Life of John Brainerd, the Brother of David Brainerd, and his Successor as Missionary to the Indians of New Jersey.* Philadelphia: Presbyterian Publication Committee, 1865.

Brand, Irene. "Dunmore's War." *West Virginia History* 40.1 (1978): 28–46.

Brooks, James, ed. *Confounding the Color Line: The Indian-Black Experience in North America.* Lincoln: U Nebraska P, 2002.

Brooks, Joanna. *American Lazarus: Religion and the Rise of African-American and Native American Literatures.* New York: Oxford UP, 2003.

———. "Six Hymns by Samson Occom." *Early American Literature* 38.1 (2003): 67–88.

Brooks, Lisa. *The Common Pot: Indigenous Writing and the Reconstruction of Native Space in the Northeast.* Ph.D. diss., Cornell UP, 2004.

Buell, Samuel. *The Excellence and Importance of the Saving Knowledge of the Lord Jesus Christ in the Gospel-preacher . . . preached . . . at the ordination of Mr. Samson Occum.* New York: James Parker, 1761.

Bureau of Indian Affairs. "Final Determination that the Mohegan Tribe of Connecticut, Inc., Does Exist as an Indian Tribe." *Federal Register* 59.50 (1994): 12140.

Burke, Thomas, Jr. *Mohawk Frontier: The Dutch Community of Schenectady, New York, 1661–1710.* Ithaca: Cornell UP, 1991.

Bushman, Richard, ed. *The Great Awakening: Documents on the Revival of Religion, 1740–1745.* New York: Atheneum, 1970.

Calloway, Colin. *The American Revolution in Indian Country: Crisis and Diversity in Native American Communities.* New York: Cambridge UP, 1995.

Chamberlain, Ava. "The Execution of Moses Paul: A Story of Crime and Contact in Eighteenth-Century Connecticut." *New England Quarterly* 72 (September 2004): 414–450.

Connecticut, Governor and Company of. *Governor and Company of Connecticut, and*

Moheagan Indians, by their Guardians. Certified Copy of Book of Proceedings before Commissioners of Review, 1743. London, 1769.

Conroy, David W. "The Defense of Indian Land Rights: William Bollan and the Mohegan Case in 1743." *Proceedings of the American Antiquarian Society* 103.2 (1993): 395–424.

Cook-Lynn, Elizabeth. "American Indian Intellectualism and the New Indian Story." *American Indian Quarterly* 20.1 (1996): 57–77.

Cronon, William. *Changes in the Land: Indians, Colonists, and the Ecology of New England.* New York: Hill and Wang, 1983.

Darlington, James. "Peopling the Post-Revolutionary New York Frontier." *New York History* 74.4 (1993): 340–381.

DeForest, John. *History of the Indians of Connecticut from the Earliest Known Period to 1850.* Hartford: Hamersley, 1851.

Dierks, Konstantin. "'Let Me Chat a Little': Letter Writing in Rhode Island Before the Revolution." *Rhode Island History* 53.4 (1995): 120–133.

———. "Letter Writing, Masculinity, and American Men of Science, 1750–1800." *Pennsylvania History* 65 (1998): 167–198.

Divine Hymns, or Spiritual Songs, for the use of religious assemblies and private Christians: being a collection by Joshua Smith, Samson Ockum and others. Troy, New York: Moffit & Lyon, 1803.

Dowd, Gregory. *A Spirited Resistance: The North American Struggle for Unity, 1745–1815.* Baltimore: Johns Hopkins UP, 1992.

Edwards, Jonathan. "Observations on the Language of the Muhhekaneew Indians." [1788]. *Massachusetts Historical Society Collections* (1823): 81–160.

Eels, Edward. "Indian Missions on Long Island." 1939. In *The History and Archeology of the Montauk.* Vol. 3 of *Readings in Long Island Archeology and Ethnohistory.* Ed. Gaynell Stone. 2nd ed. Stony Brook, NY: Suffolk County Archeological Association, 1993. 155–190.

———. "Indian Missions on Long Island: Part 5: Samson Occom." *Journal of the Department of History of the Presbyterian Church in the U.S.A.* 19.3 (September 1940): 99–109.

Elliot, Emory. *Power and the Pulpit in Puritan New England.* Princeton: Princeton UP, 1975.

Elliot, Michael. "'This Indian Bait': Samson Occom and the Voice of Liminality." *Early American Literature* 29.3 (1994): 233–253.

Elrod, Eileen. "'I Did Not Make Myself So . . .': Samson Occom and American Religious Autobiography." In *Christian Encounters with the Other.* Ed. John Hawley and Erick Langer. New York: New York UP, 1998. 135–149.

Fabend, Firth. *Zion on the Hudson: Dutch New York and New Jersey in the Age of Revivals.* New Brunswick, NJ: Rutgers, 2000.

Farrell, James M. "Letters and Political Judgement: John Adams and Cicero's Style." *Studies in Eighteenth-Century Culture* 24 (1995): 137–153.

Fea, John. "Wheelock's World: Letters and the Communication of Revival in Great Awakening New England." *Proceedings of the American Antiquarian Society* 109 (April 1999): 99–144.

Fenton, William. *The Great Law and the Longhouse: A Political History of the Iroquois Confederacy.* Norman: U Oklahoma P, 1998.

Fielding, Stephanie. Personal e-mail communication. March 4, 2005.

———. Personal e-mail communication. December 14, 2005.

Flavell, Julie M. "Government Interception of Letters from America and the Quest for Colonial Opinion in 1775." *William and Mary Quarterly* 58.2 (2001): 403–430.

Flexner, James. *Mohawk Baronet: A Biography of Sir William Johnson.* 1979. Rpt. Syracuse: Syracuse UP, 1989.

Foote, Henry Wilder. *Three Centuries of American Hymnody.* Cambridge: Harvard UP, 1940.

Frazier, Patrick. *The Mohicans of Stockbridge.* Lincoln: U Nebraska P, 1992.

Gausted, Edwin. *The Great Awakening in New England.* New York: Harper, 1957.

Gelles, Edith. "Bonds of Friendship: The Correspondence of Abigail Adams and Mercy Otis Warren." *Proceedings of the Massachusetts Historical Society* 108 (1996): 35–71.

Gewehr, Wesley M. *The Great Awakening in Virginia, 1740–1790.* Durham: Duke UP, 1930.

Gillies, John. *Memoirs of the Rev. George Whitefield.* Hartford: Edwin Hunt & Son, 1853.

Goen, C. C. *Revivalism and Separatism in New England, 1740–1800: Strict Congregationalists and Separate Baptists in the Great Awakening.* New Haven: Yale UP, 1972.

Graymont, Barbara. *The Iroquois in the American Revolution.* Syracuse: Syracuse UP, 1972.

———. "The Tuscarora New Year's Festival." 1969. Rpt. http://tuscaroras.com/pages/history/new_years.html.

Greene, Lorenzo. "Slaveholding New England and Its Awakening." *Journal of Negro History* 13.4 (October 1928): 492–533.

Griffin, Richard W. "An Origin of the Industrial Revolution in Maryland: The Textile Industry, 1789–1826." *Maryland Historical Magazine* 61.1 (1966): 24–36.

Grumet, Robert S., ed. *Northeastern Indian Lives, 1632–1815.* Amherst: U Massachusetts P, 1996.

Hamilton, Milton, ed. *Sir William Johnson Papers.* 14 vols. Albany: U State of New York P, 1962.

Hauptman, Laurence M. *Conspiracy of Interests: Iroquois Dispossession and the Rise of New York State.* Syracuse: Syracuse UP, 1999.

Hauptman, Laurence M., and Jack Campisi, eds. *The Oneida Indian Experience: Two Perspectives.* Syracuse: Syracuse UP, 1988.

Hauptman, Laurence M., and L. Gordon McLester III, eds. *The Oneida Indian Journey: From New York to Wisconsin, 1784–1860.* Madison: U Wisconsin P, 1999.

Hauptman, Laurence M., and James D. Wherry, eds. *The Pequots in Southern New England.* Norman: U Oklahoma P, 1990.

Heckewelder, John. *A Narrative of the Mission of the United Brethren among the Delaware and Mohegan Indians.* 1820. Rpt. Cleveland: Burrows Brothers, 1907.

Higginson, Stephen A. "A Short History of the Right to Petition Government for the Redress of Grievances." *Yale Law Journal* 96.1 (November 1986): 142–166.

Holmes, A. A. "Memoir of the Mohegans." *Collections of the Massachusetts Historical Society,* ser. 1, 9 (1804): 75–99.

Hopkins, Samuel. *Historical Memoirs Relating to the Housatonic Indians.* 1753. Rpt. in *Magazine of History with Notes and Queries,* extra no. 17 (1911).

Huden, John. "Samson Occum: Indian Missionary." *Long Island Forum* (November 1941): 259–262.

Humez, Jean M., ed. *Mother's First-Born Daughters: Early Shaker Writings on Women and Religion.* Bloomington: Indiana UP, 1993.

Hunter, Lois. *The Shinnecock Indians.* Islip, NY: Buys Brothers, 1950.

Jakoski, Helen, ed. *Early Native American Writing: New Critical Essays.* New York: Cambridge UP, 1996.

Jefferson, Thomas, and James Madison. *The Republic of Letters: The Correspondence between Thomas Jefferson and James Madison, 1776–1826*. Ed. James Morton Smith. 3 vols. New York: Norton, 1995.

Jennings, Francis. *The Invasion of America*. New York: Norton, 1976.

Kelly, Eric P. "The Dartmouth Indians." *Dartmouth Alumni Magazine* (December 1929): 122–125.

Kerby, Robert. "The Other War in 1774: Dunmore's War." *West Virginia History* 36.1 (1974): 1–16.

Kirkland, Samuel. *The Journals of Samuel Kirkland: Eighteenth-Century Missionary to the Iroquois, Government Agent, Father of Hamilton College*. Ed. Walter Pilkington. Clinton, NY: Hamilton College, 1980.

King, Thomas. *The Truth About Stories: A Native Narrative*. Toronto: Anansi, 2004.

Krupat, Arnold. *The Voice in the Margin: Native American Literature and the Canon*. Berkeley: U California P, 1989.

Lambert, Frank. *Inventing the Great Awakening*. Princeton: Princeton UP, 1999.

Lawson, Russell M. "Essays on Man: The Belknap-Hazard Correspondence." *Historical New Hampshire* 52.1–2 (1997): 18–27.

Lehman, J. David. "The End of the Iroquois Mystique: The Oneida Land Cession Treaties of the 1780s." *William and Mary Quarterly* 47.4 (1990): 523–547.

Levinson, David. "An Explanation for the Oneida-Colonist Alliance in the American Revolution." *Ethnohistory* 23.3 (Summer 1976): 265–289.

Love, W. DeLoss, Jr. *Fast and Thanksgiving Days of New England*. New York: Houghton and Mifflin, 1895.

———. *Samson Occom and the Christian Indians of New England*. 1899. Rpt. Syracuse: Syracuse UP, 2003.

Mancall, Peter. "Change and Continuity in a Native American Community: Eighteenth-Century Stockbridge." M.A. thesis. U Virginia P, 1982.

———. *Deadly Medicine: Indians and Alcohol in Early America*. Ithaca: Cornell UP, 1995.

Mandell, Daniel. "Shifting Boundaries of Race and Ethnicity: Indian-Black Intermarriage in Southern New England, 1760–1880." *Journal of American History* 85.2 (September 1998): 466–501.

Mann, Bruce. *Republic of Debtors: Bankruptcy in the Age of American Independence*. Cambridge: Harvard UP, 2002.

Marini, Stephen. "Rehearsal for Revival: Sacred Singing and the Great Awakening in America." *JAAR Thematic Studies* 50.1 (1983): 71–91.

McBride, Kevin. "Desirous to Improve After the European Manner: The Mashantucket Pequots and the Brotherton Movement." Unpub. ms., 1996.

McCallum, James Dow, ed. *Letters of Eleazar Wheelock's Indians*. Hanover, NH: Dartmouth College Publications, 1932.

McClure, David, and Elijah Parish. *Memoirs of the Rev. Eleazar Wheelock*. Newburyport, 1811.

McCourt, Thomas. *The Matter and Manner of Praise: The Controversial Evolution of Hymnody in the Church of England, 1760–1820*. Lanham, MD: Scarecrow, 1998.

McLoughlin, William G. *Isaac Backus and the American Pietistic Tradition*. Boston: Little, Brown, 1967.

Melish, Joanne Pope. *Disowning Slavery: Gradual Emancipation and Race in New England, 1780–1860*. Ithaca: Cornell UP, 2000.

Menschel, David. "Abolition without Deliverance: The Law of Connecticut Slavery, 1784–1848." *Yale Law Journal* 111.1 (October 2001): 183–222.

Miller, Perry. *The New England Mind: The Seventeenth Century.* 1939. Cambridge, MA: Belknap, 1982.

Montgomery, Florence M. "Fortunes to be Acquired: Textiles in Eighteenth-Century Rhode Island." *Rhode Island History* 31.2–3 (1972): 53–63.

Mook, H. Telfair. "Training Day in New England." *New England Quarterly* 11 (December 1938): 675–697.

Mullin, Michael. "Personal Politics: William Johnson and the Mohawks." *American Indian Quarterly* 17.3 (1993): 350–358.

———. "Sir William Johnson's Reliance on the Six Nations at the Conclusion of the Anglo-Indian War of 1763–65." *American Indian Culture and Research Journal* 17.4 (1993): 69–90.

Murray, David. *Forked Tongues: Speech, Writing, and Representation in North American Indian Texts.* Amherst: U Massachusetts P, 1991.

———. *Indian Giving: Economies of Power in Indian-White Exchanges.* Amherst: U Massachusetts P, 2000.

Murray, Laura. "'Pray, Sir, Consider a Little': Rituals of Subordination and Strategies of Resistance in the Letters of Hezekiah Calvin and David Fowler to Eleazar Wheelock, 1764–1768." *Studies in American Indian Literatures* 4 (Summer–Fall 1992): 48–74. Rpt. in *Early Native American Writing: New Critical Essays.* Ed. Helen Jakoski. New York: Cambridge UP, 1996. 15–41.

———. *To Do Good to My Indian Brethren: The Writings of Joseph Johnson, 1751–1776.* Amherst: U Massachusetts P, 1998.

Nelson, Dana. "'(I speak like a fool but I am constrained)': Samson Occom's Short Narrative and Economies of the Racial Self." In *Early Native American Writing: New Critical Essays.* Ed. Helen Jakoski. New York: Cambridge UP, 1996. 42–65.

Oberg, Michael Leroy. *Uncas: First of the Mohegans.* Ithaca: Cornell UP, 2003.

O'Brien, Jean. *Dispossession by Degrees: Indian Land and Identity in Natick, Massachusetts, 1650–1790.* Lincoln: U Nebraska P, 1997.

O'Brien, Susan. "A Transatlantic Community of Saints: The Great Awakening and the First Evangelical Network, 1735–1755." *American Historical Review* 91.4 (1986): 811–832.

Occom, Samson. "An Account of the Montauk Indians, on Long-Island." 1761. *Collections of the Massachusetts Historical Society* 10 (1809): 106–10.

———. *A Choice Collection of Hymns and Spiritual Songs.* New London, Connecticut: Timothy Green, 1774.

———. *A Sermon, Preached at the Execution of Moses Paul, an Indian.* New Haven: T. Green, 1772.

Ottery, Jim. "Samson Occom's Diary and D'Arcy McNickle's 'Train Time': The Real Imperative of 'Native' Education in American Indian Literature." *SAIL,* ser. 2, 13.4 (Winter 2001): 24–49.

———. "Samson Occom's Diary and D'Arcy McNickle's 'Train Time': The Real Imperative of Indian Education in Native American Literature." http://work.colum.edu/ ~jottery/IntroCW/NAC/OccumMcNicklePres.htm. August 27, 2004.

Ottery, Will. *A Man Called Sampson.* Camden, ME: Penobscot, 1989.

Parkman, Francis. *Empire of Fortune: Crowns, Colonies, and Tribes in the Seven Years' War in America.* New York: Norton, 1988.

Peyer, Bernd. "Samson Occom: Mohegan Missionary and Writer of the Eighteenth Century." *American Indian Quarterly* 6.3–4 (Fall–Winter 1982): 208–217.

———. *The Tutor'd Mind: Indian Missionary-Writers in Antebellum America.* Amherst: U Massachusetts P, 1997.

Perdue, Theda. "Native Women in the Early Republic: Old World Perceptions, New World Realities." In *Native Americans in the Early Republic*. Ed. Ronald Hoffman and Frederick Hoxies. Charlottesville: UP of Virginia, 1999. 85–122.

Plane, Ann Marie. *Colonial Intimacies: Indian Marriage in Early New England*. Ithaca: Cornell UP, 2000.

Pomedi, Michael. "Eighteenth-Century *Treaties:* Amended Iroquois Condolence Rituals," *American Indian Quarterly* 19.3 (1995): 319–339.

Pratt, Mary Louise. *Imperial Eyes: Travel Writing and Transculturation*. New York: Routledge, 1992.

Prince, J. Dyneley, and Frank G. Speck. *A Vocabulary of Mohegan-Pequot*. 1904. Rpt. Southhampton, PA: Evolution, 1999.

Quinones Kerber, Eloise. *Codex Telleriano-Remensis: Ritual, Divination, and History in a Pictorial Aztec Manuscript*. Austin: U Texas P, 1995.

Rabasa, Jose. "The Problem of the Background in Comparative Studies." Paper delivered at the *(In)Comparable Americas* conference, U Chicago, May 1, 2004.

Rabito-Wyppensenwah, Philip. "Discovering the Montauketts in Rediscovered Documents." In *The History and Archeology of the Montauk*. Vol. 3 *of Readings in Long Island Archeology and Ethnohistory*. Ed. Gaynell Stone. 2nd ed. Stony Brook, NY: Suffolk County Archeological Association, 1993. 423–427.

———. "The Hannibals: A Montaukett Family History." In *The History and Archeology of the Montauk*. Vol. 3 of *Readings in Long Island Archeology and Ethnohistory*. Ed. Gaynell Stone. 2nd ed. Stony Brook, NY: Suffolk County Archeological Association, 1993. 349–358.

Rabito-Wyppensenwah, Philip, and Robert Abiuso. "The Montaukett Use of Herbs: A Review of the Recorded Material." In *The History and Archeology of the Montauk*. Vol. 3 of *Readings in Long Island Archeology and Ethnohistory*. Ed. Gaynell Stone. 2nd ed. Stony Brook, NY: Suffolk County Archeological Association, 1993. 585–588.

Rawley, James. "The World of Phillis Wheatley." *New England Quarterly* 50.4 (December 1977): 666–677.

Richardson, Leon. *An Indian Preacher in England*. Hanover: Dartmouth College Publications, 1933.

Robertson, Thomas. "'Then Wee Were Called Brethren': The Iroquois and Leisler's Rebellion, 1689." *Halve Maen* 68.3 (1995): 54–64.

Ronda, James, and Jeanne Ronda. "'As They Were Faithful': Chief Hendrick Aupaumut and the Struggle for Stockbridge Survival, 1757–1830." *American Indian Culture and Research Journal* 3.3 (1979): 43–55.

Ruoff, LaVonne Brown. "Introduction: Samson Occom's *Sermon Preached by Samson Occom at the Execution of Moses Paul, an Indian*." *Studies in American Indian Literatures* 4.2–3 (1992): 75–105.

Salisbury, Neal. *Manitou and Providence*. New York: Oxford UP, 1982.

"Samson Occom." *The Religious Intelligencer . . . Containing the Principal Transactions of the Various Bible and Missionary Societies, with Particular Accounts of Revivals of Religion* 7.24 (November 9, 1822): 378–382.

Seaburg, Alan. "Recent Scholarship in American Universalism: A Bibliographical Essay." *Church History* 41.4 (December 1972): 513–523.

Sergeant, John. *Letter from the Rev'd Mr. Sergeant of Stockbridge to Dr. Colman of Boston*. Boston, 1743.

Shields, David. "The Religious Sublime and New England Poets of the 1720s." *Early American Literature* 19.3 (1984–1985): 231–248.

Silko, Leslie Marmon. "Language and Literature from a Pueblo Indian Perspective." In *English Literature: Opening Up the Canon*. Ed. Leslie Fiedler. Baltimore: Johns Hopkins UP, 1981. 54–72.

Silverman, David. "The Impact of Indentured Servitude on the Society and Culture of Southern New England Indians, 1680–1810." *New England Quarterly* 74.4 (December 2001): 622–666.

Simmons, William. "Red Yankees: Narragansett Conversion in the Great Awakening." *American Ethnologist* 10.2 (May 1983): 253–271.

———. *Spirit of the New England Tribes: Indian History and Folklore, 1620–1984*. Hanover: UP of New England, 1986.

Simmons, William, and Gertrude Simmons. *Old Light on Separate Ways: The Narragansett Diary of Joseph Fish, 1765–1776*. Hanover: UP of New England, 1982.

"Sketch of the life of Samson Occom." *The Religious Intelligencer . . . Containing the Principal Transactions of the Various Bible and Missionary Societies, with Particular Accounts of Revivals of Religion* 7.25 (November 16, 1822): 393–397.

"Sketch of the life of Samson Occom." *The Religious Intelligencer . . . Containing the Principal Transactions of the Various Bible and Missionary Societies, with Particular Accounts of Revivals of Religion* 7.26 (November 23, 1822): 409–415.

Speck, Frank. "Notes on the Mohegan and Niantic Indians." *Anthropological Papers of the American Museum of Natural History* 3 (1909): 183–210.

Spiess, Mathias. *The Indians of Connecticut*. New Haven: Yale UP, 1933.

Sprague, William Buell. *Annals of the American Pulpit*. Vol. 3. New York: Robert Carter and Brothers, 1858.

Stein, Stephen J. *The Shaker Experience in America*. New Haven: Yale UP, 1992.

Stevenson, Robert. "American Tribal Musics at Contact." *Inter-American Music Review* 14.1 (Spring–Summer 1994): 29.

St. Jean, Wendy. "Inventing Guardianship: The Mohegan Indians and Their 'Protectors.'" *New England Quarterly* 72.3 (1999): 362–387.

Stout, Harry. *The New England Soul: Preaching and Religious Culture in Colonial New England*. New York: Oxford UP, 1986.

Strong, John. "Azariah Horton's Mission to the Montauk, 1741–1744." In *The History and Archeology of the Montauk*. Vol. 3 of *Readings in Long Island Archeology and Ethnohistory*. Ed. Gaynell Stone. 2nd ed. Stony Brook, NY: Suffolk County Archeological Association, 1993. 191–220.

———. "How the Land Was Lost: An Introduction." In *The Shinnecock Indians: A Culture History*. Vol. 6 of *Readings in Long Island Archeology and Ethnohistory*. Ed. Gaynell Stone. Stony Brook, NY: Suffolk County Archeological Association, 1983. 53–64.

———. "How the Montauk Lost Their Land." In *The History and Archeology of the Montauk*. Vol. 3 of *Readings in Long Island Archeology and Ethnohistory*. Ed. Gaynell Stone. 2nd ed. Stony Brook, NY: Suffolk County Archeological Association, 1993. 77–120.

———. *The Montaukett Indians of Eastern Long Island*. Syracuse: Syracuse UP, 2001.

Szasz, Margaret Connell, ed. *Between Indian and White Worlds: The Cultural Broker*. Norman: U Oklahoma P, 1994.

Tantaquidgeon, Gladys. *Folk Medicine of the Delaware and Related Algonquian Indians*. Philadelphia: Pennsylvania Historical & Museum Commission, 1972.

Tantaquidgeon Zobel, Melissa Fawcett. *The Lasting of the Mohegans. Part 1: The Story of the Wolf People*. Uncasville, CT: Mohegan Tribe, 1995.

———. *Medicine Trail: The Life and Lessons of Gladys Tantaquidgeon*. Tucson: U of Arizona P, 2000.

————. Personal e-mail communication. December 6, 2004.

————. "Sociocultural Authority: The Mohegan Case." In *Rooted like the Ash Trees: New England Indians and the Land*. Naugatuck, CT: Eagle Wing, 1987. 52–53.

Toulouse, Teresa. *The Art of Prophesying: New England Sermons and the Shaping of Belief.* Athens: U Georgia P, 1987.

Turner, Victor. *The Ritual Process: Structure and Anti-Structure*. Chicago: Aldine, 1969.

Ulrich, Laurel Thatcher. "An Indian Basket." In *The Age of Homespun: Objects and Stories in the Creation of an American Myth*. New York: Knopf, 2001. 41–74.

Valone, Stephen. "Samuel Kirkland, Iroquois Missions and the Land, 1764–1774." *American Presbyterians* 65.3 (1987): 187–194.

Warrior, Robert Allen. *Tribal Secrets: Recovering American Indian Intellectual Traditions*. Minneapolis: U Minnesota P, 1995.

Weaver, Jace. *That the People Might Live: Native American Literatures and Native American Community*. New York: Oxford UP, 1997.

Weber, Donald. *Rhetoric and History in Revolutionary New England*. New York: Oxford UP, 1988.

Weinstein, Laurie. "Samson Occom: Charismatic Eighteenth-Century Mohegan Leader." In *Enduring Traditions: The Native Peoples of New England*. Ed. Laurie Weinstein. Westport, CT: Bergin & Garvey, 1994. 91–102.

Wheatley, Phillis. *The Poems of Phillis Wheatley*. Ed. Julian D. Mason, Jr. Chapel Hill: U North Carolina P, 1989.

Wheeler, Rachel. *Living Upon Hope: Mahicans and Missionaries, 1730–1760*. Ph.D. diss., Yale, 1999.

Wheelock, Eleazar. *A Continuation of the Narrative of the Indian Charity School, in Lebanon, in Connecticut*. Boston, 1765.

————. *A Continuation of the Narrative . . .* Hartford, 1771.

————. *A Continuation of the Narrative . . .* [n.p.], 1772.

————. *A Continuation of the Narrative . . .* Hartford, 1773.

————. *A Continuation of the Narrative. . . .* Hartford, 1775.

————. *A Plain and Faithful Narrative*. Boston, 1763.

Williams, Roger. *A Key into the Language of America*. 1643. Ed. John J. Teunissen and Evelyn Hinz. Detroit: Wayne State UP, 1973.

Wonderley, Anthony. "Brothertown, New York, 1785–1796." *New York History* 81.4 (2000): 456–492.

————. "'Good Peter's Narrative of Several Transactions Respecting Indian Lands': An Oneida View of Dispossession, 1785–1788." *New York History* 84.3 (2003): 236–273.

Wyss, Hilary. *Writing Indians: Literacy, Christianity, and Native Community in Early America*. Amherst: U Massachusetts P, 2000.

Wyss, Hilary, and Kristina Bross, eds. *Early Native Literacies in New England: A Documentary and Critical Anthology* Amherst: U Massachusetts P, 2006.

INDEX

CPSIA information can be obtained
at www.ICGtesting.com
Printed in the USA
BVHW011034110122
625896BV00002BA/159

9 780195 170830